Fourth Edition

S0-BZN-543

Sadlier-Oxford

Building an Enriched Vocabulary

Teacher's Annotated Edition
With Answer Key to Supplementary Testing Program

Senior Consultant

John Heath, Ph.D.
Santa Clara University

Sadlier-Oxford
A Division of William H. Sadlier, Inc.

Reviewers

The publisher wishes to thank for their comments and suggestions the following teachers, who read portions of the book prior to publication.

Eileen Bacha
English Department Chair
Cardinal Mooney High School
Youngstown, Ohio

Carole Tatem
English Teacher
Paul VI High School
Haddonfield, New Jersey

Elizabeth Bradstreet
English Teacher
Lower Richland High School
Hopkins, South Carolina

t the Fourth Edition

first published in 1983, BUILDING AN ENRICHED VOCABULARY has come to be recognized as an effective tool for stimulating systematic vocabulary growth and for helping students prepare for standardized tests. The Fourth Edition of BUILDING AN ENRICHED VOCABULARY introduces two new features designed to enhance these key elements of the program:

- In every other lesson there appears a new set of exercises titled *Related Forms in Context*. These exercises ask students to recognize and use words related in form to those they have studied in depth in the lessons. The "Related Forms in Context" exercises give students abundant practice in applying an important principle of vocabulary instruction: that in learning one word, students are often adding a family of words to their reading and writing vocabulary.

- In every review there is provided a new set of exercises titled *Choosing the Right Meaning*. In these exercises students must use context to determine which of two or more legitimate meanings is the one most appropriate to the given sentence or short passage. "Choosing the Right Meaning," then, gives students practice with the kind of usage-discrimination questions that appear in the reading sections of standardized tests.

In addition, the entire text of the Student Text and Teacher's Edition have been reviewed and updated as follows:

- All *definitions* have been checked to ensure that they reflect the present-day meanings of the words they go with. The same procedure has been applied to the *pronunciations, synonyms, antonyms, phrases,* and other materials included in the initial presentation of each word.

- All *sentences* have undergone a thorough scrutiny, and those that reflected out-of-date situations have been revised to reflect the state of the world at present.

- Sections devoted to *Working with Context Clues* have been revised to reflect current practice on standardized tests, especially the SAT I. It is hoped that this particular change will greatly help students dealing with the word-omissions or words-in-context strands of such tests.

- In a few places, exercises in the *Enriching the Lesson* sections have been updated by providing more recent examples of the type of words involved in the exercise. For example, the section on "Pormanteau Words (Blends)" on page 47 of the Student Text has been refreshed by the additon of a few newer coinages—e.g., *heliport* and *infomercial.*

- *Photographs* and other visual aids have been examined and replaced as necessary with more modern or more culturally pluralistic materials.

- The *Teacher's Annotated Edition* has also been revised and brought up to date in light of the revisions made in the Student Text.

With the introduction of two new features and the thoroughgoing updating of the text, the aim of the Fourth Edition is to make BUILDING AN ENRICHED VOCABULARY an even more useful and current resource for college-bound students.

Foreword to the
TEACHER'S ANNOTATED EDITION

This *Teacher's Annotated Edition* has been prepared for the convenience of teachers using the Fourth Edition of BUILDING AN ENRICHED VOCABULARY and the accompanying SUPPLEMENTARY EXERCISE AND TESTING PROGRAM in their classes. It is designed to give teachers direct and practical assistance in preparing lessons, correcting homework assignments, and providing answers to questions posed by students. It is hoped that teachers will find this *Teacher's Annotated Edition* of value in using both BUILDING AN ENRICHED VOCABULARY and the accompanying exercise/testing program with maximum effectiveness in the classroom.

The *Teacher's Annotated Edition* provides answers to all questions of a specific, objective type in BUILDING AN ENRICHED VOCABULARY. Answers involving only a word or two appear as annotations on the appropriate pages of the student text; more complicated or longer answers have been collected into an Answer Key that begins on page 541. In addition, answers have been provided for all questions in the SUPPLEMENTARY EXERCISE AND TESTING PROGRAM. These are contained in a special Answer Key that begins on page 628.

Teachers should note the following points when using the *Teacher's Annotated Edition.*

- Illustrative sentences have not been provided. For the great majority of questions calling for such answers, the teacher must judge individual student sentences on their own merits.

- For questions involving long or complicated replies, only "model answers" have been provided, and these have been kept as brief as possible. For that reason, student answers may differ widely in wording or scope from those provided and still be right. This is especially true for questions calling for synonyms or antonyms. Accordingly, teachers should always judge student answers to such questions on their own merits and regard the answers provided as nothing more than rough guides.

Contents

The Structure and Organization of BUILDING AN ENRICHED VOCABULARY, Fourth Edition

The primary aim of the Fourth Edition of BUILDING AN ENRICHED VOCABULARY is essentially the same as that of previous editions: to prepare college-bound students to meet the challenges ahead by familiarizing them with the vocabulary of Modern English.

In BUILDING AN ENRICHED VOCABULARY, this goal is achieved in three ways:

- in-depth study of 400 key words (the Basic Word List)

- intensive preparation for specialized question types frequently used on standardized vocabulary tests assessing college readiness

- supplementary survey of a broad but varied segment of the vocabulary students will meet at the college level or on standardized vocabulary tests

- instruction and practice in key vocabulary-building skills

Over twenty years have passed since BUILDING AN ENRICHED VOCABULARY was first published. During that time the United States and the world have seen extraordinary changes. The Fourth Edition of BUILDING AN ENRICHED VOCABULARY has taken these changes into account by thoroughly updating and modernizing the Student Text and the *Teacher's Annotated Edition*. Details of these changes, including the introduction of two new features in the Student Text, can be found in "About the Fourth Edition," which precedes the Table of Contents. Although the Fourth Edition has been designed to enhance the effectiveness of the book in the classroom of the early twenty-first century, it should be borne in mind that the basic goal of the Fourth Edition is entirely in keeping with that of the original edition.

The Introductory Chapter. An introductory chapter entitled "Learning Words" (pages 1–20) is the first item that meets the student's eye in BUILDING AN ENRICHED VOCABULARY. It reviews key technical terms or concepts relating to the study of vocabulary; it introduces the dictionary and the thesaurus; and it surveys the chief stages in the development of the vocabulary of Modern English. The historical survey has been included in order to supply the student with enough background information to make effective use of the various exercises and other materials relating to etymology or word origins that are interspersed throughout the book. Each of the three subsections of the introductory chapter concludes with a short but practical reinforcement exercise.

The Basic Word List. The key element in the structure of BUILDING AN ENRICHED VOCABULARY is the Basic Word List of 400 essential vocabulary items (pages 21–25). This list was developed from many sources, including traditional and contemporary literature, newspapers, magazines, films, radio, and television. Due attention was also paid to the spelling and vocabulary lists which have gained wide recognition as valid bases for teaching language skills on the secondary level. Current subject-area textbooks and glossaries were also examined, and the standard word-frequency studies by Dolch, Thorndike-Lorge, Dale-O'Rourke, Johnson, Hillerich, Harris, Jacobson, Carroll-Davies-Richman, and others were used to evaluate and revise the word list.

The primary criterion for the selection of entries on the Basic Word List was their frequent appearance in printed materials. The words were also chosen for their frequency on standardized vocabulary tests. In this connection, there is an unavoidable element of subjective judgment. Accordingly, the editors have had to rely to some extent on their feel for the language and for the words that are likely to be most useful to, and rewarding for, students preparing to enter college.

LESSON FORMAT. The 400 key words on the Basic Word List have been put in alphabetical order into 30 lessons, each containing 10 or 15 words. Each of these lessons consists of the following parts:

- A set of *word entries*, in dictionary-like form

- "*Using the Words*," a set of exercises providing practical reinforcement of the material presented in the word entries

- "*Dissecting the Words*," a section on word origins, or "*Completing Verbal Analogies*," a section dealing with the type of analogy questions usually found on standardized vocabulary tests

- "*Working with Context Clues*," a section introducing the student to the type of word-omission question found on standardized tests

- "*Enriching the Lesson*," a set of advanced dictionary/thesaurus exercises that enrich the material presented in the word entries and round out the presentation

The Word Entries. Each lesson in BUILDING AN ENRICHED VOCABULARY begins with a set of word entries consisting of three parts:

- the *headline*, which includes the key word in syllabicated form, the part of speech of the key word, the pronunciation, and a brief etymology

- the *body* of the entry, containing the definition or definitions; one or more illustrative sentences or passages; related forms of the key word; phrases showing the range of applicability of the key word; and usage notes regarding tone, connotation, look-alikes, and so forth

- the *supplement* to the entry, consisting of a group of synonyms and antonyms of the key word or its related forms; a selection of phrases involving these synonyms and antonyms or related in some other way to the general idea expressed by the key word; and appropriate usage notes referring to these items

The following remarks explain more fully the nature of the word entries:

- The *pronunciation* is indicated by means of a simple set of diacritical marks explained at the beginning of the book (page 26). Usually the commonly accepted pronunciation is indicated, though alternate pronunciations may be sanctioned by some dictionaries. However, exceptions to this general rule do occur occasionally when a word changes its pronunciation upon becoming a different part of speech.

- The *etymology* has been kept as simple as possible. Usually it attempts to account only for the present spelling of the key word (insofar as that is possible) and to break the word up into its basic component parts without indicating intermediate stages in its development.

- The *definitions* provided are for the most part brief and clear. Usually only the common meaning is given. Additional meanings may be given if they are of equal value, or if the key word is used as more than one part of speech. If there is any uncertainty as to what a given word means, students should be encouraged to consult an unabridged dictionary.

- The *illustrative sentences or passages* have been especially designed to show how the key word is normally used in a typical context. Where more than one illustrative sentence accompanies a single definition, a literal use of that meaning is given in the first sentence and a figurative or extended application in the second. The illustrative sentences involve situations that are familiar to the average high-school student while at the same time selectively introducing college-level subject matter or sentence structure.

- For the most part, only a selection of appropriate *synonyms* and *antonyms* of maximum usefulness has been provided. Students should be encouraged to consult a thesaurus or other "word-finder" for more complete listings.

- *Usage notes and phrases* have been kept to a minimum so as not to overload the entry or confuse the student with too much detail.

- The items included in the supplement ("Synonyms," "Antonyms," "Related Phrases") are normally not defined or explained. This was done in part to provide material for Exercise V in "Using the Words" (see below). Accordingly, students should be instructed to make use of a dictionary when studying this section of the word entry. (The items in the headline and body of a word entry are, of course, self-explanatory, and no dictionary work is required for them.)

Using the Words. Immediately after the last word entry in each lesson you will find a varied group of practical exercises entitled "Using the Words." These exercises review and reinforce the material presented in the word entries in a brief but highly effective way. Since they call on the student to use and reuse the key words in a variety of situations, the exercises extend and supplement the discussion contained in the word entries themselves.

Each of the exercises contained in "Using the Words" deals with one part of the preceding set of word entries. Nonetheless, the particular type of exercise that is included varies somewhat, depending on whether the section appears in an odd- or even-numbered lesson, as the following chart indicates:

Odd-Numbered Lesson	Even-Numbered Lesson
I. Syllabication and Pronunciation	I. Parts of Speech
II. Words Out of Context	II. Words in Phrases
III. Completing Sentences	III. Completing Sentences
IV. Synonyms and Antonyms (First Format)	IV. Synonyms and Antonyms (Second Format)
V. Word Roundup	V. Word Roundup
VI. Framing Sentences	VI. Framing Sentences

A careful examination of this sequence against a typical word entry will show that Exercise I relates to the headline, Exercises II and III to the body, and Exercises IV and V to the supplement. (See above for definitions of these terms.) Exercise VI acts as a final check on the learning experience by asking students to use the key words or their related forms in sentences of their own devising.

The following comments may prove helpful when trying to make effective use of "Using the Words":

• The sentences in Exercise III, "Completing Sentences," require the student to choose a word that fits logically and meaningfully into a given blank. If students have a good grasp of the meanings of the key words, they should have no trouble making the correct selections. Context clues of one type or another have been carefully sewn into the sentences to insure that the correct word is selected. In the earlier lessons the literal meanings of the key words are all that is involved in the sentences. Note that Exercise III makes use of only those words that have not already been used in Exercise II, so that Exercises II and III form a complementary pair of tests covering all the key words in the lesson.

• The activities in Exercise V, "Word Roundup," are designed to cover the diverse materials contained in the "Usage Notes," "Phrases," and "Related Phrases" sections of the word entry. Since many of these items are not explained in the text, the student may have to consult a dictionary or thesaurus to answer the questions about them. Thus, Exercise V acts as a simple dictionary/thesaurus exercise that is in part designed to lead up to the more advanced and complicated dictionary/thesaurus exercises contained in "Enriching the Lesson."

Dissecting the Words. The reader will no doubt have noticed that the etymological material contained in each word entry is not covered by any of the exercises in "Using the Words." That is because a special section, entitled "Dissecting the Words," has been provided. This concentrated presentation should meet the practical needs of the average college-bound student better than a more piecemeal approach would have done.

"Dissecting the Words" appears immediately after "Using the Words" in *odd-numbered* lessons. Important word elements occurring in the key word—prefixes, roots, and suffixes—are analyzed to show what each means, where it comes from, and how it is employed in other useful words not on the Basic Word List.

A short but lively exercise involving the use of a dictionary or thesaurus concludes each of the etymology sections, so that the learning exercise is reinforced in as effective a manner as possible.

Completing Verbal Analogies. Earlier it was remarked that BUILDING AN ENRICHED VOCABULARY in part attempts to prepare students for the type of standardized vocabulary test that is frequently used to assess college readiness. The next two sections of the lesson—"Completing Verbal Analogies" and "Working with Context Clues"—have this practical aim.

"Completing Verbal Analogies," appears immediately after "Using the Words" in *even-numbered* lessons. As teachers are well aware, analogy questions are valuable and revealing not merely as a kind of mental gymnastics but also as a means of pinning down the exact meanings of words and of remedying misconceptions or uncertainties about the ways in which they are used. For that reason, analogy questions are both functional and effective pedagogical tools.

The treatment of analogy questions in BUILDING AN ENRICHED VOCABULARY is organized but succinct, and a wealth of examples has been provided to give students adequate practice in handling these verbal brainteasers. Two different kinds of analogy-completion questions frequently met with on standardized tests are analyzed in detail (see pages 70 and 180), and about 15 basic word relationships (e.g., "*A* means the same as *B*," "*A* is an example of *B*," and "If a person is *A*, he/she lacks *B*") are highlighted. Each analogy section is divided into three parts in order to reinforce and help master the style or the kind of analogy taught in the lesson. Starting in Lesson 20, special review exercises not only recapitulate the kinds of word relationships that the students are already familiar with but also introduce a few others that they have not been formally taught to recognize. (The latter were included in order to provide the teacher with a useful check of student mastery of the material under real testing conditions.)

The analysis of a representative set of analogy situations in BUILDING AN ENRICHED VOCABULARY is to be considered as introductory to the whole field of verbal logic. The teacher may feel it pedagogically necessary to simplify the concepts or upgrade the level of the exercises in order to meet the special needs of the students. In any event, the study of analogies as presented in this book is certain to provide a practical test of the challenges students will confront on college-entrance aptitude tests and other such vocabulary situations.

Working with Context Clues. The other special section in the lesson that aims at preparing students for standardized vocabulary tests is called "Working with Context Clues." It first appears in Lesson 11 and occurs in every lesson thereafter.

"Working with Context Clues" has been designed to familiarize students with the type of word-omission question that frequently appears on standardized vocabulary tests. In this type of question, the student is given a short passage of connected prose from which (usually) two words have been removed and replaced by blanks. The passage is followed by four or five pairs of words from which the student is to select the pair that correctly completes the passage. Context clues are provided within the passage to guide students to the correct choice.

BUILDING AN ENRICHED VOCABULARY addresses the problem of preparing students for this type of testing device by providing a systematic pedagogical program based on the recognition of three broad categories of context clues. These may be conveniently described as *restatement clues* (page 183), *contrast clues* (page 219), and *inference clues* (page 254). Each of these clues is first introduced and explained in the context of a *one-word* omission question and then extended to the type of *two-word* omission questions that the student can expect to meet on an actual test. Extensive exercise materials have been provided to reinforce the learning experience at every stage, and a wide variety of review items has been included.

Many of the basic words taught in BUILDING AN ENRICHED VOCABULARY appear as the answers in the exercises accompanying the "Working with Context Clues" sections. This was intentionally done to tie these sections more closely to the rest of the lesson.

Though the present treatment of two-word omissions cannot be considered exhaustive, the coverage is certainly as full an introduction as the teacher is likely to find in any comparable vocabulary book. Indeed, in many ways it is fuller and more thorough than what is currently available.

Enriching the Lesson. The final section of every lesson is called "Enriching the Lesson." It contains a group of advanced dictionary/thesaurus exercises that spin off from something that has been noted in the word entries and is intended to enrich and round off the lesson. For example, Lesson 1 contains the word *academic,* which is derived from an ancient Greek place name. Accordingly, the "Enriching the Lesson" section that concludes Lesson 1 contains an exercise relating to other place names that have become familiar, everyday words in Modern English.

The material included in the exercises is organized around a number of important themes that throw light on the character and history of our vocabulary. These themes include the technical vocabulary of English (*e.g.,* The Language of the Mind, page 258), the sources of our vocabulary (*e.g.,* Loan Words from Faraway Places, page 257, and Eponyms, page 108), word formation (*e.g.,* Curious Compounds, page 133), advice on the use of words (*e.g.,* Clichés, page 95), humor (*e.g.,* the various "Verbal Diversions" included in the text), and others.

New to this edition is an exercise titled "Related Forms in Context." In this exercise students are required to use context to identify words related in form to those they have studied in depth in the lessons and then to use these related forms to complete sentences.

THE REVIEWS. The treatment of vocabulary contained in the 30 lessons is rounded out by the inclusion of three *periodic reviews* (after Lessons 10, 20, and 30, respectively) and one *final cumulative review* (at the end of the book). Each of these items covers the material presented in the word entries and "Dissecting the Words" sections only and does not draw upon the specialized features dealing with standardized vocabulary tests or the advanced dictionary/thesaurus exercises in "Enriching the Lesson." For use as either review or testing devices, these supplementary sections combine familiar testing techniques with some new and interesting question types.

Among these types is a set of exercises, new to this edition, titled "Choosing the Right Meaning." In this exercise students are called upon to choose from among two or more correct meanings of a given word the meaning that best suits the context within which the given word appears. This new exercise gives students practice in using context to distinguish shades of meaning and proper usage, as well as practice in the usage-discrimination items that appear in the reading sections of standardized tests.

ILLUSTRATIONS. Ample use of photographs and other visuals has been made to illustrate and enrich the text. Two groups of illustrative materials deserve special notice: The *Wordsmiths,* which focus on some of the people who have made significant contributions to the development of the modern dictionary and thesaurus; and *Careers for Word Buffs,* which highlights some of the careers that a person who is good at vocabulary might profitably pursue. These items and the other illustrations in the text make a unique contribution to the particular pedagogical approach taken in BUILDING AN ENRICHED VOCABULARY.

SUPPLEMENTARY MATERIALS. For the convenience of the teacher using BUILDING AN ENRICHED VOCABULARY in the classroom, a *Teacher's Annotated Edition* of the Student Text and a 96-page *Supplementary Exercise and Testing Program* have been prepared. The former provides answers to all questions in both the Student Text and the Supplementary Testing Program; the latter supplies additional exercise materials that can be used for review or testing. The *Teacher's Annotated Edition* offers a ready resource in one easy-to-use product.

Using the Program. It is believed that the program presented here can be used with profit and enjoyment by the vast majority of students in our secondary schools. The rate of progress will depend, naturally, on both the grade and ability levels of particular classes or students. The book may be used as a regular class text, as a supplementary resource, or as a self-teaching text by individual students.

Teacher Resources

The following titles may prove useful to teachers and students who wish to study in greater depth the vocabulary, history, and usage of the English language.

I. DICTIONARIES

Recommended

Merriam-Webster's Collegiate Dictionary [Eleventh Edition] (Springfield, MA: Merriam-Webster, 2003)

Webster's Third New International Dictionary (Springfield, MA: G. & C. Merriam, 1993)

American Heritage Dictionary (Boston: Houghton Mifflin, 2000)

Oxford English Dictionary [Compact Edition] (Oxford: Oxford University Press, 1971)

Skeat, W.W. *A Concise Etymological Dictionary of the English Language* (NY: G.P. Putnam, 1980)

Supplemental

12,000 Words [A Supplement to *Webster's Third International Dictionary*] (Springfield, MA: Merriam-Webster, 1993)

The Random House Dictionary of the English Language [Unabridged Edition] (NY: Random House, 1987)

II. THESAURI

Recommended

Roget's II The New Thesaurus (Boston: Houghton Mifflin, 1995)

Random House Roget's Thesaurus (NY: Random House, 2001)

Rodale, J. [Revised by Urdang, L. and La Roche, N.] *The Synonym Finder* (Emmaus, PA: Rodale Press, 1979)

Supplemental

Chapman, R.L. (Ed.). *Roget A to Z* (NY: Harper Perennial, 1994)

Laird, C. *Webster's New World Thesaurus* (NY: Warner Books, 1990)

Roget's International Thesaurus [Fifth Edition] (NY: HarperCollins, 1992)

Abate, F. *The Oxford Dictionary and Thesaurus: The Ultimate Language Reference for American Readers* (NY: Oxford University Press, 1996)

III. OTHER REFERENCE WORKS

Recommended

Carroll, J., Davies, P., and Richman, B. *Word Frequency Book* (Boston: Houghton Mifflin, 1971)

Dale, E. and O'Rourke, J. *The Living Word Vocabulary* (Chicago: Scott & Fetzer, 1981)

Supplemental

Harris, A. and Jackson, M. *Basic Reading Vocabularies* (NY: Macmillan, 1982)

Thorndike, E. and Lorge, I. *The Teacher's Book of 30,000 Words* (NY: Teachers College Press, Columbia University, 1968)

IV. HISTORY

General

Baugh, A.C. and Cable, T. *A History of the English Language* [Third Edition] (Englewood Cliffs, NJ: Prentice-Hall, 1992)

Carver, C. *A History of English in Its Own Words* (NY: HarperCollins, 1991)

Jespersen, O. *Growth and Structure of the English Language* (Chicago: University of Chicago Press, 1982)

McCrum, R., Cran, W., and MacNeil, R. *The Story of English* (NY: Penguin, 1993)

Myers, L.M. *The Roots of Modern English* (Boston: Little, Brown, 1961)

Pyles, T. *The Origins and Development of the English Language* [Fourth Edition] (NY: Harcourt, Brace, Jovanovich, 1993)

Robinson, O. *Old English and Its Closest Relatives* (Stanford, CA: Stanford University Press, 1993)

American English

Dillard, J.L. *All-American English* (NY: Random House, 1975)

Dillard, J.L. *American Talk* (NY: Random House, 1976)

Flexner, S.B. *I Hear America Talking* (NY: Simon & Schuster, 1976)

Mencken, H.L. *The American Language* (NY: Alfred A. Knopf, 1979)

V. OTHER USEFUL RESOURCES

A Dictionary of American Idioms (Woodbury, NY: Barron's Educational Series, Inc., 1995)

Bryson, B. *A Dictionary of Troublesome Words* (NY: Viking Penguin, 1988)

Carroll, D. *Dictionary of Foreign Terms in the English Language* (NY: Hawthorn Books, 1973)

Dixson, R. *Essential Idioms in English* (Englewood Cliffs, NJ: Pearson ESL, 1993)

Room, Adrian. (Ed.) *Brewer's Dictionary of Phrase and Fable* [Sixteenth Edition] (NY: HarperCollins, 1999)

Harrison, G. *Vocabulary Dynamics* (NY: Warner Books, 1992)

Hendrickson, R. *The Dictionary of Eponyms* (NY: Stein and Day, 1985)

Morris, W. and M. *Morris Dictionary of Word and Phrase Origins* [Second Edition] (NY: HarperCollins, 1988)

Paxson, W. *New American Dictionary of Confusing Words* (NY: NAL-Dutton, 1990)

Room, A. *Dictionary of Contrasting Pairs* (NY: Routledge Educational Series Inc., 1988)

Room, A. *The Penguin Dictionary of Confusibles* (NY: Penguin Books, 1989)

Shipley, J. *Dictionary of Word Origins* (Glenville, IL: Greenwood Press, 1988)

Smith, R. *Dictionary of English Word-Roots* (Totowa, NJ: Littlefield, Adams & Co., 1980)

Spears, R. *Slang and Euphemisms* (NY: NAL-Dutton, 1991)

Webster's Word Histories (Springfield, MA: Merriam-Webster, 1989)

Fourth Edition

Sadlier-Oxford

Building an Enriched Vocabulary

Senior Consultant

John Heath, Ph.D.
Santa Clara University

Sadlier-Oxford
A Division of William H. Sadlier, Inc.

Reviewers

The publisher wishes to thank for their comments and suggestions the following teachers, who read portions of the book prior to publication.

Eileen Bacha
English Department Chair
Cardinal Mooney High School
Youngstown, Ohio

Carole Tatem
English Teacher
Paul VI High School
Haddonfield, New Jersey

Elizabeth Bradstreet
English Teacher
Lower Richland High School
Hopkins, South Carolina

Contents

Learning Words

An Introduction for the Student

I. The Vocabulary of Vocabulary

Before you begin learning the words presented in this book, it might be useful to review what you know about the "vocabulary of vocabulary." Accordingly, a number of key concepts or technical terms relating to the study of words are discussed below. Some of these items—*synonyms*, for instance—will no doubt be familiar, but the discussion may help to bring their meaning and use into sharper focus. Others—*connotation*, for example—may be entirely new to you.

Denotation and Connotation.   It would be fair to say that words basically convey meaning in two distinct ways, for which the terms *denotation* and *connotation* have been devised.

The **denotation** of a word is its specific meaning as given in a dictionary. For example, the denotation of the adjective *scholarly* is "learned." Similarly, the denotation of the adjective *grasping* is "overly eager for material gain," and the denotation of the verb *travel* is "make a journey." The verb corresponding to *denotation* is *denote.*

Connotation, on the other hand, relates to the tone of a word—that is, the emotions or associations that the word arouses in the listener or reader. If a word—*scholarly*, for instance—arouses positive emotions, its tone or connotation is said to be favorable or positive. If it arouses negative emotions (the way *grasping* does), its tone or connotation is said to be negative, unfavorable, or pejorative (pronounced pə-jôr′-ə-tĭv). A word that does not arouse any strong feeling, either good or bad, is said to be neutral. The verb *travel* is such a word. The verb corresponding to *connotation* is *connote.*

Literal and Figurative Meaning.   It would also be fair to say that, generally speaking, words may be used on two quite distinct planes of meaning, which for convenience can be termed *literal* and *figurative* (or *metaphorical*).

When a word is being used in a **literal** sense, it is being employed in its strict or primary dictionary meaning in a situation (or context) that makes sense from a purely logical point of view. For example, if someone says that there are logs floating in the river, he or she is using the verb *float* literally because logs can actually float in water.

If, however, the person says that a famous actress "floated" into the room, he or she is using *float* in a nonliteral way and in a context that does not make sense from a purely logical point of

1

view. People can't really float into a room except by artificial means. In other words, the person has applied the verb *float* to an unusual context in order to create a vivid and forceful image of the grace and elegance with which the actress *walked* into the room. Notice that now *float* no longer means "be buoyed up by" but, rather, something closer to "move gracefully or as if on air." We call this extended or nonliteral application of a word a **figurative** or **metaphorical** usage.

Another example may help clarify this distinction. If you read an old tale about a knight who slew a fire-breathing dragon, the word *fire-breathing* in this context is being used quite literally. Dragons were indeed believed to breathe real fire. If, however, your best friend says that her father rushed into the room "breathing fire," the expression *breathing fire* is being used figuratively or metaphorically in order to convey a vivid picture of the man's state of mind. In other words, your friend is simply saying that her father was very angry or upset, but she is saying it more colorfully and dramatically than the words "in a very angry/upset frame of mind" could possibly convey. It is this added dimension that makes the figurative use of language so striking and appealing.

One final note: Though all words, of course, have literal meanings and can be used literally, only a fraction of the vocabulary can normally be applied figuratively. Such words are often referred to as *resonant*. One must be careful, therefore, not to try to use nonresonant words in a figurative way.

Parts of Speech.   Lexicographers (dictionary writers) and grammarians classify the words and other expressions that make up our language as different parts of speech, depending upon the function or functions they perform. Knowing what these classifications are and what they signify helps a person use a word correctly. For that reason, it might be well at this point to review some of the more common classifications that appear in this book.

A **noun** is a word or phrase that names a person, place, thing, or idea. Examples include *astronaut, library, trowel,* and *justice.* Nouns are usually divided into *common nouns* (e.g., *girl, day*) and *proper nouns* (e.g., *Jane, Wednesday*). All the nouns on the Basic Word List in this book (see pages 21–25) are common nouns.

An **adjective** is a word that is used to describe a noun (or pronoun). It changes (or modifies) the meaning of the word to which it refers by answering such questions as: How many? Which one? What kind? Examples include *yellow, old, first,* and *many.* As with nouns, adjectives are divided into *common adjectives* (e.g., *tall, earliest*) and *proper adjectives* (e.g., *Spanish, Elizabethan*). All the adjectives on the Basic Word List in this book (see pages 21–25) are common adjectives.

A **verb** is a word that expresses some kind of action or indicates some state of being. Examples include *run, think, enjoy, remain,* and *be.* Verbs are further subdivided into those that can take an object (*transitive* verbs) and those that cannot (*intransitive* verbs). *Shoot* is an example of a transitive verb; *sleep,* an illustration of one that is intransitive.

An **adverb** is a word that modifies a verb, an adjective, or another adverb. Adverbs usually answer such questions as: Where? When? How? How much? How long? Examples include *there, sometimes, badly, forever,* and *almost.*

One final note: Some words perform a number of different functions and are, therefore, classified as more than one part of speech. For example, *hope* is both a noun and a verb, *exact* is both a verb and an adjective, and *corporal* is both a noun and an adjective.

Synonyms and Antonyms. Over the centuries English has absorbed a great many words that mean more or less the same thing as other words in the language. Two words that are similar in meaning are called **synonyms**. For example, *fragile* and *delicate* are more or less synonyms. So are *thief* and *robber.* The adjective form of *synonym* is *synonymous.*

Of course, no two words in English ever really convey exactly the same meaning, have exactly the same tone or connotation, or apply to exactly the same situations. They may be very close to one another, but they are rarely identical twins. That is because usage over a long period of time has shaped and molded a special character for most words, and it is this character that makes a word unique. For example, *hate* and *detest* mean much the same thing except that *detest* conveys a stronger or more intense feeling of loathing than *hate* does. Accordingly, a person who says that he or she "detests" spinach is registering a stronger dislike of the vegetable than is the person who merely says that he or she "hates" it. Usually a dictionary provides much useful information about such fine distinctions of meaning and usage, but it cannot cover everything. For that reason, the student must often learn such subtleties by observation—that is, by noticing how and when other people use a given word, both in speaking and in writing.

Just as some words mean more or less the same thing, others indicate opposites. A word that means the opposite of another word is called its **antonym**. For example, the verbs *relish* and *detest* are antonyms. So are the adjectives *wet* and *dry.* The adjective form of *antonym* is *antonymous.*

Frequently, the term *antonym* is used not so much for the opposite of a given word as for its *counterpart.* For example, *doctor* doesn't really have an opposite, but it does have *counterparts—nurse* and *patient.* Similarly, *actor* doesn't have an opposite, but it does have a counterpart—*actress.* These are the items that people mean when they speak of the antonym of *doctor* or the antonym of *actor,* and the student should bear this in mind when dealing with antonym questions on various kinds of standardized tests.

3

The Parts of a Word. As you probably already know, words are made up of various parts or elements, for each of which a general name has been devised. The most important of these are:

prefix—a syllable or syllables placed at the beginning of a word. Examples include *in* (as in *inspect*), *pre* (as in *predict*), and *post* (as in *postpone*).

root or **base**—the main part of a word to which prefixes and suffixes (see below) are attached. Examples include *spect* (as in *inspector*), *dict* (as in *prediction*), and *pone* (as in *postponement*).

suffix—a syllable or syllables placed at the end of a word. Examples include *or* (as in *inspector*), *ion* (as in *prediction*), and *ment* (as in *postponement*).

Exercise

The following questions are designed to help you apply your knowledge of the vocabulary of vocabulary to real situations.

1. With or without the aid of a dictionary, supply the *denotation* of each of the following adjectives. Then indicate whether its *connotation* is favorable, unfavorable, or neutral. (There are two examples of each.)

   a. valiant   c. sudden   e. enchanting
   b. malevolent   d. puritanical   f. parallel

2. Indicate whether the connotation of the *italicized* word in each of the following sentences is *positive, negative (pejorative),* or *neutral.* (There is one example of each.)

   a. Though his answers are technically correct, they are invariably routine and *mechanical.* negative (pejorative)

   b. We are looking for students with outstanding *scholastic* records. neutral

   c. The candidate's *rugged* honesty made a strong appeal to the voters. positive

3. Indicate whether the *italicized* word in each of the following sentences is being used in a *literal* or a *figurative* way. (There are two examples of each.)

   a. Dawn *tiptoed* silently across the meadow and drummed her rosy fingers on my windowpane. figurative

   b. I *danced* with the most beautiful girl in the class last night. literal

   c. Stella *tiptoed* across the room so as not to disturb her sleeping brother. literal

   d. All kinds of delightful images *dance* across the pages of that wonderful novel. figurative

4. In each of the following groups, select the *synonym* of the lettered word. Consult a dictionary, if necessary.

   a. petty
      unusual   slight   foreign   dry   visible

   b. neat
      sloppy   strong   tidy   foolish   loud

   c. rebellion
      failure   defeat   uprising   change   courtesy

   d. conceal
      burn   show   plunge   answer   hide

   e. quarrel
      doubt   work   order   excite   argue

5. In each of the following groups, select the *antonym* of the lettered word. Consult a dictionary, if necessary.

   a. cheerful
      noisy   soft   sad   pleasant   dangerous

   b. graceful
      awkward   polite   colorful   anxious   hard

   c. fix
      disturb   please   enjoy   reply   break

   d. bravery
      intelligence   cowardice   wealth   beauty   strength

   e. amateur
      beginner   pupil   farmer   professional   volunteer

6. With or without the aid of a dictionary, divide each of the following words into its component parts. Some of the words may lack one or more of these parts.

	Prefix	*Root*	*Suffix*
a. reporter	re	port	er
b. interrupt	inter	rupt	—
c. confusion	con	fus	ion
d. description	de	script	ion
e. mindful	—	mind	ful

II. The Tools of Vocabulary Building

The Dictionary.   The dictionary is the most important reference book and guide for the student who wishes to increase his or her vocabulary and acquire the ability to use words accurately and effectively. An entry in a good dictionary provides a wide range of information about the word being considered. Though the treatment is usually concise, the information is reliable. For that reason, you should regard the dictionary as your bible of the English language and its vocabulary.

Of course, most dictionaries come in two basic versions: a large *unabridged* edition designed for scholarly use and a smaller *compact* edition designed to meet everyday needs. The difference between the two lies not so much in the fact that words have been left out of the smaller book but, rather, in the fact that the entries are much briefer and more succinct in the compact edition.

Thus, a typical entry in an unabridged dictionary provides the reader with the following information:

- the spelling and syllabication of the word
- its pronunciation
- an indication of the part of speech of the word
- information regarding inflectional endings
- the etymology or origin of the word
- its definition or definitions, both past and present
- illustrative phrases utilizing the word
- idiomatic expressions involving the word (when applicable)
- special or technical uses of the word
- related or derivative forms of the word
- a selection of synonyms and antonyms, often with explanatory notes clarifying subtle distinctions of meaning, tone, or usage

Study the following example of a typical entry from an unabridged dictionary. It is taken from the Unabridged Edition of *The Random House Dictionary of the English Language* (New York: Random House, 1967). Try to determine where each of the items listed above appears in the entry.

> **a·bate** (ə-bāt'), *v.,* **a·bat·ed, a·bat·ing.** —*v.t.* **1.** to reduce in amount, degree, intensity, worth, etc.; lessen; diminish: *to abate a tax; to abate one's enthusiasm.* **2.** *Law.* **a.** to put an end to or suppress (a nuisance). **b.** to suspend or extinguish (an action). **c.** to annul (a writ). **3.** to deduct or subtract: *to abate part of the cost.* **4.** to omit: *to abate all mention of names.* **5.** to remove, as in stone carving, or hammer down, as in metalwork, (a portion of a surface) in order to produce a figure or pattern in low relief. —*v.i.* **6.** to decrease or diminish in intensity, violence, amount, worth, etc.: *The storm has abated. The pain in his shoulder finally abated.* [late ME ⟨ MF *abat(re),* equiv. to *a-* A-⁵ + *batre* ⟨ LL *batere* for L *batuere* to beat] —**a·bat'·a·ble,** *adj.* —**a·bat' er;** *Law.* **a·ba'tor,** *n.*
> —**Syn. 6.** subside. —**Ant. 1, 6,** increase, intensify.

Here is the way a compact dictionary treats the same word. The entry is taken from the College Edition of *The American Heritage Dictionary* (Boston: Houghton Mifflin Company, 1982). Which of the items listed above appear in both the unabridged and the compact dictionaries? Which appear only in the unabridged dictionary?

> **a·bate** (ə-bāt') *v.* **a·bat·ed, a·bat·ing, a·bates.** —*tr.* **1.** To reduce in amount, degree, or intensity; lessen. **2.** To deduct from an amount; subtract. **3.** *Law.* **a.** To put an end to. **b.** To make void. —*intr.* **1.** To subside. **2.** *Law.* To become void. [ME *abaten* ⟨ OFr. *abattre,* to beat: *a-,* to ⟨(Lat. *ad-*) + *batre,* to beat ⟨ Lat. *battuere.*]

For the vast majority of the exercises in this vocabulary book, you will need to make use of a compact dictionary. Occasionally you will also need to consult an unabridged dictionary or another reference book, such as a thesaurus.

The Thesaurus. Do you own a thesaurus? No student should be without this useful reference book.

The word *thesaurus* is derived from the Greek *thesauros,* meaning "treasure" or "treasury." Although the word is sometimes used in the general sense of "dictionary" or "encyclopedia" —as a "thesaurus of quotations"—it more commonly denotes a special kind of wordbook. The words are presented (not defined) in groups of related-idea categories according to a distinctive logical pattern. An index tells the reader, by a system of reference numbers, where a certain word, together with its associative words, is to be found in the main part of the thesaurus.

Writers have found this kind of reference book to be a valuable memory prodder. And the word *writer,* as used here, means not only a professional author or journalist but also anyone who is trying to use English with force and precision and who needs help in finding the right word.

How to Use a Thesaurus. Before you can make effective use of the thesaurus, you will need to do the following things:

1. Read the Preface or Introduction. It discusses in detail the special principles on which the thesaurus is based.

2. Read the Synopsis of Categories, which will give you an idea of the order and general range of the various related categories.

3. Read the introductory section, "How to Use the Book," which tells the reader, among other things, how to find:

   a. the most fitting word for a given idea
   b. the correct word for something vaguely remembered in its associations
   c. words suggestive of new ideas on a given subject

4. Always *turn first* to the Index Guide, which lists alphabetically the words you are looking for in the book.

Exercise

The following activities have been designed to help you improve your ability to use a dictionary or thesaurus.

1. Using the unabridged dictionary entry for *abate* that is printed on page 6, answer the following questions.

   a. Define *abate.*
   b. Give one phrase that illustrates its meaning.
   c. Give the etymology of *abate.*
   d. Give three special meanings *abate* has when used as a legal term.
   e. Give one synonym and two antonyms for *abate.*
   f. Syllabicate *abate,* and place the major stress mark (') after the syllable that is accented when the word is pronounced.

2. Read the Preface (Introduction), Synopsis of Categories, and Index Guide in your thesaurus. Then answer the following questions.

   a. In what specific writing situations or problems can the thesaurus serve as a helpful reference book?

   b. In what respects is the thesaurus different from an ordinary dictionary?

   c. Name five different cleaning devices listed under "Cleanliness." Answers will vary.

   d. Give five synonyms suggested in the category under the word *corrective*. Answers will vary.

   e. From the sections captioned "Obedience" and "Disobedience," select three adjective synonyms for *revolt*, and three verb synonyms for *disobey*. Answers will vary.

   f. The thesaurus lists more than twenty forms of government. Define five such terms. Answers will vary.

III. The Development of Our Vocabulary

Since many of the exercises contained in this book relate to the origins or sources of the vocabulary of present-day English, it might be wise at this point to review briefly the development of the language. Doing this will help you make sense out of much of the isolated information scattered throughout the pages of this book. It may even give you a few new insights into the character and history of the language.

The Family Tree of English. English belongs to the Indo-European family of languages. **Indo-European** is thought to have developed 5000 or more years ago somewhere in central Europe or western Asia. Quite a few modern English words appear to have their origins in Indo-European. Examples include *wolf* and *snow*.

Eventually, the people who spoke this parent language or group of related languages split up and went off in different directions. From these separate groups of people, a number of related branches of Indo-European developed. These branches include Celtic (now chiefly represented by Welsh, Irish, and Scottish Gaelic), Hellenic (that is, Greek), Italic (Latin and its Romance offshoots—French, Italian, Spanish, Portuguese, etc.), and Germanic.

It is to the **Germanic** branch of Indo-European that English specifically belongs. Germanic, however, is divided into three large groups of related languages. These are North Germanic (that is, the Scandinavian languages except Finnish), East Germanic (which consists only of an extinct language called Gothic), and West Germanic (to which a number of languages, including English, belong).

The **West Germanic** group of languages is usually further subdivided into High and Low German. High German includes

Modern German and Yiddish. **Low German** (named for the relative lowness of the area in which it is spoken) consists of Frisian (spoken in parts of Holland), Dutch and Flemish (also spoken in the Low Countries), Plattdeutsch (spoken in northern Germany), and English. Note, however, that English and Frisian are sometimes grouped separately between High German and the other Low German languages.

Angles, Saxons, Jutes, and Old English. The history of the English language and its vocabulary can be said to start around A.D. 450. About then, a number of Germanic tribes (the Angles, the Saxons, the Jutes, and probably some Frisians) began to invade and conquer the island of Britain.[1] For more than a century, these peoples poured in from Denmark, north Germany, and the Low Countries. Eventually they occupied all of present-day England, a bit of Wales, and part of southern Scotland.

The newcomers brought with them a number of closely related West Germanic dialects, out of which **Old English** (sometimes called Anglo-Saxon) developed. Old English is the earliest form of English that can be documented. In use until perhaps 1150, Old English represents the basic Germanic foundation upon which Modern English has been built.

[1]Previously, Britain had been occupied by Celtic-speaking peoples (from ca. 900 B.C.). In A.D. 43, the Romans invaded the island and made it part of their empire. However, they withdrew in 410, before the first Germanic settlers arrived. Thus, the population that these settlers found in Britain was basically a mixture of romanized and unromanized Celts. From this population, however, the Germanic settlers picked up very little in the way of vocabulary, except for place-names (e.g., *Avon*).

Alfred the Great (849–899), the most famous Anglo-Saxon king of England, was an influential patron of the language and literature of the Old English period.

Many Old English words have survived into Modern English. For example, *man, wife, child, house, ship, sheep, wrath, mirth, strong, good, well, drink, fight, to, after, and, if, we, us,* and many other common words derive from Old English. Nonetheless, these survivors constitute only a fraction of the vocabulary of Modern English. That is because much of the Old English element has long since dropped out of the language in favor of words from other sources.

Christianity, Latin, and Greek.   In 597, the Church of Rome began to convert the Anglo-Saxon peoples of England to Christianity. This was one of the most important events in English history for the development of vocabulary. The adoption of Christianity paved the way for the introduction of a good many **Latin** words into English.[2] Most of these borrowings related, of course, to religion (e.g., *altar, mass, creed*). However, others referred to household items (*candle*), clothing (*cap*), food (*radish*), medicine (*fever*), and a host of other things. These words and others like them represent the beginning of Latin's influence on English. It would be hard to overemphasize this influence. Modern English probably owes more of its vocabulary, either directly or indirectly, to Latin than to any other language.

[2]While still on the Continent, the Germanic peoples of England had already picked up a few Latin words. For the most part, these relate to military, commercial, or culinary matters (e.g., *wall, street, pound, cheap, kitchen, cup, wine, cheese*), though other areas of life are also represented. Before the advent of Christianity, a few Latin words may also have come into Old English via Celtic (e.g., *port* and the place-name element *-c(h)ester* or *-caster*).

The Christian missionary St. Augustine of Canterbury lands in Kent in southeast England in 597.

In addition, these naturalized Latin words represent the first installment in a long series of borrowings from many languages including French and Greek. Over the centuries, such borrowings (called **loan words**) have greatly altered and enriched the vocabulary of English. Indeed, without them, English would not be what it is today.

With the coming of Christianity, a number of words that Latin had borrowed from **Greek** also entered Old English, usually in their Latin forms. These include *monk, deacon, psalm, oyster, chest,* and *school.* Earlier, when the Germanic peoples of England were still on the continent, they had borrowed a few other Greek expressions via Latin. These include *bishop, anchor, dish, copper, chalk,* and *pepper.*

Vikings and Old Norse. In 787, Viking bands from Denmark, Norway, and other areas of Scandinavia began to raid Anglo-Saxon territory. This was the start of what proved to be a large-scale, long-term invasion. By 878, much of northern and eastern England (to say nothing of Scotland) had been overrun. In 1014, the king of Denmark seized the English throne, and Danish kings ruled the country until 1042.

The upshot of all this turmoil was the permanent settlement of large numbers of Scandinavians (mostly Danes and Norwegians) in Britain. These newcomers spoke Old Norse dialects—that is, early forms of the modern Scandinavian languages. **Old Norse** (sometimes called Scandinavian) was Germanic. For that reason, it was fairly closely related to Old English. Culturally, the Anglo-Saxons and the Vikings were also similar. Thus, it was almost a foregone conclusion that, as the two peoples fused, large numbers of Old Norse words should begin to filter into English. Of course, much of this borrowing can't actually be documented until somewhat later, in what is called the Middle English period (see page 15).

Surprisingly, most of the Old Norse vocabulary that entered English referred to everyday things for which there were usually Old English words already. Every part of speech in the language was affected. For example, the following nouns all derive from Old Norse: *axle, birth, dirt, egg, fellow, gap, girth, leg, loan, outlaw, rift, score, slaughter, snare, thrift, window.* The same is true of the following verbs: *call, cast, crawl, droop, gape, gasp, glitter, kindle, lift, nag, ransack, scare, sprint, thrust.* The same is also true about these adverbs or adjectives: *akimbo, aloft, athwart, both, flat, ill, loose, low, muggy, odd, rotten, rugged, same, weak.* The same is true of the conjunction *though* and the pronouns *they, their, them.* Even something as basic to the language as the verb *to be* was affected, since *are* derives from Old Norse.

In some instances, the Old Norse word drove the corresponding Old English word out of the language. For example, *take* displaced *niman,* and *sky* superseded *wolcen.* In other cases, the Old English word survived but took on the meaning of its Old Norse counterpart. Examples include *dream, dwell,* and *bread,* which in

Old English meant "joy," "lead or go astray," and "fragment," respectively. In still other cases, both words remained in the language, but with somewhat different meanings or uses. Examples include *craft* and *skill*, *hide* and *skin*, *rear* and *raise*, and *shirt* and *skirt*. Even a few mixed forms (or **hybrids**) were created—for example, *screech* and *shriek*, which technically should be something like *shreech* and *scriek*.

Normans and Old French.   Directly across the English Channel from Britain lies the French province of Normandy. In the 9th and 10th centuries, Vikings (called *Normanni*, or "Northmen," in Latin) occupied the area. Subsequently, these Scandinavians converted to Christianity and adopted an early form of French as their official language.

In 1066, William, Duke of Normandy, defeated Harold, the last Anglo-Saxon king of England, at the Battle of Hastings. As a result, Duke William became the first Norman king of England. Norman monarchs ruled the country until 1154, when they were succeeded by other French-speaking kings.

The Norman conquest of England was probably the most important event in English history for the development of the language. For one thing, Norman French became the official language of the royal court and upper classes. This state of affairs lasted for about 200 years, during which time English was pushed well into the background. (Of course, English remained the language of the common people and middle classes throughout the period.)

The Battle of Hastings, 1066.

In addition, the use of an early form of French at the upper levels of society led to the introduction of many **Old French** words into English. This was just the beginning of the tremendous influence that French has exerted on the language. This influence has subsequently been reinforced by later borrowings from Modern French. French and Old Norse are, after Latin, the two most important sources for the vocabulary of Modern English.

Old French altered almost every aspect of the vocabulary, and more of the Old English element dropped out of the language. For example, Old French words relating to the following broad topics entered the language during the Middle Ages:

Topic	Borrowed Word
government	*realm, royal, govern, mayor*
social rank	*prince, duchess, baron, peasant*
land and property	*manor, demesne, estate, chattels*
law	*justice, suit, jury, pardon*
religion	*saint, mercy, charity, preach*
defense	*war, peace, battle, lieutenant*
wearing apparel	*costume, robe, cape, lace, jewel*
food	*beef, gravy, cream, peach, jelly, vinegar, spice, mince, roast*
household	*chair, couch, chamber*
art and literature	*beauty, paint, treatise*

Of course, a great many other common words also derive from Old French. Here are some examples:

nouns	*city, courtesy, virtue, grace, joy, marriage, people, point, reason*
adjectives	*able, brief, chaste, debonair, fine, gay, petty, puny, rich*
verbs	*chafe, embrace, enjoy, force, pay, reply, trace*

Even the wording of many common idiomatic expressions was influenced by the corresponding French phrase—for example, *by heart* and *in vain.*

Finally, a number of hybrids were created. These "mixed" forms usually fused an Old English (that is, Germanic) suffix onto a French (or Latin) root. Examples include *courtship, faintness, dukedom, artless, princely,* and *powerful.*

Learning, Latin, and Greek.   Old French is a Romance language derived from Latin. Thus, many of the words given above can be traced back beyond Old French to Latin. During the Middle Ages, Latin (in its medieval form) was the language of the university, the church, some types of law, and many official documents. So it shouldn't be surprising that between 1066 and 1485, many words entered English directly from Latin. Examples include *adjacent, genius, index, inferior, intellect, lucrative, limbo, minor, necessary, ornate, picture, prevent, stupor,* and *tract.* As these items indicate, many of the new Latin words were abstract or technical terms. Thus, they may have first been used by professionals and only later achieved a wider circulation.

More Greek words also came into English during the Middle Ages, usually through Latin or French. Examples include *tyrant, scepter, theology, schism,* and *heresy.* As with the new Latin words, many of these Greek borrowings were technical terms that educated people may have introduced.

The Crusades and Arabic. In 1095, the First Crusade to recover the Holy Land from the Muslims got under way. Subsequently, eight other crusades were launched. These expeditions brought Europe into contact with the Arabs (who held Palestine) and Arabic civilization. The Arabs also held much of Spain during the Middle Ages.

As a result of these contacts, **Arabic** words began to make their way into English. Most of these words relate to science and mathematics (e.g., *alchemy, alkali, elixir, zenith, algebra, cipher, zero*). Others refer to food (e.g., *orange, sherbet, spinach, syrup*), clothing (e.g., *sash*), rooms and furniture (e.g., *alcove, sofa, mattress*), and many other things (e.g., *admiral, tariff, salaam*). Not all of these words, of course, came into the language during the Middle Ages; some appeared later. Also, none of them entered English directly from Arabic; instead, they came through intermediary sources (*e.g.,* Spanish, French, Medieval Latin). Some of these words can be recognized by the presence of the Arabic definite article *al* ("the") at the beginning of the English form.

The launching of the First Crusade, 1095.

Trade and the Low German Languages. During the Middle Ages, England traded extensively with the Low Countries and north Germany, especially in wool. These commercial relations continued to be close until well into the 18th century.

As a result, a good many **Dutch, Flemish,** and other **Low German** words filtered into English, either during the Middle Ages or later. Some of these words relate to shipping (e.g., *yacht, schooner, sloop, cruise, skipper, mate, swab, deck, dock*), commerce (e.g., *freight, smuggle, roster, dollar*), and textiles (e.g., *nap, ravel, cambric*). Others refer to military matters (e.g., *furlough, tattoo, plunder, beleaguer*), painting (e.g., *easel, sketch, etching, stipple, landscape*), and a good many other things (e.g., *measles, pickle, plump, poppycock, rant, slurp, snoop, spook, sputter, squirt, tattle, wiseacre, wriggle*). The Dutch settlers of North America were also responsible for some new terms (e.g., *cookie, cruller, patroon, Yankee*). And, much later, *veldt, trek,* and *apartheid* were contributed by **Afrikaans,** the form of Dutch spoken in South Africa.

Synonyms and Middle English. By the end of the Middle Ages, the process of word acquisition had provided English with a rich and varied assortment of synonyms. Often there were three or more words for the same thing. Each of these words had entered the language from a different source and at a different time. Usually the elements involved were Germanic, French, and Latin (or Greek). Here are a few examples: *kingly—royal—regal; climb—mount—ascend;* and *ask—question—interrogate.*

The vocabulary developments since 1066 and some technical changes relating to sounds and grammar resulted in the creation of **Middle English.** Roughly in use from 1150 to 1500, Middle English is the earliest form of the language that is unmistakably English. Accordingly, a speaker of Modern English can read many

A sample of Middle English. A page from *The Vision of Piers Plowman*, probably by William Langland (ca. 1330–ca. 1400), one of the greatest works of Middle English literature.

Middle English texts, especially those written in the 1400s, without a great deal of difficulty. For example, college students frequently study the poems of Geoffrey Chaucer (died 1400) in the original language. To do this, they receive relatively little special training.

During the early years of its existence, Middle English was not the dominant language in England. Norman French held that position and kept it for about 200 years after 1066. Still, Middle English made steady advances during this period and by the mid-1300s was well on its way to becoming the dominant language of the country, a position it finally secured in the 1400s.

Neither Old nor Middle English was a single, monolithic language; each was a group of related dialects. For that reason, there was nothing in either period that could be considered standard English. Toward the end of the Middle Ages, however, London English had moved a long way in this direction, but a standard form of the language wasn't completely achieved until later.

Early Modern English, 1500–1660. The 16th and 17th centuries were an eventful period in the history of English. The invention of printing from movable type, the tremendous revival of interest in classical Greece and Rome that occurred during the Renaissance, the Protestant Reformation, and other developments helped to introduce the use of English into fields of learning where Latin had formerly reigned supreme and also did much to establish a more uniform spelling of the language. The great voyages of discovery and the creation of British colonies in North America and elsewhere spread the language beyond the confines of England and enriched it by introducing new words from all sorts of faraway places.

As a result of these developments, together with a number of technical changes relating to the sounds and grammar of the language, **Modern English** was born. Modern English, of course, is the form of the language that is used today throughout the English-speaking world. It is with this form of the language that this vocabulary book is concerned and in which it is written.

The creative genius that shaped events during the early modern period also affected the vocabulary of English. During the 16th and 17th centuries, thousands of new words entered the language. Most of them were from Latin (e.g., *create, dexterity, notorious, transition, vindicate*), but others came from Greek (e.g., *atmosphere, anachronism*), French (e.g., *essay*), Italian (e.g., *argosy, charlatan, gala*), and Spanish or Portuguese (e.g., *palisade, desperado, armada*). Purely English resources were also called on in the coining of new words—for example, *freshman.*

Some of the new words that entered the language at this time retained their original form (e.g., *climax, epitome*); others underwent some modification or simplification. Often this took the form of dropping a foreign ending—for example, *consult* from the Latin *consultare.* Sometimes a word that had already been borrowed was borrowed a second time with a slightly different form or meaning. Examples include *dish* and *disc.*

Since so many strange new words were entering English, the first dictionaries began to appear. These were usually very modest publications that confined themselves to the hard new words in the language. For example, *The Table Alphabeticall of Hard Words,* by Robert Cawdry, published in 1604, contained only about 3000 entries and did not deal with everyday words that even a child would understand. Also, most early dictionaries only defined the words they included and did not contain the other useful information that a modern dictionary provides.

Finally, it was during this period that **American English,** the particular brand of Modern English used in the United States, had its beginnings. While this was happening, a number of words from the languages used by the Native Americans began to filter into English. Examples include *hickory, moccasin, opossum, powwow, skunk, tomahawk, totem,* and *wigwam.*

The language of the early English settlers in America also absorbed a good many words from the languages used by other colonizing nations, notably Dutch (e.g., *cookie, waffle, boss, Yankee*), French (e.g., *chowder, prairie, buccaneer*), and Spanish (e.g., *banana, cockroach*). Words from the African languages used by the slaves who were brought to America from 1619 on also probably began to enter American English at this time, though most of these contributions (e.g., *voodoo, gumbo, cooter*) cannot be documented until much later. The foregoing examples and others like them reflect the English colonists' need for new words to describe what was unfamiliar to them.

The founding of Philadelphia by William Penn, 1681.

Developments Between 1660 and 1800. Between 1660 and 1800, the spirit of creativity that had marked the early modern period gave way to a desire for system, regularity, and conformity to a standard based upon reason and buttressed by authoritative example from the classical past. This led to efforts to standardize, refine, and fix the English language. Thus, for the first time grammar books laying down rules for the proper use of English (*e.g.*, William Loughton's *Practical Grammar of the English Language* [1734]), style manuals (*e.g.*, George Campbell's *Philosophy of Rhetoric* [1776]), and a dictionary in the modern sense of the word (Dr. Samuel Johnson's *A Dictionary of the English Language* [1755]) began to appear.

Despite somewhat misguided attempts to purify and control the language during the 18th century, the vocabulary of English continued to grow. Since France was at the height of her power as a cultural force, more French expressions came into the language. Examples include *ballet, champagne, coiffure, connoisseur,* and a host of other familiar words.

At the same time, Great Britain was building up a vast overseas empire in such places as North America, Australia, and India. This development not only led to an expansion of the use of English

A scene from Tchaikovsky's ballet *Swan Lake. Ballet* is one of the words that English has borrowed without change from French. French, of course, had originally borrowed the word from Italian.

18

throughout the world but also encouraged many exotic words to enter the language. For example, India contributed such items as *bungalow, cashmere, jungle, thug,* and *verandah*; the West Indies supplied *barbecue, hurricane,* and *tobacco*; and Australia provided *boomerang* and *wombat.* The influence of Great Britain's overseas territories continued through the 19th century, when some of the items listed above came into the language, and it is still felt today.

The period also saw significant developments in American English. All kinds of new expressions were being introduced to fill the needs of life in colonial America and later the United States. Examples include *bullfrog* (which appeared around 1705), *buckshot* (1775), *sidewalk* (1765), *cent* (coined by Thomas Jefferson around 1785), *harmonica* (invented by Benjamin Franklin about 1765), and a huge number of other familiar terms. Noah Webster's *American Spelling Book* appeared toward the end of this period, and his *American Dictionary of the English Language* somewhat later.

From 1800 to 2000.   The 19th and 20th centuries witnessed the rise of an industrialized society in both Europe and America. The various technological advances that accompanied this development contributed greatly to the enrichment of our vocabulary. Scarcely any phase of life or language was untouched. Not only were new words and phrases relating to technological progress invented (e.g., *automobile, telephone, television, computer*), but a good many old expressions took on new meanings (e.g., *park* a car, a radio *broadcast*).

The growth of science during the 19th and 20th centuries also had a tremendous impact on the vocabulary. Thousands of new technical or scientific terms entered the language (e.g., *stethoscope, carbohydrate, psychoanalysis, cyberspace*), and new concepts appeared on the scene (e.g., *relativity, evolution, automation*). Though much of this new scientific vocabulary was used only by specialists, a good part of it filtered into the everyday language, usually as the result of popularization by our greatly improved means of mass communication. Startling new scientific developments, such as the exploration of space, also channeled some of the vocabulary of science into the popular language (e.g., *countdown, astronaut*).

A new science devoted to the study of language appeared on the scene during the 19th century. It is called **linguistics** (or sometimes **philology**). The contributions of philologists greatly increased our knowledge of language and also furnished new and improved tools for its study—for example, the multivolume *New (Oxford) English Dictionary.* As a result, popular interest in language continued to grow.

New social, political, or economic philosophies (*e.g.,* communism) left their mark on our language, and the two great world wars of the 20th century also enriched it (e.g., *blitzkrieg, camou-flage, Iron Curtain*). The same is true of countless social, political, economic, and cultural developments in our country (e.g., *consumerism, environmentalist, integration*).

Finally, the tremendous influx of immigrants to our shores beginning in the late 19th and early 20th centuries also made our language richer. Certainly it would be hard to do without the contributions of these new Americans—for example, the yiddishisms listed on page 85 of this book.

Into the Future. English will certainly continue to grow in the 21st century. New developments, new problems, new needs, and new interests will require new terminology. Keep your eyes peeled for new expressions. It is a rewarding experience.

Exercise

The following questions will help you review what you have learned about the development of our vocabulary.

1. To which branch of the Indo-European family of languages does English belong? Germanic

2. Define each of the following terms relating to the development of English, and state when this phase of our language was in use.

   a. Old English   b. Middle English   c. Modern English

3. Give **one** example of a word or phrase that English has borrowed from each of the following foreign languages. Then define your example, and use it in a short illustrative sentence.

   a. Latin   c. Old Norse   e. Arabic
   b. Greek   d. Dutch   f. French

4. Explain how each of the following historical events contributed to the growth of the vocabulary of English.

   a. conversion to   c. Norman conquest of
      Christianity   England
   b. Viking invasions of   d. colonization of North
      England   America

5. Briefly explain the impact of each of the following on the growth of our vocabulary.

   a. industrialization   b. science

Basic Word List

Lesson 7

61. bleak	64. boisterous	68. brash
62. blight	65. bombastic	69. bravado
63. blithe	66. boorish	70. brusque
	67. boycott	

Lesson 8

71. bungle	74. cajole	78. cantankerous
72. bureaucracy	75. callous	79. captious
73. buttress	76. calumny	80. catholic
	77. candid	

Lesson 9

81. caustic	84. chagrin	88. circumspect
82. censor	85. charlatan	89. circumvent
83. censure	86. chronic	90. clandestine
	87. circuitous	

Lesson 10

91. coerce	94. collaborate	98. condone
92. cogent	95. compatible	99. confrontation
93. cohere	96. complacent	100. conjecture
	97. concise	

Lesson 11

101. connoisseur	106. corpulent	111. crucial
102. consensus	107. corroborate	112. culpable
103. construe	108. counsel	113. cursory
104. consummate	109. credibility	114. curtail
105. copious	110. criterion	115. cynical

Lesson 12

116. dapper	121. delineate	126. desultory
117. defect	122. delinquent	127. deviate
118. defer	123. delude	128. devoid
119. dejected	124. demure	129. devout
120. delete	125. denouement	130. dexterous

Lesson 13

131. dilapidated	136. discourse	141. divulge
132. dilatory	137. discriminate	142. docile
133. diligent	138. disparage	143. dormant
134. dire	139. disparity	144. drastic
135. discomfit	140. distraught	145. duplicity

Lesson 14

146. eclectic	151. elite	156. empathy
147. effete	152. emaciated	157. emulate
148. efficacious	153. emanate	158. enclave
149. effrontery	154. embellish	159. endemic
150. elicit	155. eminent	160. enigma

Lesson 15

161. entice	166. equitable	171. euphemism
162. entreat	167. erudite	172. exacerbate
163. envisage	168. esoteric	173. exalt
164. epithet	169. ethical	174. exemplary
165. equanimity	170. ethnic	175. exigency

Lesson 16

176. exodus	181. fabricate	186. fatuous
177. exotic	182. facetious	187. feasible
178. expedient	183. facsimile	188. feign
179. exploit	184. fallacy	189. felicitous
180. expound	185. fathom	190. fetish

Lesson 17

191. fiasco	196. flaunt	201. formidable
192. fickle	197. flout	202. fortuitous
193. filch	198. fluctuate	203. frugal
194. finesse	199. foible	204. fulsome
195. flagrant	200. forestall	205. futile

Lesson 18

206. gape	211. gratuitous	216. gruesome
207. garble	212. gregarious	217. gullible
208. gloat	213. grimace	218. haggard
209. goad	214. grope	219. harangue
210. graphic	215. grueling	220. harbinger

Lesson 19

221. haughty	226. immunity	231. implacable
222. heinous	227. immutable	232. implicit
223. ignominy	228. impasse	233. impugn
224. illicit	229. impediment	234. incarcerate
225. immaculate	230. impervious	235. incense

Lesson 20

236. inception	241. instigate	246. irony
237. indigent	242. insuperable	247. jeopardize
238. ingenious	243. intervene	248. jettison
239. inherent	244. intrepid	249. judicious
240. innovation	245. inveigh	250. justify

Lesson 21

251. kudos	256. litigation	261. malapropism
252. lackadaisical	257. lucid	262. malice
253. legacy	258. lucrative	263. mammoth
254. liability	259. lurk	264. mandatory
255. libel	260. lush	265. medium

Lesson 22

266. mercenary	271. myriad	276. nomadic
267. moot	272. narcissistic	277. nominal
268. morass	273. nebulous	278. nostalgia
269. motley	274. negligible	279. novice
270. mundane	275. nepotism	280. nuance

Lesson 23

281. obscene	286. ominous	291. paradox
282. obsequious	287. opportune	292. paraphrase
283. obsession	288. ostensible	293. parochial
284. obsolete	289. ostracize	294. parody
285. officious	290. pandemonium	295. pensive

Lesson 24

296. peremptory	301. phobia	306. precarious
297. perjure	302. plagiarism	307. precocious
298. permeate	303. plaintive	308. predatory
299. pernicious	304. plethora	309. prelude
300. persevere	305. poignant	310. premise

Lesson 25

311. prerogative	316. promulgate	321. pseudonym
312. probity	317. propensity	322. purge
313. procrastinate	318. propitiate	323. pusillanimous
314. prodigious	319. protracted	324. quell
315. proliferate	320. prowess	325. quixotic

Lesson 26

326. raze	331. redundant	336. repercussion
327. recalcitrant	332. relent	337. replenish
328. recant	333. reminiscence	338. reprisal
329. reciprocate	334. remorse	339. rescind
330. recrimination	335. renegade	340. resilient

Lesson 27

341. reticent	346. ritual	351. sacrilegious
342. retribution	347. rudiment	352. salient
343. retroactive	348. ruminate	353. sanctimonious
344. reverberate	349. ruse	354. sanguine
345. revere	350. sabotage	355. satellite

Lesson 28

356. scapegoat	361. solace	366. stipulate
357. schism	362. sordid	367. strategy
358. scrutinize	363. stamina	368. strident
359. secular	364. stereotype	369. surveillance
360. senile	365. stigmatize	370. syndrome

Lesson 29

371. tacit	376. thwart	381. ubiquitous
372. taciturn	377. tranquil	382. urbane
373. tangible	378. traumatic	383. usurp
374. tenable	379. trenchant	384. vagary
375. tentative	380. turbulent	385. venal

Lesson 30

386. veneer	391. vie	396. wrath
387. venerable	392. vindictive	397. yoke
388. veracity	393. vitiate	398. zany
389. versatile	394. volatile	399. zeal
390. veto	395. wane	400. zenith

Pronunciation Key

The authorities used for the pronunciation of words in the Basic Word List include the *Random House Dictionary*, *Webster's Third New International Dictionary*, and the *American Heritage Dictionary*. In the relatively few cases where these authorities are not in agreement, the editors have chosen the pronunciation that appears to be representative of the actual preference of most educated people in the American speech community. In some instances, several equally acceptable pronunciations are given.

Diacritical Marks. The following diacritical marks are used in this book to indicate the pronunciation of all the vowel sounds and one consonant in the words of the Basic Word List:

ā as in f*a*ce	ō as in c*o*de
ă as in m*a*t	ŏ as in c*o*d
ä as in f*a*ther	ô as in f*o*r
â as in c*a*re	o͞o as in sp*oo*n
	o͝o as in l*oo*k
ē as in f*e*ver	ou as in *ou*t or c*ow*
ĕ as in s*e*nd	
ē̃ as in p*e*rfect	yo͞o as in p*u*re
ə as in *a*lone	ŭ as in *u*p
	û as in l*u*rk
ī as in b*i*te	
ĭ as in b*i*ll	th as in clo*the*
î as in p*ier*	th as in clo*th*

The Schwa. In a great many English words, the vowel sounds of unstressed syllables are faint or indistinct. These neutral vowel sounds, for all practical purposes, are identical, regardless of the letter that may be used to represent them. In most modern dictionaries, the pronunciation of such vowel sounds is indicated by the symbol ə (an inverted *e*). This is designated by the term *schwa*—pronounced *shwa* or *shva*.

The schwa should be used to indicate the pronunciation of the unstressed vowel sound (*italicized*) in each of the following words: form*a*l, partn*e*r, vis*i*ble, hum*o*r, circ*u*s, paral*y*sis. A schwa is usually pronounced as the *a* in *a*lone or the *u* in *u*p.

Lesson 1

1. abdicate — 10. addiction[1]

---

1. **ab·di·cate** *verb* ăb'-dĭ-kāt
[*ab* (Latin), "away" + *dicare, dicatus* (Latin), "proclaim"]

Definition: To give up formally, as an office, duty, power, or claim.

The first Romanov czar of Russia was crowned in 1613; the last was forced to **abdicate** in 1917.

However heavy the burden may be, you cannot **abdicate** your responsibilities as the head of this household.

Related Form: (*noun*) abdication

Synonyms: (*verbs*) resign, renounce, relinquish, divest oneself of; (*nouns*) resignation, renunciation, relinquishment

Antonyms: (*verbs*) retain, hold on to

Related Phrases: renounce a claim or title, relinquish (or waive) a right, resign from a job, divest oneself of power

Usage Note:
Abdicate is usually used of a *crowned* head of state; *resign* is used of an *elected* official. Thus, Edward VIII *abdicated*, but Richard Nixon *resigned*.

2. **a·bet** *verb* ə-bĕt'
[*a*, from *ad* (Latin), "to" + *beter* (Germanic), "bait or incite"]

Definition: To encourage or assist, especially in wrongdoing.

In Shakespeare's *Richard III* Buckingham knowingly **abets** Gloucester's plans to seize the throne.

At that memorable concert the great singer's efforts were ably **abetted** by her accompanist.

Phrase: to aid and abet

Synonyms: (*verbs*) egg on; promote, further, advance, help, aid

Antonyms: (*verbs*) dissuade, discourage, deter, restrain, curb, inhibit, hinder, block, frustrate, thwart (Word 376)

Related Phrases: with the connivance of, in league with

---

[1]For a full listing of the basic words in each lesson, see the Basic Word List, pages 21–25.

3. **ab-hor**   *verb*   ăb-hôr′

[*ab* (Latin), "from; at" + *horrere* (Latin), "shiver, shudder"]

Definition: To regard with horror and loathing; to hate intensely.

Religious prejudice is something decent people **abhor**.

Related Forms: (*adjective*) abhorrent; (*noun*) abhorrence

Usage Note:

Because *abhor* implies strong *moral* condemnation, it should properly be reserved for attitudes or actions that really do offend a person's sense of right and wrong (*e.g.*, racism, child abuse). This, of course, is not to say that the word *cannot* be applied to other things. On the contrary, it is frequently used of trifling matters that normally would not be thought to grate on one's *moral* sensibilities—for example, spinach or TV game shows.

Synonyms: (*verbs*) loathe, despise, detest, abominate; (*noun*) aversion

Antonyms: (*verbs*) like, fancy, relish, love, cherish, delight in, be fond of, dote on

Related Phrases: look askance at, make a wry face at, turn up one's nose at, turn thumbs down at

Usage Note:

Do not confuse the verb *loathe*, meaning "dislike intensely," and the adjective *loath*, meaning "reluctant, disinclined." Note the following pair of sentences:

The human vice I *loathe* most deeply is insincerity.

I am *loath* to sign your petition.

4. **ab-ject**   *adjective*   ăb′-jĕkt   *or*   ăb-jĕkt′

[*ab* (Latin), "down; from" + *jacere, jactus* (Latin), "throw"]

Definition:

a.   Wretched, miserable; degrading, humiliating.

Many people around the world live in such **abject** poverty that they cannot afford even the most essential items of food and clothing.

b.   Mean-spirited, base; despicable, contemptible.

Only an **abject** coward would stand idly by as a defenseless person was mugged.

c.   Complete and unrelieved.

At the slightest sound of thunder, my dog dives under the bed in a state of **abject** terror.

Phrases: an abject flatterer, an abject liar, an abject imitator, abject surrender, abject apologies

Synonyms: (*adjectives*) disheartening, debasing, hopeless, helpless; vile, shameless, ignoble, craven; utter, sheer, downright, thoroughgoing

5. **ab·solve**   *verb*   ăb-sŏlv'

[*ab* (Latin), "from" + *solvere* (Latin), "loosen; release"]

Definition: To clear of guilt or blame.

"The evidence I will present," the lawyer told the jury, "clearly **absolves** my client of any complicity in the crime."

The most effective way we can **absolve** our society of the charges of racism and prejudice is to remedy the injustices of the past.

Related Form: (*noun*) absolution

Usage Note:

In a religious sense, *absolve* and *absolution* refer to granting a pardon, especially for a sin.

Synonyms: (*verbs*) acquit, exonerate, exculpate, vindicate; (*nouns*) acquittal, exoneration, vindication

Antonyms: (*verbs*) incriminate, inculpate; indict, impeach; convict, condemn; (*nouns*) indictment; conviction, condemnation

6. **ab·stain**   *verb*   ăb-stān'

[*abs*, a form of *ab* (Latin), "from" + *tenere* (Latin), "hold; keep"]

Definition: To refrain completely and voluntarily.

Only ten members of the Security Council voted on the resolution; the others **abstained**.

If you want to lose some weight, you'll have to **abstain** from eating those rich desserts you love so much.

Related Forms: (*nouns*) abstinence, abstention; (*adjective*) abstinent

Usage Note:

Abstain and *abstinence* are often used in reference to strong drink, with the meaning "refrain completely from drinking." A common synonym for *abstinence* in this sense is *temperance*. Persons who never drink intoxicating beverages are sometimes referred to as *teetotalers*.

Synonyms: (*verbs*) forgo, forbear, avoid, shun, eschew; (*nouns*) self-restraint, self-denial, forbearance, abstemiousness; (*adjectives*) abstemious, forbearing, temperate, sparing, moderate; ascetic

Antonyms: (*verbs*) indulge (in), partake (of); (*noun*) indulgence; (*adjectives*) self-indulgent, intemperate, immoderate

Usage Notes:

a.   *Abstemious, forbearing, temperate,* and *sparing* all indicate moderation in indulging one's appetites. *Abstinent,* on the other hand, indicates a total avoidance of the thing in question.

b.   Be careful not to confuse the verb *forbear,* meaning "to restrain oneself," with the noun *forebear,* meaning "ancestor." The noun, which is usually plural, has a slightly different pronunciation, with the accent on the *first* syllable (fôr'-bâr).

7. ac-a-dem-ic   *adjective*   ăk-ə-dĕm'-ĭk

[From *Akademia*, the name of the ancient Greek philosopher Plato's school outside Athens. It was located in a grove or park dedicated to the hero Akademos.]

Definition:
- a. Pertaining to a college or other institution of learning; scholarly.

  The role of a scholar in modern society is a subject of abiding concern in **academic** circles everywhere.
- b. Theoretical rather than practical; unrealistic.

  What we need to do is develop a solid plan of action, not engage in **academic** debates over purely theoretical questions.

Related Forms: (*nouns*) academy, academician; (*adverb*) academically

Phrases: academic freedom, the halls of academe; an academic question

Synonyms: (*adjectives*) scholastic; speculative

An academic procession during the graduation exercises at an American university.

From the Halls of Academe

Academy applies to institutions of higher learning, secondary schools, or any place where special subjects, arts, and skills are taught (*e.g.*, military academies, riding academies). The word is also used to refer to societies of learned individuals who have united to advance learning, literature, the arts, and the sciences (*e.g.*, the National Academy of Sciences, the Academy of Motion Picture Arts and Sciences).

The phrase *academic freedom* refers to the freedom of a teacher or student to discuss or express his or her views on political, social, or economic issues without interference from public or school officials.

An *academician* is a member of a learned society.

An *academic question* is one that is purely theoretical and has little or no bearing on practical problems or real situations.

8. **ac·cede**   *verb*   ăk-sēd′

[*ad* (Latin), "to" + *cedere* (Latin), "go; yield"]

Definition:
   a.   To yield to; to agree to.
        It took no little persuasion to get my parents to **accede** to my plan
        for a trip to California on my own.
   b.   To enter upon an office or dignity.
        Queen Elizabeth II **acceded** to the throne of Great Britain upon
        the death of her father, George VI, in 1952.

Related Forms: (*nouns*) access, accession, accessory; (*adjective*) accessible

Synonyms: (*verbs*) agree, assent, consent, concur, acquiesce, comply

Antonyms: (*verbs*) dissent, demur, balk at

9. **ac·cli·mate**   *verb*   ə-klī′-mĭt   *or*   ăk′-lə-māt

[*acclimater* (French), "get used to"]

Definition: To get used to (usually an environment or situation).

Coming from the Pacific Northwest, we found it difficult to **acclimate**
ourselves to the heat and humidity of a New York summer.

Related Forms: (*verb*) acclimatize; (*nouns*) acclimation, acclimatization

Synonyms: (*verbs*) adjust, adapt, orient, orientate, familiarize, accustom,
habituate; (*noun*) orientation

10. **ad·dic·tion**   *noun*   ă-dĭk′-shən

[*addictus* (Latin), "given over to"; from *ad* (Latin), "to" + *dicere, dictus* (Latin),"say"]

Definition: A habit-forming practice or pursuit, usually one that is bad
   for a person's health or morally objectionable; habitual use of, or devotion to, something.

   Cigarette smoking is an **addiction** that may prove difficult to overcome.

   The speaker at last Thursday's assembly discussed a number of problems relating to young people, including drug **addiction**.

Related Forms: (*noun*) an addict; (*adjectives*) addictive, addicted to

Usage Note:
Addiction and *addicted to* are much used today in connection with
drugs, but neither expression is limited to that area alone. One may, for
example, be addicted to gambling, television, or coffee. In addition, both
terms may be employed semihumorously, as in "addicted to detective
stories" or "an addiction to chocolate marshmallow sundaes."

Using the Words

Exercise I
1. ad-dic'-tion
2. ab'-ject, ab-ject'
3. ac-a-dem'-ic
4. ac-cli'-mate, ac'-cli-mate
5. ac-cede'
6. ab-solve'

Exercise I. Syllabication and Pronunciation

Syllabicate the following words correctly, and place the major stress mark (') after the syllable that is accented when the word is pronounced. Two answers are correct in some instances.

Example: a-bet'

1. addiction
2. abject
3. academic
4. acclimate
5. accede
6. absolve

Exercise II. Words Out of Context

In each of the following groups, select the item that best expresses the meaning of the numbered word at the left.

1. abstain   a. transfer   b. refrain   c. indulge
   d. vote

2. abhor   a. relish   b. release   c. frustrate
   d. detest

3. abet   a. encourage   b. initiate   c. deplore
   d. hamper

4. accede   a. offer   b. renew   c. demur
   d. yield

5. abject   a. proud   b. temperate   c. wretched
   d. scholarly

Exercise III. Completing Sentences

Complete each of the following sentences by selecting the most appropriate word from the group of words given below. Make whatever adjustments are necessary to fit the words into the sentences properly.

absolve   academic   acclimate

abject   addiction   abdicate

1. I chose an _academic_ career rather than business because I felt that I was better suited to the life of a teacher and scholar.

2. Convinced by the evidence presented by the defense, the jury _absolved_ the defendant of all wrongdoing.

3. Long accustomed to their own traditional way of life, the refugees found it difficult to _acclimate_ themselves to a new language and strange customs.

4. Many a crime is committed by someone who has developed an <u>addiction</u> to drugs and must have large sums of money to support this habit.

5. "I'd rather resign from my job," Professor Harris declared, "than <u>abdicate</u> my right to speak out publicly on such an important social problem."

Exercise IV.   Synonyms and Antonyms

Classify each of the following pairs of words as **S** for **synonyms** or **A** for **antonyms**.

A 1.   absolve—convict
S 2.   familiarize—acclimate
A 3.   relinquish—retain

S 4.   accede—consent
S 5.   abet—encourage
A 6.   relish—abhor

Exercise V.   Word Roundup

1. What is the difference between an *abstemious* person and a person who is *abstinent?* Complete each of the following with one of these words.

   a.   Henry takes a drink once in a long while. He is <u>abstemious</u>.
   b.   Henry never touches liquor. He is <u>abstinent</u> .

2. Define each of the following phrases. Consult a dictionary or other reference book if necessary.

   a. academic robes
   b. a riding academy

   c. academic freedom
   d. an academic question

3. Explain the difference in meaning between the terms in each of the following word pairs.

   a. forbear—forebear
   b. loathe—loath

Exercise VI.   Framing Sentences

A.   Use each of the following words in a short illustrative sentence.

1. abet
2. abject

3. accede
4. addiction

B.   Give a **noun** form of each of the following words, and use it in a short illustrative sentence.

1. abdicate abdication
2. abhor abhorrence
3. absolve absolution
4. abstain abstinence, abstention
5. academic academy, academician
6. acclimate acclimation, acclimatization

Dissecting the Words

At this point in half the lessons in this book, there is a section devoted to etymology. **Etymology** is the study of where words come from and how they are formed or change. Accordingly, each of these sections focuses attention on some of the prefixes, roots, and suffixes that make up the bulk of the words on the Basic Word List. The reason for studying these word elements is simple: They form the backbone of a substantial proportion of the English words in current use. For that reason, one effective way to expand your word power is to learn the meanings of such word elements and to use them as "keys" to a wider understanding of new words that crop up in your reading and school studies.

Prefix

The Latin prefix **ab**, **abs**, meaning "away from, off," is found in numerous English words. A few of them, including *abdicate* and *abject*, appeared in this lesson. Here are some more:

abduct (literally, "to lead away")—to take away by force

abscond—to depart secretly

abrupt—(literally, "broken off")—sudden or hasty

abstract—to draw from. The noun *abstract* means "a brief summary or a shorter form of the original."

Other English words containing this prefix include *abrasion*, *absent*, *abrogate*, and *absurd*.

Sir James A. Murray (1837–1915), the editor of the multivolume *New (Oxford) English Dictionary*, probably the most authoritative and certainly the most complete English dictionary in existence.

1. **Ced** is a Latin root meaning "go" or "yield." It provides the core meaning of many English words, including *accede*, studied in this lesson. (Note that this root appears as **ceed** in some English words.) Here are some other words from the same root:

concede—to grant or admit. Noun: *concession*

secede—to break away from; to withdraw from membership in. Noun: *secession*

exceed—to go beyond what is necessary or proper. Noun: *excess*; adjective: *excessive;* adverbs: *exceedingly, excessively*

recede—to go back, to withdraw. Noun: *recession*

proceed—to go forward. Noun: *procession*

antecedent—going before. A person's *antecedents* are his ancestors or forerunners.

procedure—the regular, definite order by which something is done.

   Other words from this root are *intercede, precedent, cession.*

2. The root **dic, dict,** which is found in the Latin verb *dicere,* "to say," and in the related verbs *dicare,* "to indicate, consecrate, devote, dedicate," and *dictare,* "to declare; to order," is the basis of the words *abdicate* and *addiction,* studied in this lesson. Note the following English words also formed from this root:

contradict (literally, "to speak against")—to oppose, to deny

valedictory (literally, "saying *be well*")—farewell

indict (literally, "to declare against")—to charge with guilt

interdict (literally, "to say between")—to prohibit

dictum (literally, "a thing said")—an authoritative statement

   Other English words containing this root include *edict, dedicate, benediction, predict, malediction* (a curse), *predicament, indicate, dictionary,* and *dictator.*

Exercise

1. Select the word that does not contain the prefix *ab.*

    a. abhor   b. abscond   c. abide   d. abject

2. Give **three** English words that are derived from the same root as *accede.* Use each in a short illustrative sentence.

3. Explain the origin of each of the following words: *indict, dictum, contradict, benediction.*

4. Explain the meaning of each of the following phrases, with particular reference to the etymology of the word in *italics*. Consult a dictionary or other reference book if necessary.

    a. the class *valedictorian*   c. *abstract* art
    b. a *receding* hairline   d. the *antecedent* of a pronoun

Enriching the Lesson

Exercise I.   It's the Law!

This lesson includes a number of legal terms, such as *absolve* and *accessory*. The following exercise may help you widen your knowledge of the language of the law. Consult a dictionary or other reference book for the meanings of the words indicated; then do the exercises.

A. Match the legal term in Column A with the phrase that defines it in Column B.

	Column A	*Column B*
c	1. indictment	a. a law passed by a duly authorized law-making body
e	2. subpoena	b. one who is guilty of a crime
a	3. statute	c. a formal written accusation of a crime
b	4. culprit	d. a temporary delay in carrying out a sentence
h	5. affidavit	e. a written order summoning a person to a court to give testimony
i	6. plaintiff	f. to call before a court to answer a formal charge
d	7. reprieve	g. to expel from the practice of law
f	8. arraign	h. a written statement made under oath
j	9. contraband	i. the person who makes the complaint in a lawsuit
g	10. disbar	j. smuggled goods

B. Now complete each of the following.

1. What is the difference between an *accessory before the fact* and an *accessory after the fact*?

2. What is a *quitclaim?* Show how *quit* in this word is related etymologically to *acquit.*

3. Why would a respected lawyer object to being called a *shyster?* In which country is the term *barrister* used?

4. What is a *writ?* Define *writ of habeas corpus* and *writ of mandamus.*

5. What is the difference between *impeach* and *convict?* Which branch of Congress has the power to *impeach* a president of the United States? Which is authorized to *try and judge* him?

6. What is a *plea*? Define *plea bargaining* and *to cop a plea*.

7. Legally speaking, what is a *misdemeanor*? a *felony*? What is the difference between the two? Define *tort*.

8. If the defendant in a criminal case is seeking a *change of venue*, what is he or she asking for? Why might a judge grant such a request?

9. Define the following: *petit jury, grand jury, hung jury*.

10. What principle of constitutional law is usually referred to by the phrase *double jeopardy*?

Exercise II. Place Names in Common Use

A fair number of common English words—for example, *academic*, studied in this lesson—are derived from the names of places. Some of these expressions are listed below. With or without the aid of a dictionary, define each as it is used in present-day English. Then give the place name from which the word is derived. Finally, choose any **five** of the items, and for each compose an original sentence that clearly illustrates the expression's meaning.

1. limerick	6. hackneyed	11. blarney
2. varnish	7. limousine	12. mayonnaise
3. mecca	8. bedlam	13. gasconade
4. cologne	9. sybaritic	14. tawdry
5. bunkum	10. donnybrook	15. sardonic

Exercise III. Expanding Your Word Power

The words listed below are not on the Basic Word List, but they were mentioned in passing in Lesson 1. All of them would make useful additions to your working vocabulary. Define each, give its etymology, list **two** synonyms and **two** antonyms (where possible), and use in a short sentence that clearly illustrates its meaning.

1. waive	5. connive	9. acquiesce
2. deter	6. incriminate	10. orientation
3. aversion	7. ascetic	11. indulge
4. ignoble	8. eschew	12. demur

Lesson 2

11. adjourn — 20. agile

---

11. **ad-journ**   *verb*   ə-jûrn′
[*a*, from *ad* (Latin), "to" + *diurnum* (Late Latin), "day"]

Definition:
- a. To close formally.

  Congress is scheduled to **adjourn** in two days, but pressing business will probably delay its closing for at least a week.

- b. To put off to another time; to move to another place.

  "This meeting is **adjourned** until ten o'clock tomorrow morning," the chairwoman declared, rapping her gavel smartly on the table.

  In view of clear community prejudice against the defendant, the judge **adjourned** the trial to another county.

  After dinner we **adjourned** to the living room for a quiet chat.

Related Form: (*noun*) adjournment

Synonyms: (*verbs*) conclude, terminate; defer (Word 118), postpone; suspend; transfer

12. **ad-verse**   *adjective*   ăd′-vûrs   *or*   ăd-vûrs′
[*ad* (Latin), "to; against" + *vertere, versus* (Latin), "turn"]

Definition: Hostile in purpose or effect; unfavorable.

Although the novel received much **adverse** criticism in the press, it became a national best-seller.

Related Forms: (*adverb*) adversely; (*nouns*) adversary, adversity

Usage Note:
Do not confuse *adverse* with the related adjective *averse*, meaning "opposed" or "disinclined." *Adverse* (with the *d*) is used of things to indicate that they have gone contrary to a person's wishes. *Averse* (without the *d*), on the other hand, indicates opposition on the part of the person himself or herself. Note the following pair of sentences:

The Supreme Court handed down an *adverse* decision on censorship.

The Supreme Court showed itself *averse* to censorship laws.

Synonyms: (*adjectives*) unfavorable, unfriendly, negative, antagonistic, antipathetic, inimical

Antonyms: (*adjectives*) favorable, friendly, propitious

13. ad·vo·cate   *verb:* ăd'-və-kāt   *noun:* ăd'-və-kĭt

[*ad* (Latin), "to" + *vocare, vocatus* (Latin), "call"]

Definition:
   a. (*verb*) To speak or argue in favor of; to give active public support to.

     In his TV address to the nation, the president **advocated** a series of measures that he believed would stimulate the economy.

   b. (*noun*) A person who pleads in the interest of a cause or individual.

     I have become her **advocate** because I honestly believe in her ideas.

Related Form: (*noun*) advocacy

Synonyms: (*verbs*) champion, support, espouse, uphold, recommend; (*nouns*) proponent, backer, defender, spokesman

Antonyms: (*verbs*) denounce, condemn, oppose, attack; (*nouns*) critic, opponent, adversary, antagonist

A scene from *The Devil's Disciple* (1897), a play about the advocates and opponents of the American Revolution by George Bernard Shaw (*inset*).

Devil's Advocate

In the Roman Catholic procedure of canonization, by which a person is elevated to sainthood, arguments are heard pro and con regarding the proposed measure. A church official is selected to pick flaws in the record or character of the candidate—to present arguments against the canonization. This official is given the title *advocatus diaboli*, "devil's advocate." The idea is that any candidate who can survive the onslaughts of a skilled devil's advocate probably does have authentic credentials for sainthood.

   The expression has been widened to embrace anyone who expresses the opposition point of view as a means of arriving at the truth, even though, in fact, he may not be in disagreement with his opponent. Thus one might say: "I am not necessarily in disagreement with your plan, but I am going to serve as a *devil's advocate* and point out its possible flaws."

14. **aes·thet·ic**   *adjective*   ĕs-thĕt'-ĭk

[*aisthetikos* (Greek), "perceptible to the senses"]

Definition: Pertaining to a sense of beauty; artistic.

Though the picture did not have much **aesthetic** appeal, it had considerable commercial value.

In 1756 the English philosopher Edmund Burke wrote an influential book on **aesthetic** theory.

Related Forms: (*adverb*) aesthetically; (*nouns*) aesthete, aesthetics

Usage Notes:
   a.   *Aesthetic* is sometimes spelled *esthetic*. Do not confuse the word with *ascetic*.
   b.   An *aesthete* is a person who is sensitive to, or has a love of, the beautiful in art or nature. However, the term is often used with an unfavorable tone to indicate someone who makes overmuch of his or her sensitivity to beauty.
   c.   *Aesthetics* is a branch of philosophy dealing with theories and principles of beauty in art and literature.

15. **af·fa·ble**   *adjective*   ăf'-ə-bəl

[*ad* (Latin), "to" + *fari* (Latin), "speak" + *abilis, abile* (Latin), "able to"]

Definition: Courteous and agreeable in manner; easy to talk to or approach.

It's fun to spend an hour or two chatting with my next-door neighbor because she is one of the most **affable** people I know.

Related Forms: (*adverb*) affably; (*nouns*) affableness, affability

Synonyms: (*adjectives*) sociable, genial, amiable, friendly, good-natured
Antonyms: (*adjectives*) unsociable, surly, testy, ill-tempered

16. **af·fec·ta·tion**   *noun*   ăf-ĕk-tā'-shən

[*affectare, affectatus* (Latin), "strive after"]

Definition: A pretentious display of manners or sentiments that are not genuine; a peculiar habit of dress or behavior that has been adopted to impress others.

Beneath his **affectation** of elegance and refinement, I could easily recognize the crude and awkward youth I had known years before.

Related Forms: (*adjective*) affected: (*verb*) affect

Phrases: an affected style of speaking; to affect an air of sophistication

Synonyms: (*nouns*) pose, pretense; mannerism
Related Phrase: to put on airs

17. **af-flu-ent**   *adjective*   ăf'-loo-ənt

[*ad* (Latin), "to" + *fluens, fluentis* (Latin), "flowing," from *fluere* (Latin, "flow"]

Definition: Prosperous, wealthy.

A good friend of mine is constantly borrowing money from his more **affluent** relatives.

The German writer Thomas Mann's novel *Buddenbrooks* details the lives of generations of **affluent** Hamburg merchants.

Related Forms: (*noun*) affluence; (*adverb*) affluently

Synonyms: (*adjectives*) flourishing, well-to-do, opulent

Antonyms: (*adjectives*) indigent (Word 237), destitute, penniless, poverty-stricken

Related Phrases:

living high off the hog — This phrase of rural American origin suggests that a person is in good circumstances because he or she is eating the more desirable cuts of meat from a slaughtered hog.

as rich as Croesus — This phrase goes back to Croesus, king of Lydia, an ancient country in western Turkey. Croesus had a reputation among the Greeks for being extremely rich, and he became the personification of limitless wealth.

to serve Mammon — The word *mammon* means "riches" in Aramaic, an ancient Semitic language related to Hebrew. Among the Hebrews of biblical times, *mammon* was personified as the god Mammon, who represented not merely wealth but materialism and an excessive concern with acquiring riches.

well-heeled — In the old days only wealthy people could afford shoes with heels on them. Since they were wealthy, they could also afford to keep those heels in good condition. Hence, to be *well-heeled* came to mean "to be wealthy or affluent." The opposite is *down-at-heel*, meaning "poor" because run-down heels were a sign of poverty. As Shakespeare says in *King Lear*: "A good man's fortune may grow out at heel."

A depiction of Croesus (*top right*) displaying his wealth to the Greek philosopher Solon. Solon admonished Croesus by pointing out that happiness was based on good fortune, not great wealth.

18. **a·gen·da**   *noun*   ə-jĕn′-də

[*agere* (Latin), "do"]

Definition: A list or program of things to be done or acted upon.

"Have you any idea what is on the **agenda** for today's meeting?" she asked.

Poland had top priority on Adolf Hitler's **agenda** of military conquest in the fall of 1939.

Usage Note:

Agenda was originally a Latin plural noun meaning "things to be done" (singular, *agendum*). However, it is generally treated in English today as a collective noun taking a singular verb, as in the following example:

The *agenda* includes the question of raising money for the dance.

On the other hand, it is certainly not wrong—although it may seem a bit pedantic—to treat *agenda* as a plural form. In that case, the Latin singular form *agendum* may be used to indicate one particular item among several included in the agenda.

Synonyms: (*nouns*) schedule, docket

Usage Note:

A *docket* is literally a list of cases awaiting action in a court of law, but the word is often used figuratively of any list of things to be done.

"Winter Carnival is the next item on today's *docket*," the head of the planning committee announced.

19. **ag·gre·gate**   *noun and adjective:* ăg′-rə-gĭt
verb: ăg′-rə-gāt

[*ad* (Latin), "to" + *grex, gregis* (Latin), "herd"]

Definition:

a.   (*noun*) The total amount or sum total of the individual parts.

The United Nations is no more than a loose **aggregate** of nations, each of which retains full sovereignty.

b.   (*verb*) To gather or merge into a single whole; to amount to.

The merger of the two great banks **aggregated** working capital totaling several trillion dollars.

c.   (*adjective*) Total, collective.

The **aggregate** effect of misguided monetary policies is usually financial chaos.

Related Form: (*noun*) aggregation

Usage Note:

Perhaps the widest current use of *aggregate* as a noun occurs in the prepositional phrase *in the aggregate*, meaning "collectively."

Synonyms: (*nouns*) mass, assemblage, amalgamation, conglomeration, cluster; (*verbs*) amalgamate, consolidate; (*adjectives*) net, composite

42

20. ag-ile   *adjective*   ăj′-əl

[*agilis* (Latin), "busy; active," from *agere* (Latin), "do")

Definition: Swift and light in action, movement, or thought.

Despite his sixty-odd years, the circus clown was as energetic and **agile** as any of the younger members of the troupe.

It certainly takes a very **agile** mind to do some kinds of crossword puzzles.

Related Form: (*noun*) agility

Synonyms: (*adjectives*) nimble, limber, alert, brisk, supple, lithe, spry

Antonyms: (*adjectives*) torpid, sluggish, lethargic; awkward, clumsy

Related Phrases: to limber up one's muscles, to look chipper

Usage Note:
Some distinctions should be drawn among the synonyms listed above: *alert* refers to quickness of mind; *brisk* suggests liveliness; *supple* means "pliant" or "bending and twisting easily"; and *spry* indicates agility despite age or infirmity.

Using the Words

Exercise I.   Parts of Speech

Indicate the part of speech of each of the following words. Two answers are possible in one instance; three in another.

1. agenda n.
2. adjourn v.
3. advocate n., v.
4. agile adj.
5. affluent adj.
6. aggregate adj., v., n.

Exercise II.   Words in Phrases

In each of the following groups, select the item that best expresses the meaning of the *italicized* word in the introductory phrase.

1. *adjourned* the meeting promptly at three o'clock
   a. planned   b. opened   c. suspended   d. attended

2. very *agile* for her age
   a. ignorant   b. clumsy   c. popular   d. spry

3. *advocated* changes in the tax laws
   a. considered   b. rejected   c. supported   d. ignored

4. came from a very *affluent* family
   a. obscure   b. poverty-stricken   c. brilliant   d. wealthy

5. the *aggregate* opinion of the jury
   a. collective   b. informed   c. far-reaching   d. mistaken

Exercise III. Completing Sentences

Complete each of the following sentences by selecting the most appropriate word from the group of words given below.

| aesthetic | advocate | agenda |
| affectation | adverse | affable |

1. We are determined to succeed in spite of all the __adverse__ conditions affecting this project.

2. The first item on the __agenda__ at the convention was the selection of a temporary chairperson.

3. Our personnel manager is a very __affable__ woman whose friendly, informal manner immediately puts a person at ease.

4. While the Romans were essentially practical in their approach to building design, the Greeks were deeply concerned with beauty for its own sake and worked hard to produce structures of high __aesthetic__ appeal.

5. Throwing an obscure French expression into the middle of an English sentence just to show that you've been to Paris is an __affectation__ that really irritates me.

Exercise IV. Synonyms and Antonyms

A. Match each word in Column A with its **synonym** in Column B.

Column A   *Column B*

d 1. terminate adjourn   a. amiable

f 2. nimble agile   b. consolidate

e 3. opulent affluent   c. pretense

c 4. pose affectation   d. conclude

b 5. fuse aggregate   e. luxurious

                                 f. spry

Now indicate which of the basic words taught in this lesson (Words 11–20) is most nearly **synonymous** with each of the words in Column A.

B. In each of the following groups, select the two words that are most nearly **antonyms**.

1. a. agile   b. filthy   c. hostile   d. sincere   e. awkward

2. a. civilian   b. opponent   c. foreigner   d. advocate   e. aesthete

3. a. ascetic   b. sluggish   c. propitious   d. adverse   e. neat

4. a. artificial   b. testy   c. penniless   d. aesthetic   e. affable

5. a. wealthy   b. insincere   c. indigent   d. lithe   e. illegal

Exercise V.   Word Roundup

1. Explain the derivation of *agenda*. Give the singular form of the word. How do you explain the fact that *agenda* itself may be used as a singular form?

2. Define each of the following phrases.
   a. a devil's advocate
   b. living high off the hog
   c. the affluent society
   d. to put on airs
   e. to serve Mammon
   f. in the aggregate

Exercise VI.   Framing Sentences

Use each of the following words in an original sentence that clearly illustrates its meaning.

1. adjourn
2. adverse
3. advocate
4. affable
5. affluent
6. agenda
7. agile
8. affectation
9. aesthetic

Completing Verbal Analogies

What Is a Verbal Analogy?   Today, practically every standardized test in vocabulary contains at least one section dealing with verbal analogies. A **verbal analogy** is a kind of equation that uses words rather than numbers. This equation indicates that the relationship between two words or expressions is the **same** as the relationship between two other words or expressions.

Here is a simple verbal analogy:

boy : man = girl : woman

This is to be read, "The word *boy* is to the word *man* as the word *girl* is to the word *woman*"—or, simply, "*Boy* is to *man* as *girl* is to *woman*." What the analogy is saying is that the relationship between the word *boy* and the word *man* is the same as the relationship between the word *girl* and the word *woman*.

And what is that relationship? Well, a boy grows into a man. In other words, the word *boy* refers to the immature version of the male human being, while the word *man* indicates the fully adult specimen.

In the same way, a girl grows into a woman. In other words, the word *girl* refers to the immature version of the female human being, and the word *woman* indicates the adult.

Now, if the four words in the original analogy are replaced by what they mean (as indicated above), the new analogy will read:

immature male : adult male = immature female : adult female

This makes it clear that the relationship between the pair of words on each side of the equals sign is the same. That relationship can be expressed as "A boy becomes a man, just as a girl becomes a woman." This is essentially what the analogy is saying.

In the analogy sections of standardized tests, students are asked to complete analogies just like the one given above. They are to do this by selecting one or two (or a group of two) items from a possible four or five choices. The format varies a bit from test to test, and, of course, the number of word relationships involved is as infinite as a human being's capacity to manipulate words and ideas.

Exercise I

Three common word relationships that occur in analogy questions on standardized tests are listed below. (In this list, A means the first word or expression in the analogy, B the second, and so forth.)

    a. A means the same as B; C means the same as D.
    b. A means the opposite of B; C means the opposite of D.
    c. A is an example of B; C is an example of D.

And here are five complete analogies taken from typical standardized tests. The four expressions that make up each have been marked A, B, C, and D. Look at each analogy carefully. Then indicate which of the three word relationships on the list it illustrates.

        A   *B*   *C*   *D*
b 1. gigantic : tiny = wet : dry

      A   *B*   *C*   *D*
c 2. oak : tree = rose : flower

      A   *B*   *C*   *D*
a 3. stop : halt = rest : relax

        A   *B*   *C*   *D*
c 4. Rembrandt : painter = Beethoven : composer

      A   *B*   *C*   *D*
a 5. abet : aid = fuse : merge

Exercise II

Below are five complete analogies. Three of them are correctly constructed; the other two are not. Read each analogy carefully. Then indicate which **three** are correctly constructed. Explain why the other two are not.

1. affluent : indigent = wealthy : poor correct

2. advocate : support = accede : dissent

3. Asia : continent = Sri Lanka : island correct

4. fire : hot = ice : cold correct

5. renounce : retain = abhor : loathe

2. *Accede* means opposite of, not same as, *dissent.*
5. *Abhor* means same as, not opposite of, *loathe.*

Enriching the Lesson

Exercise I.   Specialized Knowledge

There are many terms in English that indicate specialized skills or knowledge and the people who possess them—for example, *academician* (studied in Lesson 1) and *aesthete* (studied in Lesson 2). A number of these terms are listed below. With or without the aid of a dictionary, define each. Then choose any **five**, and for each compose an original illustrative sentence.

1. conjurer
2. chiropractor
3. disc jockey
4. therapist
5. environmentalist
6. consumer advocate
7. spin doctor
8. podiatrist
9. comptroller
10. programmer
11. anthropologist
12. sociologist
13. pediatrician
14. obstetrician
15. ophthalmologist
16. veterinarian
17. optometrist
18. acrobat
19. neurosurgeon
20. meteorologist

Exercise II.   Portmanteau Words

A **portmanteau word** (sometimes called a **blend**) is a word that has been coined by combining elements of two other words. For example, the portmanteau word *brunch* is made up of *breakfast* and *lunch*.

Read the following excerpt from Lewis Carroll's *Through the Looking-Glass*. It deals with portmanteau words.

> "You seem very clever at explaining words, Sir," said Alice to Humpty Dumpty. "Would you kindly tell me the meaning of the poem called 'Jabberwocky'?"
>
> > 'Twas brillig, and the slithy toves
> > Did gyre and gimble in the wabe;
> > All mimsy were the borogoves,
> > And the mome raths outgrabe.
>
> "That's enough to begin with," Humpty Dumpty interrupted. "There are plenty of hard words there. *Brillig* means four o'clock in the afternoon—the time when you begin broiling things for dinner."
>
> "That's very well," said Alice—"and *slithy?*"
>
> "Well, *slithy* means *lithe* and *slimy*. *Lithe* is the same as *active*. You see, it's like a portmanteau [a kind of large suitcase]—there are two meanings packed up into one word."

Below are a number of portmanteau words. Define each, and indicate the elements that went into its formation.

1. chortle
2. splatter
3. simulcast
4. happenstance
5. squawk
6. infomercial
7. telecast
8. smog
9. motel
10. guesstimate
11. advertorial
12. cablegram
13. telethon
14. sitcom
15. heliport

Exercise III.   Exploring the Dictionary

1. What is a business *conglomerate*? How does it differ from an ordinary business organization?

2. Consult a dictionary or other reference book for the specific meaning of each of the following "group" words. Then use each in a sentence that clearly illustrates its meaning.

    a. federation   d. bloc   g. consortium
    b. confederation   e. cartel   h. alliance
    c. cabal   f. coalition   i. junta

3. Define *federalism.* What does the term *world federalism* mean?

4. Explain the meaning of each of the following expressions involving the word *devil.*

    a. in a devil-may-care mood   e. a devilish expression
    b. giving the devil his due   f. a printer's devil
    c. deviled eggs   g. a devil's food cake
    d. between the devil and the   h. bedeviled by misfortune
       deep blue sea

Exercise IV.   Expanding Your Word Power

The words listed below are not on the Basic Word List, but they were mentioned in passing in Lesson 2. All of them would make useful additions to your working vocabulary. Define each, give its etymology, list **two** synonyms and **two** antonyms (where possible), and use in a short sentence that clearly illustrates its meaning.

1. adversary   5. surly   9. composite
2. adversity   6. genial   10. lethargic
3. inimical   7. destitute   11. antipathetic
4. espouse   8. amalgamate   12. nimble

Related Forms in Context

Beneath each sentence below are four words introduced in Lesson 1 or 2. Review the related forms for these words, and choose the one that best completes the sentence. Write that related form in the space provided.

1. The _abdication_ of King Edward VIII in December 1936 stunned the British people.

    a. advocate   b. absolve   c. abdicate   d. aggregate

2. Thanks to translations provided in the form of subtitles, foreign-language films are _accessible_ to a wide audience.

    a. acclimate   b. adjourn   c. aggregate   d. accede

3. Prejudice in all its forms is __abhorrent__ to those who believe in a just and democratic society.

   a. abhor   b. accede   c. abdicate   d. advocate

4. Someone who is very fashion conscious is likely to devote a great deal of attention to choosing the perfect _accessories_ to complete an outfit.

   a. adjourn   b. aggregate   **c. accede**   d. acclimate

5. The determined __advocacy__ of many groups lobbying for equal opportunities for the disabled led to the enactment of the Americans with Disabilities Act of 1990.

   a. addiction   b. agenda   c. affectation   **d. advocate**

6. The U.S. Census Bureau offers numerous options for the _aggregation_ of data — for example, making it possible for a researcher to access totals by region, country, or year.

   a. aggregate   b. agenda   c. advocate   d. addiction

7. Each year the National __Academy__ of Sciences honors eminent scientists and engineers for their significant original research.

   a. abject   b. affluent   **c. academic**   d. adverse

8. On June 22, 1937, African Americans cheered as Joe Louis, great-grandson of a slave, knocked out his __adversary__ to win the World Heavyweight Championship, which he held until 1949.

   a. affable   **b. adverse**   c. affluent   d. academic

9. Although tai chi was developed as a martial art, it improves posture, mental focus, balance, and __agility__.

   a. affluent   b. aggregate   **c. agile**   d. aesthetic

10. At Pilgrim Hall Museum, we could see evidence of the __affluence__ of some colonial families—works by local silver-smiths and artists and luxury goods imported from England.

    a. affable   b. adverse   **c. affluent**   d. agile

11. A strict vegan diet requires __abstinence__ from all animal foods and dairy products.

    a. accede   b. absolve   c. adjourn   **d. abstain**

12. Many travelers to Denver, the Mile High City, find that it takes them a day or two to _acclimatize_ to the altitude.

    a. accede   **b. acclimate**   c. abet   d. abhor

13. People who owe a great deal of money may seek __absolution__ from their debts by declaring bankruptcy.

    a. abstain   b. accede   c. acclimate   **d. absolve**

14. Mrs. Young complains that the Internet is definitely __addictive__, for Soo Mee spends most of her waking hours on-line, frequently forgetting to eat or do her homework.

    a. advocate b. addiction c. aggregate d. agenda

15. Whenever he returns from visiting his family in Atlanta, Georgia, my Boston cousin Ron ___affects___ a southern accent.

    a. affectation b. aggregate c. addiction d. advocate

16. My anger quickly faded as the customer service representative politely and ___affably___ responded to my complaints.

    a. affluent b. adverse c. academic d. affable

17. Which of these portraits by the seventeenth-century Dutch artist Jan Vermeer do you find more aesthetically pleasing—*The Milkmaid* or *Girl with a Pearl Earring*?

    a. academic b. affable c. aesthetic d. affluent

18. Despite a backlog of bills waiting to be dealt with, the state legislature refuses to postpone its adjournment, which is scheduled for Friday of next week.

    a. abstain b. absolve c. abdicate d. adjourn

19. During the Great Depression of the 1930s, a time of economic __adversity__, people flocked to the movies, seeking a respite from their troubles.

    a. affluence b. adverse c. affable d. aggregate

20. The controversial bill narrowly squeaked past the Senate with forty-nine votes in favor, forty-eight against, and three abstentions.

    a. absolve b. abstain c. adjourn d. abdicate

Lesson 3

21. alienate — 30. anecdote

---

21. al·ien·ate   *verb*   āl'-yə-nāt   *or*   ā'-lē-ə-nāt
[*alienare, alienatus* (Latin), "estrange," from *alius* (Latin), "other"]

Definition: To cause hostility or indifference where love, friendliness, or interest formerly existed.

> During the years before the Russian Revolution, the increasingly rigid and oppressive policies of the czarist government **alienated** many of those who formerly supported it.

Related Forms: (*noun*) alienation; (*noun and adjective*) alien; (*adjectives*) alienable, inalienable

Usage Note:
Alienation denotes a state of estrangement, disaffection, or isolation. In psychology, the word is used in a special sense to indicate a state of estrangement between a person and the outside world or between the different parts of the personality.

Synonyms: (*verbs*) estrange, disaffect, antagonize

Antonyms: (*verbs*) befriend; captivate

Related Phrases: sever (or break off) relations with; the generation gap; catch someone's fancy, ingratiate oneself with

22. al·lege   *verb*   ə-lĕj'
[*ad* (Latin), "to; toward" + *legare* (Latin), "depute, grant, bequeath"]

Definition: To claim that something is true but without offering any proof.

> The men now being held in police custody are **alleged** to have robbed eight supermarkets in the past year.

> As an excuse for refusing to lend me the money, she **alleged** that she had financial troubles of her own.

Related Forms: (*noun*) allegation; (*adjective*) alleged

Usage Note:
The use of the word *allege* often implies that there is some doubt about the truth of a statement—for example, in the second sentence above. At other times, the word *allege* is used because the speaker wishes to disclaim all responsibility for the truth of whatever follows—for example, in the phrases "an alleged miracle" or "the alleged visitor from Mars."

Synonyms: (*verbs*) claim, contend; declare, assert, affirm, avow, asseverate, aver

51

23. **al·lude**   *verb*   ə-lōōd′ *or* ăl-yōōd′
[*ad* (Latin), "to" + *ludere* (Latin), "play"]

Definition: To refer to indirectly.

During the course of the evening, he **alluded** to the fact that he had attended Harvard.

Related Forms: (*noun*) allusion; (*adjective*) allusive

Usage Note:
Take care not to confuse the following words:

allude (refer indirectly to) and *elude* (evade, escape)
allusion (an indirect reference) and *illusion* (a false perception or impression)
allusive (containing allusions; suggestive) and *illusory* (tending to deceive) or *elusive* (difficult to find or grasp)

Synonyms: (*verbs*) hint at, suggest, insinuate, intimate

24. **am·bi·ence**   *noun*   ăm′-bē-əns
[*ambi* (Latin), "around" + *iens* (Latin), "going," from *ire* (Latin), "go"]

Definition: The surrounding or pervading atmosphere; the tone and spirit of an environment.

In the 1920s, the literary and artistic **ambience** of the Latin Quarter in Paris attracted many young American writers, such as Ernest Hemingway and F. Scott Fitzgerald.

Related Form: (*adjective*) ambient

Synonyms: (*nouns*) surroundings, milieu, setting; character, flavor

25. **am·biv·a·lent**   *adjective*   ăm-bĭv′-ə-lĕnt
[*Ambivalenz*, a German word coined by Sigmund Freud from *ambi* (Latin), "both" + *valens, valentis* (Latin), "worth"]

Definition: Wavering or uncertain because of an inability to make a choice between two contradictory feelings or viewpoints in regard to a person, a thing, or a course of action.

My parents have **ambivalent** feelings about the college I have chosen. On the one hand, they are favorably impressed by its academic standards; on the other, they are unhappy about its great distance from our home.

Related Form: (*noun*) ambivalence

Phrases: ambivalent emotions, an ambivalent position

Synonyms: (*adjectives*) contradictory, opposing, conflicting, equivocal; vacillating

Antonyms: (*adjectives*) definite, firm, unwavering, steady; clear-cut, unequivocal

26. **am‑nes‑ty**   *noun*   ăm′‑nəs‑tē
[*a* (Greek), "not" + *mnasthai* (Greek), "remember"]

Definition: An official pardon granted to offenders against the government, especially for political offenses.

A new government, seeking to restore normal conditions after a bitter civil war, may grant an **amnesty** to all who had been guilty of political offenses.

Synonyms: (*nouns*) forgiveness, immunity (Word 226), remission (of punishment), absolution (of sin)

27. **a‑nach‑ro‑nism**   *noun*   ə‑năk′‑rə‑nĭz‑əm
[*ana* (Greek), "backwards" + *chronos* (Greek), "time"]

Definition: The misplacing of an object or event in a period to which it cannot possibly belong; anything out of its proper time frame.

Cassius's reference to mechanical clocks in Shakespeare's *Julius Caeser* is an **anachronism** because such devices were unknown in Roman times.

Someone who lives too much in the past is bound to be considered something of an **anachronism** by her or his contemporaries.

Related Forms: (*adjective*) anachronistic

Synonyms: (*nouns*) incongruity, inconsistency, contradiction; throwback

28. **an‑ar‑chy**   *noun*   ăn′‑ər‑kē
[*anarchia* (Greek), "anarchy," from *an* (Greek), "without" + *archos* (Greek), "ruler"]

Definition: Absence of governmental authority; general political and social disorder.

During the famous Year of the Four Emperors (A.D. 69), the Roman Empire was thrown into a state of almost total **anarchy**.

A sloppy clerk can easily reduce a filing system to complete **anarchy** in no time at all.

Related Forms: (*nouns*) anarchism, anarchist

Usage Note:
Anarchism is a political doctrine that advocates the abolition of all forms of government as being oppressive and undesirable. The word is also used in an extended sense to indicate active resistance to the state, including terrorism and guerrilla warfare. An *anarchist* is a person who favors the ideas of anarchism or engages in activities aimed at the violent overthrow of an existing government.

Synonyms: (*nouns*) disorder, chaos, lawlessness, pandemonium (Word 290), turmoil

29. a-nath-e-ma   *noun*   ə-năth'-ə-mə

[*anathema* (Late Latin), "a curse," from *anathema* (Greek), "a votive offering"]

Definition:
- a. A curse or strong denunciation.

  Many an Old Testament prophet did not hesitate to hurl stinging **anathemas** at the wayward children of Israel.

- b. The person or thing cursed; more generally, any object of intense dislike.

  Red meat is usually **anathema** to a vegetarian.

Usage Note:
When *anathema* occurs without modification after the verb *to be* (as in the second example above), it functions more as an adjective than as a noun. For that reason, it may properly be replaced by such adjectives as *repugnant* or *abhorrent*, rather than by the corresponding nouns (*repugnance, abhorrence*). Thus, the second example above could also read:

  Red meat is usually *repugnant/abhorrent* to a vegetarian.

One of the few nouns that can replace *anathema* in this situation is *abomination* (with the indefinite article).

  Red meat is usually *an abomination* to a vegetarian.

Related Forms: (*verb*) anathematize; (*noun*) anathematization

Synonyms: (*nouns*) malediction, execration, imprecation; abomination

Antonyms: (*nouns*) blessing, benediction, eulogy, encomium; (*verbs*) bless, glorify, praise, extol, cherish

30. an-ec-dote   *noun*   ăn'-ĭk-dōt

[*anekdota* (Greek), "unpublished things," from *an* (Greek), "not" + *ek* (Greek), "out" + *dotos* (Greek), "given"]

Definition: A brief account of some interesting or amusing incident, especially one containing biographical or historical details.

  The *Oxford Book of Royal **Anecdotes*** contains amusing true-life stories about the men and women who have worn the English crown.

Related Forms: (*adjective*) anecdotal; (*nouns*) anecdotist, anecdotage

Usage Note:
Anecdotal means "containing anecdotes." An *anecdotist* is a person who tells anecdotes, especially as a hobby or profession. *Anecdotage*, a blend of *anecdote* and *dotage*, indicates the kind of old age that is accompanied by a tendency to ramble on endlessly about the past.

Synonyms: (*nouns*) tale, story, vignette, sketch, narrative, reminiscence, memoir; episode; storyteller, raconteur

An Amusing Anecdote

Louis Armstrong (1901–1971), known familiarly as "Satchmo," was one of this nation's great jazz musicians. As a bandleader and soloist, he did much to popularize jazz across America during his long career. He also starred in several films and was noted for his sense of humor.

Many amusing anecdotes are told about this colorful figure. Once, for instance, he was asked if he objected to his fellow performers imitating his exuberantly extroverted musical style. "No," he replied. "A lot of cats copy the Mona Lisa, but people still stand in line to see the original!"

Louis Armstrong

Exercise I
1. am'-nes-ty
2. al-lude'
3. am'-bi-ence
4. al'-ien-ate
5. an'-ar-chy
6. an'-ec-dote

Using the Words

Exercise I.   Syllabication and Pronunciation

Syllabicate the following words correctly, and place the major stress mark (') after the syllable that is accented when the word is pronounced.

Example: al-lege'

1. amnesty
2. allude
3. ambience
4. alienate
5. anarchy
6. anecdote

Exercise II.   Words Out of Context

In each of the following groups, select the item that best expresses the meaning of the numbered word at the left.

1. ambience
   a. formula   b. concern   c. atmosphere
   d. schedule

2. ambivalent
   a. discourteous   b. imaginary
   c. wealthy   d. conflicting

3. anathema
   a. a throwback   b. an abomination
   c. a champion   d. an illusion

4. anarchy
   a. chaos   b. poverty   c. fear   d. danger

5. amnesty
   a. assemblage   b. gap   c. mannerism
   d. pardon

Exercise III.   Completing Sentences

Complete each of the following sentences by selecting the most appropriate word from the group of words given below. Make whatever adjustments are necessary to fit the words into the sentences properly.

allege	anachronism	alienate
anecdote	allude	anarchy

1. During a speech a politician may repeatedly ___allude___ to "pressing economic problems" without actually specifying what he or she has in mind.

2. A modern-dress production of one of Shakespeare's tragedies may be full of the most absurd anachronisms but still be quite convincing.

3. The people now being held in police custody are ___alleged___ to have committed a series of spectacular bank heists over the past year.

4. The English writer Fanny Burney's diaries and journals are full of the most interesting stories and ___anecdotes___ involving people who were prominent in her lifetime.

5. A supervisor who treats the members of his or her staff with contempt or indifference will soon ___alienate___ each and every one of them.

Exercise IV.   Synonyms and Antonyms

Classify each of the following pairs of words or phrases as **S** for **synonyms** or **A** for **antonyms**.

S 1. alienate—antagonize
S 2. milieu—ambience
A 3. anathema—blessing
S 4. anecdote—yarn
S 5. claim—allege

A 6. unequivocal—ambiguous
S 7. allude to—hint at
A 8. order—anarchy
S 9. anachronism—throwback
S 10. immunity—amnesty

Exercise V.   Framing Sentences

A. Use each of the following words in an original sentence that clearly illustrates its meaning.

1. alienate
2. allude

3. amnesty
4. ambivalent

B. Give an **adjective** form of each of the following words, and use it in an original sentence that clearly illustrates its meaning.

5. anecdote anecdotal
6. anarchy anarchistic

7. anachronism anachronistic
8. allege alleged

Exercise VI.   Word Roundup

Explain the difference in meaning between the words in each of the following groups.

1. allude—refer
2. allusion—illusion
3. allusive—elusive
4. elusive—illusory

Dissecting the Words

Prefixes

1.   The Latin prefix **ad**, meaning "to, toward," appears in countless English words. Sometimes it is disguised when it precedes a root beginning with a consonant. In such cases, the *d* in *ad* is often dropped, and the following consonant doubles. For example, *affluent*, meaning "prosperous," studied in Lesson 2, comes from *ad* and the Latin verb *fluere*, meaning "flow." When the two parts are joined, the *d* of *ad* is replaced by an *f* (because *fluere* begins with an *f*). Similarly, *ad* and *knowledge* merge to become *acknowledge*; *ad* and *grandize* become *aggrandize*, meaning "to increase in power or rank."

Thus, *ad* may appear in an English word as **ac-, af-, ag-, al-, an-, ap-, ar-, as-,** or **at-**. This merging, or fusion, of consonants is technically called **assimilation**.

2. The Greek prefix **a, an,** meaning "not," "without," or "opposed to," is found in two words studied in this lesson: *anarchy* and *anecdote*. (Note that the prefix takes the form **an** before a root beginning with a vowel and usually before *h*.) Other words derived from this prefix include:

anonymous (from *an*, "without" + *onuma*, "name")—of unknown authorship

atypical—not typical

amorphous (from *a*, "without" + *morphe* "form")—shapeless, formless

asymmetrical—not symmetrical

amoral—without moral quality (that is, neither moral nor immoral); lacking a sense of morals

Roots

1. The Greek root **arch** (the *ch* is pronounced as a *k*) has a variety of meanings. One of them is "government" or "ruler." It appears in *anarchy*, studied in this lesson. Other English words containing *arch* with the same meaning include:

monarchy (from *monos*, "sole" + *archos*, "ruler")—a government in which one person is the sole and absolute ruler

oligarchy (from *oligos*, "few" + *arche*, "rule")—a government which is entirely in the hands of a small group of people or families

patriarch (from *pater*, "father" + *archos*, "ruler")—a father who is the head of a family or tribe

As a prefix, **arch** (here the *ch* is pronounced *tch*) means "principal" or "of the highest rank." English words in which this meaning of **arch** appears include:

archbishop—bishop of the highest rank

archenemy—chief enemy

archduke—a nobleman whose ceremonial or social status is the same as that of a reigning monarch

archfiend—chief fiend (a name for the devil)

Be careful not to confuse the Greek prefix/root **arch** with the English word *arch*, which means "*sly*" or "*mischievous*" (as in "an *arch* smile").

2. The Latin root **voc, voke,** meaning "call," forms the basis of the word *advocate* (Word 13). Other words containing this root include:

vocation—a profession, trade, or calling

avocation—a hobby (that is, something that a person pursues for pleasure in addition to his or her regular job)

revoke (literally "to call back")—to withdraw. Noun form: *revocation*

convoke (literally "to call together")—to assemble. Noun form: *convocation*

invoke—to call upon ("*invoke* God's blessing") or ask for ("*invoke* aid"). Noun form: *invocation*

provoke—to stir up or cause. Noun form: *provocation;* adjective form: *provocative*. An *agent provocateur* is a person who deliberately stirs up trouble or dissension.

vociferous—loud-voiced

evoke—to call forth or elicit

A sample of Old English. A page from the only surviving manuscript of the great Anglo-Saxon epic poem *Beowulf,* which was probably written in the 8th century. (The manuscript, however, only dates from around A.D. 1000.) *Beowulf,* which blends both Christian and pagan elements, gives a remarkable picture of the life and customs of the early Germanic peoples.

Exercise

1. How does the prefix *ad* change when added to a root beginning with a consonant? What is the technical name for this phenomenon? Give **six** words studied in Lessons 1–3 that illustrate it.

2. Complete the following activities relating to *arch*.

    a. What is an *archdiocese*? What church official resides in an archdiocese? Give the adjective form of *archdiocese*.

    b. What is a *patriarch*? Name the three patriarchs mentioned in the Bible.

    c. What does the word *arch* mean in such phrases as *an arch smile*? What does the prefix *arch* mean in such phrases as *an archenemy*?

    d. Add *arch* to each of the following, and explain how the addition adds stature or dimension to the original word: *angel, duke, duchess, priest, deacon.*

    e. Match the word in Column A with its meaning in Column B.

Column A	*Column B*
b 1. monarchy	a. government by the few
c 2. hierarchy	b. rule by a single sovereign
a 3. oligarchy	c. a ruling body arranged into series of grades

3. In place of the blank space in each of the following sentences, supply a word or phrase that clearly shows that you know the meaning of the Latin root *voc, voke*.

    a. To deliver the *invocation* at the beginning of your school's graduation exercises is to ____call____ upon God for divine favor.

    b. If something you have done has *provoked* an argument with your kid brother, it has _____. called it forth

    c. If your bus pass has been *revoked*, it has been _called back_ .

    d. If a statement by the president of the United States has *evoked* a lot of comment, it has _____.
        called forth (brought out) much discussion

    e. If you attended a *vocational* school, you would expect the school to prepare you for your ___calling___ in life.

4. For each of the following definitions, supply a word beginning with the Greek prefix *a, an*.

    a. shapeless or formless amorphous
    b. the condition of a country without an effective government anarchy
    c. of unknown authorship anonymous
    d. lacking a sense of morals amoral
    e. a short narrative, often containing biographical details anecdote

5. Occasionally *ad* appears in a Latin phrase that English has borrowed without change. A few such phrases are listed below. Define each.

   a. ad libitum (*or* ad lib, *for short*)   d. ad nauseam
   b. ad hoc   e. ad infinitum
   c. ad hominem   f. ad valorem

Enriching the Lesson

Exercise I.   Parlez-Vous Français?

The word *milieu*, mentioned in this lesson, is taken wholly and without change from French. English has many other such words and phrases. A few of them are listed in Column A below. With or without the aid of a dictionary, match each of these expressions with its meaning in Column B.

		Column A		*Column B*
e	1.	carte blanche	a.	appetizers
g	2.	fait accompli	b.	an object of strong dislike
f	3.	savoir-faire	c.	a meeting or meeting place
j	4.	chef d'oeuvre	d.	a small specialty shop
b	5.	bête noire	e.	full power to act as one sees fit
i	6.	faux pas	f.	knowing the right or proper thing to do
a	7.	hors d'oeuvres	g.	something that cannot be reversed
d	8.	boutique	h.	a blind alley or dead end
c	9.	rendezvous	i.	a social blunder
h	10.	cul-de-sac	j.	a masterpiece

Exercise II.   Stating the Case

1. Lesson 3 contains two words, *allege* and *allude*, that indicate particular ways of giving information in speech or writing. A number of other such terms are listed below. With or without the help of a dictionary, define each in such a way as to bring out its distinctive meaning.

   a. intimate (*verb*)   e. assert   i. avouch
   b. expatiate   f. declaim   j. aver
   c. avow   g. enunciate   k. cite
   d. insinuate   h. asseverate   l. imply

2. What is the distinction between a *soliloquy* and a *colloquy*? What is a *colloquium*? a *monologist*? *dialogue*?

3. Each of the following colloquial expressions has to do with talking or keeping silent. Define each.

   a. rap   d. talk back   g. badmouth
   b. chew the fat   e. spiel   h. talk big
   c. clam up   f. gab   i. blurt out

Exercise III.   Telling a Story

1. What is a *fable*? How does it differ from an *anecdote*? an *allegory*? Give the names of two authors who are famous for writing fables. In a short paragraph, retell a fable by one of these authors. Why do you think these stories are called fables?

2. Define the following: *tall story*, *memoir*, *yarn*, *parable*. How does each differ from the other? Recount a *yarn* you have heard; a *parable* from the Bible; a *tall story*.

3. What is a *quip*? *retort*? *bon mot*? Define each of these words, and, if possible, supply an anecdotal illustration of the definition.

4. The noted American painter James McNeill Whistler is as famous for his witty retorts as for his artistic achievement. The following anecdote shows Whistler in top form:

   > At a dinner attended by Oscar Wilde and Whistler, Whistler is said to have remarked: "People will forgive anything but beauty and talent. So I am doubly unpardonable." Everybody roared at this observation except Wilde. Wilde, a noted wit in his own right, looked rather chagrined at Whistler's "score" and muttered, "I wish I'd said that." To this, Whistler retorted, "You will, Oscar—you will!"

   Now recount an anecdote by Benjamin Franklin; a witticism by James Thurber; an example of repartee by Dorothy Parker; an anecdote about Will Rogers. To do this, you will probably have to consult biographies and other books dealing with these witty writers.

5. What does the Latin word *fabula* mean? How does the Latin word contribute to the meaning of the English word *fabulous*? Explain what *fabulous* means in the following phrases: *a man of fabulous wealth, fabulous exploits, a fabulous party.*

Exercise IV.   Expanding Your Word Power

The words listed below are not on the Basic Word List, but they were mentioned in passing in Lesson 3. All of them would make useful additions to your working vocabulary. Define each, give its etymology, list **two** synonyms and **two** antonyms (where possible), and use in a short sentence that clearly illustrates its meaning.

1. alien	5. chaos	9. episode
2. estrange	6. encomium	10. extol
3. vacillate	7. affirm	
4. contend	8. vignette	

Lesson 4

31. anomaly — 40. assimilate

---

31. **a·nom·a·ly**   *noun*   ə-nŏm'-ə-lē
[*an* (Greek), "not" + *homalos* (Greek), "even," from *homos* (Greek), "same"]

Definition: A deviation from what is normal or expected.

Charles Darwin wrote that there was no greater **anomaly** in nature than a bird that could not fly.

Related Form: (*adjective*) anomalous

Phrases: an anomalous situation, in an anomalous position; an anomaly in the world of politics

Synonyms: (*nouns*) abnormality, peculiarity, oddity, freak, misfit; incongruity; (*adjectives*) abnormal, irregular, freakish, deviant, atypical; incongruous

Antonyms: (*noun*) the norm; (*adjectives*) normal, usual, commonplace, ordinary, regular, typical; congruous

32. **ap·a·thy**   *noun*   ăp'-ə-thē
[*a* (Greek), "without" + *pathos* (Greek), "feeling; suffering"]

Definition: Lack of feeling, emotion, or interest.

I hoped that my idea for the class project would be greeted with some enthusiasm. Instead, it met with complete **apathy.**

Fewer people turned out to vote this year. This is indicative of the growing **apathy** with which the general public seems to regard political campaigns.

Related Forms: (*adjective*) apathetic; (*adverb*) apathetically

Synonyms: (*nouns*) indifference, unconcern, aloofness, detachment, impassivity; (*adjectives*) indifferent, uninterested, aloof, detached, stolid, impassive, unfeeling, emotionless

Antonyms: (*nouns*) enthusiasm, ardor, fervor, zeal (Word 399); concern, interest; (*adjectives*) interested, concerned; ardent, fervent, keen, zealous, passionate

Usage Note:
Be careful not to confuse *uninterested* and *disinterested.* A person is said to be *uninterested* when he or she takes no interest in something; a person is said to be *disinterested,* however, when he or she has no self-interest involved in the matter. Thus, *uninterested* is a synonym of *apathetic,* but *disinterested* means the same as *impartial.*

33. **ap·pall**   *verb*   ə-pôl′

[*ap(p)alir,* (Old French), "grow pale," from *ad* (Latin), "at" + *pallere* (Latin), "be pale"]

Definition: To fill with intense horror, fear, or dismay.

The huge number of soldiers killed during the bloody battle of Antietam **appalled** the entire nation, both North and South.

I was **appalled** to learn that a fistfight had broken out on the floor of the State Senate yesterday.

Related Form: (*adjective*) appalling

Phrases: an appalling sight; appalling disclosures

Usage Note:
Appall, also spelled *appal,* implies a strong sense of helplessness in the face of something truly enormous or monstrous.

Synonyms: (*verbs*) horrify, shock, astound, stupefy, stun, dismay; (*adjectives*) horrifying, shocking, stunning, horrific, frightful, dreadful, fearful

Antonyms: (*verbs*) please, cheer, gladden, exhilarate, elate; (*adjectives*) cheering, gratifying, exhilarating

Related Phrase: be aghast at

34. **ap·pre·hend**   *verb*   ăp-rĭ-hĕnd′

[*ad* (Latin), "to" + *prehendere* (Latin), "seize"]

Definition:
   a.   To arrest or take into custody.

      The police **apprehended** the escaped convict about three blocks from the prison.

   b.   To perceive or understand the meaning of.

      One cannot fully **apprehend** the principles of our Constitution without studying the Federalist Papers.

   c.   To look forward to with fear or anxiety.

      The doctor assured his patient that there was nothing to **apprehend** in the forthcoming operation.

Related Forms: (*nouns*) apprehension, apprehensiveness; (*adjective*) apprehensive; (*adverb*) apprehensively

Usage Notes:
   a.   The noun *apprehension* has several meanings: (*1*) anxiety about the future; (*2*) an arrest; (*3*) understanding. *Apprehensiveness,* on the other hand, indicates merely uneasiness about the future.

   b.   *Apprehensive* means "fearful of what may be coming."

Synonyms: (*verbs*) seize, capture, nab, collar; grasp, comprehend, discern, fathom (Word 185); dread, fear, have misgivings about, anticipate the worst, have a foreboding of; (*noun*) discernment

35.   **ar-bi-trar-y**   *adjective*   är'-bə-trĕr-ē *or* är'-bĭ-trâr-ē

[*arbiter* (Latin), "judge" + -*arius* (Latin), "connected with"]

Definition:

    a.   Subject to or determined by one's judgment; random.

        "The example I have used is purely **arbitrary**," the speaker told her audience. "I'm sure all of you could come up with others that would be just as illuminating."

    b.   Arrived at by an exercise of the will, personal preference, or whim, as opposed to being based on reason or justice.

        The sentence a judge hands down should be based firmly on - accepted principles of law and justice. It should not be a purely **arbitrary** decision.

    c.   Given to willful decisions or demands; tyrannical or dictatorial.

        He wouldn't make a good supervisor because he is so **arbitrary** and overbearing in his dealings with others.

        During the reign of Czar Nicholas I (1825–1855), the Russian government became increasingly **arbitrary** and repressive.

Related Forms: (*adverb*) arbitrarily; (*noun*) arbitrariness

Synonyms: (*adjectives*) judgmental, discretionary; capricious, irrational; prejudiced, partial; unreasonable; high-handed, overbearing, despotic, autocratic, authoritarian

Antonyms: (*adjectives*) objective, fair, just, equitable (Word 166)

Related Phrase: a judgment call

36.   **ar-bi-trate**   *verb*   är'-bə-trāt

[*arbitrari, arbitratus* (Latin), "give judgment," from *arbiter* (Latin), "judge"]

Definition: To act as an impartial judge in a dispute; to settle.

Both the union and the employer have confidence in Mr. Donelli's fair-mindedness and knowledge of the industry. That is why he was chosen to **arbitrate** the contract dispute.

Related Forms: (*nouns*) arbitration, arbitrament; arbitrator, arbiter; (*adjectives*) arbitrational, arbitrable

Phrases: submit to arbitration, binding arbitration; an arbiter of taste, *arbiter elegantiae* (or *elegantiarum*)

Usage Note:

An *arbitrator* (or *arbiter*) is the person who is chosen to settle a dispute. *Arbitration* is the process by which a settlement is reached. *Arbitrament* is the act of settling the dispute or the settlement that is finally made. *Arbitrable* means "open to arbitration." For example, if the president of a union says that certain demands are not arbitrable, he/she means that they are not negotiable. An *arbiter elegantiae* is a judge of what's tasteful and what isn't.

Synonyms: (*verbs*) adjudicate, mediate

A collective bargaining session under the direction of a mediator.

37. **ar-ray**   *verb and noun*   ə-rā′

[*arayer* (Old French), "arrange," possibly from *arredare* (Vulgar Latin), "arrange"]

Definition:

a. (*verb*) To line up; to dress up.

Scouts first brought the general news that the entire enemy force was **arrayed** along a series of hills not two miles distant.

The various crews and contingents participating in the Mardi Gras parade were **arrayed** in the most fantastic and elaborate outfits.

b. (*noun*) An imposing grouping; rich and beautiful attire.

The defendant entered the courtroom accompanied by an impressive **array** of lawyers and other legal advisers.

Soldiers in full battle **array** patiently awaited inspection by their commanding officer.

Usage Note:

Originally *array* meant "to ready for battle," though the word is rarely used in this sense today. Nonetheless, something of this association with the military still clings to the word's more modern usages. A careful inspection of the examples given above will reveal this.

Synonyms: (*verbs*) align; assemble, draw up, marshal, muster; deploy; adorn, deck out, doll up, gussy up; equip, outfit, accoutre; (*nouns*) alignment, lineup; finery; equipment, accoutrements

Antonyms: (*verbs*) disperse, disband, dismiss

38. **ar-tic-u-late**   *verb:* är-tĭk'-yə-lāt   *adjective:* är-tĭk'-yə-lĭt

[*articulare, articulatus* (Latin), "say clearly," from *articulus* (Latin), "division; part"]

Definition:
   a. (*verb*) To pronounce distinctly; to express well in words.

   The speaker couldn't be understood because he slurred and mumbled his words instead of **articulating** them clearly.

   One of the duties of a president is to **articulate** the policies and programs of his administration in a forceful and convincing way.

   b. (*adjective*) Expressed clearly and forcefully; able to employ language easily and fluently.

   The president's statement in defense of his economic program was unusually **articulate** and effective.

   Helen was chosen to present our petition to the mayor because she is the most **articulate** speaker in the class.

Related Forms: (*nouns*) articulation, articulateness

Synonyms: (*verbs*) enunciate; clarify, expound (Word 180), elucidate, explicate; (*adjectives*) fluent, eloquent, silver-tongued, glib

Antonyms: (*verbs*) mumble, mutter, maunder, swallow one's words; (*adjectives*) slurred, unintelligible, garbled; inarticulate, incoherent

39. **a-skew**   *adjective and adverb*   ə-skyoo'

[Derivation uncertain but probably *a* (Middle English), "on" + *skew*]

Definition:
   a. (*adjective and adverb*) Out of line or position; turned to one side.

   The drawers had been pulled out of the bureau, the lamps had been knocked over, and every picture on the wall was **askew.**

   b. (*adverb*) Disapprovingly; scornfully.

   "Why is the principal looking **askew** at me?" I wondered. "Do I have my shirt on backwards or something?"

Synonyms: (*adjectives*) crooked, cockeyed, uneven, unsymmetrical, awry; (adverbs) disdainfully, contemptuously, askance, derisively

Antonyms: (*adjectives*) straight, symmetrical; (*adverbs*) approvingly, benignly

Usage Notes:
   a. Note the somewhat subtle difference in the use of *askew* and *awry* (pronounced ə-rī'). *Askew* is usually reserved for concrete objects such as lampposts and hats. *Awry*, on the other hand, is generally used for more abstract things such as plans, arrangements, or actions.

   b. Also note the distinction between *askew* and *askance*, meaning "sideways" or "oblique(ly)." *Askew* usually implies simple disapproval or scorn. *Askance* (variant, *askant*), however, implies mistrust and suspicion as well as disapproval.

40. **as-sim-i-late**   *verb*   ə-sĭm′-ə-lāt
[*ad* (Latin), "to" + *similis* (Latin), "like; same"]

Definition:

a. To absorb fully or make one's own; to adopt as one's own.

Some children **assimilate** new information more quickly than others.

The body may **assimilate** some foods more easily than others.

America has **assimilated** the cultural traditions of many different peoples, and this process has greatly enriched our national life.

b. To adapt fully or to make like.

High school students are often under a great deal of pressure to **assimilate** their manner of dressing to that of their peers.

Related Form: (*noun*) assimilation

Usage Note:
The word *assimilation* is much used by sociologists to indicate the process by which individuals belonging to a minority group adopt the living habits and standards of the dominant group in the society. The process is also called *acculturation*. (For the use of *assimilation* in linguistics, see page 57.)

Every year thousands of immigrants from all over the world become naturalized citizens of our country.

Synonyms: (*verbs*) integrate, homogenize; fuse, merge; naturalize, acculturate; digest; incorporate, appropriate; adjust, transform

Antonyms: (*verbs*) segregate, isolate, insulate

Related Phrases: a process of naturalization; in the mainstream; a separatist movement, a standoffish attitude

Using the Words

Exercise I. Parts of Speech

Indicate the part of speech of each of the following words. Two answers are possible in some instances.

1. apathy n.
2. askew adj., adv.
3. array n., v.
4. arbitrary adj.
5. apprehend v.
6. articulate adj., v.

Exercise II. Words in Phrases

In each of the following groups, select the item that best expresses the meaning of the *italicized* word in the introductory phrase.

1. *apprehended* the suspect
   a. accused   b. protected   c. caught   d. released   e. tried

2. an *articulate* proponent of the plan
   a. long-standing   b. unexpected   c. well-known
   d. eloquent   e. self-appointed

3. an *anomaly* in today's world
   a. adage   b. issue   c. element   d. ideal   e. abnormality

4. with the bedclothes all *askew*
   a. crooked   b. faded   c. clean   d. torn   e. neat

5. a totally *arbitrary* group of numbers
   a. meaningless   b. random   c. unlikely   d. useful
   e. unworkable

Exercise III. Completing Sentences

Complete each of the following sentences or pairs of sentences by selecting the most appropriate word from the group of words given below. Make whatever adjustments are necessary to fit the words into the sentences properly.

appall	apathy	arbitrate
assimilate	anomaly	array

1. "Randy must be totally uninterested in politics," Tony observed. "Lately I've noticed that an expression of profound ___apathy___ and boredom comes over his face every time the subject comes up."

2. In the face of my opponent's formidable ___array___ of facts and figures, I was forced to concede that I was wrong.

3. "The only practical way to settle this dispute," the attorney remarked, "is to call in an impartial third party to ___arbitrate___ it."

4. It may take long hours of hard work to _assimilate_ all the technical data you need to become a computer programmer.

5. The devastation and suffering wrought by the meteorological phenomenon called *El Niño* _appalled_ the entire country.

Exercise IV. Synonyms and Antonyms

A. Match each word in Column A with its **synonym** in Column B.

Column A	*Column B*
e 1. comprehend apprehend	a. askance
d 2. mediate arbitrate	b. horrify
a 3. disapprovingly askew	c. despotic
b 4. dismay appall	d. referee
c 5. tyrannical arbitrary	e. grasp

Indicate which of the basic words taught in this lesson (Words 31–40) is **synonymous** with each of the words in Column A.

B. In each of the following groups, select the two words that are most nearly **antonyms**.

1. a. adorn   b. mediate   c. muster   d. instill   e. disperse
2. a. inarticulate   b. ordinary   c. objective   d. eloquent   e. scornful
3. a. boredom   b. oddity   c. process   d. norm   e. umpire
4. a. keen   b. dreadful   c. apathetic   d. partial   e. straight
5. a. equip   b. appall   c. manage   d. elate   e. capture

Exercise V. Word Roundup

1. Explain the difference in meaning between *disinterested* and *uninterested.*

2. What special meaning does the word *assimilation* have for a sociologist? for a linguist? Give a synonym for *assimilation* as used in sociology and one for the word as used in linguistics.

3. What is an *arbiter*? an *arbiter elegantiae* (or *elegantiarum*)?

Exercise VI. Framing Sentences

Use each of the following words in an original sentence that clearly illustrates the word's meaning.

1. anomalous
2. apathetic
3. appall
4. apprehensive
5. arbitrary
6. arbitration
7. array
8. articulate
9. askew

Completing Verbal Analogies

Analogy Question Type I.   Perhaps the simplest type of analogy question used on standardized tests (and also the easiest word relationship met with) is shown below. For convenience, the four elements involved in this sample have been labeled *A, B, C,* and *D.*

Type 1

A	B	C	_____D_____
absolve : exonerate	= abstain :		(*indulge, acquit, forgo, impeach, abet*)

What the student is being asked to do in this type of question is complete an analogy that is three-quarters finished. The student is to do this by selecting one of the five choices offered under *D.* Note that these choices are italicized within a pair of parentheses.

Completing Type-I Analogy Questions Correctly.   There are three basic steps involved in the correct completion of Type-I analogy questions.

Step 1:   Look at items *A* and *B,* and determine the relationship between them. *A* and *B* represent the two words that are in the **key** or **given relationship.** The key or given relationship usually comes before the equals sign (or before the word *as*) in an analogy question. It indicates which word relationship is being used on both sides of the equals sign in the particular analogy under consideration. (In this book the words in the key or given relationship are printed in **boldface type** so they can be spotted easily.)

In the sample analogy given above, the relationship between *A* and *B* (*absolve, exonerate*) is clearly sameness. *Absolve* and *exonerate,* as indicated in Lesson 1 (page 29), are synonyms; they mean the same thing.

This means that the relationship between *C* and *D* must also be one of sameness. In other words, the answer selected from the group of five choices given under *D* must mean the same as *C.*

Step 2:   Now look at *C,* and determine what it means. In the sample, *C* is *abstain,* which, as indicated in Lesson 1 (page 29), means "refrain."

Step 3:   Finally, look at the group of choices offered under *D,* and select the word that means the same as *abstain.* This is the item that is needed to complete the analogy correctly.

And what is the word wanted? It is *forgo,* which was listed as a synonym of *abstain* on page 29.

The other choices offered under *D* are clearly wrong. *Indulge* means the opposite of *abstain,* and the other words (*acquit, impeach,* and *abet*) bear no relation to it whatsoever. (Note, however, that *acquit* is a synonym of *absolve* and *exonerate,* while *impeach* means the opposite of these two words. These items were intentionally included in the group in order to confuse the student. When doing analogy questions, always keep an eye out for such traps.)

"A Means the Same as B.*"*   Thus, the complete analogy reads:

absolve : exonerate = abstain : *forgo*

Note that the word relationship involved in this sample is *sameness.* We can express this relationship in abstract terms as "A means the same as B; C means the same as D." This relationship is one of the most frequently used on standardized tests.

Exercise I

Complete, the following analogies.

1. **agenda : schedule** = affectation : (*sincerity, adversity, mannerism, conclusion, aesthetics*)

2. **ambivalent : uncertain** = equivocal : (*illusory, abominable, eventful, ambiguous, unanimous*)

3. **advocate : champion** = critic : (*accessory, opponent, teetotaler, flatterer, bystander*)

4. **anomaly : misfit** = anarchy : (*setting, freak, chaos, denunciation, yarn*)

5. **academic : theoretical** = opulent : (*civil, destitute, natural, unsociable, luxurious*)

Exercise II Answers will vary.

Write **three** complete analogies of your own to illustrate the word relationship "*A* means the same as *B*; *C* means the same as *D*." In **two** of your original analogies, use at least **one** of the basic words studied in Lessons 3–4 (Words 21–40).

Noah Webster

In 1828, Noah Webster (1758–1843), America's first scientific lexicographer, published a two–volume *American Dictionary of the English Language*. This work and its successors down through the years have made the name Webster synonymous with dictionary in American households. What got Webster started on the dictionary project was his profound dismay over the continued use of British textbooks and dictionaries in American schools after the United States had become independent from Great Britain. Thus, Webster began his great work in a spirit of national pride. When he was finished, his dictionary contained more than 12,000 words that were not listed in any other dictionary then

available. Many of these new items were "Americanisms"—that is, expressions coined and used by Americans. Sales of the dictionary were tremendous, and the work did much to shape and standardize the spelling and pronunciation of American English. Webster produced a second edition of his dictionary in 1840, and the work has been revised and updated many times since then. Indeed, Webster's dictionary (in its revised form) is still a staple item in libraries and households in the United States.

Enriching the Lesson

The words *apathy* (Word 32) and *anarchy* (Word 28) are but two of the numerous English words based on Greek originals. Some other words of the same type are listed below. With or without the aid of a dictionary, define each, and indicate what the original Greek word or word elements meant.

1. archaic
2. cacophony
3. neophyte
4. paragon
5. phobia
6. stratagem
7. misanthropic
8. philanthropy
9. dogmatic
10. dynamic
11. epidemic
12. panegyric
13. sophistry
14. monopoly
15. cataclysm
16. dynasty
17. pedantic
18. pedagogy
19. didactic
20. orthodox

Exercise II.   Order and Chaos

1. In Lesson 3 you learned that *anarchy* denotes the chaos resulting from a lack of effective government. The following words indicate different types of government. (An anarchist is opposed to them all.) Define each term in such a way as to bring out the distinctive characteristics of the type of government involved.

    a. democracy
    b. theocracy
    c. socialism
    d. communism
    e. fascism
    f. oligarchy

2. Answer the following questions, or supply the information requested.

    a. What is a *nihilist*? *nihilism*?

    b. What is a *subversive* interested in doing? Give a verb related to this word, and tell what it means.

    c. What is meant by *sedition*? Give an adjective related to this word, and tell what it means.

Exercise III.   Expanding Your Word Power

The words listed below are not on the Basic Word List, but they were mentioned in passing in Lesson 4. All of them would make useful additions to your working vocabulary. Define each, give its etymology, list **two** synonyms and **two** antonyms (where possible), and use in a short sentence that clearly illustrates the word's meaning.

1. stolid
2. indifference
3. aghast
4. elate
5. discern
6. misgiving
7. capricious
8. adjudicate
9. deploy

Related Forms in Context

Beneath each sentence below are four words introduced in Lesson 3 or 4. Review the related forms for these words, and choose the one that best completes the sentence. Write that related form in the space provided.

1. Can you explain why the striking clock in Act II, scene i, of Shakespeare's *Julius Caesar* is anachronistic ?

    a. amnesty   b. anecdote   **c. anachronism**   d. ambience

2. Filled with apprehension , I let the six-inch black snake coiled on Shoshi's outstretched hand slither onto my arm.

    a. allude   b. alienate   c. articulate   **d. apprehend**

3. Supporters of Nicola Sacco and Bartolomeo Vanzetti, Italian immigrants executed in 1927, claimed they did not receive a fair trial because they were anarchists .

    a. amnesty   **b. anarchy**   c. anecdote   d. anomaly

4. Doctors caution that exposure to ambient sound greater than 120 decibels may result in hearing loss caused by damage to sensitive hair cells in the inner ear.

    a. apathy   **b. ambience**   c. anachronism   d. anathema

5. The researcher could offer only anecdotal evidence from several interviews to support her claim.

    a. anecdote   b. array   c. anathema   d. anomaly

6. In Arthur Miller's *The Crucible*, based on the Salem witch trials of 1692, ordinary citizens are anathematized and tried as witches.

    a anarchy   b. anachronism   c. amnesty   **d. anathema**

7. The arbitrator, arbiter demanded that both parties listen respectfully, without interrupting, as each side stated its case.

    a. assimilate   b. apprehend   **c. arbitrate**   d. alienate

8. Next week several local political groups will sponsor a symposium on what can be done to combat the apathetic voter turnout in local elections.

    a. anarchy   **b. apathy**   c. anomaly   d. anecdote

9. A grand jury is investigating an alleged money-laundering scheme involving ten banks in three countries.

    a. allege   b. allude   c. arbitrate   d. apprehend

73

10. At the lecture, we learned of the _appalling_ events of December 29, 1890, at Wounded Knee, South Dakota, when 29 U.S. soldiers and about 200 Sioux men, women, and children were killed.

    a. alienate   b. allude   c. assimilate   **d. appall**

11. If your goal is the _assimilation_ of a vast store of knowledge, you must read extensively about a wide range of subjects.

    a. alienate   b. allude   **c. assimilate**   d. appall

12. The Universal Declaration of Human Rights, passed by the U.N. General Assembly in December 1948, lists the _inalienable_ rights of all human beings.

    a. allude   **b. alienate**   c. assimilate   d. apprehend

13. Compared with animals born in the wild, zoo-bred animals may exhibit _anomalous_ patterns of behavior.

    a. anomaly   b. anarchy   c. amnesty   d. anathema

14. Jed claims it will take _arbitration_ to decide whether his family will visit the Pro Football Hall of Fame (his choice) or the National Baseball Hall of Fame and Museum (his sister's choice).

    a. alienate   **b. arbitrate**   c. assimilate   d. articulate

15. In his three-minute Gettysburg Address, President Lincoln presented a brief, eloquent _articulation_ of the Union's goals.

    a. allude   b. assimilate   **c. articulate**   d. allege

16. *My Favorite Martian*, a 1960s TV sitcom, featured a human-looking _alien_ with retractable antennae at the back of his head.

    a. array   b. arbitrate   c. assimilate   **d. alienate**

17. Can you identify any of the literary _allusions_ in T.S. Eliot's poem "The Hollow Men"?

    a. allege   **b. allude**   c. apprehend   d. appall

18. The lead story in today's paper is about two whistle-blowers' _allegations_ of waste and outright theft in the city administration.

    a. apprehend   b. assimilate   **c. allege**   d. allude

19. We waited _apprehensively_ for the latest forecast on where and when the hurricane would make landfall.

    a. apprehend   b. appall   c. articulate   d. arbitrate

20. Whenever his mother nags him about cleaning his room, Jim looks up at her _apathetically_ and then continues reading.

    a. anecdote   b. anarchy   c. ambience   **d. apathy**

Lesson 5

41. **astute** — 50. **authentic**

---

41. **a-stute**   *adjective*   ə-stoot' *or* ə-styoot'
[*astutus* (Latin), "cunning," from *astus* (Latin), "craftiness"]

Definition: Keen of mind and judgment, especially in practical matters; cunning.

>   The novelist Jane Austen was an **astute** observer of life and manners in the English countryside at the beginning of the 19th century.

>   More than one clever money manager has been able to amass a tremendous fortune by **astute** speculation in the stock market.

Related Forms: (*noun*) astuteness; (*adverb*) astutely

Phrases: an astute analysis, an astute criticism; astute advertising

Synonyms: (*adjectives*) shrewd, perceptive, sharp, acute; sagacious, judicious (Word 249); farsighted, perspicacious; quick-witted, clever; wily, cagey; (*nouns*) perceptiveness, discernment, acumen, sagacity

Antonyms: (*adjectives*) obtuse, unperceptive, undiscerning; empty-headed, stupid, foolish, doltish, vacuous, inane

Related Phrases: sharp practice; acute perceptions; cunning as a fox; shrewd insights into human nature; a shrewd investor

42. **a-sy-lum**   *noun*   ə-sī'-ləm
[*asylon* (Greek), "place of refuge," from *a* (Greek), "without" + *sylon* (Greek), "right of seizure"]

Definition:
a. An institution that shelters and cares for mentally unbalanced, aged, or homeless persons.

>   The eighteenth-century poet Christopher Smart spent a good deal of his life in the infamous London insane **asylum** commonly called Bedlam.

b. Any place offering protection or security.

>   Ever since early colonial days, the United States has served as an **asylum** for the oppressed and downtrodden of the world.

c. Protection against a legal or social penalty.

>   Many Cubans escaping from the oppressive regime of Fidel Castro have been granted political **asylum** in the United States.

Synonyms: (*nouns*) sanctuary, refuge, haven

Related Phrases: seek sanctuary; take refuge; protective custody; a safe house

Sanctuary

Literally, the word *sanctuary* (from *sanctus* [Latin], "sacred") denotes a holy place, usually the most sacred part in a church, often referred to as "the holy of holies" In biblical times, the sanctuary sheltered the Ark of the Covenant.

The word *sanctuary* is imbedded in historical tradition. In ancient and medieval times, churches and monasteries served as a place of asylum or sanctuary for persons fleeing violence or penalties of the law. Once inside such a refuge, a fugitive would claim "the right of sanctuary"—that is, immunity from arrest or injury. To injure such a protected person or to remove him by force was regarded as a sacrilege. Eventually the abuse of the privilege led to its general abolition, though it survives in modern times in certain situations.

43. **a-tone**   *verb*   ə-tōn'

[from the English phrase "to be *at one* with," the idea being that a person who atones for a misdeed is brought back together with God and made whole (or one with himself) in conscience]

Definition: To make up for or repent.

"You made an honest mistake," Wanda said. "Don't feel that you have to **atone** for it."

The plot of the novel is awfully contrived, but the wonderfully vivid descriptions of the setting do much to **atone** for this weakness.

Related Form: (*noun*) atonement

Usage Note:

The *Day of Atonement* (from the Hebrew *Yom Kippur*) is a day set aside by Jews for fasting and prayer as penance for sins and misdeeds committed during the year just past.

Synonyms: (*verbs*) expiate, redeem, offset; (*nouns*) penance, expiation; compensation, reparation, restitution, redress

Related Phrases: make amends for; do penance for

44. a-troc-i-ty   *noun*   ə-trŏs'-ə-tē
[*atrox, atrocis* (Latin), "cruel" + *-ox, -oc-* (Latin), "looking"]

Definition: A savagely cruel, brutal, or inhuman deed; a monstrosity.

For days after the city had fallen to the enemy, bands of drunken soldiers wandered the streets, committing one **atrocity** after another on the helpless and terrified population.

"*You* may call that thing a hat," Al exclaimed. "*I* call it an **atrocity**."

Related Forms: (*adjective*) atrocious; (*noun*) atrociousness

Usage Note:

Atrocious (pronounced ə-trō'-shəs) means not only "extremely cruel or brutal" (as in the phrase "an atrocious crime") but also "extremely poor or bad" (as in the phrases "atrocious behavior" and "atrocious taste"). *Atrociousness*, the noun form, is used in exactly the same way.

Synonyms: (*nouns*) enormity, outrage; (*adjectives*) barbarous, barbaric, sadistic; grisly, gruesome (Word 216), ghastly; heinous (Word 222), outrageous; horrible, dreadful, abominable

Antonyms: (*nouns*) kindness, good deed, act of charity; (*adjectives*) clement, benevolent, kindhearted, merciful, humane; impeccable, flawless, irreproachable, unimpeachable

Related Phrases: war crimes, a crime against humanity

45. at-ro-phy   *noun and verb*   ă'-trə-fē
[*a* (Greek), "without" + *trophe* (Greek), "nourishment"]

Definition:

a.   (*noun*) A failure to develop normally; a progressive wasting away or decline.

> Medical experts state that almost every case of muscle and tissue **atrophy** is the result of changes in cell nutrition, disease, or prolonged disuse.

> The tremendous influx of wealth, luxuries, and slaves that resulted from the acquisition of foreign lands was in part responsible for the moral **atrophy** of the Roman ruling class.

b.   (*verb*) To waste away.

> "Well, here I am," Mr. Kravitz thought to himself sadly on the morning of his 40th birthday, "a middle-aged man whose talents are beginning to **atrophy**."

Related Form: (*adjective*) atrophic

Synonyms: (*nouns*) deterioration, degeneration, decay; (*verbs*) decay, deteriorate, degenerate, shrivel, wither, shrink, rot, stunt

Antonyms: (*nouns*) growth, development, maturation; (*verbs*) grow, develop, mature, flourish, prosper

46. at·tri·tion   *noun*   ə-trĭsh'-ən

[*attritio, attritionis* (Latin), "a rubbing against," from *ad* (Latin), "against" + *terere* (Latin), "rub"]

Definition:

a. A gradual wearing down or weakening of resistance resulting from constant friction, pressure, or harassment.

> Guerrilla warfare achieves its ends through a slow but steady process of **attrition**, rather than by victory in a quick, winner-take-all campaign.

> "A heavyweight boxing match is not so much a pitched battle as a war of **attrition**," the sportscaster observed. "For that reason, the winner is usually the fighter who is not too battered and exhausted to go on."

b. A gradual, often natural decrease in size, strength, or number as a result of resignation, retirement, death, or the like.

> "The sales department is a bit overstaffed," the firm's personnel manager remarked. "However, the normal rate of **attrition** around here should solve that problem fairly quickly."

Synonyms: (*nouns*) abrasion, erosion; exhaustion, enervation; reduction, diminution

Antonyms: (*nouns*) increase, augmentation, expansion, enlargement

47. aug·ment   *verb*   ôg-mĕnt'

[*augmentum* (Latin), "an increase," from *augere* (Latin), "to increase"]

Definition: To make greater; to become greater.

> If we are to contend with the population explosion, we must **augment** the world's food supply.

> Traffic noises in the street outside my window **augment** appreciably during rush hour.

Related Form: (*noun*) augmentation

Synonyms: (*verbs*) increase, enlarge, expand, extend, magnify

Antonyms: (*verbs*) decrease, lessen, reduce, curtail (Word 114), diminish; contract, shrink, shrivel, abate, slacken, dwindle

48. au·gur   *noun and verb*   ô'-gûr

[*augur* (Latin), "soothsayer, diviner"]

Definition:

a. (*noun*) Someone who can forecast the future by spotting various signs or indications of what is to come.

> "I know you claim to be a reliable **augur** of future trends and developments in the economy," Mike remarked. "Still, your predictions are usually no more accurate than other people's."

78

b. (*verb*) To predict or foretell through signs; to point to or be an omen of.

> The Aztecs of Mexico believed that comets **augured** impending disaster, even the end of the world.

> The enthusiasm with which our candidate has been greeted all over the country certainly **augurs** well for success in the upcoming election.

Related Form: (*noun*) augury

Usage Note:
The noun *augury* (pronounced ô'-gyə-rē) means a number of things: (1) "the art of forecasting the future," (2) "a prophecy," and (3) "a sign or omen." Accordingly, words that mean the same thing include both *divination* and *prediction*, as well as *portent, premonition,* and *harbinger.*

Synonyms: (*nouns*) soothsayer, diviner, prophet, seer; (*verbs*) prophesy, divine, prognosticate; portend, forebode, presage, bode, foreshadow

The second inauguration of Abraham Lincoln, January 1, 1865.

Augur

In ancient Rome, the *augurs* were a group of priests who sought to discover, by observing certain signs, whether or not the gods approved of a proposed policy or action. The sign most often used for this purpose was the flight of birds, although the augurs also depended on such phenomena as lightning, comets, and the appearance of the entrails of animals. The "taking of the auguries" preceded every important public action, and especially in the early days of Rome, was widely used by private individuals.

From *augur*, we get the word *inaugurate*, meaning "to begin formally; to induct into office," and the corresponding noun, *inauguration*. The hope is, of course, that the omens will be favorable for such an important beginning.

A specialist among soothsayers or diviners in ancient Rome was the *auspex*, who depended specifically on the flight of birds. From this title, we get the word *auspicious*, meaning "favorable, under good omens." and its opposite, *inauspicious*.

79

49. aus-tere   *adjective*   ô-stēr′
[*austeros* (Greek), "harsh, rough, bitter, unadorned"]

Definition: Rigidly severe; severely simple or bare.

My grandfather was an **austere** man whom I never knew to laugh or smile.

During World War II, living conditions in England were extremely **austere** because of severe shortages of food, fuel, and consumer goods.

The Puritans practiced an **austere**, cheerless form of religion.

Caesar's simple, even **austere**, style of writing contrasts greatly with the complicated and ornate manner of Cicero.

Related Forms: (*nouns*) austereness, austerity, austerities; (*adverb*) austerely

Phrases: austere surroundings, an austere manner, an austere diet; a life of austerity; the austerities imposed by want

Synonyms: (*adjectives*) stern, strict, straitlaced; abstemious, sober, puritanical, ascetic; solemn; harsh, forbidding; somber, gloomy; plain, unadorned, undecorated

Antonyms: (*adjectives*) gentle, mild, kindly; affable (Word 15), tolerant; self-indulgent; elaborate, involved; orotund, florid; gaudy, flamboyant

50. au-then-tic   *adjective*   ô-thĕn′-tĭk
[*authentikos* (Greek), "genuine"]

Definition: Genuine, trustworthy.

"The painting the salesman showed you has to be a fake," Vera informed me. "You can't buy an **authentic** Rembrandt for five dollars."

Related Forms: (*noun*) authenticity; (*verb*) authenticate

Phrases: an authentic record, an authentic document, an authentic account

Synonyms: (*adjectives*) real, true, actual, veritable, bona fide, legitimate, kosher; indisputable, indubitable

Antonyms: (*adjectives*) counterfeit, fraudulent, fake, forged, spurious, phony, bogus, apocryphal; dubious, untrustworthy, fishy

Usage Notes:

a. The synonyms and antonyms listed above include a number of colloquial or slang terms, including *fake, phony, bogus,* and *fishy. Kosher,* a colloquial term meaning "legitimate or proper," has come into English (via Yiddish) from the Hebrew word *kasher,* meaning "in accordance with Jewish dietary laws and, therefore, clean or proper."

b. *Bona fide,* literally meaning "in good faith," is one of a large group of words and phrases that English has borrowed without change from Latin. In English it means "genuine" or "sincere."

Using the Words

1. a-stute'
2. a-tone'
3. a-troc'-i-ty
4. at-tri'-tion
5. aug-ment'
6. au-then'-tic

Exercise I. Syllabication and Pronunciation

Syllabicate the following words correctly, and place the major stress mark (') after the syllable that is accented when the word is pronounced.

1. astute
2. atone
3. atrocity
4. attrition
5. augment
6. authentic

Exercise II. Words Out of Context

In each of the following groups, select the item that best expresses the meaning of the numbered word at the left.

1. asylum
   a. prison   b. booth   c. arena   <u>d. haven</u>
   e. office

2. atrocity
   a. natural talent   <u>b. inhuman act</u>
   c. outstanding accomplishment
   d. grievous fault   e. kind deed

3. augment
   a. imagine   b. solidify   c. belittle
   d. curtail   <u>e. enlarge</u>

4. augur
   a. accumulate   <u>b. bode</u>   c. expiate
   d. compensate   e. refine

5. authentic
   a. phony   b. gross   <u>c. kosher</u>   d. cagey
   e. rotten

Exercise III. Completing Sentences

Complete each of the following sentences by selecting the most appropriate word from the group of words given below. Make whatever adjustments are necessary to fit the words into the sentences properly.

atone	attrition	austere
astute	atrophy	augment

1. The reason why premed programs have such a high rate of __attrition__ is simple: A great many students find the course of study too demanding and turn to something easier.

2. Protestant churches in New England tend to be __austere__ structures with little or no architectural adornment.

3. It was never clear whether the defendants had been acquitted because they were innocent or because they had an __astute__ lawyer who found a clever way to get them off the hook.

81

4. I have heard it said that many people no longer know right from wrong and have, in effect, sunk into a profound state of moral __atrophy__.

5. Paying for the repairs that are necessary seems to be an effective way to __atone__ for the damage you have done.

Exercise IV.   Synonyms and Antonyms

Classify each of the following pairs of expressions as **S** for **synonyms** or **A** for **antonyms**.

S 1. erosion—attrition   S 6. sanctuary—refuge
S 2. gaudy—flamboyant   A 7. flourish—wither
A 3. perceptive—dense   A 8. magnify—minimize
S 4. seer—prophet   S 9. impeccable—flawless
A 5. bona fide—bogus   A 10. humane—barbaric

Exercise V.   Framing Sentences

A. Use each of the following words in an original sentence that clearly illustrates its meaning.

1. asylum   3. atrophy   5. augment
2. atrocity   4. attrition   6. augur

B. Give a **noun** form of each of the following words, and use it in an original sentence that clearly illustrates its meaning.

1. astute astuteness   3. authentic authenticity
2. atone atonement   4. austere austerity

Dissecting the Words

Roots

1. The Greek root **auto(s)**, meaning "self" or "same," is found in numerous English words, including *authentic,* studied in this lesson. Here are some other words in which this root appears:

autocrat (literally "self-ruling")—a ruler with unlimited or unrestricted power; a tyrant or despot. Noun: *autocracy*; adjective: *autocratic*

autopsy (literally "seeing with one's own eyes")—the examination of a dead body to determine the cause of death

autonomy—independence; self-government. Adjective: *autonomous*

autograph—a person's own signature or handwriting

autodidact—a person who is self-taught

automatic—self-operating; running or working by itself

2. The Latin root **ag, act** (as in the Latin verb *agere, egi, actus*) means "act, drive." It occurs in such words as *agenda* (Word 18) and *agile* (Word 20). Other words derived from the same root include:

exigency—a driving need

agitate—to stir up

coagulate—to form into a compact mass; to congeal

enact—to make into law; to act out on the stage. Noun: *enactment*

cogent—forceful; convincing

cogitate (literally "drive about in one's mind")—to ponder or consider intently

Suffix

The suffix **-ize** (British variant, **-ise**) has the general meaning of "make or make into." It has proved to be a handy tool for making a verb out of a noun or an adjective. For example:

popular + ize = *popularize*—to make popular

deputy + ize = *deputize*—to make into a deputy

Sometimes, of course, the spelling of the form to which -*ize* is attached is modified in some way in the new word. For example:

pole + ize = *polarize* (not *polize*!)—to concentrate around two conflicting or contrasting positions

fraternity + ize = *fraternize* (not *fraternitize*!)—to be sociable with

Exercise

1. Answer the following questions regarding words containing the root *auto(s)*.

   a. The word *autointoxication* may be used in both a physical and a psychological sense. Explain the two senses in which the word may properly be used.

   b. Explain the italicized word in this sentence: "The remaining colonies in Africa demanded *autonomy*."

   c. What part of the human nervous system is referred to as *autonomic*? Why is this word appropriate?

   d. What does *autosuggestion* mean? Explain its origin.

2. With or without the aid of a dictionary, define each of the nouns or adjectives listed below, and convert it into a related verb form by adding -*ize*. (Make any spelling changes that are necessary.)

a. victim	f. eulogy	k. social
b. dogma	g. civil	l. plagiarism
c. politics	h. legitimate	m. theory
d. trauma	i. proselyte	n. radical
e. deputy	j. tyranny	o. normal

83

Enriching the Lesson

Exercise I. Latin Phrases in English

As indicated earlier in this lesson, *bona fide* is just one of a large group of phrases that English has borrowed without change from Latin. Some other examples are listed below. What does each mean in present-day English? What is its literal meaning in Latin?

1. alter ego
2. quid pro quo
3. de facto
4. persona non grata
5. obiter dictum
6. amicus curiae
7. de jure
8. status quo
9. pro tempore *(often shortened to* pro tem)
10. prima facie
11. modus operandi *(often shortened to* MO)
12. ex officio
13. alma mater
14. sub rosa
15. in absentia
16. vice versa
17. casus belli
18. non sequitur
19. sine qua non
20. deus ex machina

Exercise II. "Newsworthies"

A number of the basic words studied in this lesson, including *atrocity, attrition,* and *asylum,* frequently crop up in newspaper and magazine articles and on radio-TV news programs. Each gained a currency that made it newsworthy. A number of other examples of newsworthy expressions are listed below. With or without the aid of a dictionary, explain what each of these items means. Then use it in a phrase or sentence of your own.

1. détente
2. an activist
3. deficit spending
4. elitist
5. a police state
6. dumb down
7. a pluralistic society
8. a welfare state
9. a civil libertarian
10. permissiveness
11. a status symbol
12. urban renewal
13. disinformation
14. a reactionary
15. sexist
16. the establishment
17. gentrification
18. insider trading
19. rapprochement
20. a conservative
21. downsizing
22. neoconservative
23. a grass-roots movement
24. open diplomacy
25. software
26. a third-world nation
27. the feminist movement
28. a liberal
29. the inner city
30. human rights

Can you think of any others to add to this list?

Exercise III.   Yiddish in English—Is It Kosher?

Yes, today it certainly is kosher (a Yiddish word meaning "clean" or "proper") to use the word *kosher* colloquially. All dictionaries sanction such usage. A word or phrase that is Yiddish in origin and has been assimilated into our daily language is called a **yiddishism**.

Many of us use yiddishisms without being aware of their origin. Here are a few familiar expressions that are actually translations from Yiddish: *O.K. by me! How come? He knows from nothing. It shouldn't happen to a dog. What's with the jokes?*

It should be noted that since many of these adopted expressions are identified as either *slang* or *informal* by the dictionaries, they must be handled with care. One should not use them in formal writing. Some of the words fill a language need. For example, we have no equivalent English word or phrase to pinpoint the kind of annoying meddler that the yiddishism *kibitzer* denotes.

The American writer Leo Rosten (1908–1997) made a comprehensive study of Yiddish in English. Two of the words that he analyzes in detail are *chutzpah* ("unbelievable gall") and *megillah* ("a long, boring, overdetailed account"). The yiddishism *shtik*—meaning "a stylized or arch piece of acting overused by a performer"—is widely used, especially among actors and theater people generally.

The yiddishisms listed below are in common use. How many of them can you define?

1. yenta	5. schlock	9. schmaltz
2. mensch	6. kvetch	10. nosh
3. kvell	7. schlemiel	11. schlepp
4. klutz	8. schmooze	12. maven

Can you suggest any other words or phrases that would be appropriate for a lexicon of yiddishisms?

Exercise IV.   Expanding Your Word Power

The words listed below are not on the Basic Word List, but they were mentioned in passing in Lesson 5. All of them would make useful additions to your working vocabulary. Define each, give its etymology, list **two** synonyms and **two** antonyms (where possible), and use in a short sentence that clearly illustrates the word's meaning.

1. acumen	5. redress	9. clement
2. obtuse	6. impeccable	10. foreshadow
3. enormity	7. deteriorate	11. flamboyant
4. grisly	8. enhance	12. spurious

Lesson 6

51. avarice — 60. bland

---

51. av·a·rice   *noun*   ăv'-ə-rĭs
[*avarus* (Latin), "greedy," from *avere* (Latin), "desire"]

Definition: An excessive desire to acquire and possess wealth; a combination of greed and stinginess.

> Few novels portray the dehumanizing effects of avarice as vividly and forcefully as George Eliot's *Silas Marner*.

Related Forms: (*adjective*) avaricious; (*noun*) avariciousness

Synonyms: (*nouns*) acquisitiveness, cupidity, covetousness, rapacity; miserliness, parsimony, niggardliness; (*adjectives*) acquisitive, greedy, covetous, rapacious, grasping; stingy, miserly, niggardly, tightfisted

Antonyms: (for the miserly side of *avarice*): (*nouns*) generosity, liberality, openhandedness; (*adjectives*) generous, liberal, openhanded

52. av·id   *adjective*   ăv'-ĭd
[*avidus* (Latin), "craving; greedy," from *avere* (Latin), "desire"]

Definition: Extremely eager, anxious, or enthusiastic.

> Your mom and dad may be **avid** readers of spy novels.

> Your little brother may be an **avid** baseball fan.

Related Forms: (*noun*) avidity; (*adverb*) avidly

Phrases: an avid sportsman, an avid moviegoer, avid for adventure

Synonyms: (*adjectives*) zealous, ardent, keen, fervent, fervid, voracious, insatiable, rabid, fanatical, passionate, gung ho

Antonyms: (*adjectives*) indifferent, apathetic, unresponsive; (*nouns*) apathy (Word 32), indifference

53. bad·ger   *verb*   băj'-ēr
[Origin uncertain, possibly from the name of the animal]

Definition: To tease; to annoy with a constant string of petty torments.

> A curious child may **badger** his or her parents with an endless string of almost unanswerable questions.

> A judge may reprimand an overly aggressive attorney for **badgering** a witness.

Synonyms: (*verbs*) harass, torment, pester, plague, vex, irritate, hassle, bait, harry

Antonyms: (*verbs*) leave in peace; soothe, calm, pacify

54. **baf-fle** *verb* băf'-əl
[Origin uncertain]

Definition:
a. To puzzle completely.

"How you manage to do well on tests when you never seem to crack a book completely **baffles** me," Jerry remarked.

b. To prevent from achieving a goal.

Despite several clues that at first seemed promising, the police were eventually **baffled** in their attempt to solve the murder.

Related Forms: (*adjective*) baffling; (*noun*) bafflement

Synonyms: (*verbs*) perplex, mystify, bewilder, nonplus, confound; thwart (Word 376), foil, balk, frustrate, stymie, stump; (*adjectives*) mystifying, bewildering, enigmatic; perplexed, mystified, quizzical

Antonyms: (verbs) understand, comprehend, fathom (Word 185); help, aid, assist

55. **ba-nal** *adjective* bə-näl' *or* bā'-nəl
[*banal* (French), "commonplace," from *ban* (Old French), "summons to military service"]

Definition: Made stale by constant use or repetition.

I expected dialogue by such a well-known writer to sparkle with wit. Unfortunately, it proved to be **banal** and flat.

Related Forms: (*noun*) banality; (*adverb*) banally

Synonyms: (*adjectives*) trite, hackneyed, stereotyped, prosaic, commonplace, pedestrian, insipid, vapid, fatuous (Word 186), jejune, corny; (*nouns*) triteness, insipidity; cliché, platitude, bromide

Antonyms: (*adjectives*) novel, fresh, original, innovative, provocative, striking, sparkling, scintillating, piquant; (*nouns*) novelty, originality

Usage Note:
a. *Trite* and *hackneyed* indicate staleness or dullness due to overuse. *Stereotyped* suggests a lack of originality and an overheavy reliance on conventional ideas, images, or forms. *Pedestrian* and *prosaic* simply indicate that something is quite ordinary. *Vapid* and *fatuous* suggest a lack of substance or perceptivity. *Jejune* adds to this the idea of childishness. *Corny* is a slang expression that can designate anything from triteness to oversentimentality.
b. Do not confuse *banal* with *baneful*, which means "harmful" or "destructive."

56. **bel·lig·er·ent**   *adjective and noun*   bə-lĭj'-ər-ĕnt

[*bellum* (Latin), "war" + *gerens* (Latin), "waging," from *gerere* (Latin), "wage"]

Definition:

a. (*adjective*) Warring, actually engaged in a war; warlike or hostile.

> Between 1915 and 1917, Italy, Bulgaria, Romania, Greece, Turkey, and the U.S.A. all entered World War I. This increased the total number of **belligerent** nations to a dozen, though that many were never involved in the conflict simultaneously.

> How can we hope to arrive at a fair settlement or even discuss the situation calmly when your attitude is so **belligerent**?

b. (*noun*) A party (for example, a nation or organization) engaged in a war.

> The Security Council called upon the **belligerents** to halt all military operations and send representatives to an emergency peace conference.

Related Forms: (*nouns*) belligerence, belligerency; (*adverb*) belligerently

Synonyms: (*adjectives*) martial, combative, bellicose, quarrelsome, contentious, militant, pugnacious, hawkish

Antonyms: (*adjectives*) pacific, peaceable, conciliatory, dovish

Usage Note:

Though *belligerent* and *bellicose* are often used interchangeably, they are really quite different. Both words of course mean "warlike or hostile," but only *belligerent* also means "warring" or "actually engaged in a war." In addition, *bellicose* tends to be used of a natural or inborn inclination toward aggressiveness, whereas *belligerent* tends to be reserved for a hostile attitude that is not innate but, rather, the result of some quite specific external cause.

Mars and Martial

Mars was the Roman god of war. His name is the source of our word *martial*, meaning "warlike" or "military," and also of the name of the month of March, during which the chief festivals of Mars occurred. The planet Mars is also named after this deity.

57. be-nign   *adjective*   bĭ-nīn′

[*bene* (Latin), "well" + *genus* (Latin), "birth; race"]

Definition:
   a. Gentle and kindly.

   Though a bear cub may look friendly and **benign**, it is still dangerous.

   b. Wholesome or favorable.

   On the whole, the years she spent abroad had a **benign** effect on the development of her personality.

Related Forms: (*noun*) benignity (pronounced bĭ-nĭg′-nə-tē); (*adjective*) benignant (pronounced bĭ-nĭg′-nĕnt); (*adverb*) benignly

Usage Note:
In medicine, *benign* means "not a threat to a person's health or life" — for example, in the phrase "a benign tumor." Its opposite is *malignant*.

Synonyms: (*adjectives*) benevolent; favorable, auspicious, beneficial, salutary, salubrious

Antonyms: (*adjectives*) malevolent; pernicious (Word 299), deleterious, injurious, inimical, noxious, detrimental

58. bick-er   *verb*   bĭk′-ēr

[*bikeren* (Middle English), "thrust; attack"]

Definition: To engage in petty quarreling.

The conference soon degenerated into an ugly dispute as the participants began to **bicker** over minor details of procedure.

Related Form: (*noun*) bickering

Synonyms: (*verbs*) squabble, wrangle, haggle, dicker

Antonyms: (*verbs*) agree, concur

59. bi-zarre   *adjective*   bĭ-zär′

[*bizarre* (French), "strange," originally "gallant": from *bizarro* (Spanish), "handsome, manly"; from *bizar* (*Basque*), "beard"]

Definition: Weird or fantastic.

Wearing **bizarre** masks and costumes on Halloween is a tradition that goes back many centuries.

The emperor Caligula's behavior was so **bizarre** that many Romans doubted his sanity.

Related Form: (*noun*) bizarreness

Synonyms: (*adjectives*) grotesque, outlandish, freakish, odd, queer, singular, far-out, unconventional, eccentric

Antonyms: (*adjectives*) normal, conventional, orthodox, straight, square; sedate, conservative, sober, staid

60. **bland**   *adjective*   blănd
[*blandus* (Latin), "smooth; soft-spoken"]

Definition:
   a. Mild or gentle. (When used in this sense, the word is usually neutral in tone.)

   The doctor prescribed a **bland** diet for the patient suffering from ulcers.

   b. Lacking interest or liveliness; flat. (When used in this sense, the word is distinctly pejorative.)

   He expressed his opinion in language so ordinary and **bland** that he made little or no impression on his audience.

Related Forms: (*noun*) blandness; (*adverb*) blandly

Phrases: bland food, a bland personality, a bland smile, a bland style

Synonyms: (*adjectives*) calming, soothing, nonirritating; dull, boring, unexciting, insipid, vapid, lifeless; nondescript, mediocre, run-of-the-mill

Antonyms: (*adjectives*) irritating, harsh; spicy, pungent, piquant, racy, colorful, florid, scintillating, lively, sprightly

Using the Words

Exercise I.   Parts of Speech

Indicate the part of speech of each of the following words. In one case, two answers are correct.

1. benign adj.   3. avid adj.   5. avarice n.
2. bicker v.   4. belligerent adj., n. 6. bizarre adj.

Exercise II.   Words in Phrases

In each of the following groups, select the item that best expresses the meaning of the *italicized* word in the introductory phrase.

1. a *benign* countenance
    a. beautiful   b. scarred   c. kindly   d. surly

2. motivated by *avarice*
    a. vengeance   b. fear   c. greed   d. ambition

3. *bizarre* behavior
    a. weird   b. aggressive   c. laudable   d. ordinary

4. a *bland* writing style
    a. curious   b. nondescript c. florid   d. original

5. *badgered* me with questions
    a. thrilled   b. puzzled   c. flattered   d. pestered

Exercise III.   Completing Sentences

Complete each of the following sentences by selecting the most appropriate word from the group of words given below.

banal	avarice	belligerent
baffle	bicker	avid

1. Though Queen Victoria sympathized deeply with the Southern cause, she had no intention of allowing Great Britain to become a(n) _belligerent_ in the American Civil War.

2. "We will never be able to present a united front in the upcoming election if we continue to ___bicker___ among ourselves about matters of no importance," the politician warned.

3. Ordinary detectives are often unable to solve the crimes they're investigating, but no mystery—no matter how complicated or puzzling—ever seems to ___baffle___ the great Sherlock Holmes.

4. "I've been a(n) ___avid___ sportsman all my life," the movie star told the reporter, "and I rarely miss a day on the golf links or the tennis court."

5. Some of the incidental ideas expressed in the film are novel and interesting, but the overall handling of the theme is terribly ___banal___ and flat.

Exercise IV.   Synonyms and Antonyms

A. Match each of the words in Column A with its synonym in Column B.

Column A		Column B	
c 1.	mediocre bland	a.	harass
d 2.	beneficial benign	b.	fantastic
a 3.	pester badger	c.	run-of-the-mill
e 4.	foil baffle	d.	salutary
b 5.	outlandish bizarre	e.	frustrate

Now indicate which of the basic words in this lesson (Words 51–60) is **synonymous** with each of the words in Column A.

B. In each of the following groups, select the two words that are most nearly **antonyms**.

1. a. terminate   b. squabble   c. concur   d. atrophy
2. a. triteness   b. bafflement   c. miserliness   d. generosity
3. a. piquant   b. freakish   c. swift   d. vapid
4. a. quarrelsome   b. conciliatory   c. typical   d. inane
5. a. fervent   b. peaceful   c. orderly   d. apathetic

91

Exercise V.   Word Roundup

1. Explain the difference in meaning and usage between *bellicose* and *belligerent*. Use each in an original sentence that clearly shows its meaning.

2. By means of illustrative sentences, show how *bizarre* may be applied to each of the following.

   a. human behavior   b. physical objects   c. ideas or points of view

3. What is a *benign* tumor? Give an antonym for *benign* in the medical sense.

4. A number of the expressions mentioned in the Synonyms and Antonyms sections of the word entries in this lesson are *slang*. Make a list of these items.

Exercise VI.   Framing Sentences

Use each of the following words in an original sentence that clearly illustrates its meaning.

1.	avaricious	6.	belligerence
2.	avidity	7.	benignly
3.	badger	8.	bickering
4.	baffling	9.	bizarre
5.	banality	10.	blandness

Completing Verbal Analogies

"A *Means the Opposite of* B." Analogy questions involving opposites (antonyms) occur frequently on standardized vocabulary tests. This type of analogy can be expressed in abstract terms as "*A* means the opposite of *B*; *C* means the opposite of *D*." Look at the following example of such an analogy question, and try to figure out the answer.

A   B   C ┌──────────────── D ────────────────┐

affluent : indigent = equitable : (*florid, destitute, arbitrary, opulent, bland*)

The answer is *arbitrary*. Here's why: The words in the key relationship (*A*, *B*) are *affluent* and *indigent*. They are opposites or antonyms. So, an antonym for *C*, *equitable*, is needed to complete the analogy correctly. The only word available for this purpose from among the five choices given is *arbitrary*. Hence, *arbitrary* is the correct answer.

Note, however, that *destitute* is both an antonym of *affluent* and a synonym of *indigent*. Similarly, *opulent* is both an antonym of *indigent* and a synonym of *affluent*. In addition, *florid* is something of an antonym of *bland*. All these words were included among the five choices in order to confuse the student and make selecting the right answer more difficult.

Note also that in analogy questions involving opposites (antonyms), the positive or desirable quality often comes first.

Whoopi Goldberg (born 1949) has been performing since the age of eight. Her many Hollywood roles have highlighted her skill as both an accomplished dramatic actress and a talented comedian. She has also appeared on the Broadway stage, in nightclubs, and on television. Her one-woman stand-up comedy act has become legendary.

An ability to use words well, combined with a well-developed sense of humor, has catapulted many an American into fame and fortune in this country's ever-growing entertainment industry.

Whoopi Goldberg

Exercise I

Complete each of the following analogies.

1. **augment : decrease** = wax : (*polish, wane, declare, frustrate, accelerate*)

2. **piquant : bland** = generous : (*ardent, dull, amiable, miserly, liberal*)

3. **absolve : incriminate** = acquit : (*liberate, mystify, convict, resolve, exclude*)

4. **conciliatory : belligerent** = astute : (*passionate, sagacious, indifferent, bellicose, obtuse*)

5. **authentic : spurious** = austere : (*flamboyant, bogus, puritanical, reliable, wily*)

6. **relish : abhor** = agile : (*lithe, contradictory, clumsy, zealous, commonplace*)

Exercise II   Answers will vary.

Write **three** original analogies involving opposites (antonyms). In your analogies use at least **three** of the basic words presented in Lessons 1–6 (Words 1–60).

Exercise III

The following items review what you have so far learned about analogy questions. Complete each.

1. **anarchy : chaos** = avarice : (*indulgence, mannerism, provocation, cupidity, encouragement*)

2. **hackneyed : innovative** = pedestrian : (*original, quarrelsome, auspicious, prosaic, grisly*)

3. **badger : harass** = abstain : (*pester, indulge, pacify, champion, forbear*)

4. **haven : sanctuary** = aggregate : (*anomaly, pretense, cluster, refuge, misdemeanor*)

5. **malevolent : benign** = adverse : (*noxious, weird, mediocre, favorable, covetous*)

6. **assiduous : indolent** = diligent : (*inconsolable, lethargic, abstemious, charitable, rapacious*)

Enriching the Lesson

Exercise I.   Fighting Words

With or without the aid of an unabridged dictionary, complete the following exercises.

1. Define the following expressions.

a.	war of nerves	i.	mobilization
b.	amphibious operation	j.	guerrilla
c.	blitzkrieg	k.	armistice
d.	pacification	l.	skirmish
e.	preemptive strike	m.	hostage
f.	pacifist	n.	ordnance
g.	hostilities	o.	broadside
h.	maneuvers	p.	hold out the olive branch

2. What is an *Armageddon*? Explain the story behind this word, and indicate where it comes from.

3. What is a *Pyrrhic victory*? Explain the story behind this phrase.

4. What is *martial law*? When is it usually imposed? What are *martial arts*? Name a movie star or other celebrity who is a noted *martial artist*.

5. The Latin word *bellum* means "war." What does *antebellum* mean? In what connection is this Latin phrase used in American history?

Exercise II.   Clichés

A **cliché** is simply an expression that has grown stale and flat as a result of overuse. Some good examples of clichés are *enjoy the fruits of one's labor, wolf down one's food, go like a house afire,* and similar hand-me-down metaphors and similes. Every cliché was presumably once fresh and original, but such expressions have been so overworked that today they strike us as being trite and corny.

This, however, is not to say that clichés should be avoided altogether. Countless clichés, such as *bend over backwards, cut corners,* and *turn a new leaf,* are still serviceable, even if they are overly familiar. In fact, it would be hard, if not impossible, to carry on a conversation or otherwise communicate without calling on clichés.

For that reason, a sound principle to follow in regard to clichés is this: Don't be a fanatic about avoiding them, but don't overuse them either. Also, bear in mind the literal meaning of the cliché, and try to use it only where it will be appropriate and effective. For example, a 12th grader who has just mailed out a batch of college applications might sum up his or her hopes for them by using a familiar cliché in this novel way: "Well, I've cast my bread upon the waters," the student might observe. "Now all I can do is pray that some of it comes back sandwiches!"

Now complete the following group of exercises involving clichés.

1. Some of the sentences below contain clichés; others have a measure of freshness and originality in them. Write the identifying letter of each sentence containing a cliché. Then replace the cliché with language that is more distinctive and effective.

   a. On that hot summer afternoon, the garden sizzled with bees.

   b. When we arrived back at camp, we were as hungry as bears.

   c. Her mere presence on the platform turned a routine gathering into a once-in-a-lifetime event.

   d. She left no stone unturned in her search for the missing papers.

   e. The news we received this morning was like a bolt from the blue.

   f. The fullback drove through the line like a knife going through soft cheese.

2. Substitute a fresher, more original expression for each of the clichés listed below.

a.	worked like a Trojan	d.	prostrate with grief
b.	a sumptuous repast	e.	lost his shirt at the track
c.	slept like a log	f.	paint the town red

3. Draw up a list of **twenty** clichés that you have heard or seen in the last week.

4. Complete each of the following comparisons with a word or phrase that is not a cliché.

   a. as fat as _____   d. as pretty as _____
   b. as mad as _____   e. as quiet as _____
   c. as old as _____   f. as big as _____

Exercise III.   A Verbal Diversion

Modern English is rich in colloquial expressions involving the names of members of the animal kingdom. Two such expressions are *chicken feed* (meaning "a woefully insufficient sum of money") and to *smell a rat* (meaning "to suspect that something is not quite as it should be"). A number of similar items, all of them widely used today in informal speech and writing, are listed below. With or without the aid of a dictionary or other reference book, define each. Then choose any **five**, and use each in a short sentence that clearly illustrates the expression's meaning.

1. a red herring	13. a bookworm
2. a round-robin	14. to let the cat out of the bag
3. a stool pigeon	15. to go to the dogs
4. a loan shark	16. a harebrained scheme
5. an eager beaver	17. to throw to the wolves
6. to dovetail	18. a paper tiger
7. to play possum	19. to take the bull by the horns
8. a white elephant	20. a sacred cow
9. to handle with kid gloves	21. to get one's goat
10. a dark-horse candidate	22. a wild-goose chase
11. a kangaroo court	23. a sheepish grin
12. a lame-duck session of Congress	24. to have a frog in one's throat

Can you add to this list from your own knowledge?

Exercise IV.   Expanding Your Word Power

The following words are not on the Basic Word List, but they were mentioned in passing in Lesson 6. All of them would make useful additions to your working vocabulary. Define each, give its etymology, list **two** synonyms and **two** antonyms (where possible), and use in a short sentence that clearly illustrates the word's meaning.

1. niggardly	5. platitude	9. haggle
2. voracious	6. insipid	10. militant
3. bait	7. grotesque	11. sedate
4. quizzical	8. foil	12. eccentric

Related Forms in Context

Beneath each sentence below are four words introduced in Lesson 5 or 6. Review the related forms for these words, and choose the one that best completes the sentence. Write that related form in the space provided.

1. The county commission authorized the purchase of six new school buses, a significant _augmentation_ of the current fleet.

    a. augur   b. atrophy   c. augment   d. baffle

2. According to Greek mythology, _avaricious_ King Midas, when granted a single wish, made the mistake of wishing that everything he touched would turn into gold.

    a. atrophy   b. avarice   c. augur   d. attrition

3. To collect data on the movements of schools of fish, biologists use different kinds of tags that _benignly_ identify individual fish.

    a. bizarre   b. benign   c. austere   d. banal

4. The world was appalled to learn of the _atrocious_ conditions in the refugee camps.

    a. avarice   b. atrocity   c. asylum   d. attrition

5. To Anya's astonishment, the expert _authenticated_ her copy of the Declaration of Independence, which she bought at a garage sale for a few dollars.

    a. astute   b. authentic   c. avid   d. bizarre

6. Before conducting public or private business, ancient Romans consulted _auguries_ such as thunder and lightning or the songs and flight of birds.

    a. augur   b. avarice   c. atrophy   d. atrocity

7. Ninety-two-year-old Uncle Albert complains about age-related _atrophic_ changes in his body that make it difficult for him to get around.

    a. avarice   b. belligerent   c. asylum   d. atrophy

8. Every stockbroker boasts of the _astuteness_ of his or her investment advice, but good results are never guaranteed.

    a. banal   b. avid   c. astute   d. belligerent

9. In Shirley Jackson's shocking story "The Lottery," each year one resident of a New England village is chosen by lottery as a scapegoat for the _atonement_ of the other villagers' sins.

    a. augment   b. atone   c. bicker   d. baffle

10. The guest of honor's after-dinner speech perfectly matched the _blandness_ of the meal, which was uninspired and tasteless.

    a. bland   b. benign   c. authentic   d. avid

11. Sir Arthur Conan Doyle's Sherlock Holmes, who easily solves the most __baffling__ crimes, made his debut in the novel *A Study in Scarlet* in 1887.

    a. atrophy   b. bicker   c. baffle   d. badger

12. A panel of paleontologists was called in to assess the authenticity of a fossil found in China that appeared to be the missing link between dinosaurs and birds.

    a. avid   b. astute   c. austere   d. authentic

13. The weekly magazine's TV critic frequently attacks the networks' programming for the __banality__ of most soap operas, talk shows, and daytime TV in general.

    a. banal   b. astute   c. avid   d. benign

14. To stop the constant __bickering__ between Janie and her brothers, their parents have instituted a weekly family meeting at which they welcome suggestions from everyone.

    a. atone   b. augur   c. augment   d. bicker

15. An annual contest celebrates the complexity and bizarreness of Rube Goldberg's cartoon "inventions" by challenging students to draw complex contraptions that use everyday materials and involve at least 20 steps to accomplish a simple task.

    a. belligerent   b. bizarre   c. avid   d. bland

16. United Nations peacekeeping forces have been dispatched to countries all over the world to stop acts of belligerence and protect civilians.

    a. austere   b. bizarre   c. benign   d. belligerent

17. Most years Marc, a veterinarian, __astutely__ predicts the Best in Show in the Westminster Kennel Club show from among the winners of the seven categories of show dogs—herding, hound, nonsporting, sporting, terrier, toy, and working.

    a. astute   b. avid   c. bizarre   d. bland

18. Stranded for years on a desert island, Robinson Crusoe stoically endures his life of __austerity__ and loneliness until he discovers human footprints that aren't his own.

    a. astute   b. authentic   c. austere   d. belligerent

19. Although my supervisor spoke __blandly__, his words were shocking: "Pack up your things and turn in your key. You've been laid off, and today is your last day."

    a. authentic   b. bland   c. banal   d. avid

20. Teresa has been reading __avidly__ since childhood and is never without a book.

    a. bizarre   b. avid   c. austere   d. benign

Lesson 7

61. bleak — 70. brusque

---

61. bleak   *adjective*   blēk

[*ble(i)kke* (Middle English), "pale," from *bleikr* (Old Norse), "white; pale"]

Definition:
a. Desolate, windswept, and bare.

Much of the coast of northern Alaska is **bleak** and uninviting.

b. Cold and gloomy; unpromising.

The funeral cortege moved off slowly and silently through the chill air of the **bleak** November day.

Unless we can raise fresh capital, the outlook for the survival of this company is exceedingly **bleak**.

Related Form: (*noun*) bleakness

Synonyms: (*adjectives*) barren; raw, harsh, chilling, forbidding; dour; dismal, dreary, drab, somber, grim, cheerless, depressing

Antonyms: (*adjectives*) lush (Word 260), verdant; balmy, mild, rosy, temperate; cheerful, blithe (Word 63), joyful, joyous; positive, upbeat; promising, encouraging, bright, sunny

62. blight   *verb and noun*   blīt

[Origin unknown]

Definition:
a. (*verb*) To check or destroy the growth of.

According to the paper, an unexpectedly early frost has **blighted** a sizable part of the Florida citrus crop.

High interest rates **blighted** the manufacturer's plans to borrow the capital he needed to modernize his operation.

b. (*noun*) Something that impairs growth or causes ruin.

A truly nationwide effort is needed if we are going to check the **blight** that is slowly destroying our inner cities.

Phrases: blighted hopes, urban blight

Synonyms: (*verbs*) nip, wither, shrivel; blast, ruin, devastate, efface; frustrate, foil, dash; (*nouns*) bane, scourge, plague; eyesore

Antonyms: (*verbs*) foster, nourish, promote, stimulate; (*nouns*) stimulus, stimulant

Related Phrases: dry rot; put a damper on; urban renewal

63. **blithe**   *adjective*   blī<u>th</u>   *or*   blīth

[*blithe* (Old English), "sweet; happy"]

Definition:
- a.   Merry and carefree.

  The **blithe** and sunny personality that had made her so popular in school was unaffected by the passage of years.
- b.   Overly unconcerned; reckless.

  Their **blithe** lack of concern for the safety of the children in their charge disturbed me greatly.

Related Forms: (*noun*) blitheness; (*adverb*) blithely

Synonyms: (*adjectives*) lighthearted, jolly, jocund, jovial, buoyant, sprightly, mirthful, happy-go-lucky; light-minded, heedless, indifferent, nonchalant, blasé

Antonyms: (*adjectives*) morose, saturnine, gloomy, despondent, morbid, melancholy; pensive (Word 295); solemn, dour

64. **bois-ter-ous**   *adjective*   boi'-stər-əs   *or*   boi'-strəs

[*boistres* or *boistous* (Middle English), "violent; fierce"]

Definition: Noisy and rowdy.

It is only natural to expect small children to be a bit **boisterous** and high-spirited.

Related Forms: (*noun*) boisterousness; (*adverb*) boisterously

Phrases: boisterous students, boisterous laughter

Synonyms: (*adjectives*) loud, obstreperous, vociferous, clamorous; unruly, disorderly, riotous, uproarious, disruptive, turbulent (Word 380), tempestuous

Antonyms: (*adjectives*) quiet, peaceful, tranquil (Word 377), halcyon; calm, orderly; muted, hushed, muffled, sedate

Halcyon

The adjective *halcyon* (hăl'-sē-ən), meaning "calm and peaceful" or "prosperous," has an interesting history. It comes from the Greek word *halkyon,* meaning "kingfisher" (a kind of seabird; see drawing). In Greek mythology, the kingfisher was reputed to have the power to calm the wind and the waves while it nested on the sea during the winter solstice (December 22). Accordingly, *halcyon days* are the days of fine weather that occur about that time and, by extension, any period of peace or tranquility.

65. **bom-bas-tic**   *adjective*   bŏm-băs'-tĭk

[*bombax* (Late Latin), "cotton (often used for padding)," related to *pambuk* (Turkish), "cotton"]

Definition: Pompous or inflated in language.

Lincoln's short, subdued address at Gettysburg is far more moving than Hale's lengthy and **bombastic** oration on the same occasion.

Related Form: (*noun*) bombast

Synonyms: (*adjectives*) grandiloquent, grandiose, hyperbolic, high-sounding, high-flown, highfalutin, extravagant; swollen, bloated, turgid; (*nouns*) fustian, rant, claptrap

Antonyms: (*adjectives*) plain, direct, straightforward; lean, spare; unvarnished, unembellished; artless, unpretentious; terse, succinct; muted

Usage Note:
Bombast indicates overly padded and pretentious language. *Fustian* applies to inflated language that is absurdly out of keeping with its quite ordinary content. *Rant* (also a verb) emphasizes the expression of strong emotions together with extravagance of language and violence of delivery. *Claptrap* is pretentious, insincere, or empty language designed to attract applause.

66. **boor-ish**   *adjective*   boŏr'-ĭsh

[*boer* (Dutch), "farmer"]

Definition: Rude or unrefined.

Fortunately, the loud and generally **boorish** behavior of a few of the guests did not spoil the party for the rest of us.

Related Forms: (*nouns*) boor, boorishness

Usage Notes:
a. Do not confuse a *boor* (that is, a rude or unrefined person) with a *bore* (that is, a dull or tedious person). An easy way to keep the two straight is to remember that *bore* is related to *boring* and *boredom*.

b. Also keep *boor* separate from the proper noun *Boer*. You may recall from your study of history that the Boers were South Africans of Dutch descent who engaged in an unsuccessful war with Great Britain from 1899 to 1902. Their descendants are the *Afrikaners* of today.

Synonyms: (*adjectives*) vulgar, uncouth, gauche, crude, crass, churlish, ill-bred, lowbred, ill-mannered, unmannerly; (*nouns*) vulgarian, lout, yahoo

Antonyms: (*adjectives*) urbane (Word 382), suave, polished; tactful, discreet, diplomatic; (*nouns*) savoir faire, social savvy, finesse (Word 194), class, style

67. **boy-cott** *verb and noun* boi'-kŏt

[After Charles C. Boycott, a land agent in County Mayo, Ireland, who was subjected to this form of treatment in 1880 for refusing to lower rents on the lands he managed]

Definition:

a. (*verb*) To refuse to buy, use, or deal with as a way to protest (or force acceptance of) some form of behavior.

During the civil rights movement of the 1950s and 1960s, both black and white Americans **boycotted** segregated lunch counters, bus depots, schools, and the like.

b. (*noun*) An instance of such treatment.

Many forms of nonviolent protest, including sit-ins, picket lines, and **boycotts**, have become common in today's United States.

Synonyms: (*verbs*) ban, proscribe, ostracize (Word 289), blacklist, blackball; (*nouns*) ban, embargo

Antonyms: (*verbs*) patronize, fraternize with, support; endorse, sanction, approve

Charles C. Boycott

In 1873, a retired English army officer, Captain Charles C. Boycott (1832–1897), became the rent collector on the estates of an aristocrat called Lord Erne. These estates were in Country Mayo, Ireland, and the tenants on them were Irish small farmers who paid an annual rent for the use of the land. Unfortunately, Captain Boycott took his job too seriously; and as a result, a new word, *boycott,* entered the language.

This is what happened. A series of poor harvests in the late 1870s caused widespread suffering among Lord Erne's tenants. Accordingly, in 1880 they asked for a 25% reduction in their rents. To these pleas Captain Boycott turned a deaf ear. As a matter of fact, he attempted to evict some of the tenants for nonpayment of their rent. In reply, the tenants and other people who sympathized with them decided to have nothing whatsoever to do with the captain. He was refused lodgings when he traveled, frequently did not receive his mail, and had to make special arrangements to get food and other necessities. These tactics worked so well that Captain Boycott was forced to give up his job and return to England. He left Ireland late in 1880, and shortly thereafter the verb *boycott,* meaning "to refuse to deal with as a means of protest," first appeared in English.

68. brash *adjective* brăsh

[Origin unknown, possibly *brisk* + *rash*]

Definition: Overly bold, hasty, and thoughtless.

Nature and experience have a way of turning a **brash** and tactless youngster into a thoughtful and considerate adult.

Related Form: (*noun*) brashness

Phrases: a brash comedian, brash behavior

Synonyms: (*adjectives*) rash, reckless, foolhardy, impetuous, precipitate; impudent, saucy, impertinent, brazen, shameless; tactless, gauche

Antonyms: (*adjectives*) cautious, prudent, circumspect (Word 88), wary; tactful, considerate

69. bra·va·do *noun* brə-vä'-dō

[*bravada* (Spanish), "boastfulness," from *bravo* (Spanish), "brave; boastful"]

Definition: A boastful or swaggering show of false bravery; false courage in general.

His challenge to fight was pure **bravado**; inwardly he hoped that no one would take him on.

Synonyms: (*nouns*) braggadocio, swagger, bluster, cockiness, bluff

Antonyms: (*nouns*) fearlessness, intrepidity, gallantry, audacity, bravery, valor, pluck, daring, stoutheartedness, dauntlessness

Related Phrases: put up a bold front; call someone's bluff

70. brusque *adjective* brŭsk

[*brusque* (French), "fierce; harsh," from *brusco* (Italian), "sharp; sour"]

Definition: Overly short or abrupt.

He is so courteous and affable that I was totally taken aback by his unaccountably **brusque** answer to my question.

Related Form: (*noun*) brusqueness

Phrases: a brusque reply, a brusque tone, a brusque manner

Usage Notes:
a. *Brusque* is also spelled *brusk*. This applies to *brusqueness* as well.
b. Do not confuse *brusque* (*brusk*) with *brisk*, meaning "lively or energetic."

Synonyms: (*adjectives*) curt, blunt, terse; gruff, rough, sharp, harsh; uncivil, impolite

Antonyms: (*adjectives*) civil, polite, cordial, affable (Word 15); voluble, effusive

Using the Words

Exercise I
1. boy'-cott
2. bom-bas'-tic
3. bra-va'-do
4. brusque
5. bois'-ter-ous
6. boor'-ish

Exercise I.   Syllabication and Pronunciation

Syllabicate the following words correctly, and place the major stress mark (') after the syllable that is accented when the word is pronounced.

Example: a-bet'

1. boycott
2. bombastic
3. bravado
4. brusque
5. boisterous
6. boorish

Exercise II.   Words Out of Context

In each of the following groups, select the item that best expresses the meaning of the numbered word at the left.

1. brusque   a. pompous   <u>b. curt</u>   c. energetic   d. obscure   e. unwieldy

2. bombastic   a. fearful   b. reckless   c. mild   d. sprightly   <u>e. inflated</u>

3. boisterous   a. tranquil   b. bloated   c. dismal   <u>d. rowdy</u>   e. exhausted

4. blight   a. bluster   b. merriment   <u>c. eyesore</u>   d. claptrap   e. curiosity

5. brash   a. overly sensitive   <u>b. overly forward</u>   c. overly critical   d. overly tired   e. overly stingy

Exercise III.   Completing Sentences

Complete each of the following sentences by selecting the most appropriate word from the group of words given below. Use the words exactly as they are printed in this list.

| bleak | blight | boorish |
| boycott | bravado | blithe |

1. The speeches of both Hitler and Mussolini were full of the kind of overblown bluster and __bravado__ that today strikes us as pathetic.

2. Her __blithe__ and sunny disposition is clearly the product of a happy childhood spent amid pleasant surroundings and among caring relatives.

3. I know they think they're being suave and sophisticated, but I consider their conduct downright __boorish__.

4. They are depressing people to be around because their attitude toward life is so ___bleak___ and cheerless.

5. Since most of the country continued to buy the product to which the small group of protesters objected, the ___boycott___ failed.

Exercise IV.   Synonyms and Antonyms

Classify each of the following pairs of words as **S** for **synonyms** or **A** for **antonyms**.

A 1. bleak—rosy
S 2. lighthearted—blithe
A 3. boycott—patronize

A 4. halcyon—tempestuous
S 5. reckless—brash
A 6. brusque—civil

Exercise V.   Word Roundup

1. Distinguish between the words in each of the following pairs.

   a. brusque—brisk   b. boor—bore

2. Explain the meaning of the *italicized* element in each of the following phrases.

   a. *bleak* prospects   d. *blighted* hopes
   b. urban *blight*   e. a *brash* comedian
   c. *boisterous* laughter   f. a *brusque* reply

3. Define each of the following terms.

   a. bombast   c. rant
   b. claptrap   d. fustian

   What do these words have in common?

4. Explain the story behind the phrase *halcyon days*. Then retell the myth of Alcyone and Ceyx, and relate it to the history of the phrase. (If you don't know the myth, look it up in Robert Graves's *The Greek Myths* or *Bulfinch's Mythology*.)

Exercise VI.   Framing Sentences

A. Use each of the following words in an original sentence that clearly illustrates its meaning.

1. blight   3. boycott
2. blithe   4. bravado

B. Give a **noun** form of each of the following words, and use it in an original sentence that clearly illustrates its meaning.

1. bleak bleakness   4. boorish boor, boorishness
2. boisterous boisterousness 5. brash brashness
3. bombastic bombast   6. brusque brusqueness

105

Dissecting the Words

Prefixes

1. The Latin prefix **ambi** means "both" or "around." It occurs in *ambience* (Word 24) and *ambivalent* (Word 25). Other words using this prefix include:

ambidextrous (literally, "with a right hand on both sides")—able to use both hands equally well

ambient (literally, "going around")—surrounding or encompassing

ambiguous (literally, "going in both directions at once")—unclear or uncertain

ambition (literally, "a going around [to canvass for votes]")—a strong desire to achieve some goal

The corresponding Greek prefix is **amphi.** It occurs in the following English words:

amphitheater—a kind of theater or stadium that has seats going all around the stage or arena

amphibious (literally, "living both lives")—able to live or operate on land *and* in the water

2. The prefix **be**, meaning "thoroughly" or "completely," is of Germanic origin. It appears in many words that have come down to us from Old and Middle English. Today it is used for the following purposes:

a. To give greater force or thoroughness to an action.

    be + smirch = *besmirch*—to soil thoroughly

b. To make an intransitive verb (*i.e.*, one that cannot take a direct object) transitive.

    be + moan = *bemoan*—to moan and groan about

c. To form a verb or participial adjective from a noun.

    be + witch = *bewitch*—to enchant; *bewitching*—enchanting; *bewitched*—enchanted

Samuel Johnson

The eminent 18th-century writer and critic Samuel Johnson (1709–1784) published his two-volume *Dictionary of the English Language* in 1755. It surpassed earlier dictionaries in the precision of its definitions and the wealth of its examples of usage. Though the work had its flaws and revealed much about Johnson's personal prejudices, it soon became a staple item in most private libraries.

Root

The Latin root **vert**, **vers** means "turn." It is found in many English words, including *adverse* (Word 12). Here are a few other words from this root:

advert—to refer to

animadversion—a strong criticism; a hostile remark

averse—disinclined, reluctant, or opposed to

avert—to turn away from; to prevent. Noun: *aversion*

divers—several

diverse—varied. Another adjective with the same meaning is *diversified*.

invert—to turn over or in on itself. Noun: *inversion*

convert—to transform, exchange, or adopt. A *convert* is a person who adopts (turns to) a new religion or other doctrine. Noun: *conversion*

revert—to turn or go back to. Noun: *reversion*

subvert (literally, "turn from under") —to overthrow; to seek to undermine (as, for example, a government or institution). Adjective: *subversive*; noun: *subversion*

vertigo (literally, "a turning about") —a sensation of dizziness and a feeling that one is about to fall

Exercise

1. Define each of the following words using the prefix *be*, and use the word in a short sentence that clearly illustrates its meaning. Then give the etymology of the word, and explain the function that *be* performs.

   a. beseech
   b. bespeak
   c. bedizen
   d. belie
   e. beleaguer
   f. betroth
   g. beguile
   h. berate
   i. begrudge
   j. behoove
   k. bereave
   l. befall
   m. belittle
   n. befriend
   o. belabor

2. Complete each of the following sentences by supplying a word or phrase which clearly shows that you know the meaning of the <u>underscored</u> root or prefix.

   a. To di<u>vert</u> a person is to _____turn_____ his or her mind aside from the business at hand.

   b. A sub<u>vers</u>ive movement is one that seeks to ___overturn___ the existing government or social order.

   c. An <u>amphi</u>bious military operation is one that will take place _____. on both land and sea

   d. In an <u>amphi</u>theater the seats go all ___around___ the stage or arena.

Enriching the Lesson

Exercise I.   Eponyms

A good many English words derive from the names of the people who were originally associated with the object, practice, or attitude that the word indicates. Such words are called **eponyms**. A good example of an eponym is *boycott*, studied in this lesson.

Below are listed a number of other useful eponyms. With or without the aid of a dictionary or other reference book, define each, and give the name of the person from whom the word comes. Then choose any **five** items on the list, and for each write a short sentence that clearly illustrates its meaning.

1. bowdlerize
2. quisling
3. shrapnel
4. mesmerize
5. lynch

6. maverick
7. sadistic
8. gerrymander
9. chauvinist
10. sandwich

11. silhouette
12. galvanize
13. martinet
14. nicotine
15. masochistic

Exercise II.   Classical Contributions to English

A. *"O Ye Immortal Gods!"*   Surprisingly, the names of a number of Roman (or sometimes Greek) gods live on in present-day English words. Some of these words are listed below in Column A. With or without the aid of a dictionary, match each with its meaning in Column B. Then give the name of the god from which the modern English word derives, and explain how the deity in question is connected with the current meaning of the word.

Column A	*Column B*
c 1. jovial	a. warlike or military
d 2. bacchanalian	b. sullen and gloomy
e 3. mercurial	c. jolly or merry
b 4. saturnine	d. riotous and drunken
a 5. martial	e. fickle or changeable

B. *Gifts from the Greeks.*   The geography, history, and mythology of ancient Greece have contributed much to the richness and variety of modern English. Below are listed a few samples of this remarkable heritage. Define the *italicized* item in each of the following phrases, and explain its connection with the ancient Greeks.

1. a *titanic* struggle
2. a *herculean* task
3. a *laconic* reply
4. to run in a *marathon*
5. a *colossal* mistake

6. an *Achilles' heel*
7. a *spartan* lifestyle
8. a *tantalizing* glimpse
9. an *atlas* of the world
10. to deliver a *philippic*

Exercise III.   Spanish Borrowings

Present-day English contains a number of words borrowed with little or no change from Spanish. *Bravado*, studied in this lesson, is a good example of such a word. A number of others are listed below. Define each as it is used in English today. Then use it in an original sentence that clearly illustrates its meaning.

1. aficionado
2. bonanza
3. peccadillo
4. macho
5. embargo
6. armada
7. desperado
8. cargo
9. incommunicado

Exercise IV.   Short, Sturdy Words

According to an old saying, "the shorter the word, the harder the push." This lesson has presented a number of short, sturdy words with a lot of "push" (e.g., *blight, bleak, blithe*). These items, of course, do not exhaust the list. On the contrary, English abounds in forceful one-syllable expressions. Many of them have come down to us from Old and Middle English; others are derived from Old Norse, the language of the Vikings.

1. With or without the aid of a thesaurus, list **ten** forceful, one-syllable synonyms for the humble and rather bland word *hit*. Then define each of your choices so as to bring out its distinctive qualities, and use it in an original sentence. (Hint: You might do well to start with *thwack* or *cuff*.)

2. With or without the aid of a dictionary, define the following words that were in use long before Chaucer died in 1400 and are still alive today. Then use each in an original sentence.

   a. goad
   b. bliss
   c. meek
   d. quake
   e. throng
   f. craft
   g. wail
   h. bleat
   i. rend
   j. grim
   k. skulk
   l. cram

Exercise V.   Expanding Your Word Power

The words listed below are not on the Basic Word List, but they were mentioned in passing, in one form or another, in Lesson 7. All of them would make useful additions to your working vocabulary. Define each, give its etymology, list **two** synonyms and **two** antonyms (where possible), and use in a short sentence that clearly illustrates the word's meaning.

1. dour
2. stimulus
3. blasé
4. obstreperous
5. hyperbole
6. turgid
7. sanction
8. impertinent
9. crass
10. jocund
11. efface
12. voluble

Lesson 8

71. bungle — 80. catholic

---

71. bun·gle   *verb*   bŭn'-gəl

[Origin unknown, perhaps from *bangla* (Swedish), "work poorly"]

Definition: To mismanage or make a mess of.

They **bungled** the job so badly that it took me days to straighten out the mess.

Related Form: *(noun)* bungler

Synonyms: *(verbs)* botch, butcher, mangle, mar, spoil, foul up, bollix up; *(nouns)* butcher, klutz; *(adjectives)* incompetent, inept; clumsy, awkward

Antonyms: *(nouns)* expert, whiz, ace; *(adjectives)* competent, workmanlike, skillful, adroit, deft, dexterous

Usage Note:

Some of the items included among the synonyms for *bungle*—for example, *bollix up* and *klutz*—are slang expressions that should be avoided in formal speech and writing. The same is true for the antonyms provided. For example, neither *ace* nor *whiz* would be considered appropriate in formal contexts.

72. bu·reauc·ra·cy   *noun*   byo͞o-rŏk'-rə-sē

[*bureau* (French), "desk; office" + *kratos* (Greek), "rule"]

Definition: A complicated system of administrative agencies and officials; the officials themselves.

"I don't know whether the people being helped by our federally funded social programs are eating up too much of the taxpayer's money," the senator remarked. "However, the **bureaucracy** that administers such programs may be."

Related Forms: *(noun)* bureaucrat; *(adjective)* bureaucratic

Usage Note:

Today *bureaucracy*, *bureaucrat*, and *bureaucratic* are used most frequently of government, especially the federal government, to suggest too much formalism or red tape. As a result, the terms are almost always pejorative (unless, of course, the context indicates otherwise). Note, too, that all three expressions may properly be used of nongovernmental institutions, since private organizations are run in much the same way as the government. Indeed, *bureaucracy* and its derivatives can justly be applied to any administrative setup that has become overgrown or that insists upon following complex rules and procedures that seem to hinder or stifle quick and effective action.

Charles Dickens

Thomas Carlyle

Red Tape

The term *red tape* is used critically to describe bureaucratic procedures that are considered unnecessarily rigid, complicated, and time-consuming. When we say that something "is tied up in red tape," we mean that there are so many regulations, so many papers to be filled out, so many technicalities to observe that it is difficult to get anything done.

The term is said to have been introduced by Charles Dickens and popularized by Thomas Carlyle, the English historian. It originated from the common use of pieces of red tape to tie together bundles of legal papers in English courts and governmental offices.

Today, official papers are more likely to be processed by a computer than tied together by a clerk, but people still complain about the delays and frustrations caused by too much red tape.

---

73. but-tress   *noun and verb*   bŭt'-rĭs

[*bo(u)terez* (Old French), "thrusting," from *bo(u)ter* (Old French), "strike against, butt"]

Definition:

a. (*noun*) A support or reinforcement.

The towering walls of many medieval cathedrals are prevented from falling down by huge flying **buttresses** on the outside of the building.

b. (*verb*) To support or reinforce.

The speaker **buttressed** her arguments with a solid presentation of relevant facts and figures.

From time to time, Congress has considered a number of measures designed to **buttress** and protect the economy against the ravages of inflation.

Synonyms: (*nouns*) prop, brace; mainstay, cornerstone, pillar; (*verbs*) prop up, brace, bolster, shore up, strengthen

Antonyms: (*verbs*) weaken, impair, undermine

74. ca-jole   *verb*   kə-jōl′ *or* kă-jōl′
[*cajoler* (French), "chatter like a jay in a cage"]

Definition: To persuade or obtain by flattery or deceit.

Like most people, I enjoy flattery, but I can't be **cajoled** into doing something that I know in my heart is foolish.

He's so tight with his money that it's just about impossible to **cajole** a nickel out of him, no matter how worthy the cause.

Related Forms: (nouns) cajolery, cajoler

Synonyms: (verbs) wheedle, inveigle, coax, beguile, induce, flatter

Antonyms: (verbs) dissuade, deter, discourage

Related Phrases: soft-soap, sweet-talk; curry favor with; apple-polishing

75. cal-lous   *adjective*   kăl′-əs
[*callosus* (Latin), "thick-skinned," from *callus* (Latin), "hard skin"]

Definition: Unfeeling or insensitive.

The sight of children starving slowly and horribly to death brought tears of rage and indignation to the eyes of even the most **callous** and thick-skinned observer among us.

Related Forms: (noun) callousness; (adverb) callously

Usage Note:

Do not confuse the adjective *callous* with either the noun *callus*, meaning "a hardened or thickened part of the skin" (e.g., "had a callus on his hand"), or the adjective *callow*, meaning "untried or inexperienced" (e.g., "a callow youth").

Synonyms: (adjectives) indifferent, unresponsive, unsympathetic; thick-skinned, hard-hearted, hard-boiled, hard-nosed

Antonyms: (adjectives) compassionate, tenderhearted, softhearted, kindhearted; thin-skinned, sensitive

76. cal-um-ny   *noun*   kăl′-əm-nē
[*calumnia* (Latin), "trickery; slander"]

Definition: A false statement deliberately made up to injure a person.

"It is one thing to make honest criticisms of my administration and its methods," the president observed. "It is quite another to repeat **calumnies** and slanders that simply have no basis in fact."

Related Forms: (verb) calumniate; (adjective) calumnious

Synonyms: (nouns) lie, falsehood; slander, libel; slur, aspersion

Antonyms: (nouns) flattery, adulation

Related Phrases: do a hatchet job on, hurl brickbats at; mudslinging

77. **can-did**   *adjective*   kăn'-dĭd

[*candidus* (Latin), "white; pure," from *candere* (Latin), "glisten"]

Definition:

a. Fair and impartial.

"Only a disinterested observer of a traffic accident can give you a **candid** account of what actually happened," the officer told the reporter.

b. Frank or outspoken.

"You can't expect diplomats to be as **candid** and forthright as you might wish," she observed.

c. Informal or unposed.

"Why do I always look so awful in **candid** photos?" my little brother asked plaintively.

Phrases: a candid opinion, a candid interview, a candid critic

Related Forms: (*nouns*) candor, candidness; (*adverb*) candidly

Synonyms: (*adjectives*) objective, disinterested, unbiased, unprejudiced, balanced; forthright, unreserved, straight-from-the-shoulder; spontaneous, impromptu

Antonyms: (*adjectives*) partial, biased, prejudiced; reserved, reticent (Word 341); disingenuous, artful, evasive, equivocal, ambiguous

Candidate

In ancient Rome a man who wished to be elected to public office wore a white robe or toga while canvassing for votes. That way, he could be recognized more easily wherever he went. Since the Latin word for "white" is *candidus*, the would-be official came to be known as a *candidatus*, meaning "one clothed in white." From this we get our English word *candidate*.

78. can-tan-ker-ous   *adjective*   kăn-tăng'-kĕr-əs

[Probably *contekour* (Middle English), "brawler," from *contek* (Norman French), "strife"]

Definition: Foul-tempered and quarrelsome.

"Having to put up with a surly and **cantankerous** boss can sometimes make life pretty miserable," Betty Lou said. "Still, I like working in an office."

"When I was a young man I tried to be as agreeable as possible," Dad remarked. "But now that I'm getting on in years, I find that I have become surprisingly **cantankerous**."

Related Forms: (*noun*) cantankerousness; (*adverb*) cantankerously

Usage Note:
Though *cantankerous* is normally used of people who are determined to be nasty or disagreeable (*e.g.,* "the cantankerous leader of the opposition party"), the word may also be applied to animals or things. In that case, it means "irritating or difficult to deal with." Examples of such usage include "a cantankerous washing machine" and "a cantankerous camel."

Synonyms: (*adjectives*) peevish, contrary, cross-grained, irritable, irascible, perverse, choleric, bearish, testy, crabby, grouchy, cranky; intractable, unamenable, ornery; (*nouns*) curmudgeon, grouch

Antonyms: (*adjectives*) good-natured, sweet tempered, amiable, lovable, affable (Word 15), genial; even tempered, unexcitable, imperturbable, equable; docile (Word 142), tractable, amenable

79. cap-tious   *adjective*   kăp'-shəs

[*captieux* (French), "hypercritical," from *captio* (Latin), "seizure; deception"]

Definition:

   a.   Quick to find petty faults or raise trifling objections; overly demanding or fussy.

     Though they found a lot to disagree with in my plan, most of their objections were **captious** and niggling.

   b.   Intended to trap, confuse, or show up.

     "A president has to be pretty alert when talking to the press," the aide observed. "After all, a careless answer to a **captious** question could land him in a great deal of political hot water."

Phrase: a captious critic

Related Forms: (*noun*) captiousness; (*adverb*) captiously

Synonyms: (*adjectives*) hypercritical, caviling, carping, censorious; niggling, pettifogging, hairsplitting, picky, picayune, nit-picking; artful, tricky, loaded

Antonyms: (*adjectives*) unexacting, uncritical, undiscriminating; straightforward; laudatory, complimentary

80. cath-o-lic   *adjective*   kăth'-ə-lĭk   *or*   kăth'-lĭk

[*katholikos* (Greek), "general," from *kata* (Greek), "according to + *holos* (Greek), "(the) whole" + *ikos* (Greek), "pertaining to"]

Definition:

a. Broad or widely inclusive.

Painting and sculpture, architecture and engineering, mathematics and music—these were just a few of Leonardo da Vinci's truly **catholic** interests.

b. General or universal; worldwide.

Even though living standards in many parts of the world have noticeably improved since 1900, poverty, hunger, and unemployment are still **catholic** concerns for humankind more than one hundred years later.

Related Form: (*noun*) catholicity

Usage Note:

Be sure to distinguish carefully between *catholic* (with a *c*) and *Catholic* (with a *C*). The word with the capital letter is a proper adjective that refers to the ancient universal (that is, undivided) Christian church or to its present-day representatives. Frequently, of course, *Catholic* is used as an abbreviation for *Roman Catholic*—that is, in reference to the Church of Rome, its beliefs and practices, or its members.

Synonyms: (*adjectives*) comprehensive, wide, liberal; ecumenical, global

Antonyms: (*adjectives*) narrow, provincial, parochial (Word 293)

Using the Words

Exercise I.   Parts of Speech

Indicate the part of speech of each of the following words. In one case, two answers are correct.

1. bungle v.
2. buttress v., n.
3. callous adj.
4. cajole v.
5. calumny n.
6. catholic adj.

Exercise II.   Words in Phrases

In each of the following, select the item that best expresses the meaning of the *italicized* word in the introductory phrase.

1. nothing more than a blatant *calumny*

a. trick   b. crime   c. mistake   d. joke   e. falsehood

2. a *cantankerous* lawn mower

a. useful   b. ornery   c. complicated   d. expensive   e. new

3. unusually *candid* comments
   a. learned   b. tactful   c. sour   d. frank   e. amusing

4. *catholic* tastes in music
   a. broad   b. strange   c. ordinary   d. austere   e. narrow

5. tried to *buttress* her position at the office
   a. undermine   b. clarify   c. strengthen   d. eliminate
   e. utilize

Exercise III.   Completing Sentences

Complete each of the following sentences or pairs of sentences by selecting the most appropriate word from the group of words given below.

callous	captious	bureaucracy
buttress	bungle	cajole

1. If you focus your attention too single-mindedly on trifles, as some overly _captious_ critics do, you may lose sight of the more important aspects of the thing you are considering.

2. "I'd hoped that my proposal for reducing our overgrown federal bureaucracy would have passed the House by now," the representative told the press. "Unfortunately, it is still all tied up in congressional red tape."

3. "If you keep telling your uncle what a superb driver he is," Marv advised me, "you may be able to ___cajole___ him into giving you driving lessons in his new car."

4. Anyone who can look at photos from Auschwitz or Buchenwald and not be moved deeply is indeed ___callous___ and insensitive.

5. "Just how am I supposed to get quality work out of a staff that manages to ___bungle___ the simplest job?" the production chief asked ruefully.

Exercise IV.   Synonyms and Antonyms

A. In each of the following numbered groups, select the **two** words that are most nearly **synonyms**.

1. a. discourage   b. butcher   c. mangle   d. attend   e. retain

2. a. bolster   b. impair   c. pretend   d. brace   e. convene
   bungle

3. a. patronize   b. magnify   c. inveigle   d. boycott
   e. wheedle   cajole
   buttress

4. a. mannerism   b. libel   c. chaos   d. slander   e. order
   calumny

5. a. objective   b. grisly   c. spurious   d. lethargic
   e. impartial   candid

116

Now, for each of the pairs of synonyms that you have selected, supply a word from the Basic Word List for this lesson (Words 71–80) that means the **same** or **almost the same** thing.

B. In each of the following numbered groups, select the **two** words that are most nearly **antonyms**.

1. a. cantankerous   b. penniless   c. genial   d. authentic
   e. workmanlike

2. a. spry   b. captious   c. illegal   d. chipper   e. unexacting

3. a. deft   b. inept   c. academic   d. collective   e. inimical

4. a. illusory   b. atrocious   c. catholic   d. narrow   e. gaudy

5. a. smooth-talking   b. glib   c. brand-new   d. callous

   e. tenderhearted

Exercise V.   Word Roundup

1. Two groups of expressions with related meanings are given below. Indicate the items in each that would be classified as *slang* or *overly colloquial.*

   ### A.   Ability

   a. expert   c. competent   e. klutz
   b. inept   d. ace   f. adroit

   ### B.   Persuasion

   a. coax   c. inveigle   e. wheedle
   b. sweet-talk   d. cajole   f. soft-soap

2. Define *callous, callus,* and *callow.* Use each in an original illustrative sentence.

3. What is the difference between *catholic* and *Catholic*? Use each in a sentence that clearly illustrates its meaning.

4. Define *red tape,* and use the phrase in an original sentence.

5. Explain the story behind the word *candidate.* How is the word related to *candid*?

Exercise VI.   Framing Sentences

Use each of the following words in an original sentence that clearly illustrates its meaning.

1. bungle   6. calumniate
2. bureaucrat   7. candor
3. buttress   8. cantankerous
4. cajole   9. captious
5. callously   10. catholic

Completing Verbal Analogies

"A Denotes the Lack of B."   Another word relationship frequently encountered on standardized vocabulary tests may conveniently be expressed as "*A* denotes the lack of *B*." An example of an analogy question utilizing this word relationship is given below. See if you can figure out the correct answer.

| A | B | C | D |

cowardly : courage = awkward :(*fear, honor, grace, kindness, intelligence*)

The answer, of course, is *grace*. An *awkward* person lacks *grace* (or gracefulness), just as a *cowardly* person lacks courage.

Exercise I

Complete the following analogies based on the word relationship "*A* denotes the lack of *B*."

1. **biased : objectivity** = callous : (*ambition, experience, compassion, malice, humor*)

2. **boorish : manners** = blithe : (*skills, morals, funds, friends, cares*)

3. **indigent : money** = lethargic : (*wisdom, energy, talent, family, schooling*)

Exercise II   Answers will vary.

Write **three** original analogies based on the relationship "*A* denotes the lack of *B*." In your analogies use at least **one** of the basic words studied in Lessons 1–8 (Words 1–80).

Exercise III

The following items review what you have so far learned about analogy questions. Complete each.

1. **affable : cantankerous** = catholic : (*liberal, genial, critical, provincial, abnormal*)

2. **bungle : botch** = defame : (*flatter, slander, ignore, praise, persuade*)

3. **bleak : warmth** = brash : (*caution, frankness, pride, greed, enthusiasm*)

4. **grasping : rapacious** = generous : (*miserly, ardent, liberal, bellicose, grotesque*)

5. **buttress : undermine** = foster : (*sanction, foreshadow, promote, redress, blight*)

Enriching the Lesson

Exercise I.   The Language of Government and Politics

The word *bureaucracy,* studied in this lesson, often comes up in discussions of government and politics. A number of other words and phrases connected with the workings of our government or political system are listed below. Define each.

1. checks and balances
2. political machine
3. revenue sharing
4. civil rights
5. merit system
6. pocket veto
7. executive privilege
8. separation of powers
9. lobby *or* interest group
10. reapportionment
11. referendum
12. party platform
13. executive order
14. popular sovereignty
15. regulatory agency
16. due process of law
17. judicial review
18. civil service
19. bipartisan
20. franchise
21. eminent domain
22. senatorial courtesy
23. pork barrel
24. conflict of interest
25. filibuster
26. political patronage

Can you think of any others? List and define them.

Exercise II.   Gobbledygook

Gobbledygook is the name by which people commonly refer to the inflated, involved, and unnecessarily obscure language that is characteristic of bureaucratic pronouncements. The word was coined by Maury Maverick, chairman of the Smaller War Plants Corporation during World War II. As head of this government agency, Maverick was subjected to a seemingly endless flow of trite, tortured, or pompous language, for which he devised the name *gobblebygook.* Here is an example of the kind of writing (and speaking) that Maverick had in mind. It is taken from an administrative order issued by the federal Food and Drug Administration.

> References in this order to any order shall be construed as referring to that order as amended by any subsequent order, whether made before or after the making of this order, and if any order referred to in this order is replaced by any such subsequent order, the references shall be construed as referring to that subsequent order.

As you know, the purpose of language is to communicate ideas and information clearly and concisely. Needless to say, this sentence and the kind of writing it represents defeat that purpose. To begin with, the sentence is oppressively long (58 words) and involved. This makes it almost impossible for the reader to grasp what is being said without rereading the sentence several times.

(A simple way to begin correcting this problem would be to break the sentence in two just before the words *and if*.)

In addition, the phrasing is awkward and unnatural. Notice, for instance, the number of passive constructions, the use of the single word *order* to indicate several different sets of instructions issued at different times, and the presence of clumsy or tortured expressions (*e.g.,* "shall be construed as referring to," "the making of this order," "any such subsequent order"). These items add to the difficulties the reader already faces in trying to make something meaningful out of this muddle.

By now the point of this discussion should be clear to you: Write as clearly, simply, and concisely as you can. Don't let your sentences become unduly long and involved. Don't overload them with highfalutin expressions or bizarre turns of phrase. Use the active voice of the verb rather than the passive. And, finally, try not to string together too many Latinate words; such expressions tend to weigh down a sentence and produce a ponderous effect. As Maury Maverick wrote to his staff in a now-famous memo about writing style: "Say what you're talking about" as clearly and directly as possible.

One final note: Needless to say, gobbledygook is not the exclusive preserve of government. Indeed, anyone who has been in the armed forces, tried to make sense out of the fine print in an insurance policy, or had occasion to inspect business documents knows just how pervasive it can be.

1. Read the following statement from an official report issued by one of the administrative departments of the government of New Zealand. The statement concerns the possible use of a certain piece of land for recreational purposes. Then try your hand at rephrasing the statement in comprehensible English.

   > It is obvious from the difference in elevation with relation to the short depth of the property that the contour is such as to preclude any reasonable development potential for active recreation.

2. A federal agency that was considering the accuracy of a label used on a certain brand of bottled beer said that the label *"retained a tendency to mislead."* Rephrase the *italicized* words in intelligible English.

Exercise III.   Expanding Your Word Power

The words listed below are not on the Basic Word List, but they were mentioned in passing, in one form or another, in Lesson 8. All of them would make useful additions to your working vocabulary. Define each, give its etymology, list **two** synonyms and **two** antonyms (where possible), and use in a short sentence that clearly illustrates the word's meaning.

1. deft	4. adulation	7. irascible
2. impair	5. impromptu	8. amenable
3. cavil	6. disingenuous	9. curmudgeon

Related Forms in Context

Beneath each sentence below are four words introduced in Lesson 7 or 8. Review the related forms for these words, and choose the one that best completes the sentence. Write that related form in the space provided.

1. At the end of the second debate, which lasted an hour, one of the candidates observed that his opponent's remarks were all ___bombast___ and no substance.

   a. bleak   **b. bombastic**   c. captious   d. catholic

2. The tight end, a notorious ___bungler___, recovered the fumble and took off running—in the wrong direction.

   a. blight   b. boycott   **c. bungle**   d. cajole

3. In Act I, scene iii, of *Hamlet,* Polonius advises his son Laertes, "Virtue itself [e]scapes not <u>calumnious</u> strokes."

   a. bravado   b. bureaucracy   c. buttress   **d. calumny**

4. The author was extremely upset by the <u>captiousness</u> of the critic's review of her first novel.

   a. captious   b. bleak   c. catholic   d. blithe

5. In Guy de Maupassant's short story "The Necklace," Monsieur Loisel is a minor <u>bureaucrat</u> in the Ministry of Education and cannot afford the luxuries his wife desires.

   a. boycott   **b. bureaucracy**   c. bravado   d. calumny

6. Despite the ___cajolery___ of her mother and the photographer, the little girl refused to look at the camera and smile.

   a. bungle   **b. cajole**   c. boycott   d. buttress

7. In Anton Chekhov's one-act play *The Brute*, a rudely impatient landowner challenges a beautiful widow to a duel, but his <u>boorishness</u> disappears when he suddenly falls in love with her.

   a. catholic   b. bombastic   **c. boorish**   d. candid

8. W. C. Fields, an American comic actor with a reputation for <u>cantankerousness</u>, wrote his own epitaph: "On the whole, I'd rather be in Philadelphia."

   a. cantankerous   b. blithe   c. bleak   d. candid

9. When we tried to collect on an insurance claim for flood damage to our house, we found ourselves caught in a <u>bureaucratic</u> nightmare.

   a. boycott   b. blight   **c. bureaucracy**   d. calumny

10. We frequently have to complain to the police about the boisterousness of our neighbors' parties, which last until the small hours of the morning.

    a. bleak   b. blithe   c. callous   d. boisterous

11. The Brontë sisters—Charlotte, Anne, and Emily—must surely have been affected by the bleakness of the dark, windy moors near their Yorkshire home, especially in winter.

    a. brash   b. bleak   c. brusque   d. bombastic

12. Hunters callously slaughtered the great herds of American buffalo that were central to the lives of the Plains Indians.

    a. candid   b. cantankerous   c. callous   d. captious

13. During soccer matches fans boisterously sing and chant, urging their teams to victory.

    a. boisterous   b. callous   c. cantankerous   d. candid

14. The brashness of her behavior suggests that when she gets her driver's license, she may be reckless behind the wheel.

    a. blithe   b. brusque   c. callous   d. brash

15. An elderly woman stepped to the mike at the city council meeting and pointedly announced, "We voters have a right to expect both candor and responsibility from all our elected officials."

    a. boisterous   b. brash   c. candid   d. cantankerous

16. From the brusqueness of Marty's reply and the look on his face, I could tell that he had been deeply hurt by what was intended to be a humorous remark.

    a. boorish   b. brusque   c. blithe   d. captious

17. When her husband could no longer travel, Eleanor Roosevelt traveled for him; and in a daily newspaper column called "My Day," she candidly reported what she had observed and felt.

    a. candid   b. cantankerous   c. boisterous   d. callous

18. To win Prince Charming, Cinderella's stepsister blithely cut off her heel and tried to force her huge foot into the dainty glass slipper.

    a. candid   b. blithe   c. captious   d. boisterous

19. At the Morgan Library, which was once financier J. P. Morgan's home, we were impressed by the catholicity of Morgan's taste in art and rare books.

    a. cantankerous   b. brusque   c. catholic   d. candid

20. African American slaves suffered greatly from the callousness of their owners and their overseers.

    a. blithe   b. callous   c. catholic   d. candid

Lesson 9

81. caustic — 90. clandestine

---

81. caus-tic   *adjective*   kôs'-tĭk

[*kaustikos* (Greek), "burnt"]

Definition:

a. Able to dissolve or eat away by chemical action.

Substances with highly **caustic** or corrosive properties are widely used in present-day commercial processes, such as the manufacture of cloth and yarn.

b. Sharp and biting.

Why is it that so many successful theater critics seem to possess sharp tongues and **caustic** wits?

Phrases: a caustic substance, a caustic agent, a caustic reply

Related Forms: (*noun*) causticity; (*adverb*) caustically

Synonyms: (*adjectives*) corrosive; keen, cutting, stinging, tart, pungent, trenchant, mordant, astringent, acidulous, sarcastic, sardonic, acrimonious, venomous; (*nouns*) asperity, acrimony, mordancy, acerbity; sarcasm

Antonyms: (*adjectives*) mild, bland (Word 60), amiable, good-natured, charitable; sweet, sugary, honeyed, saccharine

82. cen-sor   *noun and verb*   sĕn'-sər

[*censor* (Latin), from *censere* (Latin), "estimate, assess"]

Definition:

a. (*noun*) An official who examines works of literature, films, and the like for things considered to be immoral, offensive, or dangerous and who is empowered to prohibit or remove this material; anyone who acts as an arbiter of morals or reading/viewing matter.

"If it were always easy to distinguish art from obscenity," the official remarked, "the job of a **censor** wouldn't be so difficult."

b. (*verb*) To examine for and remove objectionable material.

Many parents believe that prime-time TV programs should be carefully **censored** in order to protect children from accidental exposure to "adult" material.

Related Forms: (*adjectives*) censorial, censorious; (*noun*) censorship

Synonyms: (*nouns*) expurgator, bowdlerizer; Comstockery, Grundyism; (*verbs*) expurgate, bowdlerize; excise, delete (Word 120), expunge

Anthony Comstock (*left*);
Cato the Censor (*above*)

Censors and Censorship

English has borrowed a good many words and phrases without change from Latin. One such word is *censor*. In ancient Rome there were two magistrates with this title. Their functions included taking the census of citizens (which was necessary for tax purposes), filling vacancies in the Senate (Rome's governing body), and supervising public morals and behavior. One Roman censor, Cato the Elder (234–149 B.C.), became especially well known for his stern and unyielding standards of behavior and for the overly aggressive way in which he sought to impose them on the Roman people.

The word *censor* and the powers connected with the office or the act have passed down to present-day society. Various public officials in the United States possess a limited power of censorship over moving pictures, written materials, TV programs, etc., although the word itself is likely to be avoided. Of course, censorship is limited by the First Amendment guarantees of freedom of expression.

English has a number of interesting expressions connected with censorship. One of these is *Grundyism*. Grundyism is a rigid insistence upon strict conformity to the accepted moral or social code. The word derives from Mrs. Grundy, an overly proper character in the English playwright Thomas Morton's comedy *Speed the Plough* (1798).

Another useful expression is *Comstockery*, which indicates zealous but narrow-minded (and often unfair) censorship of art, literature, or the like. The word is derived from Anthony Comstock (1844–1915), an American author and an aggressive, if somewhat bigoted, crusader against what he considered immorality.

124

83. **cen-sure**   *noun and verb*   sĕn'-shər

[*censura* (Latin), "censorship"]

Definition:

  a. (*noun*) Open and strong criticism or disapproval (often taking the shape of a formal reprimand by someone in authority).

      Perhaps my actions were hasty and ill-advised, but they certainly did not merit the kind of harsh public **censure** they received.

      The 18th-century English satirist Jonathan Swift wrote that "**censure** is the tax a man pays to the public for being eminent."

      What do you think Polonius means when he advises his son, Laertes, to "take each man's **censure** but withhold thy judgment"?

  b. (*verb*) To criticize severely; to disapprove strongly.

      I am very wary of anyone who is too quick to **censure** and too slow to forgive.

Phrases: a letter of censure, a vote of censure, a resolution of censure

Related Forms: (*noun*) censurer; (*adjective*) censurable

Synonyms: (*nouns*) rebuke, reprimand, reproof; (*verbs*) rebuke, reprimand, reprove, reprehend, condemn, upbraid, chastise; (*adjectives*) reprehensible, blameworthy

Antonyms: (*nouns*) praise, commendation; approval, approbation; (*verbs*) praise, commend, laud, extol, applaud; (*adjectives*) laudable, praiseworthy, meritorious, admirable, creditable

Related Phrases: (*expressing strong disapproval*) take to task, call on the carpet, dress down, bawl out; (*expressing mild disapproval*) let off with a slap on the wrist; (*expressing approval*) give a pat on the back

84. **cha-grin**   *noun and verb*   shə-grĭn'

[*chagrin* (French), "sadness"]

Definition:

  a. (*noun*) Irritation, embarrassment, or humiliation caused by disappointment or frustration.

      "I didn't particularly want to go to the party," Alex admitted. "Still, I felt a deep sense of **chagrin** when I realized that I wouldn't be invited."

  b. (*verb*) To cause such a feeling.

      Since Marsha prides herself on her skill as a politician, her failure to win election to the student council **chagrined** her deeply.

Synonyms: (*nouns*) vexation, annoyance, mortification; (*verbs*) vex, annoy, mortify, abash

Antonyms: (*nouns*) jubilation, exultation, delight, exhilaration, elation; (*verbs*) exult, delight, exhilarate, elate

85. char-la-tan   *noun*   shär'-lə-tən

[*ciarlatano* (Italian), a variant of *cerretano* (Italian), "an inhabitant of Cerreto," a village near Spoleto in central Italy. The place was famous for its quacks.]

Definition: Anyone who claims to have skills or knowledge that he or she doesn't possess.

> "Don't be too eager to accept the claims of every fad diet that comes along," my physician warned me. "Some of these programs may have been concocted by **charlatans** whose recommendations could do you great harm."

Related Forms: (*nouns*) charlatanism, charlatanry

Synonyms: (*nouns*) impostor, quack, mountebank, humbug, fraud, faker

Two famous charlatans and their 20th-century impersonators: Burt Lancaster as Elmer Gantry and Fernando Corena as Dr. Dulcamara ("Sweet and Sour"), the quack doctor in Gaetano Donizetti's comic opera *The Elixir of Love* (*inset*).

Quacks and Other Charlatans

A *quack* (from *quacksalver*) is a person who makes false claims about the salves and other medications that he or she sells. By extension, the word indicates anyone who makes false or exaggerated claims about his or her medical knowledge, skills, or techniques. A *mountebank* (literally, a person who "climbs on a bench") is a charlatan who uses clownish or flamboyant techniques to sell his or her wares. By extension, the word is applied to any boastful or unscrupulous salesman. A *humbug* is a self-important fraud. An *impostor* is simply someone who assumes another person's identity for the purposes of fraud or deception.

86. chron-ic   *adjective*   krŏn'-ĭk

[*chronikos* (Greek), "pertaining to time," from *chronos* (Greek), "time"]

Definition: Continuing over a long period of time or recurring often.

The poor woman suffers terribly from **chronic** arthritis.

His inability to arrive anywhere on time, at first an amusing weakness, has become a **chronic** problem.

There have been long periods when our economy has been plagued by **chronic** inflation.

Phrases: chronic insomnia, chronic attacks of asthma, chronic financial problems, chronic unemployment, a chronic complainer

Related Form: (*adverb*) chronically

Usage Note:
When used as a medical term, *chronic* indicates the kind of ailment or disease that develops slowly over a very long period of time and only gradually becomes serious or fatal—for example, heart disease. The opposite is *acute,* which indicates the kind of medical problem that comes on a person suddenly or unexpectedly and takes only a short time to become critical— for example, appendicitis.

Synonyms: (*adjectives*) long lasting, prolonged, continual, constant; habitual, inveterate, confirmed, deep-rooted, ingrained; perennial, recurrent

Antonyms: (*adjectives*) transitory, transient, evanescent, ephemeral; sporadic, occasional

Related Phrases: a hardened criminal, a lingering illness, a confirmed bachelor, sporadic fighting

87. cir-cu-i-tous   *adjective*   sẽr-kyo͞o'-ĭ-təs

[*circu(m)* (Latin), "around" + *ire, itus* (Latin), "go"]

Definition: Indirect or roundabout; long-winded.

"If I have a little time on my hands after school, I take the long way home," Marta said. "It's a **circuitous** route, but the scenery is just beautiful!"

His style of writing is so **circuitous** and diffuse that I often get lost halfway through one of his paragraphs.

Phrases: circuitous logic or reasoning, circuitous procedures

Related Forms: (*nouns*) circuitousness, circuit

Synonyms: (*adjectives*) winding, meandering, rambling, sinuous, devious, oblique; circumlocutory, periphrastic, digressive

Antonyms: (*adjectives*) direct, undeviating, unswerving, straightforward, unveering

Related Phrases: veer off at a tangent, sidetrack a discussion, beat around the bush; as the crow flies

88. cir·cum·spect   *adjective*   sûr'-kəm-spĕkt

[*circum* (Latin), "around" + *specere, spectus* (Latin), "look"]

Definition: Cautious or prudent, especially in regard to the consequences of actions or statements; tactful.

Since you don't know most salespeople personally, always be as **circumspect** as possible in your dealings with them.

Phrases: a circumspect investor, circumspect behavior

Related Forms: (*noun*) circumspection; (*adverb*) circumspectly

Synonyms: (*adjectives*) careful, watchful, vigilant, guarded, wary, chary, leery; discreet, politic, diplomatic, judicious

Antonyms: (*adjectives*) careless, imprudent, incautious, heedless; rash, reckless, foolhardy; brash (Word 68), precipitate; indiscreet, tactless

89. cir·cum·vent   *verb*   sûr-kəm-vĕnt'

[*circum* (Latin), "around" + *venire, ventus* (Latin), "come"]

Definition: To get around or avoid, especially by trickery or deception.

We planned our route so as to **circumvent** heavily congested urban areas that might slow down our progress.

If people are not in agreement with a given law, they may attempt to ignore or **circumvent** it.

Related Form: (*noun*) circumvention

Synonyms: (*verbs*) bypass, skirt, evade, sidestep, dodge, duck

Antonyms: (*verbs*) obey, observe, comply with, respect, abide by

90. clan·des·tine   *adjective*   klăn-dĕs'-tĭn

[*clandestinus* (Latin), "secret," from *clam* (Latin), "in secret"]

Definition: Concealed from view so as to hide one's purpose.

Try as they might, federal agents were unable to locate the **clandestine** printing press that had turned out the counterfeit $100 bills.

Related Forms: (*noun*) clandestineness; (*adverb*) clandestinely

Phrases: a clandestine meeting, clandestine broadcasts, clandestine activities

Synonyms: (*adjectives*) surreptitious, covert, furtive, stealthy, underhand(ed)

Antonyms: (*adjectives*) open, undisguised, overt, manifest, obvious, avowed

Related Phrases: deep cover, behind closed doors, cloak-and-dagger, an undercover agent

Using the Words

Exercise I
1. char'-la-tan   4. cha-grin'
2. cir'-cum-spect   5. cir-cu'-i-tous
3. cen'-sor   6. cir-cum-vent'

Exercise I. Syllabication and Pronunciation

Syllabicate the following words correctly, and place the major stress mark (') after the syllable that is accented when the word is pronounced.

Example: a-bet'

1. charlatan
2. circumspect
3. censor
4. chagrin
5. circuitous
6. circumvent

Exercise II. Words Out of Context

In each of the following groups, select the item that best expresses the meaning of the numbered word at the left.

1. charlatan   a. officer   b. immigrant   c. fraud   d. critic

2. clandestine   a. sharp   b. secret   c. savage   d. sensible

3. censure   a. rebuke   b. remove   c. relax   d. restore

4. circuitous   a. electrical   b. collective   c. indirect   d. foolhardy

5. caustic   a. expensive   b. final   c. responsible   d. biting

Exercise III. Completing Sentences

Complete each of the following sentences or pairs of sentences by selecting the appropriate word from the group of words given below. Use each word only once.

censor   chagrin   circumvent

charlatan   chronic   circumspect

1. The novelist felt a deep sense of __chagrin__ when the book he had worked on so long and hard received unfavorable reviews in the press.

2. "A person never knows where a friendship will lead," Mom observed. "That's why it's always best to be as circumspect as possible in choosing one's companions."

3. Unemployment is a __chronic__, rather than an occasional, problem for some members of our society.

4. I thought we should meet the problem head-on; Tom thought we should try to _circumvent_ it.

5. During a war, a government will often ___censor___ all kinds of documents in order to keep sensitive or classified material from falling into the hands of the enemy.

Exercise IV. Synonyms and Antonyms

Classify each of the following pairs of words as **S** for **synonyms** or **A** for **antonyms.**

S 1. caustic—corrosive
S 2. bowdlerize—expurgate
A 3. commend—censure
A 4. chagrin—delight
S 5. charlatan—mountebank

A 6. covert—overt
S 7. habitual—chronic
A 8. circuitous—straightforward
A 9. imprudent—circumspect
S 10. circumvent—dodge

Exercise V. Word Roundup

1. Explain the difference between a *chronic* illness and an *acute* illness.

2. Give **two** colloquial phrases that mean "censure strongly." Use each in an original sentence.

3. Define each of the following.
   a. a humbug
   b. a quack
   c. a pat on the back
   d. cloak-and-dagger
   e. an undercover agent
   f. as the crow flies
   g. a hardened criminal
   h. a confirmed bachelor

4. What is the source of the term *Grundyism?* the word *Comstockery?* What does each of these words mean?

5. Give **three** synonyms for each of the following. Consult a thesaurus if necessary.
   a. praiseworthy
   b. blameworthy

Exercise VI. Framing Sentences

A. Use each of the following in an original sentence.
   1. clandestine
   2. censor
   3. charlatan
   4. chagrin
   5. circuitous
   6. censure
   7. circumvent
   8. caustic

B. Give an **adverb** form of each of the following, and use it in an original sentence.
   1. chronic chronically
   2. circumspect circumspectly

130

Dissecting the Words

The Latin prefix **circum**, meaning "around" or "about," occurs in a number of English words, including *circuitous*, *circumspect*, and *circumvent*, all of which were studied in this lesson. Here are some other examples:

circumference (literally "a carrying around")—the boundary of a circle

circumlocution—a roundabout way of saying something. Adjective: *circumlocutory*

circumnavigate—to sail around (for example, the globe)

circumscribe (literally, "to write around"—to encircle; to confine or restrict within limits

circumstance (literally, "a standing around")—a fact or condition that accompanies an event or has some bearing on it. The related adjective *circumstantial* means "relating to the circumstances involved" or, by extension, "incidental; nonessential."

In some English words *circum* loses its *m* and becomes **circu**. Good examples of this include *circuitous* and *circuit*.

Finally, note that *circum* itself comes from the Indo-European root **(s)ker**, which means "bend" or "turn." Words from this root include *circus*, *circle*, *circulate*, *curvature*, and, surprisingly, *search* and *crown*.

Roots

1. The Greek root **chron(o)** means "time." It is found in a small number of English words, including *chronic* and *anachronism*. Here are some other words using this root:

chronology—the arrangement of events in time; a list of events in the order that they happened. Adjective: *chronological*

chronicle—a year-by-year record of historical events; to record events in this way. Noun: *chronicler*

synchronize—to occur at the same time; to cause to coincide in time.

2. English words ending in -*cracy* are derived from the Greek root **kratos** meaning "rule" or "power." One such word is *bureaucracy* (Word 72). Here are a few more:

democracy (*demos* [Greek] "people" + *kratos*, "rule")—rule by the people

plutocracy (*ploutos*, [Greek] "wealth" + *kratos*, "rule")—rule by the wealthy class of society. Noun: *plutocrat*; adjective: *plutocratic*

aristocracy (*aristos* [Greek] "best" + *kratos*, "rule")—rule by the upper or privileged classes. Noun: *aristocrat*; adjective: *aristocratic*

theocracy (*theos* [Greek] "god" + *kratos*, "rule")—a government controlled solely by the religious authorities. Adjective: *theocratic*

ochlocracy (*ochlos* [Greek], "mob" + *kratos*, "rule")—mob rule

thalassocracy (*thalassa* [Greek], "sea" + *kratos*, "rule")—domination of the sea; naval supremacy. Noun: *thalassocrat*

Exercise

1. Define the following terms or phrases, and indicate what part the prefix *circum* plays in each.

    a. circumstantial evidence
    b. a circuit breaker
    c. a circuit court
    d. a circumlocution

2. Two of the books of the Bible are called *Chronicles*. Judging by this name and your knowledge of the meaning of the root *chron(o)*, what do you think these books contain?

3. One of the most common forms of Elizabethan drama is called the *chronicle play*. Judging by this name and your knowledge of the root *chron(o)*, what do you think such a play would be about, and how would it be organized?

4. What is a person's *chronological age? mental age?*

5. Name an example, past or present, of each of the following forms of government. For instance, *Great Britain* is a good example of a *constitutional monarchy*.

    a. aristocracy
    b. democracy
    c. autocracy
    d. theocracy

Enriching the Lesson

Exercise I.   "Time on My Hands"

With or without the aid of a dictionary, define each of the following expressions involving the word *time*. Then choose any **five** of the items, and for each compose an original sentence that clearly illustrates the expression's meaning.

1. timeserver
2. timely
3. time-honored
4. behind the times
5. time deposit
6. time bomb
7. in good time
8. for the time being
9. time-out
10. timetable
11. make time
12. high time
13. timepiece
14. time clock
15. keep time

Now, using a thesaurus, supply the following information:

16. List and define **five nouns** that relate in one way or another to the concept of time. For instance, you might begin with *duration* or *infinity*.

17. List and define **five verbs** that have to do with time. For example, you might begin with *tarry* or *abide*.

18. List and define **five adjectives** involving the concept of time. For instance, you might begin with *retroactive* or *transient*.

19. List and define **five phrases** connected in some way with the concept of time. For instance, *the ravages of time* or *tide over* might top your list.

Exercise II. Our Latin Heritage

A good number of words commonly used in modern English come with little or no change from Latin. One such word, *censor*, was studied in this lesson. Some other words of this kind are listed below. With or without the aid of a dictionary, define each. Then choose any **five**, and for each compose an original sentence.

1. alias
2. quorum
3. propaganda
4. bonus
5. gratis
6. onus
7. affidavit
8. opprobrium
9. consensus
10. alibi
11. animus
12. caveat
13. ultimatum
14. verbatim
15. imprimatur

Can you think of any others? Make a list of them.

Exercise III. Curious Compounds

The way English forms compound words is fascinating. **Compound words** are words that are made up of two (or more) separate words or word elements (e.g., *standoff, takeover, kingless, fearful*). One curious group of compound words is made up of a short, usually monosyllabic verb plus its object, usually a noun, in that order. A good example of this kind of compound is *scarecrow*, which, as you already know, is a dummy set up in a field to *scare* (the verb) off *crows* and other birds (the object) looking for food.

Below are listed a number of other compound words made up of a verb and its object. The first ten items are given out of context; the others are *italicized* in a representative phrase. Define each item, and indicate which part of the word is the verb and which its object. Then choose any **five**, and for each supply an original sentence that illustrates the word's meaning.

1. scofflaw
2. pickpocket
3. turncoat
4. spendthrift
5. breakwater
6. tattletale
7. scapegrace
8. spoilsport
9. daredevil
10. cutthroat
11. at a *breakneck* pace
12. a *telltale* odor
13. a *makeshift* arrangement
14. a *lackluster* performance
15. a *stopgap* measure

Exercise IV. Expanding Your Word Power

The words listed below are not on the Basic Word List, but they were mentioned in passing in Lesson 9. All of them would make useful additions to your working vocabulary. Define each, give its etymology, list **two** synonyms and **two** antonyms (where possible), and use in a short sentence that clearly illustrates the word's meaning.

1. sarcasm
2. saccharine
3. sporadic
4. abash
5. manifest
6. inveterate
7. ephemeral
8. oblique
9. periphrastic
10. diplomatic
11. approbation
12. trenchant

Lesson 10

91. **coerce** — 100. **conjecture**

---

91. **co·erce**   *verb*   kō-ûrs′
[*co*, a form of *cum* (Latin), "together" + *arcere* (Latin), "confine"]

Definition: To force someone to do something against his or her will by using undue pressure, threats, intimidation, or physical violence.

There are far more subtle ways of **coercing** a person into doing what you want than twisting his or her arm.

"Though my parents frequently advise me about how to act in a particular situation," Rhoda said, "they never try to **coerce** me into doing what they think best."

If you seek to impose your will on others by **coercing** them, you will make many enemies.

Related Forms: (*nouns*) coercion, coerciveness; (*adjectives*) coercive, coercible; (*adverb*) coercively

Synonyms: (*verbs*) constrain, compel, pressure, bulldoze, dragoon; hector, browbeat, cow

Related Phrases: strong-arm tactics; high-pressure someone, bring pressure to bear, railroad someone into; under duress

92. **co·gent**   *adjective*   kō′-jĕnt
[*cogens, cogentis* (Latin), "driving together"; from *co*, a form of *cum* (Latin), "together" + *agere* (Latin), "drive; force"]

Definition: Forceful and convincing; to the point.

"The objections that Gloria raised to my plan were not only **cogent**," Frank admitted candidly, "they were totally unanswerable!"

One of the articles in yesterday's paper had some **cogent** and perceptive things to say about our troubled economy.

Phrases: a cogent argument; a cogent criticism, a cogent account, a cogent description, a cogent analysis, at her most cogent and compelling

Related Forms: (*noun*) cogency; (*adverb*) cogently

Synonyms: (*adjectives*) powerful, potent, effective, telling; persuasive, compelling; valid, sound; relevant, pertinent, apposite, germane, apropos

Antonyms: (*adjectives*) weak, ineffective, unconvincing, frivolous, inane; invalid, untenable; irrelevant

93. co-here   *verb*   kō-hēr'
[*co*, a form of *cum* (Latin), "together" + *haerere* (Latin), "stick, cling"]

Definition: To hold or stick together; to fit together into an orderly, logical, and unified whole.

> Add just enough water to the mixture of sand and cement to produce a gritty substance that **coheres** like oatmeal.

> If all the elements in your essay don't **cohere** properly, you won't achieve a single overall effect.

Related Forms: (*nouns*) coherence, coherency, cohesion, cohesiveness; (*adjectives*) coherent, cohesive

Usage Note:
In spoken and written English, *coherence* is the principle that requires the parts of a sentence or a longer composition to be so worded and arranged that they stick together in an orderly, logical relationship. Errors that usually produce incoherence, especially in student writing, include dangling or misplaced modifiers, faulty pronoun references, lack of an overall focus, puzzling shifts in thought, the inclusion of irrelevant details, the illogical arrangement of facts or events, and the omission of essential information.

Synonyms: (*verbs*) coalesce, combine, gel

Antonyms: (*verbs*) separate, fall apart, come apart, come asunder; diverge, disperse, dissipate, diffuse, scatter; (*noun*) incoherence; (*adjectives*) incoherent, disjointed

94. col-lab-o-rate   *verb*   kə-lăb'-ə-rāt
[*col*, a form of *cum* (Latin), "together" + *laborare, laboratus* (Latin), "work"]

Definition:
a. To work together on some kind of joint project. (In this sense the tone of the word is neutral.)

> Though Shakespeare usually worked by himself, other Elizabethan dramatists frequently **collaborated** on plays.

b. To cooperate with the enemy in some kind of treasonable activity. (In this sense the tone of the word is definitely pejorative.)

> "Make no mistake," the leader of the resistance movement declared. "A frightful punishment awaits any citizen who willingly **collaborates** with the foreign power that has occupied our country."

Related Forms: (*nouns*) collaboration, collaborator

Synonyms: (*verbs*) cooperate, team up, join forces, pool one's efforts; intrigue, collude, conspire; (*nouns*) partner, colleague, coworker; quisling, fifth columnist, fellow traveler; partnership, team effort, joint effort

Antonyms: (*verbs*) work by oneself; dissociate oneself from, part company with, take leave of

Related Phrase: in cahoots with

Quisling

In the 1930s Vidkun Quisling (1887–1945) was a respected Norwegian serving in various political and diplomatic posts. By 1945 he had become Norway's most notorious turncoat, and his surname had supplied English with a new word for *traitor*.

Trained at Norway's only military academy, Quisling became a major in the Norwegian army. After that, he served as an official at the League of Nations and was responsible for the handling of refugees fleeing Stalin's Russia.

While acting as Norway's Minister of Defense from 1931 to 1933, Quisling developed a great admiration for the Germans. When World War II broke out, Quisling helped the German military plan the invasion of his native land; and when the Nazis arrived, he used his influence to hasten Norway's collapse. Somewhat later, the Nazis appointed Quisling Premier of Norway, a position he held until the war ended. In May 1945, Quisling was arrested, tried, and executed for high treason. Because of Quisling's part in the betrayal of Norway, his name became synonymous with treachery.

95. **com-pat-i-ble**   *adjective*   kəm-păt'-ə-bəl
[*com*, a form of *cum* (Latin), "together" + *pati* (Latin), "feel; endure" + *abilis* (Latin), "able to"]

Definition:
   a. Capable of use with some other brand or model.

   A particular software program that you have seen advertised on television or in the newspaper may or may not be **compatible** with the type of home computer you own.

   b. Capable of living or getting along together.

   The two people work well together despite the fact that their personalities don't seem at all **compatible**.

Related Forms: (*nouns*) compatibility, compatibleness; (*adverb*) compatibly

Synonyms: (*adjectives*) harmonious, agreeable, like-minded; consistent, congruous; parallel

Antonyms: (*adjectives*) incompatible, antagonistic; inconsistent, incongruous

Related Phrases: in sync, in keeping with, in line with

136

96. com-pla-cent   *adjective*   kəm-plā'-sĕnt

[*com*, a form of *cum* (Latin), "with; very" + *placens, placentis*, from *placere* (Latin), "please, be satisfied"]

Definition: Overly self-satisfied; smug.

"If you had achieved as much this year as he has," I replied, "you'd be a little **complacent,** too!"

Related Forms: (*nouns*) complacence, complacency; (*adverb*) complacently

Phrases: a complacent attitude, a complacent look

Usage Note:
Do not confuse the adjective *complacent*, meaning "self-satisfied," with the related adjective *complaisant*, meaning "eager to please" or "cheerfully obliging."

Synonyms: (*adjectives*) content(ed), self-content(ed)

Antonyms: (*adjectives*) dissatisfied, discontent(ed), malcontent

Related Phrases: to rest on one's laurels, pleased with oneself; displeased with oneself

97. con-cise   *adjective*   kən-sīs'

[*concidere, concisus* (Latin), "cut up"; from *con*, a form of *cum* (Latin), "very" + *caedere, caesus* (Latin), "cut"]

Definition: Saying a lot in a few words.

Since there is a charge for every word you use in a telegram, always make your message as **concise** as possible.

Phrases: a concise account, a concise statement

Related Forms: (*nouns*) conciseness, concision; (*adverb*) concisely

Synonyms: (*adjectives*) brief, compact, succinct, terse; laconic, summary; pithy

Antonyms: (*adjectives*) wordy, prolix, verbose, garrulous, loquacious, long-winded

98. con-done   *verb*   kən-dōn'

[*condonare* (Latin), "forgive"; from *con*, a form of *cum* (Latin), "completely" + *donare* (Latin), "give away"]

Definition: To overlook or disregard an offense, thereby implying forgiveness, acceptance, or possibly approval of it.

"I'm perfectly willing to wink at a harmless practical joke," Mom remarked, "but I refuse to **condone** outright vandalism."

Today it is considered permissible for children to behave in ways that earlier generations of parents would not have **condoned.**

Related Forms: (*nouns*) condonation, condoner

Synonyms: (verbs) ignore; accept, countenance, stomach, tolerate

Antonyms: (verbs) condemn, denounce, disapprove, deprecate, castigate, decry, revile

Related Phrases: close one's eyes to, turn a blind eye to; put up with

99. con-fron-ta-tion   *noun*   kŏn-frən-tā'-shən

[*confrontare, confrontatus* (Latin), "have a common border"; from *con,* a form of *cum* (Latin), "together" + *frons, frontis* (Latin), "forehead"]

Definition: A face-to-face encounter, usually (but not always) suggesting a hostile or defiant attitude.

"Our two countries must make every effort to settle our differences peacefully," the ambassador said. "An all-out **confrontation** might ruin us both."

Related Form: (verb) confront

Synonyms: (nouns) showdown, face-off, shoot-out

Related Phrases: stand up to, square off against, throw down the gauntlet, take up the gauntlet, on the brink

Maya Angelou

The African American poet and writer Maya Angelou (born 1928) is best known for her engaging series of autobiographical books dealing with problems and issues she confronted growing up black and female in 20th-century America. Beginning with I *Know Why the Caged Bird Sings* (1970), she has given her audience a series of memorable self-portraits designed to lay bare the black experience of life in these United States. The themes she evokes in her autobiographical writing also find expression in her numerous volumes of poetry. Angelou's writing combines a rich and flexible vocabulary with a deft ear for the cadences of ordinary, everyday speech.

100. con·jec·ture   *noun and verb*   kən-jĕk'-chər

[*conjectura* (Latin), "conclusion"; from *con*, a form of *cum* (Latin), "together" + *jacere, jactus* (Latin), "throw"]

Definition:
   a. (*noun*) A conclusion based on inadequate evidence; a guess.

   Since the coroner's findings were inconclusive, the exact cause of the child's death remains for the present a matter of **conjecture**.

   b. (*verb*) To conclude from inadequate evidence; to guess.

   "I haven't enough hard evidence at hand to say for sure," the detective declared. "I can only **conjecture**, based on past experience, that this was an inside job."

Related Forms: (*adjective*) conjectural

Synonyms: (*nouns*) surmise, supposition, presumption, suspicion, inference; speculation, theory; (*verbs*) surmise, suppose, presume, suspect, infer; speculate, theorize

Antonyms: (*nouns*) fact, certainty; (*verbs*) demonstrate, substantiate

Related Phrases: an educated guess, a shot in the dark, a ballpark estimate

Using the Words

Exercise I.   Parts of Speech

Indicate the part of speech of each of the following words. In one case, two answers are correct.

1. confrontation n.
2. compatible adj.
3. conjecture n., v.
4. coerce v.
5. cogent adj.
6. complacent adj.

Exercise II.   Words in Phrases

In each of the following groups, select the item that best expresses the meaning of the *italicized* word in the introductory phrase.

1. a particularly *cogent* argument
    a. forceful   b. bizarre   c. elaborate   d. weak   e. silly

2. *compatible* interests
    a. unusual   b. conflicting   c. deep   d. parallel   e. scholarly

3. *condone* wrongdoing
    a. point at   b. flinch at   c. aim at   d. rail at   e. wink at

4. find someone with whom to *collaborate*
    a. chat   b. team up   c. disagree   d. sit down   e. sympathize

5. an interesting *conjecture*
    a. fact   b. situation   c. guess   d. development   e. history

Exercise III. Completing Sentences

Complete each of the following sentences or pairs of sentences by selecting the most appropriate word from the group of words given below.

concise	confrontation	cohere
coerce	conjecture	complacent

1. Though it omitted many details, her spare and ___concise___ account of the accident left us in no doubt as to exactly what had happened.

2. Some chemical compounds ___cohere___ readily; others are highly unstable and separate easily.

3. "I don't understand why you are walking around with that ___complacent___ grin on your face," I exclaimed. "Exactly what have you done to make you so pleased with yourself?"

4. The bitter rivals for public office met in a dramatic confrontation on TV to debate the issues of the campaign.

5. You should know better than to try to ___coerce___ me into doing something that goes against my principles.

Exercise IV. Synonyms and Antonyms

A. In each of the following numbered groups, select the **two** words that are most nearly **synonyms**.

1. a. gel   b. rebuke   c. separate   d. coalesce   cohere
2. a. disregard   b. overlook   c. redress   d. compel   condone
3. a. circumvent   b. blight   c. pressure   d. bulldoze   coerce
4. a. put-on   b. showdown   c. time-out   d. shoot-out   confrontation
5. a. terse   b. succinct   c. frivolous   d. incongruous   concise

   Now, for each of the pairs of synonyms you have selected, supply a word from the Basic Word List for this lesson (Words 91–100) that means **the same** or **almost the same** thing.

B. In each of the following numbered groups, select the **two** words that are most nearly **antonyms**.

1. a. cogent   b. agreeable   c. unique   d. frivolous
2. a. campaign   b. conjecture   c. certainty   d. chagrin
3. a. awry   b. faulty   c. discontented   d. complacent
4. a. collaborate   b. border   c. dissociate   d. recognize
5. a. joyful   b. compatible   c. frequent   d. antagonistic

Exercise V. Word Roundup

1. With or without the aid of a dictionary, define or explain each of the following expressions.
    - a. strong-arm tactics
    - b. fifth columnist
    - c. in cahoots with
    - d. in sync
    - e. rest on one's laurels
    - f. throw down the gauntlet
    - g. quisling
    - h. a shot in the dark
    - i. an educated guess
    - j. turn a blind eye to

2. Explain what principle of good writing (and speaking) is indicated by the term *coherence*. What are some of the characteristics of *incoherent* writing?

3. Explain the difference between *complacent* and *complaisant*. Use each in a sentence that clearly illustrates the word's meaning.

Exercise VI. Framing Sentences

A. Use each of the following words in an original illustrative sentence.
    - 1. conjecture
    - 2. cogent
    - 3. collaborate
    - 4. compatible
    - 5. confrontation
    - 6. condone

B. Give an **adjective** form of each of the following, and use it in an original illustrative sentence.
    - 1. cohere
      coherent
    - 2. conjecture
      conjectural
    - 3. coerce
      coercive

C. Give an **adverb** form of each of these words, and use it in an original illustrative sentence.

	cogently	complacently	concisely
	1. cogent	2. complacent	3. concise

William Safire

William Safire (born 1929) is a noted commentator on the American language. For over twenty years he has written a popular weekly column, "On Language," which investigates and spotlights development in our language. He has also written seven books on American English. An influential political columnist as well, Safire was awarded a Pulitzer Prize for political commentary.

Completing Verbal Analogies

"A Indicates the State of Being B.*"*   Another important word relationship that turns up on standardized vocabulary tests may conveniently be expressed as *"A* indicates the state of being *B."* An example of an analogy question involving this word relationship is given below. See if you can figure out the correct answer before you read the explanation of it given below.

A   *B*   *C*   *D*

chagrin : mortified = candor : (*careless, vexed, frank, reserved, hungry*)

The answer, of course, is *frank. Candor* indicates the state of being *frank* or open about one's knowledge, thoughts, or feelings, just as *chagrin* indicates the state of being *mortified* or humiliated by some kind of disappointment or frustration.

Note that, as usual, the wrong choices offered under *D* include some traps for the unwary. For example, *vexed,* which is something of a synonym of *mortified,* indicates how a person feels when overcome with *chagrin,* but it has nothing to do with *candor.* Similarly, *reserved* indicates a trait that is the opposite of the one suggested by *candor.*

Exercise I

Complete the following analogies based on the word relationship "*A* indicates the state of being *B."*

1. **complacence : smug** = vigilance : (*sweet, quarrelsome, generous, watchful, jolly*)
2. **conciseness : brief** = cogency : (*terse, forceful, elaborate, bizarre, childish*)
3. **prudence : careful** = apathy : (*indecisive, indignant, indigent, indiscreet, indifferent*)

Exercise II   Answers will vary.

Write **three** original analogies based on the relationship "*A* indicates the state of being *B."* In your analogies use at least **two** of the basic words studied in Lessons 1–10 (Words 1–100).

Exercise III

The following items review what you have so far learned about analogy questions. Complete each.

1. **anarchy : order** = apathy : (*influence, ignorance, income, interest, intelligence*)
2. **callous : compassionate** = caustic : (*forthright, bland, callow, myopic, pungent*)

3. **clandestine : openness** = compatible : (*conflict*, *direction*, *sympathy*, *meaning*, *unity*)

4. **coerce : constrain** = cohere : (*circumvent*, *censure*, *compel*, *commend*, *coalesce*)

5. **affluence : rich** = captiousness : (*hypercritical*, *hyperbolic*, *hyperactive*, *hypothetical*, *hypocritical*)

Enriching the Lesson

Exercise I. Look-Alikes

English has a great many duos or even trios of words that look alike but mean quite different things. Some of these items are paired off below. With or without the aid of a dictionary, explain the difference in meaning between the members of each pair.

1. abrogate—arrogate	11. affect—effect
2. human—humane	12. flaunt—flout
3. resound—redound	13. fallible—fallacious
4. envious—enviable	14. noisy—noisome
5. official—officious	15. founder—flounder
6. laudable—laudatory	16. ceremonious—ceremonial
7. judicial—judicious	17. fortunate—fortuitous
8. ferment—foment	18. contemptible—contemptuous
9. ingenious—ingenuous	19. progeny—prodigy
10. martial—marital	20. depredation—deprivation

Now, choose any **five** of the pairs of words listed above. For each, compose a set of **two** sentences, each of which illustrates the meaning and use of **one** of the words in the pair.

Exercise II. By the Sweat of Your Brow

Some terms and expressions used in connection with working in general and labor-management relations are listed below. With or without the aid of a dictionary or other reference book, define each.

1. labor force	11. seniority
2. skilled worker	12. real wage
3. unskilled worker	13. minimum wage
4. blue-collar worker	14. cost-of-living increase
5. white-collar worker	15. craft union
6. journeyman	16. industrial union
7. apprentice	17. right-to-work laws
8. injunction	18. automation
9. collective bargaining	19. featherbedding
10. equal employment opportunity	20. productivity

Exercise III.   Ships That Have Never Seen the Sea

Below you will find a group of "ship" words. With or without the aid of a dictionary, define each. Then illustrate its meaning by using it in an original sentence or by telling an anecdote that conveys its basic idea.

1. statesmanship
2. gamesmanship
3. horsemanship
4. wordsmanship
5. sportsmanship
6. one-upmanship
7. leadership
8. lifemanship
9. guardianship

Exercise IV.   A Verbal Diversion

A. *Doublets*   A good many common English phrases are made up of two elements connected by the word *and* or the word *or* (or sometimes a preposition). Such phrases are often called **doublets**. A good example of a doublet is *aid and abet,* mentioned in Lesson 1. Below are listed a number of other doublets. Define each.

1. flotsam and jetsam
2. null and void
3. sackcloth and ashes
4. kith and kin
5. rank and file
6. spick and span
7. by hook or by crook
8. raise a hue and cry
9. cut and dried
10. in dribs and drabs

B. *Triplets*   There is also a small group of common phrases made up of three elements. Such phrases are sometimes called **triplets**. A good example of a triplet is the phrase *ready, willing, and able.*

Below you are given the first two elements of a number of other common triplets. Supply the missing third element. Also, define any of these phrases that is not immediately intelligible to you.

1. lock, stock, and __barrel__
2. hook, line, and __sinker__
3. bell, book, and __candle__
4. healthy, wealthy, and _wise_
5. tall, dark, and _handsome_
6. any Tom, Dick, or__Harry__
7. signed, sealed, and _delivered_
8. beg, borrow, or __steal__
9. rag, tag, and __bobtail__
10. blood, sweat, and __tears__

Exercise V.   Expanding Your Word Power

The words listed below are not on the Basic Word List, but they were mentioned in passing in Lesson 10. All of them would make useful additions to your vocabulary. Define each, give its etymology, list **two** synonyms and **two** antonyms (where possible), and use in a short illustrative sentence.

1. potent
2. relevant
3. inane
4. valid
5. incongruous
6. diffuse
7. intrigue
8. malcontent
9. substantiate

Related Forms in Context

Beneath each sentence below are four words introduced in Lesson 9 or 10. Review the related forms for these words, and choose the one that best completes the sentence. Write that related form in the space provided.

1. The _collaboration_ of Richard Rodgers, composer, and Oscar Hammerstein, lyricist, produced such classics of the American musical theater as *Oklahoma!, Carousel, South Pacific,* and *The King and I.*

   a. censor   b. circumvent   c. coerce   d. collaborate

2. The federal government indicted two young men for the _circumvention_ of coding in software programs designed to protect copyrighted DVDs.

   a. censure   b. circumvent   c. cohere   d. condone

3. Did you see the movie based on a true story about the _charlatanry_ of a young man without any credentials who passes himself off as a doctor and a pilot?

   a. censor   b. charlatan   c. confrontation   d. chagrin

4. During the Cuban Missile Crisis in October 1962, the two great superpowers—the United States and the USSR— _confronted_ each other head-on over the Soviet installation of missiles in Cuba, only 90 miles from Florida.

   a. chagrin   b. conjecture   c. confrontation   d. charlatan

5. During World War II, when soldiers wrote home from the front, their letters were subject to military _censorship_.

   a. censor   b. censure   c. conjecture   d. chagrin

6. How much of a role do you think American _complacency_ played in the devastating attack on Pearl Harbor, which left more than two thousand dead and sank or damaged almost two dozen ships?

   a. compatible   b. concise   c. cogent   d. complacent

7. After a three-month investigation, the grand jury concluded that the city officials' actions were not only _censurable_ but actually indictable as criminal offenses.

   a. conjecture   b. censor   c. censure   d. confrontation

8. When writing dictionary definitions, lexicographers aim for clarity and _conciseness_.

   a. circuitous   b. concise   c. complacent   d. compatible

9. Without evidence to support it, your intriguing theory remains purely _conjectural_.

   a. chagrin   b. conjecture   c. censure   d. censor

10. "Of course you're right," she said caustically . "You always are, aren't you?"

    a. clandestine   b. compatible   c. complacent   d. caustic

11. The speaker explained Albert Einstein's general theory of relativity so cogently that even a layperson could understand its basic points.

    a. complacent   b. cogent   c. chronic   d. caustic

12. Sunshine laws in most states prohibit or restrict government groups from meeting clandestinely.

    a. cogent   b. concise   c. clandestine   d. chronic

13. A strike by workers is a type of coercion designed to bring labor and employers to the bargaining table.

    a. coerce   b. cohere   c. condone   d. circumvent

14. Can you explain what causes the cohesion of molecules in a chemical compound?

    a. collaborate   b. conjecture   c. coerce   d. cohere

15. "I have never been a condoner of sloth," Grandma said sternly to the two little boys sprawled on the couch watching TV.

    a. circumvent   b. conjecture   c. condone   d. collaborate

16. The people who score standardized tests of writing evaluate students' essays for clarity, coherence , and the development of ideas.

    a. collaborate   b. condone   c. cohere   d. coerce

17. Do you suppose that the White Rabbit in Lewis Carroll's *Alice's Adventures in Wonderland* might have been chronically late for important dates?

    a. caustic   b. chronic   c. cogent   d. compatible

18. Because of the circuitousness of the route the taxi driver took, I ended up having to pay three times the usual fare.

    a. cogent   b. concise   c. complacent   d. circuitous

19. In a 1771 speech, the American patriot Samuel Adams warned colonists, "The necessity of the times, more than ever, calls for our utmost circumspection, deliberation, fortitude, and perseverance."

    a. circumspect   b. complacent   c. caustic   d. chronic

20. After she bought her new computer, Mia was dismayed to discover that compatibility is a problem and that she might have to replace her printer.

    a. concise   b. compatible   c. complacent   d. cogent

Review

1. **abdicate** — 100. **conjecture**

Exercise I
1. ac-cli'-mate, ac'-cli-mate
2. au'-gur
3. ba'-nal, ba-nal'
4. bom-bas'-tic
5. cha-grin'
6. co-erce'

Exercise I.   Syllabication and Pronunciation

Syllabicate the following words correctly, and place the major stress mark (') after the syllable that is accented when the word is pronounced. Two answers are correct in some instances.

1. acclimate
2. augur
3. banal
4. bombastic
5. chagrin
6. coerce

Exercise II.   Parts of Speech

Indicate the part of speech of each of the following words. In some cases, two answers are correct.

1. advocate n., v.
2. atrophy n., v.
3. bicker v.
4. brash adj.
5. censure n., v.
6. conjecture n., v.

Exercise III.   Words Out of Context

In each of the following groups, select the lettered item that best expresses the meaning of the numbered word at the left.

1. abdicate — a. serve b. retain c. delete d. beg e. resign

2. appall — a. propose b. determine c. horrify d. cover e. attract

3. anarchy — a. chaos b. hostility c. support d. ignorance e. effort

4. boisterous — a. greedy b. cowardly c. ugly d. noisy e. lazy

5. bleak — a. mindless b. fearless c. aimless d. timeless e. cheerless

6. baffle — a. nurture b. puzzle c. aid d. relish e. conclude

7. captious — a. favorable b. destitute c. hypercritical d. collective e. clumsy

8. clandestine — a. opulent b. sarcastic c. furtive d. vigilant e. laudable

9. caustic   **a. cutting**   b. frivolous   c. occasional
                  d. indirect   e. lofty

10. cogent   a. loathsome   b. innocent   c. theoretical
                  d. compelling   e. endless

Exercise IV.   Words in Phrases

In each of the following groups, select the lettered item that best expresses the meaning of the *italicized* word in the introductory phrase.

1. *adjourned* the meeting
   a. suggested   **b. suspended**   c. convened   d. arranged
   e. attended

2. *chronic* financial problems
   a. occasional   b. unexpected   c. severe   **d. recurrent**
   e. temporary

3. *badger* a witness
   a. call   b. find   **c. harass**   d. question   e. excuse

4. a *brusque* reply
   a. curt   b. puzzling   c. detailed   d. timely   e. written

5. a *complacent* attitude
   a. nasty   b. foolish   c. hostile   d. dangerous   **e. smug**

Exercise V.   Completing Sentences

Complete each of the following sentences by selecting the most appropriate word from the group of words given below. Use each word only once. Make any adjustments that are necessary to fit the words into the sentences properly.

asylum	boycott	concise
collaborate	affluent	bungle

1. Though I can occasionally afford some of life's more expensive luxuries, I'd hardly describe myself as __affluent__ .

2. "Usually I don't make a mess of things," I thought in dismay as I looked at the burned muffins, "but this time I've really __bungled__ the job."

3. Traditionally, refugees from all sorts of oppression have sought __asylum__ in the United States.

4. Since there isn't much space to write on a postcard, you must make your messages as __concise__ as possible.

5. When two famous dramatists __collaborate__ on the script for a new play, the result is likely to be extraordinary.

Exercise VI. Synonyms and Antonyms

Classify each of the following pairs of words as **S** for **synonyms** or **A** for **antonyms**.

S 1. hostile—belligerent   **S** 6. estrange—alienate
A 2. abhor—relish   **S** 7. circuitous—roundabout
A 3. augment—reduce   **A** 8. reckless—circumspect
S 4. amnesty—pardon   **A** 9. affable—surly
A 5. bland—piquant   **A**10. deter—abet

Exercise VII. Framing Sentences

Use each of the following words in a short illustrative sentence of your own devising.

1. addiction   3. boycott   5. cantankerous
2. agile   4. buttress   6. charlatan

Exercise VIII. Related Forms

A. Give a **noun** form of each of the following words.
        abstinence   allegation   cajolery
    1. abstain   2. allege   3. cajole

B. Give a **verb** form of each of the following words.
        authenticate   confront   calumniate
    1. authentic   2. confrontation   3. calumny

C. Give an **adjective** form of each of the following words.
    1. apathy   2. bureaucracy   3. avarice
     apathetic   bureaucratic   avaricious

Exercise IX. Word Roundup

1. Explain the difference between the words in each of the following pairs.

    a. loathe—loath   d. callow—callous
    b. averse—adverse   e. allusion—illusion
    c. aesthetic—ascetic   f. forbear—forebear

2. Explain what each of the following means.

    a. academic freedom   c. red tape
    b. halcyon days   d. living high off the hog

3. Explain the story behind each of the following expressions.

    a. Grundyism   b. candidate

4. What principle of good writing and speaking is indicated by the term *coherence*? What are some of the characteristics of *incoherent* writing?

5. Give the singular form of the word *agenda*. Explain the fact that *agenda* itself may be used as a singular form.

Exercise X. Etymology

1. Give **three** English words that derive from the Latin root *ced* or *ceed*. What does this root mean?

2. What does the Greek prefix *a* or *an* mean? For each of the following definitions, supply an English word beginning with this prefix.

    a. shapeless or formless   b. of unknown authorship

3. How does the prefix *ad* change when it is added to a root beginning with a consonant? What is the technical name for this phenomenon?

4. Convert each of the following nouns or adjectives to a verb by adding the suffix *ize*. Make any spelling changes that are necessary. Then define the verb you have created.

    a. social   b. proselyte   c. maximum

5. Define each of the following words using the Germanic prefix *be*, and explain what function the prefix performs.

    a. bemoan   b. bewitch   c. besmirch

Exercise XI. Choosing the Right Meaning

Read each sentence carefully. Then underline the item that best completes the statement below the sentence.

1. During the late nineteenth and early twentieth centuries, millions of immigrants from western and eastern Europe sought (2) asylum in the United States. They fled from economic hardship, religious persecution, and political unrest. Many of (4) them sailed into New York Harbor, where they were welcomed by the Statue of Liberty, a gift from France. (6)

    The word **asylum** in line 3 means

    a. sanctuary   c. psychiatric hospital
    b. wealth   d. citizenship

2. The farm's owners seem to have mysteriously disappeared without making any provision for their animals. When neigh- (2) bors investigated after several days, they found the horses and cattle in abject condition. They fed and watered the ani- (4) mals and then notified the police.

    The word **abject** in line 4 means

    a. mean-spirited   c. wretched
    b. despicable   d. unhealthy

3. Voters overwhelmingly passed an amendment to the state constitution that mandates class size be decreased to a maximum of 25 students per classroom. But in a recent debate over the state's budget, one legislator denounced the plan as purely academic. "Without a drastic raise in taxes," he claimed, "no funds are available to hire the necessary teachers and build the new schools that the plan requires." (2) (4) (6)

The word **academic** in line 5 means

a. scholarly   c. expensive
b. unrealistic   d. experimental

4. Abraham Lincoln may not have been an abolitionist, but he campaigned on his opposition to extending slavery into the territories. By the time that Lincoln acceded to the presidency on March 4, 1861, seven states (South Carolina, Mississippi, Florida, Alabama, Georgia, Louisiana, and Texas) had seceded from the Union. (2) (4) (6)

The words **acceded to** in line 3 mean

a. agreed to   c. campaigned for
b. balked at   d. entered the office of

5. In 1803 President Thomas Jefferson appointed his private secretary, Captain Meriwether Lewis, head of the expedition to explore the Louisiana Territory and the West. Sacajawea, a Shoshone woman who accompanied the expedition, helped Lewis and Clark acquire horses for their circuitous journey over the high Rocky Mountains to the land of westward-flowing rivers and, finally, to the Pacific Ocean. (2) (4) (6)

The word **circuitous** in line 5 means

a. long-winded   c. strenuous
b. winding   d. terrifying

6. Studies have shown that identical twins generally have a benign influence on each other's development and personalities. As they grow, they maintain a strong bond of friendship and support each other's interests. Often, identical twins develop similar—but not identical—personality traits. (2) (4)

The word **benign** in line 2 means

a. strong   c. gentle
b. harmful   d. wholesome

7. A tangram is a Chinese puzzle designed to baffle both adults and children. Tangrams are made by cutting a square into seven smaller shapes (five triangles, a square, and a rhomboid), that can then be arranged to create various geometric shapes or designs. (2) (4)

The word **baffle** in line 1 means

a. mystify   c. thwart
b. challenge   d. annoy

8. Ansel Adams, an astute observer of nature, devoted his life to taking and developing black and white photographs of the **(2)** western and southwestern United States. His great love of nature is evident in his moving photographs—with their **(4)** stunning effects of light, clarity, and mist—taken in the Yosemite and High Sierra valleys. **(6)**

The word **astute** in line 1 means

a. perceptive
b. cunning
c. subtle
d. artistic

9. Choosing a topic for a research paper should not be arbitrary. Remember that you will spend upward of six weeks working **(2)** on your topic. That is why teachers recommend that you choose a subject that genuinely interests you. **(4)**

The word **arbitrary** in line 1 means

a. high-handed
b. compulsory
c. random
d. judgmental

10. Did you know that some household cleaners are caustic and therefore dangerous? Be careful to avoid combining bleach **(2)** with other cleaning agents, for example, because the combination may release gases that are extremely harmful if inhaled. **(4)**

The word **caustic** in line 1 means

a. sarcastic
b. malodorous
c. poisonous
d. corrosive

11. The push to have every child reading well by third grade continues to gain momentum. Reading experts advise that **(2)** families begin regularly reading aloud to children in infancy and that youngsters be encouraged to develop catholic **(4)** tastes in books and other reading matter.

The word **catholic** in line 4 means

a. religious
b. global
c. specialized
d. broad

12. In 1955 Rosa Parks triggered the Montgomery, Alabama, bus boycott by refusing to give up her seat on a bus to a **(2)** white man. In her autobiography, *Rosa Parks: My Story,* she is candid about her motivation. She wasn't old or physically **(4)** tired, she says. "The only tired I was, was tired of giving in."

The word **candid** in line 4 means

a. impromptu
b. forthright
c. impartial
d. biased

Lesson 11

---

101. **con·nois·seur**   *noun*   kŏn-ə-sûr′
[*connoisseur* (obsolete French), "expert"; from *connoistre* (Old French), "know"; from *co*, a form of *cum* (Latin), "thoroughly" + *(g)noscere* (Latin), "know"]

Definition: Someone with informed and discriminating judgment, especially in matters of art, literature, or taste.

> Though the exhibition was by no means a popular success, it caused a sensation among **connoisseurs** and scholars.

> I don't know anything about quiches or soufflés, but I'm a true **connoisseur** when it comes to pizza.

Synonyms: (*nouns*) expert, authority, specialist, pundit, savant, maven, devotee; judge, critic, arbiter; (*plural noun*) cognoscenti

Antonyms: (*nouns*) beginner, novice, neophyte, greenhorn, tenderfoot, tyro; amateur, dilettante

Usage Note:
Amateur and *dilettante* both refer to someone who studies or practices an art for his or her own amusement. *Dilettante* also suggests the idea of dabbling or not being very serious about the pursuit. A *connoisseur*, on the other hand, has sufficient knowledge or expertise to serve as a competent judge or critic.

102. **con·sen·sus**   *noun*   kən-sĕn′-səs
[*consensus* (Latin), "general agreement"; from *con*, a form of *cum* (Latin), "together" + *sentire, sensus* (Latin), "feel"]

Definition: Collective uniformity of opinion; general agreement in feeling or belief.

> Though everyone in our club agreed that we had a problem, there was no group **consensus** on how to solve it.

Usage Note:
Adding the phrase "of opinion" to *consensus* is frowned upon by most authorities because the idea that these words express is already included in the meaning of *consensus*.

Synonyms: (*nouns*) unanimity, like-mindedness, concord, harmony, accord, unity, concurrence

Antonyms: (*nouns*) discord, disagreement, disunity, disharmony, dissent, conflict, diversity, dissidence

Related Phrases: in accord with, in unison, of the same mind

153

103. con-strue   *verb*   kən-strōō'

[*con*, a form of *cum* (Latin), "together" + *struere* (Latin), "heap up"]

Definition: To analyze, explain, interpret, or understand.

As you have already learned, the word *agenda* may be **construed** as either singular or plural.

"Am I to **construe** your silence as an admission of guilt?" Dad asked.

Related Forms: (*verb*) misconstrue; (*adjective*) construable; (*nouns*) construction, misconstruction

Synonyms: (*verbs*) deduce, infer, translate, gather, take to mean

Antonyms: (*verbs*) misinterpret, misunderstand

104. con-sum-mate   *adjective:* kən-sŭm'-ĭt   *verb:* kŏn'-sə-māt

[*con*, a form of *cum* (Latin), "together" + *summa* (Latin), "highest, supreme"]

Definition:

   a. (*adjective*) Complete or perfect in the highest degree.

     The soprano may lack the **consummate** artistry of a great singing actress such as Callas, but she is still a remarkable performer.

   b. (*verb*) To bring to completion or perfection.

     Though there are still a few minor details to iron out, we expect to **consummate** the deal sometime this week.

Related Forms: (*noun*) consummation; (*adverb*) consummately

Synonyms: (*adjectives*) superlative, supreme; transcendent, surpassing, matchless; finished, total; masterful, virtuoso; (*verbs*) clinch, conclude

Antonyms: (*adjectives*) mediocre, indifferent, run-of-the-mill, ordinary; inept, incompetent, inadequate; (*verbs*) begin, start, initiate, launch

105. co-pi-ous   *adjective*   kō'-pē-əs

[*copiosus* (Latin), "plentiful," from *copia* (Latin), "plenty"]

Definition: Large in number or quantity; full.

In no time at all, the guests reduced the **copious** supply of edibles to a mere memory.

A long epic poem such as Dante's *Divine Comedy* is equally the product of a **copious** mind and a fertile imagination.

Related Forms: (*nouns*) copiousness, copiosity; (*adverb*) copiously

Synonyms: (*adjectives*) abundant, plentiful, ample, bountiful, bounteous, profuse, lavish, numerous; extensive, comprehensive

Antonyms: (*adjectives*) meager, scanty, scarce, sparse; inadequate, insufficient; empty, vacant, vacuous, barren

Cornucopia

A Greek myth tells how Zeus, having been nursed in infancy by the nymph-goat Almathea, showed his gratitude by a gift of a miraculous horn. This horn, or *cornucopia* (Latin, *cornu*, "horn" + *copiae*, "of plenty") furnished the possessor with an inexhaustible supply of food and other good things. A horn overflowing with fruits and ears of grain has come to be used as an emblem of plenty in the decorative arts, as well as a general symbol of abundance and prosperity.

106. **cor-pu-lent**   *adjective*   kôr'-pyə-lĕnt
[*corpulentus* (Latin), "fat," from *corpus* (Latin), "body"]

Definition: Fat and bulky.

As I grew older and less active, I became decidedly more **corpulent**.

On paydays my wallet becomes pretty **corpulent**; the rest of the week it looks as if it's on a very stringent diet.

Related Forms: (*nouns*) corpulence, corpulency

Synonyms: (*adjectives*) chubby, plump, husky, burly, portly, stout, rotund, obese

Antonyms: (*adjectives*) lean, lanky, thin, wiry, scrawny, gaunt

107. **cor-rob-o-rate**   *verb*   kə'-rŏb-ə-rāt   *or*   kô-rŏb'-ô-rāt
[*corroborare*, *corroboratus* (Latin), "strengthen"; from *cor*, a form of *cum* (Latin), "thoroughly" + *robur*, *roboris* (Latin), "oak; strength"]

Definition: To confirm the truth or accuracy of.

The defendant's alibi may sound far-fetched, but highly reliable evidence **corroborates** every last word of it.

Only time can **corroborate** some predictions.

Related Forms: (*nouns*) corroboration, corroborator; (*adjectives*) corroborative, corroboratory

Synonyms: (*verbs*) verify, substantiate, support, back up, bear out

Antonyms: (*verbs*) contradict, refute, rebut, confute, discredit, impugn

155

108. coun-sel   *noun and verb*   kaun'-səl

[*conseil* (French), "advice," from *consilium* (Latin), "deliberation"]

Definition:

a. (*noun*) Advice secured through consultation.

At first I ignored my grandmother's advice, but as I grew older, I came to appreciate the wisdom of her **counsel**.

b. (*noun*) An adviser, especially a legal adviser.

Under a landmark Supreme Court ruling, every defendant in a criminal case is assured of representation by legal **counsel**.

c. (*verb*) To advise or recommend as a course of action.

"Before you make your final choice," my faculty adviser **counseled**, "visit each of the colleges to which you've applied."

Usage Note:
Do not confuse *counsel* with either *council* (a group assembled to give advice or exchange opinions) or *consul* (an official appointed to represent a government in a foreign country, especially in commercial matters).

Related Form: (*noun*) counselor

Phrases: keep one's own counsel, on advice of counsel, a camp counselor

Synonyms: (*nouns*) guidance, direction, recommendation; attorney, lawyer; (*verbs*) guide, instruct, urge, exhort, admonish, caution

109. cred-i-bil-i-ty   *noun*   krĕd-ə-bĭl'-ə-tē

[*credibilis* (Latin) "believable," from *credere* (Latin), "believe" + *abilis, abile* (Latin), "able to"]

Definition: The ability to inspire belief or trust.

"The secretary's public statements are often at odds with official pronouncements," the reporter observed. "This has seriously impaired his **credibility** as a reliable spokesman for the administration."

Related Forms: (*noun*) credibleness; (*adjective*) credible; (*adverb*) credibly

Usage Notes:

a. Do not confuse *credibility*, which indicates the ability to inspire belief or trust, with *credence*, which indicates the belief or trust that has been inspired.

b. Note too the difference between *credible*, which means "worthy of *belief*," and *creditable*, which means "worthy of *praise*."

c. The phrase *credibility gap* refers to a general public skepticism about the truth or accuracy of official claims or statements.

Synonyms: (*nouns*) reliability, believability, plausibility, trustworthiness, dependability; (*adjective*) plausible

Antonyms: (*nouns*) unreliability, undependability

110. cri-te-ri-on   *noun*   krī-tîr'-ē-ən
[*kriterion* (Greek), "means of judging," from *krinein* (Greek), "judge"]

Definition: A standard or principle on which to base a judgment or decision.

Usefulness is not the only **criterion** for including words in this book, but it is the primary one.

Usage Note:
The plural of *criterion* is *criteria* (or sometimes *criterions*). Under no circumstances is the form ending in *a* acceptable as the singular.

Synonyms: (*nouns*) yardstick, touchstone, guideline, gauge, canon, rule

111. cru-cial   *adjective*   krōō'-shəl
[*crucial* (Old French), "cross-shaped," from *crux, crucis* (Latin), "cross"]

Definition: At a point that will determine the final outcome; of supreme importance.

"The next few months are **crucial**," President Harry S. Truman once said. "What we do now will affect our American way of life for decades to come."

Related Form: (*adverb*) crucially

Synonyms: (*adjectives*) critical, decisive, momentous, pivotal, vital

Antonyms: (*adjectives*) insignificant, unimportant, inconsequential

Related Phrases: the crux of the matter, reach the crisis point

112. cul-pa-ble   *adjective*   kŭl'-pə-bəl
[*culpabilis* (Latin), "blameworthy," from *culpa* (Latin), "guilt; fault"]

Definition: At fault; blameworthy.

"I should have kept a closer eye on the project," the supervisor confessed. "In this regard, I'm as **culpable** as those who actually botched the job."

Phrases: culpable stupidity, culpable neglect (or negligence)

Related Forms: (*nouns*) culpability, culpableness, culprit

Usage Note:
Culpable is stronger than *blameworthy* but less severe than *guilty*. As the example above indicates, it is usually reserved for a fault that is the result of an error of omission, lack of sound judgment, negligence, or ignorance, rather than actual criminal intent.

Synonyms: (*adjectives*) guilty, delinquent, peccant, wanting; blamable, censurable, reprehensible

Antonyms: (*adjectives*) innocent, blameless; laudable, commendable, meritorious, praiseworthy

113. **cur·so·ry**   *adjective*   kûr'-sə-rē

[*cursorius* (Late Latin), "pertaining to running," from *currere, cursus* (Latin), "run"]

Definition: Hasty and superficial.

"I was so pressed for time that I couldn't give the lengthy report more than a **cursory** reading," the busy executive confessed.

Phrases: a cursory examination, a cursory report, in a cursory fashion

Related Forms: (*noun*) cursoriness; (*adverb*) cursorily

Synonyms: (*adjectives*) hurried, perfunctory, quick, summary, careless, unmethodical, casual, slapdash

Antonyms: (*adjectives*) thorough, exhaustive, comprehensive, in-depth, systematic, painstaking, careful, meticulous

114. **cur·tail**   *verb*   kər-tāl'

[from obsolete English *to make a curtal of* (a *curtal* being a horse with shortened ears and tail); from *curtus* (Latin), "shortened"]

Definition: To shorten or reduce.

When problems arose at the office, I was forced to **curtail** my vacation and hurry back to the city.

Over the centuries, the powers of the British monarch have been greatly **curtailed**.

Related Form: (*noun*) curtailment

Synonyms: (*verbs*) abridge, abbreviate, truncate, lessen, diminish, cut short, cut back, dock, pare down, trim

Antonyms: (*verbs*) increase, enlarge, augment, amplify, expand, extend

115. **cyn·i·cal**   *adjective*   sĭn'-ĭ-kəl

[*kynikos* (Greek), "doglike, currish," from *kyon* (Greek), "dog"]

Definition: Inclined to doubt or deny the virtuousness or honesty of human motives; sneeringly bitter or negative.

"As you say, my view of the world may be far too rosy," I admitted. "On the other hand, yours is perhaps a bit too **cynical**."

Related Forms: (*nouns*) cynic, cynicism; (*adverb*) cynically

Synonyms: (*adjectives*) skeptical, suspicious, doubtful; pessimistic, misanthropic; derisive, scornful; caustic (Word 81), sardonic, acerbic

Antonyms: (*adjectives*) optimistic, sanguine, positive; naive, starry-eyed, romantic, idealistic

Related Phrase: view the world through rose-colored glasses

Diogenes of Sinope (*left*);
Alexander the Great (*above*)

Cynic

The Cynics were a group of ancient Greek philosophers who followed the teachings of Antisthenes of Athens (ca. 444–ca. 371 B.C.). Antisthenes, a pupil of Socrates, believed that virtue was the only good and that human happiness consisted in trying to be virtuous. In order to become virtuous, he argued, a person must reduce his or her dependence on the outside world. That meant living in poverty, scorning pleasure, and ignoring social conventions. As you can see, this was a high-minded but essentially negative program.

Of course, it wasn't long before the Cynics were sneering at people and their motives as well as at things. For instance, Diogenes of Sinope (ca. 412–323 B.C.), a pupil of Antisthenes, showed his contempt for worldly goods by living naked in a tub. He expressed his disdain for the average human being (and his or her motives) in an equally dramatic way. During the daytime, he went around Athens shining a lantern in people's faces and looking at them intently. When asked why he did this, he replied haughtily that he was "looking for an honest man."

Diogenes even sneered at Alexander the Great and his achievements. For instance, once Alexander asked Diogenes, "Can I do anything for you?" "Only get out of my sunshine!" Diogenes sarcastically replied.

It is from such contemptuous attitudes toward people and their motives that our modern words *cynic* and *cynical* take their meanings.

By the way, the ancient Greeks probably nicknamed these philosophers *Kynikoi* (that is, "doglike") because of the bad manners they displayed. The name was ironically appropriate because the gymnasium at which Antisthenes taught happened to be named the *Kynosarges.* To the Greeks, the first syllable of this name appeared to contain a form of the Greek word for *dog* (*kyon*).

Using the Words

Exercise I
1. con-nois-seur′
2. con-sen′-sus
3. con-sum′-mate,
   con′-sum-mate
4. cor′-rob-o-rate,
   cor-rob′-o-rate
5. coun′-sel
6. cred-i-bil′-i-ty
7. cul′-pa-ble
8. cur′sory
9. cyn′-i-cal

Exercise I.   Syllabication and Pronunciation

Syllabicate the following words correctly, and place the major stress mark (′) after the syllable that is accented when the word is pronounced. Two answers are correct in two instances.

1. connoisseur
2. consensus
3. consummate
4. corroborate
5. counsel
6. credibility
7. culpable
8. cursory
9. cynical

Exercise II.   Words Out of Context

In each of the following groups, select the item that best expresses the meaning of the numbered word at the left.

1. connoisseur   a. bystander   b. expert   c. foreigner
   d. advocate   e. beginner

2. copious   a. some   b. few   c. none   d. one
   e. many

3. counsel   a. advise   b. refuse   c. order
   d. control   e. question

4. criterion   a. needle   b. thimble   c. pincushion
   d. yardstick   e. scissors

5. culpable   a. in unison   b. on target   c. at fault
   d. by heart   e. off guard

6. consummate   a. complete   b. plump   c. empty
   d. reliable   e. mediocre

7. cursory   a. positive   b. different   c. innocent
   d. hasty   e. abundant

Exercise III.   Completing Sentences

Complete each of the following sentences or pairs of sentences by selecting the most appropriate word from the group of words given below. Use each word only once. Make any adjustments that are necessary to fit the words into the sentences properly.

corpulent   consensus   corroborate

construe   cynical   credibility

connoisseur   curtail   crucial

1. The country is so deeply divided over the issue that no national
   consensus on how to handle the matter appears likely or
   even possible.

160

2. "The facts of the matter don't appear to _corroborate_ your suspicions," Grace said. "Can you offer any evidence to back up your ideas?"

3. The official's absurd excuses for covering up his involvement in the unsavory affair have completely destroyed his _credibility_, even among his warmest supporters.

4. "I don't know what to make of their recent behavior," Jack admitted. "How should it be _construed_?"

5. Selling arms to both sides in a civil war strikes me as a heartless and _cynical_ exploitation of an unfortunate situation.

6. "I realize that this decision is by no means inconsequential," Mom told me. "Still, I don't believe it is as _crucial_ as you make out."

7. I'd describe some of my classmates as lean or lanky; others I'd call a bit _corpulent_.

8. Though her job responsibilities have been greatly enlarged this year, mine have by no means been _curtailed_.

Exercise IV. Synonyms and Antonyms

Classify each of the following pairs of words as **S** for **synonyms** or **A** for **antonyms**.

A 1. disprove—corroborate
S 2. copious—plentiful
A 3. crucial—insignificant
S 4. unanimity—consensus
A 5. untrustworthiness—credibility
A 6. culpable—blameless
S 7. portly—corpulent

A 8. connoisseur—novice
A 9. cynical—starry-eyed
S 10. infer—construe
S 11. truncate—curtail
A 12. cursory—thorough
S 13. lawyer—counsel
S 14. consummate—clinch

Exercise V. Word Roundup

1. What is the difference between a _dilettante_ and _connoisseur_?

2. Why shouldn't the phrase _of opinion_ be added to the word _consensus_?

3. What is the difference in meaning between _burly_ and _husky_? _chubby_ and _obese_?

4. Briefly explain the background behind the words _cornucopia_ and _cynic_.

5. Tell the difference between the words in the following pairs.

   a. counsel—council
   b. counsel—consul

   c. credibility—credence
   d. credible—creditable

6. Give the plural of _criterion_. (Two forms are possible.)

7. Define each of the following words or phrases.

a. greenhorn
b. credibility gap
c. in unison

d. the crux of the matter
e. view the world through rose-colored glasses

Exercise VI. Framing Sentences

A. Use each of the following words in an original illustrative sentence

1. connoisseur
2. consensus
3. construe

4. counsel
5. criterion
6. credibility

7. consummate
8. cursory
9. curtail

B. Give a **noun** form of each of these words, and use it in an illustrative sentence.

corpulence
1. corpulent

corroboration
2. corroborate

culpability
3. culpable

C. Give an **adverb** form of each of these words, and use it in an original sentence.

1. cynical
   cynically

2. crucial
   crucially

3. copious
   copiously

Amy Tan

Amy Tan is one of the most successful Asian American writers working today. Born in Oakland, California, in 1952, the daughter of Chinese parents who had fled the communist revolution in their homeland, Amy Tan earned a degree in linguistics and then began a career as a business and marketing writer. At the same time she began to create language programs for developmentally impaired children. In 1987 she and her mother visited China to explore the people and places that had played so large a part in her mother's life. Her experiences in China were so powerful that she used them and her mother's life as the basis for her first novel, *The Joy Luck Club* (1989). Since then she has published several other novels and some children's books.

Dissecting the Words

Prefix

Co, col, com, con, and **cor** are all combining forms of the Latin preposition **cum,** meaning "with," "together," or "completely." These elements appear in all the basic words studied in Lesson 10 and many of those studied in this lesson. Note how each is used.

a. **Co,** a shortened form of **com,** occurs before Latin words beginning with *h, gn,* or (usually) a vowel. It is also used to coin new words, in which case it may be attached to words beginning with other consonants.

coherent (*co,* "together" + *haerere,* "stick")—sticking together

cognizance (*co,* "completely" + *gnoscere,* "know")—conscious knowledge or recognition of something

coalesce (*co,* "together" + *alescere,* "grow")—to fuse or merge

coeducational (*co,* "together" + *educational*)—attended or participated in by both male and female students

cobelligerent (*co,* "with" + *belligerent*)—a partner in a war

b. **Col** is used before Latin words beginning with *l.*

colloquial (*col,* "together" + *loqui,* "speak")—acceptable only in familiar conversation

collusion (*col,* "together" + *ludere,* "play")—cooperation, usually secret, in some fraudulent or evil enterprise

c. **Com,** the basic combining form of **cum,** appears before Latin words beginning with *b, m, p,* and sometimes *i.*

combat (*com,* "together" + *battere,* "fight")—battle

commemorate (*com,* "completely" + *memmorare,* "mention, be mindful of")—to serve as a memorial of

commiserate (*com,* "together with" + *miserari, miseratus,* "pity")—to sympathize with; to feel pity or sorrow for

compete (*com,* "with" + *petere,* "strive")—to vie or contend with

d. **Con** is used before all consonants except *b, h, l, m, r,* and *w.*

contagious (*con,* "together" + *tangere,* "touch")—transmitted by direct or indirect contact

construct (*con,* "together" + *struere,* "pile up")—to build or erect

conjugal (*con,* "together" + *jugum,* "yoke")—relating to marriage

conform (*con,* "together" + *formare,* "shape")—to have the same form or character; to act in the same way

e. **Cor** is used before Latin words beginning with *r.*

corrode (*cor,* "completely" + *rodere,* "gnaw")—to dissolve or wear away by chemical action

correlate (*cor,* "together" + *relatus,* "carried back")—to show a logical relationship among different elements

Exercise

1. For each of the following definitions, give an English word that contains a form of the Latin preposition *cum*.

   a. work together
   b. meet together
   c. join together
   d. fall down completely
   e. unite into a compact mass
   f. existing at birth
   g. stick together
   h. agree together
   I. squeeze together
   j. destroy the virtue of

2. With or without the help of a dictionary, give the meanings of the component parts of the words listed below. Then define each word, and use it in a short illustrative sentence.

   a. coauthor
   b. commutation
   c. compatible
   d. corrugate
   e. coordinate
   f. commingle
   g. confederate
   h. coexistence
   I. compunction
   j. concurrent
   k. constrain
   I. contemplate

H. L. Mencken

H. L. Mencken (1880–1956) was one of the most colorful and influential figures in the history of American linguistics. Though Mencken was a working journalist and magazine editor all of his life, he found time to compile a monumental study of American English called *The American Language.* First published in 1919 and subsequently revised or expanded on several occasions, *The American Language* deals with all aspects of American English from its beginnings in the 17th century to developments in the 1930s and 1940s. The lively, often caustic style in which this and other works were written influenced such notable 20th-century American writers as Theodore Dreiser, Sinclair Lewis, and Sherwood Anderson. Indeed, the word *Menckenese,* coined to describe Mencken's pungent, vigorous style, has found a lasting place in our language.

Working with Context Clues

Sentence-Completion Exercises.   Today, practically every standardized vocabulary test contains at least one section involving sentence-completion exercises. A **sentence-completion** exercise (sometimes called a **cloze exercise)** asks a student to complete a sentence or group of sentences from which one or two words have been removed. The student is to do this by selecting one of the four or five possible answers that are supplied. Here is a sample sentence-completion exercise. See whether you can figure out which word belongs in the blank.

> Faithfully reading a weekly news magazine such as *Time* or *Newsweek* not only broadens my knowledge of current events but also _____ my vocabulary.
>
> a. decreases   b. fragments c. expands d. demolishes e. contains

Sentence-completion exercises test a student's ability to perceive a meaningful connection between the words in a sentence or between the sentences in a paragraph. They also test a student's knowledge of the meanings of specific words and the proper use of these words in an appropriate context. Thus, sentence-completion exercises are excellent tools for ascertaining a student's knowledge of the vocabulary of Modern English.

Of course, every sentence-completion exercise provides the student with enough information to make the correct choice without going beyond what is actually given. This is done through the use of context clues. As their name implies, **context clues** are verbal or logical hints that have been carefully sewn into the context that surrounds the blank for the missing word. Sometimes these hints are quite concrete—a word or a phrase that gives away the correct answer. Other times, they depend more on an appreciation of the whole situation that is outlined in the passage. In either case, context clues point the student unmistakably toward the correct choice. Here, for example, are the context clues in the sample sentence-completion exercise given above. They have been <u>underlined</u> so you can spot them easily.

> Faithfully reading a weekly news magazine such as *Time* or *Newsweek* <u>not</u> <u>only</u> <u>broadens</u> my knowledge of current events <u>but</u> <u>also</u> _____ my vocabulary.

Now can you figure out which of the five choices given above belongs in the blank? The answer, of course, is choice *c, expands.* Here's why.

If you look at the part of the sentence that follows the word *but,* you will realize that a verb is missing. This tells you that the kind of word you want is a verb.

Next you may notice that the sentence contains the phrase *not only . . . but also.* This is the type of conjunction that binds two parallel or similar parts of a sentence together. Accordingly, the verb that is missing after the words *but also* must mean something like the verb that follows the words *not only.* And what is the verb that follows *not only?* It is *broadens.*

Now you know that you need a verb that means more or less the same as *broadens.* And what is that verb? It is *expands,* which is the only one of the choices that means anything close to *broadens.*

As you can see, completing this type of exercise successfully boils down to a search for the context clues that point to the correct choice. This, in turn, involves knowing what general types of clues are usually employed in such exercises. These general types will be discussed in the "Working with Context Clues" sections of the next few lessons.

Exercise I

Three sample sentence-completion exercises are given below. The context clues that each contains have been underlined. Using these context clues as guideposts, choose the word that correctly completes each exercise.

1. Only one word can adequately describe the lawlessness that prevails when a government collapses: _____ .

   a. asylum   b. anarchy   c. avarice   d. bureaucracy
   e. confrontation

2. Criticism can be caring and constructive, but too often it is _____ and destructive.

   a. cogent   b. avid   c. caustic   d. banal   e. chronic

3. If you know little about art, consult a(n) _____ before paying a large sum of money for a painting.

   a. academic   b. agenda   c. charlatan   d. advocate
   e. connoisseur

Exercise II

Three more sample sentence-completion exercises are given below. The correct answer has been underlined in each case. Using the answer as a guidepost, underline the context clues that each of the samples contains.

1. When pupils are in a very _____ mood, teachers have to discipline them for their loud and rowdy behavior.

   a. copious   b. boisterous   c. bleak   d. clandestine
   e. ambivalent

2. Although politicians are not always open and accessible, they are usually _____ when campaigning for office.

   a. abject   b. concise   c. bland   d. affable   e. agile

3. If Congress wants to reduce federal government spending, it will have to _____ the expansion of already existing programs.

   a. curtail   b. abet   c. censor   d. coerce   e. accede

Enriching the Lesson

Exercise I. The Greeks Had a Word for It

Even though you have probably never studied Greek, you may actually know some. That is because English has borrowed quite a few words and phrases with little or no change from Greek (allowing, of course, for the difference in alphabets). One of these items is *criterion*, studied in this lesson. Some others are listed below. With or without the aid of a dictionary, define each. Then choose any **five,** and for each compose a short illustrative sentence.

1. pathos	11. dilemma	21. dogma
2. aroma	12. climax	22. antithesis
3. plethora	13. diagnosis	23. catharsis
4. ethos	14. psyche	24. hubris
5. panacea	15. crisis	25. trauma
6. genesis	16. catastrophe	26. hypothesis
7. phenomenon	17. stigma	27. apotheosis
8. aegis	18. acme	28. charisma
9. hoi polloi	19. metamorphosis	29. iota
10. synopsis	20. nemesis	30. paralysis

Exercise II. Linguistic Shortcuts

A. *Abbreviations.* A good many abbreviations for Latin phrases commonly turn up in written English. Some of these items are listed below. With or without the help of a dictionary, define each, and give the full Latin phrase for which the abbreviation stands. Then, choose any **five** of the items, and use each in a short illustrative sentence.

1. etc.	7. op.cit.	13. ca. *or* c.
2. et al.	8. e.g.	14. A.D.
3. q.v.	9. i.e.	15. cf.
4. ibid.	10. N.B.	16. viz.
5. loc. cit.	11. A.M.	17. fl.
6. P.S.	12. sc.	18. vs.

B. *Acronyms.* Another type of linguistic shortcut is called an acronym. **Acronyms** are pronounceable words that are made up of the initial letters (or sometimes syllables) of a multiword phrase. Since so many of our modern-day organizations, agencies, and products have fairly long formal names, acronyms are usually devised for them. This saves people the time and trouble of saying or writing the full name. For example, *NATO* (pronounced nā′-tō) is an acronym for the North Atlantic Treaty Organization. Similarly, *Nabisco* (pronounced nə-bĭ′-skō) is an acronym for the National Biscuit Company. Good acronyms become so common that soon everybody understands what is meant, and the long formal name may become quite scarce in everyday usage.

Below are listed a number of common acronyms. With or without the help of a dictionary, define each. Then give the phrase or formal name for which the acronym stands.

1. NASA	7. ASAP	13. SALT
2. CORE	8. NIMBY	14. radar
3. NOW	9. WASP	15. scuba
4. SEATO	10. AWOL	16. sonar
5. VISTA	11. ZIP code	17. laser
6. UNESCO	12. OPEC	18. ATM

Exercise III. Philosophical and Religious Positions

The word cynical, studied in this lesson, suggests a philosophical position or a general attitude toward life. English is rich in such words. Some of them are listed below. With or without the aid of a dictionary, define each. Then choose any **five**, and use each in a short illustrative sentence.

1. materialist	11. romantic	21. skeptic
2. hedonist	12. stoic	22. monotheist
3. idealist	13. humanist	23. heretic
4. empiricist	14. egotist	24. altruist
5. atheist	15. mystic	25. racist
6. agnostic	16. optimist	26. pessimist
7. pragmatist	17. realist	27. latitudinarian
8. epicurean	18. egalitarian	28. utilitarian
9. freethinker	19. misogynist	29. fundamentalist
10. misanthrope	20. humanitarian	30. iconoclast

Exercise IV. Expanding Your Word Power

The words listed below are not on the Basic Word List, but they were mentioned in passing in Lesson 11. All of them would make useful additions to your working vocabulary. Define each, give its etymology, list **two** synonyms and **two** antonyms (where possible), and use in a short illustrative sentence.

1. tyro	6. profuse	11. canon
2. discord	7. plausible	12. pivotal
3. deduce	8. gaunt	13. meticulous
4. derisive	9. rebut	14. abridge
5. initiate	10. admonish	15. acerbic

Lesson 12

116. dapper — 130. dexterous

---

116. dap-per *adjective* dăp'-ẽr
[*dapyr* (Middle English), "elegant," probably from *dapper* (Low German), "agile"]

Definition: Neatly and stylishly dressed.

I'd hardly call someone who always looks as though he's slept in his clothes a **dapper** dresser.

Related Form: (*adverb*) dapperly

Usage Note:
As the example given above suggests, *dapper* is normally reserved for *men*. Accordingly, a stylishly dressed *woman* would probably be called *chic* (pronounced shēk), not *dapper.*

Synonyms: (*adjectives*) natty, smart, spruce, stylish, chic

Antonyms: (*adjectives*) unkempt, sloppy, slovenly, shabby, seedy; dowdy, blousy, frowsy, frumpy

117. de-fect *noun:* dē'-fĕkt *verb:* dĭ-fĕkt'
[*deficere, defectus* (Latin), "fail; remove from"; from *de* (Latin), "away from" + *facere, factus* (Latin), "do; make"]

Definition:
a.   (*noun*) A flaw or shortcoming.

Members of Congress may draft new legislation to correct the **defects** in our tax laws.

b.   (*verb*) To desert one country, cause, or the like for another.

During the Cold War a good many Soviet artists and intellectuals **defected** to the West.

Related Forms: (*nouns*) defectiveness, defection, defector; (*adjective*) defective

Usage Notes:
a.   Something that is *defective* is faulty. For example, a piece of machinery or a copy of a book may be defective. Do not confuse the word with *deficient,* which means "lacking." A person may be deficient in good judgment, for instance.

b.   Someone who defects from one country or cause to another is called a *defector,* and the act of defecting is called a *defection.*

Synonyms: (*nouns*) blemish, fault, imperfection, weakness, failing, bug, kink; (*verbs*) abandon, forsake, bolt; repudiate, disown, abjure

118. de-fer   *verb*   di-fûr′

[*de* (Latin), "away" + *ferre* (Latin), "carry"]

Definition:

a. To put off or postpone.

Unfortunately, a person cannot **defer** payment of a debt indefinitely.

b. To yield courteously to the wishes or judgments of someone else.

It is usually a good idea to **defer** to the judgment of your elders in matters in which you are uncertain about what to do.

Related Forms: (*nouns*) deferment, deferral, deference; (*adjectives*) deferential, deferent

Usage Note:

The nouns *deferment* and *deferral* denote a temporary postponement of, or exemption from, something (for example, jury duty). *Deference* indicates a willing or courteous submission to another person's wishes or ideas, usually out of respect for the latter's age, wisdom, or experience. The adjectives *deferential* and *deferent* mean "respectful," as in "a deferential attitude."

Synonyms: (*verbs*) delay, table, shelve; bow (to), accede (to) (Word 8)

Antonyms: (*verbs*) expedite, facilitate, hasten; spurn, disdain, reject

Related Phrases: hold off on, put on ice, put on a back burner; give way to

119. de-ject-ed   *adjective*   dĭ-jĕk′-tĭd

[*dejicere, dejectus* (Latin), "cast down"; from *de* (Latin), "down" + *jacere, jactus* (Latin), "cast, throw"]

Definition: In very low spirits.

The whole school was very **dejected** after our team's unexpected loss of the championship.

Related Forms: (*noun*) dejection; (*verb*) deject; (*adverb*) dejectedly

Synonyms: (*adjectives*) sad, blue, depressed, gloomy, despondent, melancholy, morose, downcast, dispirited, disheartened

Antonyms: (*adjectives*) happy, merry, elated, exultant, jubilant

Related Phrases: on top of the world; down in the dumps

120. de-lete   *verb*   dĭ-lēt′

[*delere, deletus* (Latin), "wipe away"]

Definition: To strike out or remove.

When my article for the student newspaper ran a bit long, I **deleted** enough material to make it fit.

Related Form: (*noun*) deletion

Usage Note:
Do not confuse the adjective *deleterious* with forms of the verb *delete*. *Deleterious* means "physically or morally harmful."

Synonyms: (*verbs*) cancel, expunge, omit, efface, excise

Antonyms: (*verbs*) retain, include; add, insert

121. de-lin-e-ate   *verb*   dĭ-lĭn′-ē-āt
[*delineare, delineatus* (Latin), "draw lines"; from *de* (Latin), "completely" + *linea* (Latin), "thread; line"]

Definition: To make an accurate line drawing or diagram of; to portray or describe in detail.

The artist's pen-and-pencil sketch not only **delineated** the model's features accurately but also captured something of her personality.

Few writers have J. D. Salinger's remarkable ability to **delineate** the emotions, aspirations, and troubled confusion of the average teenager.

Related Forms: (*nouns*) delineation, delineator

Usage Note:
As a technical term, *delineate* and *delineation* indicate a drawing or engraving that consists of lines, as opposed to one that employs shading or tints. Note too that both words stress fullness and accuracy of detail.

Synonyms: (*verbs*) picture, depict, set forth, sketch, etch

122. de-lin-quent   *adjective and noun*   dĭ-lĭng′-kwĕnt
[*delinquens, delinquentis* (Latin), "leaving completely undone"; from *de* (Latin), "completely" + *linquere* (Latin), "leave undone"]

Definition:
a.   (*adjective*) Neglectful of a duty or obligation; seriously overdue.

Citizens who fail to vote out of indifference or laziness are **delinquent** in their civic duties.

"Pay your bills on time," Mom advised. "It's not a good idea to let any of your accounts become **delinquent**."

b.   (*noun*) A person who fails to perform a duty; an offender.

The family court deals with juvenile **delinquents**, not adult offenders.

Related Form: (*noun*) delinquency

Synonyms: (*adjectives*) remiss, derelict, negligent; owing, outstanding, unsettled; (*nouns*) scofflaw; malefactor, wrongdoer

Antonyms: (*adjectives*) punctilious, scrupulous, dutiful, conscientious, meticulous; paid up

Related Phrases: dereliction of duty, in arrears

123. de-lude   *verb*   dĭ-lōōd′

[*deludere* (Latin), "play false"; from *de* (Latin), "away (*i.e.*, from the truth)" + *ludere* (Latin), "play"]

Definition: To mislead or deceive.

More than one Roman emperor **deluded** himself into believing that he was divine rather than mortal.

Related Forms: (*nouns*) deluder, delusion; (*adjectives*) deluded, delusive, delusory

Usage Note:

A *delusion* is a false belief that usually results from trickery, self-deception, or mental disease (*e.g.*, "*delusions* of grandeur"). Do not confuse the word with *illusion*, which indicates a mistaken impression based on faulty perceptions or wishful thinking (*e.g.*, "an optical *illusion*").

Professional magicians like the one shown in this photo are always devising new and exciting illusions with which to entertain their audiences.

Synonyms: (*verbs*) dupe, gull, cozen, hoodwink, trick, beguile

Related Phrases: a complete hoax, a clever scam, a con(fidence) game, a sting operation

124. de-mure   *adjective*   dĭ-myōōr′

[*demore* (Old French), "quiet"; from *demorer* (Old French), "linger"; from *de* (Latin), "completely" + *morari* (Latin), "delay"]

Definition: Modest and reserved in dress, manner, or behavior.

The heroine of a popular action-adventure movie may be a far cry from the **demure** young women depicted in 19th-century novels.

The village is famous for its cozy thatched cottages and **demure** gardens.

Related Forms: (*noun*) demureness; (*adverb*) demurely

Usage Notes:

a. Frequently, *demure* is used disparagingly to indicate false or affected modesty. In this sense, it is a synonym of *coy*.

b. As the example given above indicates, *demure* is usually reserved for young women. Men who exhibit similar characteristics would probably be called *proper* or *staid*.

c. Do not confuse the adjective *demure* (with an *e* at the end) with the verb *demur* (without an a at the end), which means "take exception to" or "object to."

Synonyms: (*adjectives*) sedate, prim, decorous, seemly, staid; diffident, shy, self-effacing; coy

Antonyms: (*adjectives*) bold, forward, immodest; assertive, aggressive, jaunty, bumptious

Related Phrases: a wallflower, a shrinking violet

---

125. de-noue-ment   *noun*   dā-nōō-män'

[*dénouement* (French), "an untying"; from *dé* (French), "un-" + *nouer* (French), "tie"]

Definition: The point at which the plot of a novel or drama is finally resolved; the outcome or solution of a complex sequence of events.

In the **denouement** of a Victorian novel, vice is usually punished and virtue rewarded.

Their impulsive, often blundering behavior has entangled them in a series of complicated problems whose **denouement** is far from clear.

Synonyms: (*noun*) unraveling (of a plot), disentanglement, climax; final solution, final issue

---

126. des-ul-to-ry   *adjective*   dĕs'-əl-tô-rē

[*desultorius* (Latin), "relating to a jumper"; from *de* (Latin), "down" + *saltire* (Latin), "jump"]

Definition: Shifting from one thing to another without reason or purpose; haphazard or random.

The report on study habits indicated that fifteen minutes of concentrated effort produced better results than two hours of **desultory** labor.

Related Forms: (*noun*) desultoriness; (*adverb*) desultorily

Synonyms: (*adjectives*) fitful, erratic, spasmodic, intermittent; aimless, rambling; disconnected, unmethodical

Antonyms: (*adjectives*) constant, concentrated, steadfast; methodical, systematic, painstaking

Related Phrase: by fits and starts

127. de·vi·ate   *verb:*   dē′-vē-āt   *noun:*   dē′-vē-ĭt

[*deviare, deviatus* (Latin), "go off track"; from *de* (Latin), "away from" + *via* (Latin), "way, road"]

Definition:

    a.   (*verb*) To move away from, especially what is considered normal, right, or acceptable.

       "I'm afraid I'll get lost," the driver said, "if I **deviate** from the route I was told to take."

       In any society, there are those who adhere to the accepted code of behavior and those who **deviate** from it.

    b.   (*noun*) A person who differs markedly in behavior, belief, or attitude from what is accepted as normal or proper.

       Most societies not only frown upon but also proscribe the behavior of various kinds of nonconformists and **deviates**.

Related Forms: (*nouns*) deviation, deviator; (*adjective*) deviant

Synonyms: (*verbs*) diverge, veer, swerve, stray, wander, ramble, digress; (*nouns*) nonconformist, maverick, oddball, heretic

Antonyms: (*verbs*) conform to, stick to, abide by, adhere to; (*nouns*) conformist, traditionalist

Maverick

The word *maverick* is derived from Samuel A. Maverick (1803–1870), a Texas cattleman who refused to brand his calves in accordance with common procedure. At first, the word *maverick* was applied to an unbranded calf that had strayed from the herd and thus could not be readily identified and sent back where it belonged. Later, *maverick* came to mean an individual who does not follow the dictates of the majority, a political or social dissenter, one who refuses to conform to convention. Some synonyms for *maverick* follow: (*nouns*) loner, individualist, insurgent; (*adjectives*) heterodox, recalcitrant, refractory.

128. de-void   *adjective*   dǐ-void′

[*devoide* (Middle English), "rid of "; from *desvuidier* (Old French), "get rid of "; from *des* (Old French), "completely" + *vuidier* (Old French), "empty"]

Definition: Empty; lacking in.

"They are so smug and self-satisfied!" I remarked. "Rarely have I encountered people so completely **devoid** of any awareness of their own imperfections."

That slogan may sound impressive, but it is totally **devoid** of meaning.

Synonyms: (*adjectives*) destitute (of), bereft (of), wanting (in), deficient (in), barren (in)

Antonyms: (*adjectives*) replete (with), fraught (with), saturated (with), full (of), teeming (with), bursting (with), stuffed (with)

129. de-vout   *adjective*   dǐ-vout′

[*de* (Latin), "completely" + *vovere, votus* (Latin), "vow"]

Definition: Deeply religious, earnest, or sincere.

Although they make no great show of their religion, they are **devout** believers in the teachings of their faith.

For more than 50 years, her allegiance to the cause of human rights has been truly **devout**.

Related Forms: (*verb*) devote; (*nouns*) devoutness, devotion, devotee; (*adjectives*) devoted, devotional; (*adverb*) devoutly

Synonyms: (*adjectives*) pious, faithful; reverent; ardent, zealous

Antonyms: (*adjectives*) irreligious, unreligious, unfaithful; irreverent; lukewarm, tepid

130. dex-ter-ous   *adjective*   dĕk′-strəs

[*dexter* (Latin), "(on the) right; skillful"]

Definition: Skillful in using one's hands or mind; clever.

Professional jugglers are among the most **dexterous** people on the face of the earth.

Any potentially explosive situation requires extremely **dexterous** and sensitive handling by all the parties concerned.

Related Forms: (*nouns*) dexterity, dexterousness; (*adverb*) dexterously

Usage Note:
Dexterous is sometimes spelled *dextrous,* but this is not the preferred form of the word.

Synonyms: (*adjectives*) handy, adroit, deft, adept, proficient

Antonyms: (*adjectives*) awkward, clumsy, gauche, inept, maladroit

A debate in the House of Commons about 1905, showing the seating arrangement. Members of the party in power (here the Conservatives) sit to the right of the speaker (the man in the wig on the throne); members of the opposition (*i.e.*, those not in the government) sit to his left.

A Curious Case of Linguistic Prejudice

Dexterous is one of several words which show that English has a curious preference for the right side. This probably stems, at least in part, from the fact that right-handed people have always outnumbered left-handed ones.

A number of other common English words display the same prejudice. For example, *sinister*, which means "ominous" or "evil-looking," is simply the Latin word for "left." Similarly, *gauche*, which means "clumsy" or "boorish," is in fact just the French word for "left." Finally, *adroit*, which means "clever" or "skillful," comes from a French phrase meaning "to the right."

This preference for the right may even be connected with the origin of some of our most common political terms. In medieval times, the most important guest at a banquet was seated in the most favored spot. This was to the right of the host. When parliaments and similar legislative bodies began to appear in Europe, the practice was carried over into politics. Accordingly, the dominant political group (almost always the conservative element) was seated on the right of the official head of the legislature. Liberal and radical groups sat on his left.

From this arrangement modern English derives such terms as *the right* (the conservative or traditionalist element in any political party or country) and *the left* (the more liberal or radical element). The expressions *right wing*, meaning "conservative," and *leftist*, meaning "radical," also come from the same source. Variations on this theme include *rightist*, *right-winger*, *left wing*, and *left-winger*.

Using the Word

Exercise I. Parts of Speech

Indicate the part of speech of each of the following words. In some cases, two answers are correct.

1. defer v.
2. demure adj.
3. deviate n., v.
4. dexterous adj.
5. defect n., v.
6. dapper adj.
7. denouement n.
8. delinquent n., adj.
9. delete v.

Exercise II. Words in Phrases

In each of the following groups, select the item that best expresses the meaning of the *italicized* word in the introductory phrase.

1. *defer* a decision

    a. withdraw   b. overrule   c. confirm   <u>d. postpone</u>

2. in a very *dejected* frame of mind

    a. aggressive   <u>b. gloomy</u>   c. playful   d. bizarre

3. *delinquent* behavior

    a. callow   <u>b. remiss</u>   c. evasive   d. puzzling

4. in a very *demure* outfit

    a. flashy   b. odd   <u>c. staid</u>   d. elegant

5. *desultory* reading

    a. dull   b. careful   c. banal   <u>d fitful</u>

6. a truly *devout* follower of soap operas

    a. lukewarm   b. uninformed   <u>c. ardent</u>   d. sensitive

7. *deviate* from the straight and narrow

    <u>a. veer</u>   b. hale   c. infer   d. arise

Exercise III. Completing Sentences

Complete each of the following sentences or pairs of sentences by selecting the most appropriate word from the group of words given below. Make any adjustments that are necessary to fit the words into the sentences properly.

dapper	delete	delinquent
delude	denouement	devoid
defect	dexterous	delineate

1. Though the idea looked good at first glance, I soon came to the conclusion that it was __devoid__ of any real merit.

2. "The ending of this novel isn't very satisfactory," Paula observed. "The denouement just doesn't follow logically from the plot developments that lead up to it."

3. "How __dapper__ you look!" Mom exclaimed as I descended the stairs in my newly acquired finery. "You'll be the best-dressed young man at the dance!"

4. "Describing a character's outward appearance isn't enough to make the figure come alive," my creative-writing teacher told me. "You must also __delineate__ his or her inner thoughts, feelings, and motivations."

5. It takes fairly __dexterous__ manipulation of the control strings to make a marionette's movements look smooth and natural.

6. I shortened some of the overly long sentences in my essay by __deleting__ a few unnecessary words from each.

7. No one is perfect, but that doesn't mean we should completely ignore all of a person's __defects__.

8. "There is no point in __deluding__ myself that I am a great artist," Walt said. "I am only a competent copyist."

Exercise IV. Synonyms and Antonyms

A. In each of the following groups, select the **two** words that are most nearly **synonyms**.

1. a. accede b. retain c. allude d. acquiesce e. reject defer

2. a. shabby b. remiss c. respectful d. jubilant
   e. negligent delinquent

3. a. mediocre b. final c. natty d. spruce e. constant dapper

4. a. accelerate b. swerve c. elate d. infect e. veer deviate

5. a. leave b. concern c. depict d. injure e. portray delineate

Now, for each pair of synonyms that you have selected, supply a word from the Basic Word List for this lesson (Words 116–130) that means **the same** or **almost the same** thing.

B. In each of the following, select the item that is most nearly **opposite** in meaning to the numbered word at the left.

1. delete   a. cancel b. harm c. encourage
                   d. insert e. construe

2. dexterous   a. clever b. scholarly c. inept
                   d. accurate e. bold

3. devoid   a. replete b. arbitrary c. wanting
                   d. bleak e. destitute

178

4. defect   a. forsake   b. elude   c. complete
                         d. sketch   e. adhere

5. desultory   a. sober   b. concentrated   c. expensive
                         d. merry   e. awkward

Exercise V.   Word Roundup

1. What is an *optical illusion*? Give an example of the phenomenon.

2. What is the difference between *devoted* and *addicted*? Use each in a sentence that clearly shows the difference.

3. In your own words, describe the kind of person indicated by each of the following phrases.

   a devoted mother   a devout Buddhist   a devotee of the arts

4. Explain the difference between the words in each of the following pairs.

   a. defective—deficient   c. delusion—illusion
   b. deferment—deference   d. demur—demure

5. What is a *leftist*? a *right-winger*? Explain the story behind these expressions.

6. Give **three** examples of words that indicate the preference English seems to have for the right side.

7. Explain the meaning of each of the following phrases.

   a. down in the dumps   e. a con artist
   b. on top of the world   f. dereliction of duty
   c. a complete hoax   g. in arrears
   d. a sting operation   h. by fits and starts

Exercise VI.   Framing Sentences

A. Use each of the following words in an original sentence.

1. dapper   4. delineate   7. denouement
2. delete   5. delinquent   8. desultory
3. delude   6. demure   9. devoid

B. Give a **noun** form of each of these words, and use it in an illustrative sentence.

     dejection   dexterity   devotion
1. dejected   2. dexterous   3. devout

C. Give an **adjective** form of each of these words, and use it in an illustrative sentence.

1. defect   2. defer   3. deviate
   defective   deferent,   deviant
                   deferential

Completing Verbal Analogies

Analogy Question Type II This is probably the most common type of analogy question used on standardized vocabulary tests. It looks more or less like this:

Type II

A   B

maple : tree =
- a. acorn : oak
- b. hen : rooster
- c. iris : flower
- d. shrub : lilac
- e. tiger : ferocious

As you can see, in a Type-II analogy question, the student is given the two words in the key relationship (*A, B*). This pair of words is followed by five other pairs of words (*not* individual words!) labeled *a* through *e*. From this group, the student is to select the *pair of words* that will complete the analogy correctly.

Completing Type-II Analogies Correctly. There are two basic steps in the correct completion of Type-II analogy questions.

Step 1. Look at the two words in the key pair (*A, B*), and determine the relationship between them. This is the same procedure that was used to complete Type-I analogies (see page 70).

In the sample analogy question given above, the word *maple* denotes a particular kind of tree. In other words, a maple is an example of a tree. For convenience, this relationship can be expressed as "*A* is an example of *B*." This is the relationship that must appear on both sides of the equals sign if this particular analogy is to be correct.

A journalist at work on a story for a nightly news program. A job as a journalist of one type or another is an excellent career objective for someone who uses words well.

Step 2.   Inspect the five choices given, and determine which illustrates the same relationship as the key pair of words.

In the example given above, only choice *c, iris : flower*, does this. An iris is an example of a flower, just as a maple is an example of a tree.

All the other choices do not illustrate the required relationship. An acorn is not an example of an oak, nor is a hen an example of a rooster. Similarly, a shrub is not an example of a lilac, though a lilac is an example of a shrub. In other words, the two components of choice *d* are given in the wrong order. Finally, both of the words in the key relationship (*A, B*) are nouns. Thus, *tiger : ferocious* is wrong because *ferocious* is an adjective, not a noun. Always remember to observe the parts of speech involved in the key relationship and the order in which its component parts appear. Doing this will help you eliminate many wrong choices quickly and efficiently.

Two Colons.   On some standardized vocabulary tests (notably the Scholastic Assessment Test I), two colons (::) are used instead of the equals sign in the analogy questions. Thus, "maple : tree :: iris : flower" means exactly the same as "maple : tree = iris : flower." Both signs, of course, stand for the word *as*.

Exercise

The following items review what you have so far learned about analogy questions. Complete each.

Group A

1. **dexterous : clumsy** =
   a. copious : plentiful
   b. dapper : sloppy
   c. obese : cutpable
   d. devoid : lacking
   e. affluent : agile

2. **corpulence : portly** =
   a. corroboration : contradictory
   b. criterion : saturated
   c. denouement : virtuous
   d. consensus : unanimous
   e. desultoriness : methodical

3. **orange : sphere** =
   a. grapefruit : ellipse
   b. round : cylinder
   c. rug : area
   d. diameter : waist
   e. wheel : circle

4. **creditable : praiseworthy** =
   a. pivotal : crucial
   b. sanguine : cynical
   c. delinquent : consummate
   d. demure : forward
   e. sporadic : gaunt

5. **harmonious : discord** =
   a. skill : inept
   b. devout : sincerity
   c. cursory : thoroughness
   d. delusion : trickery
   e. deferential : respect

6. **deviate : stray ::**
   a. delete : include
   b. adhere : defect
   c. hasten : defer
   d. curtail : enlarge
   e. delineate : depict

7. **devotion : faithful ::**
   a. intoxication : sober
   b. warmth : bleak
   c. mistaken : illusion
   d. indigence : penniless
   e. complacence : quarrelsome

8. **covert : overt ::**
   a. verbose : laconic
   b. tactful : diplomatic
   c. stealthy : naive
   d. ephemeral : transitory
   e. frank : candid

9. **hammer : tool ::**
   a. singer : soprano
   b. horse : cow
   c. typewriter : machine
   d. continent : Asia
   e. trunk : branch

10. **ambivalent : certainty ::**
    a. plausible : reliability
    b. inane : substance
    c. pathos : feeling
    d. manifest : openness
    e. fretful : concern

Working with Context Clues

Handling Sentence-Completion Exercises Successfully. Study the following simple example of the kind of sentence-completion exercise that appears on standardized vocabulary tests:

When I told my landlord that I planned to _____ my apartment, he didn't seem too unhappy about my departure.

   a. clean   b. inspect   c. furnish   d. vacate   e. decorate

There are a number of simple steps involved in determining the answer to this or any other sentence-completion exercise you might encounter.

Step 1.   Read the sentence containing the blank carefully, and make sure you understand what it says.

In the example given above, the sentence says two things. First, it tells you that the speaker ("I") informed the landlord of something. Second, it indicates the landlord's reaction to this information.

Step 2.   Determine what you are to do, and where the clue to the correct answer is likely to be.

In the example given above, the part of the sentence indicating the landlord's reaction is complete. What you must do is finish the portion containing the speaker's initial statement.

This means that you must figure out what the speaker said *on the basis of* the landlord's reaction. Thus, the wording of this reaction is likely to contain the clue that you are looking for.

Step 3.   Isolate the clue.

In the example given above, look carefully at the landlord's reaction. It reads, "he didn't seem too unhappy about my departure."

Notice the words *about my departure*. These words don't tell you about the landlord's reaction; they tell you about what he was reacting to. In other words, they repeat or imply the gist of what the speaker ("I") said. This must have been something like "I'm moving out of the building" or "I'm giving up my apartment."

Now you know what the speaker initially said. You also know how to determine which word goes in the blank.

Step 4.   Look at the five items labeled *a* through *e*, and choose the correct answer.

In the example given above, only one of the five items has anything to do with the idea of leaving. It is choice *d*, *vacate*, which is, of course, the correct answer.

Step 5.   Insert your answer into the blank, and reread the completed sentence silently. Check carefully to see that the whole thing makes sense. If it doesn't, discard the answer you have chosen, and repeat steps 1–4.

Here is what the example given above looks like when the correct answer is in place:

> When I told the landlord that I planned to ____vacate____ my apartment, he didn't seem too unhappy about my departure.

Restatement Clues.   The example given above contains a clue that more or less *repeats* the meaning of the missing word. This type of clue is called a **restatement clue.** It is the simplest and most obvious kind of clue used in sentence-completion exercises. As the example also suggests, a restatement clue is often simply a *synonym* or *near-synonym* of the missing word. Sometimes, it may even give a short *definition* of it.

Exercise

Complete each of the following by selecting the word that makes the best sense in the sentence as a whole. Underline the clue or clues that led you to make this choice.

1.   If you will <u>agree</u> to my price, I will _____ to your schedule.

   a. defect   b. cohere   <u>c. accede</u>   d. array   e. atone

2.   A person with a(n) _____ attitude <u>doubts</u> that anyone is virtuous or honest.

   a. adverse   <u>b. cynical</u>   c. belligerent   d. bizarre
   e. complacent

3.   I would like to look like those _____ <u>male</u> models wearing <u>stylish</u> clothes in the fashion magazines.

   a. affluent   b. desultory   <u>c. dapper</u>   d. bombastic
   e. brash

4. Judges are often willing to _____ a first offense but will not <u>overlook</u> any further breaking of the law.

   a. <u>condone</u> **b.** abstain **c.** assimilate **d.** apprehend
   e. corroborate

5. The _____ of depressed people is so complete that they show <u>no interest in any of their daily activities</u>.

   a. attrition **b.** consensus **c.** credibility **d.** blight
   e. <u>apathy</u>

Enriching the Lesson

Exercise I. Borrowings from French

One of the words studied in this lesson is *denouement*, which English has borrowed more or less without change from French. A number of other French expressions that turn up in modern English are listed below. Define each. Then choose any **five**, and for each compose a short illustrative sentence.

1. ennui	11. macabre	21. sabotage
2. joie de vivre	12. nuance	22. de rigueur
3. mystique	13. tour de force	23. par excellence
4. fracas	14. nouveau riche	24. elite
5. éclat	15. charade	25. sortie
6. amour propre	16. repertoire	26. timbre
7. rapprochement	17. volte-face	27. mot juste
8. queue	18. suave	28. rapport
9. avant-garde	19. souvenir	29. sangfroid
10. pièce de résistance	20. verve	30. repartee

Exercise II. Anemic Expressions

A great many inexact or meaningless expressions turn up in the speech and writing of what might be called "lazy thinkers." Some of these items are descriptive adjectives such as *lousy, swell,* and *fabulous.* Others are empty phrases such as *or whatever, or something,* and *you know.*

What's wrong with these weak or "anemic" expressions should be obvious. They are too inexact, too nonspecific, too fuzzy, to convey more than a vague impression of what the person using them has in mind.

Here's an example of a sentence containing such anemic expressions. Study it carefully

   The special effects in that movie were *out of this world,* but the acting was *awful.*

This sentence doesn't say very much, does it? To be sure, it tells the reader how the person who wrote it felt about certain aspects of the movie. Still, it doesn't make the reasons for these feelings very clear. What, for example, do you suppose the writer means by "awful" acting? special effects that are "out of this world"?

The reader really can't tell because the wording of the sentence is too imprecise, too unfocused. Instead of using more specific words whose meanings are clear and unambiguous, the writer has chosen empty expressions that convey nothing more than generalized emotions. Thus, the reader is left to guess at what the writer really had in mind.

Now look at the same sentence when it has been reworded in a more precise and meaningful way.

> The special effects in that movie were *incredibly lifelike and convincing.* Unfortunately, the acting was *too wooden and stylized to make me believe that the characters were real human beings.*

Now the passage really tells the reader something not only about *how* the writer felt about the movie but also about *why.*

A number of sentences containing anemic expressions (printed in *italic* type) are given below. Substitute a more exact or meaningful expression for each italicized item. If you feel the sentence must be entirely rephrased in order to make it clearer, by all means rewrite it.

1. With a *terrific* quarterback, *dynamite* receivers, and a *super* defense, our team is sure to have a *fabulous* season.

2. Some of the paintings in the show were *gorgeous*; others were *blah*; still others were *just plain awful.*

3. Though I admit that his last novel was *pretty lousy,* I still think the man is a *fantastic* writer.

4. The food at the party was *heavenly: yummy* shrimp and lobster, a *lovely* salad, and a *swell* dessert.

5. Rose spent most of her vacation shopping, sightseeing, *etc.*

6. Even though the weather that day was *rotten,* we had a *great* time at the fair.

7. All their *neat* plans for improving the gym *or whatever* fell through at the last moment.

Exercise III.   Fused Phrases

The members of one group of English words were formed in a very curious way. Each is made up of a two- or three-word phrase that has been written as if it were one word. This phrase is usually of foreign origin, though in a number of cases it is just plain English. A good example of such "fused phrases" is the word *adroit,* which is simply a French phrase meaning "to the right" all run together.

Another is *alarm*, which comes from the Italian phrase *All'arme!*, meaning "To arms!"

Below are listed a number of other fused phrases used in present-day English. Define each. Then indicate the phrase from which the word comes, and translate it into English if it is of foreign origin.

1. debonair	7. nonplus	13. lagniappe
2. checkmate	8. metaphysics	14. puny
3. sinecure	9. akimbo	15. jeopardy
4. pedestal	10. apropos	16. orotund
5. legerdemain	11. pedigree	17. tantamount
6. namesake	12. vouchsafe	18. ado

Exercise IV. Expanding Your Word Power

The words listed below are not on the Basic Word List, but they were mentioned in passing in Lesson 12. All of them would make useful additions to your working vocabulary. Define each, give its etymology, list **two** synonyms and **two** antonyms (where possible), and use in a short illustrative sentence.

1. slovenly	6. hoodwink	11. intermittent
2. repudiate	7. jaunty	12. expunge
3. expedite	8. bumptious	13. digress
4. melancholy	9. systematic	14. tepid
5. scrupulous	10. dowdy	15. proficient

Related Forms in Context

Beneath each sentence below are four words introduced in Lesson 11 or 12. Review the related forms for these words, and choose the one that best completes the sentence. Write that related form in the space provided.

1. When the Wolf asked Red Riding Hood where she was going, she answered __demurely__, "I'm on my way to visit my sick grandmother."

    a. consummate   b. copious   c. demure   d. dapper

2. A pattern of __delinquency__ in paying your bills is likely to damage your credit rating.

    a. defect   b. credible   c. deviate   d. delinquent

3. The panel of judges penalized the ice dancers for major __deviations__ from the rules.

    a. delude   b. deviate   c. delineate   d. curtail

4. Was it a military tribunal, a judge, or a jury that determined Aaron Burr's _culpability_?

   a. culpable   b. cursory   c. dexterous   d. desultory

5. "Never look at a contract _cursorily_," the salesperson warned. "Be sure to read the fine print carefully."

   a. copious   b. consummate   c. dejected   d. cursory

6. As a _devotee_ of French Impressionism and Claude Monet in particular, Kathleen journeyed to Monet's home and gardens at Giverny, France.

   a. consummate   b. devout   c. dexterous   d. cynical

7. James Watson and Francis Crick's work with DNA and the double helix provides _credible_ evidence of how species replicate themselves.

   a. defect   b. counsel   c. credibility   d. delinquent

8. In Shakespeare's *Othello*, the villainous Iago plots to have Othello misconstrue the meaning of his wife's lost handkerchief.

   a. construe   b. credibility   c. consensus   d. deviate

9. We admired the pizza chef's _dexterity_ as he tossed the dough high in the air, stretching it thinner with each throw.

   a. demure   b. dejected   c. corpulent   d. dexterous

10. Doctors warn Americans that their increasing _corpulence_ is a serious health threat because it is directly associated with a high risk of heart disease and stroke.

   a. copious   b. corpulent   c. cynic   d. demure

11. Although I had six weeks to complete my research paper, for the first month I worked on it only _desultorily_.

   a. copious   b. dapper   c. demure   d. desultory

12. The Bill of Rights, the first ten amendments to the U.S. Constitution, is a _delineation_ of Americans' basic freedoms.

   a. delete   b. delude   c. delineate   d. deviate

13. From 1961 to 1989, _defectors_ from East Germany risked their lives to scale the Berlin Wall in order to seek freedom in the West.

   a. counsel   b. connoisseur   c. defect   d. credibility

14. For many Olympic athletes, winning a medal is the _____ of their hopes, dreams, and years of discipline and hard work.   consummation

   a. consummate   b. corroborate   c. defer   d. delude

15. Do you think the ending of George Orwell's *Animal Farm* is evidence of the author's ___cynicism___, or is he simply being realistic?

    a. copious **b.** culpable **c.** cursory **d. cynical**

16. Satellite photos provide definite ___corrobaration___ of environmentalists' predictions about the melting of polar ice caps.

    a. construe **b.** delude **c. corroborate** **d.** defer

17. Because of the budget constraints, the mayor had no choice but to announce the ___curtailment___ of some city services deemed nonessential.

    a. corroborate **b.** consummate **c.** delineate **d. curtail**

18. Germaine, who has volunteered to become a peer ___counselor___, is attending the first of six training sessions.

    a. consensus **b.** credibility **c. counsel** **d.** delinquent

19. In China and Japan, the elderly are treated with great ___deference___.

    a. delineate **b. defer** **c.** delude **d.** defect

20. The exhausted tennis player shook her opponent's hand but could not conceal her ___dejection___ at having failed to win the long, hard match.

    a. demure **b.** desultory **c.** devote **d. dejected**

Lesson 13

131. dilapidated — 145. duplicity

---

131. di-lap-i-dat-ed   *adjective*   dĭ-lăp′-ə-dā-tĭd
[*dilapidare, dilapidatus* (Latin), "pull apart the stones; destroy"; from *dis* (Latin), "apart" + *lapis, lapidis* (Latin), "stone"]

Definition: Fallen into disrepair or partial ruin, usually through neglect.

"That part of the city has truly become a ghost town," Mark observed. "Only the rats now seem to inhabit what few **dilapidated** or burnt-out buildings still remain."

Related Forms: (*verb*) dilapidate; (*noun*) dilapidation

Synonyms: (*adjectives*) deteriorated, run-down, decaying, decrepit, rickety, ramshackle; dingy, seedy, sleazy

Antonyms: (*adjectives*) shipshape, unspoiled, undamaged

Related Phrases: in disrepair, go to seed, go to wrack and ruin, run into the ground, go to pot; well kept up, well maintained

132. dil-a-tor-y   *adjective*   dĭl′-ə-tôr-ē
[*dilatorius* (Latin), "causing delay"; from *differre, dilatus* (Latin), "delay"; from *dis* (Latin), "apart" + *ferre, latus* (Latin), "carry"]

Definition: Inclined to put things off; intended to postpone something.

Some people always pay their bills on time; others are as **dilatory** as snails.

Uncertain whether the Spanish were gods or not, the Aztec emperor Montezuma adopted a wait-and-see attitude toward them. In the end, this **dilatory** policy actually helped Cortés conquer Mexico.

Related Forms: (*noun*) dilatoriness, (*adverb*) dilatorily

Usage Note:
Do not confuse *dilatory* with the adjective *dilated*, which means "spread out" or "widened."

Synonyms: (*adjectives*) late, tardy, slow, behindhand, laggard, dawdling, procrastinating, sluggish, lackadaisical, lethargic, dillydallying, shilly-shallying, temporizing

Antonyms: (*adjectives*) prompt, punctual; speedy, swift, quick, fast, expeditious

Related Phrases: play a waiting game, drag one's heels, as slow as molasses in winter, play for time; with alacrity, strike while the iron is hot

133. dil-i-gent   *adjective*   dĭl′-ĭ-jĕnt
[*diligens, diligentis* (Latin), "loving; attentive"; from *dis* (Latin), "apart" + *legere* (Latin), "choose"]

Definition: Hardworking; thorough and persistent.

A **diligent** student will devote a lot of time and effort to his or her studies.

They claim to have made a **diligent** search of the area, but I suspect their efforts were no more than perfunctory.

Related Forms: (*noun*) diligence; (*adverb*) diligently

Synonyms: (*adjectives*) assiduous, sedulous, indefatigable

Antonyms: (*adjectives*) lazy, slothful, indolent; perfunctory, cursory

Related Phrases: take pains with, work like a beaver

134. dire   *adjective*   dīr
[*dirus* (Latin), "horrible, frightful"]

Definition:
   a.   Dreadful or disastrous; bleak or cheerless.

     The introduction of the common European rabbit had a **dire** effect on the native plant and animal life of Australia.

     No one in Troy paid the slightest attention to Cassandra's **dire** predictions concerning the future of the city.

   b.   Urgent.

     As we use up the earth's fossil-fuel supplies, we are faced with an increasingly **dire** need to develop new energy resources.

Phrases: a dire fate, dire news, dire financial straits, a dire emergency

Related Forms: (*adjective*) direful; (*nouns*) direness, direfulness; (*adverbs*) direly, direfully

Synonyms: (*adjectives*) calamitous, fatal, woeful, grievous, horrendous; dismal, somber, gloomy; pressing, desperate, extreme

Antonyms: (*adjectives*) salutary, beneficial, salubrious; mild, gentle; inconsequential, insignificant

135. dis-com-fit   *verb*   dĭs-cŭm′-fĭt
[*desconfire, desconfit* (Old French), "rout"; from *dis* (Latin), "un-" + *com* (Latin), "together" + *facere, factus* (Latin), "do, make"]

Definition:
   a.   To defeat or frustrate completely.

     In the battle of Philippi, Mark Antony **discomfited** the republican forces under Brutus and Cassius.

The would-be burglars were thoroughly **discomfited** by the store's elaborate security system.

b. To perplex, confuse, or embarrass completely.

The sternness of his expression so **discomfited** me that I had difficulty replying to his question.

Related Form: (*noun*) discomfiture

Usage Note:
Do not confuse *discomfit* with *discomfort*. As a noun, *discomfort* indicates a feeling of uneasiness, uncomfortableness, or annoyance that is less severe and more generalized than pain. As a verb, it means "make mildly uneasy, uncomfortable, or annoyed."

Synonyms: (*verbs*) rout, trounce, drub; thwart, foil; baffle; nonplus, abash, disconcert, fluster

Antonyms: (*verbs*) lose to; reassure

---

136. **dis-course**   *noun:* dĭs'-côrs   *verb:* dĭs-côrs'

[*discursus* (Latin), "a running about; a conversation"; from *dis* (Latin), "in different directions" + *currere, cursus* (Latin), "run"]

Definition:
a. (*noun*) An oral exchange of ideas or conversation; a lengthy discussion, either written or spoken.

"Let your **discourse** with men of business be short and to the point," George Washington once advised.

My sister's last letter from abroad contained an amusing **discourse** on the problems of living in a foreign country.

In Puritan New England, a preacher would sometimes interrupt his Sunday **discourse** to chastise an inattentive member of the congregation.

b. (*verb*) To talk about or discuss at length.

She and I spent the afternoon casually **discoursing** on the state of the world and our ideas for improving it.

In a recent article in a national magazine, a noted sociologist **discoursed** ably and perceptively on the connection between drug abuse and crime.

Related Form: (*adjective*) discursive

Usage Note:
The adjective *discursive* means "rambling" or "digressive." Thus, a discursive style of writing is one that rambles aimlessly from one subject to another.

Synonyms: (*nouns*) treatise, dissertation; sermon, lecture, talk; colloquy; (*verbs*) enlarge (on), expand (on), expatiate (upon), descant (on)

Antonyms (all indicating brevity and conciseness of treatment): (*nouns*) summary, abstract, précis, synopsis; (*verbs*) summarize, synopsize, outline, sketch

137. dis·crim·i·nate   *verb*   dĭs-krĭm′-ə-nāt

[*discriminare, discriminatus* (Latin), "divide; distinguish," from *discrimen* (Latin), "distinction"]

Definition:

a. To distinguish between two or more things, often by perceiving minute differences.

Fine differences in markings or coloring often permit an expert birdwatcher to **discriminate** between two very similar species of birds.

"In some cases," the psychiatrist observed, "the human mind may become so warped that it cannot **discriminate** between fact and fancy."

b. To behave unfairly toward a person or group because of prejudice.

Laws now forbid employers to **discriminate** against anyone on the basis of race, creed, color, or sex.

Related Forms: (*noun*) discrimination; (*adjectives*) discriminating, discriminatory, indiscriminate

Usage Note:

Discrimination may properly be used in both a favorable and an unfavorable sense. In its favorable sense, the word means "the ability to make fine or acute distinctions" or "the act of making such distinctions." This meaning occurs in such phrases as "showed little *discrimination* in their use of words." The adjective corresponding to this meaning is *discriminating,* as in "*discriminating* tastes."

In its unfavorable sense, *discrimination* means "the practice of differentiating unfairly between individuals or groups because of prejudice." This meaning occurs in such phrases as "racial *discrimination.*" The adjective corresponding to this meaning is *discriminatory,* as in "*discriminatory* practices."

Synonyms: (*verbs*) differentiate, discern; (*nouns*) perspicacity, acumen, perceptiveness, discernment; favoritism, bias, prejudice, bigotry

138. dis·par·age   *verb*   dĭs-păr′-ĭj

[*desparag(i)er* (Old French), "deprive a person of his or her rank; marry a person of inferior rank"; from *dis* (Latin) "not" + *par* (Latin), "equal"]

Definition: To speak slightingly of or undervalue.

"I think your article on the basketball squad is eminently fair," I told Sandy. "It doesn't exaggerate the team's abilities, but it doesn't **disparage** them either."

Related Forms: (*noun*) disparagement; (*adjective*) disparaging; (*adverb*) disparagingly

Synonyms: (*verbs*) belittle, depreciate, derogate, decry, underrate, run down, minimize

Antonyms: exaggerate, magnify, increase, enhance; extol, laud, eulogize

139. dis-par-i-ty   *noun*   dĭs-păr'-ə-tē
[*disparitas* (Latin), "unlikeness"; from *dis* (Latin), "not" + *par* (Latin), "equal"]

Definition: Difference or inequality, as of age, character, or quality.

There may be a profound **disparity** between the abilities and talents of any two people.

The **disparity** between a country's needs and its financial resources may prove a stumbling block to effective social betterment.

The **disparity** between the amount of money one earns and its real value may increase or decrease over the years.

Related Forms: (*adjective*) disparate; (*adverb*) disparately

Synonyms: (*nouns*) disproportion, dissimilarity, inconsistency

Antonyms: (*nouns*) parity, likeness, similarity, equality

Related Phrases: the gender gap, a communications gap

140. dis-traught   *adjective*   dĭs-trôt'
[variant form of *distract* (Middle English), "distracted"; from *distrahere, distractus,* (Latin), "perplex"]

Definition: Deeply distressed or agitated.

The **distraught** parents of the missing child desperately appealed to the local population for help.

The whole town became **distraught** with grief at the news of the tragic accident.

Synonyms: (*adjectives*) frantic, anguished, overwrought, hysterical, distracted, perturbed, upset

Antonyms: (*adjectives*) calm, collected, composed, impassive

141. di-vulge   *verb*   dĭ-vŭlj'
[*divulgare* (Latin), "spread among the people"; from *dis* (Latin), "abroad" + *vulgus* (Latin), "common people"]

Definition: To make known; to make public.

More than one reporter has gone to jail for refusing to **divulge** the names of his or her informants.

I couldn't prove my suspicions, so I didn't **divulge** them to anyone.

Related Form: (*noun*) divulgence

Synonyms: (*verbs*) reveal, disclose, impart

Antonyms: (*verbs*) conceal, hide

Related Phrases: go public with, betray a confidence, leak information to the press, plug security leaks, a shocking exposé

142. **doc·ile**   *adjective*   dŏs'-əl

[*docilis* (Latin), "teachable"; from *docere* (Latin), "teach"]

Definition: Easy to manage, teach, train, or discipline.

"Some of my students are as **docile** as newborn lambs," the teacher remarked. "Others are as stubborn and headstrong as mules."

Related Forms: (*noun*) docility; (*adverb*) docilely

Synonyms: (*adjectives*) submissive, tractable, obedient, amenable, compliant

Antonyms: (*adjectives*) headstrong, willful, perverse, intractable, unmanageable, obdurate

143. **dor·mant**   *adjective*   dôr'-mənt

[*dormant* (French), "sleeping"; from *dormire* (Latin), "to be asleep, inactive, or unconcerned"]

Definition: Inactive, as if in sleep; suspended in use, growth, or development

The fact that the volcano is **dormant** does not mean that it is no longer capable of erupting.

After his talents had lain **dormant** for many years, he suddenly began to produce the great novels on which his reputation is based.

Related Form: (*noun*) dormancy

Synonyms: (*adjectives*) latent, passive, inert, quiescent, torpid

Antonyms: (*adjectives*) active, vigorous, vibrant; volatile, explosive; thriving, flourishing

Related Phrases: a latent talent, in a state of suspended animation

144. **dras·tic**   *adjective*   drăs'-tĭk

[*drastikos* (Greek), "active; efficient"; from *dran* (Greek), "do"]

Definition: Violently forceful and swift; extreme.

The problems of air and water pollution have become so severe and so pressing that they may require **drastic** measures to correct.

Defeat in the Civil War brought about **drastic** changes in the social structure of the South.

Phrases: a drastic remedy, drastic reforms

Related Form: (*adverb*) drastically

Synonyms: (*adjectives*) powerful, strong, rigorous, potent, thoroughgoing; severe, stern, draconian

Antonyms: (*adjectives*) weak, feeble, ineffectual, halfhearted; mild, gentle, restrained

145. du-plic-i-ty   *noun*   do͞o-plĭs′-ĭ-tē *or* dyo͞o-plĭs′-ĭ-tē

[*duplicitas* (Latin), "deceit"; from *duo* (Latin), "two" + *plicare* (Latin), "fold"]

Definition: Deliberate deception in speech or conduct.

"Sandy tries to be honest and upright in all her dealings with other people," I remarked. "**Duplicity** simply has no place in her character."

Related Form: (*adjective*) duplicitous

Synonyms: (*nouns*) guile, deceit, trickery, feint, dissimulation, chicanery, imposture, sharp practice, double-dealing

Antonyms: (*nouns*) honesty, integrity, uprightness, probity, plain dealing

Related Phrases: an artful dodge, a Judas kiss, under false colors, two-faced

A Judas Kiss

English has many colorful expressions that are concerned with duplicity or treachery. One of the most interesting of these is *a Judas kiss.*

As you may already know from reading the Bible, Judas Iscariot was the disciple who betrayed Jesus Christ to his enemies. The betrayal took place in the garden of Gesthsemane outside Jerusalem the day before Christ was crucified. Jesus and some of his most trusted friends had gone there to meditate. Suddenly, Judas and a band of soldiers and ruffians appeared. As arranged in advance, Judas showed the soldiers which of the people in the garden was Jesus by kissing him lightly on the cheek. This was a customary greeting in those times. On the surface, Judas's kiss appeared to be a harmless act of friendship and affection. In reality, however, it was a signal telling the soldiers whom to seize and lead off to eventual death.

The details of Judas's treachery were recorded by several of the writers of the New Testament (for example, Matt. 26:29, Mark 14:45, Luke 22:47). It is from these Biblical sources that the phrase *a Judas kiss* has come into present-day English to indicate any act that on the surface looks kindly, affectionate, or courteous but in reality is quite the opposite.

Using the Words

Exercise I
1. di-lap'-i-dat-ed
2. dil'-a-tor-y
3. dil'-i-gent
4. dis'-course, dis-course'
5. dis-par'-age,
6. dis-traught'
7. di-vulge'
8. dor'-mant
9. du-plic'-i-ty

Exercise I.   Syllabication and Pronunciation

Syllabicate the following words correctly, and place the major stress mark (') after the syllable that is accented when the word is pronounced. Two answers are correct in one instance.

1. dilapidated
2. dilatory
3. diligent

4. discourse
5. disparage
6. distraught

7. divulge
8. dormant
9. duplicity

Exercise II.   Words Out of Context

In each of the following, select the item that best expresses the meaning of the numbered word at the left.

1. discomfit
   a. minimize   b. soothe   c. rout
   d. uncover

2. duplicity
   a. deceit   b. promptness   c. disrepair
   d. composure

3. dilapidated
   a. punctual   b. run-down   c. frantic
   d. obedient

4. dormant
   a. inactive   b. cursory   c. honest
   d. agitated

5. distraught
   a. amusingly clever   b. extremely urgent
   c. deeply distressed   d. surprisingly slow

6. drastic
   a. gentle   b. willful   c. severe   d. lazy

7. divulge
   a. lessen   b. absolve   c. reveal
   d. blame

Exercise III.   Completing Sentences

Complete each of the following sentences or pairs of sentences by selecting the most appropriate word from the group of words given below. Make any adjustments that are necessary to fit the words into the sentences properly. Use each word only once.

discriminate   docile   disparage

diligent   disparity   divulge

discourse   dilatory   dire

1. "You're only supposed to present a brief, informal report at the meeting," my boss exclaimed, "not a learned scientific discourse !"

196

2. "Don't expect them to do anything but __disparage__ your abilities," my best friend warned me before my piano recital. "They never have a good word to say about anyone!"

3. "In 1900, there was a glaring __disparity__ between the lifestyles of the haves and the have-nots of this country," the speaker said. "Fortunately, since then we have done much to close that appalling gap."

4. "I have some advice for our __dilatory__ coworkers in the shipping department," my supervisor said at the meeting. "Don't put off until tomorrow what you can do today!"

5. "At the end of the month, I found myself in ___dire___ financial straits," Ed recalled bleakly. "Never before had I been in such an awful fix as far as money was concerned."

6. She is a __diligent__ student whose hard work and dedication have been richly rewarded over the years.

7. "I believe it is wrong to _____ against people who are not exactly like ourselves," Sheila declared. "None of us should allow prejudice or bigotry to creep into our attitudes toward other human beings." discriminate

8. "Charlie Tompkins is much too __docile__ and easygoing to make an effective scoutmaster," Mr. Briggs remarked. "What we need is an energetic leader, not someone who can be led around by the nose with no trouble at all."

Exercise IV. Synonyms and Antonyms

Classify each of the following pairs of words as **S** for **synonyms** and **A** for **antonyms**.

S 1. discourse—lecture
A 2. diligent—lazy
A 3. praise—disparage
S 4. discrimination—prejudice
S 5. discomfit—fluster
A 6. conceal—divulge
A 7. headstrong—docile

S 8. calamitous—dire
A 9. disparity—similarity
S 10. deception—duplicity
A 11. dilatory—prompt
A 12. mild—drastic
S 13. dormant—latent
A 14. distraught—composed

Exercise V. Word Roundup

1. Explain what is meant by "a *discursive* writing style."

2. Explain the difference in meaning between the words in each of the following pairs.

    a. discomfit—discomfort   b. discriminating—discriminatory

3. Define the word *draconian*. What famous Greek lawgiver's name is embodied in this word? Why?

197

4. Explain the meaning of each of the following phrases.

  a. go to seed
  b. play a waiting game
  c. work like a beaver
  d. go public with
  e. drag one's heels
  f. run into the ground
  g. plug security leaks
  h. suspended animation

5. Explain what is meant by *a Judas kiss.*

6. In what famous 19th-century novel does the character called *the Artful Dodger* appear? Who is the author of this novel? What do you think the author was trying to suggest about the character by using this distinctive name?

Exercise VI.   Framing Sentences

A. Use each of the following words in an original illustrative sentence.

1. dilatory
2. dire
3. dormant
4. distraught
5. divulge
6. duplicity

B. Give a **noun** form of each of these words, and use it in an illustrative sentence.   dilapidation   discomfiture   disparagement

1. dilapidated
2. discomfit
3. disparage

C. Give an **adjective** form of each of these words, and use it in an illustrative sentence.   discursive   discriminating

1. discourse
2. discriminate
3. disparity disparate

D. Give an **adverb** form of each of these words, and use it in an illustrative sentence.

1. diligent diligently
2. docile docilely
3. drastic drastically

Peter Mark Roget

Peter Mark Roget (1779–1869), an English physician with an "insatiable thirst for knowledge and an appetite for work," was the father of a new kind of word book called a *thesaurus.* Unlike a dictionary, the words in a thesaurus are neither defined nor alphabetically arranged. Instead, they are presented in groups according to related ideas. Roget also devised a slide rule, attempted to perfect a calculating machine, invented and solved difficult chess problems, and founded a society for the diffusion of knowledge.

Dissecting the Words

1. The Latin prefix **de** is found at the beginning of a good many common English words. Among them are *defer, defect,* and most of the other basic words studied in Lesson 12. **De** has two primary meanings:

a. It may mean "away," "off," or "down," as in these words:

depart (literally, "go away") — to leave or deviate from

decapitate (literally, "take the head off") — to cut off the head

devolve (literally, "roll down") — to pass or transfer from one person to another

depress (literally, "press down") — to lower physically; to cause a lowering of mood or spirit

despoil (literally, "carry away or plunder") — to plunder or rob of by force

deter (literally, "frighten away") — to prevent or discourage

b. It may have a negative force roughly like "not" or "un-," as in these words:

dethrone (literally, "unthrone") — to remove from the throne

debunk (literally, "take the bunk out of") — to expose the falseness of unsound or exaggerated claims

demerit (literally, "not a merit; an unmerit") — a black mark usually involving the loss of some privilege or right

destabilize (literally, "unstabilize") — to upset the stability of

2. The Latin prefix **dis** is related to **de**. It occurs at the beginning of a number of words studied in Lesson 13, including *disparity* and *discriminate*. As with **de**, the prefix **dis** has two basic meanings:

a. It may mean "away from" or "apart," as in these words:

dispel (*dis*, "away" + *pel*, "drive") — to scatter or dissipate

dislodge (*dis*, "apart" + *lodge*, "place") — to remove from a place that has been occupied up until then

b. It may have a negative force meaning roughly "not" or "lack of," as in these words:

dissimilar (*dis*, "not" + *similar*) — not similar or alike

disinclined (*dis*, "not" + *inclined*) — not inclined

disintegrate (literally, "make not whole") — to deteriorate or rot away

disfranchise (*dis*, "not" + *franchise*) — to take the right to vote away from

disorder (*dis*, "lack of" + *order*) — confusion; lack of order

Note that **dis** becomes **di** before the letters *f, g, l, m,* and *v,* and sometimes these letters double. For example:

$$dis + fer = \textbf{differ}$$

Root

The Latin root **cur** or **curs,** meaning "run," appears in one form or another in numerous English words. One of them is *discourse,* studied in this lesson. Here are a few other useful examples:

concur (literally, "run together") — to coincide; to agree

cursory — running over something hurriedly and superficially

curriculum — a course of study

precursor — a forerunner

discursive — passing from one subject to another in a rambling fashion

recur — to occur again

recourse — a turning to someone or something for help or protection

recurrent — happening again and again

concourse (literally, "a running together") — an assemblage; a place of meeting; an open space where several roads come together

courier (literally, "runner") — a messenger

Other words in which **cur(s)** appears include *excursion, occur, incur, current, currency,* and *course.*

Exercise

A. Complete the following activities relating to the prefixes *de* and *dis.*

1. Give the meaning of the following words containing the prefix *de.* Then choose any **five,** and for each compose a short illustrative sentence.

   a. debar
   b. demote
   c. dejection
   d. delete

   e. denounce
   f. defer
   g. depreciate
   h. delinquent

   i. deplete
   j. depose
   k. decamp
   l. decapitate

2. Define each of the following words, and show how its meaning is affected by the prefix *dis.*

   a. disorganized
   b. disparity
   c. dispraise
   d. disproportionate

   e. disqualify
   f. discord
   g. disenchant
   h. disfigure

   i. disfranchise
   j. disinherit
   k. disbar
   l. dismember

B. Now complete the following activities relating to the root *cur* or *curs.*

1. Give a synonym for each of the following words.

   a. precursor   b. courier   c. discursive

2. With or without the aid of a dictionary, define the following words. Then use each in a short illustrative sentence.

   a. recur
   b. excursion

   c. incur
   d. recurrent

   e. recourse
   f. currency

Working with Context Clues

Review the "Working with Context Clues" section in Lesson 12 (pages 182–183) before you begin this section.

Guideposts to Restatement Clues. Sometimes the linking expressions present in a sentence-completion exercise can act as guideposts to the context clues you are looking for. In other words, these linking expressions can tip you off to the nature and location of the clue.

Let's look at the linking expressions that can do this for restatement clues. They include certain types of conjunctions (e.g., *and, or, both . . . and, not only . . . but also*), adverbs (e.g., *moreover, besides*), prepositional phrases (e.g., *in addition*), and related expressions (e.g., *that is*). Each in some way binds together two parallel or similar sentences or parts of a sentence. Usually, the clue is contained in one of these tied-together elements, and the blank appears in the other. The linking expression points to the clue by drawing your eye from the element containing the blank to the element to which it is tied. And as you already know, this is the element that probably contains the clue.

Study the following simple example of a sentence-completion exercise. It contains both a restatement clue and a linking expression that points to this clue.

> As both a hardworking businessman and an _____ community leader, Joseph X. Laurelli has done much to promote the well-being of those who live in this town.
>
> **a.** ignorant   **b.** ominous   **c.** energetic   **d.** ugly   **e.** apathetic

Notice that this sentence contains the phrase *both . . . and*. This is the type of conjunction that binds together parallel or similar parts of a sentence. In this case, it connects two parallel phrases, one of which contains the blank for the missing word.

A magazine editor prepares copy for a forthcoming issue. Working for a magazine or book publisher is an excellent career objective for someone who uses words well.

The presence of *both . . . and* in this situation tips you off to the type of clue you will find and its general location in the sentence. Since *both . . . and* connects parallel or similar sentence elements, you are probably going to find a restatement clue. Since, in this instance, it connects two parallel phrases, one of which contains the blank, you are probably going to find the clue in the other phrase, which is complete.

Look at the two phrases in question. They are "a hardworking businessman" and "an _____ community leader." Notice that each contains the indefinite article (*a, an*) and a noun (*businessman*) or noun phrase (*community leader*). Notice too that one of them contains an adjective (*hardworking*), but that the blank takes the place of a corresponding adjective in the other. This tells you that an adjective meaning something like *hardworking* is what goes in the blank.

Now look at the five words from which you are to choose the word that goes in the blank. Only one of them means anything even remotely like *hardworking*. It Is choice *c, energetic.* Clearly, this is the word that goes in the blank.

As you can see from this simple example, linking expressions can be very useful in dealing successfully with sentence-completion exercises.

Exercise

Complete each of the following by selecting the word that makes the best sense in the sentence (or group of sentences) as a whole. Underline the clue or clues that led you to make your choice.

1. A really good friend would never _____ information that was given in confidence. In addition, a good friend would never reveal anything that could hurt or embarrass someone he or she cared about.

   a. articulate   b. condone   c. divulge   d. corroborate
   e. delineate

2. Most of the new television programs that appear each fall are just like many others we've seen before, with _____ plots and boring characters.

   a. banal   b. original   c. blithe   d. avid   e. bleak

3. Parents should not permit children to _____ them into buying something they do not believe the children need, no matter how much the children coax and plead.

   a. augur   b. absolve   c. delude   d. cajole   e. coerce

4. Half-hour news programs give _____ accounts of the major stories but are too short to provide much depth.

   a. broad   b. copious   c. astute   d. agile   e. concise

5. Depriving Native Americans of their ancestral hunting grounds was a(n) _____, since this cruel policy destroyed their entire way of life.

   a. consensus   b. atrocity   c. anachronism   d. calumny
   e. affectation

6. A grandparent can be a(n) _____ figure who shows <u>kindness and understanding</u> to a lonely child.

   <u>a. benign</u>   b. demure   c. cranky   d. cynical   e. agile

7. I certainly <u>looked a mess</u> after romping with my five-year-old nephew. My shirttails were tangled, my hair was <u>going in all directions,</u> and my tie was _____.

   a. bizarre   <u>b. askew</u>   c. boisterous   d. dilapidated
   e. array

8. It is sometimes difficult for immigrants to <u>adjust</u> to the customs of their adopted country, but with time and patience they will _____ themselves to their new environment.

   a. construe   <u>b. acclimate</u>   c. apprehend   d. divulge
   e. endear

9. I know that she wanted me to give her an <u>honest</u> opinion about her performance. Still, I found it difficult to be _____ about her shortcomings.

   <u>a. candid</u>   b. benign   c. demure   d. brash   e. cogent

10. Although the <u>gap</u> between men's and women's pay has narrowed, a(n) _____ in the treatment of the sexes still exists.

    a. agenda   b. array   c. asylum   <u>d. disparity</u>   e. blight

Enriching the Lesson

Exercise I.   More Look-Alikes

As you know, English has a great many duos and even trios of words that look alike but mean quite different things. Some of these look-alikes were presented in Lesson 10 (page 143). Others are paired off below. With or without the aid of a dictionary, explain the difference in meaning between the members of each pair.

1. emulate—simulate	11. delegate—relegate
2. faint—feint	12. deprecate—depreciate
3. resemble—dissemble	13. allude—elude
4. discrete—discreet	14. envious—enviable
5. boor—bore	15. complaisant—complacent
6. manners—mannerisms	16. honorable—honorary
7. capital—capitol	17. authoritative—authoritarian
8. aesthetic—ascetic	18. imperial—imperious
9. amend—emend	19. allay—ally
10. solid—stolid	20. venal—venial

Now, choose any **five** of the pairs of words listed above. For each compose a set of **two** sentences, each of which illustrates the meaning of **one** of the words in the pair.

Exercise II. Biblical Expressions

One of the phrases mentioned in connection with *duplicity* (Word 145) in this lesson is *a Judas kiss*. As you know, this phrase derives from an incident related in the New Testament of the Bible. The Bible has given English many other words and phrases. Some of these expressions are listed below. With or without the aid of a dictionary or other reference book, define or explain each. Then choose any **five**, and for each compose a short illustrative sentence.

1. see the handwriting on the wall
2. a shibboleth
3. apocryphal
4. a doubting Thomas
5. separate the sheep from the goats (*or* the wheat from the chaff)
6. a jeremiad
7. hide one's light under a bushel
8. a Good Samaritan
9. the salt of the earth
10. a Jonah
11. serve two masters
12. reap the whirlwind
13. a behemoth
14. turn the other cheek
15. apocalyptic
16. cast one's bread upon the waters
17. antediluvian
18. the promised land
19. manna from heaven
20. cast pearls before swine

Exercise III. A Verbal Diversion

A good many expressions that occur in present-day English utilize the names of foreign peoples with whom Americans may or may not have come into contact. Most of these expressions employ the foreign name quite literally. For example, the *French* in *French fried potatoes* simply indicates that the potatoes have been fried in a manner that is (or at some point was considered to be) typical of French cooking.

A few of these expressions, however, have an extended or figurative meaning that is not immediately revealed by the name of the foreign people employed. Some examples are listed below. With or without the aid of a dictionary or other reference book, define or explain each. Then choose any **five**, and for each compose a short illustrative sentence.

1. a Dutch uncle
2. Indian summer
3. a bohemian
4. a Dutch treat *or* go Dutch
5. get your Irish up
6. vandalism
7. put a little English on the ball
8. a Scotch verdict
9. a Mexican standoff
10. French leave
11. get in Dutch with
12. Siamese twins
13. an Indian giver

Notice that some of the expressions listed above are not at all complimentary to the foreign peoples whose names appear in them. What do you think this says about the ways in which our language sometimes views foreigners?

Exercise IV.   Ricochet Words

A **ricochet word** (sometimes called a **reduplicate word**) is a word consisting of two elements that are almost identical in form—for example, *dillydally* or *hurdy-gurdy*. The two elements in a ricochet word usually differ from one another only in a single vowel (e.g., *chitchat)* or consonant (e.g., *namby-pamby*). Sometimes they are separated from each other by a hyphen (e.g., *hocus-pocus*); sometimes they are not (e.g., *hubbub*).

There are several hundred ricochet words in use in present-day English. Some of them are listed below. With or without the aid of a dictionary define each.

1. shilly-shally
2. willy-nilly
3. dillydally
4. wishy-washy
5. hoity-toity
6. harum-scarum
7. hanky-panky
8. mishmash
9. voodoo
10. hobnob
11. hocus-pocus
12. razzle-dazzle
13. flimflam
14. riffraff
15. claptrap
16. folderol
17. tittle-tattle
18. hubbub
19. hurdy-gurdy
20. hugger-mugger
21. hodgepodge
22. helter-skelter

Choose any **five** of the items given above, and for each compose a short illustrative sentence.

Exercise V.   Expanding Your Word Power

The words listed below are not on the Basic Word List, but they were mentioned in passing in Lesson 13. All of them would make useful additions to your working vocabulary. Define each, give its etymology, list **two** synonyms and **two** antonyms (where possible), and use in a short illustrative sentence.

1. decrepit
2. indefatigable
3. perfunctory
4. indolent
5. disconcert
6. treatise
7. perspicacity
8. bigotry
9. depreciate
10. parity
11. impassive
12. impart
13. tractable
14. feeble
15. chicanery

Lesson 14

146. **eclectic** — 160. **enigma**

---

146. **ec·lec·tic**   *adjective and noun*   ĕ-klĕk'-tĭk

[*eklektikos* (Greek), "picked out"; from *ek* (Greek), "out of" + *legein* (Greek), "choose"]

Definition:
  a. (*adjective*) Choosing what seems best from various sources.

  Because of her **eclectic** teaching methods and "pick-and-choose" testing techniques, students enjoy Miss Curry's classes.

  b. (*noun*) One whose opinions and beliefs are drawn from various sources.

  In a sense, St. Thomas Aquinas was an **eclectic** because he attempted to reconcile ancient Greek philosophy with Christian theology.

Phrases: an eclectic philosopher, an eclectic style of architecture

Related Form: (*noun*) eclecticism

Synonyms: (*adjectives*) selective, synthesized

Antonyms: (*adjectives*) uniform, monolithic

Related Phrase: all of a piece

---

147. **ef-fete**   *adjective*   ĕ-fēt' *or* ĭ-fēt'

[*effetus* (Latin), "worn out by childbearing"; from *ex* (Latin), "out" + *fetus* (Latin), "offspring"]

Definition: Worn out or exhausted; marked by weakness, self-indulgence or decadence.

  By late imperial times, centuries of soft living had turned the once hardy Roman people into an **effete** and indolent race.

Phrases: an effete snob, an effete aristocrat, an effete society

Related Form: (*noun*) effeteness

Usage Note:
When used of males, the word *effete* often carries with it a sense of effeminacy or unmanliness.

Synonyms: (*adjectives*) spent, burned-out; decadent; barren, sterile

Antonyms: (*adjectives*) vigorous, energetic, dynamic; productive, fertile, flourishing, prolific

Edward Gibbon

The English historian Edward Gibbon (1737–1794) was the author of the multivolume *Decline and Fall of the Roman Empire*, a monumental study of the material decay and moral decline that brought about the collapse of a great civilization and turned a vigorous people into an effete and indolent race. The work, which begins with events in the second century A.D., covers almost 1300 years of history. Despite harsh criticism from some quarters, the book won Gibbon immediate acclaim as a historian and is still one of the most widely read historical studies.

148. ef-fi-ca-cious   *adjective*   ĕf-ə-kā′-shəs
[*efficax, efficacis* (Latin), "effective"; from *ex* (Latin), "out" + *facere, factus* (Latin), "do"]

Definition: Capable of producing the desired effect.

   After-school detention seems to be an **efficacious** solution to the problem of student lateness.

Related Forms: (*nouns*) efficacy, efficaciousness; (*adverb*) efficaciously

Synonyms: (*adjectives*) effective, effectual, efficient, powerful, potent

Antonyms: (*adjectives*) ineffective, ineffectual, inefficient, unserviceable, useless, inadequate

149. ef-fron-ter-y   *noun*   ĕ-frŭn′-tə-rē
[*effronterie* (French), "shamelessness"; from *effrons, effrontis* (Latin), "barefaced"; from *ex* (Latin), "out" + *frons, frontis* (Latin), "forehead"]

Definition: Shameless boldness.

   "You mean to tell me," I exclaimed in surprise, "that you had the **effrontery** to ask for a raise when your productivity has really fallen off lately?"

Synonyms: (*nouns*) audacity, impertinence, temerity, gall, nerve, cheek, chutzpah, presumption

Antonyms: (*nouns*) timidity, shyness, meekness, modesty, diffidence

Related Phrase: barefaced audacity

150. **e-lic-it**   *verb*   ĭ-lĭs'-ĭt

[*elicere, elicitus* (Latin), "draw out"; from *ex* (Latin), "out of" + *lacere* (Latin), "draw"]

Definition: To draw out or call forth.

I was surprised that the mayor's appeal for help did not **elicit** more of a response than it did.

Occasionally, a teacher's question will **elicit** only a blank stare from the entire class.

Phrases: elicit a reaction, elicit the truth

Usage Note:
Do not confuse *elicit* with the adjective *illicit*, meaning "unlawful."

Synonyms: (*verbs*) evoke, prompt, extract, educe, produce

151. **e-lite**   *noun and adjective*   ĭ-lēt'   *or*   ā-lēt'

[*elite* (French), "choice"; from *ex* (Latin), "out" + *legere, lectus* (Latin), "pick"]

Definition:
  a.   (*noun*) A highly select group of superior individuals.

     Membership in the National Honor Society indicates that a young person belongs to this country's academic **elite**.

  b.   (*adjective*) Select; superior.

     Every army has one or two **elite** forces trained to handle especially difficult or dangerous assignments.

Related Forms: (*noun*) elitism; (*adjective*) elitist

A group of aristocrats, the elite of French society, attending a reception at Versailles during the reign of Napoleon III (1852–1870).

Though *elite* is usually a favorable word, *elitist* and *elitism* are definitely not. These two words suggest undue pride in belonging to some supposedly superior group. They also imply an underlying belief in the domination of society by the people on top. Thus, they indicate attitudes that are usually considered antidemocratic and antilibertarian. For this reason, these words are distinctly pejorative in tone.

Synonyms: (*nouns*) privileged class, privileged few, aristocracy, nobility, upper crust, cream of the crop, crème de la crème; (*adjectives*) aristocratic, choice, exclusive, first-class, top-notch, top-drawer, A-one

Antonyms: (*nouns*) masses, common herd, proletariat, hoi polloi, rank and file, rabble, riffraff, dregs of society; (*adjective*) proletarian

152. e-ma-ci-at-ed   *adjective*   ē-mā'-shē-āt-ĭd
[*e* (Latin), "completely" + *maciare, maciatus* (Latin), "make lean"; from *macies* (Latin), "leanness"]

Definition: Wasted or reduced by starvation, disease, or the like.

The hollow eyes and shrunken cheeks of the **emaciated** children in the magazine ad were haunting reminders of our role in the fight against world hunger.

Nothing causes a checking account to look more **emaciated** than paying all the monthly bills.

Related Form: (*noun*) emaciation; (*verb*) emaciate

Synonyms: (*adjectives*) gaunt, haggard, shriveled, withered, skeletal, undernourished

Antonyms: (*adjectives*) fat, chubby, plump, corpulent, obese

153. em-a-nate   *verb*   ĕm'-ə-nāt
[*ex* (Latin), "out" + *manare, manatus* (Latin), "flow"]

Definition:
a. To flow out of.

When Coach Casey gives his pregame pep talk, the enthusiasm that **emanates** from him sparks the whole team.

b. To send forth.

Some radioactive substances can **emanate** dangerous radiation for many years.

Related Form: (*noun*) emanation

Synonyms: (*verbs*) flow from, proceed from, spring, originate, emerge; emit, project, give off, issue

Antonyms: (*verbs*) soak up, absorb, draw in, attract

154. em-bel-lish   *verb*   ĕm-bĕl'-ĭsh

[*embellir* (Old French), "beautify"; from *en* (Latin), "causing" + *bellus* (Latin), "beautiful"]

Definition: To decorate or enhance.

There is rarely a good reason to **embellish** the truth.

Medieval monks **embellished** the pages of the manuscripts they copied with all sorts of beautifully colored drawings called *illuminations*.

Related Form: (*noun*) embellishment

Usage Note:
Embellish is often used in the sense of adding fictitious details to a story or statement. When used in this way, the word is virtually a synonym of *fabricate* (Word 181). Thus, a story that has been *embellished* may be partially or totally untrue.

Synonyms: (*verbs*) adorn, dress up, spruce up, gussy up, garnish

Antonyms: (*verbs*) mar, deface, disfigure

155. em-i-nent   *adjective*   ĕm'-ə-nĕnt

[*eminens, eminentis* (Latin), "lofty"; from *ex* (Latin), "out" + *minere* (Latin), "stand; project"]

Definition:

a.   High in rank; distinguished.

Your best friend's father may be an **eminent** neurosurgeon.

Who would have suspected that such a soft-spoken, retiring woman was actually an **eminent** scientist with an international reputation?

b.   Outstanding; conspicuous.

Your mother may treat all her children with **eminent** fairness.

Tact and graciousness may be **eminent** among the sterling qualities you possess.

Related Forms: (*noun*) eminence; (*adverb*) eminently

Usage Notes:

a.   The legal expression *eminent domain* indicates the right of a government to take over private property for public use (after paying a reasonable compensation for it, of course).

b.   Do not confuse *eminent* with *imminent*, which means "threatening" or "impending."

c.   *Your Eminence* is the proper phrase to employ when addressing a cardinal of the Roman Catholic Church.

Synonyms: (*adjectives*) prominent, renowned, illustrious; notable, great, noteworthy; remarkable, marked

Antonyms: (*adjectives*) obscure, lowly, undistinguished; unremarkable

156. em·pa·thy   *noun*   ĕm'-pə-thē

[*empatheia* (Greek), "passion"; from *en* (Greek), "causing" + *pathos* (Greek), "suffering"]

Definition: A sympathetic understanding of, or identification with, the feelings, thoughts, and attitudes of someone or something else.

> Ellen's volunteer work at the nursing home is motivated, not by a detached sense of duty, but by a genuine **empathy** for those who are lonely.

> So strong is my **empathy** with the poems of Robert Frost that I often feel as though I could have written them myself.

Related Forms: (*adjectives*) empathic, empathetic; (*verb*) empathize

Synonyms: (*nouns*) sympathy, compassion

Antonyms: (*nouns*) insensitivity, callousness

Related Phrases: lack of understanding, lack of appreciation

157. em·u·late   *verb*   ĕm'-yə-lāt

[*aemulari, aemulatus* (Latin), "vie with, strive to be equal; be envious"]

Definition: To try to equal or excel the excellence of.

> The old fable tells us to **emulate** the industry of the ant, so that we don't wind up empty-handed beggars like the improvident grasshopper.

Related Forms: (*nouns*) emulation, emulator

Synonyms: (*verbs*) imitate, match, rival, follow, mirror, take after

Related Phrases: follow in the footsteps of, follow the example of, model one's behavior on

158. en·clave   *noun*   ĕn'-klāv' *or* än'-klāv

[*enclave* (Old French), "enclosure"; from *in* (Latin), "in" + *clavis* (Latin), "key"]

Definition:

a. A country or area lying wholly within the boundaries of another country or area.

> Though a completely independent state, Vatican City is no more than a tiny **enclave** in the heart of the great Italian capital city of Rome.

b. A separate group or community within a larger group or community.

> "All of us had dedicated our lives to the arts," I recalled. "For that reason, we thought of ourselves as an **enclave** of culture in a society concerned only with making money and having fun."

Synonyms: (*nouns*) enclosure, precinct

159. en·dem·ic   *adjective*   ĕn-dĕm′-ĭk

[*endémique* (French), "endemic"; from *endem(i)os* (Greek), "dwelling in a place"; from *en* (Greek), "in" + *demos* (Greek), "people"]

Definition: Peculiar to a particular locality or group of people.

Lemurs are primates that are **endemic** to the island of Madagascar, which is located off the coast of Africa in the Indian Ocean.

Phrases: an endemic plant or animal, an endemic disorder

Related Forms: (*adjectives*) endemical

Usage Note:

Though the use of *endemic* is normally restricted to diseases and plant or animal life, the word may occasionally be used figuratively in other contexts. For example, a problem may be said to be endemic to a particular profession, or racism endemic to a particular area or group.

Synonyms: (*adjectives*) indigenous, native

Antonyms: (*adjectives*) alien, extraneous, foreign

An Enigmatic Creature

In classical mythology, the sphinx was a monster having the head of a woman, the body of a lion, and the wings of an eagle. This odd creature was said to crouch on a block of stone outside the Greek city Thebes, where she confronted travelers with a riddle intended to stump them. The traveler who could not answer the riddle was killed. When Oedipus, a famous figure in Greek mythology, solved the riddle, the sphinx promptly killed herself. The ancient Egyptians constructed a colossal figure of a recumbent sphinx near the pyramids of Gizah (*see photo*).

Our modern word *sphinx* derives from this creature out of Greek myth. Today, the word is sometimes used to indicate a person who habitually asks unsolvable riddles, is engaged in mysterious actions, always wears an enigmatic facial expression (the proverbial poker face), or deliberately answers questions evasively.

160. **e-nig-ma**   *noun*   ĭ-nĭg'-mə

[*ainigma* (Greek), "riddle"; from *ainos* (Greek), "tale; story"]

Definition:

   a. An intentionally obscure statement; a riddle.

        Sometimes crossword-puzzle clues contain puns, **enigmas**, and other kinds of brainteasers, rather than straightforward hints to the words that are wanted.

   b. Someone or something that is puzzling or mysterious.

        Her consistently strange and unpredictable behavior has caused many people to regard her as a complete **enigma**.

        The unexpected death of a young person is one of life's most perplexing **enigmas**, especially for those who are the same age as the deceased.

Related Forms: (*adjectives*) enigmatic, enigmatical

Synonyms: (*nouns*) mystery, puzzle, conundrum, dilemma, brainteaser, mind boggler

Related Phrases: a tough nut to crack, a complete question mark, terra incognita, a sealed (or closed) book

Using the Words

Exercise I.   Parts of Speech

Indicate the part of speech of each of the following words. In one case, two answers are correct.

1. endemic adj.
2. enclave n.
3. emulate v.
4. empathy n.
5. enigma n.
6. effete adj.
7. effrontery n.
8. elite n., adj.
9. efficacious adj.

Exercise II.   Words in Phrases

In each of the following groups, select the item that best expresses the meaning of the *italicized* word in the introductory phrase.

1. an *eclectic* style of architecture
   a. excellent   b. selective   c. efficacious   d. modern
   e. popular

2. an *effete* snob
   a. greedy   b. depressed   c. inventive   d. worn out
   e. outstanding

3. the *elite* of the entertainment world
   a. retired members   b. fans   c. rank and file   d. charlatans
   e. crème de la crème

213

4. a light *emanating* from the tunnel
   a. flashing   b. hurrying   c. blinking   d. radiating
   e. stolen

5. *endemic* to the North American continent
   a. related   b. averse   c. accustomed   d. extraneous
   e. native

6. *empathy* for her patient
   a. medical attention   b. compassion   c. fear   d. apathy
   e. financial support

7. a complete *enigma*
   a. puzzle   b. fool   c. success   d. failure   e. joke

8. an *eminent* historian
   a. elderly   b. obscure   c. renowned   d. retired   e. foreign

Exercise III.   Completing Sentences

Complete each of the following sentences or pairs of sentences by
selecting the most appropriate word from the group of words given
below. Use each word only once. Make any adjustments that are
necessary to fit the words into the sentences properly.

emaciated	enclave	empathy
elicit	eminent	efficacious
effrontery	embellish	emulate

1. "I was really only on a fishing expedition," the D.A. remarked.
   "I never expected my innocent question to ___elicit___ such
   an incriminating statement from the witness."

2. Though several workable solutions to the landfill problem
   were suggested at the meeting, Mrs. Brown's appeared to be
   the most _efficacious_.

3. My dad lost so much weight during his recent illness that for a
   while he looked positively _emaciated_.

4. Paris fashions are so popular that profit-minded New York de-
   signers take pains to ___emulate___ them.

5. He had the ___effrontery___ to ask me for a recommendation
   despite the fact that I had just fired him for gross inefficiency.

6. "I know Monaco is an independent country," I replied. "Still, as
   far as territory goes, it is nothing more than a tiny ___enclave___
   in the southeast corner of France."

7. One of the candidates running for the Senate is an ___eminent___
   educator with a national reputation. The other is an obscure
   used-car salesman from Missoula.

8. "Your hat is decorated enough already," Glenda remarked.
   "You don't need to ___embellish___ it any further."

Exercise IV.　Synonyms and Antonyms

A. In each of the following groups, select the **two** words that are most nearly **synonyms**.

1.　a. spent　b. vigorous　c. inclement　d. burnt-out　effete
2.　a. audacity　b. temerity　c. timidity　d. callousness　effrontery
3.　a. evoke　b. illicit　c. produce　d. echo　elicit
4.　a. puzzle　b. enclosure　c. mind boggler　d. gall　enigma
5.　a. sympathy　b. callousness　c. compassion　d. shyness　empathy

Now for each pair of synonyms that you have selected, supply a word from the Basic Word List in this lesson (Words 146–160) that means **the same** or **almost the same** thing.

B. In each of the following, select the item that is most nearly **opposite** in meaning to the numbered word at the left.

1.　elite　　　　a. hoi polloi　b. aristocracy　c. enclave
　　　　　　　　d. affluence　e. modesty

2.　emaciated　a. uniform　b. timid　c. corpulent
　　　　　　　　d. haggard　e. barren

3.　endemic　　a. useless　b. native　c. fertile　d. alien
　　　　　　　　e. puzzling

4.　efficacious　a. selective　b. basic　c. exclusive
　　　　　　　　d. potent　e. ineffective

5.　embellish　a. fabricate　b. adorn　c. deface　d. emerge
　　　　　　　　e. imitate

Exercise V.　Word Roundup

1.　Explain the difference in meaning between the words in each of the following pairs:

　　a. imminent—eminent　　　　b. illicit—elicit

2.　With or without the aid of a dictionary, explain the meaning of each of the following phrases:

　　a.　hoi polloi　　　d.　upper crust　　　g.　a sealed book
　　b.　terra incognita　e.　all of a piece　　h.　rank and file
　　c.　eminent domain　f.　cream of the crop

3.　Who should be addressed as *Your Eminence*?

4.　With or without the aid of a dictionary, explain the story behind each of the following expressions:

　　a. sphinx　　　　　　　　b. a poker face

Exercise VI.   Framing Sentences

A. Use each of the following words in an original sentence.

1. eclectic	4. effrontery	7. enclave
2. effete	5. endemic	8. empathize
3. elite	6. elicit	9. enigmatic

B. Give a **noun** form of each of the following words, and use it in a short illustrative sentence.   embellishment   eminence   efficacy

1. embellish	3. eminent	5. efficacious
2. emulate	4. emaciated	6. emanate
emulation	emaciation	emanation

Completing Verbal Analogies

"A Causes B."   Another word relationship that frequently appears in the analogy sections of standardized tests is "*A* necessarily causes *B*; *C* necessarily causes *D*." An example of an analogy question involving this relationship is given below. See if you can figure out the correct answer before you read the rest of this section.

starvation: emaciation ::
  a. moderation : burliness
  b. gluttony : obesity
  c. fasting : corpulence
  d. abstinence : stockiness
  e. dieting : rotundity

The answer is *b. Starvation* will necessarily produce bodily *emaciation.* In the same way, *gluttony* (that is, excessive overeating) will necessarily lead to *obesity.*

None of the other choices offered exhibits the same cause-effect relationship involved in the key pair of words. *Moderation* in the consumption of food has nothing to do with *burliness* (choice *a*), nor does *abstinence* relate to *stockiness* (choice *d*). Similarly, *fasting* does not produce *corpulence* (choice *c*), and *dieting* does not lead to *rotundity* (choice *e*).

Notice, however, that two of the wrong choices exhibit a relationship that involves the *opposite* of the relationship that is wanted. *Fasting* certainly does not produce *corpulence*, but it may lead to *emaciation.* Similarly, *dieting* does not lead to *rotundity*, but *rotundity* may make a person want to go on a *diet.* These items were both purposely included to make the selection of the correct answer more difficult.

"A Will Make a Person B."   A closely related form of the word relationship "*A* necessarily causes *B*" can conveniently be expressed as "*A* will make a person *B*; *C* will make a person *D*." Here is an example of an analogy question involving this relationship. Study it carefully.

practice : proficient ::
  a. interest : apathetic
  b. experience : talented
  c. study : knowledgeable
  d. wealth : wise
  e. famous : accomplishment

The answer is *c.* Continuous *practice* of a skill or art will make a person *proficient* at it. Similarly, continuous *study* of a subject will make a person *knowledgeable* about it.

None of the other choices exhibits this cause-effect relationship. *Interest* in something does not make a person *apathetic* about it (choice *a*). *Experience* does not make a person *talented* because talent tends to be in-born (choice *b*). The possession of *wealth* has nothing to do with how *wise* a person is (choice *d*). Finally, the two words in choice *e* come in the wrong order. In the key pair of words, the adjective (*proficient*) follows the noun (*practice*); in choice *e*, however, the adjective (*famous*) precedes the noun (*accomplishment*).

"A indicates the Extreme of B."   Another common word relationship that appears on standardized vocabulary tests is "*A* indicates the extreme of *B*; *C* indicates the extreme of *D*." Here is an example of an analogy question involving this relationship. Study it carefully.

gigantic : large ::
a. cold : frigid
b. tepid : lukewarm
c. economical : frugal
d. tiny : small
e. drab : colorful

The answer is *d*. *Tiny* indicates that something is *very small*, just as *gigantic* indicates that it is *very large*.

None of the other choices exhibits this relationship. *Frigid* means *very cold*, but *cold* does not mean *very frigid* (choice *a*). Similarly, *frugal* means *very economical*, but *economical* does not mean *very frugal* (choice *c*). *Tepid* just means *lukewarm*, not *very lukewarm* (choice *c*). And finally, *drab* does not mean *very colorful*; it means the *opposite* of *colorful* (choice *e*).

Word Order.   The comments just made about choices *a* and *c* point up an important consideration to bear in mind when answering analogy questions. It is this: Always make sure that the two words in the answer you select come *in the same order* as the two words in the key pair. If, for example, the key pair contains an adjective followed by a noun (or a strong word followed by a weak one), be certain that your answer also contains an adjective followed by a noun (or a strong word followed by a weak one). If not, you've made the wrong choice.

Teachers unfold the mysteries of computers and the Internet to groups of eager students. Teaching at any level is an excellent career goal for someone who uses words well.

Exercise I

Complete the following analogies based on the word relationships studied in this lesson.

1. **relish : like ::**
   a. upset : outrage
   b. cherish : loathe
   c. leave : depart
   d. deter : abet
   e. abhor : dislike

2. **liquor : intoxication ::**
   a. food : obesity
   b. color : candor
   c. noise : blandness
   d. water : aridity
   e. sun : pallor

3. **distraught : upset ::**
   a. bleak : rosy
   b. simple : austere
   c. gaunt : thin
   d. modest : demure
   e. irritation : peevish

4. **enigma : puzzlement ::**
   a. confrontation : belligerent
   b. discomfiture : chagrin
   c. bickering : empathy
   d. enclave : dejection
   e. calumny : devotion

5. **disappointment : cynical ::**
   a. hardship : blithe
   b. insult : dormant
   c. failure : dexterous
   d. irritation : peevish
   e. pressure : calm

Exercise II   Answers will vary.

Compose **two** complete analogies based on the word relationship "*A* necessarily causes *B*" (or the related relationship "*A* will make a person *B*"), and **two** based on "*A* indicates the extreme of *B*."

Exercise III

Complete the following analogies.

1. **dexterous : gauche** = circumspect :
   (*clandestine, complacent, cogent, compatible, incautious*)

2. **alienate : estrange** = augment :
   (*atone, augur, appall, increase, curtail*)

3. **dilatory : promptness** = distraught :
   (*composure, energy, money, backbone, honesty*)

4. **dormancy : inactive** = dilapidation :
   (*impartial, rundown, dissimilar, biased, manageable*)

5. **opulent : rich** = exhausted :
   (*energetic, lazy, tired, prosperous, untidy*)

Working with Context Clues

Contrast Clues. The second general type of context clue that you are like-ly to meet in the sentence-completion section of a standardized test may conveniently be called a **contrast clue**. As you already know, a restate-ment clue more or less repeats the meaning of the missing word. A con-trast clue, on the other hand, provides an *antonym* for, or a phrase that means the *opposite* of, the word that is wanted.

Study the following example of a sentence-completion exercise carefully. It contains both a contrast clue and a linking expression that points to this clue.

> "As you say, my view of the situation may be far too rosy," I admitted. "On the other hand, yours may be a bit too _____."
>
> a. optimistic   b. scholarly   c. pious   d. concise   e. bleak

Notice the presence of the phrase *On the other hand* at the beginning of the second sentence. This is the kind of linking expression that binds together two contrasting or dissimilar sentences or sentence elements. In this case, it connects two complete sentences.

Thus, the words *On the other hand* tell you that you are about to read a sentence that in some way contrasts with the preceding sentence. In other words, the phrase pretty much tells you what kind of clue you are likely to find. It is a contrast clue.

But the phrase *On the other hand* also tells you something else. It tells you where to look for the clue. Since the blank for the missing word fol-lows (rather than precedes) the words *On the other hand,* you are likely to find your clue in the first sentence in the example.

Look at the first sentence. It tells you that the speaker ("I") has far too "rosy" a view of a particular situation. *Rosy*, of course, means "optimistic" or "confident." This implies that the person who is dealt with in the sec-ond sentence ("you") must have a view of the same situation that con-trasts with the speaker's view. In other words, it must in some way be "unrosy." Now you know the sense of the missing word.

Now look at the five words from which you are to select the item that goes in the blank. Only one of them means anything like "unrosy" or "unoptimistic." It is choice *e, bleak*, which, as you learned in Lesson 7 (page 99), can mean "gloomy." This is clearly the missing word.

Exercise I

All the following sentence-completion exercises contain contrast clues. Complete each by selecting the word that makes the best sense in the sentence (or pair of sentences) as a whole. Underline the clue or clues that led you to make your choice.

1. "There is <u>nothing bold</u> about this character," the director said. "She is as _____ as a spring flower.

    a. effete   b. delightful   c. avid   <u>d. demure</u>   e. agile

2. Although it is easy to <u>criticize</u> the failings of people you dislike, it is much harder to _____ them for their good qualities.

    <u>a. praise</u>   b. elicit   c. condone   d. abet   e. compare

3. One child in a family can be very _____ and easy to handle; while another sibling may be very troublesome and hard to manage.

   a. docile   b. diligent   c. boorish   d. affectionate   e. belligerent

4. I keep feeling responsible for our messy room, but my sister seems to _____ responsibility for the mess.

   a. assume   b. claim   c. defer   d. abdicate   e. consider

5. Some household pets gain weight as they grow older; others, however, become _____ with age and illness.

   a. chronic   b. demure   c. cantankerous   d. corpulent
   e. emaciated

Exercise II

The following exercise reviews everything that you have learned about sentence-completion questions and context clues to this point. Complete each item in the exercise by selecting the word that makes the best sense in the sentence (or pair of sentences) as a whole. Underline the clue or clues that led you to your choice.

1. I thought the meal was very _____, but my companion found it very interesting and tasty.

   a. bland   b. eclectic   c. desultory   d. delicious   e. bizarre

2. Since our accountant advised us to put off buying a house until mortgage rates declined, we agreed to _____ the purchase.

   a. abet   b. pursue   c. defer   d. expedite   e. conclude

3. The handiwork of one of the carpenters is extremely skillful and _____; the other's is clumsy and awkward.

   a. captious   b. desultory   c. callous   d. dexterous   e. arbitrary

4, Although I find his argument _____, I am not convinced he believes what he is saying so forcefully.

   a. captious   b. weak   c. dire   d. academic   e. cogent

5. When Edward VIII chose to _____ the English throne, he did not realize he would have to give up most of his power and influence as well.

   a. abdicate   b. expel   c. secure   d. exalt   e. undo

Enriching the Lesson

Exercise I.   Our Latin Heritage

A number of the English words studied in this lesson (e.g., *efficacious*, *enclave*, *emulate*) are based on Latin originals. English is rich in such Latin borrowings. As a matter of fact, they make up a huge part of the vocabulary of present-day English.

A number of words and expressions borrowed or adapted from Latin (including medieval Latin) are listed below. With or without the aid of a dictionary, define each. Then choose any **five**, and for each compose a short illustrative sentence.

1. laborious	11. nugatory	21. lapse
2. unanimous	12. punitive	22. rapacious
3. magnanimous	13. obliterate	23. negotiate
4. puerile	14. ratify	24. superfluous
5. terminate	15. malevolent	25. provoke
6. mandate	16. nullify	26. quash
7. supersede	17. juxtapose	27. militate
8. raucous	18. regress	28. literate
9. nascent	19. minimal	29. notorious
10. jocose	20. malleable	30. reiterate

Exercise II.   "Extreme" Words

The adjective *emaciated*, studied in this lesson, indicates extreme thinness. Its opposite, *obese*, noted in the synonyms under *emaciated*, indicates extreme fatness. English is rich in such extreme expressions. Do the following exercise involving a few of them.

The words in column A refer to familiar emotions or traits of personality. The words in column B refer to the same emotions or traits but in a more extreme or intense sense. Match each word in column A with its related extreme word in column B.

Column A	*Column B*
d 1. glad	a. solemn
h 2. restrained	b. adore
j 3. dislike	c. immaculate
a 4. serious	d. elated
b 5. like	e. distraught
c 6. clean	f. chaotic
g 7. wise	g. sagacious
i 8. forceful	h. austere
f 9. disorderly	i. overbearing
e 10. perturbed	j. detest
l 11. well-off	k. outrage
k 12. offend	l. opulent

Exercise III. Too Much of a Good Thing

The desire to excel is generally a healthy characteristic in a person. Experience, however, shows that it can easily go sour. Thus, under the "good" word *elite*, studied in this lesson, the negative words *elitist* and *elitism* also appear. Listed below are some other common English words that suggest a desire to be superior that is expressed in a negative or objectionable way. With or without the aid of a dictionary, define each. Then choose any **five**, and for each compose a short illustrative sentence.

1. snob	7. poseur	13. bumptious
2. moralistic	8. conceit	14. perfectionist
3. dogmatic	9. authoritarian	15. purist
4. sanctimonious	10. dilettante	16. self-righteous
5. labored	11. egocentric	17. narcissism
6. autocratic	12. preciosity	18. jingoism

Exercise IV. Forms of Direct Address

Under *eminent*, a word studied in this lesson, it was noted that *Your Eminence* is the proper phrase to use when addressing a cardinal of the Roman Catholic Church. English has a few other such phrases. They are all used when addressing royalty or persons holding certain positions in the government, the church, or the legal system. Six of these phrases are listed below. With or without the aid of a dictionary, name the person or group of people to whom each is properly applied.

1. Your Excellency	3. Your Grace	5. Your Honor
2. Your Highness	4. Your Holiness	6. Your Majesty

Exercise V. Expanding Your Word Power

The words listed below are not on the Basic Word List, but they were mentioned in passing in Lesson 14. All of them would make useful additions to your working vocabulary. Define each, give its etymology, list **two** synonyms and **two** antonyms (where possible), and use in a short illustrative sentence.

1. monolithic	6. diffidence	11. garnish
2. decadent	7. evoke	12. obscure
3. prolific	8. aristocratic	13. compassion
4. ineffectual	9. obese	14. indigenous
5. impertinence	10. originate	15. dilemma

Related Forms in Context

Beneath each sentence below are four words introduced in Lesson 13 or 14. Review the related forms for these words, and choose the one that best completes the sentence. Write that related form in the space provided.

1. The tour guide drew our attention to the _eclecticism_ of the room's decor—Japanese prints, Classical Greek sculpture, Tiffany lamps, Navajo rugs, and Mission-style furniture.

    a. dilapidated   b. effete   c. eclectic   d. eminent

2. Before trying to feed an injured eagle or hawk, an avian wildlife rehabilitator needs to determine the bird's level of _emaciation_.

    a. dilatory   b. emaciated   c. distraught   d. dire

3. Comparing its past popularity with its currently dwindling numbers, the party functionaries bemoaned the sheer _effeteness_ of their movement today.

    a. effete   b. efficacious   c. dire   d. docile

4. The sixteenth-century French writer Montaigne, who developed the essay form, wrote short nonfiction pieces in a _discursive_ style about topics that interested him.

    a. disparity   b. effrontery   c. duplicity   d. discourse

5. In Shakespeare's *King Lear*, the tragedy is set in motion when Lear's three daughters give _disparate_ responses to their father's demand for an expression of their love.

    a. discourse   b. disparity   c. elite   d. enclave

6. If you stay up all night, skip breakfast, and neglect to read the questions carefully, you will _drastically_ reduce your chances of doing well on the final exam.

    a. dilatory   b. diligent   c. docile   d. drastic

7. Eight days after the Nazis' _duplicitous_ signing of a ten-year nonaggression pact with the Soviet Union, Germany invaded Poland on September 1, 1939.

    a. disparity   b. elite   c. duplicity   d. empathy

8. Ashley chose Samuel Taylor Coleridge's _enigmatic_ poem "Kubla Khan" as the subject of her three-page essay of literary interpretation and analysis.

    a. duplicity   b. enigma   c. eclectic   d. enclave

9. While India was still a colony, Mohandas K. Gandhi led nonviolent protests—including marches, boycotts, and hunger strikes—against Britain's _elitist_ rule.

    a. elite   b. enigma   c. disparity   d. discourse

10. Medical studies have proved the ___efficacy___ and safety of immunization therapy for people who have shown extreme sensitivity to bee stings.

    a. efficacious   b. effete   c. eminent   d. elite

11. Our debaters were elated by the complete ___discomfiture___ of their opponents' team.

    a. divulge   b. emanate   c. discomfit   d. embellish

12. It was Miguel de Cervantes, not Benjamin Franklin, who first said, "___Diligence___ is the mother of good fortune."

    a. dilapidated   b. docile   c. dire   d. diligent

13. In order to carry out their work, food relief agencies try to get us to ___empathize___ with the plight of malnourished and starving people all over the world.

    a. disparity   b. elite   c. enigma   d. empathy

14. In 1972, Congress passed the Equal Rights Amendment aimed at ending ___discrimination___ on the basis of sex, but the proposed amendment subsequently failed to be ratified by the required 38 states.

    a. divulge   b. discriminate   c. emulate   d. emanate

15. In physics class, our professor demonstrated the use of the Geiger counter, which measures the ___emanation___ of radiation from cosmic rays and radioactive substances.

    a. embellish   b. emulate   c. emanate   d. elicit

16. Newspaper reporters are supposed to write accurate, objective, factual reports without any ___embellishments___ or subjective judgments.

    a. discomfit   b. discourse   c. emulate   d. embellish

17. Malaria, an infectious disease ___endemical___ to the tropics, is transmitted to humans by mosquitoes.

    a. eminent   b. endemic   c. efficacious   d. emaciated

18. After serving two terms in the House of Representatives, she is ___eminently___ qualified to run as a candidate for the U.S. Senate.

    a. drastic   b. eminent   c. diligent   d. dilatory

19. In Greek mythology, Apollo gives Cassandra the power to predict the future but then decrees that no one will believe her ___direful___ prophecies.

    a. dire   b. dilapidated   c. endemic   d. dormant

20. By a large margin, voters defeated the candidate whose TV ad campaign depended solely on the ___disparagement___ of his opponent.

    a. discriminate   b. divulge   c. disparage   d. emanate

Lesson 15

161. entice — 175. exigency

---

161. **en-tice**   *verb*   ĕn-tīs′

[*enticier* (Old French) "set on fire"; from *in* (Latin), "in" + *titio* (Latin), "firebrand"]

Definition: To lead on by arousing hope or desire.

Only the offer of a tremendous increase in salary could **entice** me into leaving my present job.

Related Forms: (*noun*) enticement; (*adjective*) enticing

Synonyms: (*verbs*) tempt, lure, allure, coax, inveigle, beguile, seduce

Antonyms: (*verbs*) repel, repulse, scare off, frighten away

Related Phrases: seductive charms, a beguiling manner, bait the hook, sweet-talk, soft-soap, rope into

162. **en-treat**   *verb*   ĕn-trēt′

[*entraitier* (Old French), "deal with; plead with"; from *en* (Old French), "in" + *traitier* (Old French), "deal, treat"]

Definition: To ask or petition earnestly.

The defense attorney **entreated** the jury to weigh *all* the evidence carefully and objectively before reaching a verdict.

Related Form: (*noun*) entreaty

Synonyms: (*verbs*) implore, beg, beseech, plead for, urge, importune, press for

Related Phrase: cap in hand

163. **en-vis-age**   *verb*   ĕn-vĭz′-ĭj

[*envisager* (French), "imagine"; from *en* (French), "in" + *visage* (French), "face"]

Definition: To have a mental image of something, especially when the thing does not yet exist; to conceive of.

I find it very difficult to **envisage** the kind of society that the Greek philosopher Plato once dreamt of creating.

From his writings it is clear that Thomas Jefferson **envisaged** an America made up of small independent farmers dedicated to hard work and egalitarian principles.

Synonyms: (*verbs*) envision, visualize, picture, imagine

225

164. ep-i-thet   *noun*   ĕp'-ə-thĕt

[*epitheton* (Greek), "an addition"; from *epi* (Greek), "on" + *tithenai* (Greek), "put, place"]

Definition:
   a. A word or phrase used to describe or characterize someone or something. (The expression need not be derogatory.)

> Some English kings, such as William the Conqueror and Richard the Lion-Hearted, are better known by their informal **epithets** than by their official titles.

> To fill out a line of verse, Homer often employs a stock **epithet**— for example, "wine-dark" for the sea.

   b. A term of abuse or contempt.

> The irate motorist shouted a few choice **epithets** at the driver of the car that had cut him off.

Synonyms: (*nouns*) characterization, designation, appellation, label, nickname, moniker, handle; curse, oath, obscenity

Related Phrases: badmouth someone, hurl brickbats at, mudslinging

165. e-qua-nim-i-ty   *noun*   ē-kwə-nĭm'-ə-tē *or* ĕk-wə-nĭm'-ə-tē

[*aequanimitas* (Latin), "evenness of temper"; from *aequus* (Latin), "even; equal" + *animus* (Latin), "mind"]

Definition: Calmness or evenness of temper.

> A true stoic, Abraham Lincoln tried to bear reverses of fortune with dignity and **equanimity**.

Synonyms: (*nouns*) composure, self-composure, placidity, tranquility, serenity, sangfroid, unexcitability, imperturbability, unflappability, self-possession, nonchalance

Antonyms: (*nouns*) excitability, fretfulness, agitation, distress, hysteria

Related Phrases: mental (or emotional) stability, presence of mind

166. eq-ui-ta-ble   *adjective*   ĕk'-wə-tə-bəl

[*equitable* (French), "fair, just"; from *equite* (Old French), "justice"; from *aequus* (Latin), "even, equal"]

Definition: Fair or just.

> The owner of the company was satisfied that the distribution of raises and bonuses had been as **equitable** as possible.

Related Forms: (*adjective*) inequitable; (*adverb*) equitably; (*noun*) equity

Usage Note:
Do not confuse *equitable* with *equable*, which means "unvarying" or "tranquil."

Synonyms: (*adjectives*) impartial, unbiased, evenhanded

Antonyms: (*adjectives*) unfair, unjust, biased, partial; unreasonable, lopsided, one-sided, uneven

167. **er-u-dite**   *adjective*   ĕr'-yŏŏ-dīt   *or*   ĕr'-ŏŏ-dīt

[*erudire, eruditus* (Latin), "take the roughness out of, polish"; from *e* (Latin), "out of" + *rudis* (Latin), "rough, rude"]

Definition: Deeply learned, especially in a specialized area.

Lord Chesterfield once advised his son never to appear more **erudite** than the people he was with.

Last night Professor Maurice Lenkowski presented an **erudite**, yet entertaining, lecture on the early history of aviation in this country.

Related Forms: (*noun*) erudition; (*adverb*) eruditely

Synonyms: (*adjectives*) scholarly, profound, knowledgeable, informed

Antonyms: (*adjectives*) ignorant, uninformed

Related Phrases: a savant, a pundit, a maven, a walking encyclopedia, highbrow, an ignoramus, lowbrow

168. **es-o-ter-ic**   *adjective*   ĕs-ə-tĕr'-ĭk

[*esoterikos* (Greek), "inner"; from *eso* (Greek), "within"]

Definition:

a.   Understood by or intended for only a select few.

Only the members of the executive committee know all the **esoteric** rites involved in the initiation ceremonies of our fraternity.

b.   Difficult to understand.

"When those two computer programmers began to talk shop, the conversation became awfully **esoteric**," Molly remarked. "Yes," I replied, "I wasn't even sure that they were still speaking English!"

Related Form: (*adverb*) esoterically

Synonyms: (*adjectives*) occult, secret, confidential, private; mysterious abstruse, recondite, arcane, incomprehensible, unfathomable, cryptic, inscrutable, impenetrable

Antonyms: (*adjectives*) popular, exoteric; intelligible, accessible, crystal clear, comprehensible

Related Phrases: not for public consumption, insiders, privileged information

Usage Note:

The adjective *exoteric,* derived from the Greek word for "external," has a number of meanings, of which "less secret or confidential" (e.g., an *exoteric* rite") and "readily comprehensible" (e.g., an *exoteric* doctrine") are perhaps the most common.

169. eth·i·cal *adjective* ĕth'-ĭ-kəl

[*ethikos* (Greek), "moral"; from *ethos* (Greek), "custom, moral character"]

Definition: In accordance with accepted principles of right and wrong.

Although we cannot say outright that their sales techniques are illegal, we are prepared to argue that they are not **ethical**.

Related Forms: (*nouns*) ethicalness, ethicality, ethics, ethic, ethos; (*adjective*) unethical

Phrases: the Puritan work ethic, ethical drugs, the ethos of a people, the revolutionary ethos

Usage Notes:
   a.   *Ethics* is the branch of philosophy concerned with the general nature of morals and the specific moral choices facing the individual. It is also sometimes called *moral philosophy.*
   b.   An *ethic* is a principle of right or moral behavior or a set of such principles. The phrase *Puritan work ethic* refers to the fundamental belief in the value of hard work that was a basic part of the Puritan outlook on life.
   c.   An *ethos* is the set of fundamental attitudes, beliefs, and values that characterize a particular group or culture. Another word for this is *mores*, though today we would probably use *mind-set* instead. *Ethos* also indicates a governing principle or central idea, as in the phrase "the revolutionary *ethos.*"
   d.   In such phrases as "*ethical* drugs," *ethical* indicates that the item is distributed solely through the medical profession.

Synonyms: (*adjectives*) moral, virtuous, honorable, decent, upright, honest, righteous, principled, correct, proper

Antonyms: (*adjectives*) unfair, unjust, immoral, unscrupulous, dishonorable, discreditable, unsportsmanlike, unprofessional

Related Phrases: fair play, a lack of principles, dirty pool, hit someone below the belt

170. eth·nic *adjective* ĕth'-nĭk

[*ethnikos* (Greek), "foreign"; from *ethnos* (Greek), "people, nation"]

Definition: Relating to a small but distinct social group within the population. (The group in question is usually distinguished from the rest of the population by its particular religious, racial, national, or cultural character.)

The population of a pluralistic society is made up of many different **ethnic** groups from many different parts of the world.

Phrases: ethnic food, ethnic pride, the ethnic vote

Related Forms: (*nouns*) ethnicity, ethnology

Usage Note:
Ethnic is sometimes used as a noun to indicate a member of a particular ethnic group. This usage, however, is decidedly informal.

228

An ethnologist at work in rural central India. *Ethnology* is the science that deals with the individual cultures that make up the human family and their socioeconomic systems. It also concerns itself with the factors that bring about cultural growth and change.

171. eu·phe·mism   *noun*   yōō'-fə-mĭz-əm

[*euphemismos* (Greek), "euphemism"; from *euphemia* (Greek), "use of good words"; from *eu* (Greek), "good, well" + *pheme* (Greek), "speech"]

Definition: The substitution of a relatively inoffensive term for one that is considered too harsh, unpleasant, or blunt.

If we know that a person has lied repeatedly, why don't we say so, instead of using **euphemisms** such as "stretched the truth"?

Related Form: (*adjective*) euphemistic

172. ex·ac·er·bate   *verb*   ĕg-zăs'-ēr-bāt *or* ĕk-săs-ēr-bāt

[*exacerbare, exacerbatus* (Latin), "make harsh"; from *ex* (Latin), "completely" + *acerbus* (Latin), "harsh, bitter"]

Definition: To increase the bitterness or severity of; to irritate.

His stubborn refusal to follow the doctor's orders has done nothing but **exacerbate** his already serious medical problems.

"I don't think the proposal will do much to alleviate our present economic woes," the senator remarked, "but it may **exacerbate** them."

Related Form: (*noun*) exacerbation

Synonyms: (*verbs*) aggravate, worsen, intensify

Antonyms: (*verbs*) lessen, moderate, temper, mitigate, mollify, allay, assuage, soothe, alleviate, palliate

Related Phrases: add fuel to the fire, stoke the flames, add insult to injury, rub salt in an open wound; pour oil on troubled waters

229

173. **ex-alt**   *verb*   ĕg-zôlt′   *or*   ĭg-zôlt′

[*exaltare* (Latin), "lift up"; from *ex* (Latin), "out, up" + *altus* (Latin), "high"]

Definition: To elevate in power, position, character, or the like.

The Old Testament tells us that righteousness **exalts** a people but that evil debases it.

From truly humble beginnings, Cardinal Woolsey rose to one of the most **exalted** positions in English politics.

Related Forms: (*adjective*) exalted; (*noun*) exaltation

Usage Note:

Do not confuse *exalt* with *exult*, which means "rejoice" or "feel a sense of joy or satisfaction over some success."

Synonyms: (*verbs*) ennoble, uplift, upgrade

Antonyms: (*verbs*) debase, degrade, demote, humble, abase

174. **ex-em-pla-ry**   *adjective*   ĕg-zĕm′-plə-rē   *or*   ĭg-zĕm′-plə-rē

[*exemplaire* (Old French), "model"; from *exemplum* (Latin), "example"]

Definition:

a.   Worthy of imitation.

The dean of students congratulated the members of the senior class on their **exemplary** behavior at the prom.

b.   Serving as a model, illustration, or warning.

"I plan to mete out **exemplary** punishment to a few of the mutineers," the general said. "That, I believe, will induce the rest to return to their duty without further resistance."

Related Form: (*noun*) exemplar

Synonyms: (*adjectives*) model, sterling; commendable, meritorious, laudable; (*nouns*) paragon, epitome, archetype, prototype

Related Phrases: ne plus ultra, beau idéal

Exemplar

An exemplar is a model that is worthy of imitation. For example, in medieval times, Sir Galahad (*see illustration*) was the exemplar of the knightly virtues, especially purity and nobility. *Exemplar* is also used to indicate both the original or archetype of something and a typical representative of it.

175. ex-i-gen-cy   *noun*   ĕk'-sə-jən-sē

[*exigens* (Latin), "demanding"; from *exigere, exactus* (Latin), "drive out; demand"]

Definition: A state of urgency or a situation demanding immediate attention; the pressing needs caused by such a crisis.

"The **exigencies** of the situation demand that we curtail all unnecessary expenditures immediately," the chairman of the board announced yesterday.

Related Forms: (*noun*) exigence; (*adjective*) exigent; (*adverb*) exigently

Usage Note:
As the illustrative sentence given above suggests, *exigency* is frequently used in the plural with the meaning "pressing needs" or "urgent requirements."

Synonyms: (*nouns*) emergency, crisis; needs, demands, requirements

Related Phrases: in a tight fix, in hot water, a hot spot, a troubleshooter

Using the Words

Exercise I

1. es-o-ter'-ic
2. eth'-nic
3. eu'-phe-mism
4. ep'-i-thet
5. er'-u-dite
6. ex-ac'-er-bate
7. ex'-i-gen-cy
8. en-tice'
9. eth'-i-cal

Exercise I.   Syllabication and Pronunciation

Syllabicate the following words correctly, and place the major stress mark (') after the syllable that is accented when the word is pronounced.

1. esoteric
2. ethnic
3. euphemism
4. epithet
5. erudite
6. exacerbate
7. exigency
8. entice
9. ethical

Exercise II.   Words Out of Context

In each of the following groups, select the item that best expresses the meaning of the numbered word at the left.

1. entice   a. repel   b. tilt   c. force   d. exist   e. tempt

2. esoteric   a. intoxicated   b. agitated   c. unfair
                d. incomprehensible   e. interesting

3. envisage   a. feature   b. deceive   c. forget   d. offer
                e. visualize

4. ethical   a. morally correct   b. mildly amusing
                c. clearly wrong   d. emotionally stable
                e. deeply learned

5. exacerbate   a. alleviate   b. intensify   c. urge   d. imagine
                e. humble

231

6. entreat   a. coddle   b. repulse   <u>c. beg</u>   d. downgrade
                  e. clarify

7. exalt   a. rejoice   <u>b. uplift</u>   c. question   d. pursue
                  e. upset

Exercise III.   Completing Sentences

Complete each of the following sentences or pairs of sentences by selecting the most appropriate word from the group of words given below. Use each word only once. Make any adjustments that are necessary to fit the words into the sentences properly.

exemplary	equitable	erudite
equanimity	euphemism	epithet
entice	exigencies	ethnic

1. "It is one thing to offer constructive criticism of me and my administration," the president remarked. "It is quite another to shower us with empty <u>epithets</u> and meaningless verbal abuse."

2. *Pass away* is a common <u>euphemism</u> for *die*.

3. The <u>exigencies</u> of an overloaded business schedule prevented my dad from taking his annual vacation last year.

4. "Emma is an <u>exemplary</u> employee," the letter of recommendation read, "whose performance over the years might well serve as a model for any budding young executive."

5. Though Renaissance history is only a hobby with him, he is as <u>erudite</u> in the subject as any professional scholar.

6. Though I think of myself as an American, my family is of Polish origin, and I am proud of my <u>ethnic</u> heritage.

7. "Someone who is wise will try to bear even the most appalling misfortune with <u>equanimity</u>," he observed. "Someone who is silly will be devastated by the slightest setback."

8. Joe seems satisfied that his present salary arrangements are <u>equitable</u>, but I don't think they're at all fair.

Exercise IV.   Synonyms and Antonyms

Classify each of the following pairs of words as **S** for **synonyms** or **A** for **antonyms**.

A 1. ethical—immoral   S 6. esoteric—abstruse
A 2. alleviate—exacerbate   A 7. uninformed—erudite
A 3. debase—exalt   A 8. equanimity—excitability
S 4. implore—entreat   A 9. unfair—equitable
S 5. lure—entice   S 10. envisage—picture

Exercise V.   Word Roundup

1. With or without the aid of a dictionary, define each of the following colorful expressions.

   a. soft-soap
   b. bad-mouth someone
   c. hit below the belt
   d. mudslinging
   e. rub salt in an open wound
   f. pour oil on troubled waters
   g. ne plus ultra
   h. in hot water

2. Explain the difference between the items in each of the following word pairs.

   a. equitable—equable
   b. exalt—exult

3. What is a *savant*? a *pundit*? an *ignoramus*? What do *highbrow* and *lowbrow* mean?

4. What is *privileged information*? Who might *insiders* be?

5. Name a *hot spot* in the world today. What does a *troubleshooter* do?

6. Both *moniker* and *handle* are slang expressions. What do they mean?

7. Define or explain each of the following:

   a. the Puritan work ethic
   b. moral philosophy
   c. the ethos of a people
   d. ethical drugs

8. With what does the science of *ethnology* concern itself? What does an *ethnologist* do?

9. What does the phrase *a pluralistic society* mean? What relationship does it have to *a melting pot*?

10. What is a *paragon*? the *epitome* of gracious living?

11. Define the expression *beau idéal*. From what foreign language does it come?

Exercise VI.   Framing Sentences

A.   Use each of the following words in an original sentence.

1. equanimity
2. equitable
3. envisage
4. ethical
5. epithet
6. esoteric
7. exemplary
8. exigency
9. exacerbate

B.   Give a **noun** form of each of these words, and use it in a short illustrative sentence.

1. entreat   entreaty
2. erudite   erudition
3. entice   enticement
4. ethnic   ethnicity

C. Give an **adjective** form of each of these words, and use it in a short illustrative sentence.

1. exalt   exalted
2. euphemism   euphemistic

233

Dissecting the Words

1. The Latin prefix **e**, **ex**, and its Greek counterpart, **ec**, **ex**, are among the most common word elements used in English. They appear in several words studied in Lessons 14 and 15, including *eclectic, elicit, effete,* and *exalt*.

The primary meanings of *e, ec, ex* are "out (of)" and "away (from)." These meanings occur in the following common English words:

expel (*ex*, "out" + *pel*, "drive")—to drive out

erupt (*e*, "out" + *rupt*, "break")—to break out

eject (*e*, "out" + *ject*, "throw")—to throw out

expire (*ex*, "out" + *spir*, "breathe")—to breathe one's last; to come to an end

efface (*ex*, "out" or "away" + *face*)—to erase; to make indistinct by rubbing

excise (*ex*, "out" or "away" + *cise*, "cut")—to cut out or remove

exegesis (*ex*, "out" + *hegeisthai*, "lead")—a critical explanation, interpretation, or analysis, especially of a part of the Bible

expropriate (*ex*, "away from" + *proprius*, "one's own" + *ate*, "make")—to deprive of what is rightfully one's own, especially for public use

exorcise (*ex*, "away" + *horos*, "oath")—to expel an evil spirit by means of a spell or magical incantation

Note that in some words such as *efface, ex* becomes **ef** before an *f*.

Other meanings of *e, ex* include "up," as in *exalt* ("to lift up") and "completely," as in *efficacious* ("completely capable of producing the desired effect") and *execute* ("to perform completely").

Other common words containing the prefix *e, ec, ex* include *excavation, exhale, emigrate, excerpt* (all from Latin), and *eclipse* (from Greek).

Archaeologists excavating a Native American village on the Snake River in the state of Washington.

2. The formative prefix **en** occurs in several words studied in this lesson, including *envisage* (Word 163). This prefix comes from the Latin word element *in*. It is called *formative* because it serves to transform nouns and adjectives into verbs that take objects. For example, when *en* is prefixed to the noun *courage*, the result is the verb *encourage*, meaning "to inspire with courage." When it is attached to the adjective *noble*, it produces the verb *ennoble*, meaning "to make noble or elevate in dignity."

Note that *en* becomes **em** before the letters *b*, *p*, and sometimes *m*, as in the words *empower* and *emboss*.

Root

The Latin root **fac, fic, fact, fect,** all meaning "do" or "make," appeared in the word *efficacious* (Word 148). This root and its derivatives occur in countless common English words, including:

benefactor—one who does good

facile—easy to do

feat—a great deed

factual—pertaining to facts ("things done"); real

edifice—a building or structure

feasible—capable of being done; workable

facilitate—to help in getting something done

Other common words containing this root and its derivatives are *infect*, *effect*, *affect*, *perfect*, and *confection*.

Suffix

The Latin root *fac, fic, fact, fect* also gives English the suffix **fy**, which appears in such words as *clarify* and *exemplify*. Note that the attachment of *fy* to a root results in a word with a sense of action or performance. For example:

beautify—to make beautiful

amplify—(literally, "make large")—to enlarge

ratify—to make valid

pacify—to make quiet or set at peace

terrify—to make to feel terror

edify—to enlighten

codify—to arrange in a code; to systematize

magnify—to enlarge or increase

deify—to worship or revere as a god

glorify—to exalt, to make more glorious than is actually the case

rectify—to correct

villify—to defame or denigrate

falsify—to misrepresent; to counterfeit

signify—to mean or betoken

Exercise

A. With or without the aid of a dictionary, select the word that best answers the following questions relating to the prefix *e, ec, ex.*

1. Which of the following might be *eclipsed*?

    <u>a. a luminary</u>   b. a contingency   c. an extension

2. Which of the following might be *excised*?

    a. a mendicant   b. an abrogation   <u>c. a paragraph</u>

3. Which of the following might be *eclectic*?

    a. an encomium   <u>b. an anthology</u>   c. an ovation

4. Which of the following might be *effaced* by time?

    a. capitulations   <u>b. recollections</u>   c. denouements

B. With or without the aid of a dictionary, define each of the following words. Then show how the prefix *e, ec, ex* affects its overall meaning.

1. emanate
2. exegesis
3. elicit
4. efficacious
5. exacerbate
6. exalt

C. Attach the formative prefix *en* to each of the following nouns or adjectives, and define the resulting combination. Then choose any **five**, and for each compose a short illustrative sentence.

1. dear
2. shrine
3. feeble
4. crust
5. trap
6. compass
7. circle
8. gulf
9. vision
10. rich
11. throne
12. danger

D. With or without the aid of a dictionary, complete each of the following exercises relating to the root *fac, fic, fact, fect.*

1. Define each of the following English words containing a form of *fac.* Then choose any **five**, and for each compose a short illustrative sentence.

    a. facsimile
    b. edifice
    c. factotum
    d. feasible
    e. facilitate
    f. factor
    g. infection
    h. faction
    i. faculty
    j. feat
    k. benefactor
    l. facile

2. What is the difference in meaning between *affect* and *effect*? Use each in a short illustrative sentence.

3. The expressions *ipso facto* (Latin) and *fait accompli* (French) both stem from the Latin root *fac.* Explain what each means.

E. Form an English verb from each of the following English or Latin words by adding the suffix *fy.* Then define the resulting combination.

1. humid
2. pretty
3. null
4. identity
5. solid
6. person
7. verse
8. magnum ("great")
9. verus ("true")

236

Working with Context Clues

Review the "Working with Context Clues" section in Lesson 14 (page 219) before you begin the following material.

Guideposts to Contrast Clues. Just as some linking expressions act as guideposts to the presence and location of restatement clues in sentence-completion exercises, so other linking expressions signal contrast clues. One such expression, *on the other hand,* was examined in Lesson 14 (page 219). Others include certain conjunctions (e.g., *but, however, though, although, even though, still*), adverbs (e.g., *not, unfortunately*), prepositions (e.g., *despite*), prepositional phrases (e.g., *in spite of*), and similar contrasting expressions (e.g., *some . . . others*).

Each of these items in some way binds together two contrasting or dissimilar sentences or sentence elements. Usually, the clue is contained in one of these contrasting elements, and the blank appears in the other. The linking expression points to the contrast clue by making the reader keenly aware of the difference between the element containing the blank and the element to which it is tied.

Study the following example of a sentence-completion exercise carefully. It contains both a contrast clue and a linking expression that points to this clue.

"A person has to have a strong stomach to work in a funeral parlor or morgue," I observed. "Handling corpses is not a job for the _____."

a. enigmatic   b. squeamish   c. indigent   d. ambitious   e. callous

Read over the two sentences carefully. The first informs you that work in a funeral parlor or morgue requires persons with a certain kind of temperament. The second says that such work is *not* for people with another kind of temperament. You are to specify what the second kind of temperament is by filling in the blank.

Thus, the word *not* in the second sentence indicates that these two sentences present contrasting information. In other words, it is your guidepost to the type of clue that you are likely to find, and that is a contrast clue.

But the word *not* does something else as well. It tells you where to look for your contrast clue. Since the blank is in the same sentence as the word *not*, you are likely to find your clue in the other sentence.

Look at this sentence. It indicates that work in a funeral parlor or morgue is only for people who have strong stomachs. Clearly, the phrase "has to have a strong stomach" is your clue. If work in a funeral parlor or morgue requires people with strong stomachs, then such work is clearly *not* for people who *don't* have strong stomachs. Now you know the sense of the word that goes in the blank. It means, roughly, "without a strong stomach."

Now look at the five items from which you are to select the word that goes in the blank. Only one of them means anything like "without a strong stomach." It is choice *b, squeamish,* which means "easily nauseated, disgusted, or offended" or "overly sensitive." This is clearly the word that goes in the blank.

None of the other choices fits the situation as outlined above. Note, however, choice *e, callous,* which, as you know, means "insensitive"—the opposite of the word you are looking for. It was intentionally included to confuse you and make selecting the right answer more difficult.

Exercise I

The following sentence-completion exercises contain contrast clues and linking expressions that point to these clues. Complete each exercise by selecting the word that makes the best sense in the sentence (or pair of sentences) as a whole. Underline the clue or clues that led you to make your choice.

1. In an angry community, an obvious and massive police presence may _____ tensions and promote violence rather than soothe tempers and restore calm.

   a. curtail   b. consummate   c. defer   d. exacerbate
   e. condone

2. Some laid-off workers manage to keep their spirits up while looking for new jobs; on the other hand, others quickly become _____ after a few disappointing attempts to find employment.

   a. dejected   b. avid   c. hopeful   d. blithe   e. callous

3. A progressive income tax is supposed to be a(n) _____ system of financing government; however, in reality the middle class bears an unfair portion of the tax burden.

   a. efficient   b. equitable   c. productive   d. cogent
   e. concise

4. Good teachers praise their students' honest efforts rather than _____ them for failing to achieve perfection.

   a. cajole   b. abhor   c. censure   d. ignore   e. baffle

5. While receiving unemployment benefits, the unemployed are supposed to be making _____ efforts to find work, but often they are sitting home idle and unmotivated.

   a. chronic   b. attrition   c. equanimity   d. diligent
   e. clandestine

Exercise II

The following exercise reviews everything you have learned about sentence-completion questions and context clues to this point. Complete each item in the exercise by selecting the word that makes the best sense in the sentence (or pair of sentences) as a whole. Underline the clue or clues that led you to your choice.

1. Although scientific research has clearly explained the causes of many diseases, the precise cause of the common cold is still a matter of _____.

   a. conjecture   b. attrition   c. equanimity   d. diligence
   e. exigency

238

2. Journalists often <u>reveal</u> what they have been told off the record, but they refuse to _____ the names of their sources.

   a. delete   <u>b. divulge</u>   c. accede   d. conceal   e. disparage

3. It is easy for a <u>hard-nosed</u> politician to become _____ to the needs of ordinary citizens.

   a. sensitive   b. attuned   <u>c. callous</u>   d. attracted
   e. enslaved

4. The heads of postrevolutionary governments often choose to <u>pardon</u> former enemies in hopes that a policy of _____ will permit all parties to focus on the future.

   <u>a. amnesty</u>   b. revenge   c. trade   d. anger   e. bravado

5. I am <u>blameless</u> in the eyes of the law, <u>but</u> in my own heart, I know I am to some extent _____ in the matter.

   a. affable   b. free   c. tired   d. sick   <u>e. culpable</u>

Enriching the Lesson

Exercise I.   Words Ending in *(o)logy*

One of the items discussed in this lesson was the term *ethnology*. This term contains the element *logy*, which comes from the Greek word *logos*, meaning "word." *Logy* and its related form *ology* have several meanings, one of which is "the study of" or "the science of." This meaning appears in many scientific and philosophical terms used in present-day English. These include *biology*, the study of life, and *etymology*, the study of word origins.

   Listed below are a number of other English words ending in *logy* or *ology*. Some of these words use these elements in their primary sense of "the science (study) of"; others employ them in different meanings. With or without the aid of a dictionary, define each of the words on the list. Then indicate what *logy* or *ology* means in that particular word.

1. ornithology	11. cosmology	21. philology
2. theology	12. penology	22. tautology
3. ecology	13. sociology	23. toxicology
4. physiology	14. astrology	24. ophthalmology
5. terminology	15. pathology	25. entomology
6. archaeology	16. trilogy	26. osteology
7. paleontology	17. geology	27. chronology
8. ontology	18. anthropology	28. tetralogy
9. teleology	19. phraseology	29. parasitology
10. psychology	20. mythology	30. methodology

Exercise II. Euphemisms: Sugarcoating the Pill

If you called your overweight friends *fat*, they would undoubtedly be offended; if you called them *pleasantly plump*, they would probably smile and feel flattered. A discreet person who wishes to be candid and yet not have such frankness cause offense will often find it desirable to substitute a **euphemism** (Word 171) to sugarcoat the harsh facts.

Euphemisms were a fetish in the Victorian era. Propriety then decreed that one should avoid referring to certain parts of the body by their natural or common names. Little Nell might well have swooned at the mention of such "coarse" words as *belly* and *corsets*, or even *legs*. In writing, the epithet *damned* appeared as *d--d*.

The death of Little Nell, the heroine of Charles Dickens's novel *The Old Curiosity Shop* (1841).

Shakespeare's plays were published in bowdlerized editions, purged of words deemed to be obscene or unrefined and thus objectionable. Understandably, the adjective *Victorian* has become synonymous with prudishness and exaggerated genteelism.

Although we are much less likely than the Victorians to be squeamish about such matters, we are still given to verbal evasions of reality. For example, a clerical assistant in an office may try to enhance his job by calling himself a "junior executive."

This "word game" has spread into many other areas. Since the existence of poverty in our society is an unwelcome fact, we may choose to refer to poor people as "disadvantaged," or "underprivileged," or "in the lower-income brackets." Elderly people are "senior citizens." Charity has become "welfare assistance." A mistake in spelling may be presented as an "orthographic irregularity."

Governmental officials and military leaders are certainly not beyond retreating into euphemisms. A breakdown in services resulting from inefficiency has been called an "organizational disruption." A military retreat after a crushing defeat may be termed a "rearrangement of forces."

At this point, a word of warning is in order. Although we may laugh at such flabby and sometimes dishonest evasions of reality, we should also realize that there *are* occasions when euphemisms and genteelisms can serve a useful purpose. They may be used to spare the feelings of people under severe strain or to soften harsh or gross realities which for some reason we are not prepared to face at a given time. Certainly, no harm is done if euphemisms are used selectively and with good judgment under such circumstances to raise the level of courtesy and consideration for others. But the key word is *selectively*. If we use euphemisms indiscriminately in place of plain, homely words, our language may become at best overrefined and at worst obscure and even ludicrous.

A. Below are two lists of corresponding words or expressions. Those in Column A are "Euphemistic or Genteel"; in Column B, "Realistic or Natural." In what context or under what circumstances might each of these expressions be appropriately used? Give examples of such usage.

Column A *Euphemistic or Genteel*	Column B *Realistic or Natural*
perspire	sweat
odor	smell
expectorate	spit
cinema	movies
financially embarrassed	broke
exaggerate	lie
boutique	shop
retire for the night	go to bed
deceased	dead

B. Each of the following expressions is sometimes used euphemistically as a substitute for a more familiar, down-to-earth term. Give a blunt equivalent in each case.

1. mortician
2. protective custody
3. hair supplementation
4. billiard academy
5. gratuity
6. cocktail lounge
7. termination of employment
8. tonsorial parlor
9. weight control
10. pugilistic encounter

Exercise III.   Expanding Your Word Power

The words listed below are not on the Basic Word List, but they were mentioned in passing in Lesson 15. All of them would make useful additions to your working vocabulary. Define each, give its etymology, list **two** synonyms and **two** antonyms (where possible), and use in a short illustrative sentence.

1. inveigle
2. repel
3. importune
4. envision
5. designation
6. stability
7. literate
8. composure
9. confidential
10. allay
11. cryptic
12. crisis
13. abase
14. commendable
15. hysteria

Lesson 16

176. exodus — 190. fetish

---

176. ex-o-dus   *noun*   ĕk'-sə-dəs

[*exodos* (Greek), "a going out"; from *ex* (Greek), "out" + *hodos* (Greek), "road, way"]

Definition: A departure, usually of large numbers of people.

The massacre in Burundi in 1994 was the main cause of the hurried **exodus** of population from that African nation.

Large-scale building projects are likely to cause the **exodus** of wildlife from a previously undeveloped area.

Synonyms: (*nouns*) flight, escape, migration, emigration, hegira

Antonyms: (*nouns*) arrival, influx, immigration

Moses, by Michelangelo

Flight Words

In both Latin and English, the second book of the Old Testament of the Bible is called Exodus. It recounts the departure of the Israelites (under the leadership of Moses) from Egypt during the time of the pharaohs, about 1260 B.C. The word *exodus* is actually Greek in origin, but the title of the Old Testament book helped it come into English. This is just one of the ways in which the Bible has influenced the growth of our vocabulary. Refer to page 204 for other examples.

In Arabic, the prophet Mohammed's departure from Mecca in A.D. 622 is called "Al Hijrat," which means "The Flight." The event is important in the Muslim world because it is regarded as the beginning of the Muslim era. It has importance in the English-speaking world as well. That is because it gave modern English a new word for "flight" or "exodus." The word is **hegira**, which is pronounced hǐ-jī'-rə or hěj'ər-ə.

177. ex·o·tic   *adjective*   ĕg-zŏt'-ĭk

[*exotikos* (Greek), "foreign"; from *exo* (Greek), "outside"]

Definition: Foreign; charmingly unfamiliar or strikingly unusual.

"Australia is a fascinating continent full of strange and **exotic** wildlife," my Canadian friend remarked.

Phrases: an exotic plant, exotic foods

Synonyms: (*adjectives*) alien; striking, extraordinary

Antonyms: (*adjectives*) native, indigenous, endemic; commonplace, familiar, ordinary

178. ex·pe·di·ent   *adjective and noun*   ĕk-spē'-dē-ĕnt

[*expediens, expedientis*, "freeing, disentangling"; from *ex* (Latin), "out of" + *pes, pedis* (Latin), "foot"]

Definition:

   a.   (*adjective*) Advantageous to one's interest or purpose.

      "In solving this problem, we cannot simply do whatever is **expedient**," I protested. "We must make sure that the course of action we adopt is also ethical."

   b.   (*noun*) An emergency course of action; a means to an end.

      "We can overcome our present financial problems in a number of ways," the personnel manager remarked. "Cutting back on the staff is by no means the only **expedient** open to us."

Related Forms: (*noun*) expediency; (*adjective*) inexpedient

Synonyms: (*adjectives*) convenient, opportune, timely, practical; (*nouns*) device, scheme, design, stratagem, maneuver, stopgap

Antonyms: (*adjectives*) disadvantageous, unserviceable, unsuitable

179. ex·ploit   *verb:* ĕk-sploit'   *noun:* ĕk'-sploit

[*exploit, explait* (Old French), "achievement"; from *ex* (Latin), "out" + *plicare* (Latin), "fold"]

Definition:

   a.   (*verb*) To use to the greatest possible advantage, often selfishly.

      Working conditions have come a long way since the "bad old days," when it was customary to **exploit** the labor of children.

   b.   (*noun*) A brilliant or heroic deed.

      Because he took such pride in his wartime **exploits**, we thought it fitting to bury my grandfather in his army uniform.

Related Forms: (*nouns*) exploitation, exploiter; (*adjective*) exploitable

Synonyms: (*verbs*) capitalize on; (*nouns*) feat, heroics, coup, tour de force, derring-do

Related Phrases: cash in on, make the most of, take advantage of

180. **ex·pound**   *verb*   ĕk-spound' *or* ĭk-spound'

[*espo(u)ndre* (Old French), "put forth"; from *ex* (Latin), "out" + *ponere* (Latin), "put, place"]

Definition: To explain in detail.

In an influential book published in 1936, the English economist J. M. Keynes **expounded** his epoch-making theory of the causes of economic collapse.

I spent most of the evening listening to her **expound** her views on all sorts of interesting topics.

Related Forms: (*nouns*) exposition, exponent; (*adjective*) expository

Synonyms: (*verbs*) clarify, elucidate, explicate, delineate (Word 121)

Antonyms: (*verbs*) summarize, abstract, synopsize

Related Phrases: air one's views, in a nutshell, a thumbnail sketch

Exposition and Expository Writing,

Basically, the word *exposition* refers to the setting forth of meaning or intent in a clear and intelligible way. Nonetheless, the word has several technical usages that are worth knowing about. For example, to musicians, *exposition* indicates the opening section of a sonata or fugue, where the various musical themes that will be developed are first introduced. To dramatists, the word indicates the part of a play where the chief characters and overall theme are first presented. And to producers of public entertainments, it indicates a public exhibition of recent artistic or industrial developments.

Expository writing is the technical term for the kind of writing that is designed to set forth ideas or describe people and events in straightforward intelligible English. This is essentially the kind of writing that is necessary in all sorts of everyday situations. For example, a book review, a newspaper article, a business letter, and a chapter in a textbook all involve expository writing of one kind or another. Students, of course, are familiar with expository writing from the compositions, reports, and term papers that they do for school courses.

181. **fab·ri·cate**   *verb*   făb'-rĭ-kāt

[*fabricari, fabricatus* (Latin), "make, build"]

Definition:

   a.   To assemble or construct from separate parts.

      Philosophers have been **fabricating** new theories of the universe for thousands of years.

   b.   To make up with the intention of deceiving.

      "I don't believe that your account of the incident has any basis in fact," Mom said. "I think you **fabricated** it in order to avoid my displeasure."

Related Forms: (*nouns*) fabrication, fabricator; (*verb*) prefabricate

244

Prefabricate refers to a manufacturing process in which standardized parts or sections are mass-produced for shipment and assembly elsewhere. Thus, a prefabricated house is constructed out of ready-made sections that were manufactured in another place.

Synonyms: (*verbs*) produce, devise, manufacture, concoct, contrive, come up with, cook up

Related Phrases: a trumped-up charge; coin an excuse; make up out of whole cloth

182. fa-ce-tious   *adjective*   fə-sē'-shəs
[*facetieux* (Old French), "joking"; from *facetia* (Latin), "joke, jest"]

Definition: Not meant seriously; playful or humorous.

"Be careful what you say to him," I warned my sister. "He is so sensitive that he takes even a **facetious** remark to heart."

I didn't pay any attention to what he said because I could see that he was being **facetious**.

Related Forms: (*noun*) facetiousness; (*adverb*) facetiously

Synonyms: (*adjectives*) waggish, whimsical, joking, comic, frivolous, droll

Antonyms: (*adjectives*) serious, grave, solemn, sober, earnest, humorless

Related Phrases: a tongue-in-cheek remark, joshing, kidding; for real

183. fac-sim-i-le   *noun and adjective*   făk-sĭm'-ə-lē

[*fac simile* (Latin), "make (it) the same"; from *facere* (Latin), "do, make" + *similis, simile* (Latin), "same"]

Definition:

   a.   (*noun*) An exact copy.

Art books often contain surprisingly accurate full-color **facsimiles** of the paintings they discuss.

   b.   (*adjective*) Reproduced exactly.

Usually, a photocopy is in every respect a **facsimile** copy of the original from which it was made.

Synonyms: (*nouns*) replica, reproduction, duplicate

Related Phrases: a carbon copy, a chip off the old block; a mirror image

184. fal-la-cy   *noun*   făl'-ə-sē

[*fallacia* (Latin), "deceit, trick"; from *fallere* (Latin), "deceive"]

Definition:

   a.   Faulty reasoning; an error in logic.

"It shouldn't be too hard to shoot holes in his argument," I observed. "After all, the **fallacies** it contains are as plain as day."

   b.   A false or mistaken notion.

It's a **fallacy** to assume that all redheaded people have quick tempers.

Related Forms: (*adjective*) fallacious; (*noun*) fallaciousness

Synonyms: (*nouns*) mistake, flaw, fault, defect (Word 117), solecism

185. fath-om   *noun and verb*   făth'-əm

[*faethm* (Old English), "the distance between two outstretched arms"]

Definition:

   a.   (*noun*) A unit of length roughly equal to six feet and used primarily in the measurement of marine depths.

It might be difficult to raise a famous wreck like the *Titanic* because its remains lie under hundreds of **fathoms** of water.

   b.   (*verb*) To get to the bottom of; to understand.

For as long as human beings have been able to think, they have attempted to **fathom** the mysteries of the universe.

Related Forms: (*adjectives*) fathomable, unfathomable, fathomless

Synonyms: (*verbs*) sound, plumb, probe, delve, penetrate; ferret out, root out; divine, grasp, comprehend

246

186. fat·u·ous   *adjective*   făch'-ōō-wəs

[*fatuus* (Latin), "silly, foolish"]

Definition: Unconsciously foolish, stupid, or absurd.

It was such a **fatuous** remark that I almost burst out laughing when I heard it.

Phrases: a fatuous expression on one's face, a fatuous monarch

Related Forms: (*nouns*) fatuousness, fatuity

Synonyms: (*adjectives*) inane, vacuous, vapid, nonsensical, laughable, silly, ridiculous, ludicrous; wacky, goofy

Antonyms: (*adjectives*) sensible, intelligent, perceptive; acute, incisive; judicious

187. fea·si·ble   *adjective*   fē'-zə-bəl

[*faisible* (Old French), "workable"; from *facere* (Latin), "do, make"]

Definition: Possible; both doable and workable.

"I would really like to invite everyone I know to my party," LeVar remarked. "Unfortunately, that idea just isn't **feasible** because my home is too small to hold all my friends."

Phrases: a feasible solution, a feasible plan, a feasible proposal

Related Forms: (*adjective*) unfeasible; (*nouns*) feasibility; feasibleness

Synonyms: (*adjectives*) practicable, practical, usable, realistic

Antonyms: (*adjectives*) impossible, unworkable, impracticable, impractical

Related Phrases: within the realm of possibility, out of the question

A Useful Distinction

Practicable indicates that something is capable of being done. *Practical* indicates that it is not only capable of being done but also sensible or worthwhile. Thus, it may be practicable to travel to and from the office by pogo stick, but the idea certainly doesn't sound practical.

Fetish

A *fetish* is an inanimate object that is believed to possess magical powers of some sort. Fetishes may be natural objects (for instance, an unusual stone) or man-made items (for example, a small carved image). Many peoples, both ancient and modern, have employed fetishes; and items thought to be fetishes of one kind or another have been found in prehistoric grave sites in many parts of the world. The use of fetishes is still fairly widespread today. Do you know someone who possesses a lucky rabbit's foot?

A group of Native American fetishes.

188. feign   *verb*   fān

[*feindre* (Old French), "pretend"; from *fingere* (Latin), "shape, form"]

Definition: To pretend or give a false appearance of.

"He wasn't really sick," I said. "He just **feigned** illness in order to get out of school early."

Phrases: feign sleep, feign authorship of, feign knowledge of

Related Forms: (*adjective*) feigned; (*noun*) feint

Synonyms: (*verbs*) fake, sham, simulate

Related Phrases: sail under false colors, pass oneself off as, pose as; a wolf in sheep's clothing, a humbug, an ignis fatuus; the real McCoy

189. fe-lic-i-tous   *adjective*   fĭ-lĭs′-ĭ-təs *or* fə-lĭs′-ə-təs

[*felicity* + *ous*; from *felicitas* (Latin), "happiness"; from *felix, felicis* (Latin), "happy"]

Definition: Agreeably suited to the purpose or occasion; aptly or gracefully expressed.

"I know you don't consider yourself much of a diplomat," Mom told me. "Still, I think you handled that very delicate problem in a truly **felicitous** manner."

"Perhaps the phrasing of your letter isn't particularly **felicitous**," I said, "but the sentiments you express are indeed appropriate."

Related Forms: (*nouns*) felicity, felicitousness; (*adverb*) felicitously; (*verb*) felicitate

Synonyms: (*adjectives*) appropriate, suitable, fitting, apropos, apposite, apt; graceful, agreeable, seemly, becoming; well chosen, well put

Antonyms: (*adjectives*) graceless, unseemly, unbecoming, unsuitable; awkward, inept

Related Phrases: to the point, on target, ad rem; wide of the mark

190. fet-ish   *noun*   fĕt'-ĭsh   *or*   fē'-tĭsh

[*feitiço* (Portuguese), "charm"; from *facere, factus* (Latin), "do, make"]

Definition:
- a.   An object believed among primitive peoples to have magical powers.

  Down in the main square, a wrinkled old peasant woman sold charms and **fetishes** to ward off the evil eye.

- b.   An object of unreasonably excessive attention or reverence.

  It is one thing to be concerned about discipline; it is quite another to make a **fetish** of it.

Synonyms: (*nouns*) charm, amulet, talisman; fixation, obsession (Word 283), preoccupation; compulsion

Related Phrases: an idée fixe; a hang-up; get a complex about; a monomaniac; a sacred cow

Using the Words

Exercise I.   Parts of Speech

Indicate the part of speech of each of the following words. In some cases, two answers are correct.

1. exotic   adj.
2. facsimile   n., adj.
3. expound   v.
4. exploit   n., v.
5. expedient   n., adj.
6. fabricate   v.
7. fathom   n., v.
8. exodus   n.
9. feasible   adj.

Exercise II.   Words in Phrases

In each of the following groups select the item that best expresses the meaning of the *italicized* word in the introductory phrase.

1. *feign* illness
   a. cure   b. prevent   c. investigate   <u>d. pretend</u>   e. cause

2. *fatuous* comments
   a. perceptive   b. interesting   <u>c. silly</u>   d. appropriate
   e. surprising

3. a *felicitous* remark
   a. well-known   b. well-worn   c. well-heeled   d. well-fed
   <u>e. well-chosen</u>

4. *exotic* dishes
   <u>a. delightfully unfamiliar</u>   b. outrageously expensive
   c. unusually sweet   d. woefully inadequate
   e. moderately priced

5. will do whatever is *expedient*

    a. fashionable   b. advantageous   c. easy   d. enjoyable
    e. correct

6. *expound* a theory

    a. attack   b. demolish   c. improve   d. investigate
    e. explain

7. *facsimile* copies of the document

    a. secondhand   b. forged   c. newly discovered   d. exact
    e. famous

Exercise III.   Completing Sentences

Complete each of the following sentences or pairs of sentences by selecting the most appropriate word from the group of words given below. Use each word only once. Make any adjustments that are necessary to fit the words into the sentences properly.

fallacy	fabricate	feasible
fathom	facetious	feign
exodus	exploit	fetish

1. "He is not interested in solving this problem quickly and intelligently," I said. "He is only interested in __exploiting__ the difficulties it has created to his own advantage."

2. "Let's get out of here," Sy said after we'd been in the museum only ten minutes. "All these strange idols and __fetishes__ give me the creeps!"

3. In *The Art of the Possible,* Golda Meir suggests that politics and diplomacy have one thing in common. They are both concerned with what is __feasible__ rather than with what is ideal.

4. Fortunately, we were able to __fabricate__ a replacement for the missing article from a few short press releases and some government statistics.

5. "I've puzzled about it for days," Mom told Dad, "but I still can't __fathom__ the motives behind young Tom's strange behavior lately."

6. The blatant anti-Semitism of the Nazi regime was wholly responsible for the tremendous __exodus__ of Jews from Germany in the 1930s.

7. "Your conclusion isn't valid," I remarked, "because the argument leading up to it contains an obvious __fallacy__ ."

8. "This is a serious conversation," Jane protested. "Why do you insist on disrupting it by constantly making __facetious__ remarks?"

Exercise IV.   Synonyms and Antonyms

A. In each of the following groups, select the two words that are most nearly **synonyms**.

1. a. overwhelm   b. clarify   c. imagine   d. elucidate
    e. manufacture   expound

2. a. devise   b. escape   c. concoct   d. stumble
    e. pretend   fabricate

3. a. solution   b. duplicate   c. salary   d. problem
    e. copy   facsimile

4. a. charm   b. hobby   c. guilt   d. profession   e. amulet   fetish

5. a. migrate   b. understand   c. comprehend   d. create
    e. summarize   fathom

   Now, for each pair of synonyms, supply a word from the Basic Word List for this lesson (Words 176–190) that means the **same** or **almost the same** thing.

B. In each of the following, select the item that is most nearly **opposite** in meaning to the numbered word at the left.

1. fatuous   a. honest   b. brave   c. intelligent
                  d. wealthy   e. famous

2. feasible   a. unworkable   b. unknown   c. unseen
                  d. unfaithful   e. unavoidable

3. facetious   a. awkward   b. usable   c. ridiculous
                  d. commonplace   e. serious

4. exodus   a. scheme   b. arrival   c. flaw   d. lie
                  e. copy

5. exotic   a. convenient   b. sensible   c. mistaken
                  d. native   e. comic

Exercise V.   Word Roundup

1. Explain the difference between the words in each of the following pairs.
    a. feint—faint   b. practical—practicable

2. What is a *hegira*? From what foreign language does the word come, and to what historical event did it originally refer?

3. Define each of the following words.
    a. solecism   c. humbug   e. monomaniac
    b. coup   d. heroics   f. exposition

4. Explain the meaning of each of the following colorful phrases.
    a. in a nutshell   d. a carbon copy
    b. a tongue-in-cheek remark   e. a tour de force
    c. deeds of derring-do   f. an idée fixe

Exercise VI.   Framing Sentences

A. Use each of the following words in an original sentence that clearly illustrates its meaning.

1. exodus
2. exotic
3. expedient
4. exploit
5. expound
6. facsimile
7. fatuous
8. felicitous
9. fetish

B. Give an **adjective** form of each of these words, and use it in an original sentence.

1. fallacy *fallacious* 2. feign *feigned* 3. fathom *unfathomable, fathomless*

C. Give a **noun** form of each of these words, and use it in an original sentence.

1. feasible
   feasibility,
   feasibleness
2. fabricate
   fabrication,
   fabricator
3. facetious
   facetiousness

Completing Verbal Analogies

"A Is Primarily Concerned with B.*"* Another word relationship that frequently appears in the analogy sections of standardized vocabulary tests is "A is primarily concerned with B; C is primarily concerned with D." Here is an example of an analogy question involving this relationship. Try to determine the correct answer before you go on to read the explanation of it.

veterinarian : animals =
   a. druggist : addicts
   b. psychology : mind
   c. disputes : arbitrator
   d. warden : prisoners
   e. theologian : angels

The answer is *d*. A *warden* is primarily concerned with *prisoners*, just as a *veterinarian* is primarily concerned with *animals.*
   None of the other choices exhibits the same relationship as the key pair of words. A *druggist* is not primarily concerned with *addicts* (choice *a*), nor is a *theologian* primarily concerned with *angels* (choice *e*). Though an *arbitrator* is certainly concerned with *disputes* (choice *c*), *disputes* are not concerned with *arbitrators*. In other words, the two items in the pair come in the wrong order. Finally, *psychology* is indeed concerned with the *mind* (choice *b*), but the items in the pair are not parallel to the items in the key pair. *Psychology* indicates a science, not a person (as *veterinarian* does), and *mind* indicates a human faculty, not a type of creature (as *animals* does). Both choices *b* and *c* were intentionally included to confuse the student and make the selection of the right answer more difficult.

"A Is a Part of B.*"* Another word relationship that appears in the analogy sections of standardized tests is "A is a part of B; C is a part of D." Here is an example of an analogy question involving this relationship. Try to determine the correct answer before you read the explanation of it.

rung : ladder =
   a. cauldron : kettle
   b. saddle : stirrup
   c. apartment : room
   d. match : lighter
   e. step : staircase

The answer is *e*. A *step* is part of a *staircase*, just as a *rung* is part of a *ladder*.

None of the other choices exhibits the same relationship. A *cauldron* is not part of a *kettle* (choice *a*); it is a kind of kettle. In other words, the two words mean roughly the same thing. A *saddle* is not part of a *stirrup* (choice *b*), though a stirrup is part of a saddle. Similarly, an apartment is not part of a *room* (choice *c*), though a room is part of an apartment or may even be an apartment. In other words, the items in choices *b* and *c* come in the wrong order. Finally, a *match* is not part of a *lighter* (choice *d*), though it serves the same function as a lighter. In other words, these items are complementary, since they indicate two different ways of producing a flame.

Parallelism. In the explanation of the example under "A is primarily concerned with B," it was pointed out that the items in the answer you select should always be as parallel as possible to the items in the key pair. If they are not, you have probably made the wrong choice and should reconsider your answer.

Exercise I

Complete each of the following analogies based on the word relationships "*A* is primarily concerned with *B*" and "*A* is a part of *B*."

1. **chapter : novel** =
   a. pen : pencil
   b. dictionary : word
   c. essay : composition
   d. act : drama
   e. paragraph : sentence

2. **dentist : teeth** =
   a. ornithologist : ears
   b. surgeon : bruises
   c. ophthalmologist : eyes
   d. feet : chiropodist
   e. pharmacy : medicine

3. **deck : ship** =
   a. church : pew
   b. field : meadow
   c. chair : table
   d. bookcase : shelf
   e. floor : house

4. **legislator : lawmaking** =
   a. lawfulness : judge
   b. citizen : law-abiding
   c. criminal : lawbreaker
   d. lawsuit : attorney
   e. police officer : law enforcement

5. **astronomy : stars** =
   a. archaeologist : antiquities
   b. zoology : animals
   c. archery : buildings
   d. philatelist : coins
   e. insects : entomology

6. **county : state** =
   a. tree : forest
   b. hive : bee
   c. voyage : trip
   d. continent : peninsula
   e. mare : stallion

Exercise II.   Answers will vary.

Compose **two** complete analogies involving the word relationship "*A* is primarily concerned with *B*" and **two** involving "*A* is a part of *B*."

Exercise III

The following items review what you have so far learned about analogy questions. Complete each.

1. **augment : increase** :: horrify :
   (*arbitrate, appall, condone, atone, deviate*)

2. **circuitous : direct** :: skimpy :
   (*culpable, scant, devoid, copious, deferential*)

3. **failure : chagrin** :: success :
   (*disgust, puzzlement, elation, apathy, frustration*)

4. **cantankerous : affability** :: disgruntled :
   (*ability, wisdom, courage, honesty, contentment*)

5. **like : adore** :: dislike :
   (*loathe, lithe, lathe, loath, lath*)

Working with Context Clues

Inference Clues. The third general type of context clue you are likely to meet in the sentence-completion sections of standardized vocabulary tests is an **inference clue**. In an inference clue, the whole situation outlined in the sentence or pair of sentences suggests the sense of the word that goes in the blank. For that reason, the reader must *infer* the word that is wanted, often by recognizing familiar situations, drawing on past knowledge and experience, or applying simple logic. As you can see, an inference clue is a broader and more indirect type of hint than a restatement clue or a contrast clue.

Here is an example of a sentence-completion exercise that involves an inference clue. Try to determine the correct answer before you read the explanation of it given below.

Ninety-year-old Annie Blakeley's *The Lowing Herd Winds Slowly O'er the Lea* presents the reader with a touching picture of life in _____ Kansas at the turn of the 20th century.

a. industrialized   b. rural   c. maritime   d. urban   e. colonial

The answer is *b. rural.* Here's why.

The position of the blank indicates that you are looking for a descriptive adjective. A quick check of the five choices you are offered confirms this impression. Now you know what you need.

But you know something else as well. The blank appears immediately before the word *Kansas.* This suggests that Kansas will be of some value in determining the word that goes in the blank.

Now read the entire sentence carefully to determine what else it offers in the way of clues to the correct choice. The sentence concerns the content of a novel or memoir by a woman who grew up in Kansas around 1900. This suggests that the title of the book will be of some help in ascertaining the correct choice. The sentence also suggests that the part of the country mentioned (Kansas) and the time frame indicated (at the turn of the 20th century) may be of some use.

Now you know where the clues are likely to be. Notice that an understanding of the sense of the sentence and the application of simple logic were the governing factors in isolating the probable clues.

Reread the title of the 90-year-old woman's book carefully. It evokes a picture that immediately eliminates three of the five choices as the correct answer.

And what is that picture? It is a picture of a herd of cows moving slowly through a meadow. *Low* means the same thing as *moo*, so you know you are dealing with a herd of cows. *Lea* is an old poetic word for *meadow*.

Now, in what sort of setting would you be likely to find a herd of cows crossing a meadow? Certainly not in an *industrialized* area (choice *a*) or an *urban* center (choice *d*) or even a *maritime* community (choice *c*). These three items are clearly wrong, and you are down to two possibilities because cows would be found in both a *rural* and a *colonial* setting (choices *b* and *e*).

To determine which of the two remaining possibilities is correct, think about each in regard to the part of the country mentioned (Kansas) and the time frame indicated (around 1900). Kansas was primarily an agricultural area at the turn of the century, so *rural* (choice *b*) seems to fit. However, Kansas was never one of the 13 colonies and by 1900 had long since become a full-fledged member of the Union. Clearly, *colonial* (choice *e*) won't work, so *rural* (choice *b*) must be the correct answer. And, of course, it is.

Notice that determining the correct answer to this sentence-completion exercise depended on a combination of utilizing the whole context, recognizing familiar situations, drawing on past knowledge, and applying simple logic. These are essentially the ingredients that go into the successful solution of the type of sentence-completion exercise that involves an inference clue.

Exercise I

The following sentence-completion exercises contain inference clues. Complete each by selecting the word that makes the best sense in the sentence (or pair of sentences) as a whole. Underline the clue or clues that led you to make your choice.

1. *Sanitary engineer* is an example of a(n) _____ for *janitor* or *garbage collector*.

   a. euphemism   b. criterion   c. qualification   d. epithet
   e. advertisement

2. As my polite request failed to _____ any response from my noisy neighbors, I decided to call the police.

   a. abet   b. buttress   c. curtail   d. stop   e. elicit

3. Self-help groups such as Narcotics Anonymous try to help people overcome their _____ to drugs.

   a. sensitivity   b. fetish   c. addiction   d. revulsion
   e. anathema

4. Only a truly _____ person could forgive a friend who deliberately spread lies about him and tried to ruin his reputation.

   a. benign   b. boisterous   c. felicitous   d. fatuous
   e. callous

5. Public officials who routinely tell half-truths to their constituents destroy their own _____.

   a. anachronism   b. equanimity   c. credibility   d. duplicity
   e. fallacy

Exercise II

The following exercises review everything you have learned about sentence-completion questions and context clues to this point. Complete each item in the exercise by selecting the word that makes the best sense in the sentence (or pair of sentences) as a whole. Underline the clue or clues that led you to make your choice.

1. Whenever I am in a lighthearted and carefree frame of mind, I find myself humming a _____ tune.

   a. banal   b. boisterous   c. blithe   d. belligerent
   e. bizarre

2. Many people cannot speak well before a large audience, but they can be surprisingly _____ when speaking in small, informal settings.

   a. effete   b. bland   c. elite   d. concise   e. articulate

3. Writers often complain that editors <u>cut out</u> important sections of their manuscripts without asking their permission to _____ the material.

   a. allude   <u>b. delete</u>   c. review   d. defer   e. deviate

4. In most corporations, you have to <u>work hard</u> to get ahead. Advancement goes to those who are most _____.

   a. efficacious   b. affable   <u>c. diligent</u>   d. erudite   e. candid

5. The corporate president observed that <u>although</u> the financial officer's proposal would <u>reduce</u> some of the company's cash-flow problems, <u>unfortunately</u> it would also _____ others.

   <u>a. exacerbate</u>   b. circumvent   c. entice   d. atrophy   e. delineate

Enriching the Lesson

Exercise I   Loan Words from Faraway Places

The inclusion of the word *exotic* in this lesson brings to mind the fact that some of the vocabulary of present-day English comes from very striking and unusual sources. Listed below are a number of these unusual loan words. With or without the aid of a dictionary, define each and tell where it comes from. Then choose any **five**, and for each compose an original sentence.

1. kowtow	8. taboo	15. juggernaut
2. amuck	9. loot	16. paradise
3. tycoon	10. mogul	17. mumbo jumbo
4. powwow	11. tariff	18. mufti
5. zombie	12. pariah	19. voodoo
6. thug	13. totem	20. nadir
7. boomerang	14. caucus	21. oasis

Exercise II.   The Language of Logic

One of the words studied in this lesson is *fallacy*, which is a technical term in the language of logic. Below are listed some other words and expressions used in the study of logic. With or without the aid of a dictionary, define each.

1. logic	6. induction
2. syllogism	7. deduction
3. major premise	8. valid
4. minor premise	9. invalid
5. conclusion	10. pathetic fallacy

Exercise III. "Diehards"

This lesson includes the word *fathom*, which might be termed a "diehard" in the sense that it goes back, practically without change, to Old English. Old English, you will recall, represents the earliest stage of our language. It was used in England in the period before the Norman Conquest of 1066.

Diehards such as *fathom* make up an important and sizable segment of the vocabulary of present-day English. A few examples of other diehard expressions are listed below. With or without the aid of a dictionary, define each.

1. mirth	6. threat	11. quench
2. seethe	7. spurn	12. forbear
3. din	8. fret	13. mood
4. slough	9. mete (*verb*)	14. beckon
5. quell	10. swarthy	15. hurdle

Exercise IV. The Language of the Mind

Fetish, studied in this lesson, is frequently used in connection with psychology, which is the science that deals with the workings of the mind and with human behavior. The 20th century witnessed major developments in the science of psychology, and for many years there has been great popular interest in it. As a result, many psychological terms have become part of everyday speech and writing.

Listed below are a number of terms and expressions drawn from the language of psychology. With or without the aid of a dictionary, define each.

1. neurotic	6. split personality	11. introvert
2. psychosomatic	7. maladjustment	12. extrovert
3. paranoid	8. psychic	13. schizophrenic
4. subconscious	9. complex	14. hypochondriac
5. extrasensory	10. psychotic	15. burnout

Exercise V. Expanding Your Word Power

The words listed below are not on the Basic Word List, but they were mentioned in passing in Lesson 16. All of them would make useful additions to your working vocabulary. Define each, give its etymology, list **two** synonyms and **two** antonyms (where possible), and use in a short illustrative sentence.

1. influx	6. synopsis	11. replica
2. preoccupation	7. explicate	12. solecism
3. stratagem	8. devise	13. delve
4. talisman	9. earnest	14. simulate
5. feat	10. whimsical	15. apposite

Related Forms in Context

Beneath each sentence below are four words introduced in Lesson 15 or 16. Review the related forms for these words, and choose the one that best completes the sentence. Write that related form in the space provided.

1. For the most part Britain ignored the colonists' urgent _entreaties_ that they should not be taxed without being represented in Parliament.

   a. entice   b. exacerbate   c. entreat   d. exploit

2. The popular mystery novels of Dorothy L. Sayers display both the author's wit and her great _erudition_.

   a. erudite   b. ethical   c. feasible   d. felicity

3. Homer's long narrative poem *The Iliad*, which recounts the deeds of heroes during the Trojan War, is a perfect _exemplar_ of the classical epic.

   a. equitable   b. ethical   c. expedient   d. exemplary

4. An ad hominem argument is a type of _fallacious_ reasoning that attacks an opponent's character and motives rather than debating the issue being discussed.

   a. fathom   b. fallacy   c. exigency   d. euphemism

5. Our Youth Center held a festival to celebrate the different _ethnicities_ that make up our community.

   a. esoteric   b. ethnic   c. equitable   d. felicitous

6. Broken treaties and forcible relocations led to the _exacerbation_ of relations between Native American tribes and the Bureau of Indian Affairs.

   a. entreat   b. exalt   c. fabricate   d. exacerbate

7. In order to lead a predator away from her vulnerable chicks, a mother bird may display a _feigned_ injury such as a broken wing.

   a. entice   b. feign   c. envisage   d. expound

8. Thanks to the Hubble telescope, some of the mysteries of deep space are proving to be _fathomable_ at last.

   a. fathom   b. euphemism   c. exigency   d. fallacy

9. The leaves of the Venus's-flytrap give off a sweet-smelling nectar that acts as an _enticement_ to insects to enter the plant's deadly trap.

   a. entreat   b. exalt   c. exploit   d. entice

10. The movement to pass federal child labor laws, designed to prevent the _exploitation_ of youngsters working in factories and mines, culminated in the passage of the Fair Labor Standards Act of 1938.

    a. exalt   b. exploit   c. expound   d. fabricate

11. Government and relief agencies agreed on the _expediency_ of airlifting emergency supplies, personnel, and equipment to the villages that were buried by mudslides.

    a. fallacy   b. euphemism   c. expedient   d. equanimity

12. College applications usually require students to provide a sample of _expository_ or persuasive writing in response to a writing prompt.

    a. expound   b. exploit   c. entice   d. feign

13. The _exaltation_ of a commoner to the rank of lifetime peer is the prerogative of the British monarch.

    a. fabricate   b. entice   c. exacerbate   d. exalt

14. Instead of using the word _die_, many people prefer _euphemistic_ terms and expressions such as "pass away" or "expire."

    a. epithet   b. euphemism   c. expedient   d. fallacy

15. The state's Department of Environmental Protection and county engineers published a detailed report on the _feasibility_ of restoring eroded beaches.

    a. fatuous   b. esoteric   c. ethnic   d. feasible

16. At the end of Shakespeare's comedy _Much Ado About Nothing_, two young couples are reunited and their friends and relatives rejoice in their _felicity_.

    a. feasible   b. fatuous   c. facsimile   d. felicitous

17. Your local Better Business Bureau can tell you if the contractor you want to hire has been accused of _unethical_ practices.

    a. ethnic   b. ethical   c. exemplary   d. esoteric

18. Some scholars write very _esoterically_ for a rarefied group of academic peers rather than for a wide audience.

    a. esoteric   b. erudite   c. felicitous   d. facetious

19. Here's an example of Mark Twain's wry _facetiousness_: "Always do right. This will gratify some people, and astonish the rest."

    a. ethical   b. exotic   c. feasible   d. facetious

20. Through relentless cross-examination, the prosecution exposed the defendant's alibi as nothing more than a very clever _fabrication_.

    a. exploit   b. exalt   c. fabricate   d. feign

Lesson 17

191. fiasco — 205. futile

---

191. **fi-as-co**   *noun*   fē-ăs′-kō
[*fiasco* (Italian), "flask; failure"]

Definition: A complete failure.

In no time at all, poor management turned what should have been a surefire success into a **fiasco**.

Synonyms: (*nouns*) disaster, debacle, mess, bomb, flop

Antonyms: (*nouns*) triumph, success, hit

Related Phrases: go over like a lead balloon, a flash in the pan; a feather in one's cap, come off with flying colors

---

192. **fick-le**   *adjective*   fĭk′-əl
[*ficol* (Old English), "false, deceitful"]

Definition: Likely to change for no apparent reason; inconstant.

All during our stay on Cape Cod that memorable summer, the weather proved exceedingly **fickle**.

As many a clotheshorse has discovered, fashion can be a notoriously **fickle** mistress.

Related Forms: (*noun*) fickleness; (*adjective*) fickle-minded

Phrases: fickle weather, fickle fortune, fickle affections

Synonyms: (*adjectives*) changeable, capricious, unstable, mercurial, erratic, variable, flighty, fitful, volatile

Antonyms: (*adjectives*) steadfast, constant, immutable, steady

Related Phrase: blow hot and cold

---

193. **filch**   *verb*   fĭlch
[*filchen* (Middle English), "take as booty"; from *fylcian* (Old English), "draw up in battle array"; from *gefylce* (Old English), "band of men"]

Definition: To steal slyly, especially small things.

Two of the youngsters acted as decoys, while a third attempted to **filch** a couple of apples from the unguarded bin.

Synonyms: (*verbs*) pilfer, purloin, shoplift, pinch, rip off, snatch, heist, swipe

194. **fi-nesse** *noun and verb* fĭ-něs'

[*finesse* (French), "delicacy"; from *fin* (French), "fine"]

Definition:

a. (*noun*) skill, delicacy, or subtlety in doing something or handling a situation.

For over an hour, the two brilliant conversationalists traded verbal blows with all the **finesse** of expert fencers.

b. (*verb*) To accomplish by subtle or skillful maneuvering.

A clever operator may soon be able to **finesse** himself or herself into an important position in a business.

Synonyms: (*nouns*) artfulness, craftiness, shrewdness, adroitness, dexterity, facility, savoir faire, know-how, savvy; (*verbs*) maneuver, contrive, finagle, manipulate

In addition to its normal uses, *finesse* is a technical term in the card game bridge. As a bridge term, it refers to an attempt to take a trick with a low card while holding a much higher card in the same suit. The point of doing this is either to take the trick as cheaply as possible or to induce your opponent to play an intermediate card that you can then top.

195. **fla-grant** *adjective* flā'-grənt

[*flagrans, flagrantis* (Latin), "burning, blazing"; from *flagrare* (Latin), "burn"]

Definition: Extremely and deliberately conspicuous; glaring.

Many people felt that the outcome of the trial constituted a **flagrant** miscarriage of justice.

Related Forms: (*nouns*) flagrancy, flagrance; (*adverb*) flagrantly

Synonyms: (*adjectives*) shocking, gross, rank, heinous (Word 222), atrocious, scandalous, disgraceful, brazen, egregious, arrant

Antonyms: (*adjectives*) negligible, insignificant, minor

Phrases: caught red-handed, in flagrante delicto

196. flaunt   *verb*   flônt

[Origin unknown; possibly akin to *flanta* (Norwegian), "gad about," and *flana* (Old Norse), "rush headlong"]

Definition: To show off in a conspicuous or offensive way.

Patriotism involves more than just **flaunting** the flag on the Fourth of July.

Synonyms: (*verbs*) display, parade, exhibit, sport, spotlight

Antonyms: (*verbs*) hide, conceal, screen, cover up; downplay, soft-pedal, de-emphasize

Related Phrase: draw attention to

197. flout   *verb*   flout

[*flouten* (Middle English), "play the flute"; from *flauter* (Old French), "play the flute," and *flaute* (Old French), "flute"]

Definition: To treat openly with scorn or contempt.

Many a monarch has been deposed for **flouting** the laws of the land.

Usage Note:

Be careful not to confuse *flout* with its look-alike *flaunt* (Word 196). Though these two words are sometimes considered to be synonyms in *nonstandard* English, they are quite different and should be kept separate.

Synonyms: (*verbs*) mock, scoff at, jeer at, deride, disparage, ridicule, sneer at, defy

Antonyms: (*verbs*) respect, observe, abide by; esteem, venerate, honor

Related Phrases: laugh up one's sleeve at, poke fun at

198. fluc-tu-ate   *verb*   flŭk'-chōō-āt

[*fluctuare, fluctuatus* (Latin), "move like a wave"; from *fluere* (Latin), "flow"]

Definition: To change continually from one position to another.

Since the moon lacks an atmosphere, temperatures on its surface **fluctuate** wildly.

Prices on the stock market may **fluctuate** on a day-to-day basis.

Related Forms: (*nouns*) fluctuation, flux

Phrases: fluctuating interest rates, fluctuating popularity

Synonyms: (*verbs*) waver, vacillate, oscillate, seesaw

Related Phrases: in a constant state of flux, ups and downs, ebb and flow, a checkered career

199. foi·ble   *noun*   foi′-bəl

[*foible* (obsolete French), "weak"]

Definition: A minor, often amusing, fault or weakness in character.

You may find your best friend's **foibles** extremely funny.

Usage Note:
When certain types of *foibles* become too pronounced, they may develop into *obsessions* (Word 283) or *phobias* (Word 301). For example, a concern for punctuality may become an obsession, or a dislike of cats a phobia.

Synonyms: (*nouns*) frailty, failing, flaw, defect (Word 117), shortcoming, idiosyncrasy, peculiarity, oddity, quirk, eccentricity, crotchet

Antonyms: (*nouns*) forte, strong point, long suit

200. fore·stall   *verb*   fôr-stôl′

[*foresteall* (Old English), "highway robbery"; from *fore* (Old English), "in front of" + *steall* (Old English), "position"]

Definition: To secure an advantage or prevent a loss by previous action.

English monarchs often **forestalled** the passage of legislation they did not like by simply adjourning Parliament.

Synonyms: (*verbs*) hinder, thwart (Word 376), frustrate, preclude, obviate, prevent, ward off, fend off, stave off, anticipate

Related Phrases: take precautionary measures, nip in the bud, cut off at the pass, steal a march on, beat to the draw, preventive medicine, a preemptive strike

201. for·mi·da·ble   *adjective*   fôr′-mĭ-də-bəl

[*formidabilis, formidabile* (Latin), "causing fear"; from *formido* (Latin), "terror, dread"]

Definition:
   a. Arousing fear or admiration because of the unusual size or superiority of the thing involved.

     To the prehistoric inhabitants of Europe, Asia, and the Americas, large mountain ranges proved a **formidable** barrier to the spread of human populations.

   b. Difficult to do because of the size of the job involved.

     The **formidable** task of cleaning up after a major hurricane or tornado cannot be accomplished without the help of all levels of government.

Phrases: a formidable opponent, a formidable intellect, a formidable memory, a formidable accomplishment

Related Forms: (*nouns*) formidability, formidableness

Synonyms: (*adjectives*) awesome, redoubtable, alarming, frightening, terrifying, horrifying; mind-boggling, impressive; huge, tremendous

Antonyms: (*adjectives*) unimpressive; inconsequential, insignificant, paltry, puny, negligible; simple, easy, undemanding

202. for-tu-i-tous   *adjective*   fôr-tōō'-ĭ-təs   *or*   fôr'-tyōō'-ĭ-təs

[*fortuitus* (Latin), "accidental"; from *fors, fortis* (Latin), "chance"]

Definition: Occurring by chance or accident.

Quite by chance I bumped into her on the street one day, and the results of that **fortuitous** meeting have changed the whole course of my life.

Related Forms: (*nouns*) fortuitousness, fortuity; (*adverb*) fortuitously

Usage Note:

Be careful not to confuse *fortuitous* with *fortunate*. *Fortuitous* means "accidental" or "happening by chance." The consequences of a *fortuitous* occurrence can be either fortunate or unfortunate, though the word tends to suggest that they are good rather than bad. *Fortunate*, on the other hand, simply means "lucky" or "happy," and the consequences of a fortunate development are always good. In other words, *fortuitous* refers to the way something happened, while *fortunate* refers to its results.

Synonyms: (*adjectives*) accidental, unplanned, inadvertent, casual, adventitious; unforeseen, unexpected, unanticipated

Antonyms: (*adjectives*) intentional, planned, deliberate, premeditated

Related Phrases: a fluke, a windfall, a chance occurrence

203. fru-gal   *adjective*   frōō'-gəl

(*frugalis* (Latin), "economical"; from *frux, frugis* (Latin), "fruit, produce")

Definition:

a.   Thrifty or economical in the use of money.

"Inflation has really put a dent in my buying power this year," I thought. "If I'm going to make ends meet, I'll have to be more **frugal**."

b.   Involving little expense; meager.

Surprisingly, the **frugal** meal we got from the old peasant woman was more satisfying than many a banquet I'd attended.

Related Forms: (*nouns*) frugality, frugalness; (*adverb*) frugally

Synonyms: (*adjectives*) sparing, careful, prudent, provident; scanty, skimpy, paltry; stingy, parsimonious, penurious, niggardly, tightfisted, penny-pinching

Antonyms: (*adjectives*) lavish, extravagant, prodigal, improvident

Related Phrases: a skinflint, penny-wise and pound-foolish

204. ful·some   *adjective*   fŏŏl'-səm

[*fulsom* (Middle English), "loathsome"; from *full*, "excess" + *some*, "characterized by"]

Definition: Excessive and, for that reason, offensive to good taste and obviously insincere.

"We know you're trying to curry favor with the boss," the note read. "Still, must you greet every last one of his bright ideas with such **fulsome** and obvious flattery?"

Related Forms: (*noun*) fulsomeness; (*adverb*) fulsomely

Synonyms: (*adjectives*) inordinate, extravagant, gross, immoderate, overdone; repulsive, disgusting, nauseating, odious, loathsome; vulgar, crass, tasteless

Antonyms: (*adjectives*) modest, understated, muted, subdued, toned down, quiet

Related Phrases: ad nauseam, in poor taste

205. fu·tile   *adjective*   fyōō-təl   *or*   fyōō'-tīl

[*futilis, futile* (Latin), "fragile; worthless"]

Definition: Incapable of producing the desired result; unsuccessful or ineffective.

Though the lifeguard made a heroic attempt to save the drowning woman's life, his efforts unfortunately proved **futile**.

Related Forms: (*nouns*) futility, futileness; (*adverb*) futilely

Synonyms: (*adjectives*) vain, fruitless, unavailing, idle, ineffectual, bootless, pointless, useless

Antonyms: (*adjectives*) effective, effectual, efficacious (Word 148), successful

Related Phrases: to no purpose, all for naught, carry coals to Newcastle

Carry Coals to Newcastle

The expression *carry coals to Newcastle* means "do something that is superfluous or unnecessary" or "supply something that is already abundant." Newcastle upon Tyne in northern England, the Newcastle of the expression, has long been the center of coal mining, so there is no need to import coal to the area.

Using the Words

Exercise I

5. fru'-gal
1. fi-as'-co
6. fluc'-tu-ate
2. fick'-le
7. foi'-ble
3. fi-nesse'
8. for'-mi-da-ble
4. fla'-grant
9. for-tu'-i-tous

Exercise I. Syllabication and Pronunciation

Syllabicate the following words correctly, and place the major stress mark (') after the syllable that is accented when the word is pronounced.

1. fiasco
2. fickle
3. finesse
4. flagrant
5. frugal
6. fluctuate
7. foible
8. formidable
9. fortuitous

Exercise II. Words Out of Context

In each of the following groups, select the item that best expresses the meaning of the numbered word at the left.

1. fickle   a. respectful   b. changeable   c. modest   d. idle

2. flagrant   a. quiet   b. prudent   c. vain   d. gross

3. flaunt   a. show off   b. steal   c. frustrate   d. laugh at

4. flout   a. cover up   b. lavish   c. sneer at   d. waver

5. forestall   a. emphasize   b. observe   c. alarm   d. prevent

6. fortuitous   a. impressive   b. wasteful   c. accidental   d. fruitless

7. fulsome   a. loathsome   b. generous   c. simple   d. unstable

Exercise III. Completing Sentences

Complete each of the following sentences by selecting the most appropriate word from the group of words given below. Use each word only once. Make any adjustments that are necessary to fit the words into the sentences properly.

finesse	frugal	fluctuate
futile	fiasco	forestall
foible	filching	formidable

1. Prices for consumer goods _fluctuate_ in accordance with the ups and downs of the economy.

2. Though the young boxer doesn't look particularly impressive in his street clothes, he is a _formidable_ opponent once he's in the ring.

3. I admire someone who can handle a delicate social situation with tact and ___finesse___.

4. Curiously, a play that "bombs" in London is a hit, while one that "bombs" on Broadway is a ___fiasco___.

5. My personality isn't all of a piece; it's a mixture of strengths and weaknesses, fortes and ___foibles___.

6. She is a ___frugal___ homemaker who delights in comparison shopping and bargain hunting.

7. Someone who starts off ___filching___ pennies may end up stealing millions.

8. The police recaptured one of the fugitives in a matter of hours, but their efforts to retake the other proved ___futile___.

Exercise IV.   Synonyms and Antonyms

Classify each of the following pairs of words as **S** for **synonyms** or **A** for **antonyms**.

S 1. flagrant—glaring
S 2. shortcoming—foible
A 3. flaunt—conceal
S 4. formidable—awesome
A 5. success—fiasco
A 6. flout—respect
S 7. capricious—fickle

A 8. lavish—frugal
S 9. finesse—dexterity
A 10. effective—futile
S 11. fluctuate—vacillate
S 12. thwart—forestall
A 13. fortuitous—premeditated
S 14. pilfer—filch

Exercise V.   Word Roundup

1. Explain the difference between the items in each of the following pairs.

   a. flout—flaunt   b. fortuitous—fortunate

2. With or without the aid of a dictionary, define each of the following colloquial or slang expressions.

   a. a heist   d. a fluke
   b. to soft-pedal   e. a skinflint
   c. a windfall   f. a flop

3. With or without the aid of a dictionary, explain the meaning of each of the following colorful phrases.

   a. blow hot and cold   f. a person's long suit
   b. caught red-handed   g. steal a march on
   c. laugh up one's sleeve at h. carry coals to Newcastle
   d. a checkered career   i. a flash in the pan
   e. go over like a lead   j. penny-wise and pound-
      balloon   foolish

4. Explain the meaning of the following Latin phrases commonly used in present-day English.

  a. ad nauseam   b. (in) flagrante delicto

5. Explain what *finesse* means in bridge.

Exercise VI.   Framing Sentences

A. Use each of the following words in an original illustrative sentence.

1. fiasco	4. flaunt	7. fortuitous
2. filch	5. flout	8. forestall
3. finesse	6. foible	9. fulsome

B. Give a **noun** form of each of the following words, and use it in an original illustrative sentence.

1. fickle *fickleness*	3. fluctuate *fluctuation*	5. frugal *frugality*
2. flagrant *flagrance, flagrancy*	4. formidable *formidability, formidableness*	6. futile *futility*

Dissecting the Words

Prefixes

1.   The Old English prefix **fore**, meaning "before," "earlier," "in advance," or "in front of," appears in the word *forestall*, studied in this lesson. Following are some other common English words in which it occurs. In each case, note how the prefix contributes to the overall meaning of the word in which it appears.

forewarn (*fore*, "before" + *warn*)—to warn in advance

forecast (*fore*, "in advance" + *cast*)—to predict; a prediction

foresee (*fore*, "before" + *see*)—to see or know beforehand

forebear (*fore*, "before" + *bear* (Old English), "a being, person")—an ancestor

forebode (*fore*, "in advance" + *bode*)—to indicate the likelihood of; portend. (Note that *forebode* usually implies that what is coming is bad rather than good.)

foreshadow (*fore*, "beforehand" + *shadow*)—to indicate or suggest beforehand

Other common English words containing the prefix *fore* include *foretaste, forefather, foreword, forerunner,* and *foretell.*

2.   Do not confuse the prefix *fore* with the Old English look-alike prefix **for** (without an *e*). *For* means "away, off" or "completely, utterly." It appears in a number of common English words, including:

forgo (*for*, "completely away" + *go*)—to abstain from completely; to do totally without

forlorn (*for,* "completely" + *lorn,* "abandoned")—wretched and pitiful; nearly hopeless

forbear (*for,* "completely away" + *bear*)—to refrain completely from

forsake (*for,* "completely" + *sake,* "deny, reject")—to leave or desert completely

Other modern English words in which the prefix *for* appears are *forbid* and *forswear.*

Root

The Latin root **flu** or **fluct**, meaning "flow," is found in the word *fluctuate,* studied in this lesson. Here are some other common English words in which the root appears.

affluent (literally, "flowing toward")—wealthy, well-to-do

confluence (literally, "a flowing together")—the junction of two rivers

flux—a constant change or flow

fluent—easily flowing; effortless, polished, or graceful

influx (literally, "a flowing in")—the arrival of great numbers of something

superfluous (literally, "flowing over and above")—superabundant, excessive, extra. Noun: *superfluity*

mellifluous (literally, "flowing with honey")—very sweet and smooth; honeyed

Exercise

1. On the basis of your knowledge of the prefix *fore*, tell what each of the following compound words means:

    a. foreword   c. foremost   e. foresight
    b. forefront   d. foreshorten   f. forehand

2. With or without the aid of a dictionary, define each of the following words containing the prefix *for*. Explain how the prefix contributes to the overall meaning of the word.

    a. forlorn   b. forbearance   c. forswear

3. For each of the following definitions, supply an English word that contains either the prefix *fore* or the prefix *for*. In some instances, two answers are possible.

    a. an ancestor   c. predict   e. see beforehand
    b. do totally   d. warn in   f. completely
       without   advance   wretched

4. Define each of the following words, and use it in an original illustrative sentence.

    a. affluent   c. influx   e. fluent
    b. fusion   d. superfluous   f. influential

Working with Context Clues

Two-Word Omissions. So far you have been dealing with sentence-completion exercises containing only one blank. The sentence-completion sections of most standardized vocabulary tests, however, contain a good many items involving the omission of *two* words, not one. These two-word omissions work in exactly the same way as one-word omissions; they are just more challenging.

Study the following example of a typical two-word omission. Try to determine the correct answer before reading the explanation of it given below.

> Florida Fats and the other _____ of McDuffy's Billiard Academy come from every walk of life. You are unlikely to find a more _____ crew assembled under any other roof in town.

> **a.** quadrupeds . . . elegant   **c.** denizens . . . motley
> **b.** employees . . . uniform   **d.** proprietors . . . aristocratic

The best way to begin dealing with this example is to determine the parts of speech of the missing words. From the position of the blanks, you seem to need a noun in the first and an adjective in the second.

Notice that the noun you need forms part of the subject of the first sentence. This suggests that it may form part of the subject of the entire passage. Accordingly, read the passage carefully to determine what it is about. It concerns the kind of people who can be found in a pool hall called McDuffy's Billiard Academy. This is confirmed by the phrase *crew assembled under any . . . roof* in the second sentence and the personal name *Florida Fats* in the first. Now you know that the noun you need means something like "customers" or possibly "employees."

Run your eye down the first item in each of the four lettered choices. Eliminate any choice that does not fit in with your conclusion about the meaning of the first missing word. Choices *b* and *c* seem to work. *Employees* (choice *b*) dovetails neatly with what you think may go in the first blank. So does *denizens* (choice *c*), which means "inhabitants" or "residents." Choices *a* and *d*, however, don't agree with your ideas, so they can be eliminated. A *quadruped* (choice *a*) is a four-legged animal, not a person; *proprietors* (choice *d*) indicates the owners of a business, not its customers or employees.

Though officially a "dead" language, Latin is still used in the modern world. For instance, carved over the entrance to the Amphitheater of Arlington National Cemetery in Virginia is the Roman poet Horace's simple but unforgettable line about patriotism, "It is satisfying and fitting to die for one's country."

Now you are down to two possibilities. However, you'll need more information before you can decide which of the two is correct. Accordingly, move on to consider the second blank, for which you need an adjective.

Notice that the missing adjective modifies the word *crew*. This suggests that it in some way describes the nature or character of the people who can be found at McDuffy's. Carefully reread the entire passage to determine what it has to say about this matter.

The passage says that the crew at McDuffy's *comes from every walk of life.* This suggests that the adjective you need means something like "extremely varied" or "richly diverse."

Run your eye over the second item in choices *b* and *c*, your two remaining possibilities for the correct answer. *Uniform* (choice *b*) does not agree with your conclusion about the meaning of the adjective you need, since the word means the opposite of *varied* or *diverse*. For that reason, it can be eliminated.

Motley in choice *c*, however, does fit, since it does mean "richly diverse" or "extremely varied." Choice *c*, therefore, must be the correct answer, and, of course, it is.

One final point: Notice that two-word omissions work on exactly the same kinds of context clues as one-word omissions. In the example given above, one of the hints was essentially a restatement clue since *crew* and *denizens* mean more or less the same thing. The other was an inference clue since *motley* is implied by the phrase *come from every walk of life*.

Exercise

Choose the pair of words that best complete the meaning of each of the following passages. Underline the clue or clues that led you to make your choice.

1. The anxious cast of young actors became _____ after several reviewers declared that their new play was a complete _____ which lacked any theatrical merit or entertainment value.

   a. affable . . . failure
   b. distraught . . . fiasco
   c. belligerent . . . surprise
   d. caustic . . . anachronism

2. We realized that the woman claiming to be a psychic was a complete _____ when she began to _____ a trance by suddenly falling to the floor and pretending to speak with spirits.

   a. anomaly . . . elicit
   b. fiasco . . . exploit
   c. harbinger . . . fabricate
   d. charlatan . . . feign

3. When the brilliant physicist talks to a group of nonscientists, he must adapt his _____ so that he can be understood by a lay audience far less _____ than he.

   a. discourse . . . erudite
   b. bravado . . . fulsome
   c. harangue . . . eminent
   d. temperament . . . academic

4. The foundations of democracy are threatened when a(n) _____ group of <u>highly privileged</u> citizens can _____ others with <u>less power</u> to accept the will of the wealthy and influential.

   a. facetious . . . delude   **c.** exotic . . . entreat
   b. ethnic . . . abet   **d.** <u>elite . . . coerce</u>

5. Because of the overlapping lines of authority in <u>a large, impersonal organization</u>, people working in a(n) _____ often fail to _____ their duties and then <u>refuse to take responsibility for their mistakes</u>.

   a. boycott . . . disparage   **c.** asylum . . . curtail
   b. <u>bureaucracy . . . fulfill</u>   **d.** enclave . . . assimilate

Enriching the Lesson

Exercise I.   Our Italian Heritage

This lesson includes *fiasco*, a word borrowed without change from Italian. Listed below are a number of other Italian words and phrases that are commonly used in present-day English. With or without the aid of a dictionary, define each expression as it is used in Modern English.

1. torso	8. quarantine	15. manifesto
2. imbroglio	9. libretto	16. solo
3. sotto voce	10. studio	17. scenario
4. vendetta	11. graffiti	18. vista
5. tempo	12. motto	19. cognoscenti
6. squadron	13. salvo	20. gala
7. prima donna	14. incognito	21. virtuoso

Exercise II.   Money Talks

The presence of *frugal* in this lesson brings to mind the fact that Modern English includes an impressive array of expressions relating to business, finance, and economics. A few of these items are listed below. With or without the aid of a dictionary or other reference book (*e.g.*, an economics textbook), define each.

1. depression	8. surplus	15. deficit
2. recession	9. monetary policy	16. monopoly
3. inflation	10. market economy	17. bull market
4. deflation	11. economic climate	18. national debt
5. boom	12. private sector	19. windfall profits
6. asset	13. free enterprise	20. liability
7. gross national product	14. medium of exchange	21. prime interest rate

Exercise III.   A Verbal Diversion

Since sports and games play such an important role in our daily lives, it is only natural that many colorful terms and expressions have spilled over from the sports world into the everyday language. A few examples of this phenomenon are given below. With or without the aid of a dictionary, define or explain each. Then indicate the sport from which the expression comes.

1. pinch-hit for
2. put on a full-court press
3. par for the course
4. parry a blow
5. a gambit
6. have an ace up one's sleeve
7. kick off a campaign
8. a Monday morning quarterback
9. a goal-line stand
10. stymied
11. hotdog (*verb*)
12. a stalemate
13. a front-runner
14. showboating
15. a long shot
16. start out with two strikes against you

Exercise IV.   Expanding Your Word Power

The words listed below are not on the Basic Word List, but they were mentioned in passing in Lesson 17. All of them would make useful additions to your working vocabulary. Define each, give its etymology, list **two** synonyms and **two** antonyms (where possible), and use in a short illustrative sentence.

1. debacle
2. erratic
3. steadfast
4. purloin
5. maneuver
6. egregious
7. defy
8. oscillate
9. forte
10. quirk
11. preclude
12. redoubtable
13. inadvertent
14. prodigal
15. inordinate

Lesson 18

206. gape — 220. **harbinger**

---

206. gape   *verb*   gāp

[*gapa* (Old Norse), "open the mouth; stare"]

Definition: To stare openmouthed in amazement; to open wide.

Survivors **gaped** in disbelief at the destruction so quickly wrought by the tornado.

Scientists believe the huge crater that **gapes** in the Arizona desert was made by a meteorite crashing into the earth.

Related Forms: (*noun*) gap; (*adverb*) agape

Synonyms: (*verbs*) gawk (at); goggle (at), rubberneck, ogle; yawn

Antonyms: (*verbs*) purse (the lips), pucker (the mouth), furrow (the brow)

207. gar·ble   *verb*   gär'-bəl

[*garbellare* (Old Italian), "sift"; from *g(h)arbala* (Arabic), "he selected"; possibly from *cribellum* (Late Latin), "sieve"]

Definition: To distort in such a way as to make unintelligible.

The message was so badly **garbled** that I didn't even know who had called.

Phrases: a garbled quotation, garbled instructions

Synonyms: (*verbs*) scramble, jumble, confuse, mangle, mutilate, butcher, misrepresent, misquote, misreport

Related Phrases: take something out of context, get something wrong; get something straight, set the record straight

208. gloat   *verb*   glōt

[Origin uncertain; possibly *glotta* (Old Norse), "grin"]

Definition: To regard with excessive or malicious satisfaction.

A good winner doesn't **gloat** over victory, just as a good loser doesn't sulk over defeat.

Synonyms: (*verbs*) revel (in), delight (in), relish, crow (over), exult (in), glory (in)

Related Phrases: lord it over, rub it in

Mahouts always carry goads with them when training, caring for, and working with their elephants. Young elephants also learn to obey foot commands from their riders.

209. **goad**   *noun and verb*   gōd
[*gad* (Old English), "spearhead"]

Definition:
   a. (*noun*) A long pointed stick used for driving animals; anything that spurs a person on.

      Customarily, mahouts use short wooden **goads** to control and direct the movements of their huge charges.

      Simple financial necessity is often the **goad** that prompts a composer or painter to produce new material.

   b. (*verb*) To drive or urge on.

      Try as he might, he could not **goad** me into doing something that I knew in my heart was foolish.

Synonyms: (*nouns*) prod, spur, stimulus, incentive, inducement; gadfly; (*verbs*) prod, spur, propel, hound, impel, incite, provoke, egg on

Antonyms: (*nouns*) restraint, curb, check, deterrent; (*verbs*) restrain, curb, check, deter, impede

Related Phrases: needle someone, fire up an audience, whip up enthusiasm

210. **graph-ic**   *adjective*   grăf'-ĭk
[*graphikos* (Greek), "able to draw or paint"; from *graphein* (Greek), "draw, paint"]

Definition:
   a. Relating to a drawn or pictorial representation; visual.

      Messages posted on our refrigerator door have become quite eye-catching since my sister began majoring in **graphic** arts.

   b. Giving a clear and effective picture; vivid.

      The book contains a **graphic** and hair-raising account of the seizure of the U.S. embassy in Iran.

Related Forms: (*nouns*) graph, graphics; (*adverb*) graphically

Synonyms: (*adjectives*) pictorial, diagrammatic; striking, telling, lively, lifelike, realistic, true to life, picturesque

Antonyms: (*adjectives*) sketchy, vague; unrealistic; colorless, bloodless, anemic, pallid, bland

276

Graphs and Graphics

There is a whole family of terms and expressions related to the adjective *graphic*, studied in this lesson. For example, a *graph*, as you probably already know, is a line drawing or similar pictorial device used to represent numerical (or other abstract) relationships. The word is constantly used (both as a noun and as a verb) in mathematics and the other arts and sciences. For example, your math teacher may ask you to graph the equation $2x + y = 16$, or your history textbook may contain a graph showing unemployment in the United States during the Great Depression. Graphs, of course, are also widely used in business and other fields as convenient devices for representing abstract relationships in concrete and eye-catching ways.

A *graphic* (plural *graphics*) is similar to a graph but broader in meaning. To businesspeople and commercial artists, it indicates a picture, chart, or similar device that is designed to illustrate something. To computer experts, it refers to a diagram that the computer generates on the screen.

Graphics has several meanings. To architects and engineers, it refers to the art of making technical drawings according to strict mathematical rules. To commercial artists, it indicates the art of making graphic illustrations. And to computer experts, it is the capability of a network of linked databases to display pictures and other images as well as printed text on such systems as the Internet.

Finally, the *graphic arts* are any of the visual arts that involve applying lines to a two-dimensional surface. Thus, drawing, lettering, photography, and printing are all examples of the graphic arts.

A gratuity is a tip, usually in the form of money, given in thanks for a service. Waiters and waitresses (like the one shown in this photo) customarily receive gratuities in this country. In Europe and other parts of the world, a standard gratuity is often built into the bill.

211. **gra-tu-i-tous**   *adjective*   grə-tōō′-ĭ-təs *or* grə-tyōō′-ĭ-təs

[*gratuitus* (Latin), "given as a favor"; from *gratia* (Latin), "favor"]

Definition:

a.   Freely given; done without recompense.

She gives people a great deal of **gratuitous** service, simply because she likes them.

b.   Uncalled-for; unjustified.

After treating them so well, we were deeply offended by their **gratuitous** insults.

Related Forms: (*nouns*) gratuitousness, gratuity; (*adjective and adverb*) gratis; (*adverb*) gratuitously

Synonyms: (*adjectives*) free, complimentary, voluntary, unsolicited; unwarranted, unfounded, groundless, baseless

Related Phrases: on the house, free of charge, a freebie; foot the bill for

212. **gre-ga-ri-ous**   *adjective*   grĭ-gâr′-ē-əs

[*gregarius* (Latin), "belonging to a herd or flock"; from *grex, gregis* (Latin), "herd"]

Definition:

a.   Tending to form or move in a herd or other group; social.

Many kinds of animals — sheep, for example — are naturally **gregarious**.

b.   Enjoying the company of others; sociable.

Whether or not a person is **gregarious** is usually the result of how she or he was brought up.

Related Forms: (*noun*) gregariousness; (*adverb*) gregariously

Synonyms: (*adjectives*) outgoing, extroverted, friendly, companionable, affable, genial

Antonyms: (*adjectives*) antisocial, misanthropic, unsociable, unfriendly, withdrawn, reserved, detached, aloof, introverted

Related Phrases: esprit de corps, birds of a feather, a social butterfly; live in an ivory tower, a loner

213. **gri·mace**   *noun and verb*   grĭm'-ĭs *or* grĭ-mās'

[*grimache* (Old French), "grimace"; related to *grima* (Old English), "mask; fear" and ultimately of Germanic origin]

Definition:
  a. (*noun*) A twisted facial expression indicating pain, disgust, or disapproval.

  The **grimace** on her face told me more eloquently than words could have that she disapproved of my decision.

  b. (*verb*) To contort the features of the face in order to indicate pain, disgust, or disapproval.

  When the doctor jabbed me with that long needle, I involuntarily **grimaced** in pain.

Synonyms: (*nouns and verbs*) frown, scowl, glower, glare, wince

Antonyms: (*nouns and verbs*) smile, grin; (*verb*) beam

Related Phrases: make a (wry) face, make faces, screw up one's face; grin from ear to ear, grin like a Cheshire cat

214. **grope**   *verb*   grōp

[*grop(i)en* (Middle English), "grope"; from *grapian* (Old English), "grasp"]

Definition: To feel around uncertainly for.

When the lights suddenly went out, I **groped** my way down the stairs with the aid of a pocket lighter.

There was a momentary pause in the conversation as I **groped** for an answer to her unexpected question.

Phrases: grope for the telephone, grope for a clue

Synonyms: (*verbs*) fumble (for), poke around (for), hunt (for), cast about (for), fish around (for), look (for), flounder around (for)

Related Phrases: pick one's way through; send out a feeler, send up a trial balloon, see how the land lies, see which way the wind is blowing

215. **gru·el·ing**   *adjective*   grōō'-ə-lĭng

[Origin uncertain; possibly *gruel* (obsolete English), "punish" + *ing*)

Definition: Extremely demanding and exhausting.

With four minutes left to play, a glorious but **grueling** eighty-yard drive put the winning points on the board for the Rams.

Synonyms: (*adjectives*) taxing, draining, fatiguing, wearying, tiring, arduous, intense

Antonyms: (*adjectives*) easy, simple, enjoyable, relaxing, invigorating

216. grue-some   *adjective*   grōō'-səm

[*grue* (obsolete English), "shudder" + *some*, "characterized by"]

Definition: Causing great shock, horror, and repugnance.

The **gruesome** sight of maimed and burned bodies was enough to disillusion me forever about the so-called glories of war.

Phrases: a gruesome murder, the gruesome details

Related Forms: (*noun*) gruesomeness; (*adverb*) gruesomely

Synonyms: (*adjectives*) horrifying, horrible, monstrous, hideous, grisly, ghastly, macabre, grotesque, lurid

Antonyms: (*adjectives*) pleasant, lovely, delightful, agreeable, attractive, charming, engaging, pleasurable

217. gul-li-ble   *adjective*   gŭl'-ə-bəl

[*gull* (English), "cheat, dupe" + *ible*]

Definition: Easily cheated or deceived.

No matter how much protective legislation we pass, there will probably always be **gullible** consumers for swindlers and con artists to prey on.

Related Forms: (*noun*) gullibility; (*noun and verb*) gull

Synonyms: (*adjectives*) credulous, naive, ingenuous, unsuspecting, exploitable, trusting, unwary, green

Antonyms: (*adjectives*) skeptical, incredulous, dubious, wary, cautious, circumspect

Related Phrases: a patsy, a soft touch, a sitting duck, a pigeon; born yesterday, still wet behind the ears; pull the wool over someone's eyes, take someone for a ride; jive; caveat emptor

218. hag-gard   *adjective*   hăg'-ērd

[*haggard* (Old French), "wild," used of a female hawk in falconry]

Definition: Worn and exhausted from anxiety, disease, hunger, or fatigue.

As soon as I saw how **haggard** his face looked, I began to realize just how much he had been through recently.

Related Form: (*noun*) haggardness

Usage Note:
As the example above indicates, *haggard* usually refers to the face or facial expression. It suggests thinness, worry, or weariness and implies severe mental or physical distress.

Synonyms: (*adjectives*) careworn, drawn, gaunt, wasted, hollow eyed, drained, wan, cadaverous, pinched

Antonyms: (*adjectives*) rosy, florid, ruddy, rubicund, glowing, radiant

The Trojan Horse

The story of the Trojan Horse, as told in Homer's *Odyssey* and Virgil's *Aeneid*, is a classic example of guile and gullibility. The Greek army besieging Troy was unable to break into the city. The wily Greeks thereupon built a huge statue of a horse and left it outside the city walls. Armed Greek soldiers were concealed inside the hollow structure. Then the Greeks pretended to depart. The jubilant Trojans regarded the statue as a parting gift from a defeated foe and, despite warnings (the Trojan priest Laocoön remarked, "I fear the Greeks, even when bearing gifts"), dragged the "gift horse" into the city. At night the Greek soldiers crept out of the horse and opened the city's gates to their comrades. In this way, the city of Troy was taken.

219. **ha-rangue**   *noun and verb*   hə-răng′
[*harenga* (Medieval Latin), "public address"]

Definition:
   a.   (*noun*) A long, emotional public address designed to arouse strong feelings or spur the audience on to action; a similar piece of writing.

   Suddenly a young man rushed onto the stage and began to deliver one of the most intemperate **harangues** I have ever heard.

   b.   (*verb*) To deliver a harangue.

   It's a truly frightening experience to watch old film clips of Adolf Hitler **haranguing** his followers at the Nuremberg rallies of the 1930s.

Synonyms: (*nouns*) tirade, diatribe, philippic, denunciation; (*verbs*) rant, hold forth, pontificate

Related Phrases: rant and rave, get up on a soapbox, ride a hobbyhorse

281

220. har·bin·ger   *noun and verb*   här'-bĭn-jər

[*herbergere, herbengar* (Middle English), "person sent to prepare lodgings"; from *herberge* (Old French but of Germanic origin), "lodging." Originally, a harbinger was a servant or messenger sent on ahead to prepare lodging and entertainment for traveling royal or titled persons.]

Definition:
   a.   (*noun*) A forerunner.

      Wild geese flying south from Canada are **harbingers** of winter.

      The brutal conflict over Kansas and Nebraska in the 1850s turned out to be a modest **harbinger** of a much bloodier struggle in the 1860s.

   b.   (*verb*) To herald the approach of.

      To most people's minds, the appearance of crocuses **harbingers** the return of spring.

      I hope tonight's easy victory over Elk Grove **harbingers** success in our bid for the state basketball championship.

Synonyms: (*nouns*) precursor, herald; omen, sign, portent; (*verbs*) presage, foreshadow, prefigure, augur (Word 48), signal; usher in

Related Phrases: a point man, an advance man

Using the Words

Exercise I.   Parts of Speech

Indicate the part of speech of each of the following words. In some cases, two answers are correct.

1. gape v.
2. garble v.
3. goad n., v.
4. gratuitous adj.
5. grimace n., v.
6. grope v.
7. gullible adj.
8. harangue n., v.
9. harbinger n., v.

Exercise II.   Words in Phrases

In each of the following groups, select the item that best expresses the meaning of the *italicized* word in the introductory phrase.

1. *gratuitous* criticisms
   a. perceptive   b. unexpected   c. mindless   d. uncalled-for

2. a very *gregarious* young lady
   a. erudite   b. outgoing   c. beautiful   d. obese

3. the *gruesome* details
   a. vague   b. significant   c. horrible   d. minor

4. a *grueling* test
   a. surprise   b. written   c. brief   d. draining

5. *grope* for a name
   a. rush   b. call   c. send   <u>d. fumble</u>

6. a *haggard* expression
   <u>a. careworn</u>   b. felicitous   c. trite   d. foreign

7. *grimaced* in reply
   a. nodded   b. winked   <u>c. scowled</u>   d. laughed

Exercise III.   Completing Sentences

Complete each of the following sentences or pairs of sentences by selecting the most appropriate word from the group of words given below. Use each word only once. Make any adjustments that are necessary to fit the words into the sentences properly.

gloat	gaping	harbinger
graphic	haggard	gullible
harangue	goad	garbled

1. It made me dizzy to lean over the edge of the precipice and peer down into the __gaping__ abyss below.

2. The report contained such a __garbled__ and misleading account of my activities that at first I didn't recognize them.

3. Even though their crowing may embarrass you a little, your parents do have some right to __gloat__ over your successes.

4. Fear and confusion may __goad__ a perfectly rational person into behaving in a most irrational way.

5. The article gave such a __graphic__ description of the catastrophe that I could almost see it occurring before my eyes.

6. Only a thoroughly __gullible__ person would be taken in by the absurd claims of some TV commercials.

7. "The man's no statesman," I declared. "He's a rabble-rouser who uses his official position as a soapbox from which to __harangue__ a captive and reluctant audience."

8. In my family, opening day at the ballpark, not the advent of warmer weather, is the __harbinger__ of summer.

Exercise IV.   Synonyms and Antonyms

A. In each of the following groups, select the **two** words that are most nearly **synonyms**.

1. <u>a. unwarranted</u>   b. unplanned   c. uncontrolled
   <u>d. unjustified</u>   e. unnamed   gratuitious

2. <u>a. rant</u>   <u>b. scramble</u>   c. douse   d. spur   <u>e. jumble</u>   garble

3. a. peasant   b. knight   c. herald   d. forerunner
    e. merchant   harbinger

4. a. grisly   b. wary   c. ghastly   d. lazy   e. sketchy   gruesome

5. a. chubby   b. gaunt   c. stately   d. radiant   e. cadaverous   haggard

Now, for each pair of synonyms you have selected, supply a
word from the Basic Word List for this lesson (Words 206–220) that
means **the same** or **almost the same** thing.

B. In each of the following, select the item that is most nearly
opposite in meaning to the numbered word at the left.

1. goad
    a. grin   b. mangle   c. rave   d. restrain
    e. prod

2. gullible
    a. energetic   b. disinterested   c. skeptical
    d. friendly   e. frightening

3. grueling
    a. fulfilling   b. undemanding   c. striking
    d. unrewarding   e. fatiguing

4. gregarious
    a. naive   b. genial   c. monstrous   d. aloof
    e. ruddy

5. grimace
    a. smile   b. yawn   c. cough   d. nod
    e. scowl

Exercise V.   Framing Sentences

A. Use each of the following words in an original illustrative
sentence.

1. gape   4. goad   7. grueling
2. garble   5. grimace   8. harangue
3. gloat   6. grope   9. harbinger

B. Give a **noun** form of each of the following words, and use it in
an original illustrative sentence.

1. gullible   2. gregarious   3. haggard
    gullibility   gregariousness   haggardness

C. Give an **adverb** form of each of the following words, and use it
in an original illustrative sentence.

1. graphic   2. gruesome   3. gratuitous
    graphically   gruesomely   gratuitously

Exercise VI.   Word Roundup

1. With or without the aid of a dictionary, explain what the fol-
    lowing phrases mean.

    a. live in an ivory tower   d. wet behind the ears
    b. get up on a soapbox   e. see how the land lies
    c. pull the wool over   f. grin like a Cheshire
       someone's eyes   cat

284

2. With or without the aid of a dictionary, define each of the following colorful terms.

   a. rubberneck   c. social butterfly   e. freebie
   b. gadfly   d. sitting duck   f. birds of a feather

3. Explain what each of the following means.

   a. a graph   c. graphics
   b. a graphic   d. the graphic arts

4. Define the following foreign expressions used in present-day English.

   a. gratis   b. esprit de corps   c. caveat emptor

5. What is an *extrovert*? How does one differ from an *introvert*?

6. Recount the story of the Trojan Horse.

Completing Verbal Analogies

"If Something Is A, a Person Can B It."   Another common word relationship that occurs in the analogy sections of standardized tests involves a state or action that is stipulated by the meaning of a given word. This relationship can be expressed in abstract terms as, "If something is *A*, a person can *B* it; if something is *C*, a person can *D* it."

Here is an example of an analogy question involving this relationship. Try to determine the correct answer before reading the explanation of it given below.

tangible : touch ::
   a. susceptible : doubt   d. pliant : enjoy
   b. affable : speak   e. mutable : show
   c. portable : carry

The answer is *c*. If something is *tangible*, a person can, *touch* it. Similarly, if something is *portable*, a person can *carry* it.

"If Something is A, a Person Cannot B It."   A related word relationship involves a state or action that is precluded by the meaning of a given word. This word relationship can be expressed in abstract terms as, "If something is *A*, a person cannot *B* it; if something is *C*, a person cannot *D* it."

Here is an example of an analogy involving this relationship. Try to figure out the correct answer before reading the explanation of it given below.

immutable : change ::
   a. insurgent : raise   d. inscrutable : see
   b. inadvertent : tame   e. indelible : erase
   c. irrevocable : examine

The answer is *e*. If something is *immutable*, a person cannot *change* it. Similarly, if something is *indelible*, a person cannot *erase* it.

One Final Note.   The two word relationships examined in this section may apply to people as well as things. In that case, they may be expressed in abstract terms as "If someone is *A*, a person can(not) *B* him/her."

Exercise I

Complete each of the following analogies based on the word relationships "If something is *A*, a person can *B* it" and "If something is *A*, a person cannot *B* it."

1. **illegible : read** =
   a. invisible : see
   b. inaudible : taste
   c. innumerable : avoid
   d. immobile : touch
   e. inflammable : imagine

2. **edible : eat** =
   a. notable : forget
   b. feasible : scare
   c. pliable : bend
   d. execrable : relish
   e. stable : shift

3. **gullible : hoodwink** =
   a. reliable : mistrust
   b. affable : reject
   c. culpable : reward
   d. sensible : mislead
   e. tractable : control

4. **insuperable : overcome** =
   a. unquenchable : swallow
   b. invincible : choose
   c. inscrutable : raise
   d. indomitable : tame
   e. infallible : duplicate

Exercise II   Answers will vary.

Compose **one** complete analogy based on the word relationship "If something is *A*, a person can *B* it" and **one** based on the word relationship "If something is *A*, a person cannot *B* it."

Exercise III

The following items review what you have so far learned about analogy questions. Complete each.

1. **treachery : revulsion** :: courage :
   (*despair, horror, admiration, boredom, indifference*)

2. **poignant : sadden** :: droll :
   (*appall, enlighten, exhaust, puzzle, amuse*)

3. **nimble : ungainly** :: blithe :
   (*facetious, lithe, exotic, morose, gratuitous*)

4. **philosopher : truth** :: aesthete :
   (*beauty, research, money, fame, controversy*)

5. **prong : fork** :: spoke :
   (*headlight, wheel, pedal, handlebar, brake*)

6. **interest : absorption** :: joy :
   (*sadness, exultation, amazement, attention, apathy*)

7. **apple : fruit** :: potato :
   (<u>vegetable</u>, mineral, animal, metal, product)

8. **affluent : indigent** :: eminent :
   (notable, genial, <u>obscure</u>, heinous, defective)

9. **epigram : witty** :: cliché :
   (prolix, <u>hackneyed</u>, piquant, rational, novel)

10. **diminutive : puny** :: mammoth :
    (specious, dapper, emaciated, <u>gigantic</u>, haggard)

Working with Context Clues

More About Two-Word Omissions. Study the following example of a typical two-word omission. Try to determine the correct answer before reading the explanation of it given below.
Though a(η) _____ master might deal kindly and generously with the slaves he owned, a cruel one would usually _____ his.

   a. brutal . . . exploit   **c.** humane . . . maltreat
   b. enlightened . . . coddle   **d.** affluent . . . emancipate

The answer is *c. humane . . . maltreat.* Here's why.
The word *though* at the beginning of the example should immediately suggest to you that the sentence will present contrasting information of some kind. It should also tip you off to the kind of clue you are likely to find—a contrast clue.
Bearing this in mind, read the sentence carefully to determine how the words that go in the blanks contribute to its meaning. The sentence does indeed present contrasting information. It says that one kind of master treated his slaves in one way, but another kind of master treated his differently. You are to supply an adjective that reveals the character of the first type of master and a verb that indicates how the second treated his slaves. To help you do this, you have been told how the first type of master behaved (*deal . . . generously*) and what the second was like (*cruel*).
You now have enough information to begin completing the sentence correctly. Accordingly, consider the first blank, for which you need an adjective that describes a person's character or personality. You know that the second type of master was cruel. This suggests that the first type was "uncruel"—that is, "kind." This conclusion is backed up by the statement that the first type treated his slaves *kindly and generously.*
Run your eye down the first item in each of the four lettered choices. Eliminate any choice that does not agree with your conclusion about the character of the first type of master. Choices *b* (*enlightened*) and *c* (*humane*) dovetail with it, so they can stay. Choice *a* (*brutal*), however, does not and can confidently be eliminated. Similarly, choice *d* (*affluent*) has nothing to do with kindness or cruelty, so it can be discarded as well.
Now you have reduced the likely possibilities for the correct answer to two. Still, you can't tell which is actually right without more help. Accordingly, turn to the second blank, for which you need a verb indicating behavior.

You know that the first type of master treats his slaves kindly and generously. This suggests that the second type of master treats his *unkindly or meanly*. This conclusion, of course, also follows from the fact that the second type of master is known to be cruel.

In light of this new conclusion, consider the second item in choices *b* and *c*, your two remaining possibilities for the correct answer. Choice *b* reads *coddle*, which does not agree with your ideas about how the cruel master treated his slaves. *Coddle* means "treat too indulgently," not "treat badly." Accordingly, choice *b* can be eliminated.

Choice *c*, however, is *maltreat*, which fits in nicely with what you think belongs in the blank. Clearly, then, choice *c* is the correct answer simply because none of the other choices produces a sensible or meaningful statement when it is inserted into the sentence.

Exercise

Complete each of the following two-word omissions by selecting the pair of words that make the best sense in the passage as a whole. Underline the clue or clues that led you to make your choice.

1. If we wish to _____ the eventual exhaustion of our fossil fuel reserves, we must _____ the use of gas-guzzling vehicles now and conserve our fuel resources for the future.

    a. defer . . . exploit
    b. forestall . . . curtail

    c. advocate . . . avoid
    d. exacerbate . . . forbid

2. When people wish to avoid speaking directly about death, they often resort to a(n) _____ in order to _____ the discomfort which that subject causes.

    a. slogan . . . flout
    b. anomaly . . . decrease

    c. boycott . . . elude
    d. euphemism . . . circumvent

3. The purpose of tales that make a(n) _____ point is to encourage listeners to _____ in their personal lives the moral behavior reflected in the stories.

    a. obvious . . . disparage
    b. circuitous . . . imitate

    c. esoteric . . . condone
    d. ethical . . . emulate

4. In the _____ of Shakespeare's *Hamlet*, a(n) _____ pile of dead bodies including that of the title character, lies on the stage as the curtain closes.

    a. denouement . . . gruesome
    b. conclusion . . . devout

    c. ambience . . . graphic
    d. manuscript . . . bleak

5. Some self-satisfied criminals have had the _____ to _____ about their crimes in television interviews and then have been rewarded for their shamelessness.

    a. courage . . . cohere
    b. effrontery . . . gloat

    c. finesse . . . discourse
    d. duplicity . . . entreat

Enriching the Lesson

Exercise I.   More Classical Contributions to English

The geography, history, and mythology of the classical world have contributed much to the richness and variety of modern English. Below are listed a few more examples of this remarkable heritage. Tell what each of the items means, and explain its connection with classical Greece or Rome. Then choose any **five** of the expressions, and for each compose an original illustrative sentence.

1. a mausoleum
2. an odyssey
3. chimerical
4. hector someone
5. a nestor
6. caught between Scylla and Charybdis
7. meander
8. a maecenas
9. a thespian
10. a nemesis
11. pile Pelion on Ossa
12. open a Pandora's box
13. a xanthippe
14. pander to
15. stentorian
16. a mentor
17. a platonic relationship
18. leave no stone unturned

Exercise II.   Expressions Old and New

A. Below are listed a number of expressions that are frequently used in present-day English. With or without the aid of a dictionary, define each. Then choose any **three**, and for each compose an original illustrative sentence.

1. hit pay dirt
2. in the limelight
3. out of kilter
4. a Johnny-come-lately
5. buy a pig in a poke
6. the pecking order
7. moonlight as a cabbie
8. old hat
9. a backhanded compliment
10. wear one's heart on one's sleeve
11. swallow one's pride
12. jump the gun
13. reach for the moon
14. get wind of
15. open a can of worms
16. a bull in a china shop
17. roll out the red carpet
18. a rule of thumb
19. fly off the handle
20. keep one's nose to the grindstone

B. Below are listed ten expressions that you are likely to encounter in a newspaper or on radio or TV. None of them, probably, would have been used, or even understood, a few generations ago. With or without the aid of a dictionary, tell what each means. Then choose any **three**, and for each compose an original illustrative sentence.

1. keep one's options open
2. a counterculture
3. follow a game plan
4. make a value judgment
5. a polarized community
6. hands-on operations
7. a lifestyle
8. prime time
9. a ballpark estimate
10. a paraprofessional

Exercise III.   From the East to the West

Present-day English has been enriched by words from the many languages spoken from the Middle East to the islands in the Pacific Ocean. These loan words have come to us via many routes, including colonization, war, trade, travel, religion, philosophy, art, architecture, film and other mass media, and cuisine. Listed below are a number of these gifts from the East. With or without a dictionary, define each and tell where it comes from.

1. honcho	11. boomerang	21. sofa
2. aloha	12. caftan	22. raj
3. turban	13. lanai	23. guru
4. tulip	14. karaoke	24. shawl
5. kimono	15. curry	25. hula
6. billabong	16. khaki	26. tofu
7. genie	17. yogurt	27. yoga
8. pukka	18. rattan	28. lei
9. sahib	19. sari	
10. sushi	20. bonsai	

Exercise IV.   Expanding Your Word Power

The words listed below are not on the Basic Word List, but they were mentioned in passing in Lesson 18. All of them would make useful additions to your working vocabulary. Define each, give its etymology, list **two** synonyms and **two** antonyms (where possible), and use in a short illustrative sentence.

1. mutilate	6. anemic	11. florid
2. revel	7. introverted	12. diatribe
3. incentive	8. lurid	13. pontificate
4. incite	9. invigorate	14. gratuity
5. impede	10. dubious	15. portent

Related Forms in Context

Beneath each sentence below are four words introduced in Lesson 17 or 18. Review the related forms for these words, and choose the one that best completes the sentence. Write that related form in the space provided.

1. On December 16, 1773, a party of angry colonists disguised as Mohawk Indians __flagrantly__ broke the law when they dumped tea into Boston Harbor to protest the British tax on tea.

    a. frugal   b. fortuitous   c. flagrant   d. graphic

2. What do you think is the income ____gap____ between someone with a high school diploma and a person with a college degree?

    a. forestall   b. gape   c. gloat   d. garble

3. Undaunted by the _formidability_ of the task of cleaning the filthy stables of King Augeas in a single day, Hercules simply diverted two rivers to run through the stables.

    a. fickle   b. frugal   c. fortuitous   d. formidable

4. Eyewitnesses must have stood ___agape___ as they watched Daedalus and his son Icarus, the first people to fly on man-made wings, soar out over the sea.

    a. fluctuate   b. grope   c. gape   d. harangue

5. By the age of 30, Harriet Tubman realized the ___futility___ of the dream of buying her own freedom and escaped to the North.

    a. gullible   b. gratuitous   c. futile   d. flagrant

6. In ninth grade, Jim did a study to determine if _fluctuations_ in the U.S. stock market could be directly tied to national and international news.

    a. finesse   b. fluctuate   c. harbinger   d. forestall

7. After he kills Tybalt, Romeo exclaims, "O! I am Fortune's fool," bemoaning the _fickleness_ of fate.

    a. fickle   b. flagrant   c. gratuitous   d. gregarious

8. Modern chaos theory builds on Heraclitus's notion that everything in nature is in a constant state of ___flux___.

    a. flout   b. harangue   c. forestall   d. fluctuate

9. For years Dennis lived ___frugally___ on his small salary so that he could save enough money to bring all of his family from Ireland to America.

    a. fulsome   b. futile   c. frugal   d. flagrant

10. Christopher Columbus discovered the New World quite _fortuitously_, for he had set out to find a passage to India.

    a. futile   b. fortuitous   c. formidable   d. fulsome

11. Both Quakers and Shakers value a life of ___frugality___ and simplicity.

    a. flagrant   b. futile   c. gruesome   d. frugal

12. Although the two archrivals complimented each other _fulsomely_, their mutual dislike was quite obvious.

    a. fulsome   b. graphic   c. fickle   d. fortuitous

13. Those who peddle potions and pills that promise eternal youth and vitality rely on the _gullibility_ of people looking for quick and easy remedies.

    a. haggard   b. fortuitous   c. gruesome   d. gullible

14. Dorothea Lange's photographs document the plight of rural Americans during the Great Depression, capturing the _haggardness_ and despair reflected in their faces.

    a. fickle   b. graphic   <u>c. haggard</u>   d. gratuitous

15. Waiters and waitresses generally receive a very small salary and depend for their livelihood on _gratuities_ that their customers leave them.

    a. fortuitous   <u>b. gratuitous</u>   c. graphic   d. flagrant

16. The fierce brushstrokes and turbulent sky of Vincent Van Gogh's *Wheat Field with Crows* _graphically_ illustrate the artist's inner turmoil.

    <u>a. graphic</u>   b. gregarious   c. flagrant   d. frugal

17. Every year when our parents celebrate their anniversary, they tell us how grateful they are for the _fortuity_ of their improbable meeting so many years ago.

    a. futile   b. gregarious   <u>c. fortuitous</u>   d. formidable

18. Jane Goodall's studies of chimpanzees on the shore of Africa's Lake Tanganyika revealed new data about their social structure and _gregariousness_.

    a. graphic   b. haggard   c. gratuitous   <u>d. gregarious</u>

19. The _graph_, which is based on statistics from the latest U.S. census, illustrates the diversity of country of origin among those who identified themselves as Hispanic.

    a. flagrant   b. formidable   <u>c. graphic</u>   d. gratuitous

20. When she offered ten dollars to the young man who'd stopped to change her tire, he smiled and said, "Thanks very much, but my help is _gratis_."

    a. gullible   <u>b. gratuitous</u>   c. fickle   d. flagrant

Lesson 19

221. **haughty** — 235. **incense**

---

221. **haugh·ty**   *adjective*   hô′-tē
[*haut* (Old French), "high," from *altus* (Latin), "high"]

Definition: Scornfully superior and aloof.

I know I wasn't born with a silver spoon in my mouth, but that's no reason for a **haughty** salesclerk to treat me as if I had just crawled out of the woodwork.

Their **haughty** manner proclaimed more eloquently than words could have that they could never associate with an obscure nobody like me.

Phrases: a haughty aristocrat, a haughty manner

Related Forms: (*nouns*) haughtiness, hauteur; (*adverb*) haughtily

Synonyms: (*adjectives*) supercilious, disdainful, contemptuous, snooty, condescending, patronizing; proud, arrogant

Antonyms: (*adjectives*) modest, diffident, unassuming, unpretentious, meek; servile, fawning, obsequious (Word 282)

Related Phrases: as proud as a peacock, look down one's nose at, get up on one's high horse

222. **hei·nous**   *adjective*   hā′-nəs
[*haineus* (Old French), "hateful," from *haine* (Old French), "hatred"]

Definition: Grossly wicked or vile.

We found it hard to believe that our mild-mannered neighbor had actually committed the **heinous** crime of which he was accused.

For ancient Greeks and Romans, throwing away one's shield and fleeing from the battlefield was the most **heinous** act of cowardice a soldier could commit.

Phrases: a heinous offense, a heinous act of treason

Related Forms: (*noun*) heinousness; (*adverb*) heinously

Synonyms: (*adjectives*) diabolic, villainous, nefarious, monstrous, infamous; odious, reprehensible, abominable, loathsome, atrocious, despicable, abhorrent, execrable

Antonyms: (*adjectives*) laudable, commendable, meritorious, estimable, admirable

Related Phrases: moral turpitude, a venial sin, a mortal sin

223. ig‑no‑min‑y   *noun*   ĭg'‑nə‑mĭn‑ē

[*ignominia* (Latin), "removal of one's good name"; from *in* (Latin), "un‑, not" + *nomen, nominis* (Latin), "name"]

Definition: Dishonor or disgrace usually resulting from some sort of shameful conduct.

He was indeed a changed young man after he had suffered the **ignominy** of expulsion from West Point for conduct unbecoming an officer and a gentleman.

Related Forms: (*adjective*) ignominious; (*adverb*) ignominiously

Synonyms: (*nouns*) humiliation, degradation; disrepute, opprobrium, odium, infamy, obloquy

Antonyms: (*nouns*) esteem, acclaim, honor, admiration, glory, fame

Related Phrases: be under a cloud, be in bad odor, a blot on the escutcheon

224. il‑lic‑it   *adjective*   ĭ‑lĭs'‑ĭt

[*ill*, a form of *in* (Latin), "not" + *licitus* (Latin), "allowed"]

Definition: Unlawful, illegal.

Each year, part of the American tax dollar goes toward stemming the flood of **illicit** narcotics pouring into the country.

Related Forms: (*noun*) illicitness; (*adverb*) illicitly; (*adjective*) licit

Synonyms: (*adjectives*) unauthorized, unsanctioned; banned, forbidden, proscribed, outlawed; under‑the‑counter, under‑the‑table

Antonyms: (*adjectives*) legal, lawful, authorized, sanctioned; permissible, admissible, allowable, legitimate

Related Phrases: contraband goods, the black market, get in by the back door, a wildcat strike, off limits; go by the book

225. im‑mac‑u‑late   *adjective*   ĭ‑măk'‑yə‑lĭt

[*im*, a form of *in* (Latin), "un‑, not" + *maculatus* (Latin), "blemished"]

Definition: Entirely free of stain, blemish, fault, or error; spotless.

Despite the heat and dirt of a summer day in the city, my mother managed to keep her clothing absolutely **immaculate**.

He was a brilliant statesman whose record remained **immaculate** throughout a long career in public office.

Related Forms: (*noun*) immaculateness; (*adverb*) immaculately

Synonyms: (*adjectives*) unsoiled, unsullied, untarnished, undefiled; flawless, impeccable, unimpeachable, irreproachable

Antonyms: (*adjectives*) stained, spotted, blemished, sullied, tarnished

Related Phrases: spick‑and‑span, lily‑white, simon‑pure, pure as the driven snow

294

Police and U.S. Treasury agents close down a bar during Prohibition.

The Black Market

Black market is the popular term for the illegal sale and purchase of various kinds of commodities in violation of official restrictions, such as price controls and rationing. The expression is also applied to the place where such transactions are carried out. Today, there are black markets for a whole host of commodities ranging from automobiles and firearms to cigarettes and drugs. Black-market operations are also common in the exchange of foreign and domestic currency, especially in countries where the government has set the official exchange rate too high. During Prohibition in the United States (1920–1933), when the manufacture and sale of alcohol were illegal, *bootlegging* became a highly lucrative business. Bootlegging, which is the illegal sale of alcohol, was essentially a black-market operation under a different name.

---

226. im·mu·ni·ty   *noun*   ĭ-myoō'-nĭ-tē

[*immunis* (Latin), "exempt from service"; from *in* (Latin), "not" + *munia* (Latin), "duty, tax"]

Definition: Exemption from something, especially a disease.

Many people are fortunate enough to possess a natural **immunity** to certain diseases.

Though we all long for security in life, none of us can acquire total **immunity** from the hazards and misfortunes of the human condition.

Related Forms: (*verb*) immunize; (*noun*) immunization; (*adjective*) immune

Phrases: immune from prosecution; immune to reason; the immunization procedure

Synonyms: (*nouns*) impunity, insusceptibility; freedom, exclusion, release, protection, safety; dispensation, amnesty

Related Phrases: handle with kid gloves, preferential treatment, with impunity, get off with a slap on the wrist, go scot-free

295

227. **im·mu·ta·ble**   *adjective*   ĭ-myōō'-tə-bəl

[*im*, a form of *in* (Latin), "not" + *mutare, mutatus* (Latin), "change" + *abilis, abile* (Latin), "able to"]

Definition: Not subject to change or modification.

"Our legal system is not an **immutable** institution," the chief justice observed. "Like all else, it grows, develops, and changes over time."

Despite a series of unforeseen setbacks and failures, her faith in her own abilities remained **immutable**.

Related Forms: (*nouns*) immutability, immutableness, mutability; (*adjective*) mutable; (*adverb*) immutably

Synonyms: (*adjectives*) unchangeable, changeless, constant, fixed, invariable, unalterable, permanent; resolute, steadfast, unwavering, inflexible, rigid

Antonyms: (*adjectives*) changeable, alterable, variable; fickle, erratic, capricious, mercurial

Related Phrases: as constant as the northern star, as solid as the Rock of Gibraltar; a house built on sand

228. **im·passe**   *noun*   ĭm'-păs

[*impasse* (French), "dead end"; from *in* (French), "not" + *passer, passé* (French), "pass"]

Definition: A deadlock or dead end.

"Since we have reached an **impasse** in these negotiations," the union official asked the representative of management, "why don't we adjourn for the night?"

Related Forms: (*adjective*) impassable; (*nouns*) impassability, impassableness

Synonyms: (*nouns*) stalemate, cul-de-sac, standstill, dilemma

Related Phrases: lead up a blind alley, paint oneself into a corner, in a fix, in a bind, a Catch-22, come to a screeching (grinding) halt, a standoff, on the horns of a dilemma

Catch-22

A *Catch-22* is a difficult problem for which the different solutions that seem to be possible are logically invalid. The expression comes from *Catch-22*, the title of a novel by American writer Joseph Heller (1923–1999) (*see photo*). The hero of *Catch-22* faces many such situations throughout the course of the novel.

229. im-ped-i-ment   *noun*   ĭm-pĕd'-ə-mĕnt

[*impedimentum* (Latin), "obstacle"; from *impedire* (Latin), "get under foot or in the way"; from *in* (Latin), "in (the way of)" + *pes, pedis* (Latin), "foot"]

Definition: A hindrance or obstruction.

Lack of computer literacy is a serious **impediment** to finding a good job in today's world.

Phrase: a speech impediment

Related Forms: (*verb*) impede; (*noun*) impedimenta

Synonyms: (*nouns*) encumbrance; obstacle, handicap, barrier, bar

Antonyms: (*nouns*) aid, help, assistance

Related Phrases: a stumbling block, a fly in the ointment, a bottleneck; without let or hindrance; pull oneself up by one's bootstraps

230. im-per-vi-ous   *adjective*   ĭm-pẽr'-vē-əs

[*im*, a form of *in* (Latin), "not" + *per* (Latin), "through" + *via* (Latin), "road, way"]

Definition: Incapable of being penetrated or affected.

Cloth raincoats are usually treated with chemicals to make them **impervious** to water.

You may know someone who is absolutely **impervious** to criticism.

Related Forms: (*noun*) imperviousness; (*adjective*) pervious

Synonyms: (*adjectives*) impenetrable, impermeable; unresponsive, unreceptive, unamenable, closed (to)

Antonyms: (*adjectives*) penetrable, permeable, responsive, receptive, amenable (to), open (to), susceptible (to)

Related Phrases: proof against, hermetically sealed, vacuum-packed; stonewall someone; a closed society, a closed mind

231. im-pla-ca-ble   *adjective*   ĭm-plăk'-ə-bəl

[*im*, a form of *in* (Latin), "not" + *placare* (Latin), "calm, soothe" + *abilis, abile* (Latin), "able to"]

Definition: Incapable of being pacified or appeased; inflexible.

An **implacable** foe of slavery, William Lloyd Garrison took an uncompromising stand in favor of its abolition as early as 1831.

Several eighteenth-century British judges were **implacably** heartless and mechanical in the administration of justice.

Phrases: an implacable disease, implacable wrath

Related Forms: (*nouns*) implacableness, implacability; (*adverb*) implacably

Synonyms: (*adjectives*) unappeasable, unrelenting, unforgiving, relentless, inexorable, remorseless, unbending, obdurate, adamant, merciless

Antonyms: (*adjectives*) conciliatory, compassionate, understanding, merciful, forbearing

232. im-plic-it   *adjective*   ĭm-plĭs'-ĭt

[*implicitus* (Latin), "entangled, involved"; from *in* (Latin), "in" + *plicare, plicatus* (Latin), "fold"]

Definition:

a. Understood, implied.

> In almost any contract, there are **implicit** duties and obligations which must be fulfilled even though they are not expressed in so many words.

b. Absolute, unquestioning.

> He is the type of officer who expects **implicit** obedience from the troops under his command. When he gives an order, he assumes that it will be carried out.

Related Forms: (*adverb*) implicitly; (*nouns*) implicitness, implication; (*verb*) imply

Synonyms: (*adjectives*) inferred, inherent; tacit, unspoken; complete, unqualified, unconditional

Antonyms: (*adjectives*) explicit, specific, express

Related Phrases: take something for granted, categorically deny something, on a person's express orders

233. im-pugn   *verb*   ĭm-pyōōn'

[*in* (Latin), "against" + *pugnare* (Latin), "fight"]

Definition: To call into question; to cast doubt on.

> "Before you **impugn** the man's motives for doing what he did," I said, "you'd better make certain that you can back up your suspicions with hard evidence."

Phrases: impugn a person's veracity or honor, impugn a claim

Related Forms: (*nouns*) impugnment, impugnation; (*adjective*) impugnable

Synonyms: (*verbs*) question, query, challenge, deny, gainsay, dispute, malign

Antonyms: (*verbs*) vindicate, acquit, exonerate, exculpate; justify, rationalize; defend, champion, vouch for; affirm, verify, substantiate, confirm, corroborate

Related Phrases: cast aspersions on, run down, take exception to, bad-mouth someone, hurl brickbats at; backbiting; stick up for, an apologist

234. in·car·cer·ate *verb* ĭn-kär′-sə-rāt

[*incarcerare, incarceratus* (Latin), "imprison"; from *in* (Latin), "in" + *carcer* (Latin), "prison"]

Definition: To put in jail or otherwise confine.

In a democratic society such as ours, people may freely express their opinions without fear of being **incarcerated** for doing so.

In the Victorian era, fashionable ladies thought nothing of **incarcerating** their waists in tight corsets in order to achieve a chic hourglass figure.

Related Form: (*noun*) incarceration

Synonyms: (*verbs*) jail, imprison, intern; cage, immure, constrain, constrict

Antonyms: (*verbs*) liberate, emancipate, set free, release

Related Phrases: mew up, coop up, keep under lock and key, keep under wraps, a shut-in

235. in·cense *verb* ĭn-sĕns′

[*incendere, incensus* (Latin), "set on fire, enrage"; from *in* (Latin), "in, on" + *candere* (Latin), "glow"]

Definition: To make violently angry.

"You rarely give me cause to become angry," Dad said, "but this time your behavior has truly **incensed** me."

Related Form: (*adjective*) incendiary

Synonyms: (*verbs*) enrage, infuriate, enflame, provoke, incite

Antonyms: (*verbs*) soothe, calm, pacify, mollify, appease, placate

Related Phrases: see red, make one's blood boil, raise the hackles on one's neck, get under one's skin; a thorn in one's side.

(*Left*) A priest prepares incense for use during the Eucharist; (*right*) sticks of incense burning in a Buddhist temple. As a noun, *incense* (pronounced ĭn′-sĕns) indicates an aromatic gum or wood that produces a pleasant aroma when burned. Incense is often used in religious ceremonies to indicate the presence of God.

Using the Words

Exercise I
1. hei'-nous
2. ig'-no-min-y
3. il-lic'-it
4. im-ped'-i-ment
5. im-mu'-ni-ty
6. im-mu'-ta-ble
7. im-pugn'
8. in-car'-cer-ate
9. im'-passe

Exercise I. Syllabication and Pronunciation

Syllabicate the following words correctly, and place the major stress mark (') after the syllable that is accented when the word is pronounced.

1. heinous
2. ignominy
3. illicit

4. impediment
5. immunity
6. immutable

7. impugn
8. incarcerate
9. impasse

Exercise II. Words Out of Context

In each of the following groups, select the item that best expresses the meaning of the numbered word at the left.

1. illicit — a. illiterate b. illustrious c. illegible d. illogical e. illegal

2. immaculate — a. harmless b. spotless c. timeless d. shameless e. pointless

3. impasse — a. solution b. viewpoint c. mistake d. deadlock e. tunnel

4. implicit — a. villainous b. constant c. implied d. legitimate e. modest

5. impervious — a. shocked by b. closed to c. fond of d. eager for e. undecided about

6. implacable — a. costly b. outlawed c. unspoken d. diabolic e. relentless

7. incense — a. enrage b. puzzle c. frighten d. bore e. elate

Exercise III. Completing Sentences

Complete each of the following sentences by selecting the most appropriate word from the group of words given below. Use each word only once.

impugn   incarcerate   impediment

heinous   incense   immutable

immunity   ignominy   haughty

1. According to the Greek philosopher Heraclitus, the only _immutable_ law of nature is, paradoxically, that everything changes.

2. Somehow or other, the convicted murderer managed to escape from the maximum-security prison in which he had been <u>incarcerated</u>.

3. Once the leader's integrity had been <u>impugned</u>, his authority began to be challenged as well.

4. It wasn't the misfortune of losing the tennis match that mortified me so much as the <u>ignominy</u> of being defeated by a mere beginner.

5. Few crimes have been so monstrous and inhuman as Adolf Hitler's <u>heinous</u> scheme to exterminate millions of innocent people in grisly death camps.

6. With a sneer of contempt and a flick of his fingers, the <u>haughty</u> young man disdainfully dismissed both me and my suggestion from his mind.

7. No matter how carefully we try to protect ourselves, none of us ever achieves complete <u>immunity</u> from sickness and disease.

8. Fear of failure can often become a formidable <u>impediment</u> to success because it inhibits the mind and paralyzes the will.

Exercise IV.   Synonyms and Antonyms

Classify each of the following pairs of words as **S** for **synonyms** or **A** for **antonyms**.

S   1. anger—incense
A   2. impervious—receptive
A   3. illicit—legal
S   4. immaculate—flawless
S   5. ignominy—disgrace
A   6. meek—haughty
S   7. heinous—loathsome

S   8. impediment—obstacle
S   9. fixed—immutable
A 10. defend—impugn
A 11. incarcerate—liberate
S 12. standstill—impasse
S 13. implacable—unrelenting
A 14. explicit—implicit

Exercise V.   Word Roundup

1. With or without the aid of a dictionary, explain the difference in meaning between the words in each of the following pairs.

    a. illicit—elicit
    b. impugn—impute
    c. impassable—impassive
    d. venal—venial

2. With or without the aid of a dictionary, explain what each of the following expressions means.

    a. impedimenta
    b. an apologist
    c. a shut-in
    d. a bottleneck
    e. stonewall someone
    f. bad-mouth someone

3. With or without the aid of a dictionary, explain what each of the following colorful phrases means.

a. look down one's nose at
b. be under a cloud
c. go by the book
d. see red

e. paint oneself into a corner
f. go scot-free
g. get up on one's high horse
h. handle with kid gloves

4. Define each of the following, and explain where it came from.

a. a Catch-22
b. simon-pure

Exercise VI. Framing Sentences

A. Use each of the following words in an original sentence.

1. impugn
2. impasse
3. incense
4. immutable
5. implacable
6. impervious

B. Give a **noun** form of each of the following words, and use it in an original sentence.

incarceration
1. incarcerate
heinousness
2. heinous
haughtiness
3. haughty

C. Give a **verb** form related to each of the following words, and use it in an original sentence.

immunize
1. immunity
impede
2. impediment
imply
3. implicit

D. Give an **adverb** form of each of the following words, and use it in an original sentence.

illicitly
1. illicit
immaculately
2. immaculate
ignominiously
3. ignominy

Dissecting the Words

Prefixes

1. The Latin prefix **in** appears in a great many common English words. Basically, this prefix has two quite distinct meanings:

a. "Not," as in these words:

indefensible (*in*, "not" + *defensible*)—not capable of being defended, justified, or excused

invalidate (*in*, "not" + *validate*)—to nullify

inactivity (*in*, "not" + *activity*)—a lack of activity; idleness

inadvertently (*in*, "not" + *advertently*)—accidentally or unintentionally

When *in* has the meaning "not," it negates the sense of the word to which it is attached. In this regard, it functions in exactly the same way as the other negative prefixes used in modern English—*non*, *un*, and *a(n)*.

b. "In, into, within," as in these words:

incarnate (*in*, "into" + *caro, carnis* [Latin], "flesh")—to invest with bodily form and nature

inauguration (*in*, "in" + *augur*)—a formal beginning or introduction

incarcerate (*in*, "into" + *carcer* [Latin], "prison")—to put in prison

Note: In a few English words, *in* acts as an intensive, with the general meaning "very" or "completely." This use of the prefix occurs, for example, in the word *incandescent*, which means "glowing very bright."

2. The prefix *in* has several variant forms which are used when the word to which *in* is attached begins with a particular consonant, as follows:

a. The form **ig** is used in a few English words starting with *n*. For example:

ignoble (*ig*, "not" + *noble*)—base or lowborn; dishonorable

ignore (*ig*, "not" + *gnarus* [Latin], "knowing, known")—to refuse to notice; to reject or throw out

b. The form **il** is used before words beginning with an *l*. For example:

illogical (*il*, "not" + *logical*)—not logical

illuminate (*il*, "in" + *lumen, luminis* [Latin], "light")—to light up. Noun: *illumination*

c. The form **im** is used before a word beginning with an *m* or a *p*. For example:

immoral (*im*, "not" + *moral*)—not in accord with the accepted moral code

immerse (*im*, "not" + *mergere, mersus* [Latin], "dip")—to submerge or absorb completely

impure (*im*, "not" + *pure*)—not pure

impede (*im*, "in" + *pes, pedis* [Latin], "foot")—to hinder or obstruct

d. The form **ir** is used before a word beginning with an *r*. For example:

irreverent (*ir*, "not" + *reverent*)—lacking in sufficient respect for

irrigate (*ir*, "in" + *rigare, rigatus* [Latin], "bring water")—to supply with water; to wash out with water or another fluid

Roots

1. The Latin word **via**, which appears in the word *impervious*, studied in this lesson, means "road" or "way." Other common English words in which *via* appears as a root element include:

viaduct (*via*, "road" + *ducere, ductus* (Latin), "lead")—a bridge supporting a road or railroad over a valley or another (rail)road

deviate (*de* [Latin], "away" + *via*, "road, way" + *ate*, an English verb-forming suffix)—to turn or move away from. Noun: *deviation*

devious (*de* [Latin], "away" + *via*, "road, way" + *ous*, "characterized by") —not straightforward; roundabout or shifty. Noun: *deviousness*

convey (*cum* [Latin], "with" + *via*, "road, way")—to transmit or transport. Noun: *conveyance*—a vehicle; the act of transporting something

By itself, the Latin word *via* is used in English as a preposition with the meaning "by way of." For example, "I drove to Chicago *via* Buffalo."

2.   The Latin root **nomin** means "name." It appears in a number of common English words, including *ignominy*, studied in this lesson. Other English words in which it is used are:

nominal (*nomen, nominis*, "name" + *alis* [Latin], "relating to")—existing in name only; insignificantly small

nominate (*nomen, nominis*, "name" + *ate*, an English verb-forming suffix) —to propose for some office, responsibility, or honor. Noun: *nomination*

denomination (*de* [Latin], "completely" + *nomen, nominis*, "name" + *ation* [Latin], "state or process of")—the name of a specific group or class; an organized religious group

misnomer (*minus* [Latin], "less, wrong" + *nomen, nominis*, "name")— an error in naming something; a name inappropriately applied to something

3.   The parallel Greek word-building element usually appears in English as **onym** or **onomy**. Like *nomin*, these word elements mean "name." They appear in a number of very familiar English words, including *synonym*, *antonym*, and *homonym*. Other English words in which they are used are:

pseudonym (*pseudes* [Greek], "false" + *onoma, onyma*, [Greek], "name")— an assumed name

anonymous (*an* [Greek], "without" + *onoma, onyma*, [Greek], "name" + *ous* [Latin] "characterized by")—of unknown authorship. Noun: *anonymity*

onomatopoeia (*onoma, onyma*, [Greek], "name" + *poiein* [Greek], "make")— the formation of a word that imitates the sound of the thing it designates; for example, *hiss* or *buzz*

It is a little-known fact that Charlotte Bronte (1816–1855), the author of *Jane Eyre*, produced many of her works under the masculine pseudonym Currer Bell.

Exercise

1. For each of the following definitions, give an English word that contains the prefix *in* or one of its variants. Consult a dictionary if necessary.

   a. base or lowborn
   b. not capable of variation
   c. not able to be defended
   d. not in motion
   e. lacking sufficient respect
   f. not valid
   g. showing no emotion
   h. spotlessly clean
   i. not logical
   j. nullify

2. Change each of the following positive words to its negative form by adding the prefix *in* or one of its variants. Consult a dictionary if necessary.

   a. apt — inapt
   b. reversible — irreversible
   c. excusable — inexcusable
   d. solvent — insolvent
   e. contestible — incontestible
   f. pious — impious
   g. redeemable — irredeemable
   h. judicious — injudicious
   i. reducible — irreducible
   j. adequate — inadequate

3. With or without the aid of a dictionary, define each of the following words and use it in a short illustrative sentence.

   a. nomenclature
   b. pseudonym
   c. nominate
   d. conveyance
   e. devious
   f. convoy
   g. deviate
   h. misnomer
   i. viaduct
   j. anonymity

Working with Context Clues

More About Two-Word Omissions. Carefully study the following example of a fairly difficult two-word omission. Try to determine the correct answer before you read the explanation of it given below.

Because a medieval castle was primarily a fortress, it was built more for _____ than for _____.

a. decoration . . . usefulness
b. aggression . . . belligerence
c. pageantry . . . protection
d. defense . . . comfort

The correct answer is *d. defense . . . comfort*, as the following explanation clearly indicates.

Notice the brevity of the sentence contained in the example. It is only 17 words long. This suggests that some kind of inference clue will play a large part in determining the correct answer. Notice too the word *Because*. It suggests that you are dealing with a cause-and-effect relationship. Finally, notice the phrase *more for . . . than for* toward the end of the sentence. It indicates that two contrasting words go in the blanks.

Bearing these considerations in mind, reread the sentence carefully to find out what you are to do and how you can go about doing it. The sentence says that a medieval castle was by nature a certain type of build-

A view of the fortress at Carcassonne, France, one of the few surviving examples of a medieval walled city.

ing and that this defined the purpose it served. You are to explain what that purpose was based upon the information the sentence gives about the nature of a castle.

And what was the nature of a castle? The sentence says it was *primarily a fortress*. As you know, a fortress can be used for several purposes. It can serve as a refuge or as a prison or as a means of holding rebellious subjects in line. This suggests that the word that goes in the first blank means something like "protection" or "security" or some related idea.

Now run your eye down the first item in each of the four lettered choices. Eliminate any choice that does not conform to your conclusion about the general meaning of the word that goes in the first blank.

Choices *a* (*decoration*) and *c* (*pageantry*) do not agree with your conclusion, so they can safely be eliminated. Choices *b* (*aggression*) and *d* (*defense*), however, do, so you still have some thinking to do before you can make the correct choice.

At this point, recall what was said about the implication of the phrase *more for . . . than for*. It suggests that two *contrasting* words go in the blanks.

Accordingly, consider choices *b* and *d* from this angle. Choice *b* (*aggression . . . belligerence*) does not contain contrasting nouns, so it can be eliminated. Choice *d* (*defense . . . comfort*), however, does, so it must be the correct answer. And, of course, it is.

Exercise

Complete each of the following two-word omissions by selecting the pair of words that make the best sense in the passage as a whole. Underline the clue or clues that led you to make your choice.

1. After <u>two difficult years</u> in the White House, a <u>few run-ins</u> with the <u>press</u>, and several long, _____ battles with a <u>stubborn Congress</u>, it is no wonder that the president looks _____ and years older than when he took office.

   a. graphic . . . demure
   <u>b. grueling . . . haggard</u>
   c. diligent . . . emaciated
   d. gregarious . . . exotic

2. Clever advertisers continue to _____ supposedly sophisticated American consumers into believing the obvious _____ that cosmetics can confer youth and beauty on anyone.

   a. badger . . . effrontery
   b. cajole . . . epithet
   c. delude . . . fallacy
   d. coerce . . . calumny

3. Since the stock market is always rising and falling, investors who want to maintain their _____ must calmly stick with their investment strategy when stock prices _____ from day to day.

   a. equanimity . . . fluctuate
   b. bravado . . . augment
   c. finesse . . . deviate
   d. empathy . . . acclimate

4. The _____ monks who chose to _____ the Book of Kells with such beautiful decoration revealed not only their deep faith but also their superb artistry.

   a. eclectic . . . flaunt
   b. benign . . . array
   c. aesthetic . . . exalt
   d. devout . . . embellish

5. In 1955, when the black citizens of Montgomery, Alabama, defiantly refused to ride the segregated city buses, their _____ was meant to _____ local law and custom.

   a. anarchy . . . goad
   b. boycott . . . flout
   c. censure . . . exploit
   d. exodus . . . abet

Enriching the Lesson

Exercise I.   The Vocabulary of Social Change

Many expressions used today are associated with movements for social or cultural change. The words that make up these expressions have usually been around for a long time, but they are now being used in a sense that gives them a new significance and relevancy. This exercise is designed to help you improve your knowledge of a few of these terms.

A. *Causes Galore.*   Our national history in recent decades has been marked by many special causes and reform movements. The terms connected with a few of these movements are listed below. With or without the aid of a dictionary or other reference book, define each.

1. consumerism
2. environmentalism
3. urban renewal
4. feminism
5. multiculturalism
6. libertarianism
7. elitism
8. regionalism
9. animal rights

B. *The Struggle for Racial Equality.* Listed below are a number of terms and expressions associated with the struggle for racial equality. One of them, *lily-white*, was mentioned in passing in this lesson. With or without the aid of a dictionary or other reference book, define each.

1. racism
2. second-class citizen
3. black power
4. segregation
5. integration
6. racial profiling
7. stereotype
8. sit-in
9. lily-white
10. pluralism
11. redlining
12. equal opportunity

Exercise II. The Heritage of Literature

A. *Contributions Old and New.* Modern English has borrowed a surprising number of words and phrases from the works of famous and not-so-famous authors. Two of these expressions, *Catch-22* and *simon-pure*, were mentioned in this lesson. A few more are listed below. With or without the aid of a dictionary or other reference book, define each. Then give the source of the expression.

1. quixotic
2. a Pollyanna
3. gargantuan
4. a Babbitt
5. braggadocio
6. a Scrooge
7. serendipity
8. a rodomontade
9. a quark
10. bite the hand that feeds you
11. a termagant
12. a yahoo
13. utopian
14. a ragamuffin
15. an Ugly Duckling

Sir Thomas More (1478–1535) was a great English statesman, humanist, and martyr. Which of the words listed in Part A of Exercise II on this page did he contribute to the English language? 13. utopian

B. *William Shakespeare.* The works of William Shakespeare (1564–1616) have had a remarkable impact on the English language, including its vocabulary. Listed below are a number of familiar expressions that all derive in one way or another from Shakespeare's plays. With or without the aid of a dictionary or other reference book, define each as it is used in present-day English. Then give the name of the play from which the expression comes.

1. salad days	4. a benedict	7. mum's the word
2. a pound of flesh	5. the primrose path	8. hoist by one's
3. the milk of human kindness	6. sleep in Abraham's bosom	own petard

Exercise III.   A Verbal Diversion

One of the interesting English expressions mentioned in passing in this lesson was *see red*, meaning "become very angry." English has a number of other useful terms and expressions employing the adjective *red*. Some of them are listed below. With or without the aid of a dictionary, define or explain each. Then choose any **five** and for each compose an original illustrative sentence.

1. a red-letter day	6. in the red
2. a red herring	7. to red-pencil
3. caught red-handed	8. to roll out the red carpet
4. a redneck	9. red tape
5. to paint the town red	10. red flag

Exercise IV.   Expanding Your Word Power

The words listed below are not on the Basic Word List, but they were mentioned in passing, in one form or another, in Lesson 19. All of them would make useful additions to your working vocabulary. Define each, give its etymology, list **two** synonyms and **two** antonyms (where possible), and use in a short illustrative sentence.

1. condescend	6. dispensation	11. rationalize
2. nefarious	7. unimpeachable	12. constrain
3. turpitude	8. encumber	13. acclaim
4. sully	9. obdurate	14. mollify
5. impunity	10. gainsay	15. query

Lesson 20

236. inception — 250. justify

---

236. in-cep-tion *noun* ĭn-sĕp′-shən

[*inceptio, inceptionis* (Latin), "beginning"; from *incipere, inceptus* (Latin), "begin"; from *in* (Latin), "in, on" + *capere* (Latin), "take"]

Definition: The beginning of something.

"I have been an active member of our local bowling association," Grand-dad proudly boasted, "since its **inception** thirty years ago."

At the time of its **inception,** politicians always predict that great things will come of a new government program, but these high hopes are rarely fully realized.

Related Forms: (*adjective*) incipient; (*nouns*) incipience, incipiency

Synonyms: (*nouns*) commencement, inauguration, initiation, outset, kickoff, origin, onset, outbreak, debut, opening

Antonyms: (*nouns*) conclusion, finale, windup, finish, termination, close, completion, consummation, culmination, climax, denouement (Word 125)

Related Phrases: the opening gun, the starting lineup; from soup to nuts; the alpha and omega

237. in-di-gent *adjective* ĭn′-dĭ-jənt

[*indigens, indigentis* (Latin), "lacking, needing"]

Definition: Impoverished; needy.

The Wall Street Crash of 1929 left many a wealthy speculator as **indigent** as the proverbial church mouse.

Though the federal government does much to help those who are **indigent**, private charities play no little part in seeing to their welfare.

Related Form: (*noun*) indigence

Usage Note:
Be careful not to confuse *indigent* with either *indigenous*, meaning "native to," or *indignant*, meaning "irate" or "incensed."

Synonyms: (*adjectives*) destitute, impecunious, penniless, poverty-stricken

Antonyms: (*adjectives*) rich, wealthy, affluent (Word 17), well-to-do, well-off, well-heeled

Related Phrases: down in the heels, on the rocks, as poor as a church mouse; keep the wolf from the door, make ends meet, down and out

310

Thomas Alva Edison (1847–1931), the "Wizard of Menlo Park," was one of the most ingenious inventors ever produced by the United States.

238. in·gen·ious *adjective* ĭn-jēn'-yəs

[*ingenieux* (French), "clever"; from *ingenium* (Latin), "inborn talent"]

Definition: Showing remarkable originality, imagination, inventiveness, or skill; clever.

In 1793, Eli Whitney invented the cotton gin, an **ingenious** device for separating the seeds from the fiber quickly and easily.

Related Forms: (*nouns*) ingeniousness, ingenuity; (*adverb*) ingeniously

Usage Note:
Be careful not to confuse *ingenious* with *ingenuous* (note the first *u*), meaning "artless and unsophisticated" or "open and frank."

Synonyms: (*adjectives*) brilliant, inventive, creative, imaginative, talented; shrewd, cunning, crafty, astute; masterly, Daedalian

Antonyms: (*adjectives*) unimaginative, uninventive, unremarkable, unoriginal, pedestrian

239. in·her·ent *adjective* ĭn-hîr'-ĕnt

[*inhaerens, inhaerentis* (Latin), "sticking to"; from *in* (Latin), "in, on" + *haerere* (Latin), "stick, adhere"]

Definition: Existing as a natural or essential part of.

Most Americans firmly believe that the advantages **inherent** in a democratic form of government far outweigh the drawbacks that such a system usually entails.

Related Forms: (*adverb*) inherently; (*verb*) inhere; (*noun*) inherence

Synonyms: (*adjectives*) intrinsic, implicit, essential, internal, inner, fundamental, built-in, immanent, organic, natural, innate

Antonyms: (*adjectives*) extrinsic, external, extraneous, outside, foreign, alien; incidental, adventitious

Related Phrases: in the blood, to the manner born; a congenital defect

240. in-no-va-tion   *noun*   ĭn-ə-vā'-shən

[*innovare, innovatus* (Latin), "renew, alter"; from *in* (Latin), "completely" + *novus* (Latin), "new"]

Definition: Something new; a change.

In our eagerness to embrace whatever is new and modern, we must not assume that all **innovations** are necessarily practical and constructive.

Related Forms: (*noun*) innovator; (*verb*) innovate; (*adjective*) innovative

Usage Notes:
- a. Do not use the word *new* to qualify *innovation* because the word *new* is redundant.
- b. *Innovation* is often followed by the preposition *in*, as in the phrase "make innovations *in* the school curriculum."

Synonyms: (*nouns*) novelty, alteration, new wrinkle

Related Phrases: give something a new look, give something a face-lift; coin a word; cosmetic alterations, the avant-garde, a neologism

241. in-sti-gate   *verb*   ĭn'-stĭ-gāt

[*instigare, instigatus* (Latin), "spur on"]

Definition: To stir up or urge on.

Troublemakers in the crowd attempted to **instigate** a riot, but fortunately their efforts proved unsuccessful.

Related Forms: (*nouns*) instigation, instigator

Synonyms: (*verbs*) provoke, incite, foment, generate, touch off, start

Antonyms: (*verbs*) quell, quash, squelch, suppress, stop; allay, pacify

Related Phrases: put the kibosh on; an agent provocateur, a stormy petrel

242. in-su-per-a-ble   *adjective*   ĭn-soō'-pĕr-ə-bəl

[*insuperabilis, insuperabile* (Latin), "unconquerable" from *in* (Latin), "not" + *super-are* (Latin), "conquer" + *abilis, abile* (Latin), "able to"]

Definition: Incapable of being overcome.

"Much as I'd love to play shortstop for the Yanks, my age is an **insuperable** barrier to realizing any such dream," Granddad remarked.

Phrases: insuperable obstacles, insuperable difficulties

Related Forms: (*nouns*) insuperability, insuperableness

Synonyms: (*adjectives*) insurmountable, overwhelming, invincible, unconquerable, indomitable

Antonyms: (*adjectives*) surmountable, conquerable, vincible

243. **in-ter-vene**   *verb*   ĭn-tĕr-vēn′

[*intervenire* (Latin), "come between"; from *inter* (Latin), "between" + *venire* (Latin), "come"]

Definition: To come between; to involve oneself in.

A great many years **intervened** between the murder of the Russian imperial family and the discovery of their remains.

However benevolent your intentions, you may do more harm than good if you **intervene** in other people's quarrels.

Related Forms: (*nouns*) intervention, interventionism

Synonyms: (*verbs*) separate; interfere, meddle, intrude, interpose; kibitz

Related Phrases: an interloper; horn in on, poke one's nose into, put one's oar in, put one's two cents' worth in; in the interim; sandwiched in between

UN troops enter a town in Bosnia. During the early 1990s a multinational UN force was dispatched to the region to help put an end to a bloody civil war.

Interventionism

Interventionism is a term that is often used in discussions of international politics to describe the behavior of one country in regard to the other countries of the world, especially the smaller, weaker, and less stable ones. What the term indicates is the intentional policy of one sovereign nation of interfering in the domestic affairs of another sovereign nation. The implication, of course, is that such a policy is undertaken for purely selfish reasons or in order to achieve some advantage over one's enemies. Accordingly, the tone of the word is decidedly negative.

313

244. in·trep·id   *adjective*   ĭn-trĕp'-id

[*intrepidus* (Latin), "fearless"; from *in* (Latin), "not" + *trepidus* (Latin), "frightened, alarmed"]

Definition: Fearless and bold.

The rows of white gravestones in Arlington National Cemetery are poignant reminders of the **intrepid** men and women who gave their lives in defense of this country.

"In carrying out new programs," the legislator remarked, "we need people who are **intrepid** enough to take a few risks, even with their lives and reputations."

Related Forms: (*nouns*) intrepidity, intrepidness; (*adverb*) intrepidly

Synonyms: (*adjectives*) valiant, daring, courageous, gallant, gutsy, stouthearted, lionhearted, audacious, valorous, heroic

Antonyms: (*adjectives*) cowardly, craven, timorous, pusillanimous

245. in·veigh   *verb*   ĭn-vā'

[*invehere* (Latin), "carry in, attack"; from *in* (Latin), "in" + *vehere* (Latin), "carry"]

Definition: To protest bitterly or vehemently.

When the train ground to a halt yet again, one passenger began to **inveigh** angrily against the transit system and the people who ran it.

Related Form: (*noun*) invective

Usage Note:
Do not confuse *inveigh* with *inveigle,* which means "to obtain by flattery or deceit."

Synonyms: (*verbs*) rail against, fulminate against, denounce, berate, decry, lambaste

Antonyms: (*verbs*) praise, commend, extol, laud

Related Phrases: jump down someone's throat, give someone a tongue-lashing

246. i·ro·ny   *noun*   ī'-rə-nē

[*eironeia* (Greek), "pretended ignorance"; from *eirein* (Greek), "say"]

Definition: Incongruity between what might be expected and what actually happens.

It was one of life's little **ironies** that a man who had condemned so many others to the gallows should himself die by the noose.

Related Forms: (*adjectives*) ironic, ironical; (*adverb*) ironically

Synonyms: (*nouns*) contradiction, paradox

Related Phrases: a backhanded compliment, damn with faint praise

Mark Antony (Marlon Brando) delivers the funeral oration in the 1953 film version of Shakespeare's *Julius Caesar.*

Verbal and Dramatic Irony

Verbal irony refers to the use of words to convey the opposite of their literal meaning. For example, a person who uses expressions of praise in order to scold someone else is employing verbal irony. The device is frequently used to achieve a humorous, sarcastic, or dramatic effect. One of the most famous examples of the use of verbal irony to achieve a dramatic effect occurs in Shakespeare's *Julius Caesar.* In his funeral oration over Caesar's body, Mark Antony repeatedly characterizes Brutus and the other conspirators as "honorable men" who did Rome a service by murdering Caesar when, of course, he intends his audience to understand that they were quite the opposite.

Dramatic irony is a related device used in plays and similar material. The term indicates an incongruity between the significance of an action on the stage and the literal meaning of the words or speeches that accompany it. The audience, of course, perceives this incongruity, but the characters in the play do not. For example, Lady Macbeth's effusive greeting of King Duncan in Shakespeare's *Macbeth* is painfully ironic because the audience knows that she and her husband plan to murder the old monarch that night. King Duncan is unaware of this, so he takes the lady's words at face value and blithely walks into the trap. To Duncan, Lady Macbeth appears to be the quintessence of hospitality; to the audience, she is more like a spider luring a fly into its web.

247. jeop·ard·ize   *verb*   jĕp'-ēr-dīz

[*jeu parti* (Old French), a game in which the chances of winning or losing are equal; from *jeu* (French), "game" + *parti* (French), "divided"]

Definition: To endanger.

High school students who settle for mediocre grades when they could be doing better are **jeopardizing** their chances of being accepted by the college of their choice.

Related Form: (*noun*) jeopardy

Usage Note:
The legal expression *double jeopardy* refers to putting a person on trial for the same crime twice. Under our system of law, this is of course illegal.

Synonyms: (*verbs*) risk, hazard, imperil, compromise, gamble with

Antonyms: (*verbs*) protect, shield, safeguard, defend; improve, better

Related Phrases: sail too near the wind, fly too close to the sun, tempt fate

248. jet·ti·son   *verb*   jĕt'-ĭ-sən   *or*   jĕt'-ĭ-zən

[*getteson(e)* (Old French), "a throwing overboard"; from *jacere, jactus* (Latin), "throw"]

Definition: To throw overboard; to discard.

The crew of the sinking freighter **jettisoned** most of the cargo in a desperate effort to keep the ship afloat.

In our eagerness to improve the quality of life in America, we should not be too quick to **jettison** old ideas simply because they are old.

Synonyms: (*verbs*) dump, throw out, junk, abandon, toss out

Antonyms: (*verbs*) conserve, preserve, keep, hold on to, retain

Related Phrases: flotsam and jetsam, give something the deep-six

249. ju·di·cious   *adjective*   jōō-dĭsh'-əs

[*judicieux* (French), "wise"; from *judicium* (Latin), "judgment"]

Definition: Having or exhibiting sound judgment.

Thanks to my broker's **judicious** advice, I refrained from making what turned out to be a very unsound investment.

Related Forms: (*noun*) judiciousness, (*adverb*) judiciously; (*adjective*) injudicious

Usage Note:
Be careful not to confuse the adjective *judicious,* meaning "having or showing sound judgment," with the related adjective *judicial.* The latter means "relating to a court, the administration of justice, or the office of a judge." For example, the *judicial* system is the court system.

316

Similarly, *judicial review* is the constitutional principle that gives the Supreme Court the right to cancel any legislative or executive act that the justices sitting on the Court consider unconstitutional.

Phrases: a judicious choice of words, a judicious mixture of elements

Synonyms: (*adjectives*) prudent, astute, discriminating, discerning, sagacious, sage, shrewd

Antonyms: unwise, imprudent, foolish, rash, unsound

250. jus-ti-fy *verb* jŭs′-tə-fī
[*justificare* (Latin), "do justice to"; from *justus* (Latin), "just" + *facere* (Latin), "do, make"]

Definition: To show to be just, right, valid, or free of blame.
"You may be able to **justify** your anger at Bill," I replied, "but you were quite wrong to hit him."
The excellent quality of the coat clearly **justifies** its high price.

Related Forms: (*adjective*) justifiable; (*adverb*) justifiably; (*nouns*) justification, justifiability, justifiableness

Synonyms: (*verbs*) defend, vindicate

Related Phrases: show just cause for, give good reasons for

Using the Words

Exercise I. Parts of Speech

Indicate the part of speech of each of the following words.

1. indigent adj.
2. innovation n.
3. insuperable adj.
4. intrepid adj.
5. inveigh v.
6. irony n.
7. jettison v.
8. judicious adj.
9. justify v.

Exercise II. Words in Phrases

In each of the following groups, select the item that best expresses the meaning of the *italicized* expression in the introductory phrase.

1. *jeopardize* one's chances of success
   a. insure b. endanger c. calculate d. doubt
   e. enhance

2. a *judicious* choice of words
   a. surprising b. silly c. novel d. painful e. prudent

3. *inveigh against* injustice
   a. champion b. ignore c. denounce d. report
   e. improve

4. an *ingenious* scheme to make money
   a. clever b. unworkable c. costly d. problematic
   e. dangerous

5. full of *inherent* problems and defects
   a. built-in b. minor c. unexpected d. knotty
   e. temporary

6. since its *inception*
   a. demise b. graduation c. marriage d. inauguration
   e. dismissal

7. "*justify* the ways of God to man"
   a. criticize b. divulge c. vindicate d. deplore
   e. conceal

Exercise III.   Completing Sentences

Complete each of the following sentences or pairs of sentences by selecting the most appropriate word from the group of words given below. Use each word only once.

intrepid	intervene	indigent
instigate	jettison	irony
innovation	inveigh	insuperable

1. The man's ragged clothing and emaciated body told me instantly that he was totally __indigent__.

2. Often a(n) __innovation__ that seems bold and inventive when it is first introduced is soon taken for granted.

3. "I will never concede defeat," I told myself, "no matter how __insuperable__ the odds against me appear to be."

4. The old adage "Don't throw the baby out with the bathwater" cautions us against inadvertently __jettisoning__ the good with the bad.

5. There is an unmistakable __irony__ in the fact that the steps the dictator took to insure his own safety proved his undoing.

6. "It is one thing to be __intrepid__," my best friend observed when I tried to ride a horse I couldn't handle. "It is quite another to be foolhardy."

7. "Are you the troublemaker who __instigated__ the food fight in the cafeteria today?" the principal asked me angrily.

8. Though I didn't start to write my report until two weeks after I had completed my research, I used the time that __intervened__ to plan it out.

Exercise IV.   Synonyms and Antonyms

A. In each of the following groups, select the **two** words that are most nearly **synonymous**.

1. a. clever   b. prominent   c. mature   d. inventive   ingenious
2. a. baffle   b. provoke   c. foment   d. divulge   instigate
3. a. inaudible   b. insurmountable   c. inconceivable
    d. invincible   insuperable
4. a. interfere   b. conclude   c. meddle   d. devise   intervene
5. a. abandon   b. discard   c. retain   d. increase   jettison

Now, for each pair of synonyms that you have selected, supply a word from the Basic Word List for this lesson (Words 236–250) that means **the same** or **almost the same** thing.

B. In each of the following, select the item that is most nearly **opposite** in meaning to the numbered word at the left.

1. judicious   a. illegal   b. wealthy   c. unwise   d. novel
    e. expert
2. inception   a. articulation   b. fabrication   c. inauguration
    d. collaboration   e. termination
3. indigent   a. dejected   b. coarse   c. blithe   d. eminent
    e. affluent
4. intrepid   a. slovenly   b. treacherous   c. ignorant
    d. cowardly   e. cruel
5. jeopardize   a. protect   b. yield   c. claim   d. delay
    e. encounter

Exercise V.   Word Roundup

1. Explain the difference in meaning between the items in each of the following pairs of words.

    a. indigent—indigenous   c. ingenious—ingenuous
    b. inveigh—inveigle   d. judicious—judicial

2. With or without a dictionary, define each of the following French expressions commonly used in modern English.

    a. agent provocateur   b. tour de force   c. avant-garde

3. With or without the aid of a dictionary, explain what each of the following means.

    a. a backhanded compliment   c. a congenital defect
    b. cosmetic alterations   d. to the manner born

4. Define or explain the following legal expressions.

    a. judicial review   b. double jeopardy

5. Define each of the following colorful expressions.

    a. keep the wolf from the door   b. jump down someone's throat

Exercise VI. Framing Sentences

A. Use each of the following words in an original sentence.

1. inception   3. insuperable   5. inveigh
2. indigent   4. intrepid   6. jettison

B. Give a **noun** form of each of the following words, and use it in a short illustrative sentence.

    instigation, instigator   intervention   jeopardy
1. instigate   2. intervene   3. jeopardize

C. Give an **adjective** form of each of the following words, and use it in a short illustrative sentence.

    innovative   ironic   justifiable
1. innovation   2. irony   3. justify

D. Give an **adverb** form of each of the following words, and use it in a short illustrative sentence.

1. ingenious   2. judicious   3. inherent
   ingeniously   judiciously   inherently

Completing Verbal Analogies

"A Is by Definition a Person Who B's." Another word relationship that frequently appears in the analogy questions on standardized vocabulary tests may be expressed as "A is by definition a person who B's; C is by definition a person who D's." Following is an example of an analogy question involving this relationship. Try to determine the correct answer before reading the explanation of it given below.

fugitive : flee =
    a. critic : censor   d. doctor : operate
    b. spectator : observe   e. tyrant : prosecute
    c. advertiser : conceal

The answer is *b.* A *spectator* is by definition someone who *observes*, just as a *fugitive* is by definition someone who *flees.*

None of the other choices exhibits the same relationship as the key pair of words. A *critic* (choice *a*) may praise or censure, but he or she does not *censor.* Similarly, a *tyrant* (choice *e*) usually persecutes people, but he does not by definition *prosecute* them. (That is the job of someone like a district attorney.) Though a surgeon by definition *operates* on his or her patients, a *doctor* (choice *d*), the more general term for someone in the medical profession, is not by definition associated with such a procedure. (For choice *d* to be correct, it would have to read either *surgeon : operate* or *doctor : heal.*) Finally, an advertiser (choice *c*) makes a product or service more widely known; he or she does not *conceal* it.

Note: A related form of this word relationship may be expressed as "A is by definition someone who is B; C is by definition someone who is D." For example, *hero : valorous = knight : chivalrous.*

"The Tone of A Is B."   Another useful word relationship may be expressed as "The tone of *A* is *B*; the tone of *C* is *D*." Here is an example of an analogy question involving this relationship. Try to determine the correct answer before reading the explanation of it given below.

salubrious : favorable =
a. munificent : unfavorable
b. pernicious : favorable
c. deleterious : unfavorable
d. inimical : favorable
e. beneficial : unfavorable

The answer is *c*. The tone of *deleterious* is decidedly negative or *unfavorable*, just as the tone of *salubrious*, its antonym, is positive or *favorable*.

All of the other choices are clearly wrong. The tone of both *munificent* (choice *a*) and *beneficial* (choice *e*) is *favorable*, not unfavorable. Similarly, the tone of *pernicious* (choice *b*) and *inimical* (choice *d*) is *unfavorable*, not favorable.

Exercise I

Complete each of the following analogies based on the word relationships "*A* is a person who *B*'s" and "The tone of *A* is *B*."

1. **circumspect : favorable ::**
   a. opinionated : favorable
   b. rash : unfavorable
   c. cumbersome : favorable
   d. splendid : unfavorable
   e. erratic : favorable

2. **thief : steal ::**
   a. hoard : miser
   b. refugee : asylum
   c. researcher : investigator
   d. mendicant : beg
   e. monarch : usurp

3. **activist : militant ::**
   a. mourner : doleful
   b. proprietor : incessant
   c. accomplice : dominant
   d. peacemaker : belligerent
   e. coward : intrepid

4. **arbitrator : mediate ::**
   a. prophet : eavesdrop
   b. mason : slaughter
   c. parish : rector
   b. counselor : advise
   e. warden : prisoner

5. **murmur : low ::**
   a. mumble : clear
   b. jeer : gladden
   c. screech : piercing
   d. rasping : whine
   e. bellow : melodious

Exercise II   Answers will vary.

Compose **two** complete analogies based on the word relationship "*A* is by definition a person who *B*'s" and **two** based on "The tone of *A* is *B*." In your original analogies, use at least **two** words from the Basic Word List for Lessons 1–20 (Words 1–250).

The following items review what you have so far learned about analogy questions. Complete each.

1. **abet : encourage** = thwart :
   (connive, _frustrate_, abhor, forbear, defend)

2. **intrepid : craven** = laudable :
   (praiseworthy, illicit, _reprehensible_, timely, indigent)

3. **effrontery : audacious** = fickleness :
   (_capricious_, felicitous, adamant, fortuitous, haggard)

4. **haughty : humility** = effete :
   (duplicity, effrontery, credibility, equanimity, _vitality_)

5. **impervious : penetrate** = implacable :
   (grimace, justify, _appease_, impugn, filch)

Working with Context Clues

By now you have enough familiarity with the two-word omissions that appear on standardized tests to handle them without further guidance. Accordingly, the remaining "Working with Context Clues" sections of this book will concentrate on providing you with enough practice in dealing with two-word omissions for you to tackle those that actually appear on standardized tests with skill and confidence. In trying to apply the knowledge you now possess to practical situations, remember one important principle: Always isolate the context clues before you attempt to choose the right answer.

Exercise

Complete each of the following two-word omissions by selecting the pair of words that make the best sense in the passage as a whole. Underline the clue or clues that led you to make your choice.

1. Conservative politicians are sometimes accused by their liberal opponents of being _____ to the problems of poverty, but conservatives deny being unresponsive to the plight of the _____.

   a. dedicated . . . elite
   b. impervious . . . indigent
   c. adverse . . . belligerent
   d. ambivalent . . . frugal

2. In order not to _____ the safety of the community, a judge can refuse to grant bail and _____ a defendant when the judge believes the accused might cause harm if set free while on trial.

   a. jeopardize . . . incarcerate
   b. disparage . . . censure
   c. flout . . . absolve
   d. compromise . . . coerce

3. Some ambitious politicians will do whatever is _____ to get elected, even if that means they must abandon principles and _____ programs and policies that they once believed in and worked hard to achieve.

   a. crucial . . . justify   c. astute . . . bungle
   b. fortuitous . . . exploit   d. expedient . . . jettison

4. The shameful extent to which the federal government and the U.S. Army were willing to _____ the trust of the Native American peoples in the nineteenth century by repeatedly making and breaking treaties with them is a national _____.

   a. abuse . . . harbinger   c. exploit . . . disgrace
   b. cajole . . . anomaly   d. coerce . . . calumny

5. The nature of the crimes committed in the Nazi concentration camps was so _____ that it is hard to imagine any action redeeming enough to _____ for such terrible suffering.

   a. gratuitous . . . qualify   c. heinous . . . atone
   b. flagrant . . . grope   d. delinquent . . . abdicate

6. After hours of _____ debate, the exhausted senators were unable to resolve their differences and had to admit that they had reached a(n) _____.

   a. judicious . . . amnesty   c. facetious . . . consensus
   b. esoteric . . . boycott   d. grueling . . . impasse

7. Despite probing studies by many experts who are trying to _____ their meaning, the mysterious animal paintings on the caves of Altamira in northern Spain remain a(n) _____.

   a. fathom . . . enigma   c. divulge . . . conjecture
   b. explain . . . fiasco   d. elicit . . . irony

8. Due to the _____ efforts of courageous abolitionists, runaway slaves from the South were able to find shelter in a series of _____ way stations on their trek north to freedom on the secret Underground Railroad.

   a. frugal . . . convenient   c. astute . . . exotic
   b. illicit . . . austere   d. intrepid . . . clandestine

9. Some seasoned organizers of political demonstrations deliberately provoke a(n) _____ so they can use the face-to-face encounter to _____ the authorities into making themselves look bad.

   a. exigency . . . force   c. exodus . . . embarrass
   b. confrontation . . . goad   d. anecdote . . . harangue

10. The manufacturing sector of our economy is shrinking due to a <u>continuing flight</u> of capital investment abroad, resulting in _____ unemployment at home and obvious _____ in the number of domestic-made products.

   a. chronic . . . attrition
   b. temporary . . . growth
   c. implacable . . . duplicity
   d. arbitrary . . . apathy

Enriching the Lesson

Exercise I. Coining Words

Coinage of English words goes on all the time. A new development occurs in politics, science, business, entertainment, or elsewhere. If current language has no suitable words to define or describe it, a new word will probably be devised, or an old word (or old words in combination) will be adapted to meet the need. If the coinage is vivid or picturesque or pointedly fitting, it catches on and may enjoy some degree of permanence.

Consider the word *conglomerate.* It is by no means a newcomer to English, having been used for centuries to refer to a certain type of rock composed of fragments. It *is* relatively new, however, in its application to a type of business combination that developed in the middle of the 20th century.

The nuclear age gave birth to the word *brinkmanship* (*brink* + *manship*), linguistically structured like *penmanship* and *salesmanship,* to describe a certain type of strategy used in international politics. It suggests the act of creating a potentially explosive situation and pushing it to the very brink of war in order to intimidate other nations and force them to make concessions.

In the 1950s, the novelist Jack Kerouac used the common word *beat* in a new phrase, *beat generation,* to identify members of the disillusioned generation following World War II who developed a new lifestyle of nonconformity and freewheeling self-expression and social criticism.

Some other more or less recent coinages include *take-home pay, astronaut, brainwash, telethon,* and *printout.*

Listed below are a number of coinages. Some are more or less recent. Others go farther back into the history of English. With or without the aid of a dictionary or other reference book, define each. Then choose any **five**, and for each compose a short illustrative sentence.

1. urbanologist
2. superstar
3. peacenik
4. telemarketing
5. debit card
6. environmentalist
7. astronaut
8. supersonic
9. brainwash
10. unisex
11. paraprofessional
12. cyberspace
13. programmer
14. brunch
15. quasar

During the 1950s, Jack Kerouac (1922–1969) was as much an "apostle" of the beat generation in prose as Allen Ginsberg was in poetry. A native of Lowell, Massachusetts, Kerouac roamed through the United States and Mexico for a number of years investigating the beatnik subculture. He published a series of novels that drew upon his travels and reflected his relentless pursuit of new experience and sensation. These include *The Town and the City* (1950), *On the Road* (1957), *The Dharma Bums* (1958), and *Big Sur* (1962).

16. virtual reality	23. prime time	30. debrief
17. biohazard	24. play-off	31. E-mail
18. miniskirt	25. motorcade	32. camcorder
19. ecosystem	26. miniseries	33. skateboard
20. anchorperson	27. fanzine	34. litterbug
21. megalopolis	28. cheeseburger	35. jet lag
22. whistle-blower	29. soap opera	36. camper

Exercise II.   Expanding Your Word Power

The words listed below are not on the Basic Word List, but they were mentioned in one form or another in Lesson 20. All of them would make useful additions to your working vocabulary. Define each, give its etymology, list **two** synonyms and **two** antonyms (where possible), and use in a short illustrative sentence.

1. culmination	6. fulminate	11. vindicate
2. impecunious	7. compromise	12. timorous
3. immanent	8. suppress	13. interpose
4. adventitious	9. hazard	14. generate
5. indomitable	10. sagacious	15. conserve

Related Forms in Context

Beneath each sentence below are four words introduced in Lesson 19 or 20. Review the related forms for these words, and choose the one that best completes the sentence. Write that related form in the space provided.

1. Ella Fitzgerald, an ___innovator___ among jazz and blues singers, pioneered scat singing, a type of vocal improvisation without words.

   a. impasse   b. inception   c. impediment   **d. innovation**

2. It is ___ironic___ that the supposedly unsinkable SS *Titanic* sank on her maiden voyage after colliding with an iceberg.

   a. immunity   **b. irony**   c. innovation   d. inception

3. Sir Thomas Malory wrote most of *The Book of King Arthur and His Noble Knights of the Round Table* during his twenty-year incarceration for violent crimes, including murder and robbery.

   a. impugn   b. instigate   **c. incarcerate**   d. intervene

4. When it came to planning King Duncan's murder, who do you think was the chief ___instigator___—Macbeth or Lady Macbeth?

   a. instigate   b. incense   c. intervene   d. jeopardize

5. During the Nuremburg trials of 1945–1946, concentration camp survivors testified to the heinousness of the Nazis' crimes.

   a. inherent   b. impervious   c. implicit   **d. heinous**

6. "I know not what course others may take, but as for me, give me liberty or give me death!" cried Patrick Henry in his ___incendiary___ speech to the Virginia Convention in March of 1775.

   a. impugn   **b. incense**   c. jeopardize   d. jettison

7. In December 1955, Rosa Parks ___justifiably___ refused to give up her seat to a white man on a Montgomery, Alabama, municipal bus, touching off a year-long bus boycott led by Dr. Martin Luther King, Jr.

   a. incense   b. jeopardize   c. inveigh   **d. justify**

8. When they built the western leg of the transcontinental railroad, the mostly Chinese laborers tunneled through mountain ranges once thought to be impassable .

   a. ignominy   **b. impasse**   c. innovation   d. immunity

9. On a number of occasions, intervention by U.N. multinational peacekeeping forces has been necessary in countries torn by civil war.

   a. incarcerate   b. instigate   **c. intervene**   d. inveigh

10. Despite his harsh __invective__ when our baseball crashed through his kitchen window, our softhearted neighbor tossed the ball back to us.

    a. instigate   b. incense   c. jeopardize   d. inveigh

11. Queen Elizabeth I of England may have had a reputation for haughtiness, but she was beloved by her people for the strong leadership she provided during her 44-year reign.

    a. haughty   b. immaculate   c. indigent   d. impervious

12. Those who __illicitly__ copy and sell movies or recordings can be prosecuted for copyright infringement.

    a. haughty   b. illicit   c. implicit   d. immutable

13. In both plants and animals, __pervious__ cell membranes regulate the flow of materials into and out of the cell.

    a. immaculate   b. implicit   c. illicit   d. impervious

14. Someone with an obsessive personality may perform mundane routines with an __implacability__ that is startling to others.

    a. illicit   b. implacable   c. implicit   d. heinous

15. __Inherently__ talented, the Austrian composer Wolfgang Amadeus Mozart was composing minuets at age five and his first symphony at age nine.

    a. indigent   b. immutable   c. implicit   d. inherent

16. The Hoover Dam, which __impedes__ the flow of the Colorado River at Black Canyon, provides hydroelectric power, water for irrigation and recreation, and flood control.

    a. inception   b. impediment   c. irony   d. ignominy

17. Pediatricians recommend that children receive immunizations for the following diseases: hepatitis B, diphtheria, whooping cough, tetanus, polio, measles, mumps, rubella, and chicken pox.

    a. ignominy   b. innovation   c. immunity   d. impasse

18. Some historians believe that the ignominious terms for German surrender in the 1919 Treaty of Versailles led directly to World War II.

    a. inception   b. ignominy   c. innovation   d. impediment

19. As a child, what I admired most about Wonder Woman, the first female comic book superhero, was her intrepidness.

    a. inherent   b. immutable   c. implicit   d. intrepid

20. Wendy is sneezing and has a scratchy throat, sure signs of an __incipient__ cold.

    a. inception   b. innovation   c. immunity   d. impasse

Exercise I

1. con-strue′	5. ec-lec′-tic	11. gri′-mace,
2. cor′-rob-o-rate,	6. em′-a-nate	gri-mace′
cor-rob′-o-rate	7. es-o-ter′-ic	12. gul′-li-ble
3. de′-fect, de-fect′	8. ex-pe′-di-ent	13. ha-rangue′
4. de′-vi-ate	9. fet′-ish	14. in-veigh′
	10. fu′-tile	15. jus′-ti-fy

Review

101. **connoisseur** — 250. **justify**

Exercise I.   Syllabication and Pronunciation

Syllabicate the following words correctly and place the major stress mark (′) after the syllable that is accented when the word is pronounced. Two answers are correct in some instances.

1.	construe	6.	emanate	11.	grimace
2.	corroborate	7.	esoteric	12.	gullible
3.	defect	8.	expedient	13.	harangue
4.	deviate	9.	fetish	14.	inveigh
5.	eclectic	10.	futile	15.	justify

Exercise II.   Parts of Speech

Indicate the part of speech of each of the following words. In some cases, two answers are correct.

1.	consensus n.	6.	discourse v., n.	11.	finesse n., v
2.	consummate v., adj.	7.	epithet n.	12.	heinous adj.
3.	counsel v., n.	8.	forestall v.	13.	impasse n.
4.	curtail v.	9.	fickle adj.	14.	impugn v.
5.	dire adj.	10.	filch v.	15.	irony n.

Exercise III.   Words Out of Context

In each of the following groups, select the lettered item that best expresses the meaning of the numbered word at the left.

1. devoid
a. saturated   b. angry   c. empty
d. foolish   e. clumsy

2. efficacious
a. effective   b. inadequate   c. extravagant
d. recent   e. lethargic

3. fabricate
a. remove   b. concoct   c. conceal
d. destroy   e. consider

4. facsimile
a. oath   b. treachery   c. skill   d. duplicate
e. fortune

5. garble
a. distort   b. clarify   c. report   d. sing
e. control

6. goad
a. suppose   b. curb   c. investigate
d. enjoy   e. prod

7. haggard
a. sunny   b. wealthy   c. gaunt   d. fat

328

8. instigate   a. snoop **b. foment** c. explore d. yawn
e. complain

9. illicit   a. invincible b. illiterate c. interminable
d. illegal e. inflexible

10. jettison   a. beautify **b. discard** c. preserve d. order

Exercise IV. Completing Sentences

Complete each of the following sentences by selecting the most appropriate word from the groups of words given below.

Group A

exacerbate	foibles	flagrant
grueling	criterion	deleted

1. Though I admire the candidate's strong points, I find his _____foibles_____ laughable.

2. In my haste to cut my essay down to size, I accidentally _____deleted_____ some essential information.

3. "Though the proposal will certainly solve some of our economic problems," the senator remarked, "it will unfortunately _exacerbate_ others."

4. A 26-mile marathon is a(n) _____grueling_____ test of any runner's strength and endurance, no matter how well prepared he or she may be.

5. Though the defense attorney was overjoyed by the outcome of the trial, the prosecutor branded it a(n) _____flagrant_____ miscarriage of justice.

Group B

fiasco	ethnic	innovation
jeopardize	gaped	dilatory

6. Having to pay a sizable fine on some overdue library books has taught me not to be so _____dilatory_____ in the future.

7. Many of the minority groups that have come to the United States have managed to preserve their _____ethnic_____ identities while at the same time becoming full-fledged Americans.

8. A combination of poor planning and bad luck turned what should have been a surefire success into an utter _____fiasco_____.

9. "Pursuing such a risky and ill-considered course of action now," I observed, "will surely _jeopardize_ all that we have so far succeeded in achieving."

10. Observers on the shore _____gaped_____ openmouthed in horror as the stricken vessel slowly sank beneath the turbulent waters of the storm-tossed sea.

Exercise V.   Words in Phrases

In each of the following groups, select the item that means the same as the *italicized* word in the introductory phrase.

1. a *crucial* moment
   a. comical   b. pivotal   c. sad   d. boring   e. wasted

2. a group of *demure* young women
   a. bold   b. pretty   c. secretive   d. arrogant   e. modest

3. a *diligent* worker
   a. sedulous   b. new   c. pleasant   d. foreign
   e. bright

4. *fatuous* remarks
   a. perceptive   b. inane   c. amusing   d. brief   e. loud

5. *fluctuate* in popularity
   a. seesaw   b. continue   c. increase   d. remain
   e. decline

6. *elicit* a response
   a. make up   b. repeat   c. call forth   d. ignore
   e. strike out

7. *formidable* opposition to the proposal
   a. negligible   b. unexpected   c. reluctant   d. tremendous
   e. recent

8. *embellish* the facts
   a. investigate   b. report   c. conceal   d. reveal
   e. improve upon

9. the *gruesome* details
   a. relevant   b. horrible   c. minor   d. important
   e. unknown

10. all kinds of *ingenious* devices
    a. clever   b. unworkable   c. costly   d. practicable
    e. dangerous

Exercise VI.   Related Forms

A. Give a **noun** form of each of the following words.
   1. cynical cynic, cynicism   3. ethical ethic(s)   5. haughty haughtiness, hauteur
   2. dormant dormancy   4. frugal frugality, frugalness   6. intervene intervention, interventionism

B. Give a **verb** form of each of these words.
   1. empathy empathize   2. immunity immunize   3. impediment impede

C. Give an **adjective** form of each of these words.
   1. enigma enigmatical   2. fallacy fallacious   3. euphemism euphemistic

D. Give an **adverb** form of each of these words.
   1. drastic drastically   2. graphic graphically   3. ignominy ignominiously

Exercise VII. Synonyms and Antonyms

Classify each of the following pairs of words as **S** for **synonyms** or **A** for **antonyms**.

A 1. dapper—slovenly
S 2. dejected—crestfallen
A 3. corpulent—skinny
A 4. eminent—obscure
S 5. divulge—reveal

S 6. fathom—comprehend
S 7. feign—pretend
S 8. harbinger—forerunner
A 9. indigent—affluent
A 10. intrepid—timorous

Exercise VIII. Framing Sentences

Use each of the following words in a short illustrative sentence of your own devising.

1. cursory
2. copious
3. dexterous
4. disparage
5. emaciated
6. emulate
7. erudite
8. elite
9. feasible
10. gloat
11. gregarious
12. inception
13. incarcerate
14. innovation
15. judicious

Exercise IX. Word Roundup

1. Explain the difference between the words in each of the following pairs.

   a. flout—flaunt
   b. indigent—indigenous
   c. demur—demure
   d. credibility—credence
   e. discomfit—discomfort
   f. counsel—council
   g. exalt—exult
   h. feint—faint
   i. fortuitous—fortunate
   j. deferment—deference

2. Define each of the following terms.

   a. a skinflint
   b. a windfall
   c. a fluke
   d. to stonewall
   e. to rubberneck
   f. to soft-soap

3. Explain the meaning of each of the following colorful phrases.

   a. down in the dumps
   b. strike while the iron is hot
   c. pour oil on troubled waters
   d. paint oneself into a corner
   e. keep the wolf from one's door
   f. drag one's heels
   g. live in an ivory tower
   h. still wet behind the ears
   i. see red
   j. pull the wool over someone's eyes

4. Explain the meaning of each of the following foreign expressions used in present-day English, and tell what language it comes from.

   a. idée fixe
   b. hoi polloi
   c. impedimenta
   d. esprit de corps
   e. ad nauseam
   f. tour de force

331

5. Explain why you would be *flattered* or *insulted* if you were described as each of the following:

   a. an ignoramus c. a connoisseur e. a patsy
   b. a greenhorn   d. a dapper Dan   f. a paragon

Exercise X. Etymology

1. For each of the following definitions, supply an English word that begins with the Latin prefix *co, col, com, con,* or *cor.*

   a. fight against c. stick together e. eat away
      combat   cohere   corrode
   b. fall down   d. build or erect f. work together
      completely   construct   collaborate
      collapse

2. Define each of the following words beginning with the Latin prefix *de* or the Latin prefix *dis.*

   a. dispel   c. depose   e. disinherit
   b. denounce   d. dismember   f. demerit

3. Form a verb from each of the following English words by adding the suffix *(i)fy.* Then define the resulting combination.

   a. null   c. identity   e. beauty
   b. person   d. solid   f. terror

4. List and define **three** English words containing the Latin root *flu* or *fluct.* What does this root mean? Answers will vary; "flow"

5. Change each of the following positive words to its negative form by adding the Latin prefix *in* or one of its variants. Then define the resulting combination.

   a. reverent   c. moral   e. noble
   b. validate   d. logical   f. excusable

Exercise XI. Choosing the Right Meaning

Read each sentence carefully. Then underline the item that best completes the statement below the sentence.

1. The 9-1-1 telephone number for reporting dire emergencies had its origins in 1957, when an organization of fire chiefs rec- (2) ommended that there be a national, easy-to-remember phone number for reporting fires. Ten years later, the Federal Trade (4) Commission and the American Telephone and Telegraph Company (AT&T) met to establish a universal emergency telephone (6) number—9-1-1.

   The word **dire** in line 1 means

   a. gloomy   c. desperate
   b. unusual   d. suspicious

2. To Americans, the game of cricket, Britain's most popular sport, is decidedly esoteric compared with baseball. Cricket is (2) played with a paddle-shaped bat and a hard leather ball.

Eleven players on each team come up to bat as a bowler throws (4)
the ball to the batsman in the middle of the field. The rules are
complicated, and a two-inning game may take several days to (6)
complete.

The word **esoteric** in line 2 means

a. antiquated   c. confidential
b. mysterious   d. humorous

3. When they framed the U.S. Constitution, the Founding Fathers
chose to defer dealing with the problem of slavery. It remained a (2)
festering issue, and there were bitter debates over the expansion
of slavery into the new territories. The Missouri Compromise, (4)
which admitted Maine (1820) and Missouri (1821) as states, was
an attempt to maintain the balance of slave and free states. (6)

The word **defer** in line 2 means

a. reject   c. investigate
b. accede to   d. postpone

4. In a radio broadcast on October 1, 1939, the year before he became prime minister of Britain, Winston Churchill noted the (2)
impossibility of predicting how the Soviet Union would act.
"I cannot forecast to you the action of Russia," Churchill said. (4)
"It is a riddle wrapped in a mystery inside an enigma."

The word **enigma** in line 5 means

a. obscure statement   c. devious player
b. dangerous game   d. something puzzling

5. An artist fabricates a collage by gluing found materials (such
as newspaper, wallpaper, magazine photos, ads, cloth, and (2)
string) onto a flat surface, creating a three-dimensional effect.
The artist may then use paint or pen and ink to add to the as- (4)
semblage. Pablo Picasso originated this new art form in 1912,
and it was soon taken up by other Cubist painters, most no- (6)
tably Georges Braque.

The word **fabricates** in line 1 means

a. creates   c. deceives
b. sketches   d. prints

6. Trapped in the cave of Cyclops, a man-eating one-eyed monster, the clever Odysseus blinds his formidable opponent. En- (2)
raged, Cyclops demands to know who blinded him, and the
wily Odysseus answers, "Noman." Then Odysseus devises a (4)
shrewd plan to free himself and his remaining men from the
monster's cave.

The word **formidable** in line 2 means

a. huge   c. terrifying
b. drunken   d. brutal

7. Among the Zuni people, animal fetishes carved from rock or
semiprecious stone represent the animal's spirit. A bear fetish, (2)
for example, is said to symbolize strength and health. Many
bear fetishes have small bundles of stones tied to their backs. (4)
These medicine bundles are offerings to the animal's spirit and
make the fetish more powerful.

The word **fetish** in line 2 means

a. obsession   c. talisman
b. sand painting   d. folk dance

8. Henry David Thoreau, the nineteenth-century American naturalist and writer, championed the frugal, simple life. For two (2) years and two months, he lived alone in a house he built himself in the woods at Walden Pond near Concord, Massachu- (4) setts, his birthplace. In *Walden*, the book he wrote about his thoughts and experiences there, he warns: "Beware of all (6) enterprises that require new clothes."

The word **frugal** in line 2 means

a. stingy   c. rural
b. thrifty   d. natural

9. Shakespeare's *Hamlet* opens on an ominous, mysterious note. A ghost—looking very like the late King of Denmark—appears, (2) and sorrow seems to emanate from this ghastly figure. The ghost appears and exits twice in the play's first scene. It (4) seems about to speak when the cock crows, and it vanishes.

The words **emanate from** in line 3 mean

a. flow from   c. surround
b. send forth   d. draw in

10. In 1855, Walt Whitman self-published his revolutionary book of free verse, *Leaves of Grass*, and mailed copies to writers he (2) admired. Ralph Waldo Emerson, the most eminent essayist and poet of his time, sent Whitman a congratulatory letter: "I (4) find [in *Leaves of Grass*] incomparable things said incomparably well. . . . I greet you at the beginning of a great career. . . ." (6)

The word **eminent** in line 3 means

a. conspicuous   c. distinguished
b. talented   d. original

11. Behavioral biologists study the social patterns and interactions of nonhuman primates, such as monkeys, chimpanzees, apes, (2) and baboons. These gregarious animals live within a distinct structure, with identifiable patterns of interaction between— (4) and among—the genders and between young and old.

The word **gregarious** in line 3 means

a. affable   c. social
b. territorial   d. living alone

12. There are several different types of color blindness, or color-vision deficiency. The most common type involves an inability (2) to discriminate between red and green. Someone with this type of color blindness looks at a rainbow and sees red, or- (4) ange, yellow, and green as a single color (yellow) and the other half of the rainbow as blue. Color blindness is genetic and (6) almost twenty times more prevalent in men than in women.

The word **discriminate** in line 3 means

a. distinguish   c. treat prejudicially
b. carefully observe   d. treat fairly

Lesson 21

---

251. ku-dos   *noun*   kyōō'-dōs *or* kōō'-dōz
[*kudos* (Greek), "fame, glory"; originally English university slang but popularized in the United States some years ago by *Time* magazine]

Definition: The prestige or acclaim that results from some noteworthy achievement or position.

> An "unsung hero" is a person whose achievements have never been accorded the **kudos** they deserve.

Usage Note:
Since *kudos* is singular, it takes a singular verb. *Kudo* (without the *s*) is sometimes mistakenly used as the singular, but it is not considered correct.

Synonyms: (*nouns*) glory, honor, acclamation, credit, recognition, renown; accolade, plaudit

Antonyms: (*nouns*) odium, opprobrium, obloquy, contempt, disdain

Accolade

During the Middle Ages, an *accolade* was the ceremony in which a king or other overlord conferred knighthood upon a deserving subject. During part of this elaborate ceremony, usually conducted in the presence of the notables of the land, the king officially elevated the subject to the rank of knight by embracing him around (*ad* [Latin]) the neck (*collum* [Latin]) and tapping him lightly on the shoulder with the flat of a sword. The ceremony still survives in countries (*e.g.,* Great Britain) that have a titled nobility or where knighthood is customarily bestowed as an official token of thanks for outstanding personal service to the nation. It is from this connection with knighthood that the word *accolade* has now come to mean not only the formal bestowal of important honors and awards but also the simple granting of praise or approval.

Queen Elizabeth II makes a deserving subject a knight.

252. lack-a-dai-si-cal   *adjective*   lăk-ə-dā'-zĭ-kəl

[*lackaday* (obsolete English), "Woe is me," an archaic expression of sorrow or regret derived from *Alack* (= Woe) *the day*]

Definition: Sorely lacking in spirit, energy, or purpose.

"No matter how bright a youngster is," the child psychologist observed, "a **lackadaisical** attitude toward studying will result in poor grades."

Related Forms: (*noun*) lackadaisicalness; (*adverb*) lackadaisically

Synonyms: (*adjectives*) lethargic, listless, sluggish, torpid, indolent, lazy, supine, slothful; blasé, nonchalant, indifferent; perfunctory

Antonyms: (*adjectives*) energetic, vigorous, dynamic, spirited, animated

Related Phrases: a devil-may-care attitude, a fainéant administration, a drone

253. leg-a-cy   *noun*   lĕg'-ə-sē

[*legatia* (Medieval Latin), "office of deputy; bequest"; from *legare, legatus* (Latin), "send as a deputy; bequeath"]

Definition: Something left to a person in a will; something handed down from the past.

In her will, Grandmother left me a sizable cash **legacy,** which I have wisely used to further my education.

It is our duty to preserve and augment the **legacy** of freedom that we have received from earlier generations of Americans.

Synonyms: (*nouns*) bequest, inheritance, endowment; present, gift

Related Phrases: a family heirloom, a hand-me-down

254. li-a-bil-i-ty   *noun*   lī-ə-bĭl'-ə-tē

[*ligare, ligatus* (Latin), "tie, bind" + *abilis, abile* (Latin), "able to" + *itas, itatis* (Latin), "state or condition of"]

Definition:

a.   A debt or obligation, especially of a financial nature.

"When we balanced this company's assets against its **liabilities**," the executive remarked, "we found that we had turned a handsome profit this year."

b.   A hindrance or handicap.

Sometimes the traits of character that make people successful in the business world can prove to be **liabilities** in their personal lives.

My failure to learn how to type in high school later proved to be a **liability** when I applied for a secretarial position at a large Chicago firm.

Related Form: (*adjective*) liable

Synonyms: (*nouns*) indebtedness, debit, minus; disadvantage, drawback, obstacle

Antonyms: (*nouns*) asset, plus, advantage

Related Phrases: have an albatross around one's neck, have a cross to bear, have a millstone around one's neck, a stumbling block

---

255. li·bel   *noun and verb*   lī′-bəl
[*libellus* (Latin), "little book, petition"; from *liber* (Latin), "book"]

Definition:
  a. (*noun*) A public statement or picture that damages a person by falsely impugning his or her character, motives, or actions or by unjustly exposing the person to public censure or ridicule.

   "The laws of this land do not shield public figures from just criticism," the lawyer remarked, "but they do protect them against **libel**."
  b. (*verb*) To slander publicly.

   "Reliable witnesses can prove beyond the shadow of a doubt that the defendant has scurrilously **libeled** my client," the prosecutor told the jury.

Related Form: (*adjective*) libelous

Synonyms: (*nouns*) calumny, slander; (*verbs*) calumniate, defame, traduce, bad-mouth

Antonyms: (*verbs*) whitewash, gloss over, cover up

Related Phrases: hurl brickbats at, do a hatchet job on, drag someone's name through the mud; defamation of character; character assassination; a muckraker

---

256. lit·i·ga·tion   *noun*   lĭt-ĭ-gā′-shən
[*litigare, litigatus* (Latin), "sue"; from *lis, litis* (Latin), "lawsuit" + *agere, actus* (Latin), "bring, incite"]

Definition: Legal action; a lawsuit.

   "You are perfectly free to take your case to court," the lawyer told her client, "but if you do, the matter may be tied up in **litigation** for years."

Related Forms: (*noun*) litigant; (*adjective*) litigious; (*verb*) litigate

Usage Notes:
  a. *Litigation* usually indicates that a civil, as opposed to a criminal, action is involved.
  b. *Litigious* means "given to engaging in lawsuits" or, more broadly, "quarrelsome, pugnacious."

Synonyms: (*noun*) legal proceedings

Related Phrases: initiate legal proceedings against, bring an action against, file suit against, press charges against, go to court over, bring to book

257. lu-cid   *adjective*   lo͞o'-sĭd
[*lucidus* (Latin), "clear, bright"; from *lucere* (Latin), "shine"]

Definition: Clear and intelligible to the understanding; mentally competent.

The speaker gave such a **lucid** explanation of the complicated medical procedure that even a nonprofessional like me could understand it.

Though George III was declared permanently insane in 1810, he occasionally had brief periods when he was quite **lucid**.

Related Forms: (*nouns*) lucidity, lucidness; (*adverb*) lucidly

Synonyms: (*adjectives*) crystal clear, understandable, comprehensible; sane, rational

Antonyms: (*adjectives*) unintelligible, confused, puzzling; ambiguous, equivocal; mad, insane, irrational

Related Phrase: (non) compos mentis

258. lu-cra-tive   *adjective*   lo͞o'-krə-tĭv
[*lucrativus* (Latin), "profitable"; from *lucrum* (Latin), "profit, gain"]

Definition: Profitable.

"Running a popular pizza parlor may not be the most elevated occupation in the world," he replied, "but it certainly is **lucrative**."

Elizabethan opposition to the growth of Spanish power in Europe and the Americas proved far more **lucrative** than originally anticipated.

Related Forms: (*nouns*) lucrativeness, lucre

Synonyms: (*adjectives*) gainful, remunerative, rewarding, worthwhile; productive, fruitful, advantageous

Antonyms: (*adjectives*) unprofitable, unrewarding, unremunerative; unproductive, barren

Related Phrase: the profit motive

259. lurk   *verb*   lûrk'
[*lurka* (Old Norse), "sneak away slowly"]

Definition: To sneak; to lie hidden or in wait.

The police officer stopped to question the seedy-looking man who had been **lurking** around the corner drugstore for hours.

Who would have imagined that such a subtle thought could **lurk** in that innocent-looking head!

Synonyms: (*verbs*) skulk, prowl, slink, loiter

Related Phrases: a prowler, a stalking-horse

Filthy Lucre

Lucre, meaning "monetary profit or gain," has a decidedly negative connotation, perhaps because its most common use occurs in the phrase *filthy lucre*, which is derived from the New Testament. In his first letter to his disciple Timothy, the apostle Paul mentions that a bishop should not be "greedy of filthy lucre" (1 Timothy 3:2). In this context, *filthy* means "sordid" or "dishonorable," and Paul is saying that a bishop should not be open to bribes and other questionable ways of acquiring money. Accordingly, the phrase *filthy lucre* has come to be a highly contemptuous synonym for "ill-gotten gains," though it is also sometimes applied to people who are simply overly interested in making and amassing money, whatever their means.

St. Paul

260. lush   *adjective*   lŭsh′
[*lusch* (Middle English), "lax, soft"]

Definition:

   a. Luxuriant, plentiful; luxurious, opulent.

> The **lush** vegetation of the Hawaiian Islands is home to countless species of exotic birds and other animals.

> The walls of medieval castles were covered with **lush** tapestries and other hangings to keep out drafts.

   b. Overelaborate or overripe.

> What a contrast between George Orwell's lean, understated prose and the **lush**, overblown style of some of his contemporaries!

Phrases: lush farmland, lush surroundings, a lush orchestral texture

Related Forms: (*noun*) lushness; (*adverb*) lushly

Synonyms: (*adjectives*) dense, thriving, flourishing, profuse, lavish, prodigal, extravagant; ornate, sumptuous

Antonyms: (*adjectives*) simple, restrained, spartan; bleak, barren

261. mal-a-prop-ism   *noun*   măl'-ə-prŏp-ĭz-əm
[*mal à propros* (French), "out of place, inappropriate"]

Definition: An unconscious and usually ludicrous misuse of a word.

In one of his typical **malapropisms**, my landlord informed me on the hottest day of the year that he didn't mind the heat so much as the humility.

Synonyms: (*nouns*) flub, gaffe, solecism

Related Phrases: a play on words, a pun, an Irish bull, a spoonerism

262. mal-ice   *noun*   măl'-ĭs
[*malitia* (Latin), "wickedness"; from *malus* (Latin), "bad, evil"]

Definition: A desire to cause harm or suffering; deep-seated ill will.

In a famous passage in his Second Inaugural Address (1865), Abraham Lincoln suggested that national unity could never be restored if the defeated South were treated with **malice** rather than magnanimity.

Phrase: malice aforethought

Related Forms: (*adjective*) malicious; (*noun*) maliciousness

Synonyms: (*nouns*) malevolence, spite, rancor, animosity, vindictiveness, malignity, enmity, resentment

Antonyms: (*nouns*) benevolence, beneficence, goodwill, generosity, charity, magnanimity

263. mam-moth   *noun and adjective*   măm'-əth
[*mammot* (Russian), "a mammoth"]

Definition:

a.   (*noun*) An extinct form of elephant; a giant or colossus.

     During the Ice Age, woolly **mammoths** and other huge elephant-like creatures were common in much of North America.

     According to legend, Paul Bunyan, America's most celebrated lumberjack, was a **mammoth** of a man whose proudest possession was a gigantic blue ox named Babe.

b.   (*adjective*) Gigantic.

     The popular British singing group capped off its tour of the United States with a **mammoth** rock concert at Yankee Stadium.

Synonyms: (*nouns*) mastodon, behemoth; (*adjectives*) colossal, titanic, vast, gargantuan, enormous, monstrous, prodigious, stupendous

Antonyms: (*adjectives*) minute, minuscule, diminutive, Lilliputian, microscopic, tiny

340

The English actress Mary Boland as Mrs. Malaprop in Richard Brinsley Sheridan's comedy *The Rivals*.

Malapropisms, Irish Bulls, and Puns

The 18th-century Anglo-Irish playwright Richard Brinsley Sheridan (1751–1816) took the French phrase *mal à propos*, meaning "out of place" or "inappropriate," as the basis for the name of one of his most inspired comic creations, Mrs. Malaprop in *The Rivals* (1775). Mrs. Malaprop's most outstanding quality is her propensity to confuse words in a way that yields unintentionally comic effects. For example, she says, "I would have her instructed in geometry [*i.e.*, geography] that she might know something of the boundaries of contagious [*i.e.*, contiguous] countries" and "He is as headstrong as an allegory on the banks of the Nile." Such incongruous misusages, dubbed *malapropisms* in the lady's honor, are scattered like buckshot throughout *The Rivals*.

Movie mogul Sam Goldwyn achieved a certain amount of notoriety for his malapropisms. He was "credited" with such verbal gaffes as "A verbal agreement isn't worth the paper it's written on" and "I'll answer you with a definite maybe." Baseball great Yogi Berra had a similar gift for gaffes. He is credited with saying "If people don't want to come out to the ball park, nobody's going to stop them" and "When you come to a fork in the road, take it." This kind of self-contradictory statement is sometimes called an *Irish bull*.

Finally, it has been said that a *pun* (an intentionally comic play on words) is a "deliberate" or "controlled" malapropism. If you analyze a typical pun, you will see that this is true.

341

Larger Than Life

Modern English is rich in interesting expressions that indicate tremendous size. One of the most useful of these is *colossal*, which comes from the Greek word *kolossos* and its Latin equivalent, *colossus*. To the ancient Greeks and Romans, a kolossos or colossus was a gigantic statue. For example, the Colossus of Rhodes, one of the Seven Wonders of the World, was a gigantic statue erected about 280 B.C. by the inhabitants of Rhodes, an island republic off what is now southwest Turkey, to commemorate their deliverance from a siege. The statue, which represented the sun god Helios, the patron deity of the republic, was made entirely of bronze and rose to a height of 105 feet. It is from this connection with one of the most famous tourist attractions of the ancient world that we get our words *colossus*, meaning "anything of great size or impressiveness," and *colossal*, meaning "immense."

Our word *coliseum* also comes from the same source. It is a variant of the Latin word *Colosseum*, the name of the huge sports stadium that the Flavian emperors built in Rome about A.D. 80 (see photo). It is interesting to note, however, that many modern coliseums are not, strictly speaking, colosseums in the ancient sense because they are not open-air structures and were not primarily designed for sporting events.

Another useful expression relating to great size is *gargantuan*, which comes from the title of a famous novel by François Rabelais (c. 1483–1553), a French comic writer who lived during the Renaissance. Gargantua, the hero of this book, is described by Rabelais as a giant with enormous vitality and unlimited appetites. Accordingly, the English adjective *gargantuan* usually suggests an enormous capacity for food and pleasure, as in the phrase "a *gargantuan* appetite."

The 18th-century English satirist Jonathan Swift (1667–1745) also contributed two interesting "size" words to our vocabulary. Lemuel Gulliver, the hero of Swift's classic novel, *Gulliver's Travels*, visits the kingdom of Lilliput, where the inhabitants are only six inches tall and everything else is correspondingly small. On a later voyage, he travels to the land of Brobdingnag, where everything is gigantic. Swift's description of Gulliver's adventures in these two fantastic places was so memorable that soon the adjectives *Lilliputian*, meaning "extremely small in size or outlook," and *Brobdingnagian*, meaning "gigantic and correspondingly gross or boorish," had found permanent places in the vocabulary of English.

264. **man·da·to·ry** *adjective* mǎn'-də-tôr-ē

[*mandatum* (Latin), "command" + *orius* (Latin), "having the effect of"; from *manus* (Latin), "hand" + *dare, datus* (Latin), "give, place"]

Definition: Required, obligatory.

In this state, attendance at school is **mandatory** for children between the ages of six and seventeen.

Related Form: (*noun and verb*) mandate

Phrases: a mandatory life sentence, the mandate of the court, mandated services, a mandated territory, a writ of mandamus

Usage Notes:
a. In politics, the word *mandate* is sometimes used to express the authorization that the voters have presumably given to public officials by electing them. The following sentence illustrates this use of the word:

"The overwhelming victory I have won," the governor-elect said, "is a clear **mandate** to carry out my program."

b. After World War I, the League of Nations used the term *mandate* to describe a colonial territory that had been taken from one of the defeated belligerents and assigned to the administrative control of one of the victors. For example, Great Britain had a mandate over Palestine, which formerly belonged to the Turkish Empire. Under the UN, *trusteeship* is used for much the same arrangement.

Synonyms: (*adjectives*) compulsory, requisite; imperative

Antonyms: (*adjectives*) optional, discretionary, voluntary

Related Phrases: de rigueur, an elective course

265. **me·di·um** *noun* mē'-dē-əm

[*medium* (Latin), "the middle"; from *medius* (Latin), "middle"]

Definition: The means by which some goal is achieved or the person through whom it is realized.

Modern-day activists advocate strong political action as the most effective **medium** of social change.

Carlos was the **medium** through whom we made our views known to the student council.

Usage Notes:
a. Among those involved in the occult, a medium is a person who is believed to have the power to communicate with the dead.

b. The plural of *medium* is *media*. This plural form has come to be used to refer collectively to means of mass communication, particularly newspapers, radio, and television. Note: Since *media* is a plural form, it takes a *plural* verb, though some modern authorities sanction the use of the singular.

Synonyms: (*nouns*) agency, channel, vehicle

Using the Words

Exercise 1
1. ku'-dos
2. lack-a-dai'-si-cal
3. li-a-bil'-i-ty
4. lu'-cid
5. lu'-cra-tive
6. mal'-ice
7. mam'-moth
8. man'-da-to-ry
9. me'-di-um

Exercise I.   Syllabication and Pronunciation

Syllabicate the following words correctly, and place the major stress mark (') after the syllable that is accented when the word is pronounced.

1. kudos
2. lackadaisical
3. liability
4. lucid
5. lucrative
6. malice
7. mammoth
8. mandatory
9. medium

Exercise II.   Words Out of Context

In each of the following groups, select the item that best expresses the meaning of the numbered word at the left.

1. kudos
   a. lawsuit   b. glory   c. agency
   d. calumny   e. inheritance

2. lackadaisical
   a. obscure   b. unrewarding   c. energetic
   d. obligatory   e. lethargic

3. lucrative
   a. daily   b. intelligible   c. eager
   d. profitable   e. average

4. malice
   a. charity   b. sensitivity   c. animosity
   d. indifference   e. idleness

5. liability
   a. refuge   b. advantage   c. environment
   d. commencement   e. drawback

6. mammoth
   a. gigantic   b. kindly   c. optional
   d. shabby   e. evil

7. libel
   a. murder   b. slander   c. famine
   d. chaos   e. disaster

Exercise III.   Completing Sentences

Complete each of the following sentences by selecting the most appropriate word from the group of words given below. Use each word only once.

lucid	legacy	mandatory
litigation	malapropism	lush
lurk	libel	medium

1. Deteriorating climatic conditions eventually transformed what had been a __lush__ tropical paradise into a barren and inhospitable wasteland.

2. Though slavery has long since passed from the scene, the ___legacy___ of guilt and fear it left behind still affects our national life.

3. Fortunately, we were able to avoid a great deal of costly ___litigation___ by settling the dispute out of court.

4. Though he worked in a variety of materials, stone was the ___medium___ through which Michelangelo preferred to express his artistic ideas.

5. Her prose is as ___lucid___ and direct as mine is muddled and digressive.

6. Who can ever accurately predict what evil schemes ___lurk___ like sneak thieves in the dark recesses of a criminally insane person's mind?

7. The senator's command of English is so uncertain that his public utterances are full of bizarre ___malapropisms___ such as "make a bee dive for the door" and "the boy who cried, 'Woof'!"

8. Though high school students are no longer required to study Latin and Greek, English is still a ___mandatory___ subject.

Exercise IV.   Synonyms and Antonyms

Classify each of the following pairs of words as **S** for **synonyms** or **A** for **antonyms**.

S 1. lush—opulent
A 2. lackadaisical—energetic
S 3. libel—slander
S 4. skulk—lurk
A 5. liability—asset
S 6. channel—medium
S 7. litigation—lawsuit

A 8. lucrative—unprofitable
A 9. lucid—unintelligible
S 10. compulsory—mandatory
S 11. kudos—acclaim
A 12. benevolence—malice
S 13. legacy—bequest
A 14. diminutive—mammoth

Exercise V.   Word Roundup

1. Give the plural of *medium*, explain how it is used in contemporary English, and use it in a short illustrative sentence.

2. Explain the story behind each of the following expressions.

   a. accolade
   b. filthy lucre
   c. Lilliputian
   d. gargantuan

3. With or without the aid of a dictionary, define each of the following.

   a. a drone
   b. a hand-me-down
   c. a muckraker
   d. a stalking-horse

4. What is a *mandate*?

5. With or without the aid of a dictionary, explain what each of the following means.

   a. an elective course
   b. a family heirloom

   c. defamation of character
   d. malice aforethought

6. With the help of a dictionary, define each of the following foreign phrases used in modern English.

   a. non compos mentis

   b. de rigueur

7. Define each of the following expressions.

   a. a pun
   b. a spoonerism

   c. an Irish bull
   d. a malapropism

Exercise VI.   Framing Sentences

A. Use each of the following words in an original illustrative sentence.

1. kudos
2. legacy

3. lurk
4. malapropism

5. mammoth
6. medium

B. Give a **noun** form of each of the following words, and use it in an original illustrative sentence.

mandate

1. lush lushness
2. mandatory
3. lucrative lucre

C. Give an **adjective** form of each of these words, and use it in an original illustrative sentence.

1. litigation litigious 2. libel libelous
3. liability liable

D. Give an **adverb** form of each of these words, and use it in an original illustrative sentence.

lackadaisically

1. lucid lucidly
2. lush lushly
3. lackadaisical

Dissecting the Words

Prefix

The Latin prefix **inter**, meaning "between" or "among," occurs in a great many English words, including *intervene* (Word 243). Here are a few other useful English words in which it appears:

interpose (*inter*, "between" + *ponere, positus* [Latin], "place")—to place between, to come between

interject (*inter*, "between" + *jacere, jactus* [Latin], "throw")—to thrust abruptly between. Noun: *interjection*

intermediary (*inter*, "between" + *medius* [Latin], "middle")—a go-between

interstice (*inter*, "between" + *sistere, status* [Latin], "cause to stand")—a space between two things *intersperse* (*inter,* "among" + *spargere, sparsus* [Latin], "scatter")—to scatter or distribute among other things

interrogate (*inter,* "between" + *rogare, rogatus* [Latin], "ask")—to question formally. Nouns: *interrogation* and *interrogator*

intersect (*inter,* "between" + *secare, sectus* [Latin], "cut")—to cut across or through. Noun: *intersection*

intercept (*inter,* "between" + *capere, captus* [Latin], "seize")—to stop or interrupt the intended progress of. Noun: *interception*

Do not confuse the prefix **inter** with the prefix **in** when the latter occurs before the syllable **ter.** For example, the word *interminable* begins with what looks like the prefix **inter** but is in fact the prefix **in** (meaning "not") followed by the word *terminable* (meaning "capable of being ended" or "having an end").

Roots

1. The Latin and French roots **mal(e)** have a number of meanings: (*a*) "bad, badly"; (*b*) "evil, ill"; and (*c*) "abnormal, abnormally." These word elements occur in many common English words, including *malice,* studied in this lesson. For example:

malefactor (*male,* "evil" + *facere, factus* [Latin], "do")—a person who commits a crime or other offense

malevolent (*male,* "evil, ill" + *volens, volentis* [Latin], "wishing")—showing ill will; having an evil influence. Noun: *malevolence*

maladroit (*mal,* "ill, badly" + *adroit* [French], "skillful")—clumsy or inept

malodorous (*mal,* "badly" + *odor* [Latin], "smell")—foul smelling

malign (*mal,* "evil" + *gignere, genitus* [Latin], "bear, bring forth")—to speak evil or ill of

malaise (*mal,* "ill" + *aise* [French], "comfort, ease")—a vague, undefined feeling of illness or discomfort

malformation (*mal,* "abnormal" + *formation*)—an abnormal structure or formation

Other words that contain the word element **mal(e)** include *malcontent, malpractice, malfunction, malediction, malignant,* and *malnutrition.*

2. The Latin word element **ben(e)** indicates the opposite of *mal(e)*; that is, "good" or "well." It occurs in several useful English words, including *benign* (Word 57). Here are a few others in which it appears.

benefactor (*bene,* "good" + *facere, factus* [Latin], "do")—a person who confers some kind of good on another. Nouns: *benefactress, benefaction*

benediction (*bene,* "good, well" + *dicere, dictus* [Latin], "say")—a blessing

benevolent (*bene,* "good, well" + *volens, volentis* [Latin], "wishing")—kindly and generous. Noun: *benevolence*

benign (*bene,* "well" + *gignere, genitus* [Latin], "bear, bring forth")—gentle and mild; beneficial; not dangerous. Noun: *benignity*

Other words in which **ben(e)** appears include *benefit, beneficial, beneficiary, benefice, beneficent,* and *benignant.*

3. The Latin and Greek word element **gen** or **gene** has a number of meanings: (*a*) "give birth"; (*b*) "born" and; (*c*) "race or kind." Among the many words in which this element appears is *ingenious* (Word 238). Here are a few others.

genesis ([Greek], "beginning")—the origin of something. Adjective: *genetic*

generate (*genus* [Latin], "birth" + *ate* [from Latin *-atus*], "make")—to produce or bring into being. Noun: *generation*

genocide (*genos* [Greek], "race" + *caedere, caesus* [Latin], "kill")—the systematic destruction of a racial or cultural group

genealogy (*genea* [Greek], "family, kin" + *logy* [Greek], "study, science")— a record of the ancestry of a person or family; the study of family ancestry; lineage or descent. Adjective: *genealogical*

generic (*genus, generis* [Latin], "kind, sort")—characteristic of an entire group or class

progeny (*pro* [Latin], "forward" + *gignere, genitus* [Latin], "beget")— offspring, descendants

Other words in which **gen(e)** appears include *gentle, genteel, gentile, gender, general, generous, genre, congenial, heterogeneous, indigenous,* and *primogeniture.*

Exercise

1. Add the prefix *inter* to each of the following words. Then define the new word that results, and explain how *inter* contributes to its meaning.

   a. cede
   b. collegiate
   c. denominational
   d. lock
   e. marry
   f. national

2. With or without the aid of a dictionary, define each of the following words. Then choose any **five**, and for each compose a short illustrative sentence.

   a. intercession
   b. intermittent
   c. interloper
   d. interlude
   e. interval
   f. interpolate

3. For each of the following definitions, supply a word beginning with the root *mal(e)*. You may need to use a dictionary.

   a. a vague feeling of discomfort malaise
   b. a lawbreaker malefactor
   c. foul smelling malodorous
   d. clumsy or inept maladroit
   e. to speak ill or evil of malign
   f. ill will or spite malevolence, malignity

4. For each of the following definitions, supply a word beginning with the root *ben(e)*. You may need to use a dictionary.

   a. a blessing benediction
   b. gentle and mild benign
   c. an heir beneficiary
   d. advantageous beneficial

5. With or without the aid of a dictionary, explain what each of the following words means.

   a. engender   d. genus   g. genesis
   b. degenerate   e. ingenuous   h. congenial
   c. homogeneous   f. heterogeneous i. progeny

Working with Context Clues

With or without the aid of a dictionary, complete each of the following two-word omissions by selecting the pair of words that make the best sense in the passage as a whole. Underline the clue or clues that led you to make your choice.

1. In order to reduce the ever-growing number of <u>civil suits</u> being filed each year in American courts, some legislators are calling for _____ ceilings on the amounts of money that juries can award <u>plaintiffs</u>. Their hope is that these <u>legally binding</u> limits will stem the tide of costly _____.

   a. judicious . . . liability   c. lucid . . . arbitration
   b. <u>mandatory . . . litigation</u>   d. reasonable . . . insurance

2. In today's technological marketplace, a lack of computer skills is a(n) _____ when searching for a job. However, it is not a(n) _____ drawback because it <u>can be overcome</u> by further education.

   a. anomaly . . . implicit   c. ignominy . . . chronic
   b. foible . . . graphic   d. <u>liability . . . insuperable</u>

3. Legitimate businesses may not be as _____ as _____ activities, such as <u>gambling or drug selling</u>, but the profits from <u>a legal enterprise</u> are far more secure than money made from <u>criminal activity</u>.

   a. <u>lucrative . . . illicit</u>   c. feasible . . . callous
   b. exotic . . . clandestine   d. frugal . . . unethical

4. In the aftermath of a(n) _____, <u>such as flood or famine</u>, in a developing country, there is an urgent need for <u>sustained and systematic, rather than</u> _____, relief efforts by the international community.

   a. impasse . . . gratuitous   c. fiasco . . . austere
   b. <u>exigency . . . desultory</u> d. anathema . . . futile

5. A preacher who delivers a <u>long emotional speech hoping</u> that such a(n) _____ will <u>spur</u> the congregation into right-eousness may discover that it is difficult to _____ people into being good with words alone.

   a. legacy . . . coerce   c. <u>harangue . . . goad</u>
   b. irony . . . deceive   d. argument . . . cajole

6. Public figures who sue for _____ must prove that those who spread lies about them are prompted by _____, not just mistaken or careless.

   a. fraud . . . bravado   c. libel . . . malice
   b. atrocity . . . jealousy   d. damages . . . apathy

7. The old adage "Money is the root of all evil" is a wise _____ against _____.

   a. anachronism . . . greed   c. appeal . . . empathy
   b. anecdote . . . malice   d. counsel . . . avarice

8. New ideas in art and politics tend to _____ from a(n) _____ such as Greenwich Village in New York or the Left Bank in Paris, where artists and intellectuals gather together to live and work. Often, the original source of these ideas is forgotten, and they are eventually accepted by the general public.

   a. emanate . . . enclave   c. gape . . . legacy
   b. deviate . . . anomaly   d. defect . . . aggregate

9. The instinct to nest in huge colonies is _____ in seabirds such as penguins and puffins. Such _____ behavior is inborn and helps these species to survive.

   a. boorish . . . implicit   c. endemic . . . lucid
   b. inherent . . . gregarious d. widespread . . . gratuitous

10. Some writers passionately hate publicity and _____ the limelight, while others love to _____ their talents in front of any audience who will listen to them read from their works or talk about their lives.

   a. flout . . . disparage   c. court . . . array
   b. allude . . . censure   d. abhor . . . flaunt

Enriching the Lesson

Exercise I.   More Words from Literary Sources

A few useful expressions derived from the names or works of famous and not-so-famous authors are listed below. With or without the aid of a dictionary or other reference book, define each.

1. Machiavellian	6. Rabelaisian	11. Barmecidal
2. a Lothario	7. a Frankenstein	12. Pecksniffery
3. namby-pamby	8. a pamphlet	13. euphuism
4. a Tartuffe	9. a Sherlock	14. a Micawber
5. tilt at windmills	10. a Simon Legree	15. a panjandrum

Exercise II.   Russian Loan Words in English

In this lesson, you have studied a word derived from Russian: *mammoth* (Word 263). Listed below are a number of other English words that have been borrowed from Russian. With or without the aid of a dictionary, define each.

1. pogrom	4. ukase	7. czar
2. cossack	5. steppe	8. samovar
3. intelligentsia	6. tundra	9. dacha

Many Russian words that have made their way into English have to do with life under Communism in the USSR. This is scarcely surprising in view of the fact that Communism, whether perceived as a promise or a menace, was such an important factor in the politics and history of the twentieth century.

A few of the more common Russian words of this type are given below. With or without the aid of a dictionary, define each. Note, however, that you may have to consult an unabridged dictionary for some of them.

10. commissar	12. gulag	14. glasnost
11. perestroika	13. apparatchik	15. soviet
12. kulak	15. tovarish	18. kolkhoz

Exercise III.   Plurals in *A*

A number of useful English words form their plurals in the same way as *medium* (Word 265) does. A few of these items are listed below. With or without the aid of a dictionary, define each and give its plural form.

1. addendum	3. agendum	5. bacterium
2. erratum	4. datum	6. stratum

Exercise IV.   Expanding Your Word Power

The words listed below are not on the Basic Word List, but they were mentioned in one form or another in Lesson 21. All of them would make useful additions to your working vocabulary. Define each, give its etymology, list **two** synonyms and **two** antonyms (where possible), and use in a short illustrative sentence.

1. disdain	6. traduce	11. enmity
2. supine	7. rational	12. diminutive
3. equivocal	8. sumptuous	13. remuneration
4. endowment	9. skulk	14. imperative
5. liable	10. solecism	15. vehicle

Lesson 22

---

266. mer·ce·nar·y   *noun and adjective*   mûr'-sə-nĕr-ē

[*mercenarius* (Latin), "hired, paid" from *merces* (Latin), "wages, salary"]

Definition:
  a. (*noun*) A hireling, especially a hired professional soldier.

   The Roman army of Republican times was essentially a citizen militia, though foreign **mercenaries** were sometimes used as auxiliary troops.

  b. (*adjective*) Motivated solely by a desire for material gain.

   Once the war had been won, the victors laid aside the high-minded ideals for which they had fought and became embroiled in a deplorably **mercenary** squabble over the spoils.

Related Form: (*noun*) mercenariness

Synonyms: (*nouns*) hired hand, freelancer, soldier of fortune, condottiere; (*adjectives*) greedy, avaricious, acquisitive, grasping, rapacious

Antonyms: (*adjectives*) altruistic, disinterested

267. moot   *adjective and verb*   mo͞ot

[*mot* (Old English), "a meeting for discussion"]

Definition:
  a. (*adjective*) Debatable and therefore unresolved.

   The seemingly incontestable right that a person has to direct his or her own life becomes a **moot** point when it interferes with the rights of others.

  b. (*verb*) To bring up for discussion.

   "I rejected the idea when it was first **mooted** years ago," the governor said, "and I haven't regretted my decision yet."

Phrases: a moot question, a moot court

Usage Note:
A *moot court* is a mock court in which law students try hypothetical cases in order to obtain experience under fire.

Synonyms: (*adjectives*) arguable, disputable; questionable, doubtful; (*verbs*) broach, raise, pose, put forward

Antonyms: (*adjectives*) incontrovertible, indisputable, irrefutable

Related Phrases: a Gordian knot, a foregone conclusion

352

268. mo-rass   *noun*   mə-răs' *or* mô-răs'

[*moeras* (Dutch), "marsh"; from *maresc, mareis* (Old French), "swamp"; of Germanic origin and related to *mersc, merisc* (Old English), "marsh"]

Definition: A swamp or bog; a confused or degrading situation that is difficult to get out of.

> Heavy rains had transformed the unpaved road into a miniature **morass**, and we were soon up to our knees in mud.

> "Our once-great city," the candidate complained, "is slowly sinking into a **morass** of waste, corruption, and decay."

Synonyms: (*nouns*) marsh, fen, quagmire

269. mot-ley   *noun and adjective*   mŏt'-lē

[Origin uncertain; perhaps from *mot* (Old English), "speck"]

Definition:
a.   (*noun*) A kind of multicolored cloth; a garment made from this cloth, especially the costume worn by a court jester or clown.

> Shakespeare's players were a versatile crew; even the great tragic actor Richard Burbage donned **motley** now and then.

b.   (*adjective*) Multicolored; diverse or varied.

> In no time at all, she turned a **motley** assortment of leftovers into an elegant and tasty dinner.

> As W. S. Maugham once observed, the human personality is a **motley** collection of strengths and weaknesses, foibles and fortes.

Related Forms: (*adjective*) mottled; (*verb*) mottle

Synonyms: (*adjectives*) polychrome, polychromatic, piebald; variegated, heterogeneous, miscellaneous

Antonyms: (*adjectives*) monochrome, monochromatic; monolithic, homogeneous, uniform

Related Phrases: a pluralistic society, a diversified economy, a checkered career

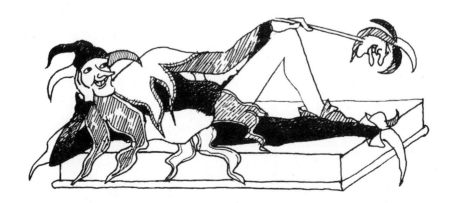

270. mun-dane   *adjective*   mŭn-dān' *or* mŭn'-dān

[*mundanus* (Latin), "relating to the world"; from *mundus* (Latin), "world"]

Definition: Worldly (as opposed to spiritual); humdrum or everyday.

"May I interrupt this esoteric discussion of interpersonal relationships," I asked, "and turn your attention to more **mundane** matters—like what's for dinner?"

Most people I know are too busy dealing with such **mundane** concerns as paying off the mortgage or meeting deadlines at the office to have much time for abstruse philosophical speculation.

Related Form: (*adverb*) mundanely

Synonyms: (*adjectives*) earthly, terrestrial; secular, temporal; material, physical; ordinary, prosaic, routine, commonplace, banal (Word 55)

Antonyms: (*adjectives*) celestial, heavenly, cosmic; unworldly, spiritual; metaphysical, transcendental; extraordinary, unique

Related Phrases: worldly goods, worldly wisdom; a man of the world

271. myr-i-ad   *adjective*   mîr'-ē-əd

[*myrias, myriadis* (Greek), "ten thousand"; from *myrios* (Greek), "countless"]

Definition: Countless, innumerable.

During the East Coast blackout of 1966, the **myriad** lights by which New York City is normally illuminated at night suddenly went out.

Can any one man or woman reasonably be expected to deal with the **myriad** problems and predicaments that now face a president of the United States?

Usage Note:
Occasionally, *myriad* is used in older writing as a noun—for example, in the phrases "a *myriad* of stars" and "a *myriad* of possibilities." In such cases, the word means "a vast number" or "a great multitude."

Synonyms: (*adjectives*) multitudinous, multifarious, manifold, infinite

Antonyms: (*adjectives*) finite, limited

272. nar-cis-sis-tic   *adjective*   när-sə-sĭs'-tĭk

[*Narcissus*, see caption on page 355 + *istic* (from Greek *istikos*), "like"]

Definition: Dominated by an excessive love or admiration of oneself.

"Is a constant need to admire oneself in the mirror a sign that someone is developing a **narcissistic** personality?" I asked.

Narcissistic tendencies can perhaps be excused as an inevitable phase in a teenager's struggle to achieve an identity, but they are alarming in an adult.

Related Forms: (*nouns*) narcissism, narcissist

Synonyms: (*adjectives*) egotistic(al), egoistic, egomaniacal, self-centered, conceited, vain

Antonyms: (*adjectives*) self-deprecating, self-deprecatory, self-critical, self-destructive

Related Phrase: amour propre

Narcissus and Narcissism

Narcissism is a psychological term derived from the ancient Greek mythological figure of Narcissus. Narcissus was a beautiful young man who steadfastly refused to fall in love with anyone, including the lovely mountain nymph Echo. As a punishment for this attitude, the gods made Narcissus fall in love with his own reflection in a mountain pool. Since he was unable to consummate this love, Narcissus pined away with grief. Eventually, he was transformed into the white or yellowish flower that we know by the name of narcissus. Echo, by the way, also pined away from unrequited love until all that was left of her was her voice, which, as you may suspect, was the first echo.

People who suffer from narcissism have exalted feelings of self-importance, personal success, and attractiveness. They generally feel a strong need to be the center of attention. They are dominated by fantasies of gaining great wealth and power, displaying dazzling creative talents, and achieving ideal love relationships. Of course, all people share symptoms of this type, but in the *narcissist* they become dominant to the point where reality blurs into fantasy. Accordingly, the narcissist is typically preoccupied with his or her own needs and feelings and shows little or no capacity to relate constructively and warmly to other people.

Adapted in part from *Psychology for You*, by Sol Gordon (New York: William H. Sadlier, Inc., 1983), page 59.

273. neb-u-lous *adjective* něb′-yə-ləs

[*nebulosus* (Latin), "cloudy, misty"; from *nebula* (Latin), "cloud"]

Definition: Hazy, vague, or indistinct.

Neither the police force nor the justice system can act on **nebulous** rumors and vague suspicions.

Physicians most always act with caution because the line between what is proper procedure and what is not is sometimes extremely **nebulous** and uncertain.

Phrases: a nebulous recollection of an event, nebulous fears and suspicions

Related Forms: (*nouns*) nebulousness, nebulosity, nebula

Synonyms: (*adjectives*) amorphous, opaque, shapeless, fuzzy, indefinite

Antonyms: (*adjectives*) clear, distinct, well-defined, unambiguous

Nebulae

In astronomy, *nebula* (plural, *nebulae*) is the name given to a discrete mass of matter and gases that appears in the sky. Sometimes these formations are illuminated; sometimes they are not. They also have several different shapes. Some are cloudlike or spiral-shaped. Others are long, irregular veils or thin hazes stretched across the sky. Still others look something like planets because they consist of an outer envelope of gassy material completely surrounding a star. Though our galaxy, the Milky Way, contains a number of nebulae, other important examples of the formation can be found outside it. One nebula is even thought to be a separate galaxy of its own. This is the Great Spiral Nebula of Andromeda (*shown at the left*).

274. neg-li-gi-ble *adjective* něg′-lĭ-jə-bəl

[*neglegere* (Latin), "ignore" + *abilis, abile* (Latin), "able to"]

Definition: Too small to be significant.

Though the product does indeed contain a **negligible** amount of a harmful chemical, it poses absolutely no threat to anyone's health or longevity.

The effect of an unexpected downturn in the economy on a national election will probably be far from **negligible**.

Related Forms: (*nouns*) negligibility, negligibleness

Synonyms: (*adjectives*) insignificant, inconsequential, trivial, piddling, trifling, nugatory

Antonyms: (*adjectives*) significant, considerable; telling, meaningful; critical, crucial, pivotal

Related Phrases: small potatoes, trivia

275. **nep-o-tism** *noun* něp′-ə-tĭz-əm

[*nepotismo* (Italian), "favoritism to nephews"; from *nepote* (Italian), "nephew"; from *nepos, nepotis* (Latin), "nephew; descendant"]

Definition: Unwarranted favoritism shown to relatives or friends by someone in high office.

"If your brother-in-law is really the best available candidate for the job you have to offer," I told my boss, "no one will accuse you of **nepotism**."

Some **nepotism** is unavoidable in a small, family-run business such as a mom-and-pop candy store.

Related Forms: (*noun*) nepotist; (*adjectives*) nepotistic(al)

Synonyms: (*nouns*) partisanship, bias, partiality, patronage

Related Phrases: a client state, the spoils system; the merit system

Alexander VI   Cesare Borgia

During the Middle Ages and Renaissance, the rulers of the Roman Catholic Church were occasionally accused of showing special consideration for their nephews and other relatives when making appointments to high ecclesiastical office, such as the cardinalate. For example, Pope Alexander VI (1492–1503) was notorious for the blatant favoritism he showed to his relatives Cesare (1475–1507) and Lucrezia (1480–1519) Borgia.

276. no-mad-ic   *adjective*   nō-măd′-ĭk

[*nomas, nomados* (Greek), "wanderer in search of pasturage" (from *nemein* [Greek], "pasture") + *ikos* (Greek), "pertaining to"]

Definition: Wandering, roving.

About 5000 B.C., the peoples of the Near East began to make the transition from the **nomadic** existence of a hunter to the more settled life of a farmer.

Related Form: (*noun*) nomad

Phrase: urban nomads

Synonyms: (*adjectives*) itinerant, migratory, peripatetic

Antonyms: (*adjectives*) settled, fixed, stationary

Related Phrases: footloose and fancy-free; a fly-by-night operation, a roving reporter, a Peripatetic philosopher, a migrant farmworker; wanderlust

The Peripatetics

Aristotle

The *Peripatetic* school of ancient Greek philosophy owed its name in part to the unusual teaching habits of its founder, the famous philosopher Aristotle of Stagira (384–322 B.C.). Aristotle, a pupil of Plato, preferred to teach or lecture while walking about rather than while sitting or standing still. (His students, of course, would follow him as he moved around.) One of his favorite places for doing this kind of nomadic pedagogy was a covered walkway called the Peripatos ("Walkabout"), which formed part of a gymnasium in Athens called the Lykeion or Lyceum. Accordingly, the school of philosophy that Aristotle founded came to be called *peripatetikos*—that is, "the one founded in the Peripatos."

Initially, the members of the Peripatetic school were almost exclusively students or followers of Aristotle and his empirical approach to philosophy. These men spent most of their time writing commentaries on Aristotle's works, attempting to refine his philosophic system, or composing specialized treatises on the natural sciences. Later, however, some of the Peripatetics developed more independent lines of philosophic thought.

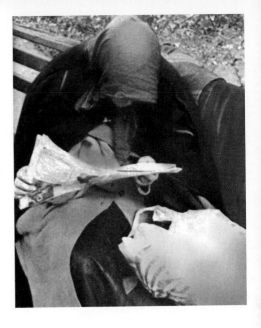

Urban Nomads

Pathetic reminders of our dim nomadic past, bag ladies (like the one in this photo) and other homeless persons now roam the streets of some of our largest cities.

277. nom-i-nal   *adjective*   nŏm'-ə-nəl

[*nominalis* (Latin), "relating to a name"; from *nomen, nominis* (Latin), "name"]

Definition:
  a. Existing in name only.

Since the prime minister actually directs the British government, the reigning monarch is really only the **nominal** head of state.

  b. Insignificantly small.

Most government-funded medical centers charge only **nominal** fees so that even the poorest member of the community can afford their services.

Phrases: a nominal Christian, nominal representation on the board

Related Forms: (*adverb*) nominally; (*nouns*) nominalism, nominalist

Synonyms: (*adjectives*) titular; token, symbolic; trifling, inconsequential

Antonyms: (*adjectives*) real, actual; exorbitant, excessive

Related Phrase: a puppet ruler

278. nos-tal-gia   *noun*   nŏ-stăl'-jə *or* nə-stăl'-jə

[*nostos* (Greek), "a return home" + *algos* (Greek), "pain"; actually a learned translation of *Heimweh* (German), "homesickness"]

Definition: A longing to return to a sentimentalized past; homesickness.

Around Christmas, I always get a feeling of **nostalgia** for the days of my youth and the friends I grew up with.

Related Form: (*adjective*) nostalgic

Synonyms: (*nouns*) yearning, pining, hankering; wistfulness, sadness, sentimentality, sorrow, regret; lonesomeness

279. nov-ice   *noun*   nŏv'-ĭs

[*novicius* (Medieval Latin), "probationary member of a religious order"; from *novus* (Latin), "new"]

Definition:

a. A person who has just entered a religious order on a probationary basis.

Many **novices** find their first days in a religious community difficult, but usually they become accustomed to the lifestyle relatively quickly.

b. A beginner of any kind.

Show jumping is an aspect of the art of horseback riding that an experienced rider can tackle, but not a **novice**.

"He's such a consummate master of the art of politics that he makes even a seasoned veteran look like a **novice**," I remarked.

Related Form: (*noun*) novitiate

Usage Note:

Occasionally *novice* is used as an adjective before another noun or a noun phrase—for example, "a *novice* swimmer."

Synonyms: (*nouns*) postulant; neophyte, tyro, fledgling, trainee, rookie, probationer, greenhorn, tenderfoot

Antonyms: (*nouns*) expert, pro, veteran, old hand, past master, virtuoso

Related Phrases: still wet behind the ears; a babe in the woods, a freshman senator; a black belt in karate

280. nu-ance   *noun*   n(y)o͞o-äns' *or* n(y)o͞o'-äns

[*nuance* (French), "shade, hue"; from *nubes* (Latin), "cloud"]

Definition: A slight or subtle variation in meaning, expression, tone, feeling, color, or the like.

Two synonyms are never exactly alike because **nuances** of tone or applicability make each of the words unique.

Music can sometimes express a **nuance** of mood or feeling that would be difficult to put into words.

Her colorful outfit contained every imaginable **nuance** of red—from the palest pink to the deepest burgundy.

We may hope that our friends will understand the **nuances** of feeling implied in our words, but we shouldn't expect them to be mind readers.

Synonyms: (*nouns*) subtlety, nicety, overtone, gradation, refinement, delicacy

Related Phrases: a fine point; read between the lines, read the small print

Using the Words

Exercise I.   Parts of Speech

Indicate the part of speech of each of the following words. In some cases, two answers are correct.

1. mercenary n., adj.
2. moot adj., v.
3. motley n., adj.
4. mundane adj.
5. myriad adj.
6. nebulous adj.
7. nepotism n.
8. nominal adj.
9. nuance n.

Exercise II.   Words in Phrases

In each of the following groups, select the item that best expresses the meaning of the *italicized* word in the introductory phrase.

1. at a *nominal* cost to the consumer
   a. guaranteed   <u>b. token</u>   c. sizable   d. fair

2. *nebulous* plans
   a. radical   b. detailed   c. costly   <u>d. vague</u>

3. *mundane* pursuits
   <u>a. commonplace</u>   b. sensible   c. odd   d. interesting

4. a *motley* group
   a. snobbish   b. penniless   c. enthusiastic   <u>d. diverse</u>

5. for purely *mercenary* reasons
   a. practical   <u>b. monetary</u>   c. social   d. personal

6. *nuances* of tone and shading
   <u>a. subtleties</u>   b. theories   c. uses   d. problems

7. the *myriad* leaves on an oak
   a. edible   b. uniform   <u>c. countless</u>   d. colorful

Exercise III.   Completing Sentences

Complete each of the following sentences by selecting the most appropriate word from the group of words given below. Use each word only once.

narcissistic	nepotism	nuance
novice	negligible	morass
nostalgia	nomadic	moot

1. Understandably, many of those who suffered through the hard economic times of the 1930s don't remember that particular era with much <u>nostalgia</u>.

2. "Twenty-five dollars may be a <u>negligible</u> amount of money to you," I replied, "but it's sizable to me."

3. Whether or not Lincoln could have bound up the nation's wounds by being merciful is a ___moot___ question simply because he was assassinated before he got the chance to try.

4. Since most people cannot resist sneaking a peek at their reflections in a plate-glass window, is it fair to say that human beings generally have a _narcissistic_ streak in them?

5. Trying to work my way through the ___morass___ of complicated paperwork involved in the project was like trying to swim through shark-infested custard.

6. "Once you have mastered the basics of the game and can play with some degree of skill and confidence," my instructor said, "you will cease to be a ___novice___."

7. I chose the ___nomadic___ life of a traveling salesperson simply because I felt too tied down by a nine-to-five office job.

8. "The appointment of your son to the job may have been based solely on merit," I told the mayor, "but your critics will surely see it as ___nepotism___."

Exercise IV.   Synonyms and Antonyms

A. In each of the following groups, select the **two** words that are most nearly **synonymous**.

1. a. precipice   b. quagmire   c. grove   d. bog   morass

2. a. conceited   b. affluent   c. vengeful   d. egotistic   narcissistic

3. a. prosaic   b. humdrum   c. gullible   d. slovenly   mundane

4. a. biased   b. infinite   c. hazy   d. vague   nebulous

5. a. ace   b. greenhorn   c. tenderfoot   d. hillbilly   novice

Now, for each pair of synonyms that you have selected, supply a word from the Basic Word List for this lesson (Words 266–280) that means **the same** or **almost the same** thing.

B. In each of the following, select the item that is most nearly **opposite** in meaning to the numbered word at the left.

1. moot   a. incredible   b. invaluable   c. interminable
               d. insoluble   e. indisputable

2. nomadic   a. pleasant   b. itinerant   c. awkward
               d. stationary   e. theatrical

3. motley   a. trite   b. uniform   c. charitable
               d. ambiguous   e. miscellaneous

4. nominal   a. exorbitant   b. genial   c. abject
               d. prompt   e. human

5. mercenary   a. arduous   b. aggressive   c. altruistic
               d. arbitrary   e. ambitious

362

Exercise V.   Word Roundup

1. With or without the aid of a dictionary, explain the meaning of each of the following terms indicating kinds of people.

   a. a soldier of fortune
   b. a freelancer
   c. a puppet ruler
   d. a roving reporter
   e. a Peripatetic philosopher
   f. a man of the world
   g. a freshman senator
   h. an urban nomad
   i. a migrant farmworker
   j. a nominal Christian

2. With or without the aid of a dictionary, explain the meaning of each of the following expressions indicating things.

   a. a moot court
   b. a fly-by-night operation
   c. a client state
   d. a checkered career
   e. a diversified economy
   f. a pluralistic society

3. What is a *Gordian knot*? Tell the story behind the phrase.

4. With or without the aid of a dictionary, explain what each of the following foreign expressions means, and tell what language it comes from.

   a. condottiere   b. amour propre   c. wanderlust

5. With or without the aid of a dictionary, explain the meaning of each of the following colorful English expressions.

   a. wet behind the ears
   b. read between the lines
   c. small potatoes
   d. a babe in the woods

6. Tell the story of Echo and Narcissus. How does this story relate to the meaning of the psychological term *narcissism*? What is a *narcissist*?

7. What is *the spoils system*? *the merit system*? How do the two systems differ?

8. What is a *nebula*? In what science is this term used?

Exercise VI.   Framing Sentences

A. Use each of the following words in an original illustrative sentence.

1. mercenary
2. moot
3. morass
4. myriad
5. mundane
6. motley
7. nominal
8. novice
9. nuance

B. Give a **noun** form for each of the following words, and use it in an original illustrative sentence.

narcissism   nomad   negligibility
1. narcissistic   2. nomadic   3. negligible

C. Give an **adjective** form for each of these words, and use it in an original illustrative sentence.

1. nostalgia   2. nepotism   3. motley
   nostalgic   nepotistic(al)   mottled

Completing Verbal Analogies

By now you should be familiar enough with how verbal analogies work to handle them on your own. Accordingly, the remaining "Completing Verbal Analogies" sections of this book will concentrate on providing you with ample practice in dealing with them. That way, you will acquire the skill and confidence needed to tackle those that actually appear on standardized vocabulary tests. However, since many of the word relationships that you will meet, both in the remaining analogy sections in this book and on standardized tests, will be new to you, in the sense that you have not formally studied them, bear one important principle in mind: Always identify the relationship between the words in the key or given pair before you attempt to choose your answer.

Exercise

Complete each of the following analogies.

Group A

1. **momentous : trivial =**
   a. opportune : negligible
   b. year : decade
   c. temporary : ephemeral
   d. moot : nomadic
   e. significant : inconsequential

2. **ship : nautical =**
   a. subterranean : tunnel
   b. helicopter : lunar
   c. automobile : terrestrial
   d. horse : marine
   e. skateboard : celestial

3. **philatelist : stamps =**
   a. spendthrift : profits
   b. numismatist : coins
   c. charity : philanthropist
   d. speculation : philosopher
   e. astrologer : books

4. **behemoth : puny =**
   a. mammoth : massive
   b. gargantuan : carnivore
   c. mastodon : huge
   d. leviathan : minuscule
   e. colossus : gigantic

5. **cat : feline =**
   a. equine : horse
   b. cow : bovine
   c. rooster : hen
   d. dog : mongrel
   e. sheep : amphibian

Group B

1. **callow : experience ::**
   a. predatory : intelligence
   b. pensive : aplomb
   c. petulant : imagination
   d. self-esteem : narcissistic
   e. provincial : sophistication

2. **lax : stringent ::**
   a. circuitous : straight
   b. errant : nightly
   c. nominal : meritorious
   d. decadent : motley
   e. nebulous : hazy

364

3. **pickpocket : filch ::**
   a. cutthroat : deface
   b. spendthrift : hoard
   c. daredevil : lurk
   d. spoilsport : incarcerate
   e. scofflaw : flout

4. **avarice : grasping ::**
   a. humility : bare-knuckled
   b. liability : tightfisted
   c. nepotism : light-fingered
   d. generosity : openhanded
   e. nostalgia : double-jointed

5. **palace : opulence ::**
   a. mansion : austerity
   b. shack : affluence
   c. hovel : indigence
   d. cottage : luxury
   e. skyscraper : poverty

Working with Context Clues

Complete each of the following two-word omissions by selecting the pair of words that make the best sense in the passage as a whole. If necessary, consult a dictionary for the meaning of any word with which you are not familiar.

1. American democracy is in trouble if the only people running for office are either <u>wealthy</u> or <u>motivated by a desire to become rich</u>. The danger of such a situation is that the _____ may ignore the needs of the poor and the _____ may rob them.

   a. indigent . . . ambitious
   b. affluent . . . mercenary
   c. brash . . . delinquent
   d. erudite . . . gregarious

2. When a third of the members of a leader's inner circle are <u>relatives</u>, it is tempting to _____ the practice of _____ without any further solid evidence.

   a. allege . . . nepotism
   b. instigate . . . effrontery
   c. construe . . . euphemism
   d. delineate . . . demagoguery

3. When an ordinary citizen makes an embarrassing <u>slip of the tongue</u>, the effect is usually _____, <u>but</u> an ill-timed _____ by a candidate in a televised debate can have a <u>serious impact</u> on election results.

   a. facetious . . . remark
   b. brash . . . calumny
   c. grueling . . . accusation
   d. negligible . . . malapropism

4. When <u>listening to old songs</u>, I often find myself slipping into a <u>confused state</u> of <u>joy and sadness</u> that is hard to shake. I am not sure why I sink into such a(n) _____ of _____ at these times.

   a. morass . . . nostalgia
   b. ambience . . . despair
   c. legacy . . . apathy
   d. state . . . nuance

5. Children learn best when their parents are neither too quick to praise them nor too ready to _____ their efforts. _____ parents are too easily satisfied, and overly critical ones are too hard to please.

   a. exploit . . . Docile
   b. flout . . . Formidable
   c. condemn . . . Delinquent
   d. disparage . . . Complacent

6. When you _____ someone to give you a serious response to an important question and instead you are given a _____ reply, you are bound to be sorry you ever asked.

   a. cajole . . . brash
   b. entreat . . . facetious
   c. entice . . . candid
   d. goad . . . gratuitous

7. After a major earthquake, rescue workers are faced with an awesome challenge. Just removing the tons of debris is a(n) _____ task, and the huge effort may seem _____ when no survivors are found.

   a. gruesome . . . frugal
   b. formidable . . . futile
   c. insuperable . . . graphic
   d. grueling . . . fortuitous

8. If you invest cautiously and in a variety of investment vehicles, you should be able to ride out a major failure in the stock market. Investors who are _____ can usually avoid the huge losses that often accompany a Wall Street _____.

   a. prudent . . . bravado
   b. frugal . . . impasse
   c. circumspect . . . fiasco
   d. brash . . . collapse

9. When children are guilty of breaking the rules, they often make up stories to explain their _____ behavior. Usually, they give up this tendency to _____ excuses as they get older.

   a. brash . . . instigate
   b. heinous . . . gloat
   c. exemplary . . . alienate
   d. culpable . . . fabricate

10. The _____ bedouin are a tribe who move continually over the sands of Saudi Arabia, stopping occasionally at the _____ oases where the desert blooms.

   a. nomadic . . . lush
   b. formidable . . . blithe
   c. dilatory . . . exotic
   d. primitive . . . bleak

11. Sometimes when I am alone at night, I have horrible fears that _____ monsters _____ in the dark, waiting to pounce on me.

   a. implacable . . . toil
   b. intrepid . . . grope
   c. myriad . . . inveigh
   d. gruesome . . . lurk

Enriching the Lesson

Exercise I.   Our German Heritage

Modern German has contributed a number of useful words to the vocabulary of present-day English. One such expression, *wanderlust*, was mentioned in passing in this lesson. A few others are listed below. With or without the aid of a dictionary, define each. Then choose any **three**, and for each compose a short illustrative sentence.

1. strafe
2. ersatz
3. leitmotif
4. wunderkind
5. blitz(krieg)
6. putsch
7. seminar
8. flak
9. kitsch

Exercise II.   The Clothes We Wear

One of the meanings noted for the word *motley*, studied in this lesson, was "a kind of multicolored cloth" or "a garment made from this cloth." This brings to mind the fact that there is a great deal of interesting history involved in the names of some of our most familiar fabrics and articles of clothing.

Listed below are the names of some common fabrics or articles of wearing apparel. With or without the aid of a dictionary or other reference book, identify each, and explain where the name comes from.

1. raglan
2. jeans
3. knickerbockers
4. mackintosh
5. Levi's
6. muslin
7. madras
8. lisle
9. dungarees
10. Stetson
11. cardigan
12. denim
13. calico
14. oxfords
15. fedora

Exercise III.   Words from the Sciences

One of the items mentioned in passing in this lesson was the term *nebula*, which comes from the science of astronomy. This brings to mind the fact that a good many scientific terms have been borrowed for use in a broad social sense. A few such expressions are listed below. With or without the aid of a dictionary, define each as it is used in the sciences and as it is used in more everyday situations. Then choose any **three**, and for each compose an original illustrative sentence.

1. catalyst
2. polarize
3. hybrid
4. eclipse
5. erosion
6. symbiosis
7. parasite
8. inertia
9. satellite

Exercise IV.   What's in a Name?

Listed below are a number of expressions for different kinds of names. With or without the aid of a dictionary, define each. Then choose any **four**, and for each compose an original illustrative sentence.

1. epithet
2. surname
3. alias
4. stage name
5. honorific
6. sobriquet
7. misnomer
8. appellation
9. moniker
10. toponym
11. pen name
12. nickname
13. pseudonym
14. patronymic
15. diminutive

Exercise V.   Number Words

Earlier in this lesson it was noted that *myriad* (Word 271) comes directly from the Greek term meaning "ten thousand." The English word, however, has lost this precise numerical denotation and is used to suggest (connote) the idea of "a very large number."

There are many other words in English derived from specific numbers. Some of them are listed below. Identify the number in each case. Then tell what the word means in present-day usage. In some cases, the original number meaning has been retained. In others, an entirely new meaning has been assumed. Try to account for the change. An unabridged dictionary will help.

1. millennium
2. quintet
3. decade
4. centurion
5. septuagenarian
6. bicentennial
7. trio
8. Pentecostal
9. trivial
10. unique
11. triumvirate
12. pentagon
13. trilogy
14. monolithic
15. decathlon
16. monogamy
17. monopoly
18. pentathlon
19. decimal
20. quadruped
21. decimate

Exercise VI.   Expanding Your Word Power

The words listed below are not on the Basic Word List, but they were mentioned in one form or another in Lesson 22. All of them would make useful additions to your working vocabulary. Define each, give its etymology, list **two** synonyms and **two** antonyms (where possible), and use in a short illustrative sentence.

1. altruistic
2. incontrovertible
3. fledgling
4. temporal
5. manifold
6. egotistical
7. opaque
8. finite
9. nugatory
10. patronage
11. itinerant
12. titular
13. partisanship
14. wistfulness
15. refinement

Related Forms in Context

Beneath each sentence below are four words introduced in Lesson 21 or 22. Review the related forms for these words, and choose the one that best completes the sentence. Write that related form in the space provided.

1. In *Brown* v. *Board of Education*, the landmark civil rights case, Brown, the __litigant__, sued the Board of Education of Topeka, Kansas; and on May 17, 1954, the U.S. Supreme Court unanimously ruled the concept of "separate but equal" public schools unconstitutional.

   a. novice **b. litigation** c. mercenary d. libel

2. The Ethics Committee is holding a hearing to determine whether the city manager's appointment of his second cousin by marriage is __nepotistic__.

   a. libel b. malice c. nostalgia **d. nepotism**

3. In "Pied Beauty," the English poet Gerard Manley Hopkins counters the traditional notion of beauty by celebrating all things that are __mottled__.

   a. malice **b. motley** c. mercenary d. novice

4. If the promised _____ of an investment scheme seems too good to be true, you would be wise to think twice before risking your life's savings on it. lucrativeness

   a. lucrative b. lush c. nebulous d. negligible

5. In just a few paragraphs, a skillful columnist can __lucidly__ state her or his opinion and support it with convincing reasons and evidence.

   a. lackadaisical b. lush c. mundane **d. lucid**

6. He moved through life _____, displaying little enthusiasm either for work or for play. lackadaisically

   a. lucrative b. nominal **c. lackadaisical** d. mercenary

7. Determined to remain "the fairest of them all," the __malicious__ queen disguises herself as an old woman and offers Snow White a poisoned apple.

   a. malapropism b. motley c. libel **d. malice**

8. If someone falls and is injured on a sidewalk in front of your house, are you __liable__ for that person's medical expenses?

   a. liability b. libel c. litigation d. nostalgia

9. In *A Christmas Carol*, Charles Dickens makes it clear that Ebenezer Scrooge's _____ prevents him from leading a happy, fulfilling life. mercenariness

   a. lucrative **b. mercenary** c. lackadaisical d. nominal

10. Many movie stars have sued tabloid newspapers for their __libelous__ headlines and stories.

 a. mercenary b. liability c. libel d. motley

11. Although her voice was well past its prime, __nostalgic__ fans cheered her renditions of her greatest hits.

 a. nostalgia b. nepotism c. malice d. litigation

12. Paul Gauguin's paintings of Tahiti are remarkable for the beauty of their composition and the __lushness__ of their colors.

 a. mundane b. nominal c. lush d. mammoth

13. A candidate who wins an election by a landslide may be justified in believing that he or she has received a __mandate__ from the voters.

 a. mercenary b. narcissistic c. mandatory d. nebulous

14. Although it is a thousand light years away, the bright __nebula__ in the constellation Orion is visible to the naked eye.

 a. myriad b. nebulous c. narcissistic d. nomadic

15. Given the __negligibility__ of the differences between the performance ratings of the two automobiles, I will probably choose the one that looks sportier.

 a. mandatory b. lucid c. narcissistic d. negligible

16. I was surprised that she spoke so __mundanely__ of her travels to places that seem to me to be so exotic.

 a. mundane b. lucrative c. negligible d. nomadic

17. It may be said that __narcissists__ hold themselves in much higher esteem than anyone else does.

 a. motley b. lucrative c. nomadic d. narcissistic

18. Traditionally, the Inuit, like other __nomads__, erected temporary shelters—igloos in winter, tents in summer—near their food source.

 a. narcissistic b. nominal c. nomadic d. mundane

19. Though the nine-year-old was __nominally__ king of Egypt, all the real power rested with his advisors.

 a. mandatory b. nominal c. lucid d. mundane

20. Several candidates criticized the __nebulousness__ of the front-runner's plan for stimulating the nation's faltering economy.

 a. nominal b. nebulous c. mandatory d. lackadaisical

Lesson 23

281. obscene — 295. pensive

---

281. ob-scene   *adjective*   ŏb-sēn' *or* əb-sēn'

[*obsc(a)enus* (Latin), "foul, repugnant"; perhaps from *ob* (Latin), "on account of" + *sc(a)enum* (Latin), "dirt, filth"]

Definition: Offensive to accepted standards of decency; repulsive.

Federal regulations forbid the use of **obscene** language in programs broadcast over the airwaves.

Concerned citizens may complain that the misuse of our national resources verges on the **obscene**.

Phrases: an obscene gesture, an obscene dance, an obscene picture

Related Forms: (*noun*) obscenity, (*adverb*) obscenely

Synonyms: (*adjectives*) indecent, lewd, salacious, smutty, bawdy, scatological, pornographic; risqué, suggestive; vulgar, crude, coarse; disgusting, abominable, reprehensible, loathsome

Antonyms: (*adjectives*) decent, refined, modest; laudable, meritorious

Related Phrases: an X-rated (or R-rated) film, an off-color joke

---

282. ob-se-qui-ous   *adjective*   ŏb-sē'-kwē-əs

[*ob* (Latin), "to, toward" + *sequi* (Latin), "follow, yield" + *osus* (Latin), "characterized by, full of"]

Definition: Excessively submissive to another person's wishes or ideas, often for purely self-interested reasons.

During imperial times, the Roman Senate was little more than a collection of **obsequious** yes-men, intent on preserving their own lives by gratifying the emperor's every whim.

At an autocrat's court, free speech is usually replaced by the **obsequious** twaddle of self-seeking toadies and flunkies.

Related Forms: (*nouns*) obsequiousness, obsequy; (*adverb*) obsequiously

Usage Note:

The noun *obsequy*, usually used in the plural, means "a funeral rite."

Synonyms: (*adjectives*) servile, fawning, subservient, groveling, mealymouthed, sycophantic, unctuous, compliant, deferential

Antonyms: (*adjectives*) independent; frank, candid, outspoken; self-assertive, aggressive, bumptious

Related Phrases: a yes-man, a rubber stamp; toe the line, knuckle under to

283. **ob·ses·sion**   *noun*   ŏb-sĕsh'-ən   *or*   əb-sĕsh'-ən
[*ob* (Latin), "in front of, before" + *sedere, sessus* (Latin), "sit"]

Definition: An irrational preoccupation with an idea or feeling that usually results in severe anxiety.

> Fear of falling victim to some dread disease can become such an **obsession** that it actually drives a person into a nervous breakdown.

Related Forms: (*verb*) obsess; (*adjective*) obsessive

Phrases: obsessed by a sense of one's own importance, obsessed with an idea, an obsessive need for reassurance

Synonyms: (*nouns*) compulsion, fixation, mania, phobia, hang-up

Related Phrases: an idée fixe; have a one-track mind; have a bee in one's bonnet, have an ax to grind, ride a hobbyhorse; a perfectionist, a monomaniac, a paranoiac, a megalomaniac, a compulsive gambler

Have a Bee in One's Bonnet

The colloquial expression *have a bee in one's bonnet* means "have some fixed idea or obsession that other people find odd or eccentric."

284. **ob·so·lete**   *adjective*   ŏb-sə-lēt'   *or*   ŏb'-sə-lēt
[*obsolescere, obsoletus* (Latin), "grow old; wear out"]

Definition: No longer in use; outmoded.

> "I'm interested in the present-day meaning of the word," I exclaimed, "not in one that has been **obsolete** for over 200 years!"

> The automobile made many older forms of land transportation, such as the horse and buggy, **obsolete**.

Phrases: an obsolete expression, obsolete equipment, an obsolete idea

Related Forms: (*nouns*) obsolescence, obsoleteness; (*adjective*) obsolescent

Usage Note:
Be careful to distinguish between *obsolete*, which indicates that something has already become outmoded, and *obsolescent*, which indicates that it is still in the process of becoming antiquated.

Synonyms: (*adjectives*) old-fashioned, antiquated, dated, out-of-date, passé, old hat, superannuated; archaic, defunct, extinct

Antonyms: (*adjectives*) up-to-date, new, novel, fresh, newfangled, avant-garde, ultramodern

Related Phrases: behind the times, past one's prime; a discontinued model, a has-been, a thing of the past; au courant, dernier cri, still on the drawing board, hot off the presses

285. **of-fi-cious**   *adjective*   ə-fĭsh′-əs

[*officiosus* (Latin), "dutiful"; from *officium* (Latin), "duty, obligation"]

Definition: Excessively forward in offering unwanted or unnecessary help or advice; meddlesome.

"I'm not going to get this job done any faster," I objected, "just because you shout unnecessary instructions at me and otherwise make an **officious** nuisance of yourself."

Related Forms: (*noun*) officiousness; (*adverb*) officiously

Usage Note:
Be careful to distinguish between *officious* and *official*, which as an adjective means "authoritative" or "formal" and as a noun means "a person in authority." Of course, an official may be officious (annoyingly meddlesome), but the two words are not related in meaning.

Synonyms: (*adjectives*) intrusive; prying, nosy; forward, pushy, bossy; importunate

Related Phrases: a busybody, a gadfly, a self-appointed watchdog of the government

286. **om-i-nous**   *adjective*   ŏm′-ə-nəs

[*ominosus* (Latin), "ill-omened"; from *omen, ominis* (Latin), "sign, portent" + *osus* (Latin), "full of"]

Definition: Foreshadowing evil; menacing or threatening.

The **ominous** silence that greeted the proposal presented by one of the members clearly foretold the plan's eventual defeat.

If we had paid some attention to the **ominous** sounds coming from the engine, we would have not been so surprised when the car stopped dead in the middle of nowhere.

Phrases: an ominous pause, ominous clouds

Related Forms: (*nouns*) ominousness, omen; (*adverb*) ominously

Synonyms: (*adjectives*) portentous, ill-omened, foreboding, untoward, unpromising, sinister

Antonyms: (*adjectives*) lucky, happy, felicitous (Word 189), auspicious propitious

Related Phrase: a bird of ill omen

287. op-por-tune *adjective* ŏp-ēr-to͞on′ *or* ŏp-ēr-tyo͞on′

[*opportunus* (Latin), "suitable, favorable"; from the phrase *ob portum veniens* (Latin), "coming (*i.e.*, blowing) toward the harbor"; from *ob* (Latin), "to, toward" + *portus* (Latin), "harbor"]

Definition: Suitable, appropriate, or timely.

Someone with a natural sense of timing can usually select the most **opportune** moment to ask his or her boss for a raise.

Related Forms: (*nouns*) opportunity, opportunism, opportunist; (*adjectives*) inopportune, opportunistic

Usage Note:

An *opportunist* is a person who takes advantage of events to further his or her own purposes regardless of the principles involved. Similarly, *opportunism* is the policy or practice of letting circumstance, rather than principle, dictate a person's behavior or course of action.

Synonyms: (*adjectives*) convenient, seasonable, apt, fitting, propitious, fit, auspicious, advantageous

Antonyms: (*adjectives*) inappropriate, untimely, unsuitable, ill timed, inconvenient, inauspicious

Related Phrases: a timeserver, take time by the forelock

288. os-ten-si-ble   *adjective*   ŏ-stĕn′-sə-bəl

[*ostensibilis* (Medieval Latin), "apparent"; from *ostendere* (Latin), "to reveal; appear" + *abilis, abile* (Latin), "able to"]

Definition: Apparent or professed.

Though a commendable concern for the average wage earner's welfare was the **ostensible** reason for the candidate's proposal, I suspect that his real motives were more self-serving.

Related Form: (*adverb*) ostensibly

Synonyms: (*adjectives*) purported, alleged, avowed, nominal (Word 277), supposed, reputed, evident, manifest

Antonyms: (*adjectives*) true, real, actual, authentic (Word 50), genuine

289. os-tra-cize   *verb*   ŏs′-trə-sīz

[*ostrakizein* (Greek), "banish"; from *ostrakon* (Greek), "potsherd; shell"]

Definition: To banish or exclude from a group; to shun.

Once the details of his scandalous behavior became public knowledge, the entire community **ostracized** him.

Will the day ever come when Americans finally agree to **ostracize** industrial pollution of the environment once and for all?

Related Form: (*noun*) ostracism

374

Synonyms: (*verbs*) expel, exile; blacklist, blackball, snub; boycott (Word 67); bar, repudiate, reject; proscribe, outlaw

Antonyms: (*verbs*) accept, welcome, embrace; associate with

Related Phrases: give someone the cold shoulder, cut someone dead, drum out of the army, send someone to Coventry; a pariah

Ostraka from the marketplace in Athens. Among the names that appear on these broken bits of pottery are Aristeides and Themistokles.

Ostracism

In the ancient Greek city of Athens, it became customary to banish any citizen who was considered to be dangerous to the welfare of the state. Just who should be banished was decided by voting. On the day that the vote was taken, each citizen scratched the name of the person he wished to banish on a bit of broken pottery and deposited this curious ballot in one of the official voting urns set up for the purpose. These broken pieces of crockery were called *ostraka* (singular, *ostrakon*) in Greek. They were used as ballots because great numbers of them lay scattered about the marketplace (or *agora*), where the voting took place. Once all the ballots had been cast, the officials supervising the voting sorted them out. The man who received the largest number of votes was banished from Athenian territory, usually for a period of ten years. The voting was declared invalid, however, if fewer than 6000 votes (total) were cast.

The first *ostracism*, as the Greeks called this curious "unpopularity poll," took place in 487 B.C. and the last about 416 B.C. By the way, many famous Athenians, including Themistokles and Aristeides "the Just," two of Athens's greatest generals and statesmen, were the victims of ostracism, and no particular shame or disgrace was attached to it. In fact, ostracism became such a useful political tool that a number of other Greek city-states adopted it. In Syracuse, the institution was called *petalism* because the names were written on olive leaves (*petala*), not potsherds.

290. pan-de-mo-ni-um   *noun*   păn-də-mō'-nē-əm

[*pas, pan* (Greek), "all" + *daimon* (Greek), "spirit; deity." For further details, see the caption and illustration on page 377.]

Definition: General disorder, confusion, noise, and commotion.

When the verdict of the jury was announced, **pandemonium** broke loose in the courtroom.

The trading floor of the Commodities Exchange was a scene of unbelievable **pandemonium**, unlike anything I had ever witnessed before.

Related Form: (*adjective*) pandemoniac

Synonyms: (*nouns*) chaos, bedlam, turmoil, tumult, din, cacophony, hubbub, hullabaloo, ruckus, racket, rumpus

Antonyms: (*nouns*) order, silence, calm, tranquility, placidity, repose, peace

Related Phrases: raise a hue and cry, a three-ring circus, a brouhaha

291. par-a-dox   *noun*   păr'-ə-dŏks

[*paradoxos* (Greek), "incredible"; from *para* (Greek), "beyond" + *doxa* (Greek), "thought, opinion, expectation"]

Definition:

  a. A seemingly self-contradictory statement that, on closer examination, proves worthy of belief.

      At some time in our lives, all of us discover the truth of the ancient **paradox** that by giving freely to others, we gain more for ourselves.

  b. Someone or something that is full of contradictions and inconsistencies.

      That terrible instruments of war should in fact prove useful as guardians of the peace was one of the **paradoxes** of the Cold War.

Related Forms: (*adjective*) paradoxical; (*adverb*) paradoxically

Synonyms: (*nouns*) riddle, enigma, anomaly

Related Phrases: caught on the horns of a dilemma, a Gordian knot, an oxymoron, a contradiction in terms

Some Famous Paradoxes

Whosoever shall exalt himself shall be abased; and he that shall humble himself shall be exalted.

—The Bible

In this world there are only two tragedies. One is not getting what one wants, and the other is getting it.

—Oscar Wilde

Pandaemonium, by the 19th-century French illustrator Gustave Doré.

Pandemonium

The word *pandemonium* was originally coined by the English poet John Milton (1608–1674) as the name of the capital city of Hell, where much of the action of Milton's great epic poem *Paradise Lost* (1667) takes place. The following extract from this poem shows how Milton originally used the word and also how he spelled it:

> The rest were all
> Far to the inland retir'd, about the walls
> Of Pandaemonium, city and proud seat
> Of Lucifer. . . .
>
> *Paradise Lost*, X, 422–425

Milton also used the word as the name of the palace of Lucifer (or Satan), the ruler of Hell.

Later, the word came to mean Hell itself and, finally (now shorn of its capital letter and second *a*), any place that was like Hell—that is, any scene of wild commotion, general disorder, and noise. This more extended meaning is normally what the word denotes in present-day English.

292. par-a-phrase   *verb and noun*   păr'-ə-frāz

[*paraphrazein* (Greek), "restate"; from *para* (Greek), "alongside" + *phrazein* (Greek), "show, tell"]

Definition:

   a. (*verb*) To restate in other words or another form, often in order to clarify meaning or avoid difficulties.

      She didn't quote the passage verbatim; she **paraphrased** it.

   b. (*noun*) A restatement in other words or another form.

      Some of the most famous passages in Shakespeare's plays turn out to be loose **paraphrases** of Holinshed's *Chronicles* or North's translation of Plutarch.

Related Forms: (*adjective*) paraphrastic; (*noun*) paraphrasis

Usage Note:
Do not confuse the adjective *paraphrastic*, meaning "in the nature of a paraphrase," with the look-alike adjective *periphrastic*, which means "circumlocutory" or "roundabout."

Synonyms: (*verbs*) reword, rephrase; (*nouns*) rewording, rephrasing, free rendering, version

Antonyms: (*verbs*) quote, duplicate, reproduce; (*noun*) quotation

Related Phrase: a word-for-word (or literal) translation

293. pa-ro-chi-al   *adjective*   pə-rō'-kē-əl

[*parochia* (Latin), "parish" + *alis, ale* (Latin), "relating to"; from *paroikos* (Greek), "neighbor, Christian"; from *para* (Greek), "alongside" + *oikos* (Greek), "house"]

Definition:

   a. Located in, or supported by, a parish (a type of ecclesiastical district).

      The Roman Catholic Church maintains a system of **parochial** schools that provide students with religious instruction in addition to their regular academic education.

   b. Restricted in scope or range; narrow or limited.

      I found it hard to believe that a person who had read and traveled so extensively should have such a **parochial** outlook on life.

Related Form: (*noun*) parochialism

Usage Note:
When used of a school or school system, *parochial* is confined to establishments maintained by the Roman Catholic Church. Though other religious organizations certainly maintain schools of their own, these institutions are not normally referred to as parochial schools.

Synonyms: (*adjectives*) local, regional, district; narrow-minded, insular, provincial, hidebound, myopic

Antonyms: (*adjectives*) broad-minded, cosmopolitan, liberal

Related Phrase: wear blinders (or blinkers)

294. par-o-dy   *noun and verb*   pär′-ə-dē

[*paroidia* (Greek), "burlesque poem"; from *para* (Greek), "alongside; subsidiary to" + *oide* (Greek), "song, poem"]

Definition:

a. (*noun*) A comic imitation of the style, form, or content of a serious piece of work.

> Satirical magazines often contain amusing **parodies** of popular movies and TV shows.

> *MacBird* is an amusing **parody** of Shakespeare's *Macbeth* set during the Johnson administration.

b. (*noun*) A performance that is so bad as to constitute a mockery of the thing it is intended to represent.

> The famous show trials that Joseph Stalin mounted in the 1930s were little more than a **parody** of justice.

c. (*verb*) To imitate in a mocking or unworthy way.

> Several popular entertainers are noted for their ability to **parody** the words and gestures of prominent Americans.

> The constitutions of some third world countries do little more than **parody** the principles of Western democracy.

Related Form: (*noun*) parodist

Synonyms: (*nouns*) spoof, takeoff, lampoon, caricature, burlesque, travesty, satire; (*verbs*) spoof, lampoon, satirize, mock, ridicule

Caricature

A *caricature* is a distorted representation of a person in which a characteristic physical feature, mannerism, or other peculiarity is exaggerated in order to produce a comic effect. Often certain physical features provide the focus of the caricature. Other times, the subject's style, attitudes, or ideas are the central feature, as the accompanying cartoon of Theodore Roosevelt reveals. By the way, a caricature need not be a drawing; it may also take the form of a written composition.

295. pen-sive   *adjective*   pĕn'-sĭv

[*pensif, pensive* (French), "thoughtful"; from *penser* (French), "think"; from *pensare* (Latin), "to weigh; ponder, consider"]

Definition: Immersed in deep, often melancholy, thought.

Usually Mary is overflowing with good cheer, but today she is rather **pensive** and withdrawn.

Related Forms: (*noun*) pensiveness; (*adverb*) pensively

Synonyms: (*adjectives*) meditative, reflective, contemplative, introspective; sad, melancholy, wistful, heavyhearted, mournful, doleful

Antonyms: (*adjectives*) lighthearted, blithe, cheerful, gay, mirthful, merry, jocund

Related Phrases: mull over, ruminate on, be lost in thought

Using the Words

Exercise I

1. ob-se'-qui-ous
2. ob-so-lete', ob'-so-lete
3. of-fi'-cious
4. os-ten'-si-ble
5. pan-de-mo'-ni-um
6. par'-a-dox
7. par'-a-phrase
8. pa-ro'-chi-al
9. pen'-sive

Exercise I.   Syllabication and Pronunciation

Syllabicate the following words correctly, and place the major stress mark (') after the syllable that is accented when the word is pronounced. Two answers are correct in one instance.

1. obsequious
2. obsolete
3. officious
4. ostensible
5. pandemonium
6. paradox
7. paraphrase
8. parochial
9. pensive

Exercise II.   Words Out of Context

In each of the following groups, select the item that best expresses the meaning of the numbered word at the left.

1. obsequious   a. lively b. courteous <u>c. deferential</u>
d. vague e. profitable

2. obsolete   a. required b. insignificant c. daring
d. costly <u>e. outmoded</u>

3. officious   <u>a. meddlesome</u> b. changeable c. gigantic
d. exciting e. clever

4. ostensible   a. outrageous b. economical c. graphic
<u>d. apparent</u> e. luxurious

5. ostracize   a. steal <u>b. shun</u> c. seal d. sham
e. stun

6. paradox   <u>a. enigma</u> b. consensus c. anathema
d. kudos e. facsimile

7. paraphrase   a. recall   b. return   c. repulse   d. renew
                   <u>e. restate</u>

8. pensive   a. theoretical   b. crucial   c. disorderly
                   <u>d. contemplative</u>   e. foolhardy

Exercise III.   Completing Sentences

Complete each of the following sentences by selecting the most appropriate word from the group of words given below. Use each word only once. Make any adjustments that are necessary to fit the words into the sentences properly.

parody	pensive	ostracize
obsession	opportune	parochial
ominous	pandemonium	obscene

1. Today, films containing <u> obscene </u> language or nudity are usually given an "R" rating in order to alert potential viewers to the sensitive nature of the material presented.

2. Since I was desperately in need of funds, Mom's check arrived at a most <u> opportune </u> moment.

3. *Omlet, the Great Dane* is both an amusing <u> parody </u> of Shakespeare's *Hamlet* and an irreverent commentary on American politics.

4. Some of my friends went to public school; others attended private or <u> parochial </u> schools.

5. Somehow or other, the speaker managed to make herself heard above the <u>pandemonium</u> that reigned in the convention hall.

6. It is one thing to be concerned about punctuality; it is quite another to allow it to become a(n) <u> obsession </u>.

7. One look at the <u> ominous </u> black clouds rolling in from the west, and I knew we were in for a storm.

Exercise IV.   Synonyms and Antonyms

Classify each of the following pairs of words as **S** for **synonyms** or **A** for **antonyms**.

S	1.	bedlam—pandemonium	**A**	7.	paraphrase—quote
S	2.	fixation—obsession	**A**	8.	cosmopolitan—parochial
A	3.	ominous—auspicious	**S**	9.	obscene—smutty
S	4.	ostensible—alleged	**A**	10.	blithe—pensive
A	5.	newfangled—obsolete	**S**	11.	ostracize—blackball
S	6.	parody—lampoon	**S**	12.	opportune—timely

Exercise V. Word Roundup

1. With or without the aid of a dictionary, explain what each of the following means.

    a. a yes-man
    b. a megalomaniac
    c. a monomaniac
    d. a has-been

    e. an opportunist
    f. a paranoiac
    g. a timeserver
    h. a perfectionist

2. With or without the aid of a dictionary, define each of the following colorful idiomatic expressions.

    a. raise a hue and cry
    b. knuckle under to
    c. wear blinders
       (or blinkers)

    d. give someone the
       cold shoulder
    e. take time by the forelock
    f. have a one-track mind

3. Explain what each of the following means. Consult a dictionary if necessary.

    a. a Gordian knot
    b. an off-color joke

    c. a rubber stamp
    d. an R-rated film

4. The following expressions have been borrowed from French. What does each mean?

    a. avant-garde   b. idée fixe   c. au courant

5. Explain the difference between the items in each of the following pairs of words.

    a. obsolete—obsolescent   b. officious—official

6. Explain the story behind the word *ostracize*. From what foreign language does it come? Name two famous statesmen who were subjected to ostracism.

Exercise VI. Framing Sentences

A. Use each of the following words in an original illustrative sentence.

1. obsequious
2. obsolete
3. obsession

4. opportune
5. pandemonium
6. paraphrase

7. parochial
8. parody
9. pensive

B. Give a **noun** form of each of the following words, and use it in an original illustrative sentence.

1. obscene / obscenity
2. ostracize / ostracism
3. officious / officiousness

C. Give an **adverb** form of each of the following words, and use it in an original illustrative sentence.

1. ostensible
   ostensibly
2. paradox
   paradoxically
3. ominous
   ominously

Dissecting the Words

Prefixes

1. The Latin prefix **ob** occurs, in one form or another, in a great many common English words, including *obsequious, obsession,* and *obscene,* all of which were studied in this lesson. This prefix has a variety of meanings, depending upon how it is used in the word in which it appears. These meanings include:

a. "To, toward," as in these words:

objective (*ob,* "to, toward" + *jacere, jactus* [Latin], "throw")—(*noun*) an aim or goal; (*adjective*) real or actual; uninfluenced by personal feeling or prejudice

obverse (*ob,* "to, toward" + *vertere, versus* [Latin], "turn")—the part of something that is turned toward the viewer; the front

b. "Against, in opposition to," as in these words:

obstacle (*ob,* "against" + *stare, status* [Latin], "stand")—someone or something that is in a person's way

obloquy (*ob,* "against" + *loqui* [Latin], "speak")—abuse; the discredit resulting from such abuse

obstruct (*ob,* "against" + *struere, structus* [Latin], "pile up")—to block, hinder, or impede. Noun: *obstruction*

obtuse (*ob,* "against" + *tundere, tu(n)sus* [Latin], "beat")—dull or blunt

c. "In front of, before," as in these words:

obsess (*ob,* "in front of, before" + *sedere, sessus* [Latin], "sit")—to haunt, harass, or bedevil. Noun: *obsession* (Word 283)

obstetrics (*ob,* "in front of" + *stare, status* [Latin], "stand"; in Latin a midwife was called an *obstetrix,* literally, "a woman who stands before [the bed]")—the branch of medicine dealing with care of women before, during, and just after childbirth. Adjective: *obstetric.* Noun: *obstetrician*

d. "Down, over," as in this word:

obituary (*ob,* "down, over" + *ire, itus* [Latin], "go")—a death notice

e. "Out of, away from," as in this word:

obliterate (*ob,* "out of, away from" + *littera* [Latin], "letter" + *atus* [Latin], "make, do"; in Latin the verb for "delete" was *oblitterare*)—to do away with completely. Noun: *obliteration*

f. "Completely," as in these words:

obdurate (*ob,* "completely" + *durare, duratus* [Latin], "harden")—unyielding, inflexible, or intractable

obfuscate (*ob,* "completely" + *fuscare, fuscatus* [Latin], "darken")—to darken, muddy, or confuse. Noun: *obfuscation*

oblong (*ob,* "completely" + *longus* [Latin], "long")—having one dimension (length or width) much longer than the other

2. The prefix **ob** changes form, depending upon the first letter of the root to which it is attached. These changes include the following:

a. *Ob* becomes **o** before *m*, as in this word:

omit (*ob*, "away from" + *mittere*, *missus* [Latin], "send")—to leave out. Noun: *omission*

b. *Ob* becomes **oc** before *c*, as in these words:

occident (*ob*, "down" + *cadere*, *casus* [Latin], "fall, go")—the west (because that is where the sun sets). Adjective: *occidental*

occlude (*ob*, "completely" + *claudere*, *clausus* [Latin], "close")—to cause to close; to shut in, out, or off. Noun: *occlusion*

occult (*ob*, "completely" + *cul(t)*, a Latin root meaning "conceal")—secret, beyond the understanding of most people

c. *Ob* becomes **of** before an *f*, as in these words:

offend (*ob*, "against" + *-fendere*, *-fensus* [Latin], "strike")—to insult or outrage. Noun: *offense*. Adjective: *offensive*

offer (*ob*, "to, toward" + *ferre* [Latin], "bring")—to put forward or present. Noun: *offering*

Note, however, that *ob* remains unchanged in the word *obfuscate*, studied above.

d. *Ob* becomes **op** before *p*, as in these words:

oppose (*ob*, "against" + *ponere*, *positus* [Latin], "put")—to combat or resist. Nouns: *opposition*, *opponent*. Adjective: *opposite*

oppress (*ob*, "against" + *premere*, *pressus* [Latin], "press")—to weigh heavily on; to persecute. Adjective: *oppressive*

opprobrium (*ob*, "against" + *probum* [Latin], "reproach")—the disgrace that arises from shameful behavior. Adjective: *opprobrious*

3. The Greek prefix **par(a)** appears in a number of useful English words, including *paradox*, *paraphrase*, *parochial*, and *parody*, all of which were studied in this lesson. This prefix has a number of meanings, including:

a. "Alongside, by the side of, beside," as in these words:

parable (*parabola* [Greek], "comparison"; from *para*, "beside" + *ballein*, "throw")—a simple story of everyday life illustrating a moral or religious principle. Related noun: *parabola*

paradigm (*paradeigma* [Greek], "model; from *para*, "alongside" + *deiknynai*, "show, exhibit")—an example or model

paragon (*parakone* [Medieval Greek], "whetstone"; from *para*, "alongside" + *akonan*, "sharpen")—a model or pattern of excellence

paraprofessional (*para*, "alongside"+ *professional*)—a person who is not a member of a given profession but who helps those who are

parapsychology (*para*, "alongside" + *psychology*)—the study of phenomena that cannot be explained by known natural laws—for example, mental telepathy

Other words in which this meaning of *para* is used include *paraplegia*, *paragraph*, *parameter*, *parasite*, and *parenthesis*.

b. "Beyond," as in these words:

paralogism (*para*, "beyond" + *logos* [Greek], "logic")—faulty or illogical reasoning

paranoia (*paranoos* [Greek], "demented"; from *para*, "beyond" + *nous*, "mind")—a mental illness characterized by delusions of being persecuted or being greater than one is. Adjective: *paranoid.* Noun: *paranoiac*

paraphernalia (*para*, "beyond" + *pherne* [Greek], "dowry")—the gear or equipment used in some activity; one's personal belongings

c. "Wrongly, harmfully," as in this word:

paralysis (*paralyein* [Greek], "disable"; from *para*, "wrongfully" + *lyein*, "loosen, release")—loss or impairment of the ability to move or feel; a general stoppage of activity. Verb: *paralyze*

d. "Completely," as in this word:

paroxysm (*paroxysmos* [Greek], "irritation, stimulation"; from *para*, "completely, very" + *oxynein*, "whet, sharpen")—a sudden outburst of feeling or emotion (*e.g.*, laughter)

Note that in a few military words, such as *paratrooper*, the element *para* is not the Greek prefix but a shortened form of the word *parachute*.

Exercise

1. With or without the aid of a dictionary, define each of the following words containing the Latin prefix *ob*, and explain what the prefix means in that particular word. Then choose any **five** of the words, and for each compose an original illustrative sentence.

a. obliterate	**e.** obstruct	**i.** obsess
b. oblong	**f.** obverse	**j.** obdurate
c. obloquy	**g.** obituary	**k.** obtuse
d. obviate	**h.** obnoxious	**l.** obtrude

2. With or without the aid of a dictionary, define each of the following words containing the Greek prefix *para*, and explain what the prefix means in that particular word. Then choose any **five** of the words, and for each compose an original illustrative sentence.

a. paranoid	**d.** parasite	**g.** parameter
b. parabola	**e.** paraphernalia	**h.** paraplegic
c. paralyze	**f.** paroxysm	**i.** paragon

3. Add the prefix *para* to each of the following English words, define the resulting combination, and explain how *para* has altered the meaning of the original word.

a. military	**c.** medical
b. psychology	**d.** professional

Working with Context Clues

Complete each of the following two-word omissions by selecting the pair of words that make the best sense in the passage as a whole. If necessary, consult a dictionary for the meaning of any word with which you are not familiar.

1. <u>Rather than promptly paying his taxes</u>, Greg is always _____. Every year he tries to <u>put off</u> the inevitable by asking the government to _____ the date on which he must submit his completed tax forms.

   a. demure . . . postpone
   b. frugal . . . confirm
   c. <u>dilatory . . . defer</u>
   d. diligent . . . arbitrate

2. It is irresponsible for a community leader to _____ a crowd that is already <u>angry</u> at a verdict it considers unjust. If a <u>riot</u> breaks out, the leader will bear some of the responsibility for the _____.

   a. ostracize . . . atrocity
   b. exploit . . . morass
   c. goad . . . duplicity
   d. <u>incense . . . pandemonium</u>

3. <u>Few</u> audiences today <u>will welcome</u> "<u>Polish</u> jokes" or any other type of humor that insults particular _____ groups. Such _____ remarks merely reveal the comic's <u>prejudice</u> and <u>lack of imagination</u>.

   a. <u>ethnic . . . gratuitous</u>
   b. elite . . . brash
   c. coherent . . . austere
   d. motley . . . opportune

4. When local politicians are elected to Congress, they are expected to balance the _____ concerns of <u>their home district</u> with a more _____ outlook that takes the good of <u>the whole nation</u> into account.

   a. dire . . . felicitous
   b. <u>parochial . . . catholic</u>
   c. pressing . . . narcissistic
   d. nominal . . . mercenary

5. After I glued the two halves of the antique vase back together, the _____ was <u>no longer visible</u>. In fact, to the naked eye, there was no _____ <u>flaw</u> to lower its resale value.

   a. impediment . . . fickle
   b. foible . . . gaping
   c. grimace . . . implicit
   d. <u>defect . . . ostensible</u>

6. All attempts to <u>reword</u> Shakespeare are _____ since any _____ of his poetry, no matter how polished, is <u>arguably</u> inferior to the original.

   a. futile . . . parody
   b. <u>moot . . . paraphrase</u>
   c. obsolete . . . translation
   d. nominal . . . attrition

7. It is hard to know who is more undesirable: a(n) _____ assistant who <u>does far more than you ask</u> or a(n) _____ one who <u>does almost nothing at all</u>.

   a. lucid . . . ominous
   b. haggard . . . fatuous
   c. <u>officious . . . lackadaisical</u>
   d. diligent . . . cynical

8. The <u>conceited</u> anchorman featured on several television <u>comedies</u> is <u>a takeoff</u> on one or more actual network anchors whose _____ personalities lend themselves to _____.

   a. intrepid . . . irony   **c.** ominous . . . humor
   b. flagrant . . . cynicism   <u>**d.** narcissistic . . . parody</u>

9. Alexander the Great was a(n) _____ foe of the Persians as long as they <u>posed a threat to Greek security</u>. Once he had _____ the danger by <u>conquering</u> them, however, he proved to be their most <u>steadfast</u> champion.

   a. effete . . . exploited   **c.** fulsome . . . exacerbated
   <u>**b.** implacable . . . forestalled</u> **d.** boorish . . . curtailed

10. It is characteristic of narrow-minded groups to <u>shun</u> everyone who is <u>unconventional</u>. Such insecure people prefer to _____ those they consider _____ <u>rather</u> than try to <u>understand</u> anyone who is <u>different</u> from themselves.

   <u>**a.** ostracize . . . outlandish</u>   **c.** goad . . . implacable
   b. exalt . . . banal   **d.** forestall . . . motley

11. "I <u>haven't had time</u> to give your report more than a _____ glance," my boss told me. "However, I plan to _____ it <u>carefully</u> before we actually sit down to discuss it.

   <u>**a.** cursory . . . scrutinize</u>   **c.** nominal . . . libel
   b. gratuitous . . . parody   **d.** quick . . . disregard

Enriching the Lesson

Exercise I.   More of Our Greek Heritage

A number of the words studied in this lesson, including *ostracize* and *paradox*, are derived with very little change from Greek. Some other useful English words derived from Greek prototypes are listed below. With or without the aid of a dictionary, define each, and give its etymology. Then choose any **five** of the words, and for each compose an original illustrative sentence.

1. protagonist	11. polyglot	21. myth
2. spasmodic	12. toxic	22. heterogeneous
3. psychotic	13. xenophobic	23. lyric
4. tyrannical	14. phantasm	24. schism
5. polemic	15. litany	25. tragedy
6. lethargy	16. autochthonous	26. tautology
7. therapeutic	17. panoply	27. phlegmatic
8. mimic	18. metaphoric	28. kaleidoscope
9. rhetoric	19. mosaic	29. category
10. calisthenics	20. kinetic	30. periphery

Exercise II.   Ecclesiastically Speaking

English is rich in words and phrases relating to the church or the clergy. One such expression, *parochial*, was studied in this lesson. A few others are listed below. With or without the aid of a dictionary or other reference book, define each, and give its etymology. Then choose any **five** of the items, and for each compose an original illustrative sentence.

1. sacrilege
2. sacrament
3. prelate
4. laity
5. ecclesiastical
6. pastoral
7. liturgy
8. ecumenical
9. diocese
10. monastic
11. canonical
12. Pentecostal
13. theology
14. rite
15. episcopal

Exercise III.   Manias

A *mania* is an exaggerated or hampering obsession, a dominating preoccupation or craving that often leads to unbalanced or irrational behavior. The word *mania* forms part of many compound words that indicate particular kinds of behavior patterns. A few of these words are listed below. With or without the aid of a dictionary or other reference book, define each, and give its etymology.

1. pyromania
2. bibliomania
3. kleptomania
4. dipsomania
5. egomania
6. megalomania

Exercise IV.   Expanding Your Word Power

The words listed below are not on the Basic Word List, but they were mentioned in passing, in one form or another, in Lesson 23. All of them would make useful additions to your working vocabulary. Define each, give its etymology, list **two** synonyms and **two** antonyms (where possible), and use in a short illustrative sentence.

1. salacious
2. unctuous
3. compulsive
4. defunct
5. intrusive
6. omen
7. untimely
8. purport
9. exile
10. tumult
11. insular
12. satire
13. duplicate
14. portentous
15. introspective

Lesson 24

296. peremptory — 310. premise

---

296. pe·remp·to·ry   *adjective*   pə-rĕmp′-tə-rē

[*peremptorius* (Latin), "final"; from *per* (Latin), "completely" + *emere, emptus* (Latin), "buy, obtain" + *orius* (Latin), "characterized by"]

Definition:

  a. Having the nature of a command in that it does not allow discussion, contradiction, or refusal.

     Good supervisors soon learn that they can get more cooperation from those under them by making polite requests than by issuing **peremptory** orders.

  b. Determined, resolute.

     "Though we are always ready to settle our differences with other countries peacefully," the official said, "we are not afraid to make **peremptory** use of force when necessary."

  c. Offensively dictatorial.

     Though his manner is **peremptory** with those below him in the office hierarchy, it is obsequious with those higher up.

Related Forms: (*noun*) peremptoriness; (*adverb*) peremptorily

Synonyms: (*adjectives*) binding, obligatory, mandatory, prescriptive; categorical, unconditional, positive, emphatic, concerted; despotic, tyrannical, high-handed

Antonyms: (*adjectives*) tentative, contingent, provisional; irresolute, indecisive, hesitant; mild, unassuming, diffident

---

297. per·jure   *verb*   pẽr′-jûr

[*per* (Latin), "harmfully, falsely" + *jurare* (Latin), "swear"]

Definition: To lie deliberately while under oath to tell the truth.

  Though there are minor inconsistencies in his testimony, there is no evidence that the witness actually **perjured** himself.

  I described my reaction to his performance at the recital as favorably as I could without actually **perjuring** myself.

Related Forms: (*nouns*) perjury, perjurer; (*adjective*) perjurious

Phrases: commit perjury, perjured testimony

Synonyms: (*verbs*) forswear, prevaricate

Related Phrases: bear false witness, give false testimony

298. per-me-ate   *verb*   pĕr'-mē-āt

[*permeare, permeatus* (Latin), "pass through"; from *per* (Latin), "through" + *meare, meatus* (Latin), "go, pass"]

Definition: To spread through; to penetrate.

Noxious fumes from the industrial accident so **permeated** the atmosphere that scores of people living nearby had to be evacuated from their homes.

During the days before Constantinople fell to the Turks in 1453, the mood of the besieged city was **permeated** by a sense of doom.

Related Forms: (*nouns*) permeation, permeability; (*adjectives*) permeable, impermeable

Synonyms: (*verbs*) pervade, infiltrate, diffuse, saturate, impregnate, imbue, filter into, seep through, soak through

Related Phrase: infiltrate enemy lines

299. per-ni-cious   *adjective*   pĕr-nish'-əs

[*perniciosus* (Latin), "destructive"; from *per* (Latin), "completely" + *nex, necis* (Latin), "violent death" + *osus* (Latin), "full of"]

Definition: Highly injurious or harmful.

Despite mounting medical evidence concerning the **pernicious** effects of fatty foods, many people categorically refuse to give up eating them on a daily basis.

Phrases: a pernicious influence, a pernicious practice

Related Forms: (*noun*) perniciousness; (*adverb*) perniciously

Synonyms: (*adjectives*) deleterious, detrimental, malignant, baneful, ruinous, destructive

Antonyms: (*adjectives*) wholesome, beneficial, salutary, salubrious

300. per-se-vere   *verb*   pĕr-sə-vîr'

[*perseverare* (Latin), "persist"; from *per* (Latin), "thoroughly" + *severus* (Latin), "serious, in earnest"]

Definition: To continue steadfastly despite obstacles or discouragment.

The old saying "If at first you don't succeed, try, try again" encourages us all to **persevere** in whatever we undertake.

Related Forms: (*noun*) perseverance; (*adjective*) persevering

Synonyms: (*verbs*) persist, endure

Antonyms: (*verbs*) quit, desist, give up on, abandon

Related Phrases: plug away at, stick something out, stop at nothing to achieve a goal, stick to one's guns; throw in the towel

301. pho·bi·a   *noun*   fō'-bē-ə
[*phobos* (Greek), "fear, flight" + -*ia* (Greek), "state of"]

Definition: An intense irrational fear of something; any strong aversion.

She attributed her pronounced **phobia** about dogs to the fact that she was nipped on the finger by an overly defensive collie when she was a child.

The legislator warned that we must not allow our natural concern for security to develop into an obsessive **phobia** about foreigners.

Related Form: (*adjective*) phobic

Usage Note:
Phobia often appears in compound words indicating particular kinds of fears or aversions. For example, *claustrophobia* (*claustrum* [Latin], "enclosed place" + *phobia*) is the proper term for an irrational fear of small, tightly enclosed places. The related word element -*phobe*, meaning "one who fears or dislikes," also appears in such words. For example, a *xenophobe* is a person who dislikes foreigners and all things relating to them. Note that -*phobe* is only used as a combining form, not as an independent word.

The Greek suffixes -*philia*, meaning "a liking or attraction for," and -*phil(e)* or -*philiac*, meaning "one who has a liking for or is attracted to," are the "antonyms" of *phobia* and -*phobe*. For example, a philosopher is someone who loves (*philos* [Greek], "loving, liking") wisdom (*sophia* [Greek], "wisdom"). Similarly, *necrophilia* is the technical name for a morbid attraction to dead bodies (*necros* [Greek], "corpse"). Note that -*philia*, -*phil(e)*, and -*philiac* are only used as combining forms, not independent words.

Synonyms: (*nouns*) dread (of), horror (of), aversion (to), distaste (for), abhorrence (of), antipathy (for), loathing (for)

Antonyms: (*nouns*) liking (for), taste (for), partiality (for), fondness (for), affinity (for), predilection (for)

Related Phrases: have a soft spot in one's heart for; have no stomach for

302. pla·gia·rism   *noun*   plā'-jə-rĭz-əm
[*plagiarius* (Latin), "kidnapper"; from *plaga* (Latin), "net"]

Definition: The use of another person's writings or ideas as one's own without acknowledging their source.

"No one is going to accuse you of **plagiarism**," the editor told the fledgling author, "just because a couple of paragraphs in a very long novel are vaguely reminiscent of Hemingway."

Far from being a retelling of one of O. Henry's best-loved short stories, as the author claims, the work is an outright **plagiarism**.

Related Forms: (*verb*) plagiarize; (*nouns*) plagiary, plagiarist, plagiarizer

Synonyms: (*nouns*) theft, piracy

Related Phrases: literary piracy, an infringement of copyright, a crib

303. **plain-tive**   *adjective*   plān'-tĭv

[*plaintif, plaintive* (Old French), "sorrowful"; from *plangere, planctus* (Latin), "lament"]

Definition: Sorrowful or melancholy; mournful.

She closed her recital with a **plaintive** little Scottish ditty entitled "The Exile's Lament."

The **plaintive** moaning of a distant foghorn accorded well with the regret I felt in my heart at leaving that fair city forever.

Related Forms: (*nouns*) plaint, plaintiveness; (*adverb*) plaintively

Phrases: the plaintive tones of an oboe, the plaintive cry of an orphan

Synonyms: (*adjectives*) doleful, dolorous, disconsolate, lachrymose, wistful, heartbroken, tearful, lugubrious

Antonyms: (*adjectives*) merry, jocund, cheerful, lighthearted

Related Phrase: shed crocodile tears

Jeremiah

Jeremiad

In modern English, a long, involved lament is sometimes called a *jeremiad*. This word has an interesting origin. It is based on the name Jeremiah. Jeremiah (*c.* 628–586 B.C.), as you may recall, was one of the major prophets of the Old Testament and the author, among other things, of a book of moving poems mourning the destruction of Jerusalem by the Babylonians. As a result, Jeremiah became associated with the elegiac mood, and this in turn gave rise to the use of a word based on his name for any kind of lengthy lament or tale of woe.

304. pleth-o-ra   *noun*   plĕth'-ə-rə

[*plethora* (Greek), "fullness"; from *plethein* (Greek), "be full"]

Definition: Superabundance or excess.

As usual, we got a **plethora** of advice about what to do but precious little help doing it.

Many Hollywood stars receive a **plethora** of fan mail every day.

Phrases: a plethora of ideas, a plethora of complaints, a plethora of food and drink

Synonyms: (*nouns*) profusion, welter, superfluity, glut, surplus, surfeit, deluge, avalanche

Antonyms: (*nouns*) scarcity, paucity, dearth, shortage, lack, want

Related Phrases: give something short shrift, a shortfall

In 1750, the poet Thomas Gray (1716–1771) published one of the most poignant poems in the English language, "Elegy Written in a Country Churchyard."

305. poign-ant   *adjective*   poin'-yənt

[*poignant*, present participle of *poindre* (Old French), "sting"; from *pungere* (Latin), "puncture, sting"]

Definition: Keenly touching or moving.

Though the play was essentially a comedy, it nevertheless contained a **poignant** moment or two.

Related Forms: (*nouns*) poignancy, poignance; (*adverb*) poignantly

Synonyms: (*adjectives*) heartbreaking, tender, heartrending, wistful, affecting, melancholy, elegiac, bittersweet

Antonyms: (*adjectives*) unaffecting; bland, vapid, insipid

306. pre-car-i-ous   *adjective*   prĭ-kâr′-ē-əs

[*precarius* (Latin), "dependent upon prayer or entreaty"; from *prex, precis* (Latin), "prayer, entreaty" + *arius* (Latin), "relating to"]

Definition: Dangerously insecure, unstable, or uncertain.

Some of the firefighters battled the blaze from a **precarious** perch atop a mobile crane called a *cherry picker*.

Even with the help of modern life-support systems, a premature baby's hold on life is often **precarious**.

Related Forms: (*noun*) precariousness; (*adverb*) precariously

Synonyms: (*adjectives*) perilous, hazardous, risky, treacherous; dubious, touch-and-go, ticklish, touchy, delicate

Antonyms: (*adjectives*) safe, secure, stable, firm, certain, impregnable

Related Phrases: skate on thin ice, walk a tightrope, hang by a thread, out on a limb, a sword of Damocles

307. pre-co-cious   *adjective*   prĭ-kō′-shəs

[*praecox, praecocis* (Latin), "ripening before its time"; from *prae* (Latin), "before" + *coquere, coctus* (Latin), "cook, boil"]

Definition: Developing unusually early.

Wolfgang Amadeus Mozart was a **precocious** youngster who wrote his first opera at the age of eleven.

Given the kinds of tools the Egyptians had to work with, raising the pyramids constituted an extraordinarily **precocious** feat of engineering.

Related Forms: (*nouns*) precociousness, precocity; (*adverb*) precociously

Phrases: at a precocious age, a precocious achievement

Synonyms: (*adjectives*) forward, gifted; advanced; premature

Antonyms: (*adjectives*) backward, retarded; underdeveloped; laggard

Related Phrases: a child prodigy; a late bloomer

308. pred-a-to-ry   *adjective*   prĕd′-ə-tô-rē

[*praedari, praedatus* (Latin), "plunder, pillage" + *orius* (Latin), "characterized by"; from *praeda* (Latin), "booty"]

Definition: Preying on, plundering, or piratical.

Though many other **predatory** creatures prefer to hunt at night, lions and leopards are active during the daytime.

Karl Marx viewed capitalists as an essentially **predatory** class of people because he felt that they lived off the labor of others.

Related Forms: (*nouns*) predator, predatoriness

Predators such as this mountain lion still inhabit the less settled areas of the western United States, where they prey on deer, horses, cattle, and other animals.

Synonyms: (*adjectives*) marauding, pillaging, looting; rapacious, voracious, avaricious, extortionate

Related Phrases: prey on, despoil the land of its resources, pirate a novel, cannibalize a manuscript; a harpy

309. **pre-lude**   *noun*   prā'-lōōd   *or*   prĕl'-yōōd
[*prae* (Latin), "before" + *ludere, lusus* (Latin), "play"]

Definition: An introductory piece of music; anything that precedes or introduces something else.

The **prelude** to the third act of Verdi's *La Traviata* is one of the most poignant pieces of music I have ever heard.

In the State Department's view, the unexpected concentration of troops along the border could be construed only as a **prelude** to invasion.

Synonyms: (*nouns*) overture, prologue, preface, curtain-raiser

Antonyms: (*nouns*) postlude, epilogue, aftermath, sequel

Related Phrases: lay the groundwork for, a dress rehearsal

310. pre-mise　　　*noun and verb*　　　prĕm'-ĭs

[*prae* (Latin), "before, ahead" + *mittere, missus* (Latin), "send"]

Definition:

a. (*noun*) A statement upon which an argument is based or from which a conclusion is drawn.

> Your suggestion that you be given the lead in the school play is based on the totally unrealistic **premise** that you are the most talented actor available.

b. (*verb*) To state or assume as the basis for something else; to offer in advance as an explanation of, or introduction to, something else.

> Much of the judge's thinking is **premised** on the proposition that, in the eyes of the law, all people are equal.

> "Let me **premise** my remarks tonight," the speaker said, "with a bit of personal history that will explain why I feel so strongly about certain subjects."

Usage Note:

When used in the plural, *premise* also indicates a building or residence, including the land upon which it stands or that is immediately adjacent to it. This use of the word occurs in such phrases as "vacate the *premises*" and "on the *premises*."

Synonyms: (*nouns*) proposition, axiom, thesis, hypothesis, assumption; (*verbs*) preface, introduce; posit, predicate; presuppose

Using the Words

Exercise I.　Parts of Speech

Indicate the part of speech of each of the following words. In one case, two answers are correct.

1. peremptory adj.
2. pernicious adj.
3. plagiarism n.
4. plethora n.
5. poignant adj.
6. precocious adj.
7. predatory adj.
8. prelude n.
9. premise n., v.

Exercise II.　Words in Phrases

In each of the following groups, select the item that best expresses the meaning of the *italicized* word in the introductory phrase.

1. a *peremptory* tone of voice
   a. hopeful　<u>b. dictatorial</u>　c. jubilant　d. discouraged

2. now *permeates* our system of justice
   a. makes better　b. investigates　<u>c. spreads through</u>
   d. ignores

3. a *pernicious* influence on society
   a. harmful   b. lasting   c. superficial   d. wholesome

4. *persevere* despite all obstacles
   a. die out   b. carry on   c. pull down   d. give up

5. the *plaintive* notes of an oboe
   a. merry   b. melodious   c. majestic   d. mournful

6. a *plethora* of problems
   a. shortage   b. creator   c. deluge   d. solver

7. *poignant* memories
   a. bittersweet   b. remarkable   c. vague   d. amusing

8. *predatory* bands of Vikings
   a. enormous   b. unexpected   c. friendly   d. piratical

Exercise III. Completing Sentences

Complete each of the following sentences by selecting the most appropriate word from the group of words given below. Use each word only once. Make any adjustments that are necessary to fit the words into the sentences properly.

perjure	precarious	persevere
pernicious	precocious	prelude
premise	phobia	plagiarism

1. My most recent acquisition is a two-disc set of overtures and __preludes__ to famous Italian operas.

2. "With a great team like the Islanders breathing down our necks," the Rangers' star goalie observed, "our hold on first place in the Eastern Conference can only be described as _precarious_."

3. Over the years, her childhood fear of the dark developed into a serious and debilitating __phobia__.

4. The judge instructed the jury to disregard the witness's testimony after the D.A. proved that the man had __perjured__ himself while on the stand.

5. "Your conclusion is clearly invalid," I replied, "simply because it is based on a false __premise__."

6. She was a gifted youngster who started college at the _precocious_ age of 15.

7. Though the United States subscribes to an international system of copyright laws designed to protect writers from _plagiarism_ and other forms of literary piracy, China does not.

Exercise IV.   Synonyms and Antonyms

A.   In each of the following groups, select the **two** words that are most nearly **synonyms**.

permeate

1.   a. pervade   b. esteem   c. saturate   d. blemish   e. resolve

2.   a. intelligence   b. reward   c. aversion   d. antipathy   phobia
      e. fondness

3.   a. unassuming   b. piratical   c. sensible   d. tarnished   predatory
      e. plundering

4.   a. treacherous   b. wistful   c. melancholy   d. feminine   poignant,
      e. obvious   plaintive

5.   a. glut   b. request   c. scarcity   d. honor   e. profusion   plethora

   Now, for each pair of synonyms you have selected, supply a word from the Basic Word List for this lesson (Words 296–310) that means **the same** or **almost the same** thing.

B.   In each of the following, select the item that is most nearly **opposite** in meaning to the numbered word at the left.

1.   persevere   a. cling   b. repair   c. quit   d. increase
                   e. steal

2.   plaintive   a. wooden   b. merry   c. puzzling   d. silent
                  e. thoughtful

3.   prelude   a. anathema   b. epilogue   c. facsimile
                d. euphemism   e. impasse

4.   pernicious   a. wholesome   b. partial   c. ruinous
                   d. shabby   e. tentative

5.   precarious   a. delicate   b. envious   c. pompous
                   d. illegal   e. secure

Exercise V.   Word Roundup

1.   The expression *a peremptory challenge* is frequently used in the courtroom. What does it mean?

2.   What is *claustrophobia*? a *xenophobe*?

3.   Define a *jeremiad*. What is the origin of this word?

4.   With or without the aid of a dictionary, define each of the following colorful idiomatic expressions.

   a.   throw in the towel   c.   skate on thin ice
   b.   stick to one's guns   d.   shed crocodile tears

5.   With or without the aid of a dictionary, define each of the following useful terms.

   a.   a child prodigy   c.   a late bloomer
   b.   a shortfall   d.   a curtain-raiser

Exercise VI.   Framing Sentences

A. Use each of the following words in an original sentence.

1. peremptory
2. permeate
3. pernicious
4. precarious
5. phobia
6. plagiarize
7. plaintive
8. plethora
9. poignant
10. precocious
11. prelude
12. premise

B. Give a **noun** form of each of the following words, and use it in an original illustrative sentence.

1. persevere
   preseverance

2. predatory
   predator

3. perjure
   perjury, perjurer

Completing Verbal Analogies

Complete each of the following analogies.

Group A

1. **durable : long life ::**
   a. unison : great variety
   b. elite : great wisdom
   c. impecunious : great wealth
   d. prodigious : great size
   e. capricious : great reliability

2. **veer : away ::**
   a. inflate : down
   b. revert : back
   c. compress : apart
   d. proceed : sideways
   e. decline : forward

3. **rabbit : burrow ::**
   a. lion : den
   b. horse : lair
   c. nest : bird
   d. cow : bovine
   e. dog : manger

4. **kindle : extinguish ::**
   a. jeopardize : hazard
   b. instigate : repress
   c. parody : ostracize
   d. perjure : prevaricate
   e. allot : spare

5. **plod : slow ::**
   a. browse : fast
   b. dash : slow
   c. scurry : fast
   d. dawdle : fast
   e. sprint : slow

Group B

6. **fruitless : result =**
   a. heartless : skill
   b. tactless : merit
   c. value : priceless
   d. tireless : energy
   e. aimless : purpose

7. **sweater : attire =**
   a. <u>sword : weapon</u>
   b. horse : tether
   c. scavenger : jackal
   d. will : legacy
   e. mammoth : fetish

8. **thin : gaunt =**
   a. clear : cryptic
   b. lush : nebulous
   c. haughty : meek
   d. <u>big : mammoth</u>
   e. ominous : pensive

9. **officious : unfavorable =**
   a. obsequious : favorable
   b. astute : unfavorable
   c. <u>precocious : favorable</u>
   d. lucrative : unfavorable
   e. narcissistic : favorable

10. **scoff : contempt =**
    a. vex : enjoyment
    b. <u>rue : sorrow</u>
    c. happiness : elate
    d. lament : levity
    e. meditate : anger

Working with Context Clues

Complete each of the following two-word omissions by selecting the pair of words that make the best sense in the passage as a whole. If necessary, consult a dictionary for the meaning of any word with which you are not familiar. Underline the clue or clues that led you to choose your answer.

1. The prosecuting attorney did <u>not</u> provide <u>many</u> arguments to <u>back up</u> her plea for a guilty verdict, but those she did present were <u>extremely well chosen</u>. A larger but less _____ selection of arguments would probably have failed to _____ the verdict she was looking for.
   a. cogent . . . defer
   b. <u>judicious . . . justify</u>
   c. esoteric . . . elicit
   d. gratuitous . . . augur

2. An <u>irrational fear</u> can <u>spread through</u> an entire town as it did in Salem, Massachusetts. A similar _____ was able to _____ the whole nation in the 1950s, with Communists, not witches, as the source of the terror.
   a. <u>phobia . . . permeate</u>
   b. parody . . . instigate
   c. foible . . . penetrate
   d. nostalgia . . . jeopardize

3. You can be accused of <u>stealing another writer's original ideas</u> even if you <u>put those ideas in your own words</u>. Therefore, to avoid charges of _____, be sure you give credit to the source of any ideas that you _____ in your writing.
   a. duplicity . . . criticize
   b. effrontery . . . expound
   c. irony . . . embellish
   d. <u>plagiarism . . . paraphrase</u>

4. Since _____ animals must <u>kill to live</u> and since their victims <u>escape them more often than not</u>, they must _____ until they succeed in getting a meal.

   a. endemic . . . persist   <u>c. predatory . . . persevere</u>
   b. exotic . . . abstain   d. pernicious . . . entreat

5. Most experienced music teachers can distinguish an <u>extraordinarily gifted</u> _____ from an ordinary <u>beginner</u> by the <u>speed and grace</u> with which the _____ student learns.

   a. virtuoso . . . eminent   c. charlatan . . . fulsome
   b. veteran . . . erudite   <u>d. novice . . . precocious</u>

6. New styles in art and music often seem <u>weird and baffling when they first appear</u>, but what seems _____ initially may come to be seen as an exciting _____.

   a. ingenious . . . anachronism   c. elite . . . medium
   <u>b. bizarre . . . innovation</u>   d. graphic . . . harbinger

7. A person who relentlessly stalks another person and cannot control or stop the _____ is in the grip of a _____ fixation that may <u>cause great harm</u>.

   <u>a. obsession . . . pernicious</u>   c. nostalgia . . . chronic
   b. pandemonium . . . poignant   d. libel . . . gratuitous

8. If you are lost and alone in the bush, signs of lions or other _____ animals are bound to seem _____, since what greater <u>evil</u> could befall you than to become the <u>prey of one of these hunters</u>.

   <u>a. predatory . . . ominous</u>   c. mammoth . . . negligible
   b. mercenary . . . gruesome   d. exotic . . . felicitous

9. If you had committed a crime and wished to conceal it, you might be tempted to _____ yourself when <u>giving testimony in a case against someone else</u>. District attorneys sometimes offer <u>protection</u> from prosecution, in hopes that this _____ will induce witnesses to <u>testify truthfully</u>.

   a. parody . . . empathy   c. protect . . . inception
   b. flaunt . . . legacy   <u>d. perjure . . . immunity</u>

10. A warm, clear night is <u>most suitable</u> for stargazing. A cold, clear night is less _____ because although the sky provides a(n) _____ of stars, you cannot watch <u>the abundant display</u> in comfort for very long.

    a. fortuitous . . . nuance   <u>c. opportune . . . plethora</u>
    b. fulsome . . . array   d. bleak . . . myriad

Enriching the Lesson

Exercise I.   Common Phobias

It is a rare human being indeed who does not have some kind of personal anxiety or phobia. Listed below are the technical terms for a number of these peculiarities. With or without the aid of an unabridged dictionary or other reference book, define each and give its etymology. Then choose any **five**, and for each compose an original illustrative sentence.

1. ailurophobia
2. monophobia
3. hydrophobia
4. acrophobia
5. agoraphobia
6. xenophobia
7. gynephobia
8. nyctophobia
9. Anglophobia
10. bibliophobia
11. triskaidekaphobia
12. cynophobia
13. arachnophobia
14. keraunophobia
15. ophidiophobia

Exercise II.   Words Based on *Philos*

English has a group of words based on the Greek root **philos**, meaning "loving" or "dear." A number of these terms are listed below. With or without the aid of a dictionary, define each, and give its etymology.

1. philosophy
2. philatelist
3. Francophile
4. hemophilia
5. philanthropy
6. philology
7. philharmonic
8. discophile
9. Anglophile
10. philander

Exercise III.   A Verbal Diversion

Modern English contains a good many adjectives that refer to members of the animal kingdom. Some of these words are sometimes applied to individual human beings to indicate that they are the possessors of whatever characteristics are associated with that particular animal. A few of these adjectives are listed below. With or without the aid of a dictionary, define each, or name the animal to which it refers. Also give any figurative or extended meanings the word may have.

1. feline
2. canine
3. equine
4. bovine
5. leonine
6. vulpine
7. lupine
8. leporine
9. ovine
10. elephantine
11. porcine
12. pavonine
13. serpentine
14. ursine
15. simian
16. taurine
17. piscine
18. anserine

Exercise IV. Colorful Phrases

A number of colorful phrases usually employed in a figurative or metaphorical sense are listed below. With or without the aid of a dictionary or other reference book, define or explain each. Then choose any **five**, and for each compose an original illustrative sentence.

1. look a gift horse in the mouth
2. a dog in the manger
3. lose face
4. rob Peter to pay Paul
5. call someone on the carpet
6. rest on one's laurels
7. a snake in the grass
8. put all one's eggs in one basket
9. split hairs
10. pocket one's pride
11. pay through the nose for
12. fly off the handle
13. in a nutshell
14. live from hand to mouth
15. buy a pig in a poke
16. put something on a back burner

Exercise V. Expanding Your Word Power

The words listed below are not on the Basic Word List, but they were mentioned in one form or another in Lesson 24. All of them would make useful additions to your working vocabulary. Define each, give its etymology, list **two** synonyms and **two** antonyms (where possible), and use in a short illustrative sentence.

1. contingent
2. categorical
3. despotic
4. imbue
5. salubrious
6. desist
7. affinity
8. lugubrious
9. surfeit
10. elegiac
11. impregnable
12. pillage
13. aftermath
14. hypothesis
15. posit

Related Forms in Context

Beneath each sentence below are four words introduced in Lesson 23 or 24. Review the related forms for these words, and choose the one that best completes the sentence. Write that related form in the space provided.

1. According to Auguste Rodin, his sculpture of a man leaning his arm and head _pensively_ on one knee represents the poet Dante planning his *Inferno*.

   a. ostensible b. peremptory c. pensive d. precocious

2. Victims of leprosy, or Hansen's disease, were once forced to live in isolated colonies, thereby suffering _ostracism_ as well as the debilitating effects of their highly contagious disease.

   a. ostracize b. permeate c. paraphrase d. perjure

3. In Act V, scene i, of *Macbeth*, the sleepwalking Lady Macbeth __obsesses__ about blood she cannot wash from her hands.

   a. pandemonium   b. plagiarism   c. parody   d. obsession

4. The general spoke paradoxically, we thought, about the need to quadruple the size of the defense budget so that the nation could mobilize for peace.

   a. paraphrase   b. parody   c. paradox   d. pandemonium

5. Which, if any, of these electronic marvels do you consider obsolescent: dial-up computer modems, fax machines, or audiocassette tapes?

   a. obsequious   b. obsolete   c. obscene   d. opportune

6. Although both defendants swore that the signature on the letter was theirs, the testimony of a handwriting expert convinced the jury that one of the defendants had committed __perjury__.

   a. ostracize   b. paraphrase   c. parody   d. perjure

7. Rush says that he used to be __phobic__ about flying in an airplane but that six months of group therapy completely cured him of his fears.

   a. plethora   b. plagiarism   c. phobia   d. paraphrase

8. To prevent her students from plagiarizing an online research paper, Ms. Applegate requires them to turn in an outline and all of their prewriting notes.

   a. plagiarism   b. parody   c. paradox   d. obsession

9. The court jester, the only member of the court from whom the king did not demand total obsequiousness, literally lost his head when he went too far.

   a. obscene   b. obsolete   c. obsequious   d. officious

10. Although the upstream face of the Kangaroo Creek Dam in South Australia is constructed of impermeable concrete, its downstream side is built from rockfill.

    a. perjure   b. persevere   c. paraphrase   d. permeate

11. In Act II, scene ii, of *Julius Caesar*, Caesar's wife begs him not to go to the Senate, for in her dream she has seen Caesar's statue gushing a fountain of blood—an evil __omen__ if ever there was one.

    a. obsequious   b. ominous   c. officious   d. parochial

12. The praying mantis is a(n) __predator__ that waits, so well camouflaged that it is practically invisible, for an insect to stray within its long reach.

    a. pernicious   b. predatory   c. peremptory   d. ominous

13. "We need to overcome our <u>parochialism</u>," proclaimed the mayor in her inauguration speech, "and make plans for the greater good of our tricounty area."

    a. pensive   b. plaintive   c. poignant   <u>d. parochial</u>

14. The consul <u>peremptorily</u> denied Wei Lan's request for a student visa despite the fact that he'd already been offered a scholarship to an American university.

    a. opportune   b. precarious   c. officious   <u>d. peremptory</u>

15. The young couple didn't mind the bride's mother's <u>officiousness</u> about the wedding plans, for she clearly had a great need to be involved in all aspects of the event.

    <u>a. officious</u>   b. precarious   c. obsequious   d. obscene

16. Had he not been a confirmed <u>opportunist</u>, Jay Gatsby, in F. Scott Fitzgerald's *The Great Gatsby*, would probably not have been able to amass a fortune, coming as he did from such humble beginnings.

    a. obsolete   b. pernicious   <u>c. opportune</u>   d. ominous

17. To celebrate the birthdays of her friends, Maya, a talented <u>parodist</u>, writes original lyrics for popular songs.

    a. paraphrase   <u>b. parody</u>   c. phobia   d. obsession

18. Rachel Carson started the environmental movement with the publication of *Silent Spring* (1962), which documents the <u>perniciousness</u> of chemicals such as DDT.

    <u>a. pernicious</u>   b. plaintive   c. poignant   d. precocious

19. Desperate with hunger, Oliver Twist walks up to the master, holds out his porridge bowl, and says <u>plaintively</u>, "Please, sir, I want some more."

    a. peremptory   b. pernicious   c. predatory   <u>d. plaintive</u>

20. Thanks to the <u>perseverance</u> of British mathematician Alan Turing and a dedicated team of analysts, the Allies succeeded in cracking the Nazi's Enigma code.

    a. permeate   b. paraphrase   <u>c. persevere</u>   d. perjure

Lesson 25

311. **pre·rog·a·tive**   *noun*   prĭ-rŏg′-ə-tĭv

[*praerogativus* (Latin), "asked to vote first"; from *prae* (Latin), "before" + *rogare, rogatus* (Latin), "ask"]

Definition: A special right or privilege that belongs to a person or group by virtue of rank, position, or the like.

In republican Rome, election to the consulship came to be the special **prerogative** of a tiny group of noble families belonging to the senatorial order.

Synonyms: (*nouns*) perquisite, advantage, benefit, birthright

312. **pro·bi·ty**   *noun*   prō′-bə-tē

[*probitas* (Latin), "honesty, uprightness"; from *probus* (Latin), "honest, upright, virtuous" + *-itas, -itatis* (Latin), "state of"]

Definition: Unquestionable honesty or uprightness.

True **probity** is not just the absence of deceit; it is a positive passion for behaving honorably and speaking the truth.

"It is the **probity** of his financial dealings that has been called into question," I replied, "not their profitableness."

Synonyms: (*nouns*) integrity, rectitude, ethicality, righteousness, honorableness, decency

Antonyms: (*nouns*) unscrupulousness, underhandedness, shadiness, knavery, chicanery, skulduggery

Related Phrases: a man or woman of principle, moral fiber; sharp practice.

313. **pro·cras·ti·nate**   *verb*   prō-krăs′-tə-nāt

[*procrastinare, procrastinatus* (Latin), "put off until tomorrow"; from *pro* (Latin), "forward" + *cras* (Latin), "tomorrow"]

Definition: To delay action.

"We must do something about the problem now," the congresswoman declared. "The longer we **procrastinate**, the worse the situation will become."

Related Forms: (*nouns*) procrastination, procrastinator

Synonyms: (*verbs*) postpone, shilly-shally, dillydally, temporize, stall

Antonyms: (*verbs and phrases*) act (on), take action (on), settle, decide, dispose of, take care of

Related Phrases: play a waiting game, table (or shelve) a bill, put something on ice (or in cold storage), mark time, keep in a holding pattern, drag one's feet about, let something hang fire

314. **pro-di-gious**   *adjective*   prə-dĭj′-əs

[*prodigium* (Latin), "omen, ominous sign, enormity" + *osus* (Latin), "full of"]

Definition: Extraordinary in size or extent; marvelous.

Given the state of technology at the time, the raising of Stonehenge was a truly **prodigious** feat of engineering.

Lord Macaulay, the English historian and essayist, had such a **prodigious** memory that he had a clear recollection of every book he had ever read.

Phrases: a prodigious appetite, a prodigious effort

Related Forms: (*nouns*) prodigiousness, prodigy; (*adverb*) prodigiously

Synonyms: (*adjectives*) tremendous, stupendous, mammoth (Word 263), vast, gargantuan, immense, massive, enormous; phenomenal, fabulous, incredible, wondrous

Antonyms: (*adjectives*) puny, tiny, minute, trivial, minuscule, negligible, infinitesimal; unexceptional, undistinguished, unimpressive, mediocre

Related Phrases: a herculean task, a gargantuan appetite

315. **pro-lif-er-ate**   *verb*   prō-lĭf′-ə-rāt

[*proles, prolis* (Latin), "offspring" + *ferre* (Latin), "bear" + *ate*, English verb-forming suffix]

Definition: To increase rapidly in size or abundance.

The use of cellular phones has **proliferated** at a tremendous rate in recent years.

It was almost a law of ancient Roman historical writing that where the facts were few, fictions **proliferated**.

Though the Cold War is over, the United States and other countries are still trying to prevent the **proliferation** of nuclear armaments throughout the world.

Related Forms: (*noun*) proliferation; (*adjective*) prolific

Synonyms: (*verbs*) burgeon, snowball, mushroom, thrive, multiply, spread, prosper, flourish, expand, escalate, accelerate

Antonyms: (*verbs*) decline, diminish, wane, taper off, decrease, peter out, subside, dwindle

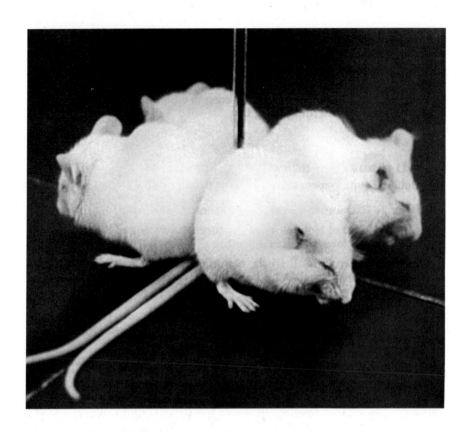

Clones and Cloning

The word *clone* (a derivative of the Greek *klon*, meaning "twig") comes from modern biological theory but has been popularized to a degree by both the social sciences and science fiction. A *clone* is a group of organisms (plants or animals) that come from a single parent and that receive exactly the same genetic makeup. Thus, all the members of the clone are, in effect, identical copies of one another. Indeed, they may be regarded, in a sense, as aspects of the same individual.

The production of clones, or *cloning*, was first limited to plants by such processes as grafting and budding. Hence the derivation from the word for "twig." However, during the 1960s and 1970s, scientists began to clone animals such as frogs and mice by physically splitting embryos. For example, a single mouse could be cloned into two or three identical mice.

For decades the possibility of cloning adult humans or animals remained largely in the realm of science fiction, but in the mid-1990s a team of Scottish researchers cloned a lamb from an adult sheep's tissue. The offspring, christened Dolly, was such an exact copy that she was, in essence, her mother's identical twin.

This ability to clone adult mammals opens many challenging possibilities, from producing organ replacements for transplant patients to propagating endangered animal species. It also presents a tremendous ethical problem.

316. prom·ul·gate   *verb*   prŏm'-əl-gāt

[*promulgare, promulgatus* (Latin), "publish"; possibly from *pro* (Latin), "before, in front of" + *vulgus* (Latin), "common people, crowd"]

Definition: To announce officially, as a law or decree.

What good will it do to **promulgate** new reforms if we lack the resources and the will to make them a reality?

Related Forms: (*nouns*) promulgation, promulgator

Synonyms: (*verbs*) proclaim, decree, broadcast, publish, disseminate

Antonyms: (*verbs*) conceal, keep secret

Related Phrases: issue a ukase, speak ex cathedra

317. pro·pen·si·ty   *noun*   prə-pĕn'-sə-tē

[*propendere, propensus* (Latin), "be inclined to" + *-itas, -itatis* (Latin), "state of"; from *pro* (Latin), "in the direction of" + *pendere* (Latin), "lean, hang"]

Definition: A natural tendency or inclination.

Someone who has a **propensity** for saying the wrong thing at the wrong time might be described as a victim of foot-in-mouth disease.

Synonyms: (*nouns*) penchant (for), proclivity (toward), capacity (for), predilection (for), bent (for), gift (for), genius (for), preference (for), fondness (for)

Antonyms: (*nouns*) aversion (to), repugnance (for), disinclination (to), antipathy (to); immunity (to)

Related Phrases: accident-prone, be allergic to something

318. pro·pi·ti·ate   *verb*   prō-pĭsh'-ē-āt

[*propitiare, propitiatus* (Latin), "appease"; from *propitius* (Latin), "favorable" + *-are, -atus* (Latin), a verb-forming suffix roughly meaning "make"]

Definition: To appease or pacify.

Before they set out, the hunters of the Ice Age performed ceremonies designed to **propitiate** the spirits of the animals they would slay.

Try as I might, I could not **propitiate** my wrathful father for having wrecked the family car.

Related Forms: (*nouns*) propitiation, propitiator; (*adjective*) propitiatory

Synonyms: (*verbs*) mollify, placate, conciliate

Antonyms: (*verbs*) antagonize, alienate (Word 21), exasperate, vex, anger, annoy, incense (Word 235)

Related Phrases: pour oil on troubled waters, hold out an olive branch, make one's peace with, defuse a situation, a scapegoat (Word 356)

319. **pro·tract·ed**   *adjective*   prō-trăk'-tĭd

[*protrahere, protractus* (Latin), "prolong, extend"; from *pro* (Latin), "forth, out" + *trahere, tractus* (Latin), "drag, draw"]

Definition: Extended or prolonged excessively.

Three great military blunders were responsible for turning World War I into a **protracted** struggle that neither side could win without outside help.

Related Forms: (*verb*) protract; (*nouns*) protraction, protractor

Synonyms: (*adjectives*) drawn-out, elongated; interminable, endless, long-winded

Antonyms: (*adjectives*) contracted, compressed, truncated, brief, foreshortened, curtailed

320. **prow·ess**   *noun*   prou'-ĭs

[*proesse* (Old French), "valor"; from *prou* (Old French), "brave"]

Definition: Superior courage, ability, or skill.

In World War I, Sergeant Alvin York of Tennessee received this country's highest decorations for his extraordinary feats of **prowess** on the battlefields of France.

Annie Oakley's **prowess** with a rifle became legendary, even in her own time.

Synonyms: (*nouns*) valor, gallantry, daring, bravery, intrepidity; mettle, pluck; expertise, facility, proficiency

Antonyms: (*nouns*) cowardice, timidity; incompetence, ineptitude

Related Phrases: feats of derring-do, a tour de force, a paladin

321. **pseu·do·nym**   *noun*   sōō'-də-nĭm

[*pseudonymos* (Greek), "having a false name"; from *pseudes* (Greek), "false" + *onyma, onoma* (Greek), "name"]

Definition: A fictitious name assumed by an author.

"Mark Twain," the **pseudonym** of Samuel Langhorne Clemens, is actually a Mississippi riverboat expression relating to the measurement of water depths.

Since the Victorians didn't think it proper for a lady to write novels, many women published their works under masculine **pseudonyms**.

Related Form: (*adjective*) pseudonymous

Synonyms: (*nouns and noun phrases*) pen name, nom de plume, nom de guerre, alias

George Sand   Mark Twain

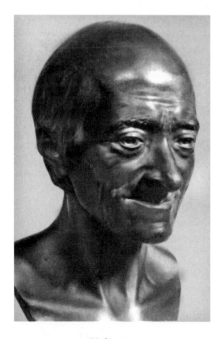

Voltaire   George Eliot

Each of the famous authors pictured on this page wrote under a
pseudonym. Find out their real names.

322. **purge**   *verb and noun*   pûrj

[*purgare* (Latin), "cleanse"; from *purus* (Latin), "pure" + *agere* (Latin), "lead, do, make"]

Definition:
   a. (*verb*) To cleanse or purify, especially to rid a group of undesirable elements.

   "The only way you can **purge** yourself of a charge of contempt," the judge admonished the refractory witness, "is to begin cooperating with this court."

   On the bloody "Night of the Long Knives," June 26, 1934, Adolf Hitler **purged** the Nazi Party of anyone who might threaten his position as absolute master of Germany.

   b. (*noun*) A medicine that cleanses; the elimination of undesirable elements from a group.

   Until relatively recent times, doctors frequently used strong **purges** designed to cure illness by removing impurities from the body.

   During the bloody **purges** of the 1930s, Josef Stalin liquidated all opposition to his rule, ideas, and methods.

Related Forms: (*nouns*) purgation, purgatory, purgative; (*adjective*) purgatorial; (*verb*) expurgate

Synonyms: (*verbs*) flush out; eject, expel, liquidate, exterminate, weed out; expiate, clear; (*nouns*) physic, laxative; pogrom

Related Phrases: wipe the slate clean, make a clean sweep of; a witch-hunt, a catharsis

Usage Note:
   A *pogrom* (from the Russian phrase meaning "like thunder") is an organized massacre or persecution of a minority group, especially the Jews.

323. **pu·sil·lan·i·mous**   *adjective*   pyo͞o-sə-lăn'-ə-məs

[*pusillus* (Latin), "very small or weak" + *animus* (Latin), "soul, spirit"]

Definition: Contemptibly cowardly or mean-spirited.

   Most people regarded the government's attempt to avert a war by buying off the aggressor as not only shameful but **pusillanimous** as well.

   He characterizes his behavior during the recent crisis as circumspect; I call it **pusillanimous**.

Related Forms: (*noun*) pusillanimity; (*adverb*) pusillanimously

Synonyms: (*adjectives*) timid, timorous, frightened, fearful, spineless, gutless, lily-livered, fainthearted

Antonyms: (*adjectives*) bold, daring, intrepid, courageous, spirited, dynamic, forceful

Related Phrases: afraid of one's own shadow; have spunk

412

A portrait of Dante Alighieri by Domenico di Michelino

Purgatory

In Roman Catholic theology, the term *Purgatory* indicates a temporary condition or state of the soul in the afterlife. It is in Purgatory that the souls of those who have died in grace and are eventually destined to enter Heaven are purged (through suffering) of whatever spiritual impurities still remain. The nature and length of this suffering varies, and the punishment is different from that of the souls in Hell. One of the most interesting descriptions of Purgatory is contained in the *Purgatorio* (Purgatory), which is the second part of the medieval Italian poet Dante Alighieri's long epic poem on salvation, *La Commedia Divina* (The Divine Comedy). It is from its connection with the theology of the afterlife that the modern English word *purgatory* (with a small *p*) has taken on the extended meaning of "any place or condition of prolonged misery and suffering."

324. **quell** *verb* kwĕl

[*cwellan* (Old English), "kill"]

Definition: To bring to an end, usually by force; to quiet or pacify.

When the handful of police officers who were on the scene were unable to **quell** the riot, reinforcements were called in.

A few kind words are often all it takes to **quell** a child's fears and soothe his or her anguished spirit.

Synonyms: (*verbs*) suppress, extinguish, subdue, stamp out, quash, squelch, crush, put down; silence, calm, allay, assuage

Antonyms: (*verbs*) instigate (Word 241), foment, provoke, incite, kindle; enflame, arouse, stir up

Related Phrases: put the kibosh on, incite to riot; an agent provocateur, a peacemaker

413

Pablo Picasso's famous depiction of Don Quixote and Sancho Panza

325. quix-ot-ic   *adjective*   kwĭk-sŏt'-ĭk

[After Don Quixote, the main character in the Renaissance Spanish writer Miguel de Cervantes's famous novel of the same name]

Definition: High-minded but impractical.

The 1920s saw the passage of several important pieces of federal legislation, including a **quixotic** scheme to prohibit the sale and use of alcohol.

Related Form: (*adverb*) quixotically

Usage Note:
Quixotic has an alternate form, *quixotical,* but this is not the preferred form of the word.

Synonyms: (*adjectives*) idealistic, visionary, fanciful, unrealistic, utopian, chimerical

Antonyms: (*adjectives*) realistic, practical, down-to-earth

Related Phrases: have one's head in the clouds; a pie-in-the-sky proposal

Using the Word

Exercise I
1. pre-rog' -a-tive
2. pro'-bi-ty
3. pro-lif'-er-ate
4. prom'-ul-gate
5. pro-pi'-ti-ate
6. prow'-ess
7. pseu'-do-nym
8. pu-sil-lan'-i-mous
9. quix-ot'-ic

Exercise I. Syllabication and Pronunciation

Syllabicate the following words correctly, and place the major stress mark (') after the syllable that is accented when the word is pronounced.

1. prerogative
2. probity
3. proliferate
4. promulgate
5. propitiate
6. prowess
7. pseudonym
8. pusillanimous
9. quixotic

Exercise II.   Words Out of Context

In each of the following groups, select the item that best expresses the meaning of the numbered word at the left.

1. probity
    a. blandness   b. knavery   c. skill
    d. integrity   e. hostility

2. prodigious
    a. immense   b. timely   c. offensive
    d. demure   e. eager

3. prowess
    a. prejudice   b. valor   c. arrogance
    d. courtesy   e. wisdom

4. promulgate
    a. disguise   b. contradict   c. foretell
    d. understand   e. proclaim

5. purge
    a. purify   b. mystify   c. edify
    d. sanctify   e. horrify

6. propitiate
    a. judge   b. bolster   c. pacify
    d. honor   e. investigate

7. pusillanimous
    a. rude   b. biased   c. expensive
    d. cowardly   e. ugly

8. quixotic
    a. practical but costly
    b. sensible but difficult
    c. inexpensive but worthless
    d. feasible but foolish
    e. high-minded but impractical

Exercise III.   Completing Sentences

Complete each of the following sentences by selecting the most appropriate word from the group of words given below. Use each word only once. Make any adjustments that are necessary to fit the words into the sentences properly.

quell	proliferate	procrastinate
protracted	propensity	quixotic
prerogative	promulgate	pseudonym

1. The old adage "Don't put off until tomorrow what you can do today" warns all of us not to __procrastinate__.

2. When she said that I "tended to view the world through rose-colored glasses," she simply meant that I had a _propensity_ for looking on the bright side of things.

3. Though the insurrection ultimately proved unsuccessful, the government was hard-pressed to __quell__ it.

4. Though it was the _prerogative_ of the head of the Senate in ancient Rome to give his opinion first, no other special privilege seems to have attached to the office.

5. I wonder why Eric Blair (1903–1950) chose to publish his novels and essays under the _pseudonym_ George Orwell.

6. As long as more and more Americans turn to home computers for entertainment, video games will continue to _proliferate_.

7. Mismanagement turned what should have been a quick and easy victory into a _protracted_ struggle that ended in stalemate.

Exercise IV.   Synonyms and Antonyms

Classify each of the following pairs of words as **S** for **synonyms** or **A** for **antonyms**.

S 1. promulgate—proclaim
A 2. propensity—aversion
S 3. utopian—quixotic
S 4. privilege—prerogative
S 5. stupendous—prodigious
S 6. prowess—intrepidity
A 7. intrepid—pusillanimous
S 8. liquidate—purge
A 9. procrastinate—act
S 10. multiply—proliferate
S 11. propitiate—appease
A 12. protracted—compressed
A 13. unscrupulousness—probity
S 14. squelch—quell

Exercise V.   Word Roundup

1. With or without the aid of a dictionary, define each of the following foreign expressions used in present-day English, and tell what language it comes from.

   a. alias
   b. ex cathedra
   c. nom de plume
   d. agent provocateur
   e. nom de guerre
   f. tour de force

2. With or without the aid of a dictionary or other reference book, name the person who used each of the following _pseudonyms_.

   a. Mark Twain
   b. O. Henry
   c. Molière
   d. Voltaire
   e. George Eliot
   f. Saki

3. Explain the story behind each of the following interesting English words.

   a. chimerical
   b. bowdlerize
   c. quixotic

4. With or without the aid of a dictionary, define each of the following words.

   a. paladin
   b. clone
   c. scapegoat
   d. catharsis
   e. spunk
   f. protractor

5. With or without the aid of a dictionary, explain the meaning of each of the following phrases.

   a. a pie-in-the-sky proposal
   b. sharp practice
   c. table a bill
   d. a witch-hunt

416

Exercise VI. Framing Sentences

A. Use each of the following words in an original illustrative sentence.

1. prerogative
2. probity
3. propensity
4. protracted
5. prowess
6. pseudonym
7. purge
8. quell
9. quixotic

B. Give a **noun** form of each of the following words, and use it in an original illustrative sentence.

1. procrastinate *procrastination*
2. prodigious *prodigiousness, prodigy*
3. proliferate *proliferation*
4. propitiate *propitiation*
5. promulgate *promulgation*
6. pusillanimous *pusillanimity*

Dissecting the Words

1. The Latin prefix **per** occurs in a great many common English words, including *peremptory* (Word 296), *perjure* (Word 297), and *permeate* (Word 298). As with many of the other word elements studied in this book, **per** has a number of meanings:

a. "Through" or "throughout," as in these words:

percolate (*per*, "through" + *colare, colatus* [Latin], "seep")—to seep or filter slowly through. Noun: *percolator*

perforate (*per*, "through" + *forare, foratus* [Latin], "bore")—to punch or pierce small holes in. Noun: *perforation*

perennial (*per*, "throughout" + *annus* [Latin], "year")—lasting throughout the year or through many years; recurring

permanent (*per*, "throughout" + *manens, manentis* [Latin], "remaining")—fixed, lasting, or unchanging. Noun: *permanence*

perambulate (*per*, "through" + *ambulare, ambulatus* [Latin], "walk")—to roam or stroll about, especially to inspect something.

pervade (*per*, "through" + *vadere* [Latin], "go")—to spread through. Adjective: *pervasive*

perspire (*per*, "through" + *spirare* [Latin], "breathe")—to sweat

perspicacious (*per*, "through" + *specere, spectus* [Latin], "look, see")—acutely perceptive. Noun: *perspicacity*

b. "Thoroughly" or "completely," as in these words:

perfect (*per*, "completely" + *facere, factus* [Latin], "do")—(*adjective*) complete or flawless; (*verb*) to bring to completion or perfection

permutation (*per*, "completely" + *mutare, mutatus* [Latin], "change")—a complete change or transformation

perpetrate (*per*, "completely" + *patrare, patratus* [Latin], "bring about or do with the authority of a father")—to carry out, perform, or commit. Nouns: *perpetration, perpetrator perplex* (*per*, "completely" + *plectere*, *plexus* [Latin], "weave, entwine")—to puzzle or bewilder. Noun: *perplexity*

pertinacious (*per*, "thoroughly" + *tenere* [Latin], "hold")—holding firmly to some purpose or belief despite all obstacles. Noun: *pertinacity*

perturb (*per*, "thoroughly" + *turbare* [Latin], "throw into disorder")—to disturb or upset greatly. Noun: *perturbation*

c. "Very," as in these words:

persist (*per*, "very" + *sistere* [Latin], "stand firm")—to continue; to hold firmly to some course or purpose. Noun: *persistence*. Adjective: *persistent*

perfervid (*per*, "very" + *fervidus* [Latin], "hot, seething, ardent")—extremely eager; impassioned or zealous

percussion (*per*, "very hard" + *quatere*, *quassus* [Latin], "strike")—the violent collision of two bodies or the sound that such a collision makes

d. "Away," as in these words:

perdition (*per*, "away" + *dare*, *datus* [Latin], "give")—eternal damnation; utter ruin

peregrination (*per*, "away" + *ager*, *agri* [Latin], "field")—a journey from place to place

perfidy (*per*, "away" + *fides* [Latin], "faith")—treachery. Adjective: *perfidious*

perish (*per*, "away" + *ire*, *itus* [Latin], "go")—to pass away, die, or disappear. Noun: *perishables*

Per also occurs as an independent word with the general meaning "by" in a number of phrases that modern English has borrowed from Latin, including:

per annum—annually   *per se*—by itself
per capita—by the head   *per diem*—by the day

2. The prefix **pre** (from Latin *prae*) occurs in a great many common English words, including *premise* (Word 310) and *prerogative*, studied in this lesson. **Pre** means "before, in front of, or ahead of in time, position, or importance," as these words show:

preamble (*prae*, "before" + *ambulare* [Latin], "walk")—an introductory statement or event

prearrange (*pre* + *arrange*)—to arrange ahead of time. Noun: *pre-arrangement*

precaution (*pre* + *caution*)—an action taken in advance to prevent a possible difficulty or danger. Adjective: *precautionary*

precede (*prae*, "before" + *cedere* [Latin], "go")—to come before in time or position. Nouns: *precedence*, *precedent*

preclude (*prae*, "before" + *claudere* [Latin], "close")—to prevent by previous action or by virtue of a previous situation

precursor (*prae*, "before" + *currere*, *curses* [Latin], "run")—a forerunner *predict* (*prae*, "before" + *dicere*, *dictus* [Latin], "say, tell")—to foretell or prophesy. Noun: *prediction*

predilection (*prae*, "before" + *diligere*, *dilectus* [Latin], "choose, prefer")—a preference

predominate (*prae*, "before" + *dominare*, *dominatus* [Latin], "rule over")—to prevail over or dominate totally. Adjective: *predominant*

preempt (*prae*, "before" + *emere*, *emptus* [Latin], "buy")—to gain possession of by advance action. Adjective: *preemptive*. Noun: *preemption*

preface (*prae*, "before" + *fari*, *fatus* [Latin], "speak")—(*noun*) an introductory statement or essay; (*verb*) to introduce

prehistoric (*pre* + *historic*)—belonging to the period before written history. Noun: *prehistory*

premature (*prae*, "before" + *maturus* [Latin], "ripe")—unexpectedly early in development; coming too soon

premeditate (*pre* + *meditate*)—to plan, arrange, or deliberate in advance. Noun: *premeditation*

premonition (*prae*, "before" + *monere*, *monitus* [Latin], "warn")—an advance warning or foreboding

preoccupy (*pre* + *occupy*)—to absorb completely or to the exclusion of all else. Noun: *preoccupation*

preponderate (*prae*, "before" + *ponderare*, *ponderatus* [Latin], "weigh")—to be greater in power, force, or importance than all others. Noun: *preponderance*. Adjective: *preponderant*

presage (*prae*, "before" + *sagire* [Latin], "perceive")—(*verb*) to warn of in advance; (*noun*) an omen or portent

presentiment (*prae*, "before" + *sentire* [Latin], "feel, perceive")—a premonition or foreboding

preside (*prae*, "before" + *sedere*, *sessus* [Latin], "sit")—to be head of or have authority over. Nouns: *president*, *presidency*

presume (*prae*, "before" + *sumere* [Latin], "take")—to suppose to be true, to take for granted; to be overbold. Adjectives: *presumptuous*, *presumptive*

prevail (*prae*, "before" + *valere* [Latin], "be strong")—to triumph over or win out against; to be in force, use, or effect. Adjective: *prevalent*

Note that **prae**, the Latin spelling of this prefix, is retained in a few words that relate to Roman history, notably *praetor* and *praenomen*.

3. The Latin prefix **pro** also occurs in numerous English words, including *procrastinate* and *propensity*, studied in this lesson. It, too, has a number of meanings:

a. "Forward," "forth," or "in public," as in these words:

proceed (*pro*, "forward" + *cedere* [Latin], "go")—to move forward or onward. Nouns: *proceedings*, *proceeds*, *process*, *procession*, *procedure*

proclaim (*pro*, "in public" + *clamare* [Latin], "cry out")—to announce or declare openly or officially. Noun: *proclamation*

The Chimaera

The *Chimaera* (from the Greek word *chimaira*, meaning "nanny goat") was a fabulous monster that, according to Homer, had the head of a lion, the body of a goat, and the tail of a dragon. It was the offspring of Typhon, the monstrous son of Gaea, and was born in Lycia in what is now southwest Turkey. (Typhon also fathered a number of other equally monstrous creatures, including Echidna, Cerberus, the Hydra, and the Sphinx.) The Chimaera was eventually killed by the Greek hero Bellerophon with the aid of his winged horse Pegasus. It is from this colorful creature out of Greek mythology that modern English gets the words *chimera* (pronounced kī-mîr′-ə), meaning "a wild and foolish fancy" or "a highly improbable and incongruous scheme," and *chimerical* (pronounced kī-mîr′-ə-kəl), meaning "given to unrealistic fantasies" or "wildly improbable."

> *produce* (*pro*, "forth" + *ducere* [Latin], "lead")—(*verb*) to bring forth or yield; (*noun*) products, especially farm products. Adjective: *productive*
>
> *profess* (*pro*, "in public" + *fateri, fassus* [Latin], "acknowledge")—to affirm openly; to claim. Nouns: *professor, profession*
>
> *profuse* (*pro*, "forth" + *fundere, fu(n)sus* [Latin], "pour")—*plentiful, extravagant.* Noun: *profusion*
>
> *progress* (*pro*, "forward" + *gradi, gressus* [Latin], "step, move")—(*noun*) forward movement; (*verb*) move forward. Noun: *progression*
>
> *promote* (*pro*, "forward" + *movere, motus* [Latin], "move")—to raise or advance to a higher rank or degree; to contribute to the advancement or success of. Nouns: *promotion, promoter*
>
> *propel* (*pro*, "forward" + *pellere* [Latin], "drive")—to cause to move forward. Nouns: *propulsion, propeller*
>
> *propose* (*pro*, "forward" + *ponere, positus* [Latin], "put")—to put forward for consideration. Nouns: *proposal, proposition*
>
> *proscribe* (*pro*, "in public" + *scribere* [Latin], "write")—to outlaw or condemn. Noun: *proscription*

b. "Away," as in these words:

   prodigal (*pro*, "away" + *agere* [Latin], "drive" + *alis* [Latin], "relating to")—(*adjective*) recklessly wasteful; (*noun*) a spendthrift. Noun: *prodigality*

   profligate (*pro*, "down and away" + *fligare, fligatus* [Latin], "strike")—dissolute, wasteful

c. "For" or "on behalf of," as in this word:

   procure (*pro*, "on behalf of" + *curare* [Latin], "take care of")—to acquire or obtain, often for another person. Noun: *procurement*

d. "Before," as in this word:

   profane (*pro*, "before, in front of" + *fanum* [Latin], "temple, sanctuary"; for the Romans, things done before [i.e., outside] a temple were neither sacred nor elevated)—(*adjective*) nonreligious, secular; vulgar, coarse; blasphemous; (*verb*) to treat with irreverence or otherwise abuse. Noun: *profanity*

e. "In favor of," as in this word:

   prorevolutionary (*pro*, "in favor of" + *revolutionary*)—in favor of revolution

   Pro also appears as an independent word with the general meaning "for" or "for the sake of" in a few phrases that English has borrowed from Latin, including:

   pro forma—purely as a matter of form
   pro tem(pore)—for the time being

4. The Greek prefix **pro**, meaning "in front of," "before," or "forward," also occurs in a few useful English words, including:

prologue (*pro*, "before" + *legein* [Greek], "say")—an introduction to a play; an introductory act or event

proboscis (*pro*, "in front" + *boskein* [Greek], "feed")—the long tubular nose of an elephant or similar animal

problem (*pro*, "forward" + *ballein* [Greek], "throw")—a difficulty. Adjective: *problematic(al)*

proem (*pro*, "before" + *oime* [Greek], "song")—a short introduction or preface

prognosis (*pro*, "before" + *gignoskein* [Greek], "know")—a prediction of the probable course or outcome of something. Verb: *prognosticate*

Exercise

1. With or without the aid of a dictionary, define each of the following words using the Latin prefix *per*, and explain what the prefix means in that particular word. Then choose any **three** of the words, and for each compose an illustrative sentence.

   a. pervade
   b. perspicacious
   c. perpetrate
   d. pertinacious
   e. persist
   f. perish

2. For each of the following definitions, supply an English word beginning with the Latin prefix *pre*.

   a. come before in time or position   precede
   b. foretell or prophesy   predict
   c. developing or occurring too early   premature
   d. an advance warning or foreboding   premonition

3. With or without the aid of a dictionary, define each of the following words using the Latin prefix *pro*, and explain what the prefix means in that particular word. Then choose any **three** of the words, and for each compose an original illustrative sentence.

   a. proclaim   c. produce   e. profane
   b. propose   d. prodigal   f. pro-Marxist

4. For each of the following definitions, supply an English word beginning with the Greek prefix *pro*.

   a. the long tubular nose of an elephant   proboscis
   b. the introductory scene of a play   prologue
   c. a difficulty or puzzle   problem
   d. a prediction of the probable course or outcome of   prognosis

5. Explain the meaning of each of the following Latin phrases commonly used in English. Then choose any **two**, and for each compose an original illustrative sentence. Consult a dictionary as necessary.

   a. per capita   c. per diem   e. pro forma
   b. per annum   d. per se   f. pro tem(pore)

Bowdlerize

In 1807 and 1818, an Englishman named Thomas Bowdler brought out editions of the works of Shakespeare in which "those words [were] omitted which [could not] with propriety be read aloud in a family." He called his edition *The Family Shakespeare*. Actually, much of the editing work on this project appears to have been done by Bowdler's sister Henrietta Maria (Harriet), but she didn't want her involvement in the matter made public "for propriety's sake." It is from the activities of Thomas Bowdler and his sister that modern English gets the verb *bowdlerize* (pronounced bōd′-lə-rīz), which means "expurgate or censor a literary work."

William Shakespeare

Working with Context Clues

Complete each of the following two-word omissions by selecting the pair of words that make the best sense in the passage as a whole. If necessary, consult a dictionary for the meaning of any word with which you are not familiar.

1. The reason contract negotiations usually <u>drag on so long</u> is that the parties <u>put off</u> talking about the major issue. If they did not _____ but tackled this issue first, the negotiations would not be so _____.

   a. arbitrate . . . cursory
   b. digress . . . poignant
   c. persevere . . . grueling
   d. <u>procrastinate . . . protracted</u>

2. The romantic _____ that children are essentially good and are corrupted by adult society is a _____ assumption that <u>does not match reality</u>.

   a. irony . . . nebulous
   b. fallacy . . . flagrant
   c. <u>premise . . . quixotic</u>
   d. paradox . . . pernicious

3. If you write a book revealing your friends' <u>faults</u>, use a(n) _____ <u>rather than your own name</u>, or be ready for anger from those whose _____ you've exposed.

   a. <u>pseudonym . . . foibles</u>
   b. medium . . . obsessions
   c. anecdote . . . nuances
   d. innovation . . . facsimiles

4. The ancients offered sacrifices to their _____ gods to <u>soften their hard hearts</u>. The people hoped that if they were able to _____ the gods, they could avoid misfortune.

   a. pensive . . . justify
   b. complacent . . . pacify
   c. immutable . . . envisage
   d. <u>implacable . . . propitiate</u>

5. What spiritual leaders such as Dr. Martin Luther King, Jr., <u>leave after</u> them is a _____ of _____ courage that young people <u>can admire and imitate</u>.

   a. phobia . . . futile
   b. <u>legacy . . . exemplary</u>
   c. prelude . . . prodigious
   d. plethora . . . dignified

6. Often the <u>unspoken</u> message of most advertising is that whoever buys the product will look or feel like the person in the ad. Since advertising does boost sales, many people must be _____ enough to <u>believe</u> this _____ promise.

   a. hopeful . . . obsequious
   b. rash . . . felicitous
   c. <u>gullible . . . implicit</u>
   d. effete . . . fatuous

7. <u>Riot police</u> are often called upon to _____ the violence that <u>rabble-rousers</u> _____ with no thought to the destruction they may be <u>setting in motion</u>.

   a. propitiate . . . suppress
   b. contain . . . exploit
   c. abet . . . expound
   d. <u>quell . . . instigate</u>

Enriching the Lesson

Exercise I.   Our Latin Heritage

A number of the English words studied in this lesson (e.g., *probity* and *pusillanimous*) are based on Latin originals. As you have already discovered in Lessons 9 (page 133) and 14 (page 221), English is rich in such Latin borrowings. A few more examples of this heritage are listed below. With or without the aid of a dictionary, define each of the items listed and give its etymology. Then choose any **five**, and for each compose an original illustrative sentence.

1. abjure	11. rabid	21. molest
2. juvenile	12. juncture	22. neutrality
3. latent	13. lethal	23. purport
4. opacity	14. magnate	24. enumerate
5. mendacious	15. luminous	25. mute
6. obtrude	16. nocturnal	26. putative
7. longevity	17. orifice	27. pulverize
8. oscillate	18. maturate	28. recluse
9. motivate	19. proxy	29. rancid
10. orbit	20. putrid	30. ordinance

Exercise II.   Verbal Pollution—the Ecology of Words

Recently, a national teachers' organization gave an award for obfuscation to a former press secretary of a national political figure. He was "honored" in this way for having sought to mislead the public over a period of years with garbled and spurious news releases. The citation hailed him as a master of dissembling whose specialty was not so much the outright misstatement of facts as the use of words to obscure the truth, give distorted impressions, and create unwarranted associations. In short, a sort of verbal pollution.

There is nothing unique about this. There are far too many examples of verbal pollution in the nation today, threatening our linguistic ecology. Euphemisms of various types are widely employed to disguise the true nature of what is happening, both here and abroad, in both civilian and military affairs. Never before has so much been obfuscated with such fogbanks of nebulous word fallout.

This is not to say the misuse of language is necessarily more rampant today than in earlier eras. Dissembling has always been with us. But technological advances, above all TV and the Internet, have greatly increased the potency of the communications media and have resulted in massive ecological disturbances in the area of language and understanding.

You know that TV announcers, especially in urban regions, give an air pollution index in connection with each weather report. It has been suggested that it might not be a bad idea to supplement this with a word pollution index to indicate just how badly our news sources are being fouled up by deliberate or inadvertent misuse of language.

Look for examples of deliberate misuse of words that threaten the wholesomeness of our verbal ecology. You may find them in statements of public figures, advertisements, speeches, publicity releases, newspaper editorials, columns, textbooks, classroom lectures, academic pronouncements, and many other sources. You may even find that you yourself are guilty of this kind of verbal pollution once in a while.

1. With or without the aid of a dictionary, define each of the following words as used in the preceding selection.

   a. obfuscation   f. unwarranted   k. nebulous
   b. spurious   g. distort   l. linguistic
   c. dissemble   h. unique   m. inadvertent
   d. pollution   i. potency   n. supplement
   e. ecology   j. fallout   o. civilian

2. Read each of the following examples of the art of dissembling in language, and then explain what is really being said.

   a. My previous statements are now inoperative.

   b. The downtrend in the economic indices may be reflected in a certain amount of drying up of employment opportunities.

   c. The inevitable tradeoff for needed industrial development may be a temporary raising of impurity levels in the atmosphere.

Exercise III.   Expanding Your Word Power

The words listed below are not on the Basic Word List, but they were mentioned in one form or another in Lesson 25. All of them would make useful additions to your working vocabulary. Define each, give its etymology, list **two** synonyms and **two** antonyms (where possible), and use in a short illustrative sentence.

1. perquisite   6. disseminate   11. expurgate
2. skulduggery   7. proclivity   12. eject
3. temporize   8. rectitude   13. expiate
4. prodigy   9. truncate   14. quash
5. burgeon   10. mettle   15. utopian

Lesson 26

326. raze — 340. resilient

---

326. **raze**   *verb*   rāz

[*radere, rasus* (Latin), "scrape, shave"]

Definition: To level to the ground; to blot out or demolish.

The atomic bomb that was dropped on Hiroshima in 1945 **razed** almost every building in the city.

Before work on the new shopping mall could begin, a group of shabby old tenements occupying the site had to be **razed**.

Usage Note:

Be careful not to confuse *raze* with its look-alike, *raise*, which means "erect" or "lift up," the opposite of what *raze* means.

Synonyms: (*verbs*) flatten, gut, fell, obliterate, eradicate, efface, tear down, dismantle, knock down, devastate

Antonyms: (*verbs*) raise, erect, set up, build

Related Phrases: lay waste to, reduce to a pile of rubble

---

327. **re-cal-ci-trant**   *adjective and noun*   rĭ-kăl′-sĭ-trĕnt

[*recalcitrans, recalcitrantis* (Latin), "kicking backwards" (used of a horse); from *re* (Latin), "back(wards)" + *calx, calcis* (Latin), "heel"]

Definition:

   a.   (*adjective*) Stubbornly resistant to reason or authority.

      Though a handful of **recalcitrant** delegates made a last-ditch effort to kill the bill, the measure was eventually passed.

   b.   (*noun*) A perverse or wayward person.

      "Cell Block R," the warden explained, "houses a group of **recalcitrants** who have so far resisted every effort we have made to rehabilitate them."

Phrases: a recalcitrant child, a recalcitrant animal, a recalcitrant motor

Related Form: (*noun*) recalcitrance

Synonyms: (*adjectives*) obstinate, perverse, intractable, unyielding, contrary, rebellious, defiant, uncooperative, contumacious, pigheaded, ornery

Antonyms: (*adjectives*) compliant, complaisant, acquiescent, tractable, cooperative, docile, amenable, accommodating, willing

Related Phrases: be at odds with; a diehard, as stubborn as a mule

328. re-cant   *verb*   rĭ-kănt′

[*re* (Latin), "back" + *cantare* (Latin), "sing, chant"]

Definition: To withdraw formally or publicly.

The theory that the earth moves around the sun was so opposed to accepted thinking during the Renaissance that many a scientist of the time was forced to **recant** his belief in it.

Related Form: (*noun*) recantation

Synonyms: (*verbs*) disown, renounce, retract, repudiate, disavow, abjure

Antonyms: (*verbs*) affirm, reaffirm, aver; hold fast to, cleave to, adhere to

Related Phrase: eat one's words

329. re-cip-ro-cate   *verb*   rĭ-sĭp′-rə-kāt

[*reciprocare, reciprocatus* (Latin), "move back and forth"; possibly from *re* (Latin), "backward" + *pro* (Latin), "forward"]

Definition: To give in return for, or in response to, something already given.

Can you blame me for being bitter when a supposed friend **reciprocated** my confidence with betrayal and slander?

Phrases: reciprocal assistance, a reciprocal relationship

Related Forms: (*nouns*) reciprocation, reciprocity; (*adjective*) reciprocal

Usage Notes:
- a. A *reciprocal trade agreement* is one in which two or more nations "swap" favors or concessions of more or less equal value. The principle involved in such an agreement is termed *reciprocity.*
- b. In mathematics, a *reciprocal* is the quotient of a quantity divided into 1. For example, the reciprocal of 7 is $1/7$.

Synonyms: (*verbs*) exchange, repay, requite, reimburse, recompense, interchange

Related Phrases: tit for tat, pay back in kind

330. re-crim-i-na-tion   *noun*   rĭ-krĭm-ə-nā′-shən

[*re* (Latin), "back" + *crimen, criminis* (Latin), "charge, accusation" + *are, atus* (Latin), a verb-forming suffix roughly meaning "make"]

Definition: The act of answering one accusation with another; a bitter reply.

Although I have been deeply wounded by their totally unfounded accusations, I am not going to reply to them with ugly and pointless **recriminations**.

Related Forms: (*verb*) recriminate; (*adjective*) recriminatory

Synonyms: (*nouns*) countercharge, counteraccusation, retort

331. **re·dun·dant**   *adjective*   rĭ-dŭn'-dĕnt

[*redundans, redundantis* (Latin), "overflowing"; from *re* (Latin), "back" + *unda* (Latin), "wave")

Definition: Unnecessarily repetitive or superfluous; more than what is normally considered adequate or necessary.

> In a way, the phrase "pizza pie" is **redundant** because, in Italian, *pizza* means "a type of pie."

> Good writers soon learn to spot **redundant** words and phrases in their writing and to remove them.

Related Forms: (*nouns*) redundancy, redundance

Usage Note:

The English verb *redound* comes from the same Latin word elements as *redundant*, but the two words are not related in meaning. *Redundant*, as you know, means "repetitive"; *redound* means "have as a consequence" or "contribute to."

Synonyms: (*adjectives*) verbose, prolix, pleonastic, wordy, tautological; superabundant, excessive

Antonyms: (*adjectives*) succinct, laconic, terse; insufficient, scarce

The *principle of redundancy* is built into spacecraft, so that there are more than enough safeguards or backup systems to keep the machine operating if the main system goes out.

332. re-lent   *verb*   rĭ-lĕnt′

[*re* (Latin), "completely; very" + *lentare* (Latin), "soften"]

Definition: To become less harsh or severe; to let up or slacken.

At first I was determined to see justice done, but her eloquent appeal for compassion and understanding touched my heart, and I **relented**.

When the wind and rain finally **relented**, I went outside to inspect the damage the storm had done.

Related Forms: (*adjective*) relentless; (*noun*) relentlessness

Synonyms: (*verbs*) yield, moderate, soften

Antonyms: (*verbs*) harden, stiffen, be adamant

Related Phrase: temper the wind to the shorn lamb

333. rem-i-nis-cence   *noun*   rĕm-ə-nĭs′-ĕns

[*reminiscens, reminiscentis* (Latin), "remembering"; from *re* (Latin) + *mens, mentis* (Latin), "mind"]

Definition: The act of recalling the past; a memory.

Grandmother's **reminiscences** of her youth may seem trivial to an outsider, but as a family member, I know how precious they are to her.

Related Forms: (*adjective*) reminiscent; (*verb*) reminisce

Usage Notes:

   a. The adjective *reminiscent*, meaning "suggestive," is normally followed by the preposition *of*. For example, the lyrics of a pop song may be *reminiscent of* one of Shakespeare's sonnets or a poem by John Keats.

   b. The plural noun *reminiscences* is often used to indicate the narrated recollections that a person has published in book or essay form. These are also sometimes called *memoirs*.

Synonyms: (*nouns*) recollection, remembrance; memoir

Related Phrases: a flashback, dwell on the past, relive the past, total recall, déjà vu

Déjà Vu

"Somehow I had the feeling that I had been in that old house before and that I was familiar with many of its contents, even though I was well aware that I could not possibly have entered it on any previous occasion."

Many of us have had the kind of strange experience suggested by this statement. Psychologists refer to it by the term *déjà vu* (dā-zhä-vōō). This comes from French and means literally "already seen." The psychological reasons for such an illusion are not entirely clear and indeed may differ widely from one case to another.

Déjà vu is also used to characterize something (*e.g.*, a film) that is supposed to be original but is actually trite and reminiscent of other works.

334. re-morse   *noun*   rĭ-môrs′

[*re* (Latin), "back; very" + *mordere, morsus* (Latin), "bite"]

Definition: Anguish, self-reproach or bitter regret for wrongdoing.

Feeling **remorse** for your thoughtlessness cannot undo the harm you have done, but it may prevent you from doing the same thing again.

The great American poet Emily Dickinson once wrote that "**remorse** is memory awake."

Related Forms: (*adjectives*) remorseful, remorseless; (*nouns*) remorse-lessness; (*adverbs*) remorsefully, remorselessly

Synonyms: (*nouns*) regretfulness, shame, contrition, sorrow, repentance, penitence

Antonyms: (*nouns*) callousness, indifference, unconcern, impenitence

Related Phrases: wear sackcloth and ashes, a twinge (or pang) of conscience, the prick of conscience; have a heart of stone

Emily Dickinson

Emily Dickinson lived most of her life in Amherst, Massachusetts, where she was born in 1830. Her lawyer father raised her in the strict Puritan tradition that was characteristic of New England in the 19th century. After 1853, she gradually became a recluse, possibly as the result of an unhappy love affair. The secluded life that she led became her chief source of inspiration as a poet and resulted in over 1000 poems of great poignancy and beauty. Many of her brief, delicate lyrics, full of startling imagery, concern nature, love, death, and immortality. Only seven of them were published during her lifetime, and the extent of her literary output—sometimes scribbled on odd bits of paper or the backs of old envelopes—was not discovered until after her death. Indeed, her recognition as a poet of immense stature did not even begin until the publication of the first collected edition of her works four years after her death in 1886. Since that time, her remarkable achievement has exerted a tremendous influence on modern American writers. (For further details consult *Emily Dickinson: An Interpretive Biography* by T. H. Johnson.)

335. ren-e-gade   *noun and adjective*   rĕn'-ə-gād

[*renegado* (Spanish), "turncoat"; from *re* (Latin), "again; very" + *negare, negatus* (Latin), "deny"]

Definition:

a. (*noun*) A person who deserts one cause or group for another.

One of history's most celebrated **renegades** is a Roman emperor by the name of Julian, who gave up his Christian faith when he came to the imperial throne.

History no longer views Geronimo as a dangerous **renegade** but rather as a patriot committed to the preservation of his people and their way of life.

b. (*adjective*) Disloyal or traitorous.

The robber bands that roamed the French countryside during the Hundred Years' War were often led by **renegade** knights.

A group of **renegade** Southern Democrats, called *boll weevils* and *gypsy moths*, consistently supported Republican President Ronald Reagan against their own party.

Related Forms: (*verb*) renege

Synonyms: (*nouns*) turncoat, traitor, defector, deserter, apostate; (*adjectives*) recreant, perfidious

Antonyms: (*noun*) loyalist; (*adjectives*) loyal, staunch, true-blue, reliable

Related Phrases: a volte-face; do an about-face

Usage Note:

During the American Revolution the *Loyalists* (note the *L*), also called *Tories*, were the colonists who opposed independence and supported the British cause. Most of the Loyalists were large landowners, Crown officials, and members of the clergy, though other groups were also represented. The Loyalists were most numerous in the far South (Georgia and South Carolina) and in the Middle Atlantic region (New York and Pennsylvania). After the revolution was over, a great many Loyalists moved permanently to Canada, the West Indies, or England.

336. re-per-cus-sion   *noun*   rĕ-pēr-kŭsh'-ən

[*re* (Latin), "back; very" + *per* (Latin), "through; very" + *cutere, cussus* (Latin), "strike (hard)"]

Definition: An indirect effect or result produced by an event or action.

The development of the computer has had far-reaching **repercussions** on the way people all over the world do business.

Even the slightest change in temperature can have profound **repercussions** on the ecosystem, just as the slightest change in the rate of inflation can have dire effects on the economy.

Synonyms: (*nouns*) aftereffect, aftermath, reverberation, backlash

337. re-plen-ish   *verb*   rĭ-plĕn'-ĭsh

[*re* (Latin), "back; very" + *plenus* (Latin), "full"]

Definition: To refill or provide a new supply of.

Just before I run out of my favorite snack food, I **replenish** my supply.

When I am most deeply discouraged, their optimism and confidence seem to **replenish** my faith in my own abilities.

Related Forms: (*nouns*) replenishment, repletion; (*adjective*) replete

Usage Notes:
  a. The noun *repletion* indicates a state of excessive fullness.
  b. The adjective *replete*, meaning "abundantly supplied," is followed by the preposition *with*—for example, an essay *replete with* glaring grammatical errors.

Synonyms: (*verbs*) restock, renew, replace

Antonyms: (*verbs*) deplete, use up, empty, exhaust

Related Phrase: devoid of

338. re-pris-al   *noun*   rĭ-prī'-zəl

[*reprisaille* (Medieval French), "retaliation"; from *reprehendere, reprehensus* (Latin), "seize, recover"]

Definition: Retaliation in kind for injuries received.

During the Cold War the Soviet Union would often expel an American diplomat in **reprisal** for our expulsion of one of theirs.

The Nazi occupiers of France usually replied to damage done by the resistance movement by taking **reprisals** on the civilian population of the country.

Synonyms: (*nouns*) retribution, requital, vengeance, revenge

Related Phrases: a vendetta; a quid pro quo; an eye for an eye, a tooth for a tooth; get a dose of one's own medicine

339. re-scind   *verb*   rĭ-sĭnd'

[*re* (Latin), "back; very" + *scindere* (Latin), "cut"]

Definition: To cancel or withdraw.

Congress has the power to **rescind** laws that prove ineffective or harmful to our national life.

When my boss saw that there was no practical way to carry out her orders, she **rescinded** them.

Phrases: rescind a contract, rescind an agreement, rescind a regulation

Related Forms: (*nouns*) rescindment, rescision

Synonyms: (*verbs*) revoke, repeal, retract, recall, abrogate, annul, nullify, countermand, invalidate

Antonyms: (*verbs*) affirm, confirm, enforce, endorse, uphold, ratify, underwrite

Related Phrase: null and void

340. re-sil-ient   *adjective*   rĭ-zĭl'-yĕnt

[*resiliens, resilientis* (Latin), "leaping back"; from *re* (Latin), "back" + *salire* (Latin), "jump, leap, spring"]

Definition:
   a.   Springy or flexible; able to resume its original shape.

   Artificial turf is a tough but **resilient** material that is ideal for long-term use as a playing surface in professional sports.

   b.   Able to recover quickly from sickness, change, or misfortune.

   Scarlett O'Hara's remarkable recovery from the disasters of the Civil War was chiefly due to her **resilient** spirit and indomitable will.

Related Forms: (*nouns*) resilience, resiliency

Synonyms: (*adjectives*) pliable, supple, malleable, buoyant

Antonyms: (*adjectives*) inflexible, rigid, stiff, obdurate, adamant

Related Phrase: roll with the punches

Using the Words

Exercise I.   Parts of Speech

Indicate the part of speech of each of the following words. In some cases, two answers are correct.

1. recalcitrant adj., n
2. recant v.
3. redundant adj.
4. reminiscence n.
5. renegade n., adj.
6. repercussion n.
7. reprisal n.
8. rescind v.
9. resilient adj.

Exercise II.   Words in Phrases

In each of the following groups, select the item that best expresses the meaning of the *italicized* word in the introductory phrase.

1. a *recalcitrant* student
   a. foreign   b. brilliant   c. perverse   d. young   e. polite

2. *recant* his beliefs
   a. discuss   b. distort   c. disclose   d. discover   e. disavow

3. exchange *recriminations*
   a. pleasantries   **b. countercharges**   c. anecdotes   d. jokes
   e. addresses

4. when she finally *relented*
   a. yielded   b. arrived   c. complained   d. answered
   e. finished

5. felt no *remorse*
   a. loneliness   b. animosity   c. hunger   **d. regret**
   e. desire

6. a *renegade* politician
   a. fledgling   **b. turncoat**   c. freshman   d. veteran
   e. expert

7. the *repercussions* of an event
   a. memories   b. reports   c. details   d. causes   **e. effects**

8. *reprisal* for an attack
   a. retaliation   b. need   c. plan   d. occasion   e. weapon

Exercise III.   Completing Sentences

Complete each of the following sentences by selecting the most appropriate word from the group of words given below. Use each word only once. Make any adjustments that are necessary to fit the words into the sentences properly.

reciprocate	raze	recalcitrant
replenish	resilient	redundant
recrimination	rescind	reminiscence

1. As part of the mayor's urban renewal program, a group of run-down inner-city buildings was ___razed___ and replaced by an ultramodern civic center.

2. To my mind, the name *Rio Grande River* is slightly _redundant_ because the word *river* appears twice, once in English and once in Spanish.

3. About a week after the Elsons had me over for dinner, I _reciprocated_ the kindness by inviting them to lunch.

4. When the legislators realized that the law they had passed simply couldn't be enforced, they _rescinded_ it.

5. Though we can replace some of the natural resources we have used up, we cannot _replenish_ our dwindling supplies of fossil fuels.

6. As its name indicates, *Recollections of My Youth* contains the author's _reminiscences_ of her girlhood and the people she grew up with.

7. People who are __resilient__ are able to bounce back quickly and easily from unexpected failures or defeats.

Exercise IV.   Synonyms and Antonyms

A. In each of the following groups, select the **two** words that are most nearly **synonymous**.

1. a. defector   b. advocate   c. beggar   d. deserter _renegade_
2. a. wordy   b. pleasant   c. verbose   d. relevant _redundant_
3. a. reply   b. renounce   c. retract   d. report _recant_
4. a. proposal   b. hunch   c. recollection   d. memory _reminiscence_
5. a. pride   b. contrition   c. stature   d. repentance _remorse_

   Now, for each pair of synonyms that you have selected, supply a word from the Basic Word List for this lesson (Words 326–340) that means **the same** or **almost the same** thing.

B. In each of the following groups, select the item that is most nearly **opposite** in meaning to the numbered word at the left.

1. replenish   a. exhaust   b. avoid   c. restock   d. contain
   e. repel
2. raze   a. allay   b. consider   c. defer   d. smolder
   e. erect
3. rescind   a. ravage   b. rival   c. ratify   d. ruffle
   e. repudiate
4. recalcitrant   a. wordy   b. accommodating   c. gorgeous
   d. affluent   e. knowledgeable
5. relent   a. collapse   b. wander   c. lend   d. stiffen
   e. protrude

Exercise V.   Word Roundup

1. Explain the difference between *raze* and *raise*.
2. What is a *reciprocal trade agreement*?
3. Explain what is meant by the *principle of redundancy* as applied to space equipment.
4. Tell what preposition usually follows each of these words:
   a. replete _with_   b. reminiscent _of_
5. With or without the aid of a dictionary, define the following words.
   a. a diehard   c. overkill   e. apostate
   b. a Loyalist   d. reciprocity   f. a flashback

6. With or without the aid of a dictionary, explain what each of the following colorful expressions means.

   a. eat one's words
   b. be at odds with
   c. give tit for tat
   d. temper the wind to the shorn lamb

   e. wear sackcloth and ashes
   f. null and void
   g. roll with the punches
   h. lay waste to

7. With or without the aid of a dictionary, define each of the following foreign expressions used in present-day English, and tell what language it comes from.

   a. quid pro quo
   b. volte-face

   c. vendetta
   d. déjà vu

Exercise VI.   Framing Sentences

A. Use each of the following words in an original illustrative sentence.

1. raze
2. recrimination
3. recalcitrant

4. remorse
5. replenish
6. reprisal

7. renegade
8. repercussion
9. rescind

B. Give a **noun** form of each of the following words, and use it in an original illustrative sentence.

recantation   resilience, resiliency   redundancy, redundance
1. recant   2. resilient   3. redundant

C. Give an **adjective** form of each of the following words, and use it in an original illustrative sentence.

1. reciprocate   2. relent   3. reminiscence
   reciprocal   relentless   reminiscent

N. Scott Momaday

The noted Native American writer, painter, and teacher N. Scott Momaday is a member of the Kiowa tribe. His novels and poems present the oral traditions of his people in a contemporary idiom. His best-known work, *House Made of Dawn*, is a long prose poem about the land and those who love and value it. The book won the Pulitzer Prize for Literature in 1969.

Completing Verbal Analogies

Complete each of the following analogies.

Group A

1. **frugal : bountiful =**
   - a. oblique : slanting
   - b. timid : audacious
   - c. churlish : expensive
   - d. willful : garish
   - e. resilient : flexible

2. **sequel : after =**
   - a. residue : behind
   - b. proximity : beneath
   - c. avalanche : between
   - d. intrigue : beyond
   - e. postlude : before

3. **busybody : meddlesome =**
   - a. grouch : genial
   - b. advocate : perverse
   - c. spendthrift : prodigal
   - d. hero : coward
   - e. faithful : renegade

4. **purge : oust =**
   - a. pulverize : cement
   - b. instill : remove
   - c. bolster : delay
   - d. reminisce : relent
   - e. replenish : refill

5. **raze : down =**
   - a. quell : up
   - b. instigate : down
   - c. erect : up
   - d. exalt : down
   - e. demolish : up

Group B

6. **hero : gallantry ::**
   - a. bully : remorse
   - b. prodigy : reprisal
   - c. mendicant : levity
   - d. renegade : disoyalty
   - e. pusillanimous : coward

7. **rant : bombastic ::**
   - a. exhort : dilatory
   - b. whine : mellifluous
   - c. inveigh : vitriolic
   - d. champion : noncommital
   - e. poignant : melodrama

8. **bovine : sluggish ::**
   - a. porcine : pig
   - b. horse : equine
   - c. feline : awkward
   - d. mammoth : mastodon
   - e. elephantine : huge

9. **reprehensible : condemnation ::**
   - a. meritorious : approbation
   - b. intrinsic : commiseration
   - c. precocious : recrimination
   - d. nominal : expiation
   - e. elongation : protracted

10. **author : pseudonym ::**
    - a. stage name : actress
    - b. criminal : alias
    - c. poet : playwright
    - d. peasant : honorific
    - e. nickname : sister

Working with Context Clues

Complete each of the following two-word omissions by selecting the pair of words that make the best sense in the passage as a whole. If necessary, consult a dictionary for the meaning of any word with which you are not familiar. Underline the clue or clues that led you to choose your answer.

1. An underline{experienced} worker doesn't normally have much trouble adapting to underline{new} methods or machinery; a _____, underline{however}, often has difficulty adjusting to _____ in the workplace.

    a. renegade . . . nuance   c. underline{novice . . . innovation}
    b. veteran . . . reprisal   d. charlatan . . . duplicity

2. Community groups have succeeded in cutting through government underline{red tape} and halting plans to _____ beautiful old buildings, proving that _____ can be defeated and architectural treasures underline{saved from the bulldozer.}

    a. buttress . . . consensus c. embellish . . . litigation
    b. underline{raze . . . bureaucracy} d. jeopardize . . . nostalgia

3. The earliest inhabitants of North America led _____ lives. Unlike farmers who underline{stay in one place} and underline{accumulate} large stores of food, these hunters had to be underline{constantly on the move} in order to _____ their small and underline{ever-dwindling} food supply.

    a. exotic . . . filch   c. precarious . . . purge
    b. benign . . . enlarge   d. underline{nomadic . . . replenish}

4. Characters such as George Eliot's underline{Silas Marner} _____ from all life's pleasures. They underline{deprive} themselves, not because they are _____, but because they refuse to spend the underline{money} they have.

    a. recant . . . pensive   c. underline{abstain . . . indigent}
    b. flinch . . . cantankerous d. withdraw . . . desultory

5. "In your essay, you underline{repeat the same} words and phrases too often," the teacher said. "To underline{trim the fat}, you will need to _____ the _____ passages."

    a. underline{delete . . . redundant}   c. purge . . . obscene
    b. rescind . . . felicitous   d. finesse . . . circuitous

6. When underline{sentimental} old friends get together to underline{talk about the past}, one fond _____ usually leads to another; and before they know it, they are awash in _____ for the good old days.

    a. anecdote . . . empathy   c. irony . . . parody
    b. epithet . . . conjecture d. underline{reminiscence . . . nostalgia}

438

7. The imagery in some contemporary poetry is so _____ that <u>confused</u> readers must _____ for the meaning of the <u>vague</u> language like a visitor <u>searching</u> for the light switch in a dark room.

    a. fatuous . . . search   **c.** esoteric . . . aspire
    <u>**b.** nebulous . . . grope</u>   **d.** cogent . . . advocate

8. In order to avoid being sued for _____, newspapers are often willing to <u>admit in print that the statement in question is untrue</u>. Usually when they agree to _____, the suit is dropped or settled.

    a. immunity . . . delete   **c.** ignominy . . . apologize
    <u>**b.** libel . . . recant</u>   **d.** reprisal . . . rescind

9. The <u>heartbreaking</u> _____ of parents who <u>regret</u> not spending enough time with their children is particularly _____ when it comes too late and the child has already developed serious problems.

    a. obsession . . . ominous   **c.** nostalgia . . . culpable
    <u>**b.** remorse . . . poignant</u>   **d.** empathy . . . flagrant

10. Our attempts to be _____ can backfire. One such _____ is an <u>outburst of impulse buying</u> if we put ourselves on <u>an overly strict budget</u>.

    <u>**a.** frugal . . . repercussion</u>   **c.** judicious . . . exigency
    b. affluent . . . effect   **d.** austere . . . propensity

Enriching the Lesson

Exercise I.   Adjectives Derived from Proper Names

If a poet or dramatist were described as *Shakespearean*, you would certainly interpret this as a very high compliment. It suggests immediately all the qualities that we associate with Shakespeare—vivid characterization, insight into human motivation, evocative use of language, and so forth. In short, the name *Shakespeare* carries so many clearly understood associations that it can serve as a useful adjective.

There are a good many other names, drawn from various cultures and different periods of history, that have been converted into adjectives. In each case, of course, the adjective suggests the qualities and accomplishments for which a particular person is famous. The words are commonly, but not always, used in a favorable or complimentary sense.

Terms of this type can be a useful part of your vocabulary. You are bound to run across some of them in your reading, and you can often introduce them into your own speech and writing to express forcefully a particular aspect of meaning that you have in mind.

Each of the words listed below is derived directly from the name of a famous person. In each case, identify the person whose name is involved. Incidentally, some of these forms may not appear in your dictionary. In that case, you may want to refer to an encyclopedia or other reference work to pin down the source of the word and the person to whom it refers.

1. Byronic	8. Kafkaesque	15. Napoleonic
2. Keynesian	9. Jeffersonian	16. Socratic
3. Chaucerian	10. Elizabethan	17. Freudian
4. Joycean	11. Platonic	18. Machiavellian
5. Marxist	12. Thomistic	19. Shavian
6. Aristotelian	13. Dickensian	20. Darwinian
7. Edwardian	14. Mosaic	21. Rabelaisian

Drawing by Ed Fisher; © 1975 *The New Yorker* Magazine, Inc.

"Ho, ho, ho! Ah, Monsieur Rabelais, there's just no word to describe that earthy humor of yours."

Exercise II.   Our Celtic Heritage

Modern English contains a number of expressions drawn from Irish, Welsh, and Scottish Gaelic, the chief modern representatives of the Celtic branch of the Indo-European family of languages. A few of these items are listed below. With or without the aid of a dictionary, define each.

1. shamrock	4. clan	7. plaid
2. banshee	5. brogue	8. slogan
3. crag	6. leprechaun	9. bog

Exercise III.   Thanks to the French

Hundreds of the expressions used in Modern English are of French origin. You have already met some of these items in Lessons 3 and 12 and elsewhere in this book. A few more are listed below. With or without the aid of a dictionary, define each. Then choose any **five**, and for each compose an original illustrative sentence.

1. communiqué
2. etiquette
3. morale
4. protégé
5. entrée
6. vis-à-vis
7. flair
8. plateau
9. reservoir
10. encore
11. penchant
12. genre
13. ensemble
14. tête-à-tête
15. liaison

Exercise IV.   Expanding Your Word Power

The words listed below are not on the Basic Word List, but they were mentioned, in one form or another, in Lesson 26. All of them would make useful additions to your working vocabulary. Define each, give its etymology, list **two** synonyms and **two** antonyms (where possible), and use in a short illustrative sentence.

1. dismantle
2. devastate
3. contumacious
4. verbose
5. requite
6. retort
7. tautological
8. contrition
9. memoir
10. buoyant
11. deplete
12. backlash
13. underwrite
14. malleable
15. apostate

Related Forms in Context

Beneath each sentence below are four words introduced in Lesson 25 or 26. Review the related forms for these words, and choose the one that best completes the sentence. Write that related form in the space provided.

1. The district attorney was known for the relentlessness with which he prosecuted members of organized crime.

   a. replenish   b. reciprocate   c. relent   d. recant

2. The recalcitrance of the temperamental chess champion, who refused to play his matches in the presence of an audience, delayed the start of the tournament for two days.

   a. renegade   b. remorse   c. recalcitrant   d. purge

3. Under the old motion picture Production Code, censors could demand that scenes deemed offensive to moral standards be expurgated from a film.

   a. propitiate   b. promulgate   c. proliferate   d. purge

4. For her science paper, Sondra plans to research the proliferation of the hoof-and-mouth disease that ravaged Britain's cattle and sheep.

   a. proliferate   b. promulgate   c. propitiate   d. procrastinate

5. Captain Ahab in Melville's *Moby Dick* pursues the great white whale remorselessly, without regard for the safety of his crew.

   a. reminiscence   **b. remorse**   c. purge   d. recrimination

6. Some screenwriters who were blacklisted during the McCarthy era created pseudonymous identities in order to continue to work.

   a. pseudonym   b. recrimination   c. reminiscence   d. remorse

7. Juneteenth, the holiday that celebrates the end of slavery, dates back to June 19, 1865, when Union soldiers rode into Galveston, Texas, and announced the promulgation—more than two years earlier—of the Emancipation Proclamation.

   a. propitiate   b. proliferate   **c. promulgate**   d. purge

8. John's research paper is due next week, but he is the world's worst procrastinator and has not begun writing it yet.

   a. proliferate   b. promulgate   c. propitiate   **d. procrastinate**

9. No 20th-century artist could rival Pablo Picasso (1881–1973) for the prodigiousness of his output and its astonishing variety.

   a. quixotic   **b. prodigious**   c. protracted   d. redundant

10. The movie I just saw runs for more than three and a half hours, and I think the director chose to _protract_ many scenes unnecessarily.

    a. prodigious   **b. protracted**   c. resilient   d. renegade

11. Once you sign a contract, you will not be able to _renege_ on the agreement; so always read carefully before you sign anything.

    a. renegade   b. recrimination   c. reminiscence   d. probity

12. Some automobiles and vans now come _replete_ with a television and DVD player for backseat passengers' viewing pleasure.

    a. recant   b. reciprocate   c. relent   **d. replenish**

13. The purpose of the Twenty-first Amendment (1933) was the _rescision_ of the Eighteenth Amendment (1919), which had prohibited the manufacture and sale of alcoholic beverages.

    a. replenish   b. reciprocate   **c. rescind**   d. relent

14. In Stephen Crane's classic novel of the Civil War, *The Red Badge of Courage*, do you think it is pusillanimity or simply fear that motivates the hero to flee from his first battle?

    a. prodigious   b. protracted   c. resilient   **d. pusillanimous**

15. When I was a child, family get-togethers began with a feast prepared by Grandma and ended with _recriminatory_ remarks as relatives rehashed old grievances.

    a. purge **b. recrimination** c. renegade d. prerogative

16. In both writing and public speaking, it is acceptable to use repetition sparingly for emphasis, but it is best to avoid redundancy.

    a. redundant b. recalcitrant c. pusillanimous d. resilient

17. In _Jane Eyre_ by Charlotte Brontë, Jane's _resiliency_ and strength of character enable her to overcome her very unhappy childhood.

    a. prodigious b. protracted **c. resilient** d. redundant

18. Galileo (1564–1642), the great Italian astronomer and physicist, was forced into a _recantation_ of his statements that Earth revolves around the Sun.

    a. procrastinate **b. recant** c. relent d. reciprocate

19. The purpose of a _reciprocal_ trade agreement between two countries is to reduce tariffs on goods imported and exported between the trading partners.

    a. promulgate b. purge c. replenish **d. reciprocate**

20. The latest fashions from the major design houses in Milan and Paris seem _reminiscent_ of popular fashions during the early 1960s.

    a. repercussion b. pseudonym c. recrimination **d. reminiscence**

Lesson 27

341. reticent — 355. satellite

---

341. **ret-i-cent** *adjective* rĕt'-ĭ-sənt

[*reticens, reticentis* (Latin), "keeping silent"; from *re* (Latin), "very; completely" + *tacere, tacitus* (Latin), "keep silent"]

Definition: Disinclined to speak out; reserved or restrained.

Though he is usually willing to talk about a wide range of general subjects, he is curiously **reticent** about his personal life.

I've always felt that a person who is **reticent** about his or her private life may have something to hide.

Understandably, diplomats must be **reticent** people, simply because what they say publicly may adversely affect delicate and complicated negotiations.

Related Forms: (*noun*) reticence

Synonyms: (*adjectives*) taciturn, tight-lipped, uncommunicative, close-mouthed, hesitant

Antonyms: (*adjectives*) voluble, prolix, garrulous, loquacious, talkative

Related Phrases: mum's the word; run off at the mouth

---

342. **re-tri-bu-tion** *noun* rĕt-rə-byoo'-shən

[*re* (Latin), "back" + *tribuere, tributus* (Latin), "pay" + *tio, tionis* (Latin), a noun-forming suffix roughly meaning "state or act of"]

Definition: Just payment for something else, especially a punishment.

Most ancient peoples looked upon plagues, famines, and other natural disasters as forms of divine **retribution** for human sin.

"I believe you all know just what kind of **retribution** you can expect if you willingly collaborate with the enemy," the leader of the resistance movement warned the crowd.

"Can any society that thinks of justice exclusively in terms of **retribution** be considered 'enlightened'?" the lawyer asked.

Related Forms: (*adjectives*) retributive, retributory

Phrases: retributive justice, in retribution for

Synonyms: (*nouns*) requital, recompense, redress, compensation, satisfaction, retaliation, reprisal (Word 338), restitution, vengeance, revenge

Related Phrase: one's just deserts

The Four Horsemen
of the Apocalypse

In the Book of Revelations (sometimes called the Apocalypse) in the New Testament, St. John the Divine describes four horsemen who issue from four seals on a closed book. These figures are usually interpreted as forms of divine retribution for human sin. They consist of pestilence (on a white horse), war (on a red horse), famine (on a black horse), and death (on a "pale" horse). Though the calamities represented by this grisly group appear regularly throughout history as the result of natural or man-made causes, St. John regards them as the instruments of God's judgment on a wayward and iniquitous human race. In the 1920s, the phrase "the four horsemen (of the Apocalypse)" was applied to a group of invincible Notre Dame football players who exacted the appropriate revenge on any opponent that attempted to score against the Fighting Irish. The Spanish novelist Vicente Blasco Ibáñez (1867–1928) called his most famous novel *The Four Horsemen of the Apocalypse* (*Los cuatro jinetes del Apocalipsis,* 1916).

The Four Horsemen of the Apocalypse by Albrecht Dürer.

---

343. ret-ro-ac-tive   *adjective*   rĕt-rō-ăk′-tĭv
[*retro* (Latin), "back" + *agere, actus* (Latin), "drive, lead"]

Definition: Applying or referring to a period prior to enactment.

Though I didn't actually receive my salary increase until the middle of February, it was **retroactive** to the first of the year.

Phrases: a retroactive order, a retroactive law, a retroactive tax hike

Related Form: (*adverb*) retroactively

Synonym: (*adjective*) retrospective

Related Phrases: an ex post facto law, an a priori argument

Usage Notes:
   a. An *ex post facto law* is one that imposes a punishment on an action that was not punishable or illegal at the time it was committed. Such laws are, of course, unconstitutional in the United States.

   b. An *a priori argument* is one in which the conclusion is deduced from a theory or hypothesis that has been stated in advance, rather than from experiment, experience, or fact.

445

344. re-ver-ber-ate   *verb*   rĭ-vûr'-bə-rāt

[*re* (Latin), "back; again" + *verberare, verberatus* (Latin), "whip, lash"; from *verber* (Latin), "a whip"]

Definition: To echo over and over again; to resound.

The majestic chords of the organ **reverberated** from the walls of the cathedral as the funeral cortege began its slow journey down the center aisle.

Lincoln's call for volunteers to fight to preserve the Union **reverberated** through the Northern states.

Related Forms: (*noun*) reverberation; (*adjective*) reverberant

Synonyms: (*verbs*) rebound, recoil, ricochet, bounce back, snap back; resonate, rumble, boom, thunder

Related Phrase: the recoil of a rifle

345. re-vere   *verb*   rĭ-vîr'

[*re* (Latin), "very; completely" + *vereri* (Latin), "respect"]

Definition: To hold in great awe, esteem, or respect.

People of all ages, races, and backgrounds **revere** the memory of Dr. Martin Luther King, Jr., and his fight for human dignity.

Even though the old man was in no way related to the little orphan, she **revered** him as a father.

People **revered** the old sage for the wisdom of his advice and the probity of his behavior.

Related Forms: (*noun*) reverence; (*adjectives*) reverent, reverential

Usage Note:
Reverend (with a capital *R*) is regularly used to address a Protestant minister or priest. *Rev.* is the usual abbreviation of the word.

Synonyms: (*verbs*) venerate, cherish, idolize, esteem, admire, honor

Antonyms: (*verbs*) ridicule, revile, execrate, disparage, belittle, denigrate

Related Phrases: hero worship, put someone on a pedestal

346. rit-u-al   *noun*   rĭch'-ōō-əl

[*ritus* (Latin), "ceremony" + *alis, ale* (Latin), "pertaining to; like"]

Definition: A prescribed form or order for some kind of ceremony; something that is regularly and faithfully practiced.

Much of the religion of the ancient Romans involved carrying out elaborate **rituals** designed to propitiate the gods and elicit their support.

Pledging allegiance to the flag can become an empty **ritual** if we fail to think of the meaning behind the words and gestures involved in it.

446

The coronation of Queen Elizabeth II at Westminster Abbey, June 2, 1953. The crowning of an English monarch is an impressive ritual full of pomp and pageantry.

Related Forms: (*nouns*) rite, ritualism; (*adjective*) ritualistic; (*adverb*) ritually

Usage Note:
Ritual is sometimes used as an adjective. In that case, it means "ceremonial" or "having the nature of a ritual." Examples of this use of the word include "pay a *ritual* call on a sick aunt" and "a *ritual* dance."

Synonyms: (*nouns*) liturgy, ceremony, formalities, service, ceremonial

Related Phrase: stand on ceremony

347. **ru·di·ment**   *noun*   rōō'-də-mĕnt
[*rudimentum* (Latin), "beginning, first attempt"; from *rudis* (Latin), "rough, raw"]

Definition: A basic principle, element, or skill.

Any good teacher will tell you that you must master the **rudiments** of a subject before you can proceed to its fine points.

Anyone who has the slightest acquaintance with the **rudiments** of economics will see that we cannot solve our financial problems simply by borrowing more and more money.

Related Forms: (*adjectives*) rudimentary, rudimental

Synonyms: (*nouns*) basics, fundamentals, ABCs, first principles

Related Phrases: a primer, in an embryonic stage of development

447

348. **ru·mi·nate**   *verb*   rōō'-mə-nāt

[*ruminare, ruminatus* (Latin), "chew the cud; ponder"; from *rumen, ruminis* (Latin), "gullet, stomach"]

Definition:

a. To chew cud. (In this sense, the word is applied to cows and other ruminants.)

  The barn was full of dairy cows contentedly **ruminating** in their stalls.

b. To ponder at length; to turn over in one's mind.

  In the corner of the garden stood a copy of Rodin's great statue of *The Thinker*, forever **ruminating** on the problems of the world.

Related Forms: (*adjective*) ruminative; (*noun and adjective*) ruminant

Ruminant

A *ruminant* is an animal that chews a cud, which is a wad of partially digested food that has been regurgitated into the mouth. Sheep, goats, cattle, oxen, deer (*e.g.*, the whitetail buck shown at the right), camels, and giraffes are all ruminants.

Synonyms: (*verbs*) masticate; mull over, reflect upon, deliberate, muse on, cogitate

Related Phrase: put on one's thinking cap

349. **ruse**   *noun*   rōōz

[*ruse* (Old French), "trick, stratagem"; ultimately from *recusare* (Latin), "reject"]

Definition: An action or device designed to confuse or mislead.

After ten long years of fruitless fighting, the Greeks finally captured Troy by resorting to a **ruse**.

Many a wily criminal has been trapped by an even more clever **ruse**.

Synonyms: (*nouns*) stratagem, ploy, subterfuge, artifice, gimmick, trick

Related Phrase: a red herring

448

350. sab-o-tage   *verb and noun*   săb'-ə-täzh

[*saboter* (French), "throw a wooden shoe into; botch"; from *sabot* (French), "a kind of wooden shoe." Supposedly, disgruntled French and Belgian factory workers threw their wooden shoes into the machinery owned by the company they worked for in order to cause damage and delay.]

Definition:

    a.   (*verb*) To hamper, injure, or destroy maliciously or stealthily.

        Members of the resistance movement tried unsuccessfully to **sabotage** an enemy munitions factory outside their native town.

        Sensing that they would be left out in the cold if the two nations actually signed a peace treaty, the extremists on both sides did everything they could to **sabotage** the negotiations.

    b.   (*noun*) Malicious damage, destruction, or hindrance of something.

        The inhabitants of that country could express their opposition to the ruthless military regime under which they lived only through **sabotage** and subversion.

Related Form: (*noun*) saboteur

Synonyms: (*verbs*) subvert, undermine, disrupt, hamstring, wreck, damage; (*nouns*) subversion, treachery

Related Phrases: throw a monkey wrench into the works, stab someone in the back, gum up the works, fifth column, a job action

Fifth Column

The term *fifth column* originated during the Spanish Civil War in the 1930s. In 1936, the insurgent (rebel) forces had an army composed of four distinct columns or units driving on Madrid (*below*). The insurgent commander, General Emilio Mola, predicted victory because, he said, he had a "fifth column" of secret sympathizers within the city, ready to engage in espionage and sabotage against the defenders. Today, the term *fifth column* is used to indicate a subversive or traitorous element within any type of organization.

351. sac·ri·le·gious *adjective* săk-rə-lē′-jəs *or* sak-rə-lĭ′-jəs
[*sacrilegus* (Latin), "one who steals sacred things"; from *sacer* (Latin), "holy, sacred" + *legere* (Latin), "gather"]

Definition: Wickedly disrespectful of sacred or revered things.

In 17th-century New England it was considered **sacrilegious** to read any book but the Bible on Sunday.

In the eyes of most Americans, those who burn or deface our flag are guilty of an intolerably **sacrilegious** act.

Related Forms: (*noun*) sacrilege; (*adverb*) sacrilegiously

Usage Note:
Sacrilege indicates the criminal abuse or misuse of something that is considered holy or sacred. Since the tone of the word is very strong, *sacrilege* is normally reserved for actions that are really reprehensible— for example, desecrating a cemetery or vandalizing a house of worship. Nonetheless, the word is occasionally used in a light or semihumorous context. For example, "he regarded my attempt to sit in his favorite chair as tantamount to *sacrilege*."

Synonyms: (*adjectives*) impious, blasphemous, ungodly, unholy, wicked, sinful, immoral, reprobate, irreverent, iconoclastic

Antonyms: (*adjectives*) pious, reverent, godly, devout

Related Phrases: accused of blasphemy, blaspheme (against), a blasphemer, an iconoclast

352. sa·li·ent *noun and adjective* sā′-lē-ĕnt *or* sā′-lyĕnt
[*saliens, salientis* (Latin), "jumping, leaping"; from *salire, saltus* (Latin), "jump, leap"]

Definition:
a. (*noun*) An outward projection in a military position; anything that protrudes beyond its surroundings.

The long Allied struggle to push back the **salient** that the Nazis had created in Belgium in 1944 is popularly known as the Battle of the Bulge.

Peninsulas can be defined as **salients** of land protruding into the sea.

b. (*adjective*) Prominent or conspicuous.

The newspaper article contained a brief synopsis of the **salient** points in the president's address.

Huge chalk cliffs projecting into the sea are the **salient** feature of the landscape around Dover.

Fair-mindedness is probably the most **salient** quality of her personality.

Phrases: a salient trait, the salient details

Related Forms: (*noun*) salience; (*adverb*) saliently; (*verb*) sally

Synonyms: (*nouns*) protuberance, protrusion, bulge, bump; (*adjectives*) outstanding, noticeable, striking, pronounced

450

Antonyms: (*nouns*) dent, depression, trough, cavity, hole, dip; (*adjectives*) inconspicuous, unobtrusive

Related Phrases: in high relief; keep a low profile

353. sanc·ti·mo·ni·ous   *adjective*   săngk-tə-mō′-nē-əs
[*sanctimonia* (Latin), "holiness"; from *sanctus* [Latin], "holy"]

Definition: Making a great but insincere show of being holy or righteous, usually for the purpose of impressing others.

> The **sanctimonious** manner in which they flaunt their faith makes me suspect that, deep down, they aren't very religious.

> I have always admired that woman because she is high-minded without being **sanctimonious** and tenderhearted without being sentimental.

Related Forms: (*noun*) sanctimony; (*adverb*) sanctimoniously

Synonyms: (*adjectives*) hypocritical, pietistic, self-righteous, canting, pompous, insincere, holier-than-thou, simon-pure

Antonyms: (*adjectives*) heartfelt, sincere

Related Phrases: a stuffed shirt, a Tartuffe

354. san·guine   *adjective*   săng′-gwĭn
[*sanguineus* (Latin), "bloody; blood-red"; from *sanguis* (Latin), "blood"]

Definition:
a. Reddish or ruddy.

> My uncle was a large man with a **sanguine** complexion that radiated good health and good cheer.

b. Cheerfully confident or optimistic.

> "Given the depressed state of the economy," I replied, "your **sanguine** assessment of this company's future doesn't appear to be very realistic."

Related Forms: (*nouns*) sanguinity, sanguineness; (*adverb*) sanguinely

Usage Note:
Be careful not to confuse *sanguine* with *sanguinary*, which means "bloodthirsty" or "murderous."

Synonyms: (*adjectives*) rosy, rubicund; florid, flushed, glowing; buoyant, sunny, bright, hopeful

Antonyms: (*adjectives*) pale, pallid, wan; pessimistic, despondent, bleak (Word 61), gloomy, glum

Related Phrases: a Pollyanna; a prophet of doom, a Cassandra

355. sat·el·lite   *noun and adjective*   sǎt'-əl-īt

[*satelles, satellitis* (Latin), "attendant"; possibly from *satnal* (Etruscan), "guard"]

Definition:

a. (*noun*) A natural or artificial body revolving around a celestial body of larger size.

> Earth has only one natural **satellite**, the Moon.

> Man-made **satellites** positioned above the Atlantic and Pacific oceans make a global system of telecommunications possible.

b. (*noun*) A country that is under the domination or influence of a larger or more powerful country.

> Although nominally independent, a number of Eastern European countries became **satellites** of the Soviet Union at the end of World War II.

c. (*adjective*) Dependent.

> Multinational corporations consisting of a number of **satellite** companies under the direct control of the parent organization exert a tremendous influence on today's economy.

Synonyms: (*nouns*) spacecraft; appendage, protectorate, client; (*adjectives*) subordinate, subject

Antonyms: (*nouns*) hegemony, dominion; (*adjectives*) dominant, parent, predominant, principal, governing

Related Phrases: a sphere of influence, a client state; a mother country, a parent organization

Rudolfo Anaya

Born in 1927, Rudolfo Anaya is both a professor at the University of New Mexico and a noted writer of novels, plays, and short stories that comment on and interpret the Hispanic way of life in the Southwest. In such novels as *Bless Me, Ultima* he weaves together folktales and questions of religious belief to produce a memorable picture of the Hispanic experience in contemporary America.

Using the Words

Exercise I
1. ret'-i-cent
2. ret-ro-ac'-tive
3. re-ver'-ber-ate
4. rit'-u-al
5. ru'-mi-nate
6. sab'-o-tage
7. sac-ri-le'-gious
8. sanc-ti-mo'-ni-ous
9. sat'-el-lite

Exercise I.   Syllabication and Pronunciation

Syllabicate the following words correctly, and place the major stress mark (') after the syllable that is stressed when the word is pronounced.

1. reticent
2. retroactive
3. reverberate
4. ritual
5. ruminate
6. sabotage
7. sacrilegious
8. sanctimonious
9. satellite

Exercise II.   Words Out of Context

In each of the following groups, select the item that best expresses the meaning of the numbered word at the left.

1. reticent
   a. colorful   b. needy   c. fortunate
   d. tremendous   e. reserved

2. reverberate
   a. honor   b. recall   c. echo   d. question
   e. ponder

3. ritual
   a. garment   b. ceremony   c. weapon
   d. development   e. profession

4. sabotage
   a. consider   b. forecast   c. scorn
   d. wreck   e. improve

5. sacrilegious
   a. judicious   b. obscure   c. impious
   d. stubborn   e. garish

6. salient
   a. elaborate   b. workable   c. prominent
   d. unexpected   e. costly

7. sanguine
   a. optimistic   b. wordy   c. useful
   d. treacherous   e. bleak

8. satellite
   a. utensil   b. principle   c. texture
   d. appendage   e. focus

Exercise III.   Completing Sentences

Complete each of the following sentences by selecting the most appropriate word from the group of words given below.

revere	retroactive	reverberate
sanctimonious	satellite	ruminate
retribution	rudiment	ruse

1. A novice swimmer is someone who is just learning the __rudiments__ of the sport.

453

2. Though the man was scorned and laughed at in his own lifetime, he is greatly __revered__ today.

3. Since the general couldn't take the enemy town by direct assault, he tried to capture it by a ____ruse____.

4. Though ordinary Greeks didn't give the nature of reality a second thought, professional philosophers like Plato and Aristotle spent their lives _ruminating_ on the matter.

5. Knowing what I do about repression in the People's Republic of China, I found Beijing's criticisms of excessive government regulation in the United States offensively sanctimonious.

6. My rent didn't actually go up until March, but the increase was _retroactive_ to the first of the year.

7. Though many of his contemporaries looked upon the destruction of Pompeii as an act of divine _retribution_, Pliny the Elder saw it as a purely natural phenomenon unconnected with questions of reward and punishment.

Exercise IV. Synonyms and Antonyms

Classify each of the following pairs of words as **S** for **synonyms** or **A** for **antonyms**.

S	1.	undermine—sabotage	S 8.	subject—satellite
A	2.	revere—revile	S 9.	fundamentals—rudiments
S	3.	ponder—ruminate	A 10.	reticent—talkative
S	4.	reverberate—resound	S 11.	ritual—rite
A	5.	sacrilegious—reverent	S 12.	ruse—stratagem
S	6.	sanctimonious—self-righteous	13.	pessimistic—sanguine **A**
S	7.	retribution—reprisal	A 14.	salient—inconspicuous

Exercise V. Word Roundup

1. Explain the difference in meaning between *sanguine* and *sanguinary*.

2. To whom is the title *Reverend* properly applied?

3. What kind of animal is referred to as a *ruminant*? Give two examples of animals that are ruminants.

4. With or without the aid of a dictionary, explain what each of the following means:

   a. an iconoclast
   b. a saboteur
   c. a stuffed shirt
   d. a fifth column

5. With or without the aid of a dictionary, explain the meaning of the following phrases:

   a. an ex post facto law
   b. an a priori argument

c. hero worship   f. a job action
d. a primer   g. a client state
e. a red herring   h. a sphere of influence

6. With or without the aid of a dictionary, explain what each of
the following colorful expressions means:

a. run off at the mouth   c. keep a low profile
b. stand on ceremony   d. stab someone in the back

Exercise VI. Framing Sentences

A. Use each of the following words in an original illustrative
sentence.

1. retroactive   4. ruse   7. sanctimonious
2. ritual   5. sabotage   8. sanguine
3. ruminate   6. salient   9. satellite

B. Give a **noun** form of each of the following words, and use it in
an original illustrative sentence.
   reticence   reverberation   sacrilege
1. reticent   2. reverberate   3. sacrilegious

C. Give an **adjective** form of each of these words, and use it in
an original illustrative sentence.

1. rudiment   2. revere   3. retribution

rudimentary,   reverent,   retributive,
rudimental   reverential   retributory

Dissecting the Words

Prefixes

1. The Latin prefix **re** appears in a great many common English words,
including *revere* and *reticent*, studied in this lesson. This prefix has a
number of different meanings, depending upon how it is used in the word
in which it appears. These meanings include:

a. "Back, backward(s)," or "behind," as in these words:

revert (*re*, "back" + *vertere, versus* [Latin], "turn")—to return to a
previous condition, subject, or practice. Noun: *reversion*

recede (*re*, "back" + *cedere, cessus* [Latin], "go")—to move back. Noun:
recession

retract (*re*, "back" + *trahere, tractus* [Latin], "draw, drag")—to take
back something that has been said, offered, or published. Noun:
retraction

remain (*re*, "back" + *manere, mansus* [Latin], "stay")—to continue
without change. Noun: *remainder*

relinquish (*re*, "behind" + *linquere* [Latin], "leave")—to give up or yield *relic* (*re*, "behind" + *linquere* [Latin], "leave")—something that has survived the passage of time; an artifact of the past

b. "Again" or "repeatedly," as in these words:

redo (*re*, "again" + *do*)—to do over

revive (*re*, "again" + *vivere, victus* [Latin], "live")—to impart new life to. Noun: *revival*

c. "Very" or "completely," as in this word:

revile (*re*, "very, completely" + *vilis, vile* [Latin], "vile")—to denounce or scorn

Occasionally **re** appears as **red**, especially before a vowel. This happens, for example, in the following word:

redeem (*red*, "back; again" + *emere, emptus* [Latin], "buy")—to rescue or recover. Noun: *redemption*

2. The Latin prefix **retro** is related to **re**. Like **re**, it means "back, backward(s), or behind." It appears in the following useful English words:

retrocede (*retro*, "back" + *cedere, cessus* [Latin], "go")—to go back or recede. Noun: *retrocession*

retrograde (*retro*, "back, backwards" + *gradi, gressus* [Latin], "walk, step")—moving backwards; reverting to an earlier condition; inverted or reversed; contrary or opposed to

retrogress (*retro*, "back, backwards" + *gradi, gressus* [Latin], "walk, step")—to move or go backwards; to return to an earlier, inferior, or less complicated state. Noun: *retrogression*. Adjective: *retrogressive*

retrospect (*retro*, "back" + *specere, spectus* [Latin], "look")—a survey or review of the past. Adjective: *retrospective*

retroversion (*retro*, "back" + *vertere, versus* [Latin], "turn")—a turning or tilting backwards

Roots

1. The Latin root **sacr** or **secr**, meaning "holy" or "sacred," appears in a a number of useful English words, including *sacrilegious*, studied in this lesson. For example:

consecrate (*con*, a form of *cum* [Latin], "very; completely" + *sacrare, sacratus* [Latin], "make holy")—to set apart as holy. Noun: *consecration*

desecrate (*de* [Latin], "away from; un-" + *sacrare, sacratus* [Latin], "make holy")—to abuse or violate the sanctity of. Noun: *desecration*

sacrament (*sacramentum* [Latin], "a holy oath or binding obligation")—one of the seven sacred rites of the Christian church; a religious rite or observance; a sacred symbol or bond. Adjective: *sacramental*

sacristy (*sacristia* [Latin], "holy place")—a room in a church for housing sacred vessels and vestments

sacrifice (*sacer, sacri* [Latin], "holy, sacred" + *facere, factus* [Latin], "make")—(*verb*) to offer to a deity as homage or in atonement for sin; to forfeit something of value for something else of greater value; (*noun*) an offering to a deity; the forfeiture of something valuable for something else of greater value. Adjective: *sacrificial*

2. The Latin root **sanct** is related to **sacr** or **sect**. It also means "holy" or "sacred." Here are a few common words in which this root appears.

sanctify (*sanctus* [Latin], "holy" + *facere*, *factus* [Latin], "make")—to consecrate; to give religious approval to

sanctity (*sanctus* [Latin], "holy" + *itas*, *itatis* [Latin], "state of")—holiness, godliness, or saintliness

sanctuary (*sanctuarium* [Latin], "a holy place")—the most holy part of a sacred place; a place of asylum or refuge

sanction (*sanctio*, *sanctionis* [Latin], "an ordaining")—(*verb*) to authorize or approve; (*noun*) authorization or approval; a measure adopted to coerce a nation or other entity into observing the law

Note the following word in which both **sacr** and **sanct** appear:

sacrosanct—sacred and inviolable

Sacrosanct may sometimes be used ironically to suggest an undeserved immunity from questioning or attack. For example, a person may say that a particular way of doing a job at his or her office is *sacrosanct*.

Exercise

1. With or without the aid of a dictionary, define each of the following words, and explain what the prefix *re* means in that particular word.

   a. reactionary c. recompense e. retrench
   b. revive   d. revere   f. relinquish

2. For each of the following definitions, supply an English word using the prefix *retro*. Two answers are correct in some instances.

   retrospective
   a. a review of the past

   retrograde, retrogressive
   c. moving backwards

   b. return to an earlier state
   retrogression, retrogress

   d. a turning or tilting backwards *retroversion*

3. With or without the aid of a dictionary, define each of the following words using the root *sacr* or *secr*. Then choose any three, and for each compose an original illustrative sentence.

   a. desecrate   c. sacrifice   e. sacrilegious
   b. consecrate d. sacrament   f. sacristy

4. For each of the following definitions, supply an English word employing the Latin root *sanct*. Then use each in an original illustrative sentence.

   sanction   *sanctuary*   *sanctity*
   a. authorize   b. refuge   c. holiness

5. With or without the aid of a dictionary, explain what each of the following means.

   a. a sacrifice hit   c. a sacred cow
   b. an inner sanctum

Working with Context Clues

Complete each of the following two-word omissions by selecting the pair of words that make the best sense in the passage as a whole. If necessary, consult a dictionary for the meaning of any word with which you are unfamiliar. Underline the clue or clues that led you to choose your answer.

1. The judge's public _____ of the way the prosecution was handling its case <u>resounded</u> throughout the courtroom and no doubt the <u>condemnation</u> will _____ in the newspapers tomorrow.

   a. reprisal . . . appear
   b. parody . . . relent
   <u>c. censure . . . reverberate</u>
   d. litigation . . . cohere

2. The people of ancient Greece <u>esteemed</u> the <u>physical bravery</u> and skill of superheroes such as Hercules just as we _____ the extraordinary _____ of celebrity athletes such as Joe DiMaggio.

   a. emulate . . . effrontery
   b. flaunt . . . empathy
   c. disparage . . . finesse
   <u>d. revere . . . prowess</u>

3, The signers of the peace treaty fear that _____ elements <u>within their own ranks</u> may try to <u>betray</u> the agreement and destroy the peace. Therefore, they are making joint plans to deal with such _____ if and when it occurs.

   a. effete . . . chagrin
   b. cynical . . . effrontery
   c. pernicious . . . prowess
   <u>d. renegade . . . sabotage</u>

4. A common <u>ploy</u> of pickpockets is to jostle or bump into you so they can _____ your wallet from your pockets or <u>snatch</u> your purse. Another _____ is to distract you by asking a question or creating a scene.

   <u>a. filch . . . ruse</u>
   b. explore . . . recrimination
   c. grope . . . enigma
   d. raze . . . propensity

5. Dieting, especially crash diets, will not necessarily make you look <u>thinner</u> and <u>more glowing</u>. <u>On the contrary</u>, the more _____ you get, the more drawn and _____ you may look.

   a. immaculate . . . pale
   <u>b. emaciated . . . haggard</u>
   c. diligent . . . austere
   d. corpulent . . . gruesome

6. Some people have <u>an inclination</u> to <u>talk happily</u> about their good fortune, while others are _____ to share good news. Perhaps the latter's _____ to keep their happiness to themselves is out of fear of losing it.

   a. distraught . . . obsession
   b. ambivalent . . . reluctance
   <u>c. reticent . . . propensity</u>
   d. eager . . . tendency

7. Since the <u>copy</u> of the Declaration of Independence that we possess is merely a(n) _____ and <u>not the real thing</u>, we cannot expect to sell it for as much money as a(n) _____ document would bring.

   <u>a. facsimile . . . authentic</u>   c. aggregate . . . elite
   b. enigma . . . antique   d. anomaly . . . copious

8. Public execution is a(n) _____ example of <u>punishment for crimes</u> against the community. Such <u>glaring</u> _____ is designed to discourage others from committing similar offenses.

   a. obscene . . . ritual   <u>c. flagrant . . . retribution</u>
   b. sanguine . . . ignominy   d. heinous . . . nepotism

9. It is the _____ of a family to arrange the funeral <u>service</u> for a loved one who dies. No one should try to take away their <u>right</u> to the kind of _____ that will give them comfort.

   a. nuance . . . remorse   c. effrontery . . . legacy
   b. privilege . . . equanimity   <u>d. prerogative . . . ritual</u>

10. I did not _____ in the dispute between my two sisters because I thought that outside <u>interference</u> would _____ <u>rather than lessen</u> the tensions between them.

   <u>a. intervene . . . exacerbate</u>   c. abdicate . . . augment
   b. participate . . . justify   d. arbitrate . . . impugn

Enriching the Lesson

Exercise I. Myth and Ritual

In this lesson, we have studied *ritual* (Word 346), meaning a prescribed way of doing things in order to satisfy some standard of a religious, intellectual, or emotional nature. Students of society and of literature have emphasized that the rituals practiced by any group of people are closely tied up with their *myths*.

The word *myth* (from the Greek *mythos*, "tale or story") is a word with many levels of meaning that has found new applications in recent years. In the most familiar and traditional sense, the word refers to an anonymous (usually ancient) story reflecting primitive beliefs and purporting to explain the mysteries of the natural universe. Thus, we have myths of the creation of the world, of the origin of a particular group of people, of heroes and gods, of cosmic catastrophes and miraculous redemptions.

The word *myth* is sometimes used in a rather pejorative sense. It suggests a belief that many people accept but that has no basis in fact and may lead to wrong and harmful judgments. Thus, we may say that writers such as James Baldwin and Ralph Ellison have devoted themselves to shattering racist *myths* about African Americans.

This has provided the basis for the word *demythologize*, which means "to strip away an accretion of legend and sentiment and to get to the hard facts underneath." We speak of historians who have sought to *demythologize* such revered figures as Thomas Jefferson and John F. Kennedy. (Of course, there is always the danger that the demythologizer, in seeking to be rigorously critical and scientific, may be propagating new myths.)

In more recent theory, a *myth* is thought of, not as a sort of harmless (or harmful) fairy tale, but rather as a symbolic projection of a people's collective values. It is a way of expressing, in a communal or instinctive fashion, how a group of people feels about life and what its ultimate values are. The rituals associated with the myth—whether religious, patriotic, aesthetic, or whatever—are a means of expressing group loyalty and acceptance of a common body of tradition.

A myth, in this extended meaning, may be embodied in a work of art that strikes some very deep chord in the collective consciousness of the group. In this sense, Hamlet, Oedipus, Captain Ahab, and Moby Dick are all *mythic* figures embodied in literary creations. Whether or not they are *literally* true is beside the point. They are *mythically* true.

A sociologist might define a myth as the imaginative interpretation of social reality. In other words, it is a way of looking at the experience of the group and of making it satisfying and familiar in common human terms. It may have great value in promoting a feeling of solidarity and in helping the group to defend itself and to survive. Indeed, it has been said that there is no successful and long-lasting grouping of human beings that does not have its accepted mythology.

The psychologist Carl Jung, a colleague and then a rival of Sigmund Freud, built his interpretation of human nature and behavior on myths. The accepted myths of the group, as Jung saw it, represent *archetypes* of the human psyche or mind. An *archetype* in this sense is a basic pattern or theme of life experience to which special details may be added to make a story. There is, for example, the archetype of the struggle between a hero and a monster, which may represent symbolically man's never-ending fight against the hostile forces of nature that seek to destroy him. Virtually all cultures of which we have any knowledge seem to possess some variation of this mythical archetype.

Modern anthropologists (*anthropology* is the "science of man") undertake, among other things, the comparative study of the mythologies of different societal groups. Much attention is given to the mythologies of primitive (that is, technologically underdeveloped) groups and to the rituals connected with them. However, anthropologists such as Margaret Mead have been quick to emphasize that the mythological traditions of such peoples are not necessarily more fanciful or childlike than the mythologies of people who consider themselves highly developed.

A. The preceding discussion contained some form of all of the following words. With or without the aid of a dictionary, define each.

1. traditional
2. purport
3. cosmic
4. catastrophe
5. redemption
6. accretion
7. demythologize
8. rigorous
9. anonymous
10. communal
11. projection
12. ultimate
13. aesthetic
14. colleague
15. solidarity
16. societal
17. fanciful
18. anthropology
19. archetype
20. racist
21. prescribed
22. propagate
23. extended
24. collective
25. symbolic
26. primitive
27. embody
28. comparative
29. psyche
30. technological

B. With or without the aid of an encyclopedia, dictionary, or other reference book, identify each of the following mythic figures.

1. Balder (Norse)
2. Quetzalcoatl (Mexican)
3. Osiris (Egyptian)
4. Cú Chulainn (Irish)
5. Shiva (Hindu)
6. Marduk (Babylonian)
7. Prometheus (Greek)
8. Romulus (Roman)
9. Paul Bunyan (American)
10. Siegfried (German)

Exercise II.   A Verbal Diversion

The inclusion of *reticent* in this lesson brings to mind the fact that modern English contains a good many compound adjectives that involve parts of the human body. A few of these items are listed below. With or without the aid of a dictionary, define each. Then choose any **five**, and for each compose an original illustrative sentence.

1. silver-tongued
2. tight-lipped
3. hard-nosed
4. flat-footed
5. hotheaded
6. openhanded
7. thin-skinned
8. sharp-tongued
9. closemouthed
10. open-faced
11. light-fingered
12. tightfisted
13. light-headed
14. wide-eyed
15. hot-blooded

Exercise III.   Expanding Your Word Power

The words listed below are not on the Basic Word List, but they were mentioned, in one form or another, in Lesson 27. All of them would make useful additions to your working vocabulary. Define each, give its etymology, list **two** synonyms and **two** antonyms (where possible), and use in a short illustrative sentence.

1. prolix
2. cogitate
3. retaliation
4. retrospective
5. recoil
6. liturgy
7. embryonic
8. ploy
9. hamstring
10. blaspheme
11. reprobate
12. cant
13. hypocritical
14. wan
15. hegemony

Lesson 28

---

356. **scape-goat**   *noun*   skāp'-gōt

[(e)*scape* + *goat*; an English translation of *ez-ozel* (Hebrew), "goat that escapes." from the allusion in Leviticus 16:8 to a goat that was let loose to perish in the wilderness after the Jewish High Priest had symbolically placed the sins of the Jewish people on its head]

Definition: Someone or something that is innocently made to bear the blame or punishment for the sins or misdeeds of others.

"I can understand why *you* don't want to take the blame for this fiasco," I said, "but why are you trying to make *me* the **scapegoat**?"

Making the Jews the **scapegoat** for the ills of Germany was part and parcel of Hitler's malevolent scheme to become master of Europe.

Synonyms: (*nouns*) victim, butt, target, patsy

Related Phrases: a whipping boy, a fall guy; pin the blame on; a witch-hunt

357. **schism**   *noun*   sĭz'-əm   *or*   skĭz'-əm

[*schisma* (Greek), "cleft, division"; from *schizein* (Greek), "split"]

Definition: A split or division within the ranks of an organization.

The split in the Roman Catholic Church that lasted from 1378 to 1417 is usually referred to as the "Great **Schism**."

The 20th century witnessed an ever widening **schism** between popular and so-called serious music.

Related Form: (*noun and adjective*) schismatic

Synonyms: (*nouns*) breach, break, cleft, rupture, rift, cleavage

Antonyms: (*nouns*) merger, fusion, union, amalgamation

Related Phrases: a falling-out among friends, a splinter group, a separatist movement; a fusion ticket

358. **scru-ti-nize**   *verb*   skrōō'-tĭ-nīz

[*scrutinium* (Latin), "search" (from *scrutari* [Latin], "search closely") + *ize*]

Definition: To examine closely or critically.

I reread my essay carefully, **scrutinizing** it for errors that I had overlooked before.

Related Forms: (*noun*) scrutiny; (*adjective*) inscrutable

Synonyms: (*verbs*) peruse, study, inspect, pore over; critique

Antonyms: (*verbs*) gloss over, skip over, scan

Related Phrases: eyeball something; give something a lick and a promise

359. **sec·u·lar**   *adjective*   sĕk'-yə-lər

[*saecularis, saeculare* (Latin), "coming once in an age"; from *saeculum* (Latin), "lifetime, age, century"]

Definition: Not religious; pertaining to worldly (as opposed to spiritual) matters; pertaining to the state.

> The program presented at last night's concert contained a fine blend of sacred and **secular** music.

> It should come as no surprise to anyone that members of the clergy have **secular** concerns and interests just like everyone else.

> During the Middle Ages, a person convicted of a crime in a religious court was sometimes handed over to the **secular** authorities for punishment.

Phrases: secular studies, the secular clergy, secular humanism

Related Forms: (*verb*) secularize; (*nouns*) secularism, secularization

Synonyms: (*adjectives*) temporal, civil, mundane (Word 270)

Antonyms: (*adjectives*) sacred, divine; spiritual; ecclesiastical, religious

The Secular Games

In ancient Rome, gladiatorial shows, chariot races (like the one from the film *Ben Hur* shown below), and other sporting events honoring the gods were given at irregular intervals. These entertainments, which lasted three days, were called the *secular games*, principally because they were supposed to be celebrated only once in a person's lifetime (*saeculum* in Latin). Theatrical entertainments, banquets, and the recitation of hymns specially composed for the occasion were also featured. One of these hymns has come down to us from antiquity. It is the "Secular Hymn" (*Carmen Saeculare*) composed by the Roman poet Quintus Horatius Flaccus (better known as Horace) for the secular games given by the Emperor Augustus about 17 B.C.

360. se-nile   *adjective*   sē'-nīl *or* sĕn'-īl

[*senilis, senile* (Latin), "relating to an old man"; from *senex, senis* (Latin), "old; old man"]

Definition: Showing the signs of old age, especially advanced mental or physical deterioration.

> "I may be getting on in years," Granddad said at his retirement party, "but I'm not **senile** yet."

> By A.D. 450, the once vigorous Roman Empire had become decidedly **senile**.

Related Forms: (*nouns*) senility, senescence; (*adjective*) senescent

Usage Notes:

   a. *Senescent* and *senescence* indicate that someone or something is in the process of becoming old; *senile*, on the other hand, indicates that he, she, or it has already reached that stage.

   b. *Senile dementia* is the technical term for the abnormally rapid deterioration of the mental and emotional faculties that sometimes comes with advanced age.

Synonyms: (*adjectives*) aged, decrepit, doddering, feebleminded, infirm, superannuated, obsolescent

Antonyms: (*adjectives*) youthful, adolescent, juvenile, infantile

Related Phrase: the science of gerontology

361. sol-ace   *noun and verb*   sŏl'-ĭs

[*solacium* (Latin), "comfort"; from *solari* (Latin), "console"]

Definition:

   a. (*noun*) Comfort or consolation in sorrow, distress, or misfortune.

> While waiting to be executed for treason, the Roman statesman Boethius sought **solace** from personal misfortune in the composition of one of the world's greatest spiritual works, *The Consolation of Philosophy.*

> It is the duty of a friend to offer congratulations in times of triumph, encouragement in times of trial, and **solace** in times of distress.

   b. (*verb*) To comfort or console.

> In his or her own way, each person who attended the funeral tried to **solace** the grieving widow.

Related Phrase: give solace to

Synonyms: (*nouns*) succor, sympathy, commiseration, condolence, cheer; (*verbs*) succor, soothe, reassure

Antonyms: (*verbs*) vex, aggravate, badger, worry, upset, alarm

Related Phrases: give someone a boost (*or* a lift), a letter of condolence; cold comfort

464

A group of seniors keeping in tip-top condition.

Some Seniors You Should Know

The English word *senior* comes from the same Latin root as *senile*. Modern English contains a good many useful expressions involving the word *senior*. For instance, a *senior citizen* is a person who has reached or gone beyond the age when many people retire from their jobs. In some places a *senior high school* is a high school that comprises grades 10 through 12. It is the counterpart of a *junior high school*, which consists of grades 7 through 9. A *senior* is a student in his or her last year of high school or college or a person who is over the retirement age. *Seniority* indicates a privileged status attained by virtue of long service in a company, institution, or other organization. The privileges that seniority brings include preferential treatment in regard to promotions and choice of work shift. The phrase *seniority rule* refers to the custom by which members of Congress choose their committee assignments according to their length of service in the House or Senate. By the way, the word *senate* is also related to *senile*. Originally, it referred to a group of old men who acted as the advisers to a king or other ruler. Now, of course, it is used of the highest lawmaking body in the land, regardless of the age or sex of its members. *Senatorial courtesy* refers to the custom of refusing to confirm a presidential appointment when both senators from the prospective appointee's state or the senior senator in the president's party oppose the idea.

362. sor-did   *adjective*   sôr′-dĭd

[*sordidus* (Latin), "filthy"; from *sordere* (Latin), "be filthy" and *sordes, sordis* (Latin), "filth"]

Definition:

a. Filthy and mean.

> Despite the great wealth and abundance this country has to offer, some Americans still live and die in **sordid** and depressing slum conditions.

b. Morally degrading or reprehensible.

> The country was dumbfounded as, little by little, the **sordid** details of the scandal came to light.

> Disgusted with what he considered the **sordid** materialism of his countrymen, the French painter Paul Gauguin fled to Tahiti to live close to nature.

Phrases: a sordid crime, sordid motives

Related Form: (*noun*) sordidness

Synonyms: (*adjectives*) foul, wretched, gross, sleazy, squalid; vile, shameful, dishonorable; crass

Antonyms: (*adjectives*) splendid, opulent, luxurious; admirable, meritorious, praiseworthy; noble, lofty

Related Phrases: a slumlord, urban blight

363. stam-i-na   *noun*   stăm′-ĭ-nə   *or*   stăm′-ə-nə

[*stamina*, the plural of *stamen, staminis* (Latin), "thread, fiber." Originally, the *stamina* were believed to be the threads of life spun by the Fates at a person's birth. These determined how long a person would live and, by extension, how much staying power he or she had.]

Definition: Endurance; the moral or physical strength required to withstand hardships or overcome obstacles.

> A runner needs a great deal of determination, as well as remarkable physical **stamina**, to complete a 26-mile marathon.

> Do you think that present-day Americans display the same amount of mental, moral, and physical **stamina** as the early pioneers?

> I agree that the candidate is a brilliant person, but I'm not sure that he has the **stamina** to serve effectively in the most trying job in the world.

Synonyms: (*nouns*) fortitude, perseverance, guts, grit, mettle, staying power, energy, vitality

Antonyms: (*nouns*) weakness, infirmity, debility, frailty, fragility, lack of strength, impotence

Related Phrases: intestinal fortitude; run out of steam

The Fates

In Greek mythology, the Fates (*Moirai*) were three sisters who were believed to determine a person's life span by spinning and cutting a slender thread that represented time. (This thread was called a *stamen* in Latin.) Clotho ("Spinner") spun the thread, Lachesis ("Allotter") measured it, and Atropos ("Inflexible") cut it. The Romans called these divinities the *Parcae*, and they are known as the *Norns* in Norse myth. One of the most interesting representations of the Norns occurs in the prologue to Richard Wagner's great music drama, *Twilight of the Gods* (*Götterdämmerung*), which was first performed in Germany in 1876.

The Three Fates by Francesco Salviati

---

364. ster-e-o-type   *noun and verb*   stĕr'-ē-ə-tīp   *or*   stîr'-ē-ə-tīp

[*stéréotype* (French), "a kind of plate used in printing"]

Definition:

a. (*noun*) A conventional, usually oversimplified, conception or representation of something.

  Though we all have a tendency to think in **stereotypes**, it would be a mistake to base our behavior on such simplistic notions.

  In recent years, the women's movement has done much to demolish the sexist **stereotypes** of a bygone age.

b. (*verb*) To force into a uniform, and usually oversimplified, mold; to develop a fixed and unvarying idea about.

  Some popular shows of TV's golden age tended to **stereotype** the average American family and its component members.

  During a war people are easily beguiled into **stereotyping** the enemy as somehow subhuman.

Related Forms: (*adjectives*) stereotypic(al), stereotyped

Synonyms: (*noun*) cliché; (*verbs*) classify, generalize about, typecast, pigeonhole, categorize

Related Phrase: force of habit

467

365. **stig·ma·tize**   *verb*   stĭg'-mə-tīz

[*stigmatizein* (Greek), "brand, mark"; from *stigma, stigmata* (Greek), "mark, brand, tattoo"]

Definition: To brand or characterize as blemished or disgraceful.

Stigmatized as a traitor by his fellow Americans, Benedict Arnold spent the last years of his life in exile in England.

Related Forms: (*nouns*) stigma, stigmata, astigmatism; (*adjective*) stigmatic

Usage Notes:
   a. A *stigma* is a mark or token of infamy, disgrace, or reproach. For example, Edgar Allan Poe bore the *stigma* of having been expelled from West Point.
   b. *Astigmatism* is a condition in which the eye does not focus properly. Glasses can usually correct this problem.

Synonyms: (*verbs*) denounce, condemn, decry, discredit, disparage, belittle; label, impute

Antonyms: (*verbs*) whitewash; compliment, extol

Stigmata

In Roman Catholicism, the term *stigmata* (the plural of *stigma*) is used to designate the impressions or marks that the Crown of Thorns and the nails left on the body of Christ during His crucifixion. Devout Roman Catholics believe that replicas of these marks have by divine favor appeared miraculously on the bodies of certain saintly men and women, including St. Francis of Assisi, on whose body the stigmata are said to have been impressed by a seraph with six wings.

366. stip-u-late   *verb*   stĭp'-yə-lāt

[*stipulari, stipulatus* (Latin), "make a specific demand for some condition in an agreement"]

Definition: To specify or demand as a condition for agreement; to guarantee or affirm.

One of the clauses in the contract **stipulates** that the agreement may be canceled if the price of oil drops below a certain level.

The lawyer for the defense **stipulated** that her client had employed the witness as a private investigator on numerous occasions.

Phrases: stipulate a price, stipulate the manner of payment

Related Form: (*noun*) stipulation

Synonyms: (*verbs*) require, contract, provide for

Related Phrases: a proviso, a must, a sine qua non; with no strings attached

367. strat-e-gy   *noun*   străt'-ə-jē

[*strategia* (Greek), "generalship"; from *strategos* (Greek), "general"; from *stratos* (Greek), "army" + *agein* (Greek), "lead"]

Definition:
a.   An overall plan of action designed to achieve a specific goal.

"The **strategy** by which we hope to win this war," the general said, "employs guerrilla tactics and avoids set battles."

Only a person with a broad knowledge of politics, social conditions, and popular attitudes throughout the country can effectively plan the **strategy** of a presidential campaign.

b.   The science of planning and directing such an operation.

Among the subjects I studied at West Point were **strategy** and tactics.

Related Forms: (*nouns*) strategist, stratagem; (*adjective*) strategic

Phrases: a strategic withdrawal, at strategic points; strategic bombing

Usage Notes:
a.   *Strategy* is sometimes used as an adjective—for example, in the phrase "a *strategy* meeting."
b.   Do not confuse *strategy* with *stratagem*. A *stratagem* is a specific scheme or device employed to gain some advantage over an opponent. In other words, it is a *tactic*. *Strategy*, on the other hand, refers to the broad, overall plan of operation.
c.   The use of *strategy* is not confined to military operations; the word may properly be applied to business, politics, sports, or other areas of life in which planning is essential.

Synonyms: (*nouns*) plan, blueprint, program, policy, approach, scenario

Related Phrases: a game plan; operational tactics; the science of logistics

368. stri-dent   *adjective*   strīd'-ĕnt

[*stridens, stridentis* (Latin), "loud and harsh"; from *stridere* (Latin), "make a loud, harsh noise"]

Definition: Loud and harsh in sound.

> On the corner a man shouting at the top of his lungs in a very **strident** voice was haranguing a throng of idle passersby.

> As election day got closer and closer, the tone of his political oratory became more and more **strident**.

Related Forms: (*nouns*) stridence, stridency; (*adverb*) stridently

Synonyms: (*adjectives*) grating, shrill, raucous, dissonant, cacophonous, jarring

Antonyms: (*adjectives*) mellifluous, euphonious, melodious, dulcet

369. sur-veil-lance   *noun*   sər-vā'-ləns

[*sur* (French), "over, on" + *veiller* (French), "watch" + *ance* (French), "state or act of"]

Definition: Close observation of a person or group considered suspicious; a continuous watch for the purpose of direction or control.

> Throughout the period that the mobster thought he had gone undetected, he was actually under close **surveillance** by the FBI.

> The disputed territory was kept under strict UN **surveillance** until peace was restored to the area.

> Observers on the ground keep close **surveillance** on air traffic at a busy international airport by means of various electronic devices, including radar.

Synonyms: (*nouns*) watch, monitoring, supervision, vigilance

Related Phrases: a stakeout, tail (*or* put a tail on) a suspect, keep tabs (*or* an eye) on, industrial espionage

370. syn-drome   *noun*   sĭn'-drōm

[*syndrome* (Greek), "combination"; from *syn* (Greek), "together" + *dramein* (Greek), "run"]

Definition: A group of traits, symptoms, or signs that collectively characterize a disease or social condition.

> A temperature, a sore throat, and a general feeling of overwhelming fatigue are characteristic of the mononucleosis **syndrome**.

> The conference sought to develop effective strategies to combat the **syndrome** of drug abuse, violence, and crime that afflicts our society.

Synonym: (*noun*) complex

Using the Words

Exercise I.   Parts of Speech

Indicate the part of speech of each of the following words. In some cases, two answers are correct.

1. schism n.
2. scrutinize v.
3. senile adj.
4. solace n., v.
5. stamina n.
6. stereotype n., v.
7. strident adj.
8. surveillance n.
9. syndrome n.

Exercise II.   Words in Phrases

In each of the following groups, select the item that best expresses the meaning of the *italicized* word in the introductory phrase.

1. a *schism* in the ranks
   a. traitor   b. movement   c. spy   <u>d. split</u>

2. *scrutinized* the report
   a. ignored   <u>b. examined</u>   c. delivered   d. questioned

3. *secular* pursuits
   a. religious   b. scholarly   c. typical   <u>d. worldly</u>

4. slowly becoming *senile*
   <u>a. feebleminded</u>   b. tight-lipped   c. ironclad   d. openhanded

5. sought *solace* in her scholarly activities
   a. payment   b. glory   c. knowledge   <u>d. comfort</u>

6. *sordid* motives
   a. unclear   <u>b. shameful</u>   c. puzzling   d. lofty

7. has no *stamina*
   a. money   b. evidence   <u>c. staying power</u>   d. job

8. a *strident* voice
   <u>a. shrill</u>   b. soft   c. clear   d. deep

Exercise III.   Completing Sentences

Complete each of the following sentences by selecting the appropriate word from the group of words given below.

stipulate	syndrome	scapegoat
strident	strategy	stereotype
stigmatize	sordid	surveillance

1. One of the clauses in the contract <u>stipulates</u> that employees are to be allowed ten sick days a year.

2. The courts have placed strict limits on secret monitoring of telephone conversations and other forms of electronic surveillance.

3. He is clever at devising temporary measures to prevent his company from going bankrupt, but he seems incapable of developing a long-term financial _strategy_.

4. "Instead of looking for a _scapegoat_ to saddle with the blame for this mess," I asked, "why don't you admit your own responsibility for it?"

5. "Though the official must, of course, bear the burden of guilt for what he has done," Angela observed, "we should not allow his misdeeds to _stigmatize_ innocent members of his family."

6. The fact that we throw away so much edible food is evidence of the _syndrome_ of wastefulness that seems to afflict modern American life.

7. Though we tend to regard racial and ethnic _stereotypes_ as relatively modern phenomena, we should not forget that the ancient world thought in such clichés as well.

Exercise IV. Synonyms and Antonyms

A. In each of the following groups, select the **two** words that are most nearly **synonymous**.

1. a. brand   b. reply   c. intrude   d. condemn   stigmatize
2. a. consider   b. inspect   c. examine   d. support   scrutinize
3. a. plan   b. blueprint   c. essay   d. novel   strategy
4. a. modern   b. sleazy   c. affluent   d. squalid   sordid
5. a. endurance   b. fortitude   c. memory   d. plight   stamina

   Now, for each pair of synonyms you have selected, supply a word from the Basic Word List for this lesson (Words 356–370) that means the **same** or **almost the same** thing.

B. In each of the following, select the item that is most nearly **opposite** in meaning to the numbered word at the left.

1. secular   a. financial   b. scientific   c. athletic
              d. political   e. sacred

2. senile   a. lush   b. wealthy   c. abrupt   d. youthful
              e. kindly

3. strident   a. mellifluous   b. obscure   c. hurried
              d. docile   e. raucous

4. schism   a. crusade   b. development   c. fusion
              d. rupture   e. prologue

5. solace   a. pay   b. upset   c. study   d. answer   e. burn

Exercise V. Word Roundup

1. Give the origin of the word *scapegoat.*
2. With what is each of the following sciences concerned?
    a. gerontology   b. logistics
3. Explain the difference in meaning between the words in each of the following pairs:
    a. senile—senescent   b. obsolete—obsolescent
4. Name the Fates, and explain how they were thought to determine a person's life span.
5. With or without the aid of a dictionary, define each of the following expressions:
    a. a whipping boy   d. a slumlord
    b. a splinter group   e. a game plan
    c. a senior citizen   f. a stakeout
6. With or without the aid of a dictionary, explain what each of the following terms means:
    a. seniority   c. astigmatism
    b. merger   d. industrial espionage
7. With or without the aid of a dictionary, define each of the following foreign expressions used in present-day English, and tell what language it comes from.
    a. sine qua non   b. scenario   c. proviso
8. With or without the aid of a dictionary or other reference book, explain what is meant by each of the following colorful phrases:
    a. to pigeonhole something   c. to eyeball something
    b. to give something a lick   d. to put a tail on
         and a promise   someone

Exercise VI. Framing Sentences

A. Use each of the following words in an original illustrative sentence.

1. scapegoat   3. solace   5. surveillance
2. secular   4. stamina   6. syndrome

B. Give a **noun** form of each of the following words, and use it in an original illustrative sentence.

1. scrutinize scrutiny   3. sordid sordidness   5. stipulate stipulation
2. senile senility,   4. stigmatize stigma,   6. strident stridence,
       senescence   stigmata, astigmatism   stridency

C. Give an **adjective** form of each of the following words, and use it in an original illustrative sentence.

1. schism   2. stereotype   3. strategy
    schismatic   stereotypic(al), stereotyped   strategic

473

Completing Verbal Analogies

Complete each of the following analogies.

Group A

1. **gibberish : meaning ::**
   a. bombast : padding
   b. clarity : exhortation
   c. innuendo : subtlety
   d. drivel : substance
   e. stamina : endurance

2. **vitriolic : acid ::**
   a. petulant : wine
   b. decadent : water
   c. <u>unctuous : oil</u>
   d. sordid : milk
   e. secular : soda

3. **expurgate : censor ::**
   a. persevere : lie
   b. <u>embezzle : steal</u>
   c. desecrate : cheat
   d. award : rob
   e. solace : murder

4. **dapper : slovenly ::**
   a. shrewd : astute
   b. quixotic : feasibility
   c. coward : pusillanimous
   d. <u>mellifluous : strident</u>
   e. precarious : perch

5. **hypocrite : sanctimonious ::**
   a. <u>showoff : ostentatious</u>
   b. glutton : abstinent
   c. avarice : miser
   d. drunkard : winsome
   e. infantile : senile

Group B

6. **egregious : mountain =**
   a. punctilious : pigsty
   b. grandiose : foxhole
   c. dispassionate : toadstool
   d. precocious : mousetrap
   e. <u>inconsequential : molehill</u>

7. **asymmetrical : balance =**
   a. anomalous : function
   b. frog : amphibian
   c. satellite : autonomous
   d. <u>amorphous : shape</u>
   e. axiom : theorem

8. **dowdy : appearance =**
   a. abstemious : background
   b. <u>gauche : behavior</u>
   c. sedentary : age
   d. debonair : build
   e. prodigious : color

9. **fox : fur =**
   a. giraffe : gist
   b. monkey : simian
   c. ruminant : gnu
   d. <u>parrot : plumage</u>
   e. colt : foal

Working with Context Clues

Complete each of the following two-word omissions by selecting the pair of words that make the best sense in the passage as a whole. If necessary, consult a dictionary for the meaning of any word with which you are not familiar. Underline the clue or clues that led you to choose your answer.

1. We can go ahead with our _____ to gain new club members if we can get the approval of the board. Otherwise, our plan of action must remain _____ until a new board is elected, and that is not scheduled to occur for at least another year and a half.

   a. innovation . . . active
   b. premise . . . nominal
   c. propensity . . . strident
   d. strategy . . . dormant

2. Some advertisers make their ads loud and insistent in the hope that the _____ tone will cause resistant consumers to _____ and buy their products, even if they really do not need them.

   a. strident . . . relent
   b. facetious . . . recant
   c. felicitous . . . grope
   d. affected . . . bicker

3. If your general attitude toward other people is so hostile and off-putting that you _____ everyone you meet, you had better think about why you are so _____.

   a. goad . . . obsequious
   b. impugn . . . benign
   c. alienate . . . belligerent
   d. stigmatize . . . cynical

4. A _____ is an oversimplified label that is used to discredit entire groups of people and to _____ individuals simply because they are members of a particular group.

   a. stereotype . . . stigmatize
   b. euphemism . . . censure
   c. paradox . . . exploit
   d. scapegoat . . . libel

5. Some senators _____ against a proposal in committee; but when it comes to the floor, they no longer protest but turn _____ and go along with the majority.

   a. inveigh . . . docile
   b. stipulate . . . reticent
   c. harangue . . . belligerent
   d. array . . . askew

6. Younger patients are more likely to recover quickly from surgery. Older patients are less _____ and may lack the _____ to endure a long operation.

   a. blithe . . . equanimity
   b. resilient . . . stamina
   c. implacable . . . bravado
   d. circumspect . . . courage

Enriching the Lesson

Exercise I.   Fairness in Language

One of the basic complaints of supporters of the women's movement was that sexist attitudes that tended to belittle and degrade women were embedded in our language. They called attention, for example, to issues such as the following:

- The use of the masculine pronoun in contexts that should apply to women fully as much as to men—for example, "Each of us should do *his* best to serve *his* community." Did this imply that men were the pivotal figures in society and that the role of women was inferior or inconsequential? Perhaps there was no such idea in the mind of the speaker or writer, but it may still have been true that the constant use of this kind of expression reflected and reinforced sexist attitudes, if only on an unconscious level. It was argued that English, unlike some other languages, doesn't have an equivalent for *he* and *his* that applies to both sexes and that we must accept this linguistic peculiarity. The answer was that one can usually get around the snag with just a little ingenuity— for example, "All of us should do *our* best to serve *our* community."

- The use of *Mrs.* and *Miss* as terms of address for married and un- married women, respectively. The term *Mr.* applies to men, whether married or not. Did this imply that a woman had no real identity aside from her marital status—that is, her relationship to men? Supporters of the women's movement recommended the title *Ms.* for all women, and this form is now in common use.

- The use of such expressions as *chairman, congressman, foreman, spokesman,* and *anchorman* to indicate positions of authority and importance. It was often said that the *man* part of such terms is simply a convention of language, with no sexist intent. However, feminists asserted that such expressions derived from a period when male dominance was taken for granted and that it was time to root them out. Suggested substitutes, such as *congressperson* and *chairperson*, seemed strange at first to some people. However, with continued use, such gender-neutral terms became the norm.

- The tendency to specify the sex of a doctor, lawyer, or some other professional person who happened to be a woman—for example, "I am being treated by a lady dentist." Would anyone say, "I am being treated by a man dentist"? Or (even more ridiculous) by a "gentleman dentist"? Surely sex was irrelevant to professional qualifications, and the specification that a dentist was a woman was male-oriented and patronizing, if not insulting. Incidentally the use of *lady* was frowned upon by many feminists because it suggested a delicate and sheltered creature, probably of the upper classes, who must be kept apart from the gross realities of real life. The more down-to-earth term *woman*—the exact equivalent of *man*—was much preferred.

476

Not everyone fully accepted such criticisms of our language habits. However, it is hard to deny that there were conventions of English usage that reflected a male-dominated society and that it was high time to make some changes that reflected the status and attitudes of women.

Listed below are some words and phrases commonly used in connection with the women's movement. Define each.

1. sexism	9. stigma	17. denigrate
2. feminism	10. male chauvinism	18. conformity
3. stereotype	11. glass ceiling	19. liberation
4. feminine mystique	12. consciousness-raising	20. male supremacy
5. conventions	13. grievance	21. dependence
6. mommy track	14. fulfillment	22. domestic
7. discrimination	15. identity	23. pink collar
8. equal rights	16. career-oriented	24. confrontation

Exercise II. "Sound" Words

This lesson includes the word *strident*, which refers to sound. A number of other useful "sound" words are listed below. With or without the aid of a dictionary, define each, and give its etymology. Then choose any **five**, and for each compose an original illustrative sentence.

1. vociferate	6. sibilant	11. purl
2. rasping	7. shrill	12. dulcet
3. sonorous	8. tremulous	13. snarl
4. bleat	9. keen (*verb*)	14. discordant
5. quaver	10. stentorian	15. clangorous

Exercise III. Expanding Your Word Power

The words listed below are not on the Basic Word List, but they were mentioned, in one form or another, in Lesson 28. All of them would make useful additions to your working vocabulary. Define each, give its etymology, list **two** synonyms and **two** antonyms (where possible), and use in a short illustrative sentence.

1. cleft	6. succor	11. scan
2. fusion	7. squalid	12. vigilance
3. critique	8. debility	13. euphonious
4. scrutiny	9. categorize	14. monitor
5. superannuated	10. denounce	15. civil

Related Forms in Context

Beneath each sentence below are four words introduced in Lesson 27 or 28. Review the related forms for these words, and choose the one that best completes the sentence. Write that related form in the space provided.

1. Those who vandalize houses of worship or damage holy objects are guilty of __sacrilege__ .

   a. retroactive   b. sanctimonious   c. sanguine   d. sacrilegious

2. After killing his brother Abel, Cain bore a __stigma__ (the "mark of Cain") that identified him as a social outcast and a murderer.

   a. stereotype   b. stipulate   c. stigmatize   d. scrutinize

3. The eponymous heroine of the novel *Pollyanna* faces every trial that life has to offer her with remarkable __sanguinity__ .

   a. sanguine   b. sacrilegious   c. secular   d. salient

4. I find the __stridency__ of television ads so grating that I hit the mute button on my remote or leave the room during commercial breaks.

   a. senile   b. sanctimonious   c. strident   d. salient

5. The 1960 television documentary *Harvest of Shame* focused public attention on the __sordidness__ of the conditions in which migrant farmworkers were forced to live.

   a. sordid   b. sanguine   c. senile   d. sanctimonious

6. The Old Testament prophet railed against his people's increasing secularization and their abandonment of traditional ways.

   a. sordid   b. senile   c. secular   d. strident

7. The great American poet Emily Dickinson, known for her __reticence__ and shyness, gave vent to her feelings in gemlike poems of great emotional power.

   a. reticent   b. retroactive   c. senile   d. sordid

8. Tsunamis, gigantic sea waves that can be 100 feet high, are caused by reverberations from underwater earthquakes or volcanic eruptions.

   a. revere   b. ruminate   c. stipulate   d. reverberate

9. A totally inscrutable facial expression, revealing not a hint of emotion, is a great asset to someone who plays poker or other card games.

   a. reverberate   b. sabotage   c. scrutinize   d. stigmatize

10. All Social Security recipients have been notified that their cost-of-living increase will be effective retroactively from January 1.

    a. salient   b. retroactive   c. santimonious   d. strident

11. Do you think the old king's madness at the end of *King Lear* is caused by ___senility___, or are we meant to view it as a tragic consequence of his actions in Act I, scene i?

    a. senile   b. sanguine   c. reticent   d. secular

12. In the earliest movies, African American actors were restricted to playing racially stereotypical roles; but in the 1920s and 1930s pioneering African American filmmakers began to cast black actors in starring roles in Westerns, mysteries, comedies, and musicals.

    a. stipulate   **b. stereotype**   c. ruminate   d. revere

13. Every Friday at sundown, Jews begin the Sabbath by ___ritually___ reciting blessings over candles, wine, and bread.

    a. salient   b. strategy   **c. ritual**   d. rudiment

14. When it comes to planning and executing football plays, Miles, the sophomore quarterback, has proved to be the best ___strategist___ the team has had in years.

    a. stereotype   b. schism   **c. strategy**   d. stamina

15. The navy sometimes uses specially trained dolphins to detect man-made objects, such as mines, that ___saboteurs___ have planted in a harbor.

    a. retribution   b. schism   **c. sabotage**   d. strategy

16. Tecumseh, chief of the Shawnee Nation, expressed his ___reverence___ for the earth when he said, "The earth is my mother—and on her bosom I will recline."

    a. solace   b. stereotype   c. reverberate   **d. revere**

17. The human appendix is a rudimentary organ that serves no useful purpose and that may become inflamed and have to be removed.

    a. ritual   **b. rudiment**   c. salient   d. schism

18. From time to time in the history of all the world's great religions, serious differences of opinion have led to the formation of ___schismatic___ cults.

    a. scapegoat   b. retribution   c. strategy   **d. schism**

19. In Dante Alighieri's "Inferno," the first part of *The Divine Comedy*, sinners suffer ___retributive___ justice, with punishments especially appropriate to their sins on earth.

    a. rudiment   **b. retribution**   c. ritual   d. syndrome

20. Some authors of whodunits give ___salience___ to intricately constructed plots, but others emphasize complexity of character.

    a. sanctimonious   b. secular   **c. salient**   d. strident

Lesson 29

---

371. **tac-it**   *adjective*   tăs'-ĭt
[*tacitus* (Latin), "silent" ; from *tacere* (Latin), "be silent"]

Definition: Unspoken; implied or inferred.

Her friendly smile of recognition was a **tacit** invitation to join the little group of admirers surrounding her.

When my proposal was returned without comment of any kind, I took it as **tacit** approval to proceed.

"Don't you think that anybody who neglects to vote is in a way giving **tacit** support to the enemies of democracy?" she asked.

Though we were still angry with each other, we had a **tacit** agreement not to let our feelings show while our parents were present.

Phrases: a tacit assumption, tacit consent, a tacit warning, a tacit arrangement

Related Forms: (*noun*) tacitness; (*adverb*) tacitly

Synonyms: (*adjectives*) understood, implicit, wordless, unexpressed, unvoiced

Antonyms: (*adjectives*) explicit, express, expressed, specific

Related Phrase: a silent partner

372. **tac-i-turn**   *adjective*   tăs'-ə-tûrn
[*taciturnus* (Latin), "silent"; from *tacere, tacitus* (Latin), "be silent"]

Definition: Habitually untalkative.

My uncle is a **taciturn** man who rarely utters more than a word or two at a time.

Some of my friends are as talkative as magpies; others are definitely on the **taciturn** side.

Jim is such a **taciturn** fellow that I sometimes forget he is even in the room.

Related Forms: (*noun*) taciturnity; (*adverb*) taciturnly

Synonyms: (*adjectives*) closemouthed, tight-lipped, laconic, reserved, uncommunicative, reticent (Word 341)

Antonyms: (*adjectives*) talkative, loquacious, garrulous, prolix, voluble

Related Phrases: economy of words, give someone the silent treatment, a silent butler

373. tan‑gi‑ble   *adjective*   tăn'‑jə‑bəl
[*tangibilis, tangibile* (Late Latin), "able to be touched"; from *tangere* (Latin), "touch"]

Definition: Capable of being touched; real or concrete.

"I need to see **tangible** proof of your identity, such as a driver's license or passport," the postal clerk said, "before I can give you this registered letter."

One **tangible** result of the administration's economic policy was a slow but steady decline in the annual rate of inflation.

Phrases: a tangible reward, a tangible benefit, a tangible gain, tangible assets

Related Forms: (*nouns*) tangibility, tangibleness; (*adverb*) tangibly; (*adjective*) intangible

Usage Notes:
a.   The legal term *tangible assets* refers to possessions that are capable of being valued in money or can be turned into cash. Similarly, the related term *tangibles* indicates material assets or property.

b.   *Intangible* means "not capable of being perceived, identified, or defined precisely." In other words, something that is intangible is *elusive*. The plural noun *intangibles* refers to things that cannot be perceived or identified, especially what cannot be perceived by the senses. For example, a person's influence on the course of events is an intangible.

Synonyms: (*adjectives*) perceptible, discernible, palpable; material, actual, physical, solid

Antonyms: (*adjectives*) imperceptible, insubstantial, immaterial, untouchable; nebulous, hazy, vague

374. ten‑a‑ble   *adjective*   tĕn'‑ə‑bəl
[*tenable* (Old French), "capable of being held"; from *tenere* (Latin), "hold"]

Definition: Capable of being defended or maintained.

When the general realized that his forward positions were no longer **tenable**, he ordered an immediate withdrawal to more defensible ground.

Modern scientific research has shown that many 19th‑century theories about the origins of language are no longer **tenable**.

Phrases: a tenable argument, a tenable idea, a tenable assumption

Related Forms: (*nouns*) tenableness, tenability; (*adverb*) tenably; (*adjective*) untenable

Synonyms: (*adjectives*) defensible, defendable, maintainable; irrefutable, incontestable, unassailable; plausible, believable, credible

Antonyms: (*adjectives*) indefensible, insupportable, unmaintainable; flawed, faulty; specious, implausible, questionable

375. ten·ta·tive   *adjective*   tĕn'-tə-tĭv

[*tentativus* (Medieval Latin), "provisional"; from *tentare*, *tentatus* (Latin), "try, attempt"]

Definition: In the nature of an experiment or trial; uncertain.

"We have made **tentative** plans to go to the shore next weekend," Randy reported, "but we will call off the trip if the weather turns bad."

A sort of **tentative**, almost apologetic smile spread over his face when I told him that I wasn't angry at him for making a first-class mess of the project.

Phrases: a tentative arrangement, tentative acceptance, a tentative schedule

Related Forms: (*noun*) tentativeness; (*adverb*) tentatively

Usage Note:
Occasionally *tentative* is used as a noun with the meaning "an experiment."

Synonyms: (*adjectives*) provisional, contingent, probationary, interim; experimental, exploratory; hesitant, unsure, doubtful; iffy

Antonyms: (*adjectives*) definite, settled, certain, finalized

Related Phrases: send up a trial balloon, a pilot program, subject to change, contingency plans, buy something on approval; finalize one's plans

376. thwart   *verb*   thwôrt

[*thwerr, thwert* (Old Norse), "oblique; across"]

Definition: To block or frustrate.

Those who dared attempt to **thwart** the bizzare schemes of the mad Roman emperor Caligula often paid for their actions with their lives and those of their families.

Our opponents' alert defense **thwarted** our efforts to score on a surprise end sweep.

"Watching too much TV has a tendency to **thwart** the natural growth of a child's reading abilities," the noted educator remarked.

Related Form: (*preposition*) athwart

Usage Note:
Athwart is an old preposition that means "across" or "crosswise." It sometimes occurs in older writing or literature—for example, in the phrase "a log lying *athwart* my path."

Synonyms: (*verbs*) foil, baffle (Word 54), neutralize, defeat, stymie, cripple; impede, inhibit

Antonyms: (*verbs*) promote, aid, help, abet (Word 2), encourage, advance, foster

Related Phrases: short-circuit something, nip something in the bud, take the wind out of someone's sails, clip someone's wings

377. tran·quil   *adjective*   trăn'-kwĭl
[*tranquillus* (Latin), "quiet"]

Definition: Peaceful and quiet; free of mental agitation.

After years of living amid the noise and hubbub of the city, we were delighted to discover the **tranquil** atmosphere of that sleepy country town.

At first I was almost hysterical with rage; but as I grew more **tranquil**, I began to perceive that the situation was not as bad as it seemed.

"Now that I have retired from the storms and stresses of the political arena," the ex-senator remarked, "my heart has become as **tranquil** as a country churchyard on an autumn afternoon."

Related Forms: (*nouns*) tranquility, tranquilness, tranquilizer; (*verb*) tranquilize

Phrase: domestic tranquility

Usage Note:
A *tranquilizer* is a drug that lessens anxiety or tension in a person or animal.

Synonyms: (*adjectives*) calm, serene, placid; cool, composed, self-possessed, unexcited, unperturbed; impassive, dispassionate

Antonyms: (*adjectives*) turbulent (Word 380), tumultuous, stormy, tempestuous, raucous; distraught, agitated, troubled, upset

Related Phrase: keep one's cool

378. trau·mat·ic   *adjective*   trô-măt'-ĭk   *or*   trou-măt'-ĭk
[*trauma* (Greek), "wound" + *ikos* (Greek), "relating to"]

Definition: So shocking as to produce a lasting psychological effect.

"Being lost in the woods for almost a day," Fred recalled, "was one of the most **traumatic** experiences of my childhood."

The sudden death or assassination of a great political leader usually has a **traumatic** effect on his or her followers.

The aftermath of the Civil War was probably as **traumatic** for most Southerners, black and white, as the war itself had been.

Related Forms: (*nouns*) trauma, traumatism; (*verb*) traumatize

Usage Note:
In medicine, *trauma* indicates a wound produced by sudden physical injury. In psychology, it refers to an emotional shock that produces substantial and lasting psychological damage. The plural of the word is either *traumas* or *traumata*.

Synonyms: (*adjectives*) shocking, paralyzing, jolting

Antonyms: (*adjectives*) beneficial, salutary, salubrious; uplifting, inspirational

379. trench-ant   *adjective*   trĕn'-chĕnt
[*trenchant* (Old French), "cutting"; from *trenchier* (Old French), "cut"]

Definition: Perceptive and forceful; cutting.

Dorothy Parker once dismissed an actress's performance of a certain role with the **trenchant** comment that she had run "the gamut of emotions from A to B."

Today's newspaper contains one of the most **trenchant** letters to the editor I have ever read.

Phrases: a trenchant reply, a trenchant pen, a trenchant imagination, a trenchant argument, a trenchant writer

Related Forms: (*noun*) trenchancy; (*adverb*) trenchantly

Synonyms: (*adjectives*) incisive, keen, acute; effective, cogent; caustic, mordant, biting

Antonyms: (*adjectives*) bland, pallid; obtuse, vacuous, vapid, inane

380. tur-bu-lent   *adjective*   tûr'-byə-lĕnt
[*turbulentus* (Latin), "stormy"; from *turba* (Latin), "turmoil, confusion"]

Definition: Violently agitated or disturbed; restless or unruly.

During a storm the normally calm waters of the lake become so **turbulent** that a small boat may easily founder.

He is well informed and has many interesting ideas, but his **turbulent** nature infuriates the people around him.

The years between 1789 and 1815 were a **turbulent** era in the history of Europe.

Related Forms: (*noun*) turbulence; (*adverb*) turbulently

Usage Note:
Do not confuse *turbulent* with the related adjective *turbid*, which means "muddy," "unclear," or "confused."

Synonyms: (*adjectives*) stormy, troubled, tumultuous, tempestuous

Antonyms: (*adjectives*) calm, peaceful, placid, tranquil (Word 377)

381. u-biq-ui-tous   *adjective*   yōō-bik'-wə-təs
[*ubiquitas* (Latin), "state of being everywhere"; from *ubique* (Latin), "everywhere"]

Definition: Being or seeming to be everywhere.

"I almost get the impression that Harry is **ubiquitous**," Roseann remarked. "No matter where or when there's a party, Harry's present."

Nowadays absolutely nothing seems to escape the **ubiquitous** eye of the closed-circuit surveillance camera.

Related Forms: (*nouns*) ubiquity, ubiquitousness

484

An airplane experiences turbulence during an electrical storm. The word *turbulence* is often used by pilots and other people connected with airplanes to indicate a highly irregular atmospheric condition produced by rapid changes in the speed and direction of the wind and the presence of up and down air currents.

Synonyms: (*adjectives*) omnipresent, pervasive, universal, ever-present

Antonyms: (*adjectives*) rare, scarce

Related Phrases: in short supply, as scarce as hen's teeth

382. ur-bane   *adjective*   ûr-bān′
[*urbanus* (Latin), "belonging to a city; refined"; from *urbs, urbis* (Latin), "city"]

Definition: Refined, elegant, and sophisticated in manner or style.

The American novelist Edith Wharton (1862–1937) usually wrote about the **urbane** gentlemen and elegant ladies who made up New York's social elite in the last quarter of the 19th century.

If these negotiations are to be successful, we need less emotionalism and more of the calm, **urbane** manner of a diplomat.

Related Forms: (*noun*) urbanity; (*adverb*) urbanely

Usage Note:
Be careful not to confuse *urbane* with its look-alike *urban*, which means "relating to, or characteristic of, the city." Synonyms of *urban* include *metropolitan* and *citified.*

Synonyms: (*adjectives*) suave, cosmopolitan, polished, genteel, smooth, bland, courtly, well-bred

Antonyms: (*adjectives*) crude, boorish, rude, discourteous, ill-bred, gauche

383. **u-surp** *verb* yōō-sûrp′ *or* yōō-zûrp′
[*usurpare* (Latin), "take possession of something simply by using or occupying it"; from *usu* (Latin), "by use" + *rapere, raptus* (Latin), "seize"]

Definition: To seize a power, office, function, or the like without any legal right to do so.

In 1399, the Duke of Hereford **usurped** the English throne and set in motion a train of events that led to civil war 56 years later.

The legislators resisted the governor's attempts to **usurp** powers specifically granted to them by the state constitution.

I was decidedly miffed when my archrival attempted to **usurp** my place in my true love's heart.

Related Forms: (*nouns*) usurpation, usurper

Synonyms: (*verbs*) expropriate, arrogate; encroach, infringe; supplant, supersede

Related Phrases: a coup d'état, steal someone's thunder, steal the show, upstage someone, make inroads into

384. **va-ga-ry** *noun* vā′-gər-ē *or* və-gâr′-ē
[*vagari* (Latin), "wander"; from *vagus* (Latin), "meandering")

Definition: A bizarre or eccentric idea, action, or condition.

Any decision to drop out of school and travel around the country is far too serious to be dismissed as a mere adolescent **vagary**.

Making a success of a small business connected with one of our beaches is unavoidably dependent on the **vagaries** of the weather.

"Say what you will," Steve remarked, "there's just no accounting for the **vagaries** of fashion."

Synonyms: (*nouns*) whim, caprice, peculiarity, quirk, crotchet, oddity, eccentricity

Related Phrases: a passing fancy, maggots in the brain, a fad, without rhyme or reason

385. **ve-nal** *adjective* vē′-nəl
[*venalis* (Latin), "for sale"]

Definition: Open to, or marked by, bribery or corruption.

Although President Ulysses S. Grant was personally incorruptible, he surrounded himself with **venal** politicians and financiers whose scandalous dealings rocked the nation.

Gaius Verres, governor of Sicily between 73 and 71 B.C., headed up one of the most **venal** and extortionate administrations ever imposed on a Roman province.

Related Form: (*noun*) venality

486

Do not confuse *venal* with *venial* (note the *i*), which means "not serious enough to merit severe criticism" or "pardonable." For example, theologians speak of "a *venial* (minor) sin."

Synonyms: *(adjectives)* corruptible, bribable, mercenary (Word 266)

Antonyms: *(adjectives)* incorruptible, scrupulous, honest, upright

Phrases: on the take, grease someone's palm

Using the Words

Exercise I
1. tac'-i-turn
2. tan'-gi-ble
3. ten'-ta-tive
4. trau-mat'-ic
5. tur'-bu-lent
6. u-biq'-ui-tous
7. ur-bane'
8. va'-ga-ry, va-ga'-ry
9. ve'-nal

Exercise I. Syllabication and Pronunciation

Syllabicate the following words correctly, and place the major stress mark (') after the syllable that is accented when the word is pronounced. Two answers are correct in one instance.

1. taciturn
2. tangible
3. tentative
4. traumatic
5. turbulent
6. ubiquitous
7. urbane
8. vagary
9. venal

Exercise II. Words Out of Context

In each of the following groups, select the item that best expresses the meaning of the numbered word at the left.

1. tacit
   a. laconic b. implicit c. general
   d. valuable e. doubtful

2. taciturn
   a. unprofitable b. unspoken c. unlikely
   d. uncommunicative e. unfortunate

3. tenable
   a. calm b. worthless c. experimental
   d. biting e. defendable

4. traumatic
   a. banal b. wealthy c. shocking
   d. faithful e. reliable

5. trenchant
   a. incisive b. specific c. muddy
   d. provisional e. inane

6. turbulent
   a. sunny b. cool c. humid d. rainy
   e. stormy

7. urbane
   a. prominent b. final c. suave
   d. affluent e. metropolitan

8. venal
   a. minor b. corruptible c. raucous
   d. sharp e. beneficial

Exercise III.   Completing Sentences

Complete each of the following sentences by selecting the most appropriate word from the group of words given below.

thwart	tentative	tranquil
tangible	vagary	traumatic
ubiquitous	venal	usurp

1. Camels may be a rare sight in the United States, but in the Sahara they are _ubiquitous_ .

2. Farmers don't lead _tranquil_ lives, free of cares and worries; they are involved in a tough and competitive business.

3. "Since my vacation plans were only _tentative_ anyway," the busy executive remarked, "I didn't mind changing them at the last minute."

4. Far from abetting his starry-eyed scheme to run off and join a traveling circus, I did everything in my power to _thwart_ it.

5. The plot of the novel concerns an evil nobleman's attempt to murder a young king and _usurp_ his throne.

6. Since stock prices fluctuate for all kinds of unexpected reasons, it is often difficult to account for the _vagaries_ of the market.

7. Though recent political polls indicate that support for candidate X has declined considerably, they also show that candidate Y has made _tangible_ gains in popularity.

Exercise IV.   Synonyms and Antonyms

Classify each of the following pairs of words as **S** for **synonyms** or **A** for **antonyms**.

S 1. thwart—foil
A 2. trenchant—obtuse
S 3. usurp—seize
A 4. incorruptible—venal
A 5. loquacious—taciturn
S 6. defensible—tenable
S 7. tentative—provisional

A 8. tempestuous—tranquil
S 9. traumatic—paralyzing
A 10. boorish—urbane
S 11. quirk—vagary
A 12. tacit—explicit
S 13. tangible—concrete
A 14. turbulent—placid

Exercise V.   Word Roundup

1. Explain the difference between the words in each of the following pairs.

   a. venal—venial   b. urban—urbane

2. Define each of the following foreign expressions used in present-day English and tell what language it comes from.

   a. gauche   b. coup d'état

3. With or without the aid of the dictionary, explain what each of the following means.

   a. a silent partner
   b. a silent butler
   c. a pilot program
   d. a tranquilizer

   e. tangible assets
   f. contingency plans
   g. maggots in the brain
   h. domestic tranquility

4. With or without the aid of a dictionary, explain what each of the following colorful expressions means.

   a. upstage someone
   b. on the take
   c. keep one's cool
   d. send up a trial balloon

   e. nip in the bud
   f. buy on approval
   g. give someone the silent treatment

Exercise VI.   Framing Sentences

A. Use each of the following words in an original illustrative sentence.

1. tacit	4. tentative	7. trenchant
2. tangible	5. tranquil	8. ubiquitous
3. tenable	6. thwart	9. vagary

B. Give a **noun** form of each of the following words, and use it in an original illustrative sentence.

1. taciturn taciturnity
2. traumatic trauma, traumatism
3. turbulent turbulence
4. urbane urbanity
5. usurp usurper usurpation,
6. venal venality

Dissecting the Words

Prefix

The Latin prefix **sub** or one of its variants appears in a great many common English words, including *subvert*, mentioned in Lesson 7. This prefix has a number of meanings, including:

a. "Under, below, or beneath," as in these words:

   subbasement—a story or floor below the main basement of a building

   subjugate—(*sub* + *jugum* [Latin], "yoke")—to conquer or subdue. Noun: *subjugation*

   subliminal (*sub* + *limen, liminis* [Latin], "threshold")—below the level of conscious perception. Noun: *sublimation*

   submerge (*sub* + *mergere* [Latin], "plunge")—to thrust fully under, or cover with, water; to hide from view *subordinate* (*sub* + *ordinare, ordinatus* [Latin], "arrange in order")—(*adjective*) secondary; (*noun*) a person who is inferior in rank or status to another person; (*verb*) to make inferior to. Noun: *subordination*

subpoena (Latin for "under penalty")—(*noun*) a legal document requiring a person to appear in a court to give testimony; (*verb*) to order or serve such a document

substratum (*sub* + *sternere, stratus* [Latin], "lie flat")—an underlying layer; the foundation or groundwork for something

subsume (*sub* + *sumere* [Latin], "take up")—to place in a more comprehensive category or under a more general heading

b. "Secondary in rank," as in these words:

subcommittee—a subordinate committee composed of some of the members of a larger committee

subculture—a distinct cultural group within the main culture

subdivide—to divide a part of something into smaller parts. Noun: *subdivision*

sublet—to rent property from someone who is himself or herself renting it from the owner

c. "Away" or "after," as in these words:

subdue (*sub*, "away" + *ducere, ductus* [Latin], "lead")—to conquer or defeat

subsequent (*sub*, "after" + *sequens, sequentis* [Latin], "following")—coming after something in time or position

d. "Down," as in these words:

subside (*sub* + *sidere* [Latin], "settle")—to sink, decrease, or abate

subsidy (*sub* + *sidere* [Latin], "settle")—financial assistance. Verb: *subsidize*

e. "Up from under," as in this word:

subsist (*sub* + *sistere* [Latin], "cause to stand")—to live or exist. (Note that this verb is often followed by the prepositions *on* or *by*.) Noun: *subsistance*

f. "Secretly," as in this word:

suborn (*sub* + *ornare* [Latin], "equip")—to induce a person to commit a wrong or illegal act. Noun: *subornation*

g. "Somewhat less than," as in these words:

subhuman—not fully human

subtropical—relating to areas adjacent to the tropics

Note that **sub** becomes **suc, suf, sug, sum, sup**, or **sur** before *c, f, g, m, p,* or *r,* respectively. **Sub** also sometimes becomes **sus** before *c, p,* or *t.* The process by which this happens is called *assimilation* (see page 57). Here are a few words illustrating these changes:

succumb (*sub*, "under" + *cumbere, cubitus* [Latin], "to lie under, give way, yield")—to yield or submit to; to give in to *suffice* (*sub*, "under" + *facere* [Latin], "do, make")—to meet present needs; to be equal to the intended task or function

suggest (*sub*, "underneath" + *gerere*, *gestus* [Latin], "carry")—to offer for consideration. Adjective: *suggestive*

summon (*sub*, "secretly" + *monere* [Latin], "warn, remind")—to send for or request. Noun: *summons*

supplant (*sub*, "up from under" + *planta* [Latin], "sole of the foot")—to take the place of; to oust

surreptitious (*sub*, "secretly" + *rapere* [Latin], "seize")—performed in secret or by stealth

susceptible (*sub*, "up from under" + *capere*, *captus* [Latin], "take")—readily subject to or influenced by. Noun: *susceptibility*

suspend (*sub*, "up from under" + *pendere* [Latin], "hang")—to hang up; to bar temporarily from a privilege or position

sustain (*sub*, "up from under" + *tenere* [Latin], "hold")—to maintain, support, or prolong; to affirm the validity of. Noun: *sustenance*

Roots

1.   The Latin root **ten** (also spelled **tain** and **tin**) means "hold." It is used in a number of common English words, including *tenable*, studied in this lesson. Here are a few more useful words in which it appears:

retain (*re* [Latin], "back" + *tenere* [Latin], "hold")—to keep or hold back; to keep in mind or remember. Adjective: *retentive*. Noun: *retention*

maintain (*manu* [Latin], "by hand" + *tenere* [Latin], "hold")—to carry on or continue; to preserve or keep up. Noun: *maintenance*

sustenance (*sub* [Latin], "up from under" + *tenere* [Latin], "hold")—support for life or health, especially food or a means of livelihood

tenacity (*tenacitas* [Latin], "perseverance")—persistence or perseverance. Adjective: *tenacious*

pertinent (*per* [Latin], "thoroughly" + *tenens*, *tenentis* [Latin], "holding")—relevant. Noun: *pertinency*. Verb: *pertain*

detain (*de* [Latin], "away" + *tenere* [Latin], "hold")—to delay; to hold in custody. Noun: *detention*

tenet (literally "he, she, or it holds")—a belief or doctrine held by a person or group

2.   The Latin root **tang**, **tact**, meaning "touch," is the source of the word *tangible*, studied in this lesson. Other useful English words in which this root appears are given below. As these words indicate, **tang**, **tact** has a number of variant forms, including **tig**, **tag**, **ting**, and **tain**.

tact (*tactus* [Latin], "sense of touch")—the ability to do or say the kindest or most appropriate thing. Adjectives: *tactful*, *tactless*

tactile (*tactus* [Latin], "sense of touch" + *ilis*, *ile* [Latin], "pertaining to")—perceptible to the sense of touch; used for feeling

tangent (*tangens*, *tangentis* [Latin], "touching")—a line touching but not intersecting another line. Phrase: *go off at* (or *on*) *a tangent tangential*—merely touching or only superficially connected with

contiguous (*cum* [Latin], "with" + *tangere* [Latin], "touch")—having the same edge or boundary as something else; adjacent. Noun: *contiguity*

contingent (*cum* [Latin], "with" + *tangens, tangentis* [Latin], "touching")—dependent on events or developments that have not yet occurred; possible. (Note that this adjective is often followed by the prepositions *on* or *upon*.) Noun: *contingency*

contagious (*cum* [Latin], "with" + *tangere* [Latin], "touch")—transmitted by direct contact. Noun: *contagion*

attain (*ad* [Latin], "to, as far as" + *tangere* [Latin], "touch, reach")—to gain, reach, or accomplish. Noun: *attainment*

Exercise

1. With or without the aid of a dictionary, define the following words using the Latin prefix *sub*, and explain what the prefix means in each.

   a. subjugate
   b. subsequent
   c. subdivide
   d. subsist
   e. suborn
   f. subpoena
   g. subtitle
   h. subsidy
   i. subhuman

2. With or without the aid of a dictionary, explain the meaning of each of the following phrases involving an *italicized* word derived from the Latin root *ten*.

   a. a *retentive* memory
   b. a *tenacious* grip
   c. have *tenure*
   d. a *retainer* fee

3. With or without the aid of a dictionary, define each of the following words using the Latin root *tang, tact* (or one of its variants).

   a. tactful
   b. attainment
   c. contagious
   d. tactile
   e. tangential
   f. contingency
   g. contiguous
   h. intangibles
   i. tactless

Walter W. Skeat

To Walter W. Skeat (1853–1912) goes the credit for creating a general interest in linguistics in both England and the United States. In 1878, Skeat became Professor of Anglo-Saxon at Cambridge, a post he retained for the rest of his life. His most important work was probably *The Etymological Dictionary of the English Language*, which first appeared in 1882. It has been said that Skeat contributed more to a sound knowledge of English linguistics than any other scholar of his time.

Working with Context Clues

Complete each of the following two-word omissions by selecting the pair of words that make the best sense in the passage as a whole. Underline the clue or clues.

1. Most dictators <u>don't speak reasonably or calmly</u> to their people; <u>instead</u> they _____ them. Far from creating a(n) _____ atmosphere, the dictator's words and manner usually <u>instill fear and anxiety</u>.

   a. instigate . . . urbane
   b. revere . . . turbulent
   c. harangue . . . tranquil
   d. deceive . . . blithe

2. Novels such as George Orwell's famous fable *1984*, written in 1949, dramatized the fear that an <u>ever-present</u> and <u>prying</u> central government, the _____ Big Brother, would _____ <u>every aspect</u> of a citizen's life.

   a. sordid . . . sabotage
   b. <u>ubiquitous . . . scrutinize</u>
   c. implacable . . . flaunt
   d. fatuous . . . exploit

3. I really appreciate the _____ that my grandmother <u>left me in her will</u>, and I intend to honor her _____ wish that I look after my younger brother, even though <u>she never made this request explicitly</u>.

   a. kudos . . . poignant
   b. retribution . . . strident
   c. propensity . . . mundane
   d. <u>legacy . . . tacit</u>

4. Many men who served in World War I suffered from a(n) _____ that was then called *shell shock*. Their <u>symptoms</u> were a result of the _____ events they experienced in the deadly trenches of France.

   a. anomaly . . . benign
   b. stereotype . . . drastic
   c. obsession . . . pernicious
   d. <u>syndrome . . . traumatic</u>

5. After the fall of Communism, <u>corruption and lawlessness</u> spread rapidly in Russia. In this _____ atmosphere, many ordinary citizens felt free to _____ the law.

   a. <u>venal . . . flout</u>
   b. secular . . . rescind
   c. precarious . . . revere
   d. mundane . . . thwart

6. Although there is often no _____ <u>monitoring of security</u> at many ATM sites, there is usually <u>hidden</u> electronic _____ by video camera.

   a. efficient . . . repercussion
   b. prodigious . . . medium
   c. <u>ostensible . . . surveillance</u>
   d. protracted . . . confrontation

7. In times of trouble or loss, a <u>comforting</u> phone call from a friend can be a <u>very concrete</u> source of _____. At such times, we need _____ signs that we are loved.

   a. <u>solace . . . tangible</u>
   b. remorse . . . ostensible
   c. empathy . . . esoteric
   d. anarchy . . . fulsome

493

8. In order to avoid a —————— between the conservatives and the liberals, the party leader proposed a —————— agreement that he firmly believed would <u>buy time</u> and avoid a <u>lasting split</u>.

   a. boycott . . . strategic   c. scapegoat . . . feasible
   b. schism . . . tentative   d. recrimination . . . graphic

9. When <u>developing a marketing plan</u>, executives want a —————— that will not only <u>promote</u> sales of their products but will also —————— their competitors' plans.

   a. paradox . . . stipulate   c. consensus . . . abet
   b. strategy . . . thwart   d. discourse . . . discomfit

10. Although my uncle was a(n) —————— man who <u>spoke very little in company</u>, he was a(n) —————— letter writer, often producing as many as <u>ten lengthy letters</u> a day. Curiously, most of these letters were addressed to friends and acquaintances with whom he would rarely share more than a word or two in public.

   a. urbane . . . agile   c. affable . . . diligent
   b. tranquil . . . dilatory   d. taciturn . . . prolific

Enriching the Lesson

Exercise I.   Is There a Doctor in the House?

The word *trauma*, discussed in this lesson, now has a wide range of applications, but its first use was in medical science. This is just one example of how medical terminology yields words of general application to enrich and enlarge the vocabulary resources of English. A few other words of this type are listed below. With or without the aid of a dictionary, define each, and give its etymology.

1. diagnosis	6. convalescence	11. fatal
2. symptom	7. psychosomatic	12. prognosis
3. therapy	8. organic	13. inoculate
4. pathology	9. epidemic	14. hysteria
5. aggravate	10. debilitate	15. cancerous

   Now complete each of the following sentences by selecting the right word from the list of words given above.

1. My point is that if we borrow money to meet our immediate obligations, we will only _aggravate_ our long-range problems.

2. His style of oratory, which you evidently admire so much, seems to depend on building up emotion to the point of _hysteria_.

3. The crisis has been overcome; the immediate danger is past. Now begins the long period of _convalescence_.

4. It is our collective task in the years ahead to clear the social organism of the cancerous growth of racial, ethnic, and religious prejudice.

5. This neighborhood has been going downhill rapidly, and it shows all the symptoms of developing into a full-fledged slum.

6. It is difficult to predict how such a simple and isolated society will react to a(n) epidemic of ideas and resources from the outside world.

Exercise II.   Some Tricky Words

Some English words are very deceptive. They seem to mean one thing but actually mean something else. Anyone, therefore, trying to guess at their proper meaning on the basis of their appearance is likely to go far afield.

Below is a list of such tricky words that merit your close attention. First indicate what you think each of these words means, based on the way it looks. Then, with or without the aid of a dictionary, define each. Finally, choose any **five** of the words, and for each compose an original illustrative sentence.

1. scarify	6. fulsome	11. adventitious
2. histrionic	7. enjoin	12. momentum
3. quizzical	8. officious	13. egress
4. noisome	9. contentious	14. bombination
5. querulous	10. meretricious	15. irenic

Exercise III.   Expanding Your Word Power

The words listed below are not on the Basic Word List, but they were mentioned in passing in one form or another, in Lesson 29. All of them would make useful additions to your working vocabulary. Define each, give its etymology, list **two** synonyms and **two** antonyms (where possible), and use in an original illustrative sentence.

1. provisional	6. neutralize	11. omnipresent
2. voluble	7. serene	12. cosmopolitan
3. palpable	8. raucous	13. arrogate
4. irrefutable	9. inspiration	14. crotchet
5. interim	10. mordant	15. upright

Lesson 30

---

386. ve‑neer   *noun and verb*   və‑nēr′

[*Furnier* (German), "veneer"; from *fournir* (French), "furnish"]

Definition:

a. (*noun*) A thin layer of fine material put on the surface of something in order to make it more attractive or cover defects; a deceptively attractive outward appearance.

The table was made of inexpensive pine that had been covered with a thin **veneer** of fine walnut.

Beneath the **veneer** of kindness and concern, I recognized the amoral opportunist I had known so long ago.

b. (*verb*) To cover something with a veneer of fine material.

Aluminum siding is one of the most popular materials with which Americans **veneer** their houses.

Synonyms: (*nouns*) facing, facade, coating, gloss, sheen, overlay, varnish, lacquer, glaze; (*verbs*) overlay, laminate, whitewash, glaze, gild; mask, screen

Related Phrases: a false facade, a false front

---

387. ven‑er‑a‑ble   *adjective*   věn′‑ẽr‑ə‑bəl

[*venerabilis, venerabile* (Latin), "revered"; from *venerari, veneratus* (Latin), "revere" + *abilis, abile* (Latin), "able to"]

Definition: Worthy of reverence or respect because of character, position, age, or religious or historical associations.

Though he had retired from public life many years before, the **venerable** old statesman was still consulted on matters of national concern.

I am glad to see that yet another **venerable** old building in this city has been declared a landmark.

"The **venerable** oak trees that line the broad avenue to the big house," the guide said, "have seen a good deal of Southern history played out beneath them."

Related Forms: (*nouns*) venerableness, venerability, veneration; (*verb*) venerate

Usage Note:

Venerable is used as a title of respect for anyone who has achieved the first degree of sainthood in the Roman Catholic Church—for example, the *Venerable* Bede.

Synonyms: (*adjectives*) time-honored, revered, esteemed, august, eminent, hallowed, hoary

Antonyms: (*adjectives*) spurned, scorned, reviled

Related Phrases: as old as the hills, hallowed ground, hallowed halls, an elder statesman

The Venerable Bede

One of the most important historians of the Old English period was a Benedictine monk whom we now call the Venerable Bede (672?–735). Bede spent the whole of his adult life in the monasteries of Wearmouth and Jarrow in northern England. One of the most learned men of his time, he wrote treatises on all sorts of theological, historical, and scientific subjects. His most famous work is *The Ecclesiastical History of the English Nation*. Originally written in Latin but soon translated into Old English, this book contains a full and reliable account of the growth of Christianity in England and the flowering of Anglo-Saxon culture. It is still an indispensable source for the history of England between 597 and 731. Bede was named a Doctor of the Church in 1899.

388. ve-rac-i-ty   *noun*   və-răs'-ə-tē
[*veracitas* (Medieval Latin), "truth"; from *verus* (Latin), "true"]

Definition: Habitual adherence to the truth; accuracy.

My judgment may be open to question, but I have told you the facts as I know them, so you have no reason to doubt my **veracity**.

The 18th-century English poet Thomas Gray once wrote that any fool could compose a valuable book if he would only put down what he had heard or seen with **veracity**.

Phrases: unshakable veracity, the veracity of a witness

Related Forms: (*adjective*) veracious; (*noun*) veraciousness

Synonyms: (*nouns*) truthfulness, honesty, integrity, reliability, credibility; authenticity, genuineness

Antonyms: (*nouns*) dishonesty, falsity, spuriousness, deceptiveness; untrustworthiness

Related Phrase: in vino veritas

389. **ver-sa-tile** *adjective* vûr′-sə-təl *or* vûr′-sə-tīl

[*versatilis, versatile* (Latin), "revolving"; from *versare* (Latin), "turn" + *abilis, abile* (Latin), "able to"]

Definition: Capable of doing many things or serving many functions.

A truly **versatile** actor or actress is at home in many different types of theater, from tragedy and drama to comedy and farce.

"This company produces a **versatile** line of products designed for a wide range of uses in the home and office," the president of the corporation boasted.

Phrases: a versatile player, a versatile speaker, a versatile painter, a versatile garment, a versatile material

Related Forms: (*nouns*) versatility, versatileness

Synonyms: (*adjectives*) all-around, all-purpose, many-sided, multipurpose; flexible, adaptable, resourceful

Antonyms: (*adjectives*) single-purpose; unadaptable, unresourceful

Related Phrases: all-purpose flour, an all-around athlete, all-purpose wear, a utility infielder

390. **ve-to** *noun and verb* vē′-tō

[*veto* (Latin), "I forbid"; from *vetare* (Latin), "forbid"]

Definition:

a. (*noun*) The right or power of the chief executive to reject measures approved by the legislative body; any authoritative prohibition.

"Even if the legislation is approved by both houses of Congress," the senator observed, "a presidential **veto** is sure to prevent it from becoming law."

The principal's **veto** put a quick end to student council plans to eliminate the school dress code.

b. (*verb*) To prevent a bill from becoming law by exercising the right of veto; to prohibit or reject.

Though the British monarch still possesses the power to **veto** bills passed by Parliament, no king or queen has actually exercised the right since the reign of Queen Anne (1702–1714).

I had planned to travel across the country this summer, but my parents **vetoed** the idea.

Phrases: a pocket veto, the veto power, a veto message

Synonyms: (*nouns*) rejection, refusal, interdiction; (*verbs*) kill, quash, turn down, forbid, interdict, rule out

Antonyms: (*nouns*) approval, consent, sanction; (*verbs*) approve, ratify, sanction

Related Phrases: turn thumbs down to, say nix to; give something one's blessing, give something the green light (*or* go-ahead)

An American president signs a bill into law. The president has the right to veto legislation passed by Congress and return it (with a statement of his or her objections) to the house in which it originated. The bill can then be repassed over the president's veto by a two-thirds vote of both houses of Congress.

391. vie   *verb*   vī

[*envier* (Old French), "challenge"; from *invitare* (Latin), "invite"]

Definition: To struggle for superiority with; to contend with.

Having recovered from a crushing defeat in World War II, Japan went on to **vie** with the world's leading manufacturing countries for dominance in the electronics and automobile markets.

Three teams are now **vying** with one another for possession of first place in the American League East.

Synonyms: (*verbs*) compete, contest

Related Phrases: neck and neck; nolo contendere

392. vin-dic-tive   *adjective*   vĭn-dĭk'-tĭv

[*vindicta* (Latin), "vengeance" + *ivus*, a Latin suffix roughly meaning "tending toward" or "performing"]

Definition: Inclined to seek revenge; intended to inflict pain or harm.

Though I am by no means a **vindictive** person, I sometimes find it very difficult not to retaliate for a particularly nasty insult.

Related Forms: (*noun*) vindictiveness; (*adverb*) vindictively

Synonyms: (*adjectives*) vengeful, revengeful, retaliatory, malevolent, spiteful, hostile

Antonyms: (*adjectives*) magnanimous, forgiving, conciliatory

Related Phrases: bear a grudge; bury the hatchet, let bygones be bygones

393. **vi-ti-ate**   *verb*   vĭsh'-ē-āt

[*vitiare, vitiatus* (Latin), "injure"; from *vitium* (Latin), "defect, flaw"]

Definition: To impair the quality, force, or value of; to debase.

Even though the effect of the article was somewhat **vitiated** by erroneous statistics and garbled quotations, the point it was making was sound.

"Be careful," the elder statesman told the would-be presidential candidate. "Every time you make a wrong choice or take a questionable stand, you **vitiate** your influence in the party."

Related Form: (*noun*) vitiation

Synonyms: (*verbs*) mar, poison, taint, contaminate, reduce, lower, lessen, weaken, depreciate, dilute, tarnish

Antonyms: (*verbs*) strengthen, buttress (Word 73), bolster, reinforce, promote, brace

Related Phrase: feet of clay

Feet of Clay

One of the most interesting expressions that present-day English has derived from the Bible is *feet of clay*. The expression comes from the Old Testament Book of Daniel. Nebuchadnezzar II, the conqueror-king of Babylon from 605 to 562 B.C., was troubled by a bad dream in which he saw a statue of himself. The Bible describes this statue as follows: "This image's head was of fine gold, its chest and arms of silver, its stomach and thighs of brass, its legs of iron, and its feet partly of iron and partly of clay." In the dream, a stone thrown by some unseen supernatural force (*i.e.*, God) hits the feet of the statue and causes it to collapse and smash to smithereens on the pavement. Daniel explains that this is a vision of the eventual destruction of Nebuchadnezzar's kingdom as the result of some fatal flaw (the feet of clay) in one of his successors. By extension, the expression *feet of clay* has now come to mean "*any* fatal personal flaw that proves to be a person's undoing."

394. vol-a-tile   *adjective*   vŏl'-ə-təl

[*volare, volatus* (Latin), "fly" + *ilis, ile* (Latin), "tending to"]

Definition:

    a. Evaporating readily at normal temperatures or pressure levels.

         Gases such as argon and helium are not very active chemically, but ammonia is extremely **volatile**.

    b. Changeable and potentially explosive.

         "I feel as though we're sitting on a powder keg," the diplomat confessed in reference to the **volatile** situation in that troubled area of the world.

         I think that "having a short fuse" aptly describes his **volatile** temperament.

Related Forms: (*nouns*) volatility, volatileness

Synonyms: (*adjectives*) volcanic, heated, supercharged; mercurial, erratic

Antonyms: (*adjectives*) stable, static, constant, settled; stagnant, torpid, sluggish, inert, quiescent, dormant; phlegmatic

Related Phrases: a short fuse, a hot spot

395. wane   *verb and noun*   wān

[*wanen* (Middle English), "decrease"; from *wanian* (Old English), "diminish"]

Definition:

    a. (*verb*) To decrease gradually in size, extent, power, or intensity.

         During the 19th century it was literally true that the sun did not set nor the full moon **wane** on the British Empire.

         As their infatuation with one another **waned**, they found themselves making excuses for not getting together as often as before.

    b. (*noun*) A gradual decline or decrease.

         "If the president's popularity continues on the **wane**," the senator remarked, "he may well lose the next election."

Usage Note:

Be careful not to confuse the verb *wane* with the adjective *wan* (pronounced wŏn), which means "pale or colorless." Two other words with which *wane* is sometimes confused are *wain* (a large heavy cart used in farming) and *vane* (a device for showing the direction of the wind).

Synonyms: (*verbs*) slacken, subside, dim, diminish, abate, taper off, ebb, fade, peter out, dwindle; (*nouns*) diminution, weakening, falloff, fading

Antonyms: (*verbs*) wax, increase, intensify, grow, swell, mushroom, expand, augment; (*nouns*) increase, augmentation, growth, expansion, increment, addition, accretion

Related Phrases: an ebb tide, a recessional

396. **wrath**   *noun*   răth

[*wraeththu* (Old English), "anger"; from *wrath* (Old English), "angry"]

Definition: Intense anger.

"My father's **wrath** will know no bounds when he sees the damage I have done to the family car," Shelly moaned.

In a blistering tirade, the old prophet called down the **wrath** of God on those who had offended against His laws.

The easternmost tip of Cuba was the first populated area to feel the **wrath** of the hurricane.

Related Forms: (*adjective*) wrathful; (*noun*) wrathfulness

Usage Note:
Be careful not to confuse the noun *wrath* with its look-alike *wraith* (pronounced rāth), which means "a specter or apparition."

Synonyms: (*nouns*) rage, fury, indignation, ire, choler, spleen

Antonyms: (*nouns*) favor, blessing, approval, pleasure

Related Phrase: in high dudgeon

397. **yoke**   *noun and verb*   yōk

[*geoc* (Old English), "yoke"]

Definition:
   a.   (*noun*) A wooden frame joining a pair of oxen or other draft animals together at the neck; any form or symbol of bondage or subjection.

   The barn had been turned into a museum of all kinds of old-fashioned implements and devices used in farming, including flails, **yokes**, and other interesting items.

   In 1776, the 13 American colonies cast off their **yoke** of subjection and declared themselves free and independent of Great Britain.

   b.   (*verb*) To join or bond together.

   Many of the pioneers crossed the Great Plains in Conestoga wagons drawn by pairs of oxen **yoked** together at the neck.

   A remarkable collaboration in the composition of light operas and other kinds of musical entertainments has forever **yoked** the names *Gilbert* and *Sullivan*.

Phrases: a yoke of oxen, the yoke of oppression

Usage Note:
In the phrase *a yoke of oxen*, sometimes encountered in older literature, the word *yoke* means "pair."

Synonyms: (*nouns*) harness, collar, oxbow; (*verbs*) hitch, link, harness, couple, unite

Antonyms: (*verbs*) sunder, separate, disconnect, dissociate, detach, split, divide

Conestoga wagons drawn by yokes of oxen brought the early pioneers into the fertile farmlands of the Great Plains.

398. **zany**   *noun and adjective*   zā'-nē

[*zanni* (Italian), "buffoon," a variant of *Gianni* (Italian), "Johnny," the pet form of *Giovanni* (Italian), "John," the name of the clownish servant in early Italian comedies]

Definition:

   a. (*noun*) A comical person given to outlandish behavior; a buffoon.

      It disturbed me to watch a person of such taste and intelligence assuming the role of a vulgar **zany**.

   b. (*adjective*) Ludicrously comic, bizarre, or absurd.

      I still enjoy watching the **zany** antics of old-time movie clowns such as the Marx Brothers or Abbott and Costello.

      Whenever a party starts to get dull, you can count on their **zany** behavior to liven things up.

Related Form: (*noun*) zaniness

Synonyms: (*nouns*) clown, fool, prankster; (*adjectives*) ridiculous, laughable, hilarious, ludicrous, inane; wacky, goofy, loony

Antonyms: (*adjectives*) sensible, serious, proper, staid, sober

Related Phrases: play the fool; high jinks; a straight man

399. **zeal**   *noun*   zēl

[*zelos* (Greek), "fervor, enthusiasm"]

Definition: Enthusiastic devotion to something; fervor.

"In our **zeal** to improve the quality of life in the United States," the speaker declared, "let us not blindly discard old ideas and institutions simply because they are old."

Related Forms: (*nouns*) zealot, zealotry; (*adjective*) zealous; (*adverb*) zealously

Synonyms: (*nouns*) ardor, gusto, eagerness, passion, intensity, alacrity, vigor, enthusiasm, relish, keenness, rapture, ecstasy

Antonyms: (*nouns*) apathy (Word 32), indifference, listlessness, uncon-cern, nonchalance

Related Phrase: gung ho

Masada

Zealot

The Zealots were a group of fervently devout Jews who organized themselves into a sort of political party or action group during the reign of Herod the Great, King of Judaea (37–4 B.C.). They derived their name from their unswerving devotion to orthodox Judaism as prescribed by the Torah, the scroll containing the first five books of the Bible. (The Torah was used for instruction during services at a synagogue.) The Zealots opposed the secularizing tendencies of Herod and other contemporary Jewish leaders. They also detested the Romans, who controlled Palestine at the time, and frequently caused minor revolts and other problems for them. After a large-scale Jewish revolt was put down in A.D. 70, a group of Zealots fled to Masada, a fortress atop an impregnable rock formation overlooking the Dead Sea. There they held out against the Romans for several years. When the Romans were on the point of taking the place, the Zealots chose to kill themselves rather than submit to the hated foreign overlords. It is from the activities of this 1st-century religious group that present-day English has derived the word *zealot*, meaning "anyone excessively or fanatically committed to some cause, idea, or belief."

400. **ze·nith**   *noun*   zē'-nĭth

[*zenit* (Old Spanish), "apex"; from *samt ar-ra's* (Arabic), "way over the head"]

Definition:
  a. The point of a celestial sphere that is directly above the observer and vertically opposite the extreme point below.

> We knew that it was close to noon because the sun was almost at its **zenith**.

  b. The highest point or state of something.

> Historians agree that Rome reached the **zenith** of her power during the reigns of the "Five Good Emperors" in the 2nd century of the Christian era.

> "If I am indeed at the **zenith** of my creative powers now," the world-famous author ruefully thought to himself, "there is no place for me to go from here but down."

Synonyms: (*nouns*) summit, apex, apogee, peak, acme, culmination, climax, pinnacle

Antonyms: (*nouns*) nadir, perigee

Using the Words

Exercise I.   Parts of Speech

Indicate the part of speech of each of the following words. In some cases, two answers are correct.

1. veneer n., v.
2. veracity n.
3. versatile adj.
4. veto n., v.
5. vie v.
6. vindictive adj.
7. volatile adj.
8. wane v., n.
9. zany n., adj.

Exercise II.   Words in Phrases

In each of the following, select the item that best expresses the meaning of the *italicized* word in the introductory phrase.

1. a *veneer* of respectability
    <u>facade</u> b. wealth c. goal d. lack e. history

2. a *vindictive* attitude
    a. puzzling b. foolish c. healthy d. modern
    <u>e. spiteful</u>

3. a very *volatile* situation
    a. heartwarming <u>b. explosive</u> c. curious d. ordinary
    e. stable

4. *vitiate* the effect of the speech
    a. analyze b. confirm <u>c. impair</u> d. measure
    e. assess

5. a *yoke* around their necks
   a. jewel   **b. oxbow**   c. medal   d. sign   e. scarf

6. a *zany* thing to do
   a. sensible   b. costly   c. sad   **d. ridiculous**   e. thoughtful

7. the *zeal* of her followers
   a. fervor   b. age   c. intelligence   d. background
   e. number

Exercise III.   Completing Sentences

Complete each of the following sentences by selecting the appropriate word from the group of words given below. Use each word only once.

zenith	vie	veracity
veto	venerable	yoke
wane	versatile	wrath

1. Toward the end of his life the champion wrestler's fabulous strength ___waned___ to the point where he could hardly walk.

2. All through high school, Laura and Peter ___vied___ energetically for first place in their class.

3. "Only a trial in a court of law can establish the ___veracity___ of the charges leveled at my client," the lawyer remarked.

4. A utility infielder has to be a ___versatile___ player because he is a jack-of-all-trades on the baseball diamond.

5. Though Spain had been at the ___zenith___ of her power during the 16th century, the 17th century saw the beginning of a long, slow decline in the country's fortunes.

6. The school I went to was a ___venerable___ old institution with a long and cherished history of outstanding accomplishment in the field of secondary education.

7. The countless religious ceremonies that the ancient Romans performed during the year were designed to gain the favor of the gods and turn away their ___wrath___.

8. "The president is still trying to decide whether to sign or ___veto___ that bill," the aide reported.

Exercise IV.   Synonyms and Antonyms

A. In each of the following groups, select the **two** words that are most nearly **synonymous**.

1. **a. hallowed**   b. emaciated   **c. revered**   d. dilapidated   venerable

2. **a. equitable**   **b. flexible**   c. culpable   **d. adaptable**   versatile

506

3. **a.** complain **b. compete** **c. contend** **d.** confer   vie
4. **a. mar** **b.** collect **c.** repeal **d. impair**   vitiate
5. **a. rage** **b. fury** **c.** terror **d.** delight   wrath

Now, for each pair of synonyms you have selected, supply a word from the Basic Word List for this lesson (Words 386–400) that means **the same** or **almost the same** thing.

B. In each of the following, select the item that is most nearly **opposite** in meaning to the numbered word at the left.

1. veto   **a.** boycott **b. sanction** **c.** permeate
                d. compete **e.** rescind

2. veracity   **a.** antiquity **b.** immunity **c.** sincerity
                d. equanimity **e. falsity**

3. wane   **a.** buff **b.** polish **c. wax** **d.** varnish
                e. glaze

4. zany   **a.** obvious **b.** weird **c.** expensive **d. sensible**
                e. ruthless

5. zenith   **a. nadir** **b.** anathema **c.** kudos **d.** plethora
                e. consensus

Exercise V.   Word Roundup

1. Explain the difference in meaning between the words in each of the following pairs:

   a. wan—wane   **b.** wrath—wraith

2. What is *a pocket veto*?

3. Who were the *Zealots*, and how are they connected with the present-day meaning of the word *zealot*?

4. With or without the aid of a dictionary or other reference book, define each of the following:

   a. a hot spot   **d.** an ebb tide
   b. a recessional   **e.** a short fuse
   c. high jinks   **f.** an elder statesman

5. With or without the aid of a dictionary or other reference book, explain what each of the following means:

   a. in high dudgeon **b.** neck and neck   **c.** gung ho

6. With or without the aid of a dictionary or other reference book, explain the meaning of each of the following colorful expressions:

   a. bear a grudge against   **d.** play the fool
   b. turn thumbs down to   **e.** feet of clay
   c. bury the hatchet   **f.** give something the green
                                      light

Exercise VI.   Framing Sentences

A. Use each of the following words in an original sentence.

1. veneer
2. venerable
3. veto
4. vie
5. vitiate
6. wane
7. yoke
8. zany
9. zealous

B. Give a **noun** form of each of these words, and use it in an original illustrative sentence.

1. **versatile**   2. **vindictive**   3. **volatile**
   versatility, versatileness   vindictiveness   volatility, volatileness

C. Give an **adjective** form of each of these words, and use it in an original illustrative sentence.

1. **veracity** veracious   2. **wrath** wrathful   3. **zeal** zealous

Completing Verbal Analogies

Complete the following analogies.

Group A

1. **lawyer : legal** =
   a. nautical : naval
   b. policeman : criminal
   c. athlete : intellectual
   d. chef : culinary
   e. wraith : wrath

2. **deluge : water** =
   a. avalanche : wind
   b. holocaust : fire
   c. hurricane : ice
   d. snow : tornado
   e. blizzard : air

3. **sponge : impervious** =
   a. glass : brittle
   b. wall : rigid
   c. umbrella : porous
   d. belt : pliable
   e. circuitous : detour

4. **sword : brandish** =
   a. string : kite
   b. flag : wave
   c. inflate : deflate
   d. airplane : train
   e. unfurl : banner

5. **malevolent : unfavorable** =
   a. deft : favorable
   b. undaunted : unfavorable
   c. unfavorable : officious
   d. ominous : favorable
   e. scrupulous : unfavorable

Group B

6. **pinnacle : high** ::
   a. strait : wide
   b. plateau : steep
   c. haven : level
   d. abyss : deep
   e. flat : mountain

7. **bear : hibernate ::**
   a. horse : mare
   b. yoke : ox
   c. scavenger : jackal
   d. cow : ruminate
   e. camel : giraffe

8. **fathom : depth ::**
   a. width : meter
   b. bushel : height
   c. knot : speed
   d. inch : yard
   e. length : breadth

9. **small : infinitesimal ::**
   a. large : small
   b. poor : beggar
   c. big : colossal
   d. wide : deep
   e. mansion : opulent

10. **poignant : sadden ::**
    a. nondescript : whet
    b. droll : amuse
    c. frighten : zany
    d. comfort : solace
    e. innocuous : appall

Working with Context Clues

Complete each of the following two-word omissions by selecting the pair of words that make the best sense in the passage as a whole. If necessary, consult a dictionary for the meaning of any word with which you are not familiar. Underline the clue or clues that led you to choose your answer.

1. On the surface, some actors may appear very breezy and _____ but behind the carefree _____, they may actually be so insecure that they must always pretend to be someone other than who they are.

   a. blithe . . . veneer
   b. bland . . . affectation
   c. effete . . . effrontery
   d. benign . . . duplicity

2. In their summations, the prosecuting and defense attorneys _____ for the minds of the jury. They compete to make their final arguments as _____ as possible, hoping to compel the jury to come up with a verdict in favor of their client through the force of their reasoning and evidence.

   a. vie . . . trenchant
   b. collaborate . . . cogent
   c. persevere . . . nebulous
   d. ruminate . . . sanguine

3. In Shakespeare's plays, there is often a parallel between what is happening in nature and in society. For example, the heavens grow _____ when the social order is disturbed by ambitious upstarts who are trying to _____ legitimate authority.

   a. tranquil . . . justify
   b. lucid . . . discomfit
   c. bleak . . . circumvent
   d. turbulent . . . usurp

4. One afteceffect of parents losing their tempers is that children learn fear but not self-control. Parents who wish to avoid that unfortunate _____ should try to control their own _____.

   a. irony . . . zeal
   b. repercussion . . . wrath
   c. nuance . . . prowess
   d. exigency . . . malice

5. In their eagerness to appear upright and moral, some politicians come across as _____, especially when their newfound-piety begins to _____ right after election day.

   a. fatuous . . . augment
   b. boorish . . . deviate
   c. sanctimonious . . . wane
   d. fulsome . . . fluctuate

6. Some Communists were so fired up with enthusiasm for their atheistic doctrine that they destroyed church property and mistreated members of the clergy. It was their revolutionary _____ that led them to commit such _____ acts.

   a. obsession . . . predatory
   b. reprisal . . . brash
   c. zeal . . . sacrilegious
   d. addiction . . . volatile

7. A jury would probably doubt the _____ of a witness who had been convicted of lying under oath. They might reason that a person willing to _____ himself once was capable of lying again.

   a. plagiarism . . . embarrass
   b. veracity . . . perjure
   c. duplicity . . . censure
   d. equanimity . . . curtail

8. Those who ponder endlessly over every decision are bound to _____ their energy and sap their ability to act. Their tendency to _____ paralyzes rather than empowers them.

   a. flaunt . . . defer
   b. propitiate . . . persevere
   c. vitiate . . . ruminate
   d. usurp . . . relent

9. A(n) _____ personality such as Shakespeare's Iago never lets go of an injury or an insult until he retaliates, and often the _____ is more harmful and cruel than the original injury.

   a. eminent . . . repercussion
   b. vindictive . . . reprisal
   c. exemplary . . . bravado
   d. formidable . . . malice

10. It is a basic legal principle that one party to a contract cannot cancel its provisions. On the contrary, all parties must agree to _____ the terms of a contract before this _____ of contract law can be set aside.

    a. rescind . . . rudiment
    b. arbitrate . . . vagary
    c. stipulate . . . strategy
    d. promulgate . . . yoke

Enriching the Lesson

Exercise I.   Misusing Words: A Look Back

In earlier lessons we have referred to various ways of using language that are usually considered weak or ineffective, even if they are not flatly wrong. These language flaws may be classified under the following headings:

Clichés (= **C**)
Malapropisms (= **M**)
Euphemisms (= **E**)
Inappropriate Connotation (= **I**)
Gobbledygook (= **G**)

At this point, you will do well to review the sections in which these concepts are analyzed and illustrated. You will note that most of these flaws are matters of *degree*. For example, it would be extremely difficult to avoid clichés entirely, and there is no point in attempting to do so; but a piece of writing that is saturated with clichés is likely to be weak, boring, and even ridiculous. Similarly, a limited amount of euphemism in speech or writing may serve a good purpose; but beyond a certain point, it almost always turns sour.

When you are confident that you have refreshed your recollection of these ideas, do the following exercise.

Each of the following sentences illustrates one of the language flaws listed above. Apply the correct identifying letter in each case. Then try your hand at rephrasing each statement in more acceptable form. (In some cases, you may be able to fit a sentence into more than one category. This really doesn't make too much difference, as long as you see what has gone wrong.)

1. *From a furniture store advertisement:* We sell the <u>cheapest</u> furniture in town. **I**

2. *Sign in government office:* Illumination by electrical facilities is hereby required to be extinguished on these premises promptly upon the termination of daily activities prior to the vacating of the area. **G**

3. We were all required to take cover during the stimulated air raid. **M**

4. What a terrific bed! No sooner had I <u>hit the hay</u> than I was in <u>the arms of Morpheus</u>, and I <u>slept like a top</u> all night. **C**

5. Alaska and Rhode Island are <u>respectfully</u> the largest and smallest of the 50 states. **M**

6. He is world famous as an interpreter of Bach's music and as an organ <u>freak</u>. **I**

7. Receiving the full weight of the enemy attack, the troops of the 5th Division broke and <u>scampered</u> to the rear at full speed. **I**

8. It is the established policy of this company to extend full cooperation to its employees in assisting them to qualify for more responsible positions within the existing organizational framework of the enterprise. **G**

9. When I saw that the doors were open, I made a <u>bee dive</u> for the exit. **M**

10. The Nazis attempted to solve their minority problems by <u>a policy of selective elimination of population elements considered undesirable</u>. **E**, possibly **G**

11. Dr. Bellman is considered an outstanding <u>maven</u> in the field of cancer research. **I**

12. With her exquisite features, magnificent eyes, flawless complexion, and long, golden hair, she was perhaps the <u>cutest</u> girl I have ever seen. **I**

13. Having made <u>every mistake in the book</u>, I found myself <u>behind the well-known eight ball</u> and was <u>in the depths of despair</u>. **C**

14. Is it any wonder that the country is in trouble when the administration has <u>flaunted</u> all the laws of sound financial management! **M**

15. We <u>worked like dogs</u> to make our <u>social function a rousing success</u>. **C**, also **E** (social function)

16. At this point in time, we hope to finalize the agreement, with full confidence that profits will be maximized and that the bottom line will be a source of satisfaction to all concerned. **G**

17. Our <u>gridiron heroes looked none the worse for wear</u> after a grueling workout in preparation for the <u>annual classic</u> against State. **C**

Exercise II.   Expanding Your Word Power

The words listed below are not on the Basic Word List, but they were mentioned in passing, in one form or another, in Lesson 30. All of them would make useful additions to your working vocabulary. Define each, give its etymology, list **two** synonyms and **two** antonyms (where possible), and use in an original illustrative sentence.

1. facade	6. ire	11. dilute
2. august	7. spiteful	12. nadir
3. deceptive	8. taint	13. hoary
4. resourceful	9. static	14. detach
5. interdict	10. increment	15. ecstasy

Related Forms in Context

Beneath each sentence below are four words introduced in Lesson 29 or 30. Review the related forms for these words, and choose the one that best completes the sentence. Write that related form in the space provided.

1. In Greek mythology, Cerberus, a three-headed dog with a serpent's tail, _zealously_ guards the gate of the Underworld to keep out all who have not yet died.

   a. veracity b. zany c. zeal d. zenith

2. It is difficult to have a lengthy conversation with Len because his _taciturnity_ often makes others feel uncomfortable.

   a. tacit b. taciturn c. traumatic d. trenchant

3. The boy had cried "Wolf!" so many times when there was no wolf that the townspeople, doubting his _____, ignored his cries when the wolf finally did appear. veraciousness

   a. vagary b. wrath c. zeal d. veracity

4. We howled at the _zaniness_ of the Marx Brothers' 1935 comedy *A Night at the Opera*, especially the scene in which dozens of people crammed into a tiny stateroom.

   a. wrath b. zeal c. zany d. veracity

5. Cindy's letter to the editor is a _wrathful_ protest against the city council's cancellation of after-school tutoring and sports at the community center.

   a. veto b. wrath c. zany d. vagary

6. The naturalist shot a _tranquilizer_ dart deep into the grizzly bear's shoulder so that the sedated animal could be transported by truck far from the populated areas of the park.

   a. tranquil b. tangible c. tenable d. tentative

7. With just a slight nod of his head, the man wearing the red tie _tacitly_ indicated to the auctioneer that he was raising his bid.

   a. tacit b. tangible c. trenchant d. venerable

8. Leora was so _traumatized_ by being taken on a roller coaster when she was a small child that she still refuses to go on any amusement park rides.

   a. ubiquitous b. tranquil c. traumatic d. vindictive

9. My friend and I _tentatively_ plan to go out to dinner once a month.

   a. tangible b. tentative c. taciturn d. trenchant

513

10. After only a dozen moves, Larry could see that White's position was ___untenable___ and predicted that White would resign in two moves.

    a. tacit b. tangible c. vindictive __d. tenable__

11. The flyer says: "Anyone with information leading to the return of a female golden retriever answering to the name of Lady will be thanked from the bottom of our hearts and ___tangibly___ rewarded, too."

    a. taciturn b. turbulent __c. tangible__ d. trenchant

12. In *As You Like It*, Shakespeare ___trenchantly___ summarizes the human life cycle—for women as well as men—in Jacques's speech about "the seven ages of man."

    __a. trenchant__ b. ubiquitous c. venal d. volatile

13. Because everyone feared the captain's ___vindictiveness___, no one dared to disobey his orders.

    a. volatile b. venerable __c. vindictive__ d. versatile

14. Pilots know that wind shear—changes in the wind's speed or direction (or both) where cold and warm air meet—is a major cause of ___turbulence___ during flight.

    a. taciturn b. tangible __c. turbulent__ d. versatile

15. The ___ubiquitousness___ of fast-food, gas, and retail chains makes every commercial street and shopping mall in America look basically the same.

    a. volatile __b. ubiquitous__ c. venerable d. trenchant

16. Dave's love of Chinese cooking led him to a lifelong ___veneration___ of Chinese art, literature, movies, and music.

    __a. venerable__ b. tranquil c. tentative d. tangible

17. Dressed in his finest, with Judy Garland on his arm, Fred Astaire ___urbanely___ tips his hat to elegantly clad passersby in the finale of the classic movie *Easter Parade*.

    a. turbulent b. trenchant c. tacit __d. urbane__

18. Switch-hitters, who can bat both right- and left-handed, are greatly valued for their ___versatility___ and their ability to hit against right- and left-handed pitchers.

    a. tangible b. turbulent c. venerable __d. versatile__

19. In the final scene, the ___usurper___ places the crown on his head and slowly ascends the steps to the throne.

    a. thwart __b. usurp__ c. vitiate d. vie

20. Since the Hindenburg disaster in 1937, hydrogen has not been used to fill blimps and other lighter-than-air craft because of its extreme ___volatility___.

    a. vindictive b. venerable c. ubiquitous __d. volatile__

514

Review

251. **kudos** — 400. **zenith**

Exercise I
1. leg'-a-cy
2. mer'-ce-nar-y
3. nep'-o-tism
4. os-ten'-si-ble
5. per'-me-ate
6. pre-co'-cious
7. pro-pi'-ti-ate
8. re-dun'-dant
9. re-sil'-ient
10. re-tri-bu'-tion
11. ster'-e-o-type
12. tac'-i-turn
13. ten'-ta-tive
14. ven'-er-a-ble
15. ve'-to

Exercise I.   Syllabication and Pronunciation

Syllabicate the following words correctly, and place the major stress mark (') after the syllable that is accented when the word is pronounced.

1. legacy
2. mercenary
3. nepotism
4. ostensible
5. permeate
6. precocious
7. propitiate
8. redundant
9. resilient
10. retribution
11. stereotype
12. taciturn
13. tentative
14. venerable
15. veto

Exercise II.   Parts of Speech

Indicate the part of speech of each of the following words. In some cases, two answers are correct.

1. libel n., v.
2. mammoth n., adj.
3. morass n.
4. narcissistic adj.
5. paraphrase v., n.
6. parody n., v.
7. peremptory adj.
8. pusillanimous adj.
9. recant v.
10. remorse n.
11. sacrilegious adj.
12. satellite n., adj.
13. surveillance n.
14. tacit adj.
15. yoke n., v.

Exercise III.   Words Out of Context

In each of the following groups, select the lettered item that best expresses the meaning of the numbered word at the left.

1. kudos — a. lawsuit b. glory c. agency d. falsehood e. inheritance

2. nebulous — a. tasty b. crazy c. lazy d. hazy e. daisy

3. obscene — a. foolhardy b. crucial c. outmoded d. frugal e. smutty

4. plaintive — a. majestic b. malicious c. melodious d. merry e. mournful

5. prowess — a. wisdom b. significance c. valor d. arrogance e. terror

6. rescind — a. repeal b. repeat c. repel d. reply e. reprove

515

7. ruse   a. fiasco   b. impasse   c. exodus
              d. stratagem   e. enigma

8. solace   a. interest   b. comfort   c. schedule
              d. report   e. ally

9. trenchant   a. experimental   b. profitable   c. fortunate
              d. hazardous   e. incisive

10. vie   a. complete   b. complain   c. compete
              d. compose   e. comply

Exercise IV. Words in Phrases

In each of the following groups, select the lettered item that best expresses the meaning of the *italicized* word in the introductory phrase.

1. a *lucrative* business venture
   a. reprehensible   b. profitable   c. risky   d. clandestine
   e. expensive

2. *nomadic* tribes
   a. primitive   b. indigent   c. numerous   d. superstitious
   e. wandering

3. an *ominous* development
   a. disturbing   b. recent   c. puzzling   d. sudden
   e. pleasing

4. a *pernicious* influence
   a. pivotal   b. salubrious   c. curious   d. detrimental
   e. welcome

5. *promulgate* a law
   a. retract   b. support   c. announce   d. oppose
   e. amend

6. a group of *renegade* Republicans
   a. loyal   b. elderly   c. turncoat   d. eminent   e. junior

7. a *sanctimonious* pronouncement
   a. pie-in-the-sky   b. holier-than-thou   c. devil-may-care
   d. fly-by-night   e. hand-me-down

8. *scrutinize* a report
   a. write   b. suggest   c. ignore   d. type   e. study

9. *tangible* evidence
   a. hidden   b. questionable   c. new   d. fabricated
   e. concrete

10. a *vindictive* attitude
    a. retaliatory   b. benign   c. disinterested   d. strange
    e. foolish

Exercise V. Completing Sentences

Complete each of the following sentences or pairs of sentences by selecting the most appropriate word from the group of words given below. Use each word only once. Make any adjustments that are necessary to fit the words into the sentences properly.

Group A

relent	procrastinate	negligible
pensive	scapegoat	phobia

1. "Why are you so __pensive__ today?" I asked. "Do you have something weighing on your mind?"

2. "Don't postpone your research until the last minute," my professor cautioned me. "Students who _procrastinate_ usually can't get their term papers done on time."

3. "Though I'm perfectly willing to take the blame for my own mistakes," I replied angrily, "I'm not about to let you make me the _scapegoat_ for yours."

4. By then the hurricane had pretty much blown itself out, and damage in the area was _negligible_.

5. Over the years, her childhood fear of heights developed into a serious and debilitating __phobia__.

Group B

stamina	volatile	lush
usurp	reminisce	pandemonium

6. It is hard to believe that such a bleak and barren wasteland had once been a(n) __lush__ tropical paradise.

7. In an interesting article called "Strolling Down Memory Lane," a world-famous actress _reminisced_ about life in the theater over 50 years ago.

8. The kind of physical, mental, and emotional __stamina__ a runner needs to complete a 26-mile marathon can justly be called "true grit."

9. In Shakespeare's *Richard III*, the villainous Duke of Gloucester has his royal nephews murdered in the Tower of London and then __usurps__ the throne.

10. "We're sitting on a volcano that is ready to erupt," the official remarked in reference to the __volatile__ situation in that turbulent part of the world.

Exercise VI.   Synonyms and Antonyms

Classify each of the following pairs of words as **S** for **synonyms** or **A** for **antonyms**.

A 1. lackadaisical—energetic
S 2. nominal—token
S 3. fixation—obsession
A 4. prelude—aftermath
A 5. quell—foment

S 6. undermine—sabotage
A 7. raze—erect
S 8. schism—rift
S 9. pervasive—ubiquitous
A 10. zenith—nadir

Exercise VII.   Framing Sentences

Use each of the following words in an original illustrative sentence.

1. mandatory
2. motley
3. novice
4. opportune
5. poignant
6. purge
7. replenish
8. ritual
9. salient
10. strident
11. sordid
12. thwart
13. vagary
14. veneer
15. zeal

Exercise VIII.   Related Forms

A. Give a **noun** form of each of the following words.
1. perjure — perjury, perjurer
2. prodigious — prodigy, prodigiousness
3. reciprocate — reciprocation, reciprocity
4. predatory — predator, predatoriness
5. ostracize — ostracism
6. versatile — versatility, versatileness

B. Give a **verb** form of each of the following words.
1. plagiarism — plagiarize
2. tranquil — tranquilize
3. traumatic — traumatize

C. Give an **adjective** form of each of the following words.
1. rudiment — rudimentary, rudimental
2. strategy — strategic
3. nostalgia — nostalgic

D. Give an **adverb** form of each of the following words.
1. mundane — mundanely
2. paradox — paradoxically
3. lucid — lucidly

Exercise IX.   Word Roundup

1. Explain the difference between the words in each of the following pairs.

a. obsolete—obsolescent
b. officious—official
c. senile—senescent
d. venal—venial
e. urban—urbane
f. turbid—turbulent
g. wrath—wraith
h. wan—wane

2. Define each of the following.

a. a muckraker
b. a drone
c. a timeserver
d. a clone
e. a has-been
f. a slumlord

3. Explain the meaning of each of the following expressions.

a. a whipping boy
b. an elective course
c. maggots in the brain
d. a hand-me-down
e. hero worship
f. a splinter group
g. sphere of influence
h. feet of clay
i. urban nomads
j. tangible assets

4. Explain what each of the following colorful phrases means.

a. wet behind the ears
b. eat one's words
c. bury the hatchet
d. keep a low profile
e. send up a trial balloon
f. shed crocodile tears
g. throw in the towel
h. put a tail on someone
i. in high dudgeon
j. give someone the cold shoulder

5. Define each of the following foreign expressions used in present-day English, and tell what language it comes from.

a. idée fixe
b. vendetta
c. non compos mentis
d. scenario
e. wanderlust
f. sine qua non
g. amour propre
h. coup d'état
i. quid pro quo

6. Explain the story behind each of the following.

a. Lilliputian
b. gargantuan
c. fifth column
d. quixotic
e. chimerical
f. zealot

Exercise X. Etymology

1. Define each of the following words utilizing the Latin prefix *inter*.

a. intercede
b. interact
c. interlude
d. interloper
e. intercept
f. interim

2. Define each of the following words utilizing the Latin prefix *ob*, and explain what the prefix means in that particular word.

a. obverse
b. obituary
c. obtuse
d. obliterate
e. obsess
f. obdurate

3. Define each of the following expressions utilizing the Latin preposition *per*.

a. per annum
b. per capita
c. per se

4. For each of the following definitions, supply an English word using the Latin root *sanct*.

a. sanction
   authorize
b. sanctuary
   refuge
c. sanctity
   holiness

5. Define each of the following words utilizing the Latin root *tang*, *tact* or one of its variants.

a. tactful
b. contagious
c. tangential
d. attainment
e. contiguous
f. contingency

519

Exercise XI.   Choosing the Right Meaning

Read each sentence carefully. Then underline the item that best completes the statement below the sentence.

1. After examining the defendant, the court-appointed psychiatrist testified that she believes the boy is lucid and capable of standing trial. The defendant's attorneys argue that he is a minor and has no idea that he committed a serious crime. It will be up to the judge to decide. (2) (4)

   The word **lucid** in line 2 means

   a. understandable
   b. sane
   c. honest
   d. reliable

2. In Fort Myers on the west coast of Florida, you can tour Thomas Edison's winter home and visit his laboratory. His lush gardens contain exotic species of tropical trees, including an enormous banyan tree more than 390 feet in diameter. (2) (4)

   The word **lush** in line 2 means

   a. flourishing
   b. overripe
   c. enormous
   d. scientific

3. The many museums that make up the Smithsonian Institution do not charge even a nominal admission fee. Some of the Smithsonian's most popular sites are the National Museum of African Art, the National Air and Space Museum, the National Portrait Gallery, and the Arthur M. Sackler Gallery. (2) (4)

   The word **nominal** in line 2 means

   a. membership
   b. monthly
   c. titular
   d. token

4. Baseball season opened on April 5, and the Swallows proceeded to lose six straight games—three of them shutouts. Pestered relentlessly by reporters, the coach held a press conference after the sixth loss. "I'm extremely sanguine about our team's chances of catching up and pulling ahead," he assured the skeptical journalists. (2) (4)

   The word **sanguine** in line 4 means

   a. optimistic
   b. pessimistic
   c. concerned
   d. ruddy

5. Go is a board game invented in China about 2000 B.C. Like chess, Go is an intellectually demanding "battle game" that requires strategy. Two players start with an empty board on which there is a 19-by-19 grid. Each player attempts to acquire territory by placing his or her stones at the intersections of the grid lines to surround empty spaces and to capture the opponent's stones. The player with the most territory wins the game. (2) (4) (6)

   The word **strategy** in line 3 means

   a. the science of planning
   b. a plan of action
   c. great intelligence
   d. great skill

6. When the dictator fled, the situation in the tiny nation became extremely volatile. There was no established line of succes- (2) sion, and analysts feared that the many factions vying for power would bring the nation to the brink of civil war. (4)

The word **volatile** in line 2 means

a. dangerous   c. evaporating readily
b. anarchic   d. potentially explosive

7. The curator's selection of objects for the exhibit of Northwest Coast American Indian art is quite parochial. Among the ob- (2) jects on display are Tlingit ceremonial shirts and baskets, Haida slate carvings, Salish blankets woven from mountain (4) goat's wool and vegetable fibers, and painted wooden face masks from various tribes. (6)

The word **parochial** in line 2 means

a. supported by a parish   c. eclectic
b. narrow in scope   d. eye-opening

8. In the process of choosing jurors for a trial, each side has a certain number of peremptory challenges. That is, after ques- (2) tioning members of the jury pool, attorneys for the defendant and for the prosecution can each eliminate a number of jurors (4) without giving cause—that is, a specific reason—based on a hunch that the potential jurors would be prejudiced against (6) their case.

The word **peremptory** in line 2 means

a. tyrannical   c. binding
b. tentative   d. resolute

9. Photos transmitted from weather satellites allow forecasters to make accurate long-range predictions. Such images are es- (2) pecially important when scientists are tracking hurricanes. You can see images of various views of Earth online at the (4) home page of the Geostationary Satellite Server, a division of the National Oceanic and Atmospheric Administration (NOAA). (6)

The word **satellites** in line 1 means

a. protectorates   c. subordinates
b. companies   d. spacecraft

10. Before clocks were invented, people measured time with sun- dials. The principle of a sundial is simple: The sun at its (2) zenith casts no shadow. From sunrise to sunset, time is indi- cated by the extent and direction of a shadow on a flat sur- (4) face marked with hours. The earliest known sundial, a flat stone with an L-shaped bar, is Egyptian and dates from the (6) 8th century B.C.

The word **zenith** in line 3 means

a. highest point directly overhead   c. height of fame
b. closest point to an observer   d. brightest moment

Exercise I
1. ac-a-dem'-ic
2. ag'-gre-gate
3. an'-ec-dote
4. a-nom'-a-ly
5. a-troc'-i-ty
6. bi-zarre'
7. bra-va'-do
8. can-tan'-ker-ous
9. cir-cu'-i-tous
10. con-fron-ta'-tion
11. cred-i-bil'-i-ty
12. de'-vi-ate
13. du-plic'-i-ty
14. em'-i-nent
15. ep'-i-thet
16. fea'-si-ble
17. for'-mi-da-ble
18. gre-ga'-ri-ous
19. hei'-nous
20. in-ter-vene'
21. lu'-cra-tive
22. nos-tal'-gia
23. os-ten'-si-ble
24. pre-car'-i-ous
25. pro-cras'-ti-nate
26. re-pris'-al
27. sac-ri-le'-gious
28. stip'-u-late
29. va'-ga-ry, va-ga'-ry
30. vin-dic'-tive

Cumulative Review

1. abdicate — 400. zenith

Exercise I.   Syllabication and Pronounciation

Syllabicate each of the following words properly, and place the major stress mark (') after the syllable that is accented when the word is pronounced. In one case, two answers are correct.

1. academic
2. aggregate
3. anecdote
4. anomaly
5. atrocity
6. bizarre
7. bravado
8. cantankerous
9. circuitous
10. confrontation
11. credibility
12. deviate
13. duplicity
14. eminent
15. epithet
16. feasible
17. formidable
18. gregarious
19. heinous
20. intervene
21. lucrative
22. nostalgia
23. ostensible
24. precarious
25. procrastinate
26. reprisal
27. sacrilegious
28. stipulate
29. vagary
30. vindictive

Exercise II.   Parts of Speech

Indicate the part of speech of each of the following words. In many cases, two answers are correct.

1. abject adj.
2. advocate n., v.
3. anachronism n.
4. array n., v.
5. atrophy v., n.
6. benign adj.
7. boorish adj.
8. buttress n., v.
9. censor n., v.
10. compatible adj.
11. consummate v., adj.
12. delinquent n., adj.
13. discourse n., v.
14. eclectic adj., n.
15. esoteric adj.
16. expedient adj., n.
17. finesse n., v.
18. harangue n., v.
19. incarcerate v.
20. jettison v.
21. mammoth n., adj.
22. mercenary n., adj.
23. obsequious adj.
24. premise n., v.
25. prowess n.
26. renegade n., adj.
27. salient adj., n.
28. stereotype n., v.
29. taciturn adj.
30. yoke n., v.

Exercise III.   Words Out of Context

In each of the following groups, select the lettered item that best expresses the meaning of the numbered word at the left.

1. abet
a. deplore   b. conclude   c. assist   d. refine
e. hamper

2. agenda
a. failure   b. battle   c. omen   d. environment
e. schedule

3. anarchy
a. chaos   b. poverty   c. throwback   d. prejudice
e. curse

4. apprehend
a. accuse   b. catch   c. protect   d. invade
e. release

5. augment   a. increase   b. scorn   c. curtail   d. expiate   e. compensate

6. bicker   a. esteem   b. measure   c. provide   d. relax   e. squabble

7. boisterous   a. bloated   b. dismal   c. friendly   d. rowdy   e. suspicious

8. candid   a. learned   b. costly   c. frank   d. sour   e. tactful

9. charlatan   a. officer   b. employee   c. fraud   d. baker   e. relative

10. condone   a. point at   b. flinch at   c. aim at   d. rail at   e. wink at

11. culpable   a. in unison   b. at fault   c. off guard   d. on target   e. by heart

12. devout   a. casual   b. ignorant   c. eccentric   d. ardent   e. polite

13. dormant   a. inactive   b. cursory   c. frantic   d. decrepit   e. obedient

14. emaciated   a. gaunt   b. gigantic   c. gleeful   d. gingerly   e. gracious

15. exacerbate   a. alleviate   b. incur   c. intensify   d. confuse   e. humble

16. feign   a. cure   b. pretend   c. honor   d. cause   e. investigate

17. fiasco   a. development   b. effect   c. reason   d. attempt   e. failure

18. garble   a. distort   b. revise   c. allow   d. concede   e. embellish

19. impasse   a. solution   b. tunnel   c. error   d. deadlock   e. viewpoint

20. ingenious   a. expensive   b. modern   c. frank   d. clever   e. dangerous

21. mandatory   a. grasping   b. lethargic   c. required   d. masculine   e. profitable

22. moot   a. debatable   b. snobbish   c. radical   d. diverse   e. monetary

23. parody   a. saloon   b. monsoon   c. pontoon   d. lampoon   e. dragoon

24. pernicious   a. welcome   b. eternal   c. fragile   d. economical   e. harmful

25. prerogative   a. privilege   b. facility   c. antipathy   d. circumstance   e. requirement

26. rescind   a. reply   b. repeal   c. reprove   d. repel   e. repeat

27. retribution   a. hostility b. discord c. pestilence
                               d. <u>vengeance</u> e. calamity

28. senile   a. openhanded b. tight-lipped c. <u>feebleminded</u>
                               d. hot-blooded e. thin-skinned

29. ubiquitous   a. incisive b. <u>omnipresent</u> c. vacuous
                               d. provisional e. specific

30. veracity   a. endurance b. wisdom c. <u>truthfulness</u>
                               d. determination e. agility

Exercise IV.   Completing Sentences

Complete each of the following sentences by selecting the most appropriate word from the groups of words given below. Make any adjustments that are necessary to fit the words into the sentences properly.

Group A

distraught	accede	ignominy
incense	pseudonym	brash

1. Though most of the committee readily __acceded__ to my request for additional funds, a few members stubbornly refused to countenance the unexpected expenditure.

2. "He is a(n)__brash__ young man," the general observed sourly, "whose reckless and precipitate actions almost cost us the battle."

3. Though one of the women received the news of the accident with remarkable composure, the other became __distraught__ with grief and worry.

4. Most writers publish their works under their own names, but a few prefer to use __pseudonyms__.

5. I could tell from the loud voices and angry words issuing from my boss's office that something had really __incensed__ him.

Group B

cajole	innovation	inherent
enigma	affluent	replenish

6. The fact that I have grown up in a(n) __affluent__ suburb does not mean that I am unaware of conditions in the inner-city slums.

7. Though we all desire to improve life in the United States, we should not blindly accept every __innovation__ that comes along simply because it is new.

8. A little sweet talk is usually a surefire means of __cajoling__ someone into doing what you want done.

9. When I realized that we were running out of potato chips, I made a hurried trip to the corner grocery store to __replenish__ our supply.

10. Just who is being described in Sir Edward Elgar's __Enigma__ *Variations* puzzled music lovers for many years.

Group C

euphemism	sabotage	ethnic
anathema	caustic	lurk

11. He is so malicious that if he cannot control the organization, he may try to __sabotage__ or otherwise hinder its operations.

12. After the nightmarish experience I had in the park last fall, I began to imagine muggers and purse snatchers __lurking__ behind every tree or bush I passed.

13. When he said, "One man's meat is another man's poison," he simply meant that what one person likes may be __anathema__ to somebody else.

14. In order to spare the feelings of relatives, funeral directors usually resort to _euphemisms_ such as "the loved one" or "the dear departed" when speaking of the person who has died.

15. She has a sharp tongue and a(n) __caustic__ wit that she uses with great skill and imagination in her televised movie reviews.

Group D

collaborate	arbitrate	fathom
myriad	surveillance	secular

16. When the contract negotiations broke down, both labor and management agreed to call in an impartial third party to __arbitrate__ the dispute.

17. One of the verses in a Shakespearean song about the sea begins, "Full __fathom__ five thy father lies; Of his bones are coral made."

18. For almost 20 years, Gilbert and Sullivan _collaborated_ on a series of world-famous light operas, including *H.M.S. Pinafore* and *The Yeoman of the Guard.*

19. The facets of the human personality are as __myriad__ as the stars in a summer sky or the grains of sand on a tropical beach.

20. Though members of the clergy must devote most of their time to their clerical duties, they are usually able to pursue __secular__ interests that have little or no bearing on their profession.

Group E

obsession	construe	fortuitous
connoisseur	traumatic	augur

21. Although he had been looking forward to retirement, he found the change in his lifestyle a disturbing, even a(n) __traumatic__ experience.

22. I have no objection to a person having a keen interest in bridge, but I am afraid that the game has become almost a(n) __obsession__ with you.

23. When Albert Einstein remarked that God does not play dice with the world, he meant that developments in nature are not purely __fortuitous__.

24. Since I didn't know how to __construe__ her unexpected remark, I asked my best friend what he made of it.

25. We might describe a promising development as something that __augurs__ well for success or victory in the future.

Group F

harbinger	grope	venerable
phobia	devoid	baffle

26. What began as a mere distaste for subway travel has developed into a full-blown __phobia__ that makes even a short trip an agonizing experience.

27. That school is a __venerable__ institution that has seen generations of students pass through its hallowed portals.

28. The proposal may look good at first glance; but if you study it carefully, you will see that it is __devoid__ of any real merit.

29. Suddenly awakened by the insistent ringing of the telephone, I __groped__ around sleepily for the receiver.

30. Ordinary detectives may be __baffled__ by a particularly ingenious crime, but the redoubtable Hercule Poirot is never stumped.

Exercise V. Words in Phrases

In each of the following groups, select the lettered item that best expresses the meaning of the *italicized* word in the introductory phrase.

1. completely *absolved* the defendant
   a. ignored   b. convicted   c. reproached   d. arrested
   e. acquitted

2. *adjourned* the meeting
   a. planned   b. suspended   c. attended   d. approved   e. opened

3. their *ambivalent* attitude
   a. scholarly   b. laudable   c. narrow-minded   d. contradictory
   e. discourteous

4. an *articulate* proponent of the plan
   a. long-standing   b. unexpected   c. well-known   d. eloquent
   e. self-appointed

5. seek *asylum* in the United States
   a. justice   b. refuge   c. wealth   d. fame   e. revenge

6. motivated solely by *avarice*
   a. hatred   b. fear   c. greed   d. ambition   e. jealousy

7. a *brusque* reply
   a. curt   b. pompous   c. interesting   d. amusing   e. silly

8. an outright *calumny*
   a. joke   b. disaster   c. blunder   d. refusal   e. falsehood

9. *clandestine* meetings
   a. unexpected   b. welcome   c. noisy   d. secret   e. important

10. an interesting *conjecture*
    a. fact   b. development   c. guess   d. book   e. history

11. my *corpulent* uncle
    a. portly   b. elderly   c. stately   d. wealthy   e. surly

12. *defer* a decision
    a. withdraw   b. overrule   c. ignore   d. confirm   e. postpone

13. *diligent* students
    a. recalcitrant   b. indolent   c. knowledgeable   d. indefatigable
    e. talented

14. the *elite* of the entertainment world
    a. retired members   b. fans   c. rank and file   d. has-beens
    e. cream of the crop

15. bore the news with *equanimity*
    a. assistance   b. composure   c. indifference   d. reluctance
    e. hysteria

16. *expound* a theory
    a. attack   b. verify   c. explain   d. demolish   e. ignore

17. *filch* an apple
    a. steal   b. polish   c. eat   d. grow   e. buy

18. a *grueling* race
    a. downhill   b. contested   c. brief   d. draining   e. surprising

19. *impugned* my motives
    a. cash doubt on   b. threw light on   c. paid attention to
    d. gave evidence of   e. took comfort in

20. "*justify* the ways of God to man"
    a. criticize   b. vindicate   c. divulge   d. deplore   e. report

21. a *lucid* account
    a. muddled   b. long   c. funny   d. brief   e. clear

22. at a *nominal* cost to the consumer
    a. guaranteed   b. legal   c. token   d. sizable   e. fair

23. in a *pensive* mood
    a. puzzling   b. thoughtful   c. elated   d. friendly   e. obstinate

24. a *peremptory* tone of voice
    a. hopeful   b. dictatorial   c. jubilant   d. discouraged
    e. plaintive

25. *promulgate* a law
    a. announce   b. oppose   c. circumvent   d. advocate   e. propose

26. felt no *remorse*
    a. loneliness   b. animosity   c. hunger   d. regret   e. desire

27. became a mere *satellite* of Alexander's empire
    a. enemy   b. friend   c. aim   d. protectorate   e. citizen

28. *scrutinize* the faces on the platform
    a. ignore   b. examine   c. draw   d. memorize   e. remember

29. *tangible* results
    a. insignificant   b. costly   c. unexpected   d. negative
    e. concrete

30. the *volatile* situation in that part of the world
   a. heartwarming   b. curious   c. explosive   d. tranquil
   e. recent

Exercise VI.   Synonyms and Antonyms

Classify each of the following pairs of words as **S** for **synonyms** or **A** for **antonyms**.

A 1. abhor—relish
S 2. amiable—affable
S 3. alienate—estrange
A 4. apathy—enthusiasm
A 5. astute—obtuse
S 6. belligerent—hostile
A 7. boycott—patronize
A 8. catholic—parochial
S 9. habitual—chronic
S 10. complacent—smug
S 11. truncate—curtail
A 12. dapper—slovenly
A 13. praise—disparage
S 14. endemic—native
A 15. ignorant—erudite

S 16. exploit—feat
S 17. fluctuate—vacillate
A 18. smile—grimace
A 19. explicit—implicit
S 20. inception—inauguration
A 21. liability—asset
S 22. nebulous—vague
S 23. bedlam—pandemonium
S 24. plaintive—mournful
A 25. quell—foment
A 26. raze—erect
S 27. ruse—stratagem
A 28. strident—mellifluous
S 29. foil—thwart
A 30. nadir—zenith

Exercise VII.   Related Forms

A. Give a **noun** form of each of the following words.
1. abdicate abdication
2. agile agility
3. allege allegation
4. banal banality
5. bombastic bombast
6. corroborate corroboration, corroborator
7. emulate emulation, emulator
8. entice enticement
9. futile futility, futileness
10. jeopardize jeopardy
11. nomadic nomad
12. prodigious prodigy, prodigiousnes
13. redundant redundancy, redundan
14. usurp usurpation, usurper
15. versatile versatility, versatileness

B. Give an **adjective** form of each of the following words.
1. coerce coercive, coercible
2. bureaucracy bureaucratic
3. defect defective
4. disparity disparate
5. rudiment rudimentary, rudimental
6. strategy strategic

C. Give an **adverb** form of each of the following words.
1. arbitrary arbitrarily
2. circumspect circumspectly
3. facetious facetiously
4. graphic graphically
5. tenable tenably
6. paradox paradoxically

D. Give a **verb** form of each of the following words.
1. authentic authenticate
2. impediment impede
3. plagiarism plagiarize

Exercise VIII.   Look-Alikes

Explain the difference in meaning between the words in each of the following pairs.

1. loath—loathe
2. averse—adverse
3. aesthetic—ascetic
4. callous—callow
5. forbear—forebear
6. flout—flaunt

7. indigent—indigenous 10. exalt—exult 13. urban—urbane
8. demur—demure 11. official—officious 14. venal—venial
9. discomfit—discomfort 12. turbid—turbulent 15. wan—wane

Exercise IX.   Framing Sentences

Compose an original illustrative sentence for each of the following words.

Group A

1. abstain
2. amnesty
3. austere
4. bleak
5. censure
6. crucial
7. divulge
8. ethical
9. foible
10. immunity
11. lackadaisical
12. ominous
13. purge
14. revere
15. tranquil

Group B

16. affectation
17. appall
18. avid
19. bungle
20. concise
21. delineate
22. effrontery
23. exodus
24. goad
25. judicious
26. motley
27. perjure
28. reciprocate
29. scapegoat
30. veto

Exercise X.   Word Roundup

1. Define each of the following words.

   a. teetotaler
   b. academician
   c. claptrap
   d. aesthete
   e. mannerism
   f. windfall
   g. rubberneck
   h. fluke
   i. dilettante
   j. greenhorn
   k. timeserver
   l. has-been
   m. clone
   n. gadfly
   o. muckraker

2. Explain what each of the following phrases means.

   a. academic freedom
   b. halcyon days
   c. red tape
   d. devil's advocate
   e. credibility gap
   f. Judas kiss
   g. mirror image
   h. hero worship
   i. feet of clay
   j. splinter group

3. Explain what each of the following colorful idioms means.

   a. living high off the hog
   b. rest on one's laurels
   c. put on airs
   d. see red
   e. paint oneself into a corner
   f. live in an ivory tower
   g. pour oil on troubled waters
   h. bury the hatchet
   i. throw in the towel
   j. shed crocodile tears

4. Explain the story behind each of the following words.

   a. boycott
   b. Comstockery
   c. jeremiad
   d. malapropism
   e. quixotic
   f. zealot

5. Explain the meaning of each of the following foreign expressions used in present-day English, and tell what language it comes from.

   a. milieu
   b. impedimenta
   c. tour de force
   d. vendetta
   e. coup d'état
   f. quid pro quo

Exercise XI.   Choosing the Right Meaning

Read each sentence carefully. Then underline the item that best completes the statement below the sentence.

1. An economics professor who appears on a weekly talk show claims
   that many people do not fully apprehend the gravity of the current sit-   (2)
   uation. Inflation is rising along with business inventories, and, she
   warns, we may be on the brink of a global recession.   (4)

   The word **apprehend** in line 2 means

   a. capture   c. comprehend
   b. fear   d. anticipate

2. Be sure to keep all caustic substances, such as lye, in tightly sealed con-
   tainers in locked cabinets. Young children, who are naturally curious,   (2)
   can be severely injured by coming in contact with these substances.

   The word **caustic** in line 1 means

   a. hazardous   c. corrosive
   b. sardonic   d. cleansing

3. This pie chart, a graphic representation of statistics from the U.S.
   Census Bureau, shows that in 1992, 40 percent of American females   (2)
   age seven and older participated in some form of aerobic exercise. Of
   these, about 32 percent ran, and about 32 percent played basketball.   (4)

   The word **graphic** in line 1 means

   a. realistic   c. factual
   b. vivid   d. visual

4. Women in the United States did not obtain the right to vote until
   1920. But advocates of woman suffrage both here and in England had   (2)
   for decades protested unequal treatment of women. No women, they
   insisted, should be discriminated against because of her sex.   (4)

   The words **discriminated against** in line 4 mean

   a. differentiated   c. criticized
   b. treated unfairly   d. isolated

5. Cattle, sheep, and other animals that ruminate exhale a sizable quantity of methane gas and thereby contribute to global warming. Scien-   (2)
   tists are researching ways to reduce ruminants' methane emissions
   by improving the kinds of feed given to livestock.   (4)

   The word **ruminate** in line 1 means

   a. contract diseases   c. ponder at length
   b. chew cud   d. roam freely

6. Betty Comden and Adolph Green collaborated for six decades, producing the lyrics and screenplays for several of Hollywood's best-loved   (2)
   musical comedies. Their many successes include *On the Town* (1949),
   Singin' in the Rain (1952), and *Bells Are Ringing* (1960).   (4)

   The word **collaborated** in line 1 means

   a. teamed up   c. conspired
   b. acted in   d. wrote

7. The course will cover works by the twentieth-century Argentine essayist, short story writer, and poet Jorge Luis Borges. Many of Borges's fictional pieces are esoteric fantasies or allegories, but he has also written detective stories.

(2)

(4)

The word **esoteric** in line 3 means

a. secret

b. popular

c. famous

d. cryptic

8. After an unusually harsh winter, spring proved to be disappointingly erratic. A string of warm and sunny April days was followed by overcast skies and bleak, snowy weather.

(2)

The word **bleak** in line 3 means

a. sunny

b. changeable

c. barren

d. cold and gloomy

9. Woods Hole, Massachusetts, on the southwestern tip of Cape Cod, is home to a prestigious enclave of marine scientists. Founded in 1930, the Woods Hole Oceanographic Institution sponsors research and education in many fields, including applied ocean physics and engineering, marine chemistry, biology, geology, geophysics, deep ocean exploration, and ocean and climate change.

(2)

(4)

(6)

The word **enclave** in line 2 means

a. separate community

b. country within a country

c. fenced-in enclosure

d. academy

10. In many states, drivers must prove that they have liability insurance before they can obtain or renew their motor vehicle registration or driver's license or obtain their vehicle safety inspection. Individual state laws mandate the minimum dollar amounts of liability coverage.

(2)

(4)

The word **liability** in line 1 means

a. hindrance or handicap

b. financial obligation

c. safety

d. medical

11. Hot pepper and curry powder give mulligatawny soup its name, for *mulligatawny* comes from the Tamil words that mean "pepper water." The soup, which is far from bland, is a popular Anglo-Indian recipe from eastern India.

(2)

(4)

The word **bland** in line 3 means

a. boring

b. spicy

c. mild

d. exciting

12. In Stephen Vincent Benét's short story "The Devil and Daniel Webster," a fictional New Hampshire farmer named Jabez Stone pleads with Webster, a real-life statesman and orator, to act as his counsel. Stone explains that ten years earlier he had sold his soul to the devil and that now the devil has come to collect it.

(2)

(4)

The word **counsel** in line 3 means

a. guidance

b. protector

c. friend

d. lawyer

13. Some county-wide services (such as parks, libraries, and schools) are gratuitous to all residents, paid for by taxes. For other services (such as garbage pickup and water), property owners pay the county directly. (2)

The word **gratuitous** in line 2 means

a. unjustified
b. expensive
c. free
d. available

14. Hansel and Gretel carefully leave a trail of breadcrumbs to mark their circuitous journey through the woods. When it's time to find their way home, they discover that birds have eaten their markers and they are lost. Soon they find themselves standing before a gingerbread house decorated with candy. (2) (4)

The word **circuitous** in line 2 means

a. roundabout
b. long-winded
c. dark and dangerous
d. steep and rocky

15. Louise Erdrich's poem "Indian Boarding School" alludes to efforts by the Federal Bureau of Indian Affairs to assimilate Native Americans into the mainstream culture. Starting in the 1870s, children from all tribes were pressured into attending boarding schools far from their homes. Once at the schools, they were prohibited from practicing any tribal rituals or speaking their native languages; only English was allowed. (2) (4) (6)

The word **assimilate** in line 2 means

a. integrate
b. separate
c. digest
d. educate

16. During the Battle of Chancellorsville in May 1863, Union forces outnumbered Confederates two to one. Nevertheless, General Robert E. Lee discomfited Major General Joseph Hooker's Union forces in a fierce battle that lasted several days. The toll was grim. More than 1,700 Confederate soldiers died and over 9,200 were wounded, while Union forces lost more than 1,600 dead and nearly 9,700 wounded. (2) (4) (6)

The word **discomfited** in line 3 means

a. soundly defeated
b. confused
c. embarrassed
d. angered

17. The United Nations Commission on Human Rights issued a resolution asking the tiny nation to allow U.N. monitors to investigate the treatment of those who openly protested the current regime. Implicit in this resolution was a criticism of the harsh crackdown on political dissidents. (2) (4)

The word **implicit** in line 3 means

a. unconditional
b. directly stated
c. emphasized
d. implied

18. Children can be exceedingly resilient. During the prolonged bombing of London during World War II, for example, most of the children who were sent for safety to strangers' homes in towns outside London adjusted to their new circumstances despite being uprooted from their family, friends, and homes. (2) (4)

The word **resilient** in line 1 means

a. able to resume original shape
b. able to recover quickly
c. able to remain cheerful
d. unable to make changes easily

19. The sun's ultraviolet rays can cause several types of skin cancer, premature wrinkles, and other signs of aging. Therefore, dermatologists   (2)
recommend that when you are out in the sun, you should apply sun-
screen liberally and frequently, especially if you have a sanguine or   (4)
pale complexion.

The word **sanguine** in line 4 means

  a. optimistic   c. freckled
  b. dark   d. ruddy

20. Here's a paradox with overtones of Washington Irving's story, "Rip Van
Winkle." Imagine that an astronaut has been in space for 25 years,   (2)
always traveling near the speed of light. When the astronaut returns
to Earth, his family and friends will have aged 25 years, but the as-   (4)
tronaut will not have aged as much. Can you explain why?

The word **paradox** in line 1 means

  a. anomaly   c. riddle
  b. scientific fact   d. humorous imitation

21. Voter apathy is a serious problem in the United States. Every year an
alarming number of registered voters do not bother to vote, even in pres-   (2)
idential elections. Some nonvoters profess a blithe attitude toward governmental matters. Others claim they are too busy to vote. Still others   (4)
say that they don't vote as a protest against the choice of candidates.

The word **blithe** in line 3 means

  a. jolly   c. blasé
  b. ambivalent   d. gloomy

22. You and a friend can take an online test to see how compatible you
are. Among other topics, the test asks about the way you like to spend   (2)
your free time, your attitude toward neatness, your spending habits,
your ambitions, your dislikes, and your fears.   (4)

The word **compatible** in line 1 means

  a. consistent   c. well-adjusted
  b. inconsistent   d. like-minded

23. In a long-running comedy, three actors perform *The Complete Works
of William Shakespeare (Abridged)* in just under 97 minutes. There is   (2)
a parody of *Hamlet,* of course, during which the actors present *Hamlet* backward.   (4)

The word **parody** in line 3 means

  a. take-off   c. condensation
  b. mockery   d. serious analysis

24. In Greek mythology, Orpheus journeys to the Underworld—a
formidable undertaking—to find and recover his beloved wife Eury-   (2)
dice. Impressed by Orpheus's great devotion, Hades promises Orpheus that his wife will be restored to him on one condition: He must   (4)
not look back at her until they reach the land of the living. But, alas,
Orpheus turns around to see if Eurydice is behind him, and she van-   (6)
ishes forever.

The word **formidable** in line 2 means

  a. tremendous   c. terrifying
  b. courageous   d. misguided

Index

The words that make up the Basic Word List are included in this Index and are printed in **boldface** type. The number following each of these words indicates the page on which the word is first introduced. Exercises and review materials in which these words also appear are not cited.

534

ob (Latin prefix) and
variants, 383–384
obscene, 371
obsequious, 371
obsequy, 371
obsession, 372
obsolescent/obsolete,
372
obsolete, 372
official/officious, 373
officious, 373
Old English, 9, 58, 109,
258
Old French, 12–13
Old Norse, 11–12, 109
(o)logy, words ending
in, 239
ominous, 373
onym, onomy (Greek
root), 304
opportune, 374
opportunist,
opportunism, 374
ostensible, 374
ostracize, 374

Pandaemonium, 377
pandemonium, 376
par, para (Greek prefix),
384–385
paradox, 376
paraphrase, 378
parochial, 378
parody, 379
parts of a word, 4
parts of speech, 2–3
pensive, 380
per (Latin preposition and
prefix), 417–418
peremptory, 389
Peripatetic, 358
periphrastic/
paraphrastic, 378
perjure, 389
permeate, 390
pernicious, 390
persevere, 390
*-philia, -phil(e),
-philiac*, 391
philos (Greek root), words
based on, 402
philosophical and
religious
positions, 168
-phobe, 391
phobia, 391
phobias, 402

phrases, fused, 185–186
place names, words
derived from, 37
plagiarism, 391
plaintive, 392
plethora, 393
poignant, 393
politics, language of
government
and, 119
pollution, verbal,
424–425
portmanteau words
(blends), 47
practical/practicable,
247
pre (Latin prefix),
418–419
precarious, 394
precocious, 394
predatory, 394
prefabricate, 245
prefix, definition of, 4
prefixes, 34, 57, 131,
163, 199, 234,
269, 346–347,
383–385, 417–
421, 455–456,
490–491
prejudice, linguistic, 176
prelude, 395
premise, 396
prerogative, 406
pro (Greek prefix), 421
pro (Latin preposition
and prefix),
419–421
probity, 406
procrastinate, 406
prodigious, 407
proliferate, 407
promulgate, 409
propensity, 409
propitiate, 409
protracted, 410
prowess, 410
pseudonym, 410
psychology, language
of, 258
pun, 340
Purgatory, 413
purge, 412
pusillanimous, 412

quack, 126
quell, 413
quisling, 136

quixotic, 414

racial equality, words
relating to
struggle for, 308
raise/raze, 426
rant, 101
raze, 426
re (Latin prefix),
455–456
recalcitrant, 426
recant, 427
reciprocal, reciprocity,
427
reciprocate, 427
recrimination, 427
red, expressions
involving, 309
red tape, 111
redound, 428
redundant, 428
reform movements,
words relating
to, 307
relent, 429
relinquish, 27
reminiscence, 429
reminiscent, 429
remorse, 430
renegade, 431
repercussion, 431
replenish, 432
replete, 432
reprisal, 432
rescind, 432
resign, 27
resilient, 433
reticent, 444
retribution, 444
retro (Latin prefix), 456
retroactive, 445
reverberate, 446
revere, 446
ricochet (reduplicate)
words, 205
right wing, right-winger,
176
ritual, 446
Roget, Peter Mark, 198
root, definition of, 4
roots, 35, 57, 82, 107,
131, 200, 235,
270, 303–304,
347–348, 456–
457, 491–492
rudiment, 447
ruminant, 448

Photo Credits

Long-Answer Key to Student Text

Learning Words (pages 1–20)

Exercise (pages 4–5)

1. a. *Denotation:* Brave; courageous.
      Connotation: Favorable.
   b. *Denotation:* Exhibiting ill will; having an evil influence.
      Connotation: Unfavorable.
   c. *Denotation:* Happening without warning; quick or hasty.
      Connotation: Neutral.
   d. *Denotation:* Marked by excessive sternness or rigor in religious observance or morality.
      Connotation: Unfavorable.
   e. *Denotation:* Having the power to delight or charm completely.
      Connotation: Favorable.
   f. *Denotation:* Being an equal distance apart at every point; having comparable parts or readily recognizable similarities.
      Connotation: Neutral.

Exercise (pages 7–8)

1. a. To lessen or diminish.
   b. To abate a tax; to abate one's enthusiasm; the storm has abated.
   c. *a* [from *ad*] (Latin), "to" + *batuere* (Latin), "beat"
   d. To suppress (a nuisance); to suspend (an action); to annul (a writ).
   e. *Synonym:* subside.
      Antonyms: increase, intensify.
   f. a-bate'
2. a. Translating; finding the right word or phrase to convey an idea; finding formal equivalents for colloquial or slang expressions (or vice versa); finding the expression one wants to use but can't quite remember.
   b. In a thesaurus, words are presented in groups of related-idea categories according to a distinctive logical pattern. The words are not defined, and no pronunciation is indicated. In a dictionary, the words are arranged in alphabetical order; they are defined, their histories and uses outlined, and their pronunciations given.

Exercise (page 20)

2. a. See page 9 of the student text.
   b. See pages 15–16 of the student text.
   c. See page 16 of the student text.
3. a. Answers will vary. See pages 10, 13–14, 16 of the student text.
   b. Answers will vary. See pages 11, 14, 16 of the student text.
   c. Answers will vary. See pages 11–12 of the student text.
   d. Answers will vary. See pages 15, 17 of the student text.
   e. Answers will vary. See page 14 of the student text.
   f. Answers will vary. See pages 12–13, 16, 18 of the student text.

4. a. See page 10 of the student text.
   b. See pages 11–12 of the student text.
   c. See page 12 of the student text.
   d. See pages 16–18 of the student text.
5. a. See page 19 of the student text.
   b. See page 19 of the student text.

Lesson 1 (pages 27–37)

Exercise V.   Word Roundup (page 33)

1. *Abstemious* indicates moderation in indulging one's appetites; *abstinent*, on the other hand, indicates total avoidance of the thing in question.
2. a. The costume (usually consisting of a cap, gown, and hood) that students, holders of academic degrees, and the faculty of a school, college, or university wear on official occasions.
   b. An establishment where the art of horsemanship is taught.
   c. The right of a teacher or student to discuss or express his or her views on current political, social, or economic issues without interference from public or school officials.
   d. A question that is purely theoretical and has little or no bearing on practical problems or real situations.
3. a. *Forbear* is a verb meaning "to restrain oneself"; *forebear* (with the extra *e*) is a noun meaning "ancestor." Also, *forbear* is accented on the second syllable; *forebear* on the first.
   b. *Loathe* is a verb meaning "dislike intensely"; *loath* is an adjective meaning "reluctant" or "disinclined." Also, the *th* in *loathe* is pronounced <u>th</u>, while the *th* in *loath* is pronounced th.

Exercise (page 35)

2. Answers will vary. See list at top of page 35 of student text.
3. *indict* ("make a formal charge against"): *in* (Latin), "against" + *dicere, dictus* (Latin), "say, speak"
   dictum ("authoritative pronouncement"): *dictum* (Latin), "something said"; from *dicere, dictus* (Latin), "say, speak"
   contradict ("express the opposite of; be contrary to"): *contra* (Latin), "against" + *dicere, dictus* (Latin), "say, speak"
   benediction ("blessing"): *bene* (Latin), "well" + *dicere, dictus* (Latin), "say, speak"
4. a. The student in the graduating class who delivers the farewell (*vale* [Latin], "farewell" + *dicere, dictus* [Latin], "say") address at commencement. Usually, the vale-

541

dictorian is the student who ranks first academically in the class.

b. A hairline that is moving backwards (*re* [Latin], "back," + *cedere* [Latin], "go") from its original position at the front of the forehead. In other words, a person with a receding hairline is beginning to go bald.

c. Nonrepresentational (*ab, abs* [Latin], "away from [*i.e.*, from concrete reality]" + *trahere, tractus* [Latin], "draw, pull, remove") art, in which intellectual and emotional meaning are conveyed solely by form.

d. The word, phrase, or clause in the preceding section (*ante* [Latin], "before" + *cedere* [Latin], "go") of the sentence or other grammatical unit to which the pronoun refers.

Exercise I. It's the Law! (pages 36–37)
B.

In addition to an unabridged dictionary, a handbook of legal terminology may prove useful in answering the questions in this section of the exercise.

1. An *accessory before the fact* is a person who knows that a crime is planned, assists in the plot, but is not present when the crime is actually committed; an *accessory after the fact* has no part in, or knowledge of, the events leading up to a crime (including its commission) but conceals or otherwise assists a criminal after he or she has committed the crime.

2. A *quitclaim* is a legal document that transfers a title, right, or claim in or to an estate from one person to another. It is sometimes used as a simple but efficient means of making a grant of land. Both *quitclaim* and *acquit* derive from *quite* (Old French, "free of"), which in turn comes from *quietus* (Latin, "calm, quiet").

3. A respected lawyer would object to being called a shyster because *shyster* is a highly offensive and pejorative slang term for an unethical or unscrupulous member of the bar. Great Britain (England); *barrister* is the British (English) term for what Americans would call a *trial lawyer*.

4. A *writ* is a written court order commanding the person or persons to whom it is addressed to perform (or cease to perform) a specific act. A *writ of habeas corpus* (Medieval Latin for "you shall have the body," the first words of such a writ) is a document that summons before a court or a judge a person who has been arrested but not formally

charged with a crime. The purpose of this writ is to compel the police to file a formal charge against the person arrested or to release him/her. A *writ of mandamus* (Latin for "we order," the first word of the writ) is a legal document issued by a superior court to a public official, public body, or lower court ordering him/her/them/it to perform a specific act.

5. *Impeach* means "charge with misconduct while in office"; *convict* means "find guilty of a crime or other form of misconduct." The House of Representatives is empowered to impeach a president of the United States; the Senate has the right to try and convict (or acquit) him/her.

6. A *plea* is the defendant's response ("guilty," "not guilty," "nolo contendere") to a charge. *Plea bargaining* refers to negotiations between prosecuting and defense attorneys to have the defendant plead guilty to a lesser charge in order to avoid standing trial for a more serious one. *To cop a plea* means "to plead guilty to a lesser charge so as to avoid standing trial for a more serious one."

7. A *misdemeanor* is a minor offense (*e.g.*, jaywalking, littering) for which the penalty is usually a fine or incarceration in a jail for less than a year; a *felony* is a serious offense (*e.g.*, murder) for which the penalty is usually capital punishment or incarceration in a penitentiary for a year or more. A *tort* is a civil (as opposed to a criminal) wrong that has been done to a person and can consequently be compensated for by cash damages (as opposed to some form of criminal punishment).

8. He or she is asking to have his/her case tried in another court. (A *venue* is the place or court where a trial is to be held.) A judge might grant such a request if the publicity surrounding the apprehension of the defendant has made it difficult or impossible to select an impartial jury.

9. A *petit jury* is the group of 12 jurors (usually plus 2 alternates) that determines whether the evidence offered at a trial proves the accused guilty or not guilty of the charge involved. A *grand jury* is a group of 12 to 23 persons convened in private session to determine whether there is probable cause to try a suspect in a court of law on a felony charge. A *hung jury* is one that is deadlocked and cannot render a unanimous verdict either for or against the defendant.

10. *Double jeopardy* refers to the constitutional principle that no person may be tried twice on the same charge or for the same offense.

Exercise II.   Place-Names in Common Use (page 37)

In addition to a dictionary, *Brewer's Dictionary of Phrase and Fable*, 16th ed. (New York: HarperCollins, 1999) and *Morris Dictionary of Word and Phrase Origins*, 2d ed. (New York: HarperCollins, 1988) may prove helpful in answering the questions in this exercise.

1. A humorous or nonsensical verse form, made up of five anapestic lines usually having the rhyme scheme aabba. County Limerick, Ireland. The name of the Irish county was first applied to the verse form (invented by Edward Lear) toward the end of the 19th century, when it became popular in barrooms to bawl out, "We'll all come up, come up to Limerick," between the verses of somewhat coarse limericks.
2. An oil-based paint used to coat a surface with a hard, glossy finish. Probably Berenike, an ancient city in Cyrenaica, Libya, where varnishes were thought to have been first used.
3. Any place regarded as the center of attraction, interest, or activity. Mecca, the birthplace of Muhammad, a city in western Saudi Arabia.
4. A scented liquid of alcohol and various fragrant oils. Cologne (Köln), a city in western Germany, where the inventor of the item, Johann Maria Farina, settled in 1709.
5. Empty or meaningless talk or claptrap, especially from a politician. Buncombe County, North Carolina; from a remark made around 1820 by Felix Walker, a U.S. congressman, who called an empty political speech he had made "a speech for Buncombe."
6. Overused and therefore trite and banal. Hackney-Stepney, a district in London where horses ("hacks") were let out for hire; such horses soon became overused and synonymous with what was stale and flat.
7. A large, luxurious passenger car, especially one with an enclosed passenger compartment and an open (but roofed) driver's seat. Limousin, a province in west-central France, where a flowing hooded garment was worn by the people. It is not certain whether the car took its name (*limousine* means "hood" in French) from the dress of the original chauffeurs or from the similarity of the enclosed passenger compartment to a hood.

8. Chaos; pandemonium. St. Mary of Bethlehem (pronounced bĕd'-ləm), a notorious hospital and insane asylum in London.
9. Devoted to pleasure and luxury. Sybaris, a Greek city on the Gulf of Taranto in southern Italy; this city became a center of luxurious living before its destruction in 519 B.C.
10. A free-for-all or brawl. The annual Donnybrook Fair, near Dublin, Ireland, where such brawls were common.
11. Smooth, flattering talk or nonsense. The Blarney Stone, Blarney Castle, County Cork, Ireland; this stone was believed to give those who kissed it the gift of eloquent flattery.
12. A dressing made of beaten egg yolk, olive oil, lemon juice or vinegar, and seasonings. Port Mahon, Minorca. According to tradition, the Duc de Richelieu's chef first prepared this concoction in honor of the Duc's capture of Port Mahon in 1756.
13. Boastfulness, swagger, or bravado. Gascony, a province in southwest France, whose inhabitants were traditionally considered to be braggarts.
14. Cheap and gaudy. St. Audrey's Fair, Isle of Ely, England, where cheap and gaudy lace neckerchiefs were sold. St. Audrey (Etheldrida), Queen of Northumbria, died in A.D. 679 of a throat tumor that was regarded as divine retribution for her overfondness for necklaces.
15. Scornfully mocking or cynical. Sardinia, where a poisonous plant (*herba Sardonica*) grew that distorted the face of the person who ate it. Another legend relates that those who ate this plant died in bitter laughter.

Exercise III.   Expanding Your Word Power (page 37)

1. *Definition:* To relinquish or give up (a claim or right) voluntarily.
   Etymology: weiven (Middle English), "abandon"; from *weyver, gaiver* (Norman French), "abandon"; from *gaif* (Old French), "ownerless property"
   Synonyms: relinquish, renounce, give up
   Antonyms: retain, hold on to
2. *Definition:* To prevent or discourage, usually by means of fear or doubt.
   Etymology: de (Latin), "away from" + *terrere* (Latin), "frighten"
   Synonyms: impede, hinder, restrain
   Antonyms: abet, aid, promote, encourage
3. *Definition:* A strong dislike, a feeling of intense repugnance.

Etymology: a (Latin), "away from" + *vertere, versus* (Latin), "turn" + *-tio, -tionis* (Latin), "state of"

Synonyms: antipathy, loathing, abhorrence, distaste

Antonyms: liking, fondness, affinity, taste, partiality

4. *Definition:* Lowborn, common, or dishonorable.

Etymology: in (Latin), "not" + *nobilis, nobile,* (Latin), "noble"

Synonyms: mean, petty, base, vile, shameful, ignominious

Antonyms: noble, lofty, elevated, honorable

5. *Definition:* To cooperate secretly in wrongdoing; to pretend ignorance of, or fail to take measures against, wrongdoing, thus implying tacit approval of what is going on.

Etymology: conivere (Latin), "close to the eyes"

Synonyms: collude, conspire; condone, turn a blind eye to

Antonyms: discourage, block, hinder, frustrate, foil, thwart

6. *Definition:* To suggest guilt or complicity in wrongdoing; to charge with or involve in a crime.

Etymology: in (Latin) "in" + *crimen, criminis* (Latin), "crime" + *-ate* (from *-atus* [Latin]), a verb-forming suffix roughly meaning "make"

Synonyms: implicate, inculpate; charge, accuse

Antonyms: exculpate, exonerate, absolve, acquit

7. *Definition: (n.)* A person who renounces creature comforts in order to lead a life of austerity and self-denial, especially as an act of religious devotion; *(adj.)* self-denying, austere.

Etymology: asketikos (Greek), "austere"; from *asketes* (Greek), "hermit"

Synonyms: (n.) celibate, puritan, anchorite; *(adj.)* abstinent, austere, puritanical, severe, harsh

Antonyms: (n.) profligate, libertine, rake, epicurean, hedonist, sybarite; *(adj.)* self-indulgent, sybaritic, debauched, dissolute, dissipated

8. *Definition:* To shun or avoid completely.

Etymology: eschiver (Old French, but ultimately of Germanic origin), "avoid"

Synonyms: abstain, steer clear of, forgo, forbear, shy away from, disdain

Antonyms: embrace, welcome

9. *Definition:* To consent to, or comply with, passively or without protest.

Etymology: acquiescere (Latin), "agree tacitly with"; from *ad* (Latin), "to" + *quiescere* (Latin), "rest; permit quietly"

Synonyms: concur, accede, assent

Antonyms: balk at, dissent, demur

10. *Definition:* The process of adjusting or adapting to a new environment or situation; a general tendency or inclination in a person's thought; introductory instruction concerning a new environment; position relative to the points of a compass.

Etymology: oriens, orientis (Latin), "rising"

Synonyms: bearings, placement; acclimation, assimilation

11. *Definition:* To yield to or gratify one's desires or whims.

Etymology: indulgere (Latin), "be kind or favorable to"

Synonyms: humor, pamper, coddle

Antonyms: curb, check, restrain

12. *Definition: (v.)* To take exception to; have scruples about; *(n.)* an objection or qualm.

Etymology: de (Latin), "very, completely" + *morari* (Latin), "delay"

Synonyms: (v.) balk at, dissent, protest; *(n.)* doubt, misgiving

Antonyms: (v.) accede, acquiesce, consent, concur, assent; *(n.)* consent, agreement, acquiescence

Lesson 2 (pages 38–50)

Exercise V.   Word Roundup (page 45)

1. *Agenda* is the plural form of the (neuter) gerund of the Latin verb *agere* ("do, make"). It means "things that are to be done." (The gerund is often used in Latin to express obligation.) The singular form is *agendum*, "that which is to be done." In English, *agenda* is often construed as singular because it is regarded as a collective noun.

2. a. See page 39 of the student text.
   b. See page 41 of the student text.
   c. See page 41 of the student text.
   d. To affect manners or a pose not one's own, but suggesting that one is more highly born, more knowledgeable, or the like, than one really is.
   e. See page 41 of the student text.
   f. See page 42 of the student text.

Exercise I.   Specialized Knowledge (page 47)

1. A magician or practitioner of sleight of hand.
2. A person who practices a system of therapy that involves the manipulation of the spinal column and other bodily structures to treat illness.
3. An announcer of a radio show featuring popular recorded music or a person who plays recorded dance music at a nightclub or party.
4. A specialist in treatment and rehabilitation.

5. A person who seeks to protect the natural environment and who has specialized knowledge of ecology.
6. A person who seeks to protect the rights of consumers by requiring such practices as honest packaging, labeling, and advertising; fair pricing; and better safety standards.
7. A person responsible for seeing that others interpret an event from a particular point of view.
8. A doctor who treats foot ailments.
9. An officer who audits the accounts and supervises the financial affairs of a corporation or a governmental body.
10. A person who prepares programs and tests for devices such as computers; a person who programs a mechanism; or a person who prepares instructional or educational programs.
11. A scientist devoted to the study of the origin and physical, social, and cultural development and behavior of human beings.
12. A scientist devoted to the study of society, social institutions, and social relationships.
13. A doctor who specializes in the care and treatment of children.
14. A doctor who specializes in the care and treatment of pregnant women before, during, and immediately after childbirth.
15. A physician specializing in the treatment of diseases or ailments of the eye.
16. A person qualified to treat or prevent disease or injury in animals.
17. A person who examines, measures, and treats visual defects by means of corrective lenses or other methods (*e.g.*, exercises) that do not require a physician's license.
18. A person who performs gymnastic feats requiring skillful or masterly control of the body and great agility.
19. A doctor who specializes in surgery performed on any part of the nervous system (*e.g.*, the brain).
20. A scientist who deals with the atmosphere and its phenomena, especially weather forecasting.

Exercise II. Portmanteau Words
(page 47)
1. (*n.*) A snorting, joyful chuckle; (*v.*) to make such a noise. *chuckle + snort*
2. (*n.*) A splash of liquid; (*v.*) to soil with splashes of liquid; to spatter. *splash + spatter*
3. (*n.*) A simultaneous broadcast on radio (for the sound) and television (for the picture); (*v.*) to make such a broadcast. *simultaneous + broadcast*
4. A chance event or circumstance. *happen + circumstance*
5. (*n.*) A harsh scream; (*v.*) to utter such a scream. *squall + squeak*
6. A lengthy TV commercial designed to appear more like an educational program or a talk show than like just another piece of advertising. *information + commercial*
7. (*n.*) A television broadcast; (*v.*) to broadcast on television. *television + broadcast*
8. Fog that has become polluted with smoke. *smoke + fog*
9. A hotel for motorists, usually with rows of rooms surrounding and opening onto a parking area. *motor + hotel*
10. An estimate made from inadequate information; a rough guess. *guess + estimate*
11. A newspaper or magazine supplement designed to appear more like a regular news piece than like a piece of advertising. *advertising + editorial*
12. A telegram sent by marine cable. *cable + telegram*
13. A long, continuous television program, usually presented to raise funds for a worthy cause. *television + marathon*
14. A situation comedy. *situation + comedy*
15. A flat space, often on top of a building, used by helicopters for take-offs and landings. *helicopter + airport*

Exercise III. Exploring the Dictionary
(page 48)
1. A conglomerate is made up of many different companies that operate in widely diversified fields. An ordinary business is a single company working in only one field.
2. a. The organization of a political or other grouping in which the various constituent units surrender their individual sovereignty to a central authority but retain limited powers over their own affairs.
   b. A political or other grouping in which the various constituent units are joined in a loose league. Usually there is a weak central authority, and the constituent units retain many of the attributes of sovereignty.
   c. A conspiratorial (and usually secret) group of plotters or intriguers.
   d. A combination of persons, groups, or nations forming a unit with a common interest or purpose.
   e. A combination of business organizations designed to limit competition.
   f. A temporary alliance of persons, parties, or states for joint action.
   g. An association of financial institutions or capitalists designed to

bring success to some business venture that requires extensive financial backing.

h. An association designed to further the interests of the constituent members (persons, parties, states); also, the bond or connection between them.

i. A group of military officers holding power in a country after a coup d'état.

3. *Federalism* indicates the doctrine or principle of the federal organization of government (see 2a above) or support or advocacy of this principle. *World federalism* indicates a program that envisages the formation of a federal union comprising all the nations of the world.

4. a. In a heedless or reckless frame of mind.

b. Admitting something good about a person one dislikes or frowns upon; owning up to favorable facts about a person, even though he or she may be somewhat distasteful.

c. Hard-boiled eggs whose yolks have been removed, mixed with mayonnaise and pungent seasonings, and then replaced in the whites.

d. Caught between two equally objectionable or hazardous alternatives or between two comparable evils.

e. A fiendish or gleefully perverse look.

f. An apprentice in a printing establishment.

g. A rich chocolate cake.

h. Harassed, annoyed, vexed, pestered, or troubled by adversity.

Exercise IV. Expanding Your Word Power (page 48)

1. *Definition:* An opponent or enemy.
Etymology: adversarius (Latin), "opponent"; from *ad* (Latin, "to; against" + *vertere, versus* (Latin), "turn"
Synonyms: antagonist, rival, foe
Antonyms: champion, proponent, defender, backer, supporter, friend

2. *Definition:* Hardship, affliction, or misfortune.
Etymology: ad (Latin), "to, toward; against" + *vertere, versus* (Latin), "turn" + *-itas, -itatis* (Latin), "state of"
Synonyms: woe, distress, misery, tribulation, calamity, disaster
Antonyms: felicity, happiness, good fortune, luck, success

3. *Definition:* Hostile or harmful.
Etymology: in (Latin), "not" + *amicus* (Latin), "friend" + *-alis, -ale* (Latin), "characteristic of, like"

Synonyms: detrimental, deleterious, pernicious, noxious, unfavorable, unfriendly
Antonyms: beneficial, salutary, salubrious, favorable, friendly

4. *Definition:* To marry; to give one's loyalty or support to.
Etymology: espouser (Old French), "marry"; from *spondere, sponsus* (Latin), "pledge solemnly"
Synonyms: wed; embrace, adopt, take up
Antonyms: divorce; reject, eschew, repudiate

5. *Definition:* Sullenly rude and ill-humored.
Etymology: sirly (obsolete English), "lordly, imperious"; from *sir* + *ly*
Synonyms: gruff, irascible, cantankerous, peevish, irritable, testy
Antonyms: friendly, affable, genial, gracious, good-natured, even-tempered

6. *Definition:* Having a pleasant or friendly disposition.
Etymology: genialis (Latin), "nuptial; joyous, festive"
Synonyms: affable, gracious, cordial, good-natured, amiable
Antonyms: surly, testy, irascible, cantankerous, peevish

7. *Definition:* Utterly penniless; altogether lacking in.
Etymology: destituere, destitutus (Latin), "desert, abandon"; from *de* (Latin), "down from; away from" + *statuere* (Latin), "place"
Synonyms: indigent, impoverished, penurious; devoid, lacking
Antonyms: affluent, well-to-do, wealthy, rich; full, abounding, replete

8. *Definition:* To blend or combine into a unified whole.
Etymology: amalgama (Medieval Latin), "mixture" + *-ate*, a verb-forming suffix roughly meaning "make"; probably from *al-jama'ah* (Arabic), "assembly"
Synonyms: fuse, merge, consolidate
Antonyms: separate, divide, partition, subdivide, disunite

9. *Definition:* (*adj.*) Made up of distinct components; (*n.*) a complex structure or entity.
Etymology: com, a form of *cum* (Latin), "together" + *ponere, positus* (Latin), "place, put"
Synonyms: (*adj.*) compound, complex; (*n.*) synthesis, blend, amalgam, pastiche, collage, mixture, hybrid
Antonyms: (*adj.*) simple, monolithic, uniform

10. *Definition:* Sluggish and indifferent.
Etymology: lethargos (Greek), "forgetful"; from *lethe* (Greek), "forgetfulness"

Synonyms: torpid, phlegmatic, supine, slothful, listless
Antonyms: active, dynamic, energetic

11. *Definition:* Having an inherent aversion to or repugnance for.
Etymology: anti (Greek), "opposite" + *pathos* (Greek), "feeling"
Synonyms: hostile, antagonistic; repugnant, abhorrent
Antonyms: friendly; pleasing, agreeable, pleasant, attractive

12. *Definition:* Quick, agile, and deft.
Etymology: nemel, nym(b)yl (Middle English), "agile"; from *naemel* (Old English), "quick-witted," and *numol* (Old English), "seizing"
Synonyms: dexterous, lithe, spry, sprightly, adroit
Antonyms: clumsy, awkward, blundering, bumbling, maladroit, slow

Lesson 3 (pages 51–61)

Exercise VI.   Word Roundup (page 57)
1. This is a somewhat subtle distinction. *Allude* usually applies to an *indirect* reference that does not name the thing being alluded to. *Refer,* on the other hand, usually means that the thing has been mentioned or named *directly.* Thus, a person might *allude* to his or her attendance at Harvard by saying something like "I really began to understand what the theater was all about as a member of the Hasty Pudding Club." (The Hasty Pudding Club is Harvard's amateur theatrical group.) However, the person would *refer* to his or her attendance at Harvard by saying something like this: "I began to understand what the theater was all about during my first semester as a drama major at Harvard."
2. See page 52 of the student text.
3. See page 52 of the student text.
4. See page 52 of the student text.

Exercise (pages 59–60)
1. The *d* of *ad* is dropped, and the following consonant doubles. This phenomenon is called *assimilation.* Basic Words showing this phenomenon in practice include the following: *accede, acclimate, affectation, affluent, aggregate, allege, allude,* and the words mentioned on page 57 of the student text.
2. **a.** An *archdiocese* is a diocese (a type of ecclesiastical district) under the jurisdiction of an archbishop. An *archbishop* resides in an archdiocese. The adjective form of archdiocese is *archdiocesan.*
   b. A *patriarch* is the paternal leader of a family, tribe, or other social grouping. The three Old Testament patriarchs are Abraham, Isaac, and Jacob, though the twelve sons of Jacob, as eponymous progenitors of the twelve tribes of Israel, are also regarded as patriarchs.
   c. The word *arch* in a phrase like *an arch smile* means "sly" or "mischievous"; the prefix *arch* in such words as *archenemy* means "principal, chief, or of the highest rank."
   d. *archangel:* a celestial being next in rank above an angel.
   archduke: a nobleman whose ceremonial or social status is the same as that of a sovereign prince and who, consequently, ranks above a simple duke.
   archduchess: the wife of an archduke, ranking higher in the social order than a simple duchess.
   archpriest: a priest holding first rank among the members of a cathedral chapter and serving as a bishop's chief assistant: accordingly, an archpriest ranks higher than a simple priest.
   archdeacon: an official (primarily of the Anglican Church) who is in charge of temporal and other affairs in a diocese; accordingly, an archdeacon ranks higher than a simple deacon.
5. **a.** At will, freely, or spontaneously.
   b. With respect to this particular thing; for this specific purpose, case, or situation.
   c. Appealing to personal interests, prejudices, or feelings rather than to reason. (This phrase is usually used of arguments.)
   d. To a disgusting or ridiculous degree; to the point of nausea.
   e. Endlessly.
   f. In proportion to the value. (This phrase is usually used of taxes or duties on goods or the like.)

Exercise II.   Stating the Case (page 60)
1. **a.** Communicate delicately or indirectly.
   b. Speak or write about at length or in great detail.
   c. Declare or confess openly.
   d. Impart or introduce artfully, stealthily, or obliquely.
   e. Declare positively, forcefully, or aggressively.
   f. Deliver in an oratorical manner or as an eloquent recitation; speak loudly and vehemently.
   g. State or set forth precisely or systematically; pronounce clearly.
   h. Declare firmly and solemnly.
   i. Assert as a confirmed truth.
   j. Declare or assert positively.

k. Quote, mention, refer to, or allude to.

l. Suggest or express indirectly or by logical necessity.

2. A *soliloquy* is a speech made while or as if alone; a *colloquy* is a conversation between two or more people. A *colloquium* is an academic seminar on some broad field of study; usually a different lecturer conducts each meeting. The word is also used to indicate an informal discussion group. A *monologist* is a comedian who delivers a continuous series of jokes or comic stories (called a *monologue*). The word is also used of a serious actor or actress who delivers sketches and other serious pieces of writing as monologues or soliloquies. *Dialogue* refers to the conversational passages in a play, novel, film, or the like.

3. a. Talk, converse frankly.

b. Talk, converse in an idle, friendly fashion; chat.

c. Become silent or uncommunicative.

d. Answer or respond rudely, disrespectfully, or impudently.

e. A voluble, often extravagant line of talk; a pitch.

f. Talk, especially idly.

g. Criticize severely or persistently.

h. Boast or talk pretentiously.

i. Utter suddenly and impulsively.

In answering the preceding question, students may find the following useful: Makkai, Boatner, and Gates: *A Dictionary of American Idioms*, 3d ed. (Barron's Educational Series: Hauppauge, New York, 1995).

Exercise III. Telling a Story (page 61)

1. A *fable* is a fictitious narrative intended to clarify and emphasize a useful truth, especially one in which animals speak and act like human beings. An *anecdote* is a short narrative telling an interesting, amusing, or curious incident of some kind; it may or may not be true. An *allegory* is a fictional narrative containing symbolic figures and actions designed to express truths or generalizations about human experience in an interesting but usually nonrealistic way. Famous authors of fables include Aesop, George Ade, and James Thurber (*Fables for Our Time*). Student answers for the remainder of this question will vary.

2. *tall story:* A narrative that, on the face of it, could not possibly be true because of exaggerated or fantastic content; the exaggeration is intended to amuse or instruct, not to deceive.

memoir: A realistic account of something noteworthy or interesting composed by the person who experienced it; a person's recollections.

yarn: A rambling narrative of adventures, experiences, etc.

parable: A short fictitious story that illustrates a religious truth or moral principle.

Differences: Yarns and tall stories are fairly similar. Yarns, however, carry the suggestion of being longer and more formless; they may also recount true happenings (which is not the case with tall stories). Parables are usually much shorter than yarns or tall stories; and the plot, characters, and incidents in a parable are usually much more realistic than in a tall story. A memoir recounts personal experiences in a realistic manner (which is not the case with a tall story, yarn, or parable).

3. A *quip* is a clever, usually taunting, reply. A *retort* is a quick, witty, or cutting reply, especially one that turns a speaker's words against him/her. A *bon mot* is a clever remark or witticism.

4. Answers will vary.

5. The Latin word *fabula* means "story" or "tale." *Fabula* is the root from which the English word *fabulous* is derived; it provides the English word with both its literal meaning ("told of or celebrated in story and fable") and its figurative meaning ("barely credible, astonishing"). In both a *person of fabulous wealth* and *fabulous exploits*, the word *fabulous* means "astonishing" or "incredible"; in a *fabulous party*, it means "extremely pleasing, successful, or enjoyable."

Exercise IV. Expanding Your Word Power (page 61)

1. *Definition:* (*adj.*) Foreign; unfamiliar; inconsistent with; (*n.*) a foreigner or outsider.

Etymology: alienus (Latin), "stranger"; from *alias* (Latin), "other"

Synonyms: (*adj.*) exotic, strange, outlandish, remote; contrary to, conflicting with; (*n.*) stranger

Antonyms: (*adj.*) native, indigenous, endemic; consistent with; (*n.*) inhabitant, native

2. *Definition:* To alienate or make hostile and unsympathetic.

Etymology: extraneus (Latin), "foreign, strange"; from *extra* (Latin), "outside, beyond" + *-neus* (Latin), "pertaining to"

Synonyms: antagonize, disaffect, part company with

Antonyms: befriend, captivate, enchant

3. *Definition:* To swing indecisively between one opinion or course of action and another.

Etymology: vacillare, vacillatus (Latin), "waver"
Synonyms: hesitate, waver, dither, hem and haw, oscillate, fluctuate
Antonyms: adhere to, remain firm, be steadfast, stick to

4. *Definition:* To strive with, as in battle, competition, or debate; to maintain.
Etymology: con, a form of *cum* (Latin), "with" + *tendere* (Latin), "strive"
Synonyms: struggle, wrestle, grapple, compete, vie, dispute; claim, assert

5. *Definition:* Total disorder and confusion.
Etymology: khaos (Greek), "empty space; confusion"
Synonyms: pandemonium, bedlam, ferment, tumult
Antonyms: order, orderliness, peace and quiet, calm, tranquility

6. *Definition:* A formal expression of lofty praise.
Etymology: enkomion (epos) (Greek), "(speech) in praise of a conqueror": from *en* (Greek), "in" + *komos* (Greek), "celebration"
Synonyms: eulogy, panegyric, tribute
Antonyms: philippic, diatribe, tirade, invective

7. *Definition:* To declare positively or firmly; to maintain to be true.
Etymology: ad (Latin), "to" + *firmare* (Latin), "give firmness"
Synonyms: assert, aver, avouch, asseverate, attest, vouch
Antonyms: impugn, cast doubt on; deny, repudiate

8. *Definition:* A decorative design along the borders of a page or at the beginning or end of a chapter or book; a literary sketch; a kind of portrait.
Etymology: vignette (French), "little vine"; from *vigne* (French), "vine"
Synonyms: headpiece, tailpiece; illumination; thumbnail sketch

9. *Definition:* An incident in a series of related events; a portion of a narrative, film, or serialized radio-TV program.
Etymology: epeisodion (Greek), "addition"; from *epi* (Greek), "besides" + *eis* (Greek), "into" + *hodos* (Greek), "road, way"
Synonyms: event, happening, occurrence; interlude; installment, chapter

10. *Definition:* To praise lavishly.
Etymology: ex (Latin), "up" + *tollere* (Latin), "raise"
Synonyms: laud, eulogize, glorify, acclaim, commend
Antonyms: disparage, belittle, depreciate, denigrate, assail, abuse, criticize

Lesson 4 (pages 62–74)

Exercise V. Word Roundup (page 69)
1. See page 62 of the student text.
2. See pages 67 and 57 of the student text.
3. See page 64 of the student text.

Exercise I. Our Greek Heritage (page 72)
1. Belonging to a much earlier time; no longer current or applicable. *arkhaikos* (Greek), "ancient"; from *arkhe* (Greek), "beginning," and *arkhein* (Greek), "begin."
2. Jarring, harsh, and discordant sound. *kakophonia* (Greek), "hubbub"; from *kakos* (Greek), "bad" + *phone* (Greek), "sound."
3. A novice or beginner; a recent convert. *neophytos* (New Testament Greek), "newly planted"; from *neos* (Greek), "new" + *phytos* (Greek), "grown."
4. A model or pattern of excellence. *parakone* (Medieval Greek), "whetstone"; from *para* (Greek), "alongside" + *akonan* (Greek), "sharpen."
5. An abnormal or illogical fear of a specific thing or situation. *phobos* (Greek), "fear; flight."
6. A maneuver designed to deceive or surprise an enemy. *stratagema* (Greek), "generalship"; from *stratos* (Greek), "army" + *agein* (Greek), "lead."
7. Hating or distrusting mankind. *misanthropos* (Greek), "hating mankind"; from *misos* (Greek), "hatred" + *anthropos* (Greek), "mankind."
8. Love of mankind; a desire to increase the well-being of mankind by charitable aid, donations, or service. *philanthropia* (Greek), "humanity"; from *philos* (Greek), "liking, loving" + *anthropos* (Greek), "human being; mankind."
9. Characterized by authoritative or arrogant assertions of unproven or unprovable principles, ideas, or doctrines; dictatorial or authoritarian. *dogmatikos* (Greek), "opinionated"; from *dogma* (Greek), "opinion, belief" + *ikos* (Greek), "full of; characterized by."
10. Characterized by continuous energy, force, or change; energetic, vigorous, or forceful. *dynamikos* (Greek), "powerful"; from *dynamis* (Greek), "power" + *ikos* (Greek), "full of; characterized by."
11. (n.) A contagious disease that spreads rapidly, especially among people; rapid spread, growth, or development; (adj.) spreading rapidly or extensively. *epidemia (nosos)* (Greek), "(illness) prevalent among

human beings"; from *epi* (Greek), "among" + *demos* (Greek), "people."

12. A formal public eulogy; elaborate praise. (*logos*) *panegyrikos* (Greek), "(speech) for a public festival"; from *pas, pan* (Greek), "all" + *agora/agyria* (Greek), "assembly; marketplace."

13. A plausible but false or misleading argument; plausible but faulty reasoning, *sophistes* (Greek), "expert, deviser"; from *sophos* (Greek), "clever, skilled, wise."

14. Exclusive control by one group over the means of producing or selling a commodity or service. *monopolion* (Greek), "sole selling rights"; from *monos* (Greek), "one, single, alone" + *polein* (Greek), "sell."

15. A violent or sudden change or upheaval. *kataklysmos* (Greek), "flood"; from *kata* (Greek), "down" + *klyzein* (Greek), "wash, pour."

16. A succession of rulers from the same family or bloodline; a family or other group that maintains power for several generations. *dynasteia* (Greek), "lordship, dominion"; from *dynastes* (Greek), "ruler."

17. Overly attentive to book learning or formal rules without having an understanding or experience of practical affairs; exhibiting learning ostentatiously. Ultimately from *paidagogos* (see below).

18. The art or profession of teaching; preparatory learning or instruction. *paidagogos* (Greek), "teacher of boys"; from *paidos* (Greek), "boy (child)" + *agein* (Greek), "lead."

19. Intended to instruct; morally instructive; inclined to teach or moralize too much. *didaktikos* (Greek), "skillful in teaching"; from *didaskein* (Greek), "'teach" + *ikos* (Greek), "full of, characterized by."

20. Adhering to the commonly accepted, traditional, or customary in practice or belief. *orthos* (Greek), "right, correct, straight" + *doxa* (Greek), "opinion, belief."

Exercise II. Order and Chaos (page 72)

1. a. A government in which the supreme power is vested in the people and exercised by them directly or indirectly through a system of representation involving periodically held free elections. *demos* (Greek), "people" + *kratia* (Greek), "rule." *Kratia* comes from the Greek root *kratos* ("rule"); it is used only in compounds.

   b. The government of a political unit by direct divine guidance or by officials regarded as divinely guided. *theos* (Greek), "god" + *kratia* (Greek), "rule."

   c. Any of the various economic and political theories advocating collective or governmental ownership and administration of the means of production and distribution of goods. *socialis* (Latin), "allied" + *ismos* (Greek), "doctrine, theory."

   d. A totalitarian system of government in which a single authoritarian party controls the state-owned means of production with the professed aim of establishing a classless society; an economic system in which goods, as well as the means of production and distribution, are owned in common and available to all as needed. *commun* (French), "common" + *ismos* (Greek), "doctrine, theory."

   e. A political philosophy, movement, or system of government that exalts the nation or race above the individual and that stands for centralized authoritarian government headed by a dictatorial leader, severe economic and social regimentation, and forcible repression of opposition. *fasces* (Latin), "bundle of rods from which an ax projects" (the symbol of the Italian Fascist movement derived from the old Roman and Etruscan symbol of kingship or power) + *ismos* (Greek), "doctrine, theory."

   f. A form of government in which a small elite group exercises control, especially for self-interested or selfish purposes. *oligos* (Greek), "(a) few" + *archia* (Greek), "rule."

2. a. In politics, *nihilism* is the belief that the destruction of all existing social and political institutions is necessary in order to bring about future improvement. In ethics, it indicates the total rejection of all distinctions in moral values. In metaphysics, it denotes the doctrine that nothing exists, is knowable, or can be communicated. A *nihilist* is a person who holds one or more of these views.

   b. A *subversive* is interested in overthrowing or undermining (*sub* [Latin], "under" + *vertere, versus* [Latin], "turn") the existing political, social, or economic institutions or systems. The verb related to *subversive* is *subvert*, which means "overthrow or undermine."

   c. *Sedition* is conduct or language that incites to rebellion or insurrection against the established authority of the state; the word also indicates the rebellion or insurrection itself. The adjective related to *sedition* is *seditious*, which means "engaged in sedition" or "characterized by sedition."

Exercise III.　Expanding Your Word Power (page 72)

1. *Definition:* Having or showing little or no emotion.
   Etymology: stolidus (Latin), "slow, dull"
   Synonyms: impassive, unemotional, dispassionate
   Antonyms: emotional, passionate, excitable
2. *Definition:* Lack of interest or concern.
   Etymology: in (Latin), "not"+ *dis* (Latin), "in different directions" + *ferre* (Latin), "carry"
   Synonyms: apathy, unconcern, disinterest, detachment
   Antonyms: enthusiasm, ardor, fervor
3. *Definition:* Thoroughly shocked by something terrible.
   Etymology: a (Middle English), "completely" + *gasten* (Middle English), "frighten"
   Synonyms: flabbergasted, astounded, nonplussed, disconcerted
   Antonyms: unmoved, unsurprised; delighted, pleased, thrilled
4. *Definition:* To excite feelings of joy, pride, or optimism.
   Etymology: efferre, elatus (Latin), "lift up"; from *e, ex* (Latin), "up, out" + *ferre, latus* (Latin), "carry"
   Synonyms: gladden, exhilarate, cheer, thrill, delight
   Antonyms: deject, discourage, dishearten, dismay, sadden
5. *Definition:* To recognize mentally; to recognize as separate and distinct.
   Etymology: dis (Latin), "apart" + *cernere* (*Latin*), "sift, separate; perceive"
   Synonyms: perceive; distinguish, discriminate
   Antonyms: overlook
6. *Definition:* A feeling of doubt, uncertainty, or apprehension.
   Etymology: mis (Middle English), "wrongly" + *give* (Middle English), "suggest"
   Synonyms: qualm, scruple; queasiness, foreboding, presentiment
   Antonyms: confidence, certainty, conviction
7. *Definition:* Subject to changes of mood or whims.
   Etymology: capriccioso (Italian), "impulsive and changeable"; from *capo* (Italian), "head" + *riccio* (Italian), "hedgehog" + *oso* (Italian), "full of." (The original meaning of the Italian word was "with the hair on the head standing up in horror like the prickles on a hedgehog"; then under the influence of the Italian word *capra* ("goat"), it developed the meaning "flighty.")
   Synonyms: fickle, changeable, flighty, erratic, mercurial
   Antonyms: constant, steadfast, dependable, reliable, steady
8. *Definition:* To hear and settle by judicial process.
   Etymology: ad (Latin), "to" + *judicare, judicatus* (Latin), "be a judge"; from *judex* (Latin), "judge"
   Synonyms: arbitrate, mediate, umpire, referee, adjudge, decide
9. *Definition:* To station systematically or spread out over an area.
   Etymology: deployer (French), "spread out"; from *dis* (Latin), "in different directions" + *plicare, plicatus* (Latin), "fold"
   Synonyms: arrange, dispose, array
   Antonym: concentrate

Lesson 5 (pages 75–85)

Exercise (page 83)

1. a. In a physical sense, *autointoxication* indicates a condition in which a person (or some other organism) has become poisoned by substances produced in the body of that individual. In a psychological sense, the word indicates a state of nervous tension or excitement (resembling drunkenness) which the individual has induced in him- or herself—for example, the reactions of the people in a mob. Here *auto(s)* means "self."
   b. *Autonomy* indicates the state of being self-governing. Here again *auto(s)* means "self."
   c. The nerves and ganglia that control vital bodily processes not subject to the will—for example, heartbeat or breathing—are termed *autonomic*. In this case, *auto(s)* means "automatic."
   d. *Autosuggestion* indicates a suggestion originating from oneself. The word is a compound of *auto(s)*, meaning "self," and *suggestion*.
2. a. Someone who is harmed or killed by some external act, agency, circumstance, or condition. victimize
   b. Something held as an established belief or doctrine; a body of such beliefs or doctrines. dogmatize
   c. The art or science of government. politicize
   d. A disordered psychic or behavioral state resulting from mental or emotional stress or physical injury; an injury to living tissue. traumatize
   e. A person appointed as a substitute; an assistant or second-in-command; a member of the lower house of some legislative bodies. deputize
   f. A formal statement or oration commending someone; high praise. eulogize
   g. Polite; pertaining to the status and rights of the citizen body in rela-

tion to the ordinary activities of everyday life; pertaining to the internal affairs of a state or nation; characteristic of the regular, lawful administration of government. civilize

h. Having full filial rights and obligations because of birth; in accord with law or established legal forms or requirements; ruling by or based on strict principles of hereditary right; relating to plays performed by professional actors. legitimize

i. A new convert. proselytize

j. A government in which absolute power is vested in a single, dictatorial ruler; oppressive power; a severe condition or effect. tyrannize

k. Marked by or passed in pleasant companionship with one's friends or associates; relating to or designed for sociability; living in more or less organized communities; relating to human society, the interaction of the individual and the group, or the welfare of human beings as members of society. socialize

l. Stealing or passing off another's words as one's own; an instance of such theft. plagiarize

m. A plausible or scientifically acceptable principle offered to explain a phenomenon; the general or abstract principles of an art or science; an unproven assumption. theorize

n. (adj.) Fundamental; extreme; (n.) a person who wants extreme changes in existing views, habits, conditions, or institutions. radicalize

o. Usual or typical. normalize

Exercise I. Latin Phrases in English (page 84)

1. A constant companion or intimate friend. Literal translation: "Another I"
2. An equal exchange or substitute. Literal translation: "Something for something"
3. (adv.) Actually; (adj.) actual. Literal translation: "According to fact"
4. An unacceptable or unwelcome person. Literal translation: "A person [whose presence is] not welcome"
5. A judicial opinion that has only incidental bearing on a case and is therefore not binding; a passing remark or observation. Literal translation: "Something said in passing"
6. A person invited to advise a court on a matter of law in a case to which he or she is not a party. Literal translation: "Friend of the court"

7. According to law; by right. Literal translation: "By right"
8. The existing state of affairs or conditions. Literal translation: "The state in which [something is/was]"
9. For the time being; temporarily. Literal translation: "For the time [being]"
10. At first sight. Literal translation: "At first glance"
11. A method of working or operating. Literal translation: "A means of doing [something]"
12. By virtue of one's office or position. Literal translation: "Because of [one's] position"
13. The school, college, or university a person has attended; the school song. Literal translation: "Nourishing mother"
14. In secret; privately or confidentially. Literal translation: "Under the rose" (from the practice of hanging a rose over a meeting place as a sign of secrecy)
15. While or as though not present. Literal translation: "In absence"
16. With the order or meaning reversed; conversely. Literal translation: "The position being reversed"
17. An act or development that justifies a declaration of war. Literal translation: "The cause of, or occasion for, a war"
18. An inference or conclusion that does not follow logically from the premises or evidence; a statement that does not follow logically from what went before. Literal translation: "It does not follow"
19. An essential or indispensable element or condition. Literal translation: "Without which [it can] not [be]"
20. In ancient Greek and Roman drama, a god who was brought onto the stage by elaborate machinery in order to resolve a difficult situation; in literature generally, any artificial or improbable character or event introduced into the plot in order to resolve a knotty problem or untangle a complicated situation. Literal translation: "A god out of a machine" (a direct Latin translation of the Greek *theos ek mekhanes*)

Exercise II. Newsworthies (page 84)

A few of the items in this exercise may be too recent to be included in most older dictionaries. Accordingly, students will have to use their knowledge of the individual words making up these expressions to arrive at a suitable definition.

1. A relaxation or easing of strained relations, as between nations.
2. A person who advocates or engages in vigorous action to achieve an

objective, usually of a social, political, or economic nature.

3. The spending of public funds raised by borrowing rather than by taxation.

4. A person who believes in or advocates rule by an elite—that is, by a group of people who are believed to be inherently superior as a result of birth, education, natural ability, or some other attribute. The word (which is both a noun and an adjective) is usually distinctly pejorative in tone, principally because an elitist is scornful of the masses or the common man.

5. A state in which the government exerts repressive controls on politics, the economy, and social life in general, usually by means of (secret) police who act arbitrarily in place of regular administrative and judicial organs.

6. To lower the level of difficulty and the intellectual content of something.

7. A society in which members of diverse racial, ethnic, religious, national, or social groups live together and make their distinctive contributions to a social order or culture that combines (but does not eliminate) these different traditions. The United States is considered a pluralistic society. The idea of a pluralistic society is different from the older idea of a melting pot, in which all the different groups were supposed to be melted down, fused, and transformed into more or less standardized Americans.

8. A social system based upon the assumption by the government of all responsibility for the welfare and security of the people.

9. A person who is firmly dedicated to the ideals and practice of personal freedom (as opposed to government regulation), in both thought and action.

10. The tendency on the part of an authority (*e.g.*, parents, school officials, the government) to allow or countenance a wide range of freedom, deviation from the norm, and perhaps undisciplined conduct on the part of the individuals in their care. The word is often used in a pejorative sense to suggest that basic and necessary controls are not being applied.

11. A tangible proof or demonstration of the position or rank of a person in the social or economic hierarchy. The term is often applied to possessions indicating wealth: for example, expensive cars or homes in particularly affluent neighborhoods.

12. Rebuilding or otherwise renovating run-down or depressed areas of a city.

13. Incorrect information deliberately spread (often secretly) in order to influence opinion or obscure the truth.

14. One who desires to turn the clock back to a prior time or an older, outmoded order. Such a person is generally opposed to change or progress of any kind. A reactionary is essentially an extreme conservative, and the word is almost always derogatory.

15. Characterized by conscious or unconscious discrimination (*adj.*), or a person who consciously or unconsciously discriminates (*n.*), against others on the basis of sex. The word almost always refers to unfair treatment of women.

16. An exclusive group of people who rule a government or society; a powerful group of people who control some field of activity. Usually, the establishment is thought of as being conservative and concerned mainly with its own interests. The word is often capitalized and sometimes used as an adjective.

17. The immigration of middle-class people into a deteriorating or newly refurbished area of a city, resulting in a general improvement of living conditions there.

18. Illegal use of inside information in order to profit from trading in stocks.

19. Establishment or state of cordial relations, as between nations.

20. A person who believes in preserving what has been established, particularly the basic social, economic, or political structure of the society.

21. The firing of employees in order to reduce the size of a company's workforce and thereby achieve savings.

22. Someone formerly a political liberal who now supports conservatism.

23. A social trend or program initiated by the people themselves, as a fundamental socioeconomic group, without control or manipulation by the centers of political leadership, power, or culture.

24. A type of international relations in which everything is out in the open, without secret negotiations or agreements.

25. The entire set of programs, procedures, and related documentation associated with a computer system; also materials for use with audiovisual equipment. Its opposite is *hardware,* which indicates the physical components that actually make up the computer or audiovisual system.

26. An underdeveloped or developing country; the world's have-not nations are now officially classified by most world economists as LDCs (less developed countries). Commonly they experience food shortages, a lack of power sources, and low gross domestic products. Many LDCs are in Africa and Asia.
27. Organized activity on behalf of women's rights and interests, especially the contemporary movement to achieve social, economic, and political equality for women in the United States. Often called the *women's movement*.
28. A person who holds political views that favor civil liberties, democratic or progressive reforms, and the use of governmental power to promote social reforms and welfare. The word is usually capitalized when it refers to members of established political parties in the United States, Great Britain, Canada, and elsewhere.
29. The older, central part of a city, especially when characterized by crowded, low-income neighborhoods.
30. The rights that are believed to accrue to a person upon birth, especially life, liberty, and the pursuit of happiness, but other political, social, or economic privileges as well.

Answers to the final question in the exercise will vary. They may include the following: military-industrial complex, accountability, role-playing, consciousness-raising, regionalism, etc.

Exercise III. Yiddish in English—Is It Kosher? (page 85)

1. A meddlesome person; a gossip or blabbermouth.
2. A person of honor and integrity.
3. To be exceptionally proud, rejoice.
4. A clumsy or bungling person.
5. (*n.*) Merchandise of obviously inferior quality; (*adj.*) inferior or third-rate.
6. (*v.*) To complain about or find fault with persistently; (*n.*) a chronic complainer.
7. A habitual bungler or dolt.
8. (*v.*) To chat idly; (*n.*) a chat.
9. Florid or sentimental art or music; sentimentality.
10. (*v.*) To snack on; (*n.*) a snack.
11. To carry with difficulty or lug; to move about slowly or laboriously.
12. A person who has specialized knowledge or experience of something; an expert or ardent fan of something.

Other yiddishisms include the following: bubkes, ganef, meshuga, bubeleh, schnozzle, schmear.

Exercise IV. Expanding Your Word Power (page 85)

1. *Definition:* Quickness, keenness, and accuracy of perception or judgment.
   Etymology: acumen (Latin), "sharpness"; from *acuere, acutus* (Latin), "sharpen"
   Synonyms: astuteness, shrewdness, penetration
   Antonyms: obtuseness, dullness
2. *Definition:* Blunt or dull.
   Etymology: obtundere, obtusus (Latin), "blunt"
   Synonyms: unperceptive, undiscerning, stupid, dumb, dense, thick
   Antonyms: acute, sharp, astute, shrewd
3. *Definition:* Outrageousness; a monstrous offense or evil.
   Etymology: e, ex (Latin), "out of, beyond" + *norma* (Latin), "the norm" + *-itas, -itatis* (Latin), "state of"
   Synonyms: atrocity, abomination, monstrosity; monstrousness, atrociousness, heinousness
   Antonyms: a petty fault, pettiness
4. *Definition:* Gruesome, horrifying, or repulsive.
   Etymology: grislic (Old English), "terrible, fearful"
   Synonyms: gory, ghastly, disgusting, sickening
   Antonyms: pleasant, delightful, congenial, agreeable
5. *Definition:* (*v.*) To remedy or set right; (*n.*) correction of, or compensation for, a wrong or damage.
   Etymology: re (French and Latin), "back" + *dresser* (French), "arrange"
   Synonyms: (*v.*) rectify, recompense, reimburse, repay; (*n.*) reparation, reimbursement, compensation, amends
6. *Definition:* Flawless, perfect.
   Etymology: in (Latin), "not" + *peccare* (Latin), "sin" + *-abilis, -abile* (Latin), "able to"
   Synonyms: immaculate, spotless, irreproachable, unimpeachable
   Antonyms: sullied, tarnished, blemished; peccant, delinquent, remiss
7. *Definition:* To lower in quality, character, or value.
   Etymology: deterior (Latin), "worse" + *-are, -atus* (Latin), a verb-forming suffix roughly meaning "make"
   Synonyms: decline, disintegrate, degenerate, go downhill *or* to seed
   Antonyms: revive, prosper, flourish, thrive; improve, better, rehabilitate
8. *Definition:* To increase or make greater, as in force, effect, or value.
   Etymology: enhauncer (Anglo-Norman), "increase"; from *in*

554

(Latin), "very; completely" + *altus*
(Latin), "high" + *-are, -atus*
(Latin), a verb-forming suffix
roughly meaning "make"
Synonyms: intensify, magnify, augment, strengthen, bolster, boost
Antonyms: reduce, lessen, detract from; mar, spoil, injure, damage

9. *Definition:* Mild, lenient, or merciful.
Etymology: clemens, clementis (Latin), "merciful, kindly"
Synonyms: compassionate, humane, kindly, benign; fair, balmy, temperate
Antonyms: cruel, ferocious, savage, brutal, inhuman, pitiless, ruthless, merciless; foul, bad

10. *Definition:* To present an indication or suggestion of beforehand.
Etymology: fore (Old English), "before" + *shadow*
Synonyms: bode, augur, presage, prefigure, portend

11. *Definition:* Richly colored; highly elaborate.
Etymology: flamboyant, the present participle of *flamboyer* (French), "blaze"
Synonyms: colorful, brilliant, resplendent; flashy, gaudy; ornate
Antonyms: subdued, staid, sober, dowdy, dull

12. *Definition:* False, forged, or invalid.
Etymology: spurius (Latin), "false; illegitimate"
Synonyms: fraudulent, counterfeit; specious, meretricious
Antonyms: genuine, authentic, bona fide; valid

Lesson 6 (pages 86–98)

Exercise V. Word Roundup (page 92)
1. See page 88 of the student text.
2. Students' sentences will vary.
3. See page 89 of the student text.
4. The slang expressions contained in Lesson 6 include the following: *gung ho* (page 86), *stymie* (page 87), *stump* (page 87), *corny* (page 87), *hawkish* (page 88), *dovish* (page 88), *far-out* (page 89), *straight* (page 89), *square* (page 89). A few others, such as *dicker* (page 89) and *stingy* (page 86), may also be considered by some to fall into this category.

Exercise I. Fighting Words (page 94)
1. a. Conflict using psychological techniques (propaganda, threats, false rumors, etc.) rather than physical force to dominate, thwart, or intimidate an enemy or opponent.
   b. A military operation by both land and naval forces against the same objective, especially an attack by troops (marines) landed from ships.
   c. A war conducted with great speed, force, and violence; specifically, a violent surprise offensive by massed air and mechanized ground forces (tanks, etc.) in close coordination; any sudden, overpowering attack intended to achieve a quick victory.
   d. The process of creating peaceful conditions by crushing all resistance in some area of military operations.
   e. An attack (such as an aerial assault) that is made on the assumption that the enemy in question is planning a similar attack and that the only way to prevent this is to strike first.
   f. A person who is opposed to war.
   g. Warlike acts; warfare.
   h. Skillful movement of troops; large-scale training operations for the armed forces.
   i. The assembling of the armed forces for war.
   j. A member of a small independent or freelance body of irregular troops using harassing tactics against (rather than engaging in pitched battles with) an enemy.
   k. A temporary halt in the fighting; a temporary cessation of hostilities.
   l. A brisk fight between small bodies of troops.
   m. A person who is kept by an enemy as a guarantee that certain conditions or terms will be met.
   n. Military supplies; military weapons and ammunition, collectively; heavy guns or artillery.
   o. United firing from one side of a warship: an explosive verbal attack or denunciation.
   p. Make an offer or gesture of good will or conciliation. (The olive branch is a symbol of peace.)

2. According to the account in Revelation 16:13–16, Armageddon is the scene of the final, apocalyptic battle between the forces of good and the forces of evil. It will take place on Judgment Day. The word *Armageddon* means the "mountains of Megiddo" (Hebrew, *har Megiddon*) and refers to the defeat sustained by King Josiah near the town of Megiddo (as recounted in 2 Kings 23:23–30). This defeat was so complete that Megiddo soon became a symbol of certain disaster (*e.g.,* in Zechariah 12:11).

3. A victory won at excessive cost to the victor. *Pyrrhic* refers to Pyrrhus, King of Epirus, who sustained heavy, almost crippling losses in victories against the Romans in the early third century B.C.

4. *Martial law* is temporary rule by the military authorities and the military

law administered by these authorities. Martial law is usually invoked by a government in an emergency, when the civilian law enforcement agencies are unable to maintain public order and welfare (*e.g.*, during a riot or rebellion of major proportions, during wartime). During this time, of course, civil law is suspended, along with whatever rights or guarantees are provided the citizen by the national constitution. Martial law is also applied to occupied territories by the occupying power.

The *martial arts* are any of the arts of combat or self-defense, such as karate and judo, usually practiced as a sport.

Students' answers to the last part of this item will vary.

5. *Antebellum* means "before the [*or* a] war"; it is usually used in special reference to the American South in the period prior to the Civil War, roughly 1790–1860.

Exercise II.   Clichés (pages 95–96)

1. The expressions in this group that are reasonably fresh and effective are contained in sentences *a, c,* and *f*. The others are stereotyped and dull. They can be improved either by simpler, more direct wording or by more distinctive comparisons. Some possibilities are as follows:
   b. We were ravenously hungry.
   d. She moved and examined everything that wasn't nailed down in her search for the missing papers.
   e. The news hit us like a bucketful of cold water in the face.
2. Answers will vary. Some possibilities include:
   a. worked very hard
   b. a delicious meal
   c. slept soundly
   d. grief-stricken; deeply upset
   e. lost all his money
   f. had an excellent time celebrating
3. Answers will vary.
4. Answers will vary. Some possibilities include:
   a. my brother after his milkshake and cream-pie binge.
   b. a waiter with a quarter tip on a ten-dollar check.
   c. a small-time comedian's jokes
   d. the most popular girl in the senior class
   e. a country churchyard on a bleak November afternoon
   f. a defensive tackle

Exercise III.   A Verbal Diversion
(page 96)
Students may find the following books (in addition to a dictionary) useful in doing this exercise: Makkai, Boatner, and Gates: *A Dictionary of American Idioms,* 3d ed. *Morris Dictionary of Word and Phrase Origins,* 2d ed.; and *Brewer's Dictionary of Phrase and Fable,* 16th ed.

1. Something that distracts attention from the real issue.
2. A tournament in which each contestant plays in turn every other contestant; a letter sent in turn to members of a group, each of whom comments on it, signs it, and forwards it; a petition on which the signatures are arranged in a circle to conceal the order of signing.
3. An informer.
4. A person who makes loans of money at exorbitant rates of interest, usually to people who cannot or do not want to get loans from more reputable sources.
5. A person who is overly eager or zealous in performing assignments.
6. To fit together neatly; to interlock harmoniously; a kind of tenon.
7. To try to avoid attention by inactivity; to feign sleep.
8. A rare and expensive possession that is financially a burden to maintain; something of dubious value that its owner no longer wants.
9. To treat very gently and carefully.
10. A candidate for elective office who is not considered likely to win at the outset of the campaign but who receives unexpected support somewhere along the line.
11. A mock court set up in violation of established legal procedures; a court characterized by incompetence and corruption.
12. A session of Congress occurring between an election and the inauguration of those who have won. During this time, those members of Congress who have failed to win reelection (and are, accordingly, going out of office) still have their seats.
13. A person unusually devoted to reading or study.
14. To let someone in on what is supposed to be a secret, either consciously or unconsciously.
15. To deteriorate or go downhill.
16. An absurdly foolish plan.
17. To sacrifice or abandon someone in order to protect oneself; to send into danger without adequate protection.
18. Something that is seemingly dangerous and powerful but is in fact impotent and weak.
19. To act directly and decisively on something despite the risks involved.
20. Something that is taboo or immune from criticism or meddling.

21. To make one angry or annoyed.
22. A hopeless pursuit of an unobtainable or imaginary goal or objective.
23. A grin that is embarrassed because one is conscious of some fault or flaw.
24. To have congestion in one's throat that inhibits clear enunciation; to be hoarse.

Exercise IV.   Expanding Your Word Power (page 96)

1. *Definition:* Stingy; scanty.
   Etymology: nigard (Middle English), "miser" + *ly*
   Synonyms: tightfisted, miserly, parsimonious
   Antonyms: openhanded, generous, liberal
2. *Definition:* Ravenous, insatiable.
   Etymology: vorax, voracis (Latin), "ravenous" (from *vorare* [Latin], "devour") + *-ious*
   Synonyms: gluttonous, unquenchable, greedy, predaceous
   Antonyms: limited, controlled
3. *Definition:* (*n.*) Food or other lure used to trap wildlife; an enticement; (*v.*) to lure or entice; to torment persistently with insult or ridicule.
   Etymology: beita (Old Norse), "hunt with dogs; food"
   Synonyms: (*n.*) lure, snare, temptation; (*v.*) entice, tempt; badger, hector, harry, harass
4. *Definition:* Puzzled, mystified; teasing, mocking.
   Etymology: quiz (English), "question" + *-ical*
   Synonyms: perplexed, baffled; derisive, mocking, sarcastic
   Antonyms: untroubled, unflustered; straightforward, serious; respectful
5. *Definition:* A trite remark or statement; triteness.
   Etymology: platitude (French); from *plattus* (Vulgar Latin), "flat," and *platos* (Greek), "broad"
   Synonyms: truism, cliché, bromide, commonplace; banality, corniness
   Antonyms: originality, freshness, novelty
6. *Definition:* Lacking flavor, zest, excitement, or interest.
   Etymology: in (Latin), "not" + *sapidus* (Latin), "tasty"
   Synonyms: bland, tasteless; dull, trite, commonplace, vapid
   Antonyms: pungent, piquant; interesting, exciting, stimulating
7. *Definition:* Distorted, extravagant, outlandish.
   Etymology: grottesca (Old Italian), "grottolike"
   Synonyms: misshapen, deformed; bizarre, weird, fantastic

Antonyms: well-proportioned, regular, normal, unexceptional
8. *Definition:* (*n.*) A flexible metal sheet; a kind of sword; anything that highlights or underscores the distinctive characteristics something else by offering a strong contrast to it; (*v.*) to thwart or frustrate.
   Etymology: (*n.*) *folium* (Latin), "leaf"; (*v.*) *foilen* (Middle English), "trample"
   Synonyms: (*n.*) plate, veneer, film; rapier; antithesis; (*v.*) hamper, impede, block, battle, checkmate, stymie
   Antonyms: (*v.*) aid, abet, promote, foster
9. *Definition:* To bargain; to argue.
   Etymology: haggen (Middle English), "bargain"; from *hoggva* (Old Norse), "cut, hew"
   Synonyms: dicker, wrangle; dispute, quibble
   Antonyms: agree, concur
10. *Definition:* (*adj.*) Combative, aggressive; (*n.*) an activist.
    Etymology: militans, militantis (Latin), "soldiering"; from *militare* (Latin), "serve as a soldier"
    Synonyms: (*adj.*) belligerent, bellicose, pugnacious, truculent; (*n.*) fighter, battler
    Antonyms: (*adj.*) pacific, peaceable, nonviolent; (*n.*) pacifist
11. *Definition:* Composed or collected in manner or behavior; staid.
    Etymology: sedare, sedatus (Latin), "settle, calm, compose"
    Synonyms: calm, quiet, serene; proper, straitlaced, decorous
    Antonyms: turbulent, tempestuous, unruly, obstreperous; zany, outlandish
12. *Definition:* (*adj.*) Departing from what is considered normal or regular; erratic; (*n.*) someone who is odd or peculiar in some way.
    Etymology: ek (Greek), "out" + *kentron* (Greek), "center" + *ikos* (Greek) "characteristic of"
    Synonyms: (*adj.*) odd, peculiar, idiosyncratic; (*n.*) oddball
    Antonyms: (*adj.*) normal, ordinary, run-of-the-mill, average; regular

Lesson 7 (pages 99–109)

Exercise V.   Word Roundup (page 105)

1. a. See page 103 of the student text.
   b. See page 101 of the student text.
2. a. grim, dismal
   b. decay, deterioration
   c. noisy, rowdy
   d. dashed, thwarted
   e. overly bold, rash
   f. abrupt, curt

3. a.–d. See page 101 of the student text. All these words refer to pretentious or overly pompous language.
4. See page 100 of the student text.

Exercise (page 107)
1. a. *Definition:* To beg.
   Etymology: besechen (Middle English), "seek"
   Use of be: To give greater force or thoroughness to the action.
   b. *Definition:* To indicate or signify.
   Etymology: bespeken (Middle English), "speak"
   Use of be: To make an intransitive verb transitive.
   c. *Definition:* To dress or adorn gaudily.
   Etymology: Perhaps *be + dise* (Middle Low German), "bunch of flax on a distaff"
   Use of be: To give greater force or thoroughness to the action.
   d. *Definition:* To misrepresent or disguise.
   Etymology: belien (Middle English), "belie"
   Use of be: To make an intransitive verb transitive.
   e. *Definition:* To besiege or harass.
   Etymology: be + leger (Middle Dutch), "camp"
   Use of be: To form a verb from a noun.
   f. *Definition:* To promise to marry.
   Etymology: be + trouthe (Middle English), "truth"
   Use of be: To form a verb from a noun.
   g. *Definition:* To deceive or lure.
   Etymology: be + gile (Middle English), "guile"
   Use of be: To form a verb from a noun.
   h. *Definition:* To scold harshly.
   Etymology: be + raten (Middle English), "scold"
   Use of be: To give greater force or thoroughness to the action.
   i. *Definition:* To concede reluctantly.
   Etymology: be + gruggen (Middle English), "grunt"
   Use of be: To give greater force or thoroughness to the action.
   j. *Definition:* To be necessary or proper for.
   Etymology: behoven (Middle English), "require"
   Use of be: To give greater force or thoroughness to the action.
   k. *Definition:* To deprive of or leave desolate.
   Etymology: bereven (Middle English), "rob"
   Use of be: To give greater force or thoroughness to the action.
   l. *Definition:* To happen.
   Etymology: befallen (Middle English), "fall, belong"
   m. *Definition:* To disparage.
   Etymology: be + litel (Middle English), "little"
   Use of be: To form a verb from an adjective.
   n. *Definition:* To act as a friend to.
   Etymology: be + frend (Middle English), "friend"
   Use of be: To form a verb from a noun.
   o. *Definition:* To assail persistently.
   Etymology: be + labor (Middle English), "exertion"
   Use of be: To form a verb from a noun.

Exercise I.   Eponyms (page 108)
The following reference books may prove useful in completing this exercise: *Morris Dictionary of Word and Phrase Origins,* 2d ed., *Brewer's Dictionary of Phrase and Fable,* 16th ed.
   1. To expurgate by omitting or modifying parts considered vulgar or obscene. Thomas Bowdler (1754–1825). (See page 422 of the student text.)
   2. A traitor or collaborator. Vidkun Quisling. (See page 136 of the student text.)
   3. Bomb, mine, or shell fragments. General Henry Shrapnel (1761–1842), an English artillery officer who invented an early type of fragmentation bomb.
   4. To hypnotize; to fascinate. Franz Mesmer (1734–1815), an Austrian physician who developed a system of treatment through hypnosis.
   5. To execute illegally, usually by hanging. Charles Lynch (1736–1796), a Virginia justice of the peace who suppressed Tory (Loyalist) activity during the American Revolution by this method.
   6. A nonconformist or dissenter. Samuel Maverick. (See page 174 of the student text.)
   7. Delighting in inflicting pain or cruelty on others. Marquis (actually Count) de Sade (1740–1814), a French soldier who wrote licentious novels featuring physical and mental abuse of their heroines.
   8. To divide an area into political units for unfair advantage of one political party during elections. Elbridge Gerry (1744–1814), the Massachusetts governor who formed such an election district in 1812.
   9. Showing or feeling undue partiality to one's own place or group; a person with this attitude. Nicholas Chauvin, a legendary French soldier who was extremely devoted to Napoleon and France.

10. Two slices of bread with a meat or other filling between them. John Montagu, the 4th Earl of Sandwich (1718–1792), an English diplomat who, reluctant to stop for a meal one day while gambling, had his chef invent something he could eat without utensils.

11. A profile drawing of someone, giving the outline only and filled in with dark color. Etienne de Silhouette (1709–1767), a French finance minister noted for his stingy monetary policies.

12. To stimulate or shock with electric current. Luigi Galvani (1737–1798), an Italian physiologist who performed electrical experiments with laboratory animals.

13. A strict disciplinarian. Jean Martinet, a 17th-century French general who followed rigid rules of discipline, even with soldiers of aristocratic background.

14. A poisonous chemical derived from tobacco. Jean Nicot, (1530–1600), a French ambassador to Portugal who introduced tobacco to France.

15. Deriving sexual or emotional stimulation or satisfaction from physical abuse or pain. Leopold von Sacher-Masoch (1836–1895), the Austrian novelist who first described the disorder.

Exercise II. Classical Contributions to English (page 108)

In addition to an unabridged dictionary, the following reference books may prove useful in doing this exercise: *Morris Dictionary of Word and Phrase Origins*, *Brewer's Dictionary of Phrase and Fable*.

A.
1. Jupiter (or Jove) was the ruler of all the Roman gods. Astrologers believed that those born under the planet named after him were merry and sociable because Jupiter was considered to be the happiest of the natal stars.

2. Bacchus was the Roman god of wine, obviously the source of drunken or rowdy behavior.

3. Mercury, the Roman messenger of the gods, was known for his speed. Those born under the planet named after him were considered to be lighthearted and volatile in nature.

4. The evil Saturn (he devoured most of his children) was the Roman god of agriculture and, according to astrologers, typified lead. Those unfortunate people born under the planet named after him were considered to be grave and gloomy.

5. Mars, the Roman god of war, is associated with military exploits.

B.
1. Having great force or magnitude. From the Titans, a race of giants in Greek mythology.

2. Tremendously difficult or powerful. From Hercules, the mythical Greek hero who performed mighty feats or "labors."

3. Terse, succinct. From Laconia, the part of Greece of which Sparta was the capital. Laconians were known for their concise and succinct habits of speech.

4. A long-distance race (in the modern Olympic Games, 26 miles). From the Battle of Marathon (490 B.C.), in which the Greeks defeated the Persians. After the battle, the courier Phidippides ran from Marathon to Athens to announce the victory.

5. Enormous in size, extent, or degree. From the Colossus. (See page 342 of the student text.)

6. A vulnerable point; a chink in one's armor. From the legend of the Greek warrior Achilles. When Achilles was an infant, his mother, Thetis, dipped him into the river Styx to make him impervious to mortal wounds. However, the heel by which she held him remained vulnerable because the waters of the Styx did not touch it. Ultimately, Achilles was slain by an arrow shot into this heel.

7. Marked by simplicity, frugality, and avoidance of luxury; austere. The people of Sparta, a city-state in ancient Greece, were known for their frugality and self-discipline.

8. To tease by keeping something in view but out of reach; to create a hope and disappoint it. From Tantalus, a mythical Greek king. As punishment for revealing secrets of the gods, Tantalus was condemned to stand in a pool of water under fruit-laden trees, but he could reach neither water nor fruit.

9. A bound collection of maps and charts. From Atlas, a Greek Titan condemned (for his part in a war against the gods) to support the world on his shoulders.

10. A speech full of invective and condemnation. From Philip II, a 4th-century king of Macedon. The Athenian orator Demosthenes delivered a series of bitter denunciations against Philip for his encroachments on Greek liberties. From this series of speeches, any harsh verbal scolding derived the name *philippic*.

Exercise III. Spanish Borrowings (page 109)

1. A devotee, fan, or enthusiast.

2. A rich vein or source of ore; a source of considerable wealth or value.
3. A slight offense.
4. Having a strong sense of masculine pride.
5. A government suspension of trade (usually with a foreign country) or of trade in a particular commodity.
6. A fleet of warships.
7. A dangerous or violent criminal or outlaw, especially in the western United States.
8. Freight carried by a ship, airplane, or other vehicle.
9. Without means of communicating with others or the outside.

Exercise IV. Short, Sturdy Words
(page 109)
1. Answers will vary; however, synonyms include: thwack, cuff, slam, bash, strike, pound, punch, smite, beat, knock, bat, poke, prod, smack, whack, swat, jab, sock, tap, pat, slap, graze, kick, boot, thump.
2. a. See page 276 of the student text.
   b. Complete happiness.
   c. Humble; submissive.
   d. To shake or tremble.
   e. (*n.*) A multitude or crowd; (*v.*) to crowd upon, into, or together.
   f. Skill in handiwork or the arts; a type of handiwork; cunning.
   g. (*n.*) A lament or cry; (*v.*) to cry mournfully; complain.
   h. (*n.*) The cry of a sheep or goat; whining or foolish talk; (*v.*) to cry or whimper.
   i. To split or tear apart violently; to distress.
   j. Unrelenting; rigid; stern.
   k. To lurk; lie in hiding.
   l. To force into an insufficient space; to study intensively for an examination.

Exercise V. Expanding Your Word Power (page 109)
1. *Definition:* Stern, gloomy.
   Etymology: Perhaps from *durus* (Latin), "hard"
   Synonyms: harsh, obstinate, unyielding
   Antonyms: cheerful, merry; flexible, adaptable
2. *Definition:* The cause of a response or action.
   Etymology: stimulus (Latin), "goad"
   Synonyms: incentive, stimulant
3. *Definition:* Lacking in capacity for enjoyment; overly sophisticated.
   Etymology: blaser (French), "cloy"; from *blasen* (Middle Dutch), "blow up"
   Synonyms: apathetic, indifferent, bored, world-weary
   Antonyms: enthusiastic, gung ho, ardent

4. *Definition:* noisily defiant; unruly.
   Etymology: ob (Latin), "against" + *strepere* (Latin), "make noise"
   Synonyms: vociferous, boisterous, unmanageable
   Antonyms: docile, quiet, peaceable
5. *Definition:* An exaggerated figure of speech or statement; exaggeration.
   Etymology: hyper (Greek), "beyond" + *ballein* (Greek), "throw"
   Synonyms: overstatement, excess
   Antonym: understatement
6. *Definition:* Swollen or distended, as from a fluid; excessively ornate in style or language.
   Etymology: turgidus (Latin), "swollen": from *turgere*, "be swollen"
   Synonyms: bloated, stuffed, inflated; ostentatious; flowery, bombastic
   Antonyms: lean, spare, unembellished, artless
7. *Definition:* (*n.*) Authoritative permission or approval; support or encouragement; a type of law or decree; a penalty for noncompliance or to ensure compliance; a coercive measure against a nation violating international law; (*v.*) to authorize, legitimize; to maintain or encourage by an indication of approval.
   Etymology: sanctio (Latin), "an ordaining," from *sanctus*, (Latin), "holy"
   Synonyms: (*n.*) certification, endorsement, imprimatur; (*v.*) approve, endorse, certify
   Antonyms: (*n.*) boycott, ban; (*v.*) ban, disapprove, invalidate
8. *Definition:* insolent; irrelevant.
   Etymology: in (Latin) "not" + *pertinens, pertinentis* (Latin), "relevant"
   Synonyms: impudent, audacious, bold, brazen
   Antonyms: tactful, considerate, circumspect; modest, demure; pertinent, relevant
9. *Definition:* So crude and unrefined as to be lacking in discrimination and sensibility.
   Etymology: crassus (Latin), "fat; gross; dense"
   Synonyms: coarse, vulgar, impolite, uncouth
   Antonyms: suave, polished, discreet, tactful
10. *Definition:* Having a cheerful disposition or quality; merry.
    Etymology: jucundus (Latin), "merry": from *juvare*, "delight"
    Synonyms: jovial, jolly, blithe
    Antonyms: morose, gloomy, despondent, negative
11. *Definition:* To wipe out.
    Etymology: effacer (French), "wipe out"; from *ex* (Latin) "out" + *facies* (Latin), "face"

Synonyms: obliterate, erase, delete
Antonyms: preserve, conserve; foster, nurture, promote

12. *Definition:* Talkative.
Etymology: volubilis (Latin), "rolling"; from *volvere,* "roll"
Synonyms: loquacious, garrulous, prolix
Antonyms: taciturn, uncommunicative, tight-lipped, closemouthed

Lesson 8 (pages 110–122)

Exercise V. Word Roundup (page 117)
2. See page 112 of the student text.
3. See page 115 of the student text.
4. See page 111 of the student text.
5. See page 113 of the student text.

Exercise I. The Language of Government and Politics (page 119)

In addition to an unabridged dictionary, a high school civics or government textbook may prove useful in doing this exercise.

1. A principle by which the powers of government are divided among different branches so that none can exercise exclusive or excessive power.
2. A term (usually derogatory) used to describe a well-disciplined political party organization, often under the control of a boss.
3. The direct disbursal of funds by the federal government to states and localities to help them meet their responsibilities more adequately.
4. The personal liberties and privileges of the individual. Under the U.S. Constitution, they are guaranteed mainly by the first ten amendments (the Bill of Rights) and by the Fourteenth Amendment.
5. The selection of government or corporate employees on the basis of demonstrated merit, usually (but not always) by competitive examinations.
6. A process by which a president may prevent a bill from becoming law by failing to act on it. This applies if Congress adjourns within less than ten days after submitting the bill to him. Some governors also have the pocket-veto power.
7. The exemption from legally enforced disclosure of communications within the executive branch when disclosure would have an adverse effect on that branch's functions and decision-making process.
8. The independence of each of the three branches of government—legislative, executive, judicial—in relation to the other two.

9. A special-interest group that tries to influence legislators to vote for measures or policies favoring its particular interests.
10. Redrawing the boundary lines of election districts so that legislative representation (for example, within a state) is redistributed to reflect recent population changes more fairly or accurately.
11. A form of direct legislation according to which a proposed legislative act requires popular approval before it becomes a law. The draft of a new state constitution or a proposed amendment to the U.S. Constitution also may require a referendum before acceptance.
12. A statement by a political party summarizing its policies and programs in regard to the main issues facing the nation (or state or city). A party appeals to the voters on the basis of its platform, as well as its candidates.
13. A decision made by the president, without congressional approval, that calls for some definite course of action. Often the purpose of such an order is to implement a law passed by Congress.
14 The doctrine or principle under which final political power is vested in the people, a basic principle of democratic government.
15. An administrative unit of the government having authority to regulate certain types of business or certain areas of activity within the nation, state, or locality. Examples are the Federal Communications Commission (FCC) and the public-service commissions of the various states.
16. The established legal procedures that provide protection against arbitrary or unreasonable infringement of private rights. In criminal procedures, this means a fair trial according to established principles of law.
17. The power of courts to nullify or invalidate statutes that, in the opinion of the judges, violate the U.S. Constitution or a state constitution.
18. The entire body of employees of a government exclusive of the military and elected officials.
19. Involving or representative of both major political parties.
20. A citizen's right to vote; a special privilege that a governmental authority grants to a private business organization: for example, the right to use city streets for a bus line.
21. The right of a governmental body to take over private property for a necessary public purpose upon

payment of fair compensation to the owner.

22. The custom prevailing in the U.S. Senate of withholding confirmation of a presidential appointment until approved by the senator (or senators) of the majority party from that state.
23. Government projects or appropriations that yield rich patronage benefits; government money, jobs, or favors given by politicians as patronage.
24. A conflict between a legislator's private interests (usually financial) and his/her public role as a representative of the people.
25. The use of obstructionist tactics to delay a vote, usually by means of extended speechmaking by a member or members of a legislative body.
26. The power to make appointments to public office.

Exercise II. Gobbledygook
(pages 119-120)
1. The land is too shallow and steep to be suitable for recreation.
2. The label was misleading.

Exercise III. Expanding Your Word Power (page 120)
1. *Definition:* Skillful; adroit.
   Etymology: defte (Middle English), "gentle; meek"
   Synonyms: dexterous, agile, proficient
   Antonyms: awkward, clumsy, unskilled, incompetent
2. *Definition:* To damage or diminish in some way.
   Etymology: in (Latin), "completely" + *pejorare* (Latin), "make worse"
   Synonyms: weaken, undermine, vitiate, injure
   Antonyms: improve, bolster, strengthen, brace
3. *Definition:* To raise unnecessary or trivial objections.
   Etymology: cavillari (Latin), "quibble"; from *cavilla* (Latin), "a jeering"
   Synonyms: carp, quibble, nitpick
4. *Definition:* Excessive praise or flattery.
   Etymology: adulari (Latin), "flatter"
   Synonyms: hero worship, idolization, adoration
   Antonyms: disparagement, denigration, vilification
5. *Definition:* Made or done as if on the spur of the moment; composed or uttered without previous preparation.
   Etymology: impromptu (French), "extemporaneously"; from *in promptu* (Latin), "in readiness"
   Synonyms: improvised, extemporaneous, unrehearsed; offhand, spontaneous

Antonyms: rehearsed, prepared; planned, premeditated
6. *Definition:* Lacking in candor; giving a false appearance of frankness or simplicity.
   Etymology: dis (Latin), "not" + *genuus* (Latin), "frank, straightforward"
   Synonyms: calculating, crafty, sly, deceitful, cunning, guileful
   Antonyms: frank, candid, guileless, honest
7. *Definition:* Prone to outbursts of temper; easily angered.
   Etymology: irasci (Latin), "become angry" + *-abilis, -abile* (Latin), "able to"; from *ira* (Latin), "anger"
   Synonyms: testy, touchy, choleric, short-tempered
   Antonyms: imperturbable, unflappable, even tempered, cool, calm
8. *Definition:* Willing to follow the advice or suggestions of others; open to.
   Etymology: a (French), "to" + *mener* (French), "lead, bring" + *-able* (French) "able to"; from *ad* (Latin), "to; at" + *minare* (Latin), "shout; threaten" + *-abilis, -abile* (Latin), "able to"
   Synonyms: agreeable, pliable, pliant, tractable, docile; responsive
   Antonyms: intractable, refractory, intransigent; unresponsive
9. *Definition:* A cantankerous person.
   Etymology: Origin unknown
   Synonyms: grouch, crank, crab, sorehead (all colloquial)
   Antonyms: doll, sweetheart, sweetie (all colloquial)

Lesson 9 (pages 123-133)
Exercise V. Word Roundup (page 130)
1. See page 127 of the student text.
2. See page 125 of the student text.
3. a. See page 126 of the student text.
   b. See page 126 of the student text.
   c. A show of sympathy or support; a word or gesture of praise or encouragement.
   d. Of or about spies and secret agents; dealing in intrigue or espionage.
   e. A spy who has been given a false identity in order to perform his/her job effectively.
   f. By the most direct way.
   g. A criminal who is unresponsive to rehabilitation.
   h. A man who is firmly settled in and contented with the single life.
4. See page 124 of the student text.
5. Answers will vary but may include the following:
   a. commendable, admirable, reputable, exemplary, laudable
   b. reprehensible, reproachable, indefensible, ignoble, shameful

Exercise (page 132)
1. a. *Definition:* Evidence not bearing directly on the fact in dispute but, rather, on various attendant circumstances from which a judge or jury might infer the occurrence of the fact.
   Meaning of circum: "around; involved"
   b. *Definition:* An automatic switch that stops the flow of electric current in a suddenly overloaded or otherwise abnormally stressed electric circuit.
   Meaning of circum: "around"
   c. *Definition:* In some states, the lowest court of record. In some instances, this court holds sessions in different places.
   Meaning of circum: "around, about"
   d. *Definition:* A roundabout way of saying something.
   Meaning of circum: "around"
2. An account of historical events in biblical history from the reign of King David to the restoration of the Jews under Cyrus I, King of Persia. The arrangement of the material conforms to the passage of time.
3. A play dealing with historical events, usually arranged chronologically into a series of short scenes or episodes. Examples include the three parts of Shakespeare's *Henry VI.*
4. *Chronological age* indicates the number of years a person has lived; *mental age,* however, reveals the measure of mental development as determined by intelligence tests.
5. Answers will vary and may include the following:
   a. Republican Rome; some of the Greek city states during the Archaic period (*e.g.*, Pisistratid Athens); the Venetian republic.
   b. United States; France; Canada; Italy; etc.
   c. Czarist Russia; the Austro-Hungarian Empire; the ancient Persian Empire; Saudi Arabia.
   d. Switzerland under Zwingli; ancient Israel; Iran under Khomeini.

Exercise I. "Time on My Hands"
(page 132)
1. An opportunist; one who conforms to the prevailing ways and opinions of the time or situation for personal advantage.
2. Occurring at a suitable or opportune time; well-timed.
3. Respected or adhered to because of age or age-old observance.
4. Old-fashioned; no longer in style.
5. A bank deposit that cannot be withdrawn before a date specified at the time of deposit.
6. A bomb with a detonating mechanism that can be set for a particular time; something with a potentially detrimental or dangerous reaction.
7. In a reasonable length of time; when or before necessary or due; quickly.
8. Temporarily; for now.
9. A short break from work or play, especially in team sports.
10. A schedule listing the time at which certain events, such as arrivals and departures at a station or depot, are expected to take place.
11. To make progress quickly; to find the time for; to make progress in pursuit of a young woman's favors.
12. Long overdue.
13. An instrument that measures, registers, or records time.
14. A clock that records the arrival and departure times of employees, usually by means of punching time cards.
15. To keep the beat; to keep the same rhythm; to keep in step; to indicate the correct time.
16. Answers will vary but may include the following: *duration* (the period of time during which something exists or persists); *calendar* (a table showing the months, weeks, and days in at least one specific year); *century* (a period of 100 years); *chronology* (the arrangement of events in time); *cycle* (a time period in which a characteristic event or sequence of events occurs; *generation* (the average time interval between the birth of parents and the birth of their offspring); *infinity* (unbounded time); *intermission* (the time period between acts of a theatrical performance); *moment* (a brief, indefinite interval of time); *eternity* (indefinite time).
17. Answers will vary but may include the following: *abide* (to wait patiently for); *chronicle* (to record historical events in order of occurrence); *date* (to mark or supply with a particular statement of time); *elapse* (to pass, slip by); *temporize* (to act evasively in order to gain time); *prolong* (to lengthen in duration); *procrastinate* (to put off doing something until a future time); *endure* (to continue in existence); *tarry* (to remain or stay temporarily in a place); *accelerate* (to cause to occur sooner than expected).
18. Answers will vary but may include the following: *abiding* (long-lasting); *continuous* (unceasing); *chronological* (arranged in order of time of occurrence); *interim* (temporary or provisional; makeshift); *permanent* (meant to last indefinitely); *perpetual* (lasting for an indefinitely long duration); *temporal* (limited by time); *temporary* (enjoyed for a lim-

ited time); *transient* (passing away with time); *retroactive* (applying to a period prior to enactment).
19. Answers will vary but may include the following: *the time is ripe* (the best time has come for doing something); *time and time again* (repeatedly); *time of one's life* (a very wonderful time); *pass the time of day* (exchange greetings); *from time to time* (occasionally); *forever and a day* (always); *turn back the clock* (relive the past); *on schedule* (at the right time); *live on borrowed time* (to live or last longer than was expected); *in good time* (in time).

Exercise II.   Our Latin Heritage
(page 133)
1. An assumed name.
2. The number of officers or members of a committee or organization (usually a majority) who must be present for the valid transaction of business.
3. The systematic spreading of a given doctrine or of allegations reflecting its views and interests.
4. Something given or paid in addition to what is usual or expected.
5. Free of charge.
6. Something that is burdensome, especially a disagreeable responsibility or necessity; a stigma.
7. A written declaration made under oath before a notary public or other authorized officer.
8. Disgrace inherent in or arising from shameful conduct; scornful contempt or reproach.
9. See page 153 of the student text.
10. A form of defense whereby a defendant attempts to prove that he or she was elsewhere when the crime in question was committed; any excuse.
11. An animating motive, intention, or purpose; hostility or animosity.
12. A warning or caution.
13. A final statement of terms made by one party to another.
14. (*adj.*) Word for word; (*adv.*) in exactly the same words.
15. Official approval or license to print or publish, especially under conditions of censorship; any official sanction or authorization.

Exercise III.   Curious Compounds
(page 133)
1. A person who habitually violates the law or fails to answer court summonses. *scoff* (verb) + *law* (object)
2. A petty thief. *pick* (verb) + *pocket* (object)
3. One who traitorously switches allegiances. *turn* (verb) + *coat* (object)

4. One who squanders money. *spend* (verb) + *thrift* (object)
5. A barrier that protects a harbor or shore from the full impact of waves. *break* (verb) + *water* (object)
6. An informer; a talebearer. *tattle* (verb) + *tale* (object)
7. An unprincipled or incorrigible person. *scape* (verb) + *grace* (object)
8. One who mars (the pleasure of others. *spoil* (verb) + *sport* (object)
9. One who is recklessly bold. *dare* (verb) + *devil* (object)
10. (*n.*) An unprincipled and ruthless person; a murderer; (*adj.*) cruel; murderous. *cut* (verb) + *throat* (object)
11. Dangerously rapid. *break* (verb) + *neck* (object)
12 Serving to indicate, reveal, or betray information intended to be kept secret. *tell* (verb) + *tale* (object)
13. Something used or assembled as a temporary expedient or substitute for something else, *make* (verb) + *shift* (object)
14. Dull and lifeless. *lack* (verb) + *luster* (object)
15. A temporary expedient; an improvised substitute for something that is lacking. *stop* (verb) + *gap* (object)

Exercise IV.   Expanding Your Word Power (page 133)
1. *Definition:* A sharply mocking or contemptuous remark intended to wound another; the quality or use of such remarks.
   Etymology: sarchasmos (Greek), "sarcasm"; from *sarkazein* (Greek), "tear flesh"; from *sarx* (Greek), "flesh"
   Synonyms: derision, scorn, ridicule; venom, asperity, mordancy
2. *Definition:* Having a sickeningly sweet character, tone, or attitude.
   Etymology: sakkharon (Greek), "sugar" + *-inos* (Greek), "pertaining to"
   Synonyms: sugary, honeyed, mawkish, maudlin
   Antonyms: sour, acerbic, tart, caustic
3. *Definition:* Occurring at irregular intervals; isolated.
   Etymology: sporadikos (Greek), "scattered, isolated"; from *sporas* (Greek), "dispersed, scattered"
   Synonyms: occasional, intermittent, periodic, spasmodic, fitful; disparate, disjointed
   Antonyms: recurrent, regular, continual, chronic, steady, continuous
4. *Definition:* To make ashamed or uneasy; to disconcert.
   Etymology: esbahier (Old French), "disconcert"; from *es* (Old French), "completely" + *baer* (Old French), "gape; yawn"

Synonyms: embarrass, chagrin, mortify, humiliate, take aback, dismay, nonplus
Antonyms: elate, delight, exhilarate

5. *Definition:* (*adj.*) Clearly apparent; (*v.*) to demonstrate plainly; (*n.*) a list of cargo, passengers, or the like.
Etymology: manifestus (Latin), "palpable"; from *manus* (Latin), "hand" + *festus* (Latin), "gripped"
Synonyms: (*adj.*) obvious, evident; (*v.*) reveal, display, exhibit; substantiate, corroborate; (*n.*) inventory, checklist, register

6. *Definition:* Deep-rooted; habitual.
Etymology: inveterare, inveteratus (Latin), "make old"; from *in* (Latin), "causing" + *vetus, veteris* (Latin), "old"
Synonyms: chronic, ingrained, confirmed, die-hard, dyed-in-the-wool, deep-seated
Antonyms: occasional, infrequent, rare

7. *Definition:* Short-lived; transitory.
Etymology: epi (Greek), "on" + *hemera* (Greek), "day" + -*alis, -ale* (Latin), "pertaining to"
Synonyms: fleeting, transient, evanescent
Antonyms: long-lasting, eternal, perpetual, everlasting

8. *Definition:* Having a slanting or sloping direction; indirect or evasive.
Etymology: obliquus (Latin), "slanting"
Synonyms: inclined, tilted, diagonal; furtive, clandestine, covert
Antonyms: straight; direct, overt

9. *Definition:* Having the nature of a circumlocution.
Etymology: peri (Greek), "around" + *phrazein* (Greek), "say"
Synonyms: circumlocutory, roundabout, indirect
Antonyms: straightforward, direct

10. *Definition:* Of, pertaining to, or involving diplomacy; characterized by tact and sensitivity in dealing with people or situations.
Etymology: diplomaticus (New Latin), "relating to documents"; from *diploma* (Latin), "document"
Synonyms: discreet, politic, tactful, statesmanlike
Antonyms: indiscreet, tactless, clumsy, maladroit

11. *Definition:* Praise; approval.
Etymology: approbatio, approbationis (Latin), "approval"; from *approbare* (Latin), "approve"
Synonyms: commendation, favor, regard, esteem; backing, endorsement, sanction
Antonyms: disapproval, disfavor; condemnation, censure

12. *Definition:* Incisive; forceful and effective.

Etymology: trenchant (Old French), the present participle of *trenchier* (Old French), "cut"
Synonyms: perceptive, keen, acute, cogent, telling
Antonyms: obtuse, fatuous, vapid, bland

Lesson 10 (pages 134–146)

Exercise V. Word Roundup (page 141)
1. a. Use of physical force or coercion.
   b. See page 449 of the student text.
   c. In secret agreement or partnership with, especially for harm.
   d. In harmony or rhythm with.
   e. To be satisfied with the success one has already won and to stop trying to win new honors.
   f. To challenge someone.
   g. See page 136 of the student text.
   h. A wild guess.
   i. A guess that is based on experience and factual knowledge.
   j. To pretend not to see something (literally or figuratively).
2. See page 135 of the student text.
3. See page 137 of the student text.

Exercise I. Look-Alikes (page 143)
1. *Abrogate:* to cancel or annul. *Arrogate:* to seize or claim without right.
2. *Human:* relating to or characteristic of human beings. *Humane:* kindly or compassionate.
3. *Resound:* to reverberate or ring loudly. *Redound:* to have as a consequence; to contribute to.
4. *Envious:* feeling or showing envy. *Enviable:* arousing envy.
5. See page 373 of the student text.
6. *Laudable:* praiseworthy. *Laudatory:* expressing praise.
7. See page 316 of the student text.
8. *Ferment:* (*v.*) to undergo a chemical change called *fermentation*; to agitate or excite; (*n.*) anything that causes fermentation (*e.g.*, yeast); a state of excitement or agitation. *Foment:* (*v.*) to instigate or incite.
9. See page 311 of the student text.
10. *Martial:* warlike. *Marital:* pertaining to marriage.
11. *Affect:* (*v.*) to exert an influence on. *Effect:* (*v.*) to bring about; (*n.*) result.
12. See page 263 of the student text.
13. *Fallible:* Capable of making a mistake. *Fallacious:* mistaken; deceptive, misleading.
14. *Noisy:* loud. *Noisome:* offensive, foul and disgusting; harmful or dangerous.
15. *Founder:* to sink or collapse; to fail utterly. *Flounder:* to struggle helplessly or hopelessly
16. *Ceremonious:* fond of ceremony or elaborately polite; rigidly formal. *Ceremonial:* (*n.*) a ceremony; (*adj.*)

relating to or characterized by ceremonies. *Ceremonious* refers chiefly to persons; *ceremonial* (*adj.*) to things.
17. See page 265 of the student text.
18. *Contemptible:* deserving contempt; despicable. *Contemptuous:* feeling contempt; scornful.
19. *Progeny:* offspring. *Prodigy:* a gifted child or person; a marvel.
20. *Depredation:* damage, destruction, or injury. *Deprivation:* privation; the act or condition of depriving.

Exercise II. By the Sweat of Your Brow
(page 143)
In addition to an unabridged dictionary, an economics textbook may prove useful in doing this exercise.
1. Everyone in the United States over 14 years old who works or is looking for work.
2. One who has received several years of training as an apprentice or on-the-job training, or a combination of these, plus special training by employers. *Skilled workers* include carpenters, plumbers, bakers, printers, and electricians, as well as secretaries, bookkeepers, computer programmers, etc.
3. An untrained worker whose only qualifications are willingness, ability to follow a simple routine, and in some cases, physical strength. Unskilled workers may include adults who have no formal education or young people just entering the workforce.
4. A person whose job is performed in work clothes and often involves manual labor (*e.g.*, a mechanic, a plumber).
5. One whose work usually does not involve manual labor and who is expected to dress with some degree of formality (*e.g.*, a teller).
6. One who has fully served an apprenticeship in a trade or craft and is a qualified worker in another's employ.
7. One who is learning a trade or an occupation, especially as a member of a labor union.
8. A judicial process or order requiring the person or persons to whom it is directed to do, or refrain from doing, a particular act.
9. Negotiations between the representatives of organized workers and their employer or employers to determine wages, hours, rules, and working conditions.
10. Equal chance to obtain work, regardless of age, race, sex, creed, national origin, or disability.

11. The priority, precedence, or status obtained as a result of a person's length of service.
12. How much a person can buy with his/her monetary wage.
13. The lowest per-hour wage that an employer may pay a worker. The minimum wage is established by law.
14. An adjustment made in wages that corresponds with an increase in the cost of living.
15. A labor union limited in membership to workers engaged in the same specific craft (*e.g.*, carpenters).
16. A labor union to which all the workers in a particular industry may belong, regardless of their craft (*e.g.*, the United Mine Workers Union).
17. Laws that prohibit a union (or closed) shop. (A *closed shop* is an establishment in which the employer agrees to hire only union workers.)
18. The automatically controlled operation of an apparatus, process, or system by mechanical or electronic devices that replace human effort, decisionmaking, and organs of observation.
19. The limitation of production or the employment of more workers than are needed as the result of safety regulations or union rules.
20. The level of output of goods or services that produce income or have value in the marketplace.

Exercise III. Ships That Have Never Seen the Sea (page 144)
1. Skill in managing public affairs.
2. Trying to win by an unsportsmanlike procedure, yet without violating any rule.
3. Skill in riding.
4. Using words self-consciously and aggressively to show off or to confuse your opponent.
5. The capacity to be fair and gracious in a competitive situation.
6. Trying to show that one is a jump ahead of a friend or rival.
7. The ability to give organization and a sense of direction to other people.
8. The art or practice of achieving superiority over other people (as in business or a conversation) by perplexing or demoralizing them.
9. Legal management or protection of a person or property.

Exercise IV. A Verbal Diversion
(page 144)
A. *Doublets*
1. Objects found floating on the sea or washed ashore.
2. Without legal force and effect.
3. In a state of repentance or sorrow.

4. Friends and neighbors.
5. The ordinary members of a group or organization, exclusive of the leaders and officers.
6. Spotlessly clean and neat.
7. By honest ways or dishonest; in any way necessary.
8. Make an excited mass protest, alarm, or outcry of any kind.
9. Decided or arranged in advance, routine, or lacking spontaneity.
10. In small and sporadic amounts.

B. *Triplets*
1. Completely; the whole lot.
2. Completely.
3. Solemnly and irrevocably. The phrase refers to the most solemn form of excommunication from the Roman Catholic Church. (See *Brewer's Dictionary of Phrase and Fable.*)
6. Anyone at all.
7. Absolutely completed or finished.
8. Get in any way possible.
9. The rabble; the hoi polloi.

Exercise V. Expanding Your Word Power (page 144)
1. *Definition:* Powerful; convincing.
   Etymology: potens, potentis (Latin), "able to; having the power to"
   Synonyms: forceful, telling, effective, cogent
   Antonyms: powerless, ineffective, ineffectual, weak
2. *Definition:* Related to the matter at hand.
   Etymology: relevans, relevantis (Medieval Latin), the present participle of *relevare* (Medieval Latin), "lift up"
   Synonyms: applicable, appropriate, germane, pertinent, apropos
   Antonyms: irrelevant, immaterial, extraneous
3. *Definition:* Lacking in sense or substance; empty or foolish.
   Etymology: inanis, inane (Latin), "empty; void"
   Synonyms: vapid, insipid, ludicrous, ridiculous, obtuse
   Antonyms: incisive, acute, trenchant, penetrating, perceptive
4. *Definition:* Sound logically, legally, or in some other way.
   Etymology: validus (Latin), "strong; effective"
   Synonyms: logical, solid, well-founded, justifiable, admissible
   Antonyms: invalid, illogical, unsound, faulty, fallacious
5. *Definition:* Not consistent or compatible with something else.
   Etymology: in (Latin), "not" + *congruus* (Latin), "meeting together"
   Synonyms: inconsistent, incompatible, anomalous
   Antonyms: consistent, compatible, harmonious, congruous
6. *Definition:* (*v.*) To spread about or scatter; to soften; (*adj.*) widely scattered; wordy.
   Etymology: dis (Latin), "apart" + *fundere, fusus* (Latin), "pour"
   Synonyms: (*v.*) disperse, dissipate; (*adj.*) dispersed, scattered; prolix, verbose
   Antonyms: (*v.*) combine, merge, fuse; (*adj.*) fused, centralized; concise, laconic
7. *Definition:* (*n.*) A secret or underhanded scheme; the use of such schemes; (*v.*) to plot secretly or underhandedly; to arouse the interest or curiosity of.
   Etymology: intrigo (Italian), "scheme"; from *intricare* (Latin), "entangle"
   Synonyms: (*n.*) plot, conspiracy; ruse, stratagem; (*v.*) conspire, scheme; interest, fascinate, attract, captivate, charm
   Antonyms: (*v.*) bore, disinterest, repel
8. *Definition:* (*adj.*) Discontented; (*n.*) a discontented person.
   Etymology: mal (French), "badly" + *content* (French), "satisfied"
   Synonyms: (*adj.*) dissatisfied, discontent, disgruntled; (*n.*) sorehead, complainer
   Antonyms: (*adj.*) satisfied, content, complacent
9. *Definition:* To make firm or solid; to support with proof or evidence; to make real or actual.
   Etymology: substantia (New Latin), "substance" + -*are*, -*atus* (Latin), "make; give"
   Synonyms: verify, confirm, validate, authenticate
   Antonyms: invalidate, disprove, refute, confute, rebut, discredit

Review (pages 147–152)

Exercise IX. Word Roundup (pages 149–150)
1. a. See page 28 of the student text.
   b. See page 38 of the student text.
   c. See page 40 and answer to III, 7, page 37 of the student text.
   d. See page 112 of the student text.
   e. See page 52 of the student text.
   f. See page 29 of the student text.
2. a. See page 30 of the student text.
   b. See page 100 of the student text.
   c. See page 111 of the student text.
   d. See page 41 of the student text.
3. a. See page 124 of the student text.
   b. See page 113 of the student text.
4. See page 135 of the student text.
5. See page 42 of the student text.

Exercise X. Etymology (page 150)
1. Answers will vary but may include: *proceed, concede, exceed, secede, recede, antecedent, cession, intercede, procedure. Ced* or *ceed* means "go" or "yield."

2. *A* or *an* means "not," "without," or "opposed to."
   a. amorphous   b. anonymous
3. See page 57 of the student text.
4. a. socialize. To make sociable; to take part in social activities.
   b. proselytize. To convert from one belief or faith to another.
   c. maximize. To increase or make as great as possible; to assign the highest possible importance to.
5. a. To moan and groan about. The prefix *be* makes the intransitive verb *moan* transitive.
   b. To enchant. The prefix *be* forms a verb from the noun *witch*.
   c. To soil thoroughly. The prefix *be* gives greater force or thoroughness to the action of *soiling*.

Lesson 11 (pages 153–168)

Exercise V.   Word Roundup
(pages 161–162)
1. See page 153 of the student text.
2. See page 153 of the student text.
3. *Burly* indicates a combination of stockiness and muscularity; *husky* suggests rugged strength. *Chubby* implies noticeable roundness; *obese* refers to excessive, unpleasing, and unhealthy overweight.
4. See pages 155, 159 of the student text.
5. See page 156 of the student text.
6. See page 157 of the student text.
7. a. An inexperienced, unsophisticated, or gullible person; a novice.
   b. See page 156 of the student text.
   c. In perfect agreement or harmony.
   d. The crucial point on which a decision or other issue depends.
   e. See only the positive side of a situation.

Exercise (page 164)
1. a. collaborate, cooperate
   b. confer
   c. conjoin
   d. collapse
   e. coalesce
   f. congenital
   g. cohere
   h. concur
   i. compress
   j. corrupt
2. a. *co*, "together; with" + *author*. (*n.*) A joint author; (*v.*) to author jointly.
   b. *com*, "with" + *mutare mutatus*, "change." A substitution or change in penalty, charge, or payment; the travel of a commuter.
   c. *com*, "with; together" + *pati*, "suffer" + *-abilis, -abile*, "able to." Capable of existing together harmoniously.
   d. *cor*, "with" + *ruga*, "wrinkle" + *-are, -atus*, "make; do." To fold into parallel alternating ridges and grooves.
   e. *co*, "with; together" + *ordinare, ordinatus*, "arrange." (*v.*) To work or act together harmoniously; to

synchronize; (*n.*) one that is equal in importance to another; (*adj.*) equal in rank or order.
   f. *com*, "together" + *menglen*, "mix." To blend harmoniously.
   g. *con*, "together" + *foedus*, "treaty; alliance" + *-are, -atus*, "make." (*n.*) An ally or accomplice; (*v.*) to band together; (*adj.*) allied.
   h. *co*, "with; together" + *ex*, "out" + *sistere*, "stand firm." Living in peace and harmony with one another.
   i. *com*, "completely" + *pungere, punctus*, "prick." Anxiety arising from a sense of guilt.
   j. *con*, "with; together" + *currere*, "run." Happening or operating at the same time.
   k. *com*, "together + *stringere, strictus*, "draw tight." To restrict or restrain; to compel by force.
   l. *com*, "completely" + *templum*, "space for observing omens; temple" + *-are, -atus*, "make; do." To consider thoughtfully.

Exercise I.   The Greeks Had a Word for It (page 167)
1. A quality arousing pity; a feeling of pity, sympathy, or tenderness.
2. A pleasant odor that is characteristic of something.
3. See page 393 of the student text.
4. See page 228 of the student text.
5. A cure-all.
6. The origin of something.
7. Any occurrence or fact perceptible to the senses; a marvel.
8. Protection; sponsorship or patronage.
9. The common people.
10. An outline or abstract.
11. A predicament calling for a choice between two equally balanced alternatives.
12. (*n.*) The point of greatest intensity in a series of events; (*v.*) to reach or bring to such a point.
13. The act of identifying a disease or malady by examining its symptoms.
14. The soul or spirit; the mind.
15. A crucial or decisive point.
16. A great or sudden calamity.
17. See page 468 of the student text.
18. The highest point.
19. A complete change; a transformation.
20. An inflictor of vengeance or retribution; an unbeatable rival.
21. A belief, principle, or idea considered to be the absolute truth; a system of such ideas or beliefs.
22. The direct opposite of something.
23. A purification or purging; a figurative release of the emotions or tension.
24. Excessive pride, arrogance, or self-confidence.
25. See page 483 of the student text.

26. A theory or assumption.
27. Deification; an exalted or glorified ideal.
28 Exceptional personal magnetism or charm.
29. A very small amount; a bit or jot.
30. Partial or complete inability to move or function.

Exercise II. Linguistic Shortcuts
(pages 167–168)
A. *Abbreviations*
1. And so forth; *et cetera.*
2. And others; *et alia.*
3. Which see; *quod vide.*
4. In the same place (used in footnotes or bibliographies to refer to the book, chapter, article, or page cited immediately before); *ibidem.*
5. In the place cited (used in footnotes or bibliographies to refer to a page, section, chapter, or book cited earlier); *loco citato.*
6. A message or additional information appended to a manuscript or a letter after the writer's signature; *postscriptum.*
7. In the work cited (used in footnotes or bibliographies to refer to a work previously cited); *opere citato.*
8. For example; *exempli gratia.*
9. That is; *id est.*
10. Note well; *nota bene.*
11. Before noon; *ante meridiem.*
12. Namely; *scilicet.*
13. Approximately; *circa.*
14. In the year of the Lord; *anno Domini.*
15. Compare; *confer.*
16. Namely; *videlicet.*
17. Flourished; *floruit.*
18. Against; *versus.*

B. *Acronyms*
1. National Aeronautics and Space Administration. One of the independent executive agencies of the federal government; in charge of the space program.
2. Congress of Racial Equality. One of the major organizations active in the civil rights movement.
3. National Organization for Women. An organization devoted to improving the lot of women in the United States.
4. Southeast Asia Treaty Organization. An organization established under the Southeast Asia Collective Defense Treaty (1954) to guarantee peace in Southeast Asia and the Southwest Pacific and to ensure them against communist aggression.
5. Volunteers in Service to America. An organization sponsored by the U.S. Office of Economic Opportunity and composed of volunteers devoted to educating and teaching skills to the poor.
6. United Nations Educational, Scientific, and Cultural Organization. A specialized agency of the UN devoted to furthering world peace by removing social, religious, and racial tensions; encouraging the free exchange of ideas; and improving and expanding education.
7. As soon as possible. Frequently used in business communications and in the workplace to indicate urgency.
8. Not in my backyard. The negative response to locating (or the plan to locate) something deemed undesirable (*e.g.,* a prison or power plant) in one's neighborhood or community.
9. White Anglo-Saxon Protestant. A somewhat derogatory expression applied to persons of northern European (especially British), Protestant decent, whose members are held by some to be the most privileged and influential group in the United States.
10. Absent without leave. A term used by the military to indicate the unauthorized absence of a soldier.
11. Zone Improvement Plan code. The five-digit or nine-digit number (determined by geographic location) assigned to each postal delivery area in the United States. Often lowercased: zip.
12. Organization of Petroleum Exporting Countries. An organization of oil producers whose members include the Arab states, Venezuela, Bolivia, Ecuador, and Mexico.
13. Strategic Arms Limitation Talks. A series of high-level diplomatic discussions between the United States and the Soviet Union for the purpose of limiting strategic arms and from which a number of important agreements resulted.
14. Radio detecting and ranging. A method of determining the existence, location, and speed of distant objects by analyzing the high frequency radio waves reflected from their surfaces.
15. Self-contained underwater breathing apparatus. An apparatus containing compressed air and used for breathing while swimming underwater.
16. Sound navigation ranging. A method of detecting and locating submerged objects by analyzing their transmitted or reflected acoustic waves.

17. Light amplification by stimulated emission of radiation. A device for amplifying light to a high degree of intensity.
18. Automated teller machine. A computerized device used for basic banking transactions such as cash withdrawals, deposits, and transfers between one's various accounts. To use an ATM, one must enter a personal identification number (PIN).

Exercise III. Philosophical and Religious Positions (page 168)

1. One who believes that physical matter constitutes the only reality; one who believes that physical well-being and worldly possessions constitute the only good in life.
2. One who believes that pleasure is the chief good in life.
3. One who pursues visionary, often impractical, ideals and whose conduct is influenced or governed by them.
4. One who believes that experience and observation (especially by the senses) provide the only basis for knowledge and who places no trust in theory or speculation.
5. One who denies the existence of God.
6. One who believes that the existence of God cannot be proved but who does not deny that God exists.
7. One who approaches situations and problems from a purely practical point of view.
8. Someone devoted to the pursuit of pleasure; someone with refined tastes, especially in food.
9. One who rejects authority or dogma (especially in religion) in favor of rational inquiry and speculation.
10. One who hates or scorns humankind.
11. One who places greater stress on subjective experience, feelings, and imagination than on facts or practical realities.
12. One who does not show any reaction to pleasure or pain.
13. One who is concerned primarily with human values, capacities, and achievements, rather than with abstract beings or theological controversy.
14. A boastful person; a conceited or self-important person.
15. One who communes with ultimate reality or God through meditation or contemplation.
16. One who always looks on the bright side of things or who expects the best-possible outcome from any situation.
17. A person who is primarily concerned with hard facts, concrete reality, the literal truth, and practical necessities.
18. One who believes in equal political, economic, or social rights for all persons.
19. One who hates women.
20. A person who is concerned with and promotes human welfare, the alleviation of suffering, and social reform.
21. One who instinctively or habitually doubts, questions, or disagrees with generally accepted ideas or beliefs.
22. A person who believes that there is only one God.
23. One who dissents from any accepted belief or doctrine, especially in religion.
24. One who is primarily concerned with the welfare of others.
25. One who believes in the superiority of his/her own racial stock.
26. One who habitually takes the gloomiest view of a situation.
27. One who favors or tolerates freedom of thought or behavior, especially in religion.
28. A person who believes that usefulness is the only criterion for judging merit and who therefore places heavier stress on practical (as opposed to aesthetic) considerations.
29. One who believes in the Bible as a factual historical document and source of incontrovertible prophecy of things to come and who, therefore, favors a strictly literal interpretation of it.
30. One who destroys religious images and opposes their veneration; one who attacks established beliefs or institutions.

Exercise IV. Expanding Your Word Power (page 168)

1. *Definition:* A beginner; an inexperienced person.
   Etymology: tiro (Latin), "recruit"
   Synonyms: novice, neophyte
   Antonyms: veteran, past master, expert
2. *Definition:* Conflict; lack of agreement.
   Etymology: dis (Latin), "apart" + cor, cordis (Latin), "heart"
   Synonyms: strife, dissension
   Antonyms: concord, harmony, agreement
3. *Definition:* To determine by reasoning or logic.
   Etymology: de (Latin), "down from; away" + ducere (Latin), "lead"
   Synonyms: conclude, infer, gather
4. *Definition:* Mocking; scoffing.
   Etymology: deridere, derisus (Latin), "mock" + -ivus (Latin). "inclined to; tending to"

Synonyms: scornful, insulting, sarcastic, disdainful
Antonyms: laudatory, flattering, complimentary

5. *Definition:* (*v.*) To begin; to induct into membership by special rites; (*n.*) one who has been initiated; a novice.
Etymology: initium (Latin). "beginning" + *-are, -atus* (Latin), "make"
Synonyms: (*v.*) commence, inaugurate; install, invest; (*n.*) neophyte, fledgling, pledge; insider
Antonyms: (*v.*) consummate, conclude, terminate

6. *Definition:* Greatly abundant; plentiful.
Etymology: pro (Latin), "forth" + *fundere, fusus* (Latin), "pour"
Synonyms: copious, lavish, prodigal
Antonyms: scanty, sparse, meager, scant

7. *Definition:* Seeming to be likely, valid, or acceptable.
Etymology: plaudere, plausus (Latin), "applaud" + *-abilis, -abile* (Latin), "able to"
Synonyms: credible, believable, likely
Antonyms: implausible, incredible, unlikely, improbable

8. *Definition:* Excessively thin and bony; pale and haggard.
Etymology: gawnt/gaunt (Middle English), "slim"; probably from Old Norse
Synonyms: lean, emaciated, scrawny, cadaverous, drawn
Antonyms: chubby, portly, plump, corpulent, obese; rosy, radiant

9. *Definition:* To refute, especially by formal argument.
Etymology: re (Old French). "back" + *buter* (Old French), "hit, push"
Synonyms: disprove, controvert, deny, contradict, discredit, confute
Antonyms: prove, validate, substantiate, verify, corroborate

10. *Definition:* To reprove kindly but seriously; to caution against.
Etymology: ad (Latin), "to; toward" + *monere, monitus* (Latin), "warn; advise"
Synonyms: rebuke, reprimand, reproach
Antonyms: praise, commend

11. *Definition:* A law, rule, or code of law or rules; a basis for judgment; the books of the Bible officially recognized by a church; a kind of priest or monk.
Etymology: kanon (Greek). "rod; rule"
Synonyms: regulation, statute; criterion, yardstick; catalog

12. *Definition:* Central or decisive.
Etymology: pivot (French), "pivot" + *al* (English suffix), "connected with"
Synonyms: crucial, critical, focal

Antonyms: peripheral, minor, inconsequential

13. *Definition:* Extremely careful and precise in regard to details; painstakingly thorough.
Etymology: metus (Latin), "fear" + *(per)iculosus* (Latin), "dangerous"
Synonyms: scrupulous, fastidious, conscientious, punctilious
Antonyms: careless, casual, perfunctory, cursory

14. *Definition:* To reduce in length or scope.
Etymology: abregen (Middle English), "shorten"; from *ad* (Latin), "to; toward" + *brevis, breve* (Latin), "short"
Synonyms: condense, abbreviate
Antonyms: expand, enlarge, lengthen, extend

15. *Definition:* Sharp or bitter in mood or tone.
Etymology: acerbus (Latin), "sour"
Synonyms: acidulous, astringent, mordant, caustic
Antonyms: saccharine, candied, sugary

Lesson 12 (pages 169–188)

Exercise V.   Word Roundup (page 179)
1. See page 172 of the student text.
2. *Devoted* means "given to" in a positive or favorable sense; *addicted* means "dependent on" or "given to" in a compulsive or obsessive (and therefore unfavorable) sense.
3. A *devoted mother* is one who feels great love and affection for her children and does everything she can for them. A *devout Buddhist* is a person who genuinely believes in the teachings of the Buddha and who tries to practice them in everyday life. A *devotee of the arts* is someone who has a deep interest in the arts and devotes much of his/her time, money, and energy to them.
4. a. See page 169 of the student text.
   b. See page 170 of the student text.
   c. See page 172 of the student text.
   d. See pages 172–173 of the student text.
5. See page 176 of the student text.
6. See pages 175–176 of the student text.
7. a. Dejected; out of spirits.
   b. Elated; carefree.
   c. A total fraud or deception.
   d. A complicated confidence game, usually conducted by undercover agents to catch criminals.
   e. An accomplished swindler who deludes a victim after first winning his or her confidence.

f. Delinquency or neglect of one's obligations or responsibilities.

g. Delinquent or behind in a payment or obligation.

h. In a desultory or intermittent manner.

Exercise I. Borrowings from French
(page 184)
1. A feeling of weariness and dissatisfaction; boredom.
2. Keen enjoyment of life.
3. An air of mystery or reverence that envelops something.
4. A noisy quarrel.
5. Brilliance of performance; notable success.
6. Self-esteem.
7. State of cordial relations, usually between nations; the reestablishment of such relations.
8. (v.) To line up; (n.) a line of people waiting for something.
9. A group that develops or applies new techniques, usually in the arts; the forefront or vanguard; (adj.) in the forefront; ahead of the times.
10. The most outstanding item or accomplishment, often in reference to gourmet food or the arts.
11. Ghastly; gruesome.
12. See page 360 of the student text.
13. A tremendous feat of strength, skill, or ingenuity.
14. A person who has recently acquired wealth (and who may tend to show it off).
15. A parlor game involving pantomine; an empty pretense or deception.
16. The complete stock of plays, operas, songs, roles, etc., performed by an artist or group; the complete range of skills, talents, or accomplishments of a person or group.
17. A complete reversal; an about-face
18. Gracious and smooth in manner; urbane.
19. A token of remembrance; a memento.
20. Liveliness, energy, or enthusiasm.
21. See page 449 of the student text.
22. Required by custom or fashion; obligatory.
23. Preeminently; regarded as the best of its kind.
24. See pages 208–209 of the student text.
25. A type of armed attack made from a defensive position; a combat mission.
26. The distinctive tone quality of a singing voice or musical instrument.
27. The most suitable word or phrase.
28. A relationship of mutual trust and understanding.
29. Self-possession or composure when under a strain.
30. A quick and witty retort or conversation.

Exercise II. Anemic Expressions
(pages 184–185)
1. *terrific:* excellent, first-rate, superb, top-notch. *dynamite:* outstanding, wily, sure-handed. *super:* excellent, invincible, powerful. *fabulous:* memorable, outstanding, victorious.
2. *gorgeous:* impressive, remarkable, masterly, inspired. *blah:* unimpressive, uninspired, uninteresting, poor, inferior, trite. *just plain awful:* incredibly ugly or inept, ludicrously bad.
3. *pretty lousy:* boring, disappointing, inferior. *fantastic:* able, skillful, gifted, talented.
4. *heavenly:* delicious, luscious. *yummy:* succulent, tasty. *lovely:* enjoyable, delectable. *swell:* mouthwatering, tempting.
5. *etc.:* going to the theater, dining out, and doing all the things a tourist does.
6. *rotten:* inclement, unpleasant, rainy, overcast and cold. *great:* enjoyable, exciting, memorable.
7. *neat:* carefully worked-out, ingenious. *or whatever:* and remodeling the cafeteria, and refurbishing the locker rooms.

Exercise III. Fused Phrases
(pages 185–186)
1. *Definition:* Suave; carefree; affable. *Phrase: de bonne aire* (French), "of good disposition"
2. *Definition:* (v.) In chess, to attack an opponent's king in a way that allows no escape; (n.) the act of checkmating; utter defeat. *Phrase: shah mat* (Arabic), "The king is dead."
3. *Definition:* An office or position that requires little or no work but provides a decent income. *Phrase: (beneficium) sine cura* (Latin), "(benefice) without cure of souls"
4. *Definition:* A support or base for a statue or other upright structure. *Phrase: piè di stallo* (Italian), "foot of a stall"
5. *Definition:* Sleight of hand; deception or trickery. *Phrase: léger de main* (French), "light of hand"
6. *Definition:* A person named after another person. *Phrase: for the name's sake*
7. *Definition:* (v.) To perplex or bewilder; (n.) a state of bafflement or perplexity. *Phrase: non plus* (Latin), "no more"
8. *Definition:* The branch of philosophy that investigates the nature of first principles and problems of ultimate reality. *Phrase: ta meta ta physika* (Greek), "the things that come after the

physics (in the medieval arrangement of Aristotle's works)"

9. *Definition:* with hands on hips and
elbows turned outward.
Phrase: probably *i keng boginn* (Old
Norse), "bent like a bow"

10. *Definition:* (*adj.*) Appropriate; pertinent; (*adv.*) pertinently; oppor-
tunely; incidentally.
Phrase: *à propos* (French), "to the
purpose"

11. *Definition:* An ancestral line, often
of a purebred animal.
Phrase: *pie de grue* (Old French),
"crane's foot," from the shape
made by the lines on a genealogical chart.

12. *Definition:* To deign to grant or
bestow.
Phrase: *vouchen sauf* (Middle
English), "warrant as safe"

13. *Definition:* A small gift by a store
owner to a customer; an extra or
bonus.
Phrase: *la ñapa* (Spanish), "the
addition"

14. *Definition:* Slight or inferior in
strength or size.
Phrase: *puis né* (Old French), "born
afterwards" (*i.e.*, younger)

15. See page 316 of the student text.

16. *Definition:* Sonorous; pompous.
Phrase: *ore rotundo* (Latin), "with
round mouth"

17. *Definition:* Equivalent in value,
significance, or effect.
Phrase: *tant amunter* (Anglo-
Norman), "amount to as much"

18. *Definition:* Fuss; bustle or bother.
Phrase: at do (Middle English), "to do"

Exercise IV. Expanding Your Word Power (page 186)

1. *Definition:* Untidy in habits or appearance; careless or slipshod.
Etymology: sloyren (Middle English), "rascal" + *ly;* perhaps from
Middle Dutch or Flemish.
Synonyms: unkempt, sloppy, messy;
lackadaisical
Antonyms: dapper, smart, spruce;
careful

2. *Definition:* To reject the validity of;
to refuse to recognize or acknowl-
edge; to disown.
Etymology: repudiare, repudiatus
(Latin), "cast off"; from *repudium*
(Latin), "divorce"
Synonyms: disavow, abjure, re-
nounce; abandon, cast off
Antonyms: adopt, accept, affirm,
acknowledge, embrace, recognize

3. *Definition:* To accelerate the pro-
gress of; to perform quickly.
Etymology: expedire, expeditus
(Latin), "free the feet; extricate,"

from *ex* (Latin), "out" + *pes, pedis*
(Latin), "foot"
Synonyms: hasten, accelerate,
facilitate
Antonyms: delay, postpone; hinder,
hamper

4. *Definition:* (*adj.*) Sad; pensive;
(*n.*) sadness or depression of the
spirits.
Etymology: melas, melanos (Greek),
"black" + *chole* (Greek), "bile"
Synonyms: (*adj.*) dejected, despondent, downcast, morose; (*n.*)
despondency, dejection
Antonyms: (*adj.*) happy, elated,
lighthearted, merry; (*n.*) elation,
euphoria, exhilaration

5. *Definition:* Having scruples; conscientious or exacting.
Etymology: scrupulus (Latin), "scruple" + *-osus* (Latin), "full of"
Synonyms: principled, punctilious,
meticulous, careful
Antonyms: unscrupulous, unethical; remiss, negligent, delinquent,
careless

6. *Definition:* To deceive.
Etymology: hood + *wink* (obsolete
English), "cover the eyes"
Synonyms: delude, dupe, trick

7. *Definition:* Natty and self-confident
in manner or appearance.
Etymology: gentil (French), "genteel;
noble"
Synonyms: buoyant, brisk, sprightly; dapper, smart
Antonyms: shy, sedate, demure,
staid; dowdy, frumpy

8. *Definition:* Offensively self-assertive.
Etymology: Perhaps a humorous
blend of *bump* and *fractious*
("unruly; cranky")
Synonyms: obtrusive, forward,
arrogant, pushy
Antonyms: self-effacing, shy, diffident

9. *Definition:* Methodical in procedure
or plan.
Etymology: syn (Greek), "together"
+ *histanai* (Greek), "stand" +
-atikos (Greek), "characteristic of"
Synonyms: orderly, well-organized,
regular, businesslike
Antonyms: unmethodical, erratic,
helter-skelter, haphazard

10. *Definition:* Drab and old-fashioned
in appearance.
Etymology: doude (Middle English),
"unattractive woman" + *y*
Synonyms: frowzy, frumpy
Antonyms: chic, smart, stylish

11. *Definition:* Stopping and starting at
intervals.
Etymology: inter (Latin), "between"
+ *mittens, mittentis,* present participle of *mittere* (Latin), "send"

Synonyms: irregular, sporadic, spasmodic, interrupted
Antonyms: incessant, continued, constant

12. *Definition:* To strike out, obliterate, or delete.
Etymology: ex (Latin), "out" + *pungere* (Latin), "prick"
Synonyms: destroy, eliminate, erase
Antonyms: retain; include, insert

13. *Definition:* To stray from the main subject.
Etymology: dis (Latin), "apart; aside" + *gradi, gressus* (Latin), "go; step"
Synonyms: deviate, diverge, stray, ramble
Antonyms: conform to, adhere to, stick to

14. *Definition:* Lukewarm.
Etymology: tepidus (Latin), "moderately warm"
Synonyms: room temperature; half-hearted, listless, lackluster
Antonyms: hot, ardent; cold, frigid, glacial

15. *Definition:* Skilled in an art, occupation, or branch of knowledge.
Etymology: proficiens, proficientis (Latin), "making progress"; from *pro* (Latin), "forward" + *facere* (Latin), "make; do"
Synonyms: expert, adept, accomplished, competent, skillful
Antonyms: inept, clumsy, awkward, unskillful

Lesson 13 (pages 189–205)

Exercise V.   Word Roundup
(pages 197–198)
1. See page 191 of the student text.
2. a. See page 191 of the student text.
   b. See page 192 of the student text.
3. Extremely harsh or severe. Draco was an Athenian lawgiver whose code of laws (issued in 621 B.C.) was noted for its harshness.
4. a. Deteriorate.
   b. Put off decisions or actions in order to see what develops.
   c. Work hard.
   d. Make public.
   e. Be dilatory.
   f. Damage or destroy.
   g. Stop the unauthorized flow of confidential information to the media or other outsiders.
   h. A temporary state of dormancy resembling death induced by the cessation of vital functions.
5. See page 195 of the student text.
6. *Oliver Twist* (1838) by Charles Dickens. By this name, Dickens seems to be implying that the character was especially clever or crafty (*artful*) at evading capture by the police (*dodging*) and in moving to and fro unhin-

dered and unnoticed. These talents would obviously be important to a professional pickpocket such as the Artful Dodger.

Exercise (page 200)
A.
1. a. To exclude or shut out.
   b. To lower in rank or grade.
   c. A state of melancholy or depression.
   d. To eliminate, omit, or strike out.
   e. To condemn, censure, or accuse formally.
   f. See page 170 of the student text.
   g. To lessen the price or estimated value of.
   h. See page 171 of the student text.
   i. To use up or exhaust.
   j. To remove from a throne, office, or other powerful position.
   k. To break camp; to depart suddenly.
   l. To behead.
2. a. *Definition:* Lacking in systematic arrangement; disordered.
      Use of dis: It negates the meaning of *organized.*
   b. *Definition:* See page 193 of the student text.
      Use of dis: It negates the meaning of *parity.*
   c. *Definition:* (v.) To censure; to express disapproval; (n.) a reproach.
      Use of dis: It negates the meaning of *praise.*
   d. *Definition:* Out of proportion relative to size or amount.
      Use of dis: It negates the meaning of *proportionate.*
   e. *Definition:* To declare ineligible or unqualified.
      Use of dis: It negates the meaning of *qualify.*
   f. *Definition:* Lack of agreement or harmony; dissension.
      Use of dis: It indicates a separation between the elements involved in the root (*cor, cordis*).
   g. *Definition:* To free from illusion or enchantment.
      Use of dis: It negates *enchant.*
   h. *Definition:* To impair by deep and persistent injuries; to mar.
      Use of dis: It negates *figure* (= "face; shape").
   i. *Definition:* To deprive of the right to vote.
      Use of dis: It negates *franchise*; it indicates a deprivation of the root (*franchise*).
   j. *Definition:* To exclude someone from an inheritance.
      Use of dis: It indicates a deprivation of the root (*inherit*); it negates *inherit.*
   k. *Definition:* To expel from the legal profession.

Use of dis: It negates *bar* (= "admit to the bar"); it indicates a separation from the bar.

l. *Definition:* To pull apart or to pieces; to break up.
Use of dis: It indicates a separation of the members of the root.

B.

1. a. Forerunner; harbinger.
   b. Messenger.
   c. Rambling; digressive.
2. a. To happen again or repeatedly.
   b. A short journey or outing.
   c. To meet with or run into; to bring upon oneself.
   d. Appearing or happening regularly or repeatedly.
   e. A turning to a person or thing for help or protection.
   f. Any form of money used for exchange; circulation.

Exercise I. More Look-Alikes
(page 203)

1. *emulate:* to try to equal or excel the excellence of; *simulate:* to imitate or feign, often for the purpose of deception.
2. A *feint* (pronounced fānt) is a misleading attack against a false target designed to draw the defense away from the real objective and so make it easier to take. Originally a military term, it is frequently used today in sports (*e.g.,* boxing) and other areas to indicate any kind of misleading movement or strategy. *Faint* as a verb means "swoon" and as an adjective means "indistinct."
3. *resemble:* to be like or similar to; *dissemble:* to disguise the real nature of; to feign.
4. *discrete:* individually distinct; *discreet:* showing good judgment; prudent.
5. See page 101 of the student text.
6. *manners:* socially correct behavior; *mannerisms:* eccentric behavioral traits or idiosyncrasies.
7. *capital:* (*n.*) the town or city that is the official seat of government in a state or country; wealth in money or property; a large letter; (*adj.*) chief or foremost; first-rate; punishable by death; *capitol:* the building in which a state legislature convenes.
8. See page 40 and answer to III, 7, page 37 of the student text.
9. *amend:* to change for the better; to rectify; *emend:* to improve or correct by critical editing.
10. *solid:* firm; well-made; substantial; *stolid:* unemotional; impassive.
11. *delegate:* (*v.*) to appoint as one's representative; (*n.*) a representative; *relegate:* send or consign to an obscure or unimportant place, position, or condition.
12. *deprecate:* to express disapproval of; to protest against; *depreciate:* to lower the price or estimated value of; to belittle.
13. See page 52 of the student text.
14. *envious:* feeling envy; resentful or jealous; *enviable:* arousing envy; highly desirable.
15. See page 137 of the student text.
16. *honorable:* upright; illustrious; *honorary:* given as a mark of honor; commemorative.
17. *authoritative:* having or arising from authority; *authoritarian:* characterized by or favoring blind submission to authority.
18. *imperial:* relating to an empire, emperor, or empress; *imperious:* acting like an emperor; commanding; domineering.
19. *allay:* to alleviate or calm; *ally:* (*v.*) to unite or associate with; (*n.*) an associate.
20. See page 487 of the student text.

Exercise II. Biblical Expressions
(page 204)

In addition to an unabridged dictionary and a concordance of the Bible, the following reference books may prove useful in completing this exercise: *Brewer's Dictionary of Phrase and Fable*, 16th ed.; *Morris Dictionary of Word and Phrase Origins*, 2d ed.

1. To recognize impending calamity or disaster. The words "Mene, mene, tekel, upharsin" appeared magically on a wall of the palace of Belshazzar, King of Babylon (Daniel 5:25–28). These were interpreted to mean that Belshazzar would shortly lose his throne to the Medes and the Persians because of his sins.
2. A password that identifies one group or class of people from another; a slogan or catchword of a particular group. The Gileadites used *shibboleth* (Hebrew, "ear of grain," "floods," or "stream") as a password to distinguish their own men from the men of Ephraim, who could not pronounce the word correctly (Judges 12:1–6).
3. Of questionable authority; false or counterfeit. The Apocrypha is a collection of 14 biblical books of doubtful authenticity. In the 5th century A.D., St. Jerome doubted their genuineness because they did not appear in the original Hebrew Old Testament.
4. A questioning or skeptical person; one who habitually has doubts. St.

Thomas was the apostle who doubted Christ's resurrection and demanded to see proof of it in the form of the wounds on Jesus' body (John 20:24–29).

5. To divide the good from the bad or the worthy from the unworthy. From the descriptions of the Judgment Day in Matthew 25:32–33 and the kingdom of heaven in Matthew 13:24–30.

6. See page 392 of the student text.

7. To conceal one's talents; to be excessively modest about one's abilities. From Christ's words to his disciples in Matthew 5:15.

8. A person who is ready to help those in distress. From the parable of the Good Samaritan (Luke 10:30–37).

9. The best of humankind; anyone regarded as the finest of his/her kind. From Christ's words to his disciples and listeners during the Sermon on the Mount (Matthew 5:13).

10. A person who brings tragedy and disaster upon his/her friends. From the story of the Old Testament prophet Jonah (Jonah 1–4).

11. To divide one's loyalties equally between two contradictory or conflicting persons or ideologies — an impossible task. From Christ's words during the Sermon on the Mount (Matthew 6:24).

12. To bring serious consequences through heedless or foolish actions. From the prophet Hosea's prediction of what would happen to the Israelites because of their impious behavior (Hosea 8:7).

13. A huge animal; something of enormous size. From the animal (most probably a hippopotamus) described in Job 40:15–24.

14. To avoid confrontation or argument; to take a pacifistic attitude. From Christ's instructions regarding the proper way to deal with hostile people (Matthew 5:39).

15. Pertaining to a prophetic disclosure or revelation; forecasting the ultimate destruction of the world. From the Apocalypse (also called the Book of Revelation), the last book of the New Testament. Attributed to St. John the Divine, it recounts a vision of the final struggle between good and evil, culminating in the triumph of God and the Christian church.

16. Not to be afraid to do something, even though you have little or no hope of immediate gain or result from it. From an expression in Ecclesiastes 9:11.

17. Very old, antiquated, or primitive. The word literally means "before (*ante* [Latin]) the flood (*diluvium* [Latin])" and refers to the era before the great flood recounted in Genesis 6–8.

18. A place or condition that provides complete satisfaction and the fulfillment of all one's hopes. The term originally referred to Canaan, which God promised to Abraham, Isaac, Jacob, and their descendants.

19. Something of value unexpectedly received. From the name of the food miraculously provided to the Israelites during their flight from Egypt (Exodus 16:4–35).

20. To offer something of value to people who are incapable of appreciating it. From Christ's warning to his disciples in Matthew 7:6.

Exercise III.   A Verbal Diversion
(page 204)

1. An honest critic or adviser; one who reproves firmly but gently. The Dutch were noted for their discipline.

2. A period of warm, mild, summerlike weather occurring in the late fall. Here *Indian* is a synonym for *bogus*, probably because the early English colonists applied *Indian* to anything that resembled, but was not really the same as, something with which they were familiar in England.

3. A somewhat derogatory label given to writers and artists who flagrantly disregard social customs and proprieties. Bohemia (in central Europe) was mistakenly thought to be the home of Gypsies, whom such people were considered to resemble.

4. A meal or social activity for which each person pays his/her own expenses; to pay one's own way. According to an obsolete English view, the Dutch were outrageously penny-pinching.

5. To become angry. The Irish were considered to have quick tempers.

6. Willful or ignorant destruction of valuables. The Vandals, a Teutonic tribe, sacked Rome in A.D. 455; their destructiveness became proverbial in the late classical world.

7. Give a ball spin by striking it to the left or right of center (as in pool) or by releasing it with a twist (as in baseball or bowling). Origin unknown.

8. An inconclusive judgment or pronouncement. Scottish law allowed a jury to hand down an inconclusive verdict in certain criminal cases.

9. A situation from which nothing at all can be expected. The phrase

stems from an earlier U.S. attitude toward Mexicans.

10. Absence or leave without announcing one's departure or receiving permission. From the 18th-century French practice (frowned upon by the English) of leaving a party without a formal farewell to the host or hostess.

11. To be in trouble, or out of favor, with someone. Origin uncertain.

12. Conjoined twins, born with their bodies joined together at some point. The first widely publicized example of the phenomenon were the twins Chang and Eng born in Siam (Thailand) in 1811.

13. One who gives a gift in expectation of something better in return; one who gives a gift and then asks for it back. The phrase originated in the early colonists' experiences with Indian gift-giving customs.

Many of the foregoing items indicate that English still contains xenophobic elements from a bygone era.

Exercise IV. Ricochet Words (page 205)

1. To show hesitation or lack of decisiveness and resolution; to dawdle.
2. Whether desired or not; without choice.
3. To dawdle; to waste time by loitering.
4. Lacking in strength, character, or determination; weak or ineffectual.
5. Pompous; marked by an air of assumed importance.
6. Reckless; rash.
7. Questionable or underhanded activity.
8. A hodgepodge; a jumble.
9. A religion derived from African ancestor worship and practiced chiefly in Haiti. It is characterized by propitiatory rites and communication with animistic spirits through trances.
10. To associate familiarly with, especially with people in a higher social sphere than one's own.
11. Nonsense words or phrases used by a magician; a magician's trick; any deception or chicanery.
12. A complex, colorful action or display, often designed to confuse an opponent.
13. (n.) Deception, fraud; questionable or deceitful activity; (v.) to trick.
14. Disreputable persons; the dregs of society.
15. Pretentious nonsense.
16. Foolishness; nonsense.
17. To gossip; to prattle.
18. Noise, uproar; confusion, turmoil.
19. A mechanical musical instrument (such as a barrel organ) operated by turning a crank.
20. Jumbled; in a confused or disordered state; secret.
21. A jumble; a disordered mixture.
22. Hurried in a confused way; haphazard or hit-and-miss.

Other ricochet words include: razzmatazz, lovey-dovey, hurly-burly, higgledy-piggledy, and loosey-goosey.

Exercise V.   Expanding Your Word Power (page 205)

1. *Definition:* Worn-out through age or use; dilapidated.
   Etymology: de (Latin), "completely" + *crepare, crepitus* (Latin), "creak; crack"
   Synonyms: deteriorated, run-down, decayed, broken-down
   Antonyms: sturdy, shipshape, well-kept-up; brand-new

2. *Definition:* Incapable of being wearied or exhausted.
   Etymology: in (Latin), "not" + *de* (Latin), "out" + *fatigare, fatigatus* (Latin), "tire" + *-abilis, -abile* (Latin), "able to"
   Synonyms: assiduous, relentless, tireless, untiring
   Antonyms: lazy, slothful, indolent, lackadaisical, sluggish, languid

3. *Definition:* Done or acting mechanically or with little care and interest.
   Etymology: perfungi, perfunctus (Late Latin), "get through (quickly)" + *-orius* (Latin), "tending toward; characterized by"; from *per* (Latin), "through" + *fungi, functus* (Latin), "do; perform"
   Synonyms: cursory, superficial, shallow, slipshod, slapdash
   Antonyms: meticulous, thorough, conscientious, painstaking

4. *Definition:* Habitually lazy.
   Etymology: in (Latin), "not" + *dolens, dolentis* (Latin), present participle of *dolere,* "give pain"
   Synonyms: slothful, shiftless, sluggish, torpid
   Antonyms: diligent, energetic, hard-working, indefatigable, assiduous

5. *Definition:* To disturb or upset the composure of.
   Etymology: des (Old French), "not; un-" + *concerter* (Old French), "bring into agreement"
   Synonyms: perturb, fluster, unsettle, ruffle
   Antonyms: reassure, calm, put/set at ease

6. *Definition:* A formal written document in which a subject is treated systematically.
   Etymology: traitier (Old French), "treat"; from *tractare* (Latin), "drag; handle"

Synonyms: dissertation, discourse, lecture

Antonyms: summary, abstract, synopsis

7. *Definition:* A high degree of perception or understanding.

Etymology: perspicax, perspicacis, (Latin), "sharp-sighted" + *-itas, -itatis* (Latin), "state of"; from *per* (Latin), "through" + *specere* (Latin), "look"

Synonyms: acumen, perceptiveness, discernment, insight

Antonyms: density, obtuseness

8. *Definition:* Strong intolerance or prejudice in matters of race, religion, politics, etc.

Etymology: bigot (Old French), "hypocrite"

Synonyms: bias, discrimination

Antonyms: open-mindedness, fair-mindedness, impartiality

9. *Definition:* To lessen the price, value, or worth of; to belittle.

Etymology: de (Latin), "down from" + *pretium* (Latin), "price" + *-are, -atus* (Latin), "make; do"

Synonyms: devalue, underrate, minimize

Antonyms: exaggerate, magnify, inflate

10. *Definition:* Equality; equivalence.

Etymology: par (Latin), "equal" + *-itas, -itatis* (Latin), "state of"

Synonyms: likeness, similiarity, correspondence, comparability

Antonyms: disparity, disproportion, dissimilarity

11. *Definition:* Devoid of emotion or expression.

Etymology: in (Latin), "not" + *pati, passus* (Latin), "suffer" + *-ivus* (Latin), "capable of"

Synonyms: unexcitable, apathetic, stolid, unemotional, emotionless, phlegmatic

Antonyms: passionate, hotheaded, excitable, zealous, ardent

12. *Definition:* To convey knowledge of; to grant a share of.

Etymology: in (Latin), "in" + *partire* (Latin), "share, divide"

Synonyms: disclose, reveal, divulge; bestow

Antonyms: conceal, withhold, keep to oneself

13. *Definition:* Easily managed or controlled.

Etymology: tractare (Latin), "pull; manage" + *-abilis, -abile* (Latin), "able to"

Synonyms: obedient, submissive; docile, malleable

Antonyms: intractable, refractory, unruly, unmanageable, recalcitrant

14. *Definition:* Lacking strength; frail or infirm.

Etymology: feble (Old French), "weak"; from *flebilis* (Latin), "lamentable"

Synonyms: weak, fragile, impotent; low, soft; ineffectual, feckless

Antonyms: strong, powerful; loud; potent, effective

15. *Definition:* Deception by trickery; a trick.

Etymology: chicaner (Old French), "quibble" + *y*

Synonyms: guile, deceit, double-dealing; stratagem, ruse, subterfuge

Antonyms: honesty, uprightness, probity; fair play

Lesson 14 (pages 206–224)

Exercise V. Word Roundup (page 215)

1. a. See page 210 of the student text.
   b. See page 208 of the student text.
2. a. The masses; the common people.
   b. Unknown land; unfamiliar territory.
   c. See page 210 of the student text.
   d. The highest social class or group.
   e. All the same.
   f. The elite; the best of the bunch.
   g. A complete enigma.
   h. The followers or ordinary members of an organization, as opposed to the leaders.
3. See page 210 of the student text.
4. a.–b. See page 212 of the student text.

Exercise I. Our Latin Heritage (page 221)

1. Requiring long, hard work.
2. Having the agreement and consent of all members of a group.
3. Noble and generous in spirit.
4. Juvenile; silly.
5. To bring to an end.
6. An authoritative command; see also page 343 of the student text.
7. To take the place of another; to replace or succeed.
8. Boisterous and disorderly.
9. Just coming into existence; in the process of emerging.
10. Given to joking; characterized by joking.
11. Of little or no value; having no power.
12. Inflicting or involving punishment; designed to punish.
13. To cause to disappear completely.
14. To give formal sanction or approval to.
15. Having or exhibiting hatred or ill will.
16. To render invalid; to annul.
17. To place side by side.
18. To go back to a previous condition.
19. Smallest in amount or degree; least possible.

20. Capable of being shaped or influenced.
21. To fall from a better or higher level to a lower or poorer one.
22. Plundering; greedy or avaricious.
23. To bring about by mutual agreement; to settle through discussion.
24. Beyond what is sufficient; extra.
25. To incite or stir up; to rouse.
26. To crush forcibly and completely.
27. To have weight, effect, or force as evidence.
28. Able to read and write; educated or cultured.
29. Well-known in an unfavorable way; infamous.
30. To say over again; to repeat.

Exercise III. Too Much of a Good Thing (page 222)

1. One who has an offensively superior air and who tries to imitate or associate with people of a higher station.
2. Characterized by or given to moralizing in a narrow way.
3. Being arrogantly overpositive in asserting what is unproven or unprovable.
4. See page 451 of the student text.
5. Done or produced with great labor; showing obvious signs of labor; lacking natural ease.
6. Offensively arrogant and domineering; tyrannical.
7. An affected or insincere person.
8. Too high an opinion of oneself; vanity.
9. Characterized by or favoring absolute obedience to authority.
10. A person who dabbles or has only a superficial interest in something.
11. Thinking or acting with the belief that one's self is the center of all experience.
12. Extreme meticulousness or over-refinement.
13. Crudely forward and self-assertive.
14. One who is displeased or dissatisfied with anything that does not meet the highest standards.
15. One who adheres rigidly to strict correctness, especially in matters of language.
16. Piously certain that one's own conduct and moral standards are the best.
17. See pages 354–355 of the student text.
18. Overenthusiastic nationalism or patriotism.

Exercise IV. Forms of Direct Address (page 222)

1. A Roman Catholic bishop; a governor; an ambassador; a viceroy.
2. A king; a queen; a prince; a princess.
3. A duke; a duchess; an archbishop.
4. The pope; the Dalai Lama.
5. A judge; a mayor.
6. A king; a queen; a reigning sovereign or his/her consort.

Exercise V. Expanding Your Word Power (page 222)

1. *Definition:* Massive, solid, and uniform.
   Etymology: monos (Greek), "one" + *lithos* (Greek), "stone"
   Synonyms: uniform, homogeneous, undifferentiated
   Antonyms: selective, synthesized, variegated, diversified, eclectic
2. *Definition:* In decay or decline.
   Etymology: de (Latin), "away, from" + *cadens, cadentis* (Latin), "falling," the present participle of *cadere* (Latin), "fall"
   Synonyms: effete, spent, sterile, barren
   Antonyms: productive, fertile, flourishing, dynamic
3. *Definition:* Producing in great abundance.
   Etymology: proles (Latin), "offspring" + *facere, factus* (Latin), "make"
   Synonyms: fruitful, fertile, profuse, rich
   Antonyms: barren, sterile, burned-out, effete
4. *Definition:* Not producing the proper or intended effect.
   Etymology: in (Latin), "not" + *efficere, effectus* (Latin), "perform" (from *ex* [Latin], "out" + *facere, factus* [Latin], "make") + *-alis, -ale* (Latin), "connected with"
   Synonyms: futile, ineffective, inadequate, useless
   Antonyms: effectual, efficient, powerful, potent, effective
5. *Definition:* Insolence. impudence; irreverence.
   Etymology: in (Latin), "not" + *pertinens, pertinentis* (Latin), "concerning," present participle of *pertinere,* "reach; concern"
   Synonyms: gall, nerve, audacity, chutzpah
   Antonyms: timidity, shyness, meekness, diffidence
6. *Definition:* lack of self-confidence; shyness.
   Etymology: dis (Latin), "not" + *fidens, fidentis* (Latin), "trusting," present participle of *fidere,* "trust"
   Synonyms: timidity, reserve, meekness
   Antonyms: assertiveness, temerity, boldness, nerve
7. *Definition:* To call forth; to produce.
   Etymology: ex (Latin), "out" + *vocare* (Latin), "call"

Synonyms: educe, elicit, prompt

8. *Definition:* Pertaining to the upper or ruling class; socially exclusive.
Etymology: aristos (Greek), "best" + *kratos* (Greek), "rule"
Synonyms: elite, noble, patrician, upper-class
Antonyms: proletarian, common, plebeian, lower-class

9. *Definition:* Excessively fat.
Etymology: ob (Latin), "away" + *edere, esus* (Latin), "eat"
Synonyms: corpulent, overweight
Antonyms: scrawny, emaciated, undernourished, lanky

10. *Definition:* To bring into being; to come into being.
Etymology: origo, originis (Latin), "beginning" + *-are, -atus* (Latin), "make"
Synonyms: inaugurate, invent, create; emanate, arise
Antonyms: abolish, terminate, conclude, end

11. *Definition:* (*v.*) To decorate or embellish, (*n.*) an ornamentation or embellishment.
Etymology: garner, garnissant (Old French), "adorn; equip"
Synonyms: adorn, dress up, enhance, gussy up
Antonyms: mar, deface, disfigure

12. *Definition:* (*adj.*) Not clearly seen or understandable; (*v.*) to darken or overshadow.
Etymology: ob (Latin), "over; against" + *-scurus* (Latin), "covered"
Synonyms: (*adj.*) vague, enigmatic, cryptic, ambiguous, indistinct; (*v.*) dim, eclipse, befog
Antonyms: (*adj.*) distinct, obvious, clear; (*v.*) illuminate, elucidate

13. *Definition:* Sympathy for the distress of others.
Etymology: cum (Latin), "with" + *pati, passus,* "bear; suffer" + *-tio, -tionis* (Latin), "state of"
Synonyms: pity, tenderness, mercy, concern
Antonyms: callousness, insensitivity, hard-heartedness

14. *Definition:* Native to a particular region or environment.
Etymology: indi (Latin), "within" + *genus* (Latin), "born"
Synonyms: endemic, aboriginal, autochthonous
Antonyms: exotic, alien, foreign; naturalized

15. *Definition:* A situation requiring the choice between equally unsatisfying alternatives.
Etymology: di (Greek), "two" + *lemma* (Greek), "proposition"
Synonyms: predicament, plight, quandary

Lesson 15 (pages 225–241)

Exercise V. Word Roundup (page 233)

1. a. To cajole or flatter.
   b. To speak ill of.
   c. To criticize or attack in an unfair or unethical manner.
   d. Making malicious charges against an opponent.
   e. To aggravate or exacerbate a situation that is already bad or sensitive; to add insult to injury.
   f. To attempt to calm down an overheated situation.
   g. The extreme or utmost point; the point of highest achievement.
   h. In trouble; in a difficult situation.

2. a. See page 226 of the student text.
   b. See page 230 of the student text.

3. *savant:* a learned scholar; a wise person. *pundit:* a learned person who frequently gives opinions in an authoritative way. *ignoramus:* an ignorant or uneducated person. *highbrow* (*n.* and *adj.*): one who has or affects great learning or cultivated tastes. *lowbrow* (*n.* and *adj.*): one with uncultivated tastes.

4. *privileged information:* confidential data available only to specially authorized persons within an organization or government. *insiders:* people with power or influence within an organization; people in the know.

5. *hot spots:* Africa, the Middle East. *troubleshooter:* a person who locates and eliminates problems or sources of trouble.

6. *moniker, handle:* personal name; nickname.

7. a.–d. See page 228 of the student text.

8. See page 229 of the student text.

9. *pluralistic society:* a society made up of various ethnic, national, or other groups that have or tend to have retained much of their original identities. *melting pot:* a society in which the various constituent ethnic or other groups have fused, thereby losing most or all of their original identities.

10. *paragon:* a model of perfection or excellence. *epitome:* the highest ideal possible.

11. *beau idéal* (French): the concept of perfect beauty; an idealized type or model.

Exercise (page 236)

B.

1. *Definition:* See page 209 of the student text.
Effect of e: It indicates the direction of movement (*out*).

2. *Definition:* A critical explanation or analysis, especially of a biblical or theological work.
   Effect of ex: It indicates the direction of movement (*out*). (*Exegesis* literally means "a showing of the way out.")
3. *Definition:* See page 208 of the student text.
   Effect of e: It indicates the direction of movement (*out, forth*).
4. *Definition:* See page 207 of the student text.
   Effect of e: It acts as an intensifier (*completely*).
5. *Definition:* See page 229 of the student text.
   Effect of ex: It acts as an intensifier (*very*).
6. *Definition:* See page 230 of the student text.
   Effect of ex: It indicates the direction of movement (*up*).

C.
1. endear: To make cherished or beloved.
2. enshrine: To enclose in a shrine; to cherish as sacred.
3. enfeeble: To make feeble; to deprive of strength.
4. encrust: To cover or overlay with a crust or crusty layer.
5. entrap: To catch in a trap; to lure into danger.
6. encompass: To enclose or envelop.
7. encircle: To form a circle about; to surround.
8. engulf: To swallow up or overwhelm.
9. envision: To picture in the mind; to foresee.
10. enrich: To make richer, fuller, or more meaningful.
11. enthrone: To seat on a throne; to invest with power and authority; to raise to a lofty position.
12. endanger: To expose to danger; to imperil.

D.
1. a. See page 246 of the student text.
   b. A building, especially a large or imposing one.
   c. An employee or assistant who has varied responsibilities.
   d. See page 247 of the student text.
   e. To make easier; to aid or assist.
   f. Something or someone that contributes to a result; an agent; an ingredient; a mathematical term.
   g. Contamination with a disease-producing agent.
   h. A cohesive group of persons within a larger group; internal dissension.
   i. An inherent power or ability; a natural aptitude; the teaching staff in an educational institution.
   j. An act of courage, skill, endurance, or the like.

k. A person who gives financial or other aid.
l. Easily or effortlessly done; acting or working effortlessly.
2. *affect:* (*v.*) to have an influence on; to make a pretense of; (*n.*) in psychology, a feeling or emotion, as opposed to a thought or action; *effect:* (*v.*) to cause to occur; to produce a result; (*n.*) a result or consequence.
3. *ipso facto:* by the fact itself; by the very fact.
   fait accompli: an already accomplished and irreversible deed or situation.

E.
1. humidify: To make humid.
2. prettify: To make pretty.
3. nullify: To make null and void; to make of no value or consequence.
4. identify: To cause to become identical; to be or become the same; to conceive as united; to establish the identify of.
5. solidify: To make or become solid, compact, or hard; to make secure, substantial, or firmly fixed.
6. personify: To conceive or represent as a person or as having the qualities or powers of a person; to be the embodiment of.
7. versify: To compose verses; to describe or relate in verse; to turn into verse.
8. magnify: To enlarge in fact or appearance; to increase in significance; to extol; to cause to be held in greater esteem or respect.
9. verify: To establish the truth, accuracy, or reality of; to confirm or substantiate in law by oath.

Exercise I. Words Ending in *(o)logy* (page 239)

1. *Definition:* The scientific study of birds.
   Meaning of (o)logy: the study of
2. *Definition:* The study of God and religious ideas.
   Meaning of (o)logy: the study of
3. *Definition:* The scientific study of the relationship between organisms and their environment.
   Meaning of (o)logy: the science of
4. *Definition:* The scientific study of the vital or characteristic life processes, activities, and functions.
   Meaning of (o)logy: the science of
5. *Definition:* Nomenclature; a system of nomenclature.
   Meaning of (o)logy: the system of
6. *Definition:* The study of human prehistory.
   Meaning of (o)logy: the study of
7. *Definition:* The study of fossils and ancient life forms.
   Meaning of (o)logy: the study of

8. *Definition:* The philosophical study of being and existence.
   Meaning of (o)logy: the study of
9. *Definition:* The study of design and purpose in nature and natural phenomena.
   Meaning of (o)logy: the study of
10. *Definition:* The study of mental processes and behavior.
    Meaning of (o)logy: the study of
11. *Definition:* The philosophical study of the origins, processes, and structure of the universe.
    Meaning of (o)logy: the study of
12. *Definition:* The theory and practice of prison management and the rehabilitation of criminals.
    Meaning of (o)logy: the science of
13. *Definition:* The study of human social behavior, particularly with respect to social development, interaction, and institutions.
    Meaning of (o)logy: the study of
14. *Definition:* The study of the positions of the stars and planets in order to predict their influence on human activities.
    Meaning of (o)logy: the study of
15. *Definition:* The scientific study of the nature of diseases and their causes, manifestations, and effects.
    Meaning of (o)logy: the science of
16. *Definition:* A series of three dramatic, literary, or musical works that are related to one subject or theme.
    Meaning of (o)logy: system, discourse
17. *Definition:* The scientific study of the origin, history, and structure of the earth and its formation.
    Meaning of (o)logy: the science of
18. *Definition:* The study of the history of human beings, particularly their origins, cultures, physical characteristics, and environmental adaptations.
    Meaning of (o)logy: the study of
19. *Definition:* The way in which words and phrases are used in speech and writing.
    Meaning of (o)logy: system
20. *Definition:* A collection of tales about gods, demigods, and legendary heroes of a people; a systematic collection and study of such tales.
    Meaning of (o)logy: system; study
21. *Definition:* The study of language and related fields.
    Meaning of (o)logy: word(s)
22. *Definition:* Needless repetition of an idea in different words.
    Meaning of (o)logy: word(s)
23. *Definition:* The scientific study of the nature, effects, and detection of poisons.
    Meaning of (o)logy: the science of

24. *Definition:* The branch of medicine dealing with the structure, functions, and diseases of the eye.
    Meaning of (o)logy: the science of
25. *Definition:* The scientific study of insects.
    Meaning of (o)logy: the science of
26. *Definition:* The anatomical study of bones.
    Meaning of (o)logy: the science of
27. *Definition:* The determination of the sequence of events or dates; the arrangement of events in time.
    Meaning of (o)logy: system
28. *Definition:* A series of four dramatic, literary, or musical works that are related to one subject or theme.
    Meaning of (o)logy: system
29. *Definition:* The scientific study of parasites.
    Meaning of (o)logy: the science of
30. *Definition:* The system of principles and procedures used in a particular field of study.
    Meaning of (o)logy: system

Exercise II. Euphemisms: Sugarcoating the Pill (pages 240–241)

A.

In some of these cases, the use of the euphemistic or genteel expression is intended to give an impression of refinement or elegance on the part of the speaker or writer. This would be true, for example, of *cinema* for *movies* or *boutique* for *shop*.

In other cases, the intent is to avoid referring too directly to a physical process or situation that may be considered somewhat crass or animal-like; for example, *perspire* in place of *sweat*, *odor* instead of *smell*, *expectorate* instead of *spit*.

Exaggerate might be used instead of *lie* to avoid a flat assertion that someone has been deliberately dishonest.

One might say *retire for the night*, rather than *go to bed*, in the belief that the latter expression is too intimate or personal.

The expression *financially embarrassed* would probably be used in the belief that any too-direct reference to money (particularly the lack of it) is in bad taste.

Deceased might be used instead of *dead* to soften a difficult loss one may not wish to face.

B.

1. undertaker	6. bar
2. arrest	7. firing
3. wig; toupee	8. barbershop
4. pool hall	9. diet
5. tip	10. fistfight

1. *Definition:* To win over or obtain by wiles or flattery.
   Etymology: *envegler* (Norman French), "blind"; from *ab* (Latin), "without" + *oculus* (Latin), "eye"
   Synonyms: entice, lure, allure, beguile
   Antonyms: repel, repulse, scare off
2. *Definition:* To drive back; to cause loathing.
   Etymology: *re* (Latin), "back" + *pellere* (Latin), "drive"
   Synonyms: repulse, beat back; disgust, revolt
   Antonyms: enchant, charm, captivate
3. *Definition:* To press or urge with persistence.
   Etymology: *importunari* (Medieval Latin), "be troublesome"; from *in* (Latin), "not" + *portus* (Latin), "harbor" + *-unus* (Latin), "relating to"
   Synonyms: implore, entreat, beg, insist
4. *Definition:* To picture in the mind; to foresee.
   Etymology: *en* (see page 235 of the student text) + *vision*
   Synonyms: envisage, imagine, visualize
5. *Definition:* A distinguishing name, title, or mark; a nomination or appointment; the act of indicating or appointing.
   Etymology: *de* (Latin), "out" + *signum* (Latin), "mark; sign" + *-are, -atus* (Latin), "make"
   Synonyms: indication, specification; appellation; selection
6. *Definition:* Resistance to sudden change; constancy; reliability.
   Etymology: *stare* (Latin), "stand (firm)" + *-abilis, -abile* (Latin), "able to" + *-itas, -itatis* (Latin), "state of"
   Synonyms: solidity, continuity, persistence, steadfastness
   Antonyms: instability, unsteadiness, shakiness; inconstancy, capriciousness
7. *Definition:* Able to read and write; educated or cultured.
   Etymology: *littera* (Latin), "letter" + *-atus* (Latin), "having"
   Synonyms: schooled, well-informed, erudite
   Antonyms: illiterate, untrained; ignorant, uninformed
8. *Definition:* Calmness of mind, manner, or appearance.
   Etymology: *compose* + *ure* (English suffix), "act; process"
   Synonyms: self-possession, equanimity, placidity, imperturbability
   Antonyms: discomposure, perturbation, excitability, fretfulness
9. *Definition:* Private; secret.
   Etymology: *cum* (Latin), "with" + *fidens, fidentis* (Latin), "trusting," present participle of *fidere* (Latin) "trust" + *-(i)alis, -(i)ale* (Latin), "pertaining to"
   Synonyms: restricted, personal, privileged
   Antonyms: open, public
10. *Definition:* To reduce the intensity of; to alleviate.
    Etymology: *a* (Old English), "completely" + *lecgan* (Old English), "lay"
    Synonyms: assuage, relieve, soothe, calm
    Antonyms: aggravate, exacerbate, worsen, intensify
11. *Definition:* Mysterious; mystifying.
    Etymology: *kryptos* (Greek), "hidden" + *-ikos* (Greek), "relating to"
    Synonyms: obscure, inexplicable, puzzling, baffling, enigmatic
    Antonyms: comprehensible, intelligible, clear
12. *Definition:* A crucial or decisive moment or situation; a turning point.
    Etymology: *krisis* (Greek), "turning point"; from *krinein* (Greek), "separate; decide"
    Synonyms: climax, emergency
13. *Definition:* To lower in rank, office, prestige, or esteem; to humble.
    Etymology: *ad* (Latin), "to" + *bassus* (Late Latin), "low"
    Synonyms: degrade, humiliate, disgrace, demote
    Antonyms: upgrade, promote
14. *Definition:* Worthy of praise.
    Etymology: *cum* (Latin), "very; completely; with" + *mandare* (Latin), "entrust" + *-abilis, -abile* (Latin), "able to"
    Synonyms: laudable, admirable; exemplary
    Antonyms: reprehensible, blameworthy; disgraceful, shameful
15. *Definition:* Uncontrollable fear or emotional distress.
    Etymology: *hysterikos* (Greek) "suffering in the womb"; from *hystera* (Greek), "womb" (because hysteria was once thought to be caused by uterine disturbances)
    Synonyms: frenzy, delirium
    Antonyms: imperturbability, composure, equanimity, serenity

Lesson 16 (pages 242–260)

Exercise V. Word Roundup (page 251)

1. a. See answer to V, I, a, page 203 of the student text.
   b. See page 247 of the student text.
2. See page 242 of the student text.
3. a. A nonstandard usage or grammatical construction; a violation of social custom; any impropriety, incongruity, or error.

b. A brilliantly executed stratagem; a masterstroke.
c. (n.) A hoax, an impostor or charlatan; nonsense; (v.) to trick, deceive, or cheat.
d. Melodramatic behavior or language.
e. A person with an exaggerated enthusiasm for, or a pathological obsession with, one idea.
f. See page 244 of the student text.
4. a. Briefly; in a few words.
b. A remark that is meant or expressed ironically or facetiously.
c. Deeds of daring and valor.
d. An exact duplicate.
e. A feat of strength, skill, or virtuosity.
f. An obsession; a fixed idea.

Exercise I.   Loan Words from Faraway Places (page 257)

1. (n.) An expression of respect or submission; an obsequious act; (v.) to show servile deference; to fawn. Chinese.
2. In a frenzy to do violence or kill; in a blind or faulty manner. Malay.
3. A wealthy and powerful businessman or industrialist. Japanese, but ultimately from Chinese.
4. A conference or meeting with. Native American (Algonquian).
5. One who looks or behaves like an automaton; a kind of strong mixed drink. African (Bantu).
6. A cutthroat, ruffian, or hoodlum. Hindi, but ultimately from Sanskrit.
7. (n.) A flat, curved wooden missile that can be hurled so that it returns to the thrower; a statement or course of action that backfires on its originator; (v.) to backfire. Australian aboriginal.
8. (n.) A prohibition excluding something from use or mention because of social custom or personal aversion; (adj.) excluded or forbidden from use or mention. Polynesian (Tongan).
9. (n.) Spoils; stolen goods; (v.) to pillage or despoil. Hindi, but ultimately from Sanskrit.
10. A very rich or powerful person (Persian, but ultimately from Mongolian); a small mound on a ski slope (Scandinavian).
11. A duty imposed by a government on imported or exported goods. Arabic via Turkish.
12. A social outcast. Tamil (India).
13. An emblem of a family or clan; any venerated emblem or symbol. Native American (Ojibwa).
14. (n.) A closed meeting of political party members to discuss questions of policy and to select candidates for office; (v.) to assemble in or hold such a meeting. Native American (Algonquian).
15. A massive force or object that crushes anything that gets in its way; anything that requires blind and destructive devotion or to which people are ruthlessly sacrificed. Hindi, from Sanskrit.
16. A place of ideal beauty or loveliness; heaven. Persian (Avestan).
17. Unintelligible or incomprehensible language; jibberish. African (Mandingo).
18. Civilian dress, especially when worn by a person who usually wears a uniform. Arabic.
19. A religious cult characterized by a belief in sorcery and fetishes and the use of trances to communicate with deceased ancestors, saints, and animalistic deities. African (Ewe).
20. The lowest point. Arabic.
21. A fertile and well-watered spot in a dry region; a refuge from surrounding unpleasantness. Ancient Egyptian (akin to Coptic *ouahe*).

Exercise II.   The Language of Logic (page 257)

1. The study of the principles of reasoning; valid reasoning.
2. A form of deductive reasoning consisting of a major premise (*e.g.*, All men are mortal), a minor premise (*e.g.*, Socrates is a man), and a conclusion (*e.g.*, Therefore, Socrates is mortal).
3. In a syllogism, the premise containing the major (*i.e.*, the general) term or assertion.
4. In a syllogism, the premise containing the minor (*i.e.*, the specific) term or assertion. The subject of the minor premise forms the subject of the conclusion.
5. In a syllogism, the proposition concluded from the major and minor premises.
6. The process of reasoning from a specific idea to a general one.
7. The process of reasoning from a general idea to a specific one.
8. Correctly inferred or deduced from a premise.
9. Falsely based or reasoned.
10. The attribution of human emotions or characteristics to inanimate objects, such as *the cruel sea* or *a raging wind*.

Exercise III.   Diehards (page 258)

1. Gladness, especially when expressed by laughter.
2. To churn and foam; to be extremely excited.
3. Clamor; loud and discordant noise.

4. (n.) A swamp or bog; a state of moral degradation or deep despair.
5. To suppress forcibly; to quiet.
6. An expression of an intention to inflict pain, injury, damage, or punishment; an indication of impending danger; something regarded as a menace.
7. To reject scornfully.
8. To be uneasy or troubled; to cause to be uneasy.
9. To allot or deal out.
10. Dark in color or complexion.
11. To put out; to put an end to; to suppress; to slake (thirst).
12. To refrain from; to desist from.
13. A state of mind or feeling; a pervading atmosphere.
14. To summon or signal with a wave, nod, or other signal.
15. (n.) A light barrier; an obstacle of any kind; (v.) to jump or leap over a barrier; to overcome.

Exercise IV. The Language of the Mind (page 258)
In addition to an unabridged dictionary, a high-school textbook in psychology may be helpful.
1. Pertaining to a mental or emotional disorder characterized by anxiety, fears, obsessions, and other similar symptoms. However, there is no serious distortion of reality, as in the case of psychosis.
2. Pertaining to disorders and other areas of life that involve both the mind (psychic) and the body (somatic). In the case of a psychosomatic illness, there are physical symptoms which appear to be psychic, rather than organic, in origin.
3. Pertaining to a psychosis (mental disturbance) characterized by delusions of persecution.
4. The area of the mind or personality which motivates an individual below the level of consciousness or awareness. For example, there may be fears and desires that manifest themselves in personality patterns, even though the person is not aware of being influenced by such emotions.
5. Pertaining to knowledge or awareness that is not gained by the ordinary or normal operation of the senses — for example, telepathy (mind reading).
6. A personality structure in which the individual shows two different sets of attitudes, temperaments, and behavior patterns. The separation is much more clearly defined and consistent than in the case of what would ordinarily be a change of mood.
7. A failure to make an effective or appropriate adaptation to the conditions under which the individual lives.
8. (adj.) Pertaining to that which lies within the mind or personality; not physical or organic; (n.) a person who is apparently sensitive to nonphysical forces in the environment.
9. A system of repressed desires and memories that exert a strong influence upon the personality.
10. Pertaining to a severe mental or emotional disorder characterized by a defective control of reality and an inability to relate to other people.
11. A person whose thoughts and interests are directed inward, rather than toward other people or the outside world in general.
12. A person whose thoughts and interests are directed outward or toward other people and things in general.
13. (adj.) Relating to a condition characterized by or resulting from a split personality, particularly a tendency to withdraw from reality.
14. A person afflicted with the persistent neurotic conviction of being ill (or likely to become ill), experiencing real pain even when illness is neither present nor likely.
15. Physical or emotional exhaustion, especially as a result of long-term stress.

Exercise V. Expanding Your Word Power (page 258)
1. *Definition:* A coming in; a flowing in.
   Etymology: in (Latin), "in" + *fluere, fluxus* (Latin), "to flow"
   Synonyms: arrival, advent; invasion, inrush
   Antonyms: departure, exodus, hegira
2. *Definition:* Extreme concern or absorption with something.
   Etymology: prae (Latin), "before" + *occupare, occupatus* (Latin), "seize; occupy"; from *ob* (Latin), "completely" + *capere* (Latin), "seize, take"
   Synonyms: engrossment, concentration, absorption; obsession, fixation
   Antonyms: inattention, disregard, unconcern
3. *Definition:* A military maneuver intended to fool or surprise the enemy; any clever deception.
   Etymology: strategema (Greek), "generalship"; from *stratos* (Greek), "army" + *agein* (Greek), "lead"
   Synonyms: device, ruse, trick, ploy
4. *Definition:* An object believed to endow its owner with supernatural powers; any charm.

Etymology: telsam, (Arabic), "charm"; from *telesma* (Greek), "consecrated object"
Synonyms: charm, amulet, fetish

5. *Definition:* A notable deed of courage or skill.
Etymology: fait (Old French), "deed"; from *factum* (Latin), "something done"; from *facere, factus* (Latin), "do"
Synonyms: exploit, achievement, coup

6. *Definition:* A brief outline or summary of a subject.
Etymology: syn (Greek), "together" + *opsis* (Greek), "view"
Synonyms: abstract, digest, précis, epitome

7. *Definition:* To make the meaning of something clear.
Etymology: ex (Latin), "out; un-" + *plicare, plicatus* (Latin), "fold"
Synonyms: explain, elucidate, expound, interpret
Antonyms: obscure, befog, muddy

8. *Definition:* To contrive or invent.
Etymology: deviser (Old French), "design"; ultimately from *dividere, divisus* (Latin), "divide"
Synonyms: concoct, design, fabricate, fashion

9. *Definition:* Serious and determined.
Etymology: eornost (Old English), "serious"
Synonyms: sincere, committed, wholehearted, dedicated
Antonyms: halfhearted, insincere, lukewarm

10. *Definition:* Playful and unpredictable.
Etymology: whimsy + ical
Synonyms: capricious, mercurial; fanciful, frivolous
Antonyms: serious, staid, sober, earnest, dour, grave

11. *Definition:* An exact copy.
Etymology: replica (Italian), "copy"; from *re* (Latin), "again" + *plicare, plicatus* (Latin), "fold"
Synonyms: reproduction, duplicate, facsimile

12. *Definition:* A nonstandard usage or grammatical contruction; a violation of social custom; any impropriety, mistake, or incongruity.
Etymology: solikos (Greek), "speaking incorrectly"; from the inhabitants of Soloi (an Athenian colony), who spoke a substandard dialect of Greek.
Synonyms: blunder, gaffe, blooper, faux pas

13. *Definition:* To dig deeply into.
Etymology: delfan (Old English), "dig (in the ground)"
Synonyms: investigate, research, probe, sound, ferret out

14. *Definition:* To have or take on the appearance of; to feign.
Etymology: simulare, simulatus (Latin), "imitate"; from *similis* (Latin), "same; alike"
Synonyms: imitate, counterfeit, sham, duplicate

15. *Definition:* Pertinent or appropriate.
Etymology: apponere, appositus (Latin), "put near"; from *ad* (Latin), "to; toward" + *ponere, positus* (Latin), "put; place"
Synonyms: fitting, suitable, apt, condign
Antonyms: inappropriate, unsuitable, incongruous

Lesson 17 (pages 261–274)
Exercise V. Word Roundup
(pages 268–269)
1. a. See page 263 of the student text.
   b. See page 265 of the student text.
2. a. (*n.*) A robbery or burglary.
   b. To make less emphatic; to play down.
   c. A sudden and unexpected gain or good fortune.
   d. An accidental stroke or piece of good luck.
   e. A miser or tightwad.
   f. A complete failure.
3. a. To vacillate; to be very changeable.
   b. Actually discovered in the act of doing something wrong.
   c. To be secretly amused.
   d. A career that has had both ups and downs.
   e. To fail completely.
   f. One's particular strength, skill, or talent.
   g. To obtain an advantage over a rival or opponent by stealth.
   h. See page 266 of the student text.
   i. A failure after a strong and impressive start.
   j. Cautious or frugal in small matters but careless in large and important ones.
4. a. To a sickening degree.
   b. In the very act; red-handed.
5. See page 262 of the student text.

Exercise (page 270)
1. a. Introductory comments at the beginning of a book; a preface.
   b. The foremost part or area; the position of greatest prominence or importance.
   c. In the first place; first in a series.
   d. To reduce or distort in order to convey an illusion of three-dimensional space; to abridge or curtail.
   e. Prudence with respect to the future.
   f. (*adj.*) Made with the hand moving palm forward; foremost or leading; (*n.*) a forehand stroke (tennis); a position of advantage.

2. a. *Definition:* Appearing sad or lonely; wretched or pitiful.
   Meaning of for: completely
   b. *Definition:* Tolerance and restraint despite provocation.
   Meaning of for: completely
   c. *Definition:* To renounce or forsake.
   Meaning of for: completely
3. a. forebear   d. forewarn
   b. forswear, forgo   e. foresee
   forbear   f. forsake
   c. foretell
4. a. Rich; wealthy
   b. A merging, union, or melting together by heat.
   c. A flowing in; an arrival.
   d. Beyond what is required; extra.
   e. Competent in the use of language; flowing easily.
   f. Able to have an effect on.

Exercise I. Our Italian Heritage
(page 273)
1. The trunk of the human body.
2. A complicated or difficult entanglement.
3. In a soft or low voice; quietly.
4. An act or attitude of vengeance; a bitter feud between families.
5. The speed at which a musical composition is played; a characteristic pace.
6. An organized military or naval unit; any organized multitude.
7. The lead female singer in an opera; any temperamental person.
8. The period of isolation (originally forty days) for persons or animals suspected of carrying disease.
9. The printed text (words only) of an opera or other musical work.
10. An artist's workroom; a photographer's establishment; an establishment where an art is taught or studied; a room or building for motion picture, radio, or TV productions.
11. Drawings, words, or statements scrawled or drawn on the surfaces of buildings, vehicles, etc.
12. A brief sentence or phrase that expresses the purpose, goals, or ideals of some person, organization, or institution.
13. The simultaneous discharge of guns (as in a military salute) or bombs; any sudden outburst (of cheers or applause, for example).
14. Having one's real identity disguised or concealed.
15. A public declaration of intentions or principles, especially when these are political in nature.
16. (*n.*) A composition or passage for one performer, voice, or instrument; (*adj.*) alone, unaccompanied.
17. The outline or synopsis of a dramatic or musicial work; a screenplay; the outline of a hypothetical chain of events.
18. A distant view as seen through a passage; a comprehensive awareness of.
19. Persons of outstanding knowledge or taste; connoisseurs.
20. (*n.*) A festive or spectacular celebration; (*adj.*) festive and spectacular.
21. (*n.*) A person, especially an artist or musician, of superior talent, technical ability, and personal style; (*adj.*) masterful; brilliant.

Exercise II. Money Talks (page 273)
In addition to an unabridged dictionary, an introductory economics textbook may prove helpful in doing this exercise.
1. A period of severe decline in the national economy.
2. A temporary and moderate decline in the national economy.
3. A sharp rise in prices due to an increase in credit and available money.
4. A decrease in prices due to reduction in credit and available money.
5. A period of rapid economic growth.
6. A valuable possession or property that can readily be converted to cash.
7. The total market value of the goods and services produced by a nation during a given period.
8. An amount or quantity that exceeds what is required; an excess.
9. The government's policy for directing and controlling the total supply of money and credit. In the United States, this policy is set by the Federal Reserve System.
10. An economic system in which private individuals own and operate most of the industry and in which economic decisions are made by individual producers and consumers through buying and selling.
11. The relative ease with which an individual can buy and sell at a profit.
12. The portion of a nation's economic activity that is in the hands of private industry and business.
13. An economic system in which an individual has the right to start, own, and operate a private business.
14. Something that everyone recognizes as money and is therefore willing to accept in exchange for goods and services.
15. A shortage; an amount spent in excess of available funds.
16. Exclusive control of ownership by one group or company of particular goods or services.
17. A stock exchange term indicating a condition of rising prices on commodities and securities.

18. The total debts and financial obligations of a national government.
19. Sudden and unexpected financial gains.
20. See page 336 of the student text.
21. The interest rate that banks offer to preferred (low-risk) customers (usually businesses) on loans. (It is usually lower than the interest rate offered to other customers.)

Exercise III.   A Verbal Diversion
(page 274)

In addition to an unabridged dictionary, consult Makkai, Boatner, and Gates, *A Dictionary of American Idioms* 3d ed.
1. To serve as a substitute for; to take over a position or responsibility in an emergency. Baseball.
2. To attempt to overcome or disconcert an opponent by harrying and contesting him/her at every possible opportunity, even where he/she might ordinarily expect to be secure. Basketball.
3. Exactly what is/was to be expected. (The expression is often ironically negative.) Golf.
4. To ward off, avoid, deflect, or escape a blow or weapon. Fencing.
5. An opening play that risks the loss of minor pieces in order to gain an early advantage. Chess.
6. Have an effective resource or factor held in reserve to be used at a strategic moment. Any of several card games in which the ace is the highest card.
7. To begin a campaign. Football.
8. An ironic expression for a person who is prepared to explain, *after* a defeat or disappointment, what went wrong and what should have been done to achieve success. Football.
9. A desperate, last-minute effort to avert defeat when one's opponent seems to be on the verge of making a decisive score. Football.
10. Blocked, frustrated, or thwarted. Golf.
11. To perform daring or ostentatious stunts or maneuvers. Skiing.
12. A situation in which further action by any of the parties involved is impossible; a deadlock. Chess.
13. The leader in a race or competition. Track.
14. Seeking attention or applause by acting ostentatiously; grandstanding. Baseball.
15. A risky bet or venture with only a slight chance of success. Horse racing.
16. To begin with a severe disadvantage or handicap. Baseball.

Exercise IV.   Expanding Your Word Power (page 274)
1. *Definition:* A sudden disaster or collapse.
   Etymology: débâcle (French), "catastrophe"
   Synonyms: fiasco, defeat, failure, breakdown
   Antonyms: success, victory, triumph
2. *Definition:* Having no fixed or regular course; irregular or inconsistent.
   Etymology: errare, erratus (Latin), "wander" + -icus (Latin), "characterized by"
   Synonyms: fitful, sporadic, changeable, capricious
   Antonyms: consistent, regular, uniform; steady; constant
3. *Definition:* Fixed or unchanging; constant or unswerving.
   Etymology: stede (Old English), "place" + faest (Old English), "fixed; fast"
   Synonyms: steady, unwavering, unflinching, unfaltering
   Antonyms: inconstant, erratic, fitful
4. *Definition:* To steal.
   Etymology: purloigner (Norman French), "put far away"; from pro (Latin), "away" + longe (Latin), "far"
   Synonyms: pilfer, rob, filch, swipe, rip off, pinch
   Antonyms: give back, restore, replace, reimburse, recompense
5. *Definition:* (n.) A tactical or strategic movement, often military; (v.) to change position or tactics for some desired end; to manipulate into position.
   Etymology: maneuver (Old French), "manual work"; from manus (Latin), "hand" + opus, operis (Latin), "work"
   Synonyms: (n.) move, gambit, tactic, play; (v.) jockey, steer, engineer, pilot
6. *Definition:* Outstandingly bad.
   Etymology: ex (Latin), "out, from" + grex, gregis (Latin), "herd" + -ius (Latin), "relating to"
   Synonyms: blatant, flagrant, glaring
   Antonyms: exemplary, notable, model; minor, insignificant, inconsequential
7. *Definition:* To stand up to; to withstand.
   Etymology: desfier (Old French), "defy"; from dis (Latin), "away; un-" + fidere (Latin), "trust"
   Synonyms: flout, slight, spurn; challenge, confront; hold out against
   Antonyms: obey, accept; give in to, succumb to

8. *Definition:* To swing back and forth; to fluctuate.
   Etymology: oscillare, oscillatus (Latin), "swing"
   Synonyms: vacillate, undulate, waver, vibrate
9. *Definition:* A person's strong point.
   Etymology: fort (Old French), "strong"
   Synonyms: long suit, cup of tea, specialty, talent, strength
   Antonyms: foible, weakness, shortcoming, blind spot
10. *Definition:* A peculiarity of behavior; an unaccountable act or event.
    Etymology: Origin unknown
    Synonyms: idiosyncrasy, crotchet, eccentricity, vagary
11. *Definition:* To make impossible by previous action; to prevent beforehand.
    Etymology: prae (Latin), "before" + *claudere* (Latin), "close"
    Synonyms: forestall, thwart, block, eliminate
    Antonyms: abet, facilitate, expedite, expediate; allow, guarantee, ensure
12. *Definition:* Arousing alarm or fear; worthy of respect.
    Etymology: re (Old French), "completely" + *doubte* (Old French), "fear" + *-able* (Old French), "able to"
    Synonyms: formidable, awesome, dreadful, fearful, awe-inspiring
    Antonyms: contemptible, despicable, mean, scurvy, vile
13. *Definition:* Accidental; not sufficiently attentive.
    Etymology: in (Latin), "not" + *ad* (Latin), "to; toward" + *vertere, versus* (Latin), "turn, pay attention" + *-ens, -entis* (Latin), "-ing"
    Synonyms: unintentional, unpremeditated; inattentive, heedless, careless
    Antonyms: intentional, purposeful, premeditated; attentive
14. *Definition:* (*adj.*) Extravagantly reckless or wasteful; profuse; (*n.*) a spendthrift or profligate.
    Etymology: pro (Latin). "forth; away" + *agere* (Latin), "drive" + *-alis, -ale* (Latin) "relating to"
    Synonyms: (*adj.*) improvident, profligate; lavish, copious, bountiful; (*n.*) wastrel
    Antonyms: (*adj.*) frugal, thrifty, parsimonious; skimpy, scant (*n.*) tightwad, skinflint
15. *Definition:* Exceeding reasonable limits.
    Etymology: in (Latin), "not" + *ordinare, ordinatus* (Latin), "set in order"
    Synonyms: exorbitant, immoderate, disproportionate, undue
    Antonyms: reasonable, just; moderate, modest

Lesson 18 (pages 275–292)

Exercise VI.   Word Roundup
(pages 284–285)

1. a. To exist in seclusion or away from everyday life, harsh reality, and practical concerns.
   b. To make an unofficial or impromtu public speech; to preach in a ranting or fanatical manner.
   c. To deceive or delude.
   d. Naive and inexperienced.
   e. To see if the situation is favorable or not.
   f. To smile broadly.
2. a. (*v.*) To stretch the neck in order to see better; to gawk; (*n.*) a gawking tourist.
   b. A person who continually criticizes established customs or institutions in a provocative way.
   c. A person who flits from one social group to another.
   d. An obvious and unmissable target; a helpless victim.
   e. Something given or received free of charge.
   f. Persons of similar type, taste, culture, or character.
3. a.–d. See page 277 of the student text.
4. a. Free; with no charge.
   b. An enthusiastic spirit of comradeship and loyalty to one another, their cause, organization, or purpose among the members of a particular group.
   c. The seller is not responsible for the quality or reliability of the product. (Latin for "let the buyer beware.")
5. An *extrovert* is a person who is interested in the people, places, and things around him/her. In contrast, an *introvert's* thoughts and interests are directed inward, toward him- or herself.
6. See page 281 of the student text.

Exercise I.   More Classical Contributions to English (page 289)

In addition to an unabridged dictionary, the following reference books may prove helpful in doing this exercise: *Brewer's Dictionary of Phrase and Fable,* 16th ed.; *Morris Dictionary of Word and Phrase Origins,* 2d ed.

1. A large building housing tombs. Mausolus was a 4th-century B.C. ruler of Caria (a region in southwestern Asia Minor), whose wife Artemisia erected a splendid monument at Halicarnassus to hold his remains.
2. An extended wandering or journey. Odysseus, the hero of Homer's epic

poem the *Odyssey*, had many fabulous adventures during his ten-year voyage home after the Trojan War.

3. See page 420 of the student text.
4. To intimidate or bully someone. Hector was the Trojan prince killed by the hero Achilles in Homer's epic poem the *Iliad*. In early drama, Hector was portrayed as a blustering bully.
5. A wise and respected old man. In the Homeric poems, Nestor is the Greek hero noted for his age and wisdom.
6. Caught between two equally dangerous situations. In the *Odyssey*, Scylla and Charybdis are two female sea monsters who lived in the Strait of Messina (between Sicily and Italy) and devoured passing sailors. They represent a large rock (Scylla) and a dangerous whirlpool (Charybdis) found in those waters.
7. To saunter: to wander around at random. The Maeander (Greek, Mainandros), a river in Phrygia (western Turkey), was noted for its excessively winding course.
8. A patron, especially one who is generous to artists. Gaius Maecenas, a Roman statesman during the reign of the emperor Augustus (27 B.C.– A.D. 14), was a noted patron of the arts.
9. An actor or actress. Thespis, a 6th-century B.C. Greek poet, was believed to be the inventor of tragedy.
10. An avenger; an unbeatable rival or challenge; an unavoidable result. Nemesis ("Allotter") was the Greek goddess of vengeance and retribution.
11. To add one difficulty or embarrassment to another. The Titans (Giants) piled Pelion and Ossa, two mountain peaks in Thessaly, on top of one another in order to climb into heaven to attack the gods.
12. To open up a can of worms; to cause a great deal of trouble. In Greek myth, Pandora was the first woman on earth. Zeus endowed her with every charm (her name means "every gift" in Greek), but he also made her curious and treacherous. As a wedding gift, Zeus gave her a box he forbade her to open. She persuaded her husband, Epimetheus, to allow her to open the box, and in this way were released all the evils (sickness, hatred, war, greed, etc.) that have since afflicted humankind. Hope alone remained inside the box.
13. An ill-tempered woman. Xanthippe, the wife of the Greek philosopher Socrates, was reputedly a very shrewish woman.
14. To cater to the low tastes or desires of; to exploit the weaknesses of. In the Roman and medieval love story of Troilus and Cressida, Pandarus acted as the lovers' go-between.
15. Very loud and resonant. Stentor was the loud-voiced Greek herald in Homer's *Iliad*.
16. A trusted counselor or advisor. In Homer's *Odyssey*, Mentor was Odysseus's trusted guide and the guardian and teacher of Odysseus's son, Telemachus.
17. One that is purely spiritual rather than physical. The Greek philosopher Plato (ca. 428–347 B.C.) advocated this form of relationship in such works as the *Symposium*.
18. To spare no time or expense in accomplishing a goal. After a battle between the Persians and the Thebans in 477 B.C., the defeated Persian general, Mardonius, was believed to have left great valuables behind, hidden under his tent. When Polycrates, the Theban general, searched for them, however, he found nothing. In frustration, he consulted the Oracle at Delphi, which told him to "leave no stone unturned" in his search. He obeyed and found the treasure.

Exercise II.   Expressions Old and New
(page 289)

In addition to an unabridged dictionary, the following may prove helpful in doing this exercise: Makkai, Boatner, and Gates, *A Dictionary of American Idioms*, 3d ed.

A.
1. To discover something profitable; to strike it rich.
2. In the public eye; at the center of attention.
3. Out of order; off balance; askew; needing repair.
4. A newcomer or upstart.
5. To buy something sight unseen.
6. The hierarchy in a group or organization.
7. To work as a taxicab driver at night, in addition to another full-time day job.
8. Old-fashioned; out-of-date.
9. An oblique or roundabout compliment, often containing a disguised insult or rebuke.
10. To show one's affections in an obvious and open way.
11. To suppress one's self-esteem; to humble oneself.
12. To begin prematurely; in a race, to start before the signal.
13. To aim too high; to have unrealistic goals.

14. To hear about, especially in advance.
15. To bring about a great deal of trouble or precipitate a difficult situation or problem.
16. A clumsy or tactless person.
17. To give a warm and generous welcome to.
18. A useful principle with wide application but not intended to be strictly accurate.
19. To lose one's temper; to become angry.
20. To work very hard and persistently at boring or tiresome work.

B.
1. To allow oneself the widest possible range of choices for one longest possible time.
2. A culture (often involving young people) whose values, standards, and attitudes run counter to those of the dominant or established society.
3. To pursue a preplanned strategy for achieving some goal, as, for example, a victory in a sporting event.
4. To assign a value (e.g., good, bad, desirable) to something on the basis of one's personal or class values.
5. A community that is broken up into sharply opposing factions over some issue, situation, or problem.
6. Projects or activities involving active physical participation.
7. The particular way of life of an individual or group of individuals.
8. The span of hours (usually in the evening) when the largest number of people are available for watching television; hence, the most desirable advertising time.
9. A guess that is approximately right; an approximation.
10. See page 384 of the student text.

Exercise III. From the East to the West
(page 290)
1. Boss, big shot. Japanese (from *hancho*, "squad leader")
2. A greeting or farewell. Hawaiian (from *aloha*, "love")
3. A headdress consisting of a long cloth wrapped around a cap. Turkish (from *tulbent*) but ultimately from Persian (*dulband*)
4. A bulbous herb of the lily family with showy flowers; the petals overlap in a way that suggests a turban. Turkish (from *tulbent*, "turban")
5. A long robe with wide sleeves and tied with a wide sash, traditionally worn by Japanese men and women; a loose jacket or dressing gown. Japanese ("clothes," from *ki*, "wearing," + *mono*, "thing")
6. A streambed that is dry except in the rainy season; a backwater forming a stagnant pool. Wiradhuri, an Australian aboriginal language (*bilaban*)
7. A magical creature that takes human form and serves the person who summons it. Arabic (from *jinniy*, "demon")
8. Authentic, genuine, first-class. Hindi (from *pakka*, "cooked, ripe, solid")
9. Master, sir; used especially in colonial India as a term of address applied to Europeans having social or official status. Hindi (*saheb*)
10. Cold rice seasoned with vinegar, formed into various shapes, and topped with raw fish or shellfish or with vegetables. Japanese
11. A flat, bent throwing club that returns near the thrower; hence, something that backfires on its originator. Dharuk, an Australian aboriginal language (*bumarin*)
12. An ankle-length garment, usually of cotton or silk, that is common throughout the countries bordering the eastern Mediterranean. Persian (*qaftan*)
13. A porch or verandah. Hawaiian
14. A machine that plays accompaniments to a selection of songs to which the user sings along and that transmits the user's voice with the music. Japanese (from *kara*, "empty," + *oke* [short for *orkesutora*], "orchestra")
15. A food, dish, or sauce originating in India, seasoned with a combination of sharp spices; a powder made from such spices. Tamil (*kari*)
16. A light yellowish brown; a cloth, usually wool or cotton, of this color, used especially for military uniforms; a garment made of this cloth. Hindi (from *khaki*, "dust-colored")
17. A fermented, acidic food made from milk. Turkish
18. A part of the stem of a rattan (a climbing palm that has very long and tough stems) used to make wicker furniture, canes, and other items. Malay (*rotan*)
19. A garment, worn by women in southern Asia, consisting of several yards of cloth draped so that one end becomes a skirt and the other covers the shoulders or head. Hindi, but ultimately from Sanskrit (from *sati*, "strip of cloth")
20. A potted tree that is dwarfed and trained to grow in an aesthetically pleasing shape. Japanese (from *bonsai*, "tray planting")
21. A long upholstered seat, usually with arms and a back. Arabic (from *suffah*, "long bench")
22. Rule, used especially of the former British rule of the Indian subconti-

nent. Hindi (*raj;* akin to the Sanskrit *rajan,* "king")

23. A religious or spiritual teacher or guide, originally in Hinduism; someone with knowledge or expertise. Hindi but ultimately from Sanskrit (from *guru,* "heavy, venerable")
24. A square or oblong fabric wrapper used to cover the shoulders or head. Persian (*shal*)
25. A type of dance, brought by Polynesians to Hawaii, involving rhythmic hip movement and narrative hand gestures, accompanied by chants and drumming. Its origin is in religious practices connected with the volcano goddess Pele. Hawaiian
26. A soft, cheeselike food made from soybean milk that is rich in protein and calcium and easily digested. Japanese and Chinese
27. A Hindu philosophy that teaches suppression of all physical and mental activity in order to achieve spiritual liberation; a system of exercise to achieve control of body and mind and thereby attain well-being. Sanskrit (from *yuga,* "yoking")
28. A wreath or necklace of flowers or leaves, considered a symbolic gift of love and friendship. Hawaiian

Exercise IV. Expanding Your Word Power (page 290)

1. *Definition:* To destroy or cut off a limb or other bodily part; to damage badly.
   Etymology: mutilare, mutilatus (Latin), "maim"
   Synonyms: disfigure, maim, mangle, butcher
   Antonyms: restore, rehabilitate, heal
2. *Definition:* (*v.*) To take great pleasure or delight; (*n.*) a noisy celebration.
   Etymology: reveler (Old French), "make noise"
   Synonyms: (*v.*) relish, savor, feast on, gloat over; (*n.*) celebration, carnival, festivity
3. *Definition:* Something that moves a person to action or effort.
   Etymology: incentivus, incentivum (Latin), "that which sets the tune; inciting"; from *in* (Latin), "very" + *canere, cantus* (Latin), "sing" + *-ivus* (Latin), "inclined to"
   Synonyms: motivation, goad, stimulus
   Antonyms: deterrent, impediment, obstacle
4. *Definition:* To move to action; to stir up or provoke.
   Etymology: in (Latin), "very" + *citare* (Latin), "put into violent motion"
   Synonyms: egg on, instigate, foment, arouse

Antonyms: dissuade, discourage, restrain, curb
5. *Definition:* To slow down the progress of.
   Etymology: impedire (Latin), "entangle; fetter"; from *in* (Latin), "in" + *pes, pedis* (Latin), "foot"
   Synonyms: obstruct, hinder
   Antonyms: facilitate, expedite, speed up
6. *Definition:* Having a deficiency of oxygen-carrying red blood cells; weak, listless, and pale.
   Etymology: an (Greek), "without" + *haima* (Greek), "blood" + *-ikos* (Greek), "relating to"
   Synonyms: wan, pallid; feeble, sluggish, enervated; lifeless
   Antonyms: ruddy, rubicund; energetic, lively, spirited
7. *Definition:* Having one's thoughts concentrated inward or on oneself.
   Etymology: intro (Latin), "inwardly" + *vertere* (Latin), "turn" + *ed*
   Synonyms: self-absorbed, introspective, aloof
   Antonyms: extroverted, outgoing, gregarious
8. *Definition:* Causing horror or revulsion; sallow in color.
   Etymology: luridus (Latin), "ghostly white"
   Synonyms: shocking, sensational; gruesome, horrible, macabre; pale, ashen
   Antonyms: pleasing, delightful; bright, colorful; ruddy
9. *Definition:* To give energy and vitality to.
   Etymology: in (Latin), "causing" + *vigor* (Latin), "force; energy" + *-are, -atus* (Latin), "make"
   Synonyms: animate, enliven, stimulate, energize, vitalize, vivify
   Antonyms: weaken, debilitate, enervate
10. *Definition:* Full of uncertainty; causing uncertainty or misgiving.
    Etymology: dubius (Latin), "doubtful"
    Synonyms: questionable, doubtful, ambiguous; unsettled, undecided
    Antonyms: certain, sure; settled, definite
11. *Definition:* Ruddy; excessively ornate or flowery.
    Etymology: floridus (Latin), "blooming"; from *flos, floris* (Latin), "flower"
    Synonyms: flushed, rosy; embellished, decorated; flamboyant, bombastic
    Antonyms: pale, ashen; stark, simple, unadorned
12. *Definition:* A bitter and abusive speech or denunciation.

Etymology: diatribe (Greek), "wearing away"; from *dia* (Greek), "completely" + *tribein* (Greek), "rub"
Synonyms: harangue, tirade, invective, philippic
Antonyms: eulogy, panegyric, encomium

13. *Definition:* (*n.*) The term of office of a pope; (*v.*) to speak or behave pompously.
Etymology: pontifex, pontificus (Latin), "pope; bishop; bridge-builder" + *-atus* (Latin), "rank; office" or *-are, -atus* (Latin), "make (like)"
Synonyms: (*n.*) primacy, prelature; (*v.*) hold forth, preach, sermonize

14. *Definition:* Something, usually money, given as a reward for a service.
Etymology: gratuitas (Latin), "gift"; from *gratus* (Latin), "pleasing"
Synonyms: tip, gift, present, bonus

15. *Definition:* Something that foreshadows a future occurrence; something amazing or marvelous.
Etymology: pro (Latin), "forth; before" + *tendere, tentus/tensus* (Latin), "stretch"
Synonyms: omen, prodigy

Lesson 19 (pages 293–309)

Exercise V.   Word Roundup
(pages 301–302)
1. a. See page 208 of the student text.
   b. *Impugn:* to call into question or cast doubt on; to attack; *impute;* to ascribe or attribute to.
   c. *Impassable:* impossible to traverse or pass through; *impassive:* incapable of physical sensation; devoid or incapable of emotion.
   d. See page 487 of the student text.
2. a. Objects that impede or hinder progress — for example, baggage.
   b. A person who argues in defense or justification of another person or cause.
   c. A person who is confined indoors, usually because of disability or illness.
   d. A narrow or congested section of a highway or the like; any obstacle to progress.
   e. To stall; to refuse to answer or cooperate with.
   f. To disparage or criticize, often spitefully or unfairly.
3. a. To treat with disdain; to regard disapprovingly.
   b. To be in disgrace or under suspicion.
   c. To act strictly according to the regulations.
   d. To become extremely angry.

e. To limit or thwart oneself by one's own action; to catch oneself in one's own trap.
f. To get away with something without penalty or punishment.
g. To become arrogant and overbearing.
h. To treat with excessive (and often undeserved) care or caution.
4. a. See page 296 of the student text.
   b. Genuinely pure; superficially or hypocritically virtuous. Simon Pure is a character in *A Bold Stroke for a Wife,* a play by the 18th-century English writer Susanna Centlivre. The character was not actually a real person but, rather, the fabrication of an unscrupulous impostor.

Exercise (page 305)
1. a. ignoble
   b. immutable, invariable
   c. indefensible
   d. inactive, inert
   e. irreverent
   f. invalid
   g. impassive
   h. immaculate
   i. illogical
   j. invalidate
3. a. A system of names or technical terms used in an art or science.
   b. An assumed or fictitious name used by a writer for purely literary purposes.
   c. To propose someone for appointment or election to an office.
   d. A means of carrying or transporting; the act of transporting something.
   e. Roundabout; cunning or deceptive.
   f. (*n.*) A protective escort of ships or other vehicles; (*v.*) to accompany for protection.
   g. (*v.*) To stray from a particular course or pattern; (*n.*) an individual who is different from the norm; (*adj.*) aberrant.
   h. An error in naming something; a name inappropriately applied to something.
   i. An elevated bridge supporting a road or railroad over obstructed terrain.
   j. The state of being unknown.

Exercise I.   The Vocabulary of Social Change (pages 307–308)
A. *Causes Galore* (page 307)
1. Concern for the promotion and protection of consumer interests, including the quality and safety of goods, price controls, truth in advertising, and reasonable financial charges.
2. Concern with preventing the deterioration of the human environment and with repairing environmental

damage. The term applies to both the natural and the man-made aspects of the environment.

3. A program to clear away slums and in general create better living conditions in urban population centers.

4. Organized activity on behalf of women's rights and interests; specifically, the movement beginning in the 19th century that sought to remove legal, political, and social restraints against women.

5. Social or educational theory that promotes interest in many cultures within a given society rather than in the mainstream culture only.

6. A firm belief in or dedication to the ideals and practice of personal freedom, both in thought and in action.

7. A belief in or advocacy of rule by people considered inherently superior as the result of birth, education, natural capacity, or some other attribute.

8. A consciousness of belonging to and feeling loyalty and affection for a particular region within a country; the development of a social or political system based on such loyalties.

9. Organized activity in support of fair and humane treatment of animals, especially the right of animals not to be exploited for human purposes.

B. *The Struggle for Racial Equality* (page 308)

1. Emphasis on race as the all-important factor in determining culture and behavior. Usually the racist believes that his/her own race is superior and should not mix with other races.

2. A person whose liberties or opportunities are restricted because he or she belongs to a particular racial, ethnic, economic, religious, or sexual group.

3. A movement emphasizing African American pride and the achievement of political and economic equality.

4. The policy and practice of separating the races (in housing, education, employment, etc.) with one race dominant; especially, discriminatory practices against nonwhites in a predominantly white society.

5. The policy or practice of bringing members of different races or other groups together on a basis of full equality. The term is used particularly to refer to the mixing of various groups in the public schools.

6. The consideration of race in a profile of someone suspected of a crime; a form of racism in which police focus on people of a particular racial group when seeking criminal suspects.

7. See page 467 of the student text.

8. The occupying of seats in a segregated establishment to protest discrimination.

9. A term used (often in a derogatory sense) to describe organizations or social groupings that exclude people who are not white. The term may be applied, for example, to a country club, a school, a place of employment, or an entire society.

10. A society in which members of diverse racial, ethnic, religious, national, and social groups live together and make their distinctive contributions to a culture that combines (but does not eliminate) these many different traditions.

11. The practice of withholding home loans or insurance from neighborhoods considered poor economic risks; the practice of discriminating against someone in housing or insurance on the basis of race.

12. Absence of discrimination in the workplace based on race, color, age, gender, national origin, religion, or disability.

Exercise II. The Heritage of Literature (pages 308–309)

In addition to an unabridged dictionary, the following reference books may prove helpful in doing this exercise: *Brewer's Dictionary of Phrase and Fable*, 16th ed.; *Morris Dictionary of Word and Phrase Origins*, 2d ed.

A. *Contributions Old and New* (page 308)

1. See page 414 of the student text.

2. A person who is overly optimistic and who sees good in everything.

3. See page 342 of the student text.

4. A member of the American middle class whose attachment to its ideals makes him/her a model of narrow-mindedness and self-satisfaction. George F. Babbitt is the main character in the American writer Sinclair Lewis's novel *Babbitt* (1922).

5. Empty and pretentious boasting; a braggart. Braggadocchio is a character in the 16th-century English poet Edmund Spenser's epic poem *The Faerie Queene*.

6. A miserly and unpleasant person. Ebenezer Scrooge is the "heavy" who later repents of his meanness in *A Christmas Carol* (1843), by Charles Dickens.

7. The ability to make fortunate and unexpected discoveries by accident. The word was coined by the 18th-century English writer Horace Walpole after the characters in the

Persian fairy tale *The Three Princes of Serendip*, who made such discoveries.
8. Boasting or bragging; bluster. Rodomonte is a boastful Moorish king in the Italian Renaissance epic poems *Orlando Inamorato* (1487) and *Orlando Furioso* (1516).
9. A hypothetical physical particle that may be the fundamental unit of matter. The word is thought to derive from the phrase "three quarks for Mr. Marks" in the 20th-century Irish writer James Joyce's stream-of-consciousness novel *Finnegan's Wake* (1939).
10. Show complete ingratitude. The phrase was first used by the 18th-century English statesman and orator Edmund Burke in reference to the public's attitude toward government. (See Morris, *op. cit.*)
11. (*n.*) A quarrelsome or shrewish woman; (*adj.*) shrewish. Termagaunt was an imaginary Muslim deity who appeared as a shrewish woman in medieval mystery plays.
12. A crude and brutish person. The Yahoos are a savage race of brutes in the 18th-century English writer Jonathan Swift's satiric novel *Gulliver's Travels.*
13. (*adj.*) Excellent or ideal but existing only in theory and not in real life; (*n.*) a zealous but impractical reformer. Utopia (*ou* [Greek], "no" + *topos* [Greek], "place") is the imaginary island that is the subject, title, and location of the action in a small book (1516) by Sir Thomas More; it was described as the seat of moral, social, and political perfection.
14. A dirty or unkempt child. Ragamoffyn is a demon in the 14th-century medieval epic poem *The Vision of Piers Plowman*, usually ascribed to William Langland.
15. An unpromising child who eventually grows into an attractive or accomplished adult; anything unprepossessing that changes with time into something attractive. The Ugly Duckling is the subject of one of the 19th-century Danish writer Hans Christian Andersen's fairy tales.

B. *William Shakespeare* (page 309)
1. One's inexperienced youth. *Antony and Cleopatra* I, v.
2. A debt or agreement harshly insisted upon; the whole of the bargain to the very last letter of the agreement. *The Merchant of Venice* IV, i.
3. Sympathy; compassion. *Macbeth* I, v.
4. A confirmed bachelor who has recently married. After Benedick, a character in *Much Ado About Nothing.*

5. The easiest way; the path of pleasure and self-indulgence (often leading to ruin or destruction). *Hamlet* I, iii and *Macbeth* II, i.
6. To die; to sleep the sleep of the blessed. *Richard III* IV, iii (but referring to Luke 16:22–23).
7. Keep what you were told secret. *Henry IV, Part 2*, I, ii.
8. Catch oneself in one's own trap. *Hamlet* III, iv.

Exercise III. A Verbal Diversion
(page 309)
1. A special or memorable day.
2. Something that draws attention away from the matter at hand; a diversion or distraction.
3. Actually discovered in the act of doing something wrong or committing a crime.
4. A Southern white rural laborer. (The term is pejorative and offensive, implying that the individual is ignorant or a segregationist.)
5. To celebrate wildly or noisily.
6. Having less money coming in than going out; operating at a loss or in debt.
7. To censor, delete, change, or correct.
8. To welcome with a formal and impressive show of hospitality.
9. See page 111 of the student text.
10. A flag used to indicate danger or as a stop signal; hence, a warning signal or something that attracts attention because it is irritating.

Exercise IV. Expanding Your Word Power (page 309)
1. *Definition:* To stoop to a level one considers beneath one's dignity.
   Etymology: cum (Latin), "with" + *de* (Latin), "down" + *scandere* (Latin), "climb"
   Synonyms: patronize, stoop, deign
   Antonym: hobnob
2. *Definition:* Extremely wicked and evil; infamous.
   Etymology: nefarius (Latin), "sinful"; from *ne* (Latin), "not" + *fas* (Latin), "divine law"
   Synonyms: diabolic, heinous, iniquitous
   Antonyms: virtuous, meritorious, honorable
3. *Definition:* Intrinsic baseness; depravity.
   Etymology: turpitudo, turpitudinis (Latin), "baseness"; from *turpis* (Latin), "base; low"
   Synonyms: wickedness, iniquity
   Antonyms: probity, goodness, virtuousness
4. *Definition:* To spoil the cleanness of.
   Etymology: souiller (Old French), "soil"

Synonyms: soil, stain, pollute, taint, tarnish

Antonyms: cleanse, purify; purge

5. *Definition:* Exemption from punishment, penalty, or harm.

Etymology: in (Latin), "not" + *poena* (Latin), "penalty" + *-itas, -itatis* (Latin), "state of"

Synonyms: immunity, freedom

Antonyms: liability, susceptibleness, vulnerability

6. *Definition:* Distribution; an exemption or release from something, a divinely appointed religious system.

Etymology: dispensatio, dispensationis (Latin), "exemption"; from *dis* (Latin), "apart" + *pendere* (Latin), "weigh"

Synonyms: allocation, apportionment; reprieve, remission

7. *Definition:* Beyond reproach; unquestionable.

Etymology: un + impeach, "challenge; accuse" (from *in* [Latin], "in" + *pedica* [Latin], "fetter" + *-are* [Latin], "make; put") + *able*

Synonyms: unexceptionable, irreproachable, blameless, faultless

Antonyms: vulnerable, questionable, assailable

8. *Definition:* To weigh down considerably; to hinder.

Etymology: en (Old French), "in" + *combre* (Old French), "hindrance"

Synonyms: burden, impede, handicap

Antonyms: unburden, unload; lighten, ease

9. *Definition:* Hardened in wickedness; resistant to persuasion.

Etymology: ob (Latin), "completely" + *durus* (Latin), "hard" + *-are, -atus* (Latin), "make"

Synonyms: impenitent, stubborn, unyielding, intractable

Antonyms: tractable, yielding, submissive

10. *Definition:* To declare false; to contradict.

Etymology: gegn (Old English), "against" + *secgan* (Old English), "say"

Synonyms: deny, dispute

Antonyms: confirm, corroborate, substantiate

11. *Definition:* To provide plausible reasons for an action or behavior.

Etymology: rational + ize

Synonyms: justify, account for, explain

12. *Definition:* To compel or restrict by force; to keep within bounds.

Etymology: constraindre (Old French), "compel"; from *cum* (Latin), "together" + *stringere* (Latin), "draw tight"

Synonyms: compel, coerce, constrict; oblige

Antonyms: release, liberate

13. *Definition:* (*v.*) To hail publicly; (*n.*) enthusiastic applause.

Etymology: ad (Latin), "to; at" + *clamare* (Latin), "shout"

Synonyms: (*v.*) cheer, applaud, praise; (*n.*) praise, kudos, approval, accolades

Antonyms: (*v.*) denounce, condemn; (*n.*) condemnation, censure, obloquy; opprobrium

14. *Definition:* To calm or allay; to soften or ease.

Etymology: mollis (Latin), "soft" + *facere* (Latin), "make"

Synonyms: placate, appease, assuage

Antonyms: exacerbate, irritate, annoy; aggravate, intensify

15. *Definition:* (*v.*) To express doubt about; to question; (*n.*) an inquiry.

Etymology: quaere (Latin), "Ask!"

Synonyms: (*v.*) doubt; inquire, ask; (*n.*) doubt; question, inquiry

Lesson 20 (pages 310–327)

Exercise V. Word Roundup
(pages 319–320)

1. a. See page 310 of the student text.
   b. See page 314 of the student text.
   c. See page 311 of the student text.
   d. See page 316 of the student text.
2. a. A secret agent hired to incite trouble designed to make an organization or its members act illegally.
   b. An achievement of great strength, skill, or ingenuity.
   c. A group of people active in inventing or applying new ideas or techniques, particularly in the arts.
3. a. A compliment that is roundabout or indirect and that often contains a disguised insult or rebuke.
   b. Surface changes or modifications made merely to improve the appearance, or enhance the beauty, of something.
   c. A flaw or deficiency that exists in something from the beginning but is not hereditary.
   d. Fitted by birth, education, or temperament to occupy a specific position; accustomed by background to a specific mode of behavior.
4. a. See page 317 of the student text.
   b. See page 316 of the student text.
5. a. To ward off hunger or want.
   b. To become very angry at someone suddenly or unexpectedly.

Exercise I. Coining Words
(pages 324–325)

1. An expert in the specialized problems (*e.g.*, race relations, housing, education) of cities, especially large ones.
2. An extremely prominent and popular larger-than-life star in sports or the arts.
3. One who opposed the war in Vietnam; one who takes part in antiwar demonstrations.
4. The marketing of products or services by telephone.
5. A card used to withdraw money or pay for purchases directly from the cardholder's bank account without incurring interest on the transaction.
6. See answer to I, A, 2, page 307 of the student text.
7. A person who is trained to pilot, navigate, or otherwise participate in the flight of a spacecraft.
8. Faster than the speed of sound (1200 feet per second).
9. To indoctrinate forcibly with the intent of changing a person's convictions or attitudes about political, religious, or social matters.
10. (*adj.*) Not distinguishable as either male or female; (*n.*) the absence of sexual distinction, especially in dress or hair styles.
11. See page 384 of the student text.
12. The online world of computer networks.
13. A person who writes, prepares, or inputs a set of instructions for a computer.
14. A late morning or early afternoon meal that combines or takes the place of breakfast and lunch.
15. A celestial object that resembles a star but is much larger and farther away.
16. An artificial environment experienced via stimuli provided by a computer, allowing the person to act in ways that affect what happens in that environment.
17. A biological condition or agent that is hazardous to people or the environment.
18. A woman's skirt that has a hemline high above the knee.
19. A community of organisms and its environment that function as a unit.
20. A broadcaster who reads the news and introduces reports by other broadcasters.
21. A large geographical area that encompasses several cities and their suburbs in sufficient proximity to be considered a single unit.
22. Someone who reveals wrongdoing to the public or to people in authority.
23. See answer to II, B, 8, page 289 of the student text.
24. A game or contest played in order to break a tie or decide a title or championship.
25. A procession of automobiles or other vehicles.
26. A television production of a story that is presented in sequential episodes.
27. A magazine written by and for fans, particularly of fantasy or science fiction.
28. A hamburger with a melted cheese topping.
29. A radio or television drama involving tangled personal relationships treated in a sentimental and melodramatic way. The name comes from the early sponsorship of such programs by soap manufacturers.
30. To interrogate someone on his or her return (*e.g.*, from a mission or conference) in order to obtain information.
31. A system for transmitting messages electronically between terminals; a message sent via such a system.
32. A small combination video camera and videocassette recorder.
33. A short board mounted on skate wheels used to coast and to perform stunts.
34. A person who drops or leaves waste materials in a public area.
35. A condition that occurs after flying through several time zones; characterized by fatigue, irritability, and other physical and psychological effects.
36. A compact vanlike motor vehicle that combines the features of an automobile and a van; usually used as a dwelling for camping or long motor trips.

Exercise II. Expanding Your Word Power (page 325)

1. *Definition:* The highest point or degree.
   Etymology: culminatus (Medieval Latin), "crown"; from *culmen, culminis* (Latin), "top" + *ion* (Latin), "act or process"
   Synonyms: cap, climax, top; finish, conclusion
2. *Definition:* Lacking money.
   Etymology: in (Latin), "not" + *pecunia* (Latin), "money; wealth" + *-osus* (Latin), "full of"
   Synonyms: poor, impoverished, indigent
   Antonyms: wealthy, rich, affluent

3. *Definition:* Existing or remaining within.
   Etymology: in (Latin), "in" + *manens, manentis,* present participle of *manere* (Latin), "remain"
   Synonyms: inherent, intrinsic
   Antonyms: external, extrinsic
4. *Definition:* Acquired by chance or accident from the outside.
   Etymology: adventicius (Latin), "arriving from the outside"; from *ad* (Latin), "to" + *venire, ventus* (Latin), "come"
   Synonyms: accidental, fortuitous
   Antonyms: predetermined, intentional, preplanned
5. *Definition:* Incapable of being overcome or tamed.
   Etymology: in (Latin), "not" + *domitare* (Latin), "tame" + *-abilis, -abile* (Latin), "able to"
   Synonyms: unconquerable, invincible
   Antonyms: conquerable, superable, vincible
6. *Definition:* To make a strong verbal attack against; to explode violently.
   Etymology: fulmen, fulminis (Latin), "lightning" + *-are, -atus* (Latin), "make"
   Synonyms: denounce, inveigh, lambaste; detonate
   Antonyms: applaud, eulogize, extol
7. *Definition: (v.)* To settle by making mutual concessions; *(n.)* a settlement of differences in such a way.
   Etymology: cum (Latin), "mutually" + *pro* (Latin), "forth" + *mittere, missus* (Latin), "send"
   Synonyms: (v.) concede, settle, come to terms; *(n.)* concession, trade-off
8. *Definition:* To crush by force; to keep from public knowledge.
   Etymology: sub (Latin), "down" + *premere, pressus* (Latin), "press"
   Synonyms: subdue, check; conceal
   Antonyms: foster, promote; expose, reveal, divulge
9. *Definition: (v.)* to expose to danger; to venture; *(n.)* a danger; an accident.
   Etymology: hazard (Old French), "a dice game"; from *yásara* (Arabic), "he plays dice"
   Synonyms: (v. and n.) chance, risk, venture, gamble
   Antonyms: (v.) protect, ensure; *(n.)* security, safety, protection
10. *Definition:* Having keen perception or judgment.
    Etymology: sagax, sagacis (Latin), "quick-witted"
    Synonyms: wise, discerning, perspicacious
    Antonyms: dense, obtuse
11. *Definition:* To clear of blame or guilt.
    Etymology: vindex, vindicis (Latin), "defender" + *-are, -atus* (Latin), "make"
    Synonyms: absolve, exonerate; confirm
    Antonyms: inculpate, incriminate, implicate; confute, controvert
12. *Definition:* Full of trepidation; lacking in confidence.
    Etymology: timor, timoris (Latin), "fear" + *-osus* (Latin), "full of"
    Synonyms: timid, aprehensive, fearful
    Antonyms: daring, courageous, bold
13. *Definition:* To place or introduce between.
    Etymology: inter (Latin), "between" + *ponere, positus* (Latin), "put"
    Synonyms: interject, insert, insinuate
    Antonyms: extract, extricate
14. *Definition:* To bring into existence.
    Etymology: genus, generis (Latin), "birth; offspring" + *-are, -atus* (Latin), "make"
    Synonyms: produce, beget, create
    Antonyms: expunge, obliterate, efface
15. *Definition:* To save or protect.
    Etymology: cum (Latin), "completely" + *servare* (Latin), "keep; guard"
    Synonyms: preserve, store, keep, guard
    Antonyms: squander, waste

Review (pages 328–334)

Exercise IX. Word Roundup
(pages 331–332)
1. a. See page 263 of the student text.
   b. See page 310 of the student text.
   c. See page 173 of the student text.
   d. See page 156 of the student text.
   e. See pages 190–191 of the student text.
   f. See page 156 of the student text.
   g. See page 230 of the student text.
   h. See answer to V, 1, a, page 251 of the student text.
   i. See page 265 of the student text.
   j. See page 170 of the student text.
2. a. See answer to V, 2, e, page 268 of the student text.
   b. See answer to V, 2, c, page 268 of the student text.
   c. See answer to V, 2, d, page 268 of the student text.
   d. See answer to V, 2, e, page 301 of the student text.
   e. See answer to VI, 2, a, page 285 of the student text.
   f. See answer to V, 1, a, page 233 of the student text.
3. a. See answer to V, 7, a, page 179 of the student text.
   b. To act while the time or opportunity presents itself.
   c. See answer to V, 1, f, page 233 of the student text.
   d. See answer to V, 3, e, page 302 of the student text.

e. See answer to V, 5, a, page 320 of the student text.
f. See answer to V, 4, e, page 198 of the student text.
g. See answer to VI, 1, a, page 284 of the student text.
h. See answer to VI, 1, d, page 284 of the student text.
i. See answer to V, 3, d, page 302 of the student text.
j. See answer to VI, 1, c, page 284 of the student text.
4. a. See answer to V, 4, f, page 251 of the student text.
   b. See answer to I, 9, page 167 of the student text.
   c. See answer to V, 2, a, page 301 of the student text.
   d. See answer to VI, 4, b, page 285 of the student text.
   e. See answer to V, 4, a, page 269 of the student text.
   f. See answer to I, 13, page 184 of the student text.
5. a. Insulted; an ignoramus is an ignorant or dense person.
   b. Insulted; a greenhorn is a novice or beginner.
   c. Flattered; a connoisseur is an expert with discriminating taste.
   d. Flattered; a dapper Dan is someone who dresses stylishly and tastefully.
   e. Insulted; a patsy is someone who has unwittingly been made the dupe of someone else.
   f. Flattered; a paragon is someone who is a model of perfection or excellence.

Exercise X. Etymology (page 332)
2. a. See page 199 of the student text.
   b. See answer to A, 1, e, page 200 of the student text.
   c. See answer to A, 1, j, page 200 of the student text.
   d. See answer to A, 2, l, page 200 of the student text.
   e. See answer to A, 2, j, page 200 of the student text.
   f. See page 199 of the student text.
3. a. See answer to E, 3, page 236 of the student text.
   b. See answer to E, 6, page 236 of the student text.
   c. See answer to E, 4, page 236 of the student text.
   d. See answer to E, 5, page 236 of the student text.
   e. See page 235 of the student text.
   f. See page 235 of the student text.
5. a. See page 303 of the student text.
   b. See page 302 of the student text.
   c. See page 303 of the student text.
   d. See page 303 of the student text.
   e. See page 303 of the student text.
   f. See answer to 2, c, page 305 of the student text.

Lesson 21 (pages 335-351)

Exercise V.   Word Roundup
(pages 345-346)
1. See page 343 of the student text.
2. a. See page 335 of the student text.
   b. See page 339 of the student text.
   c. See page 342 of the student text.
   d. See page 342 of the student text.
3. a. The male honeybee, which gathers no honey; an idle person who lives off the labor of others.
   b. Something passed along to one person after having been used by another.
   c. A person who seeks out and exposes political or economic corruption.
   d. Something used to mask or conceal one's true purpose; a candidate put forward to conceal the candidacy of another or to divide the opposition.
4. See page 343 of the student text.
5. a. An academic course that is optional rather than required.
   b. A possession of value passed down from one generation to the next.
   c. Harm done to a person's good name or reputation.
   d. The willful intent to commit an unlawful or wrongful act that will result in harm, injury, or damage to another person.
6. a. Not of sound mind.
   b. Required by fashion, custom, or tradition.
7. a. See page 341 of the student text.
   b. The unintentional transposition of sounds in two or more words (e.g., "a swell foop" for "a fell swoop").
   c. See page 341 of the student text.
   d. See page 341 of the student text.

Exercise (pages 348-349)
1. a. intercede: to mediate or plead on another's behalf. Inter indicates an intrusion ("between").
   b. intercollegiate: involving or relating to two or more colleges. Inter indicates mutuality ("among").
   c. interdenominational: involving or representing two or more religious groups. Inter indicates mutuality ("among").
   d. interlock: to unite firmly by hooking or dovetailing. Inter indicates mutuality or reciprocity ("among").
   e. intermarry: to marry a member of another group. Inter indicates a crossing over ("between; among").
   f. international: involving or relating to two or more nations. Inter indicates mutuality ("among").
2. a. Mediation or entreaty on another's behalf.
   b. Starting and stopping at intervals.

c. A person who interferes with the rights or affairs of others.

d. An intervening event or period of time; a brief episode.

e. A pause between two events.

f. To insert between other elements or parts.

5. a. To bring or come into existence.

b. (*v.*) To deteriorate from a previous and better state; (*adj.*) having declined from a better state; (*n.*) a degraded person.

c. Uniform or consistent in structure or makeup.

d. A class, kind, or group that shares common attributes.

e. Not sophisticated or worldly; open or honest.

f. Consisting of varied, dissimilar, or unrelated parts or elements.

g. The beginning or origination of something.

h. Having similar tastes and temperament; sympathetic or agreeable; friendly or sociable.

i. Children or descendants; offspring.

Exercise I.   More Words from Literary Sources (page 350)

1. Willing to use craft and deceit to obtain and hold political power, thereby denying the relevance of morality to political affairs. The Italian political theorist Niccolo Machiavelli (1469–1527) wrote a book called *The Prince* (1513) in which such views were advocated.

2. A seducer of women. Lothario is the name of the seducer in *The Fair Penitent* (1703), a play by Nicholas Rowe (1674–1718).

3. (*adj.*) Insipidly sentimental; spineless; (*n.*) such a person. *Namby-Pamby*, by Henry Carey (died 1743), is a satire on the overly sentimental pastoral poems of Ambrose Philips.

4. A religious hypocrite. Tartuffe is the religious hypocrite who is the main character in one of Molière's comedies (1664).

5. To pursue a course foredoomed to frustration. In *Don Quixote* (1605, 1615) by Miguel de Cervantes (1547–1616) the Don attacks windmills with his lance under the misapprehension that they are giants.

6. Broadly and lustily humorous; earthy and satirical. The French writer François Rabelais (c. 1483–1553) was noted for works of this type.

7. Any creation that slips from the control of, and ultimately destroys, its creator. An abbreviated form of *Frankenstein's monster* or *Frankenstein monster*. Frankenstein is the surname of the doctor who creates such a monster in Mary Wollstonecraft Shelley's romantic novel of that name (1818).

8. A booklet. From *Pamphilus seu De Amore*, a short amatory poem in Latin from the 12th century.

9. A detective. From the fictional detective Sherlock Holmes, created by Sir Arthur Conan Doyle (1859–1930).

10. A brutal or overly demanding taskmaster. Simon Legree is the name of the brutal slave dealer in Harriet Beecher Stowe's novel *Uncle Tom's Cabin* (1851–1852).

11. Plentiful or abundant in appearance only; illusory. Barmecide is the name of a noble Persian family, a member of which served a beggar an imaginary feast in *The Arabian Nights*.

12. Fatuous and hypocritical talk about benevolence and other kindly virtues. Seth Pecksniff is a character addicted to such talk in *Martin Chuzzlewit* (1843–1844) by Charles Dickens.

13. An affectedly elegant style of speech or writing. Euphues is a character with such a style in two works by John Lyly (1554?–1606).

14. An improvident person who remains optimistic about a change in his/her luck despite constant adversity. Wilkins Micawber is a character of such a kind in *David Copperfied* (1849–1850) by Charles Dickens.

15. A self-imporant or pompous official; a muck-a-muck. The Grand Panjandrum is a character in a nonsense story by the English playwright Samuel Foote (1720–1777).

Exercise II.   Russian Loan Words in English (page 351)

1. An organized, often government-encouraged massacre of a minority group, particularly Eastern European Jews.

2. A member of a group of frontiersmen from southern Russia organized as the czar's cavalry; a member of an armed unit used to suppress or break up an activity such as a demonstration or strike.

3. The intellectual class in a society.

4. An imperial edict having the force of law; any authoritative order or decree.

5. A vast semiarid, lightly wooded plain.

6. The treeless, moss- and lichen-covered area between the polar ice cap and the tree line in subarctic regions.
7. The title of the autocratic ruler of Russia before the 1917 Revolution; anyone with extensive power in a particular field.
8. A metal urn used for making tea.
9. A country cottage, especially one used during summer.
10. An official of the Communist Party in the Soviet Union in charge of indoctrination and the enforcement of party loyalty.
11. Restructuring; the policy of government and economic reform inaugurated by Mikhail Gorbachev in the mid-1980s.
12. A rich member of the Russian peasant class disenfranchised by the 1917 Revolution; a wealthy peasant in imperial Russia.
13. A labor camp; from the network of such camps that constituted the Soviet penal system.
14. A member of a Communist political organization or underground movement; any official blindly devoted to his/her superiors or organization.
15. A comrade (the term of address used by members of the Communist Party).
16. A policy of allowing open discussion of social and political issues and freer dissemination of information and news.
17. In the Soviet Union, a popularly elected legislative assembly or council existing on the local, regional, and national levels.
18. A collective farm.

Exercise III.   Plurals in A (page 351)
1. Something added; a supplement. addenda.
2. An error in printing or writing, particularly an item in a list of corrections. errata.
3. Something to be done. agenda.
4. An assumed or given fact; a piece of information. data.
5. A kind of single-celled microorganism. bacteria.
6. A horizontal bed or layer of rock, tissue, or the like. strata.

Exercise IV.   Expanding Your Word Power (page 351)
1. *Definition:* (*n.*) Scorn, contempt; (*v.*) to treat with contempt.
   Etymology: de, dis (Latin), "un-" + *dignare* (Latin), "deem worthy"
   Synonyms: (*n.*) contumely, derision; (*v.*) despise, scorn, spurn

Antonyms: (*n.*) esteem, respect, favor; (*v.*) esteem, admire, cherish
2. *Definition:* Lying on the back, face upward; inert.
   Etymology: supinus (Latin), "lying on the back; moving backward"
   Synonyms: prone, prostrate, inactive, passive
   Antonyms: upright; energetic, active
3. *Definition:* Capable of two or more explanations; of a doubtful nature.
   Etymology: aequus, aequi (Latin), "equal" + *vox, vocis* (Latin), "voice" + *-alis, -ale* (Latin), "connected with"
   Synonyms: ambiguous, cryptic, evasive
   Antonyms: unambiguous, unequivocal
4. *Definition:* Funds or property donated to an institution; a natural capacity or ability.
   Etymology: en (French), "very; completely" + *douer* (French), "provide with a dowry" + *ment* (French), "act or state of"
   Synonyms: gift, donation, grant; aptitude, talent
5. *Definition:* Subject to; likely.
   Etymology: lier (Old French), "bind" + *able* (Old French), "able to"
   Synonyms: susceptible; probable
   Antonyms: immune, exempt; unlikely, improbable
6. *Definition:* To speak ill or maliciously of.
   Etymology: traducere (Latin), "expose to ridicule"; from *trans* (Latin), "across" + *ducere* (Latin), "lead"
   Synonyms: slander, defame, malign, libel
   Antonyms: praise, extol, eulogize
7. *Definition:* Able to reason; of sound mind; based on reason.
   Etymology: ratio, rationis (Latin), "reason" + *-alis, -ale* (Latin), "connected with"
   Synonyms: reasoning, cognitive; sane, compos mentis, logical, sensible, reasonable
   Antonyms: dumb; insane, non compos mentis; irrational, illogical
8. *Definition:* Extremely rich and lavish.
   Etymology: sumptus (Latin), "expense" + *-osus* (Latin), "full of"
   Synonyms: expensive, costly; magnificent, opulent
   Antonyms: spare, sparse, mean
9. *Definition:* To lie in hiding; to move about furtively.
   Etymology: skulken (Middle English), "shirk"; ultimately of Scandinavian origin
   Synonyms: lurk, sneak, slink, prowl

Antonyms: strut, swagger

10. See answer to V, 12, page 258 of the student text.
11. *Definition:* Deep-seated hatred.
    Etymology: enemite (Old French), "hatred"; from *in* (Latin), "not" + *amicus* (Latin), "friend" + *-itas* (Latin), "state of"
    Synonyms: antagonism, ill will, hostility
    Antonyms: friendship, love, rapport
12. *Definition: (adj.)* Of very small size; *(n.)* a suffix or word indicating smallness or a smaller version of something.
    Etymology: de (Latin), "very; down from" + *minuere, minutus* (Latin), "lessen" + *-ivus* (Latin), "that which; having the power to"
    Synonyms: (adj.) tiny, minute
    Antonyms: (adj.) enormous, colossal
13. *Definition:* A payment for goods received or services rendered.
    Etymology: re (Latin), "back" + *munus, muneris* (Latin), "gift" + *-are, -atus* (Latin), "make"
    Synonyms: compensation, recompense, indemnification
14. *Definition: (adj.)* Expressing a plea or command; urgent; *(n.)* a command or order.
    Etymology: imperare, imperatus, (Latin), "command" + *-ivus* (Latin), "having the power to"
    Synonyms: (adj.) mandatory, vital; *(n.)* mandate, behest
    Antonyms: (adj.) nonessential, inconsequential, unimportant
15. *Definition:* A device for carrying passengers or equipment; any medium for conveying, transmitting, expressing, or achieving something.
    Etymology: vehiculum (Latin), "carriage"; from *vehere* (Latin), "carry"
    Synonyms: carriage, conveyance, car; means, agent, channel, instrument

Lesson 22 (pages 352–370)

Exercise V.   Word Roundup (page 363)
1. a. A soldier who will serve in any army for promise of adventure, pleasure, or profit.
   b. A person who is self-employed and sells his/her services on a short-term basis — for example, to a newspaper or magazine.
   c. A figurehead ruler who claims to be autonomous but actually acts according to the instructions of the government of another (usually neighboring) country by whom he/she is actually controlled.
   d. A newspaper or magazine journalist who moves about a great

deal in the performance of his/her duties.
   e. See page 358 of the student text.
   f. A sophisticated and worldly person.
   g. A senator who is serving his/her first term in Congress.
   h. See page 359 of the student text.
   i. An agricultural laborer who regularly moves about in search of work harvesting crops.
   j. A person who is a member of an organized Christian denomination in name only but does not regularly adhere to its practices or attend services.
2. a. See page 352 of the student text.
   b. An unreliable or transitory business establishment; a business venture of dubious legality.
   c. A country that is dependent upon the protection or patronage of a stronger country; a satellite.
   d. A career that has been filled with sudden changes and shifts of fortune.
   e. An economy that is made up of many different types of enterprise.
   f. See answer to V, 9, page 233 of the student text.
3. A difficult problem; a great difficulty. When the peasant Gordius became King of Phrygia (in western Anatolia), he dedicated his wagon to Zeus as a token of thanks. To make sure that his gift would never be stolen, he fastened it to a heavy beam with a rope so ingeniously knotted that nobody could untie it. When Alexander the Great later heard that whoever could undo the knot would rule over the whole East, he said that he could—and thereupon cut the knot in two with his sword.
4. a. A leader of mercenary soldiers; a mercenary or soldier of fortune in general. Italian.
   b. Self-esteem; self-respect. French.
   c. A strong desire to travel. German.
5. a. Inexperienced; naive.
   b. To find hidden meanings or conclusions that are not readily apparent.
   c. Something of minor significance or value.
   d. A simple and trusting person who is easily taken advantage of.
6. See page 355 of the student text.
7. *Spoils system:* The practice of choosing appointees to public office only from among the supporters of the victorious party or candidate; the term comes from the expression, "to the victor belong the spoils." *Merit system:* The practice of choosing appointees to public office by ability, as determined by competitive examinations, regardless of the appointees' political affiliations.
8. See page 356 of the student text.

Exercise I. Our German Heritage
(page 367)
1. To rake with machine-gun fire from low-flying aircraft.
2. (adj.) Substitute or artificial (and usually inferior); (n.) an inferior substitute.
3. A musical theme associated with a particular character, thing, or emotion; the dominant or recurring theme of anything.
4. A child prodigy.
5. Blitzkrieg: A sudden and forceful attack by both air and ground forces; any swift, concerted attack. Blitz: (n.) An intensive air raid or series of air raids; any intensive campaign; (v.) to subject to a blitz.
6. A secretly planned and sudden attempt to overthrow the government.
7. A small group of college and graduate students who are being guided by a professor in original research and who meet regularly for discussion; a meeting of such a group; a meeting for any exchange of ideas.
8. Antiaircraft fire; excessive criticism, abuse, or opposition.
9. Pretentious but poor taste, particularly in the arts; something that exemplifies such taste.

Exercise II. The Clothes We Wear
(page 367)
1. A loose coat or sweater with diagonally cut shoulder seams and the sleeves extending in one piece to the neckline. First worn by Lord Raglan (1788–1855), a British field marshal in the Crimean War.
2. Pants or overalls made from a sturdy cotton twill fabric, usually dark blue. Genoa, where the fabric was originally made.
3. Loosely fitting breeches, gathered and banded below the knees. After Diedrich Knickerbocker, a fictitious character who wore such trousers in a tale by the American writer Washington Irving (1783–1859).
4. A lightweight, waterproof raincoat originally made of rubberized cotton. After Charles Macintosh (1766–1843), the Scottish chemist who invented it.
5. A trademark name for a kind of denim blue jeans, reinforced with metal rivets at stress points. After Levi Strauss, a San Francisco merchant during the Gold Rush days who specialized in providing miners with sturdy work pants.
6. A sturdy, coarse, plain-weave cotton fabric, often used for sheets. After Mosul, Iraq, where it was first made.
7. A fine-textured cotton cloth usually with a plaid pattern. After Madras, India, where it is made.
8. A fine smooth thread made of long-staple cotton, used for hosiery and undergarments. After Lille, France, where it is made.
9. Pants or overalls made of a sturdy cotton twill fabric. After *dungri*, a heavy, durable Indian cotton.
10. A trademark name for a hat with a broad brim and tall crown. After John B. Stetson (1830–1906), the American hat manufacturer who originated the article.
11. A knitted sweater that buttons down the front. After James T. Brudenell, 7th Earl of Cardigan (1797–1868), who popularized the item.
12. A coarse, twilled cotton cloth, usually dark blue, used for making sturdy work trouser and overalls. From *(serge) de Nîmes*, France, where it was first made.
13. A coarse cotton cloth, usually printed with bright patterns. From Calicut, India, where it is made.
14. A low leather shoe that ties over the instep. From Oxford, England, where they were first worn.
15. A soft felt hat with a creased crown and a flexible brim. After *Fedora*, a play by the French playwright Victorien Sardou (1831–1908). The play's heroine wore such a hat.

Exercise III. Words from the Sciences
(page 367)
1. A substance that induces or accelerates a chemical reaction; someone or something that precipitates an event.
2. To cause to concentrate around two contrasting positions; to break up into two or more opposing sides.
3. (n.) The offspring of genetically different parents or stock; something of mixed origins; (adj.) of mixed origin.
4. (n.) The total or partial obscuring or covering of one celestial body by another; a fall into obscurity; (v.) to obscure or overshadow.
5. The natural processes that remove materials from Earth's surfaces, including weathering, abrasion, and corrosion; any deterioration or degeneration.
6. A relationship in which two or more dissimilar organisms live in a close, mutually beneficial association; any close relationship that is beneficial to those involved.
7. One organism that depends upon another for survival but contributes nothing to its host; a person who habitually takes advantage of another's generosity without giving anything in return.
8. The tendency or property of a body to remain at rest or to stay in the same position unless disturbed; resistance to exertion or change.
9. See page 452 of the student text.

Exercise IV. What's in a Name?
(page 368)

1. See page 226 of the student text.
2. A person's last, or family, name, as distinguished from his/her first, or given, name.
3. An assumed name, usually used by a criminal or fugitive to escape detection.
4. A name assumed for professional performing purposes.
5. A title or phrase conveying respect, usually used when addressing a superior.
6. A comic or affectionate nickname; also, an assumed name.
7. See answer to 3, h, page 305 of the student text.
8. An identifying name or title.
9. See answer to V, 6, page 233 of the student text.
10. The name of a place; a name derived from a place or region.
11. The name a writer assumes for professional purposes.
12. A descriptive name added to or replacing the proper name of a person, place, or thing; the shortened or familiar form of a proper name.
13. See page 410 of the student text.
14. A name derived from a paternal ancestor, especially one formed adding an affix (e.g., -son).
15. See answer to IV, 12, page 351 of the student text.

Exercise V. Number Words (page 368)

1. One thousand. A span of one thousand years.
2. Five. A group of five musicians or the compositions they play; any group of five persons or things.
3. Ten. A span of ten years.
4. One hundred. The commanding officer of the Roman military unit called a century, which originally consisted of one hundred soldiers.
5. Seventy. A person who is between seventy and eighty years old.
6. Two hundred. Occurring every two hundred years; a two-hundredth anniversary celebration.
7. Three. A group of three people or things.
8. Fifty. Relating to the Christian feast that takes place on the fiftieth day after Easter; relating to any of the various Christian sects that seek to be filled with the Holy Spirit.
9. Three. Of small significance or importance.
10. One. One of a kind; without equal.
11. Three. An association or group of three men sharing the administration of, or authority over, something.
12. Five. A five-sided polygon.
13. Three. A group of three dramatic, literary, or musical works.
14. One. Pertaining to a single large block of stone; solid, massive, and uniform.
15. Ten. A ten-event athletic contest.
16. One. Marriage to one person at a time.
17. One. See answer to II, 16, page 273 of the student text.
18. Five. A five-event athletic contest.
19. Ten. A linear array of integers representing a fraction; expressed or expressible as a fraction based on ten or its multiples.
20. Four. An animal with four feet.
21. Ten. To destroy a significant part of.

Exercise VI. Expanding Your Word Power (page 368)

1. *Definition:* Unselfishly concerned and devoted to the welfare of others; selfless.
   Etymology: altruisme (French), "altruism"; from *alter* (Latin), "other"
   Synonyms: unselfish, benevolent, charitable
   Antonyms: egoistical, selfish, self-centered
2. *Definition:* Incapable of being contradicted.
   Etymology: in (Latin), "not" + *contra* (Latin), "against" + *vertere* (Latin), "turn" + *-abilis, -abile* (Latin), "able to"
   Synonyms: indisputable, incontestable, unimpeachable
   Antonyms: arguable, questionable, disputable
3. *Definition:* A young bird; a young or inexperienced person.
   Etymology: flegge (obsolete English), "feathered" + *ling* (English), diminutive suffix roughly meaning "little one"
   Synonyms: novice, rookie, greenhorn
   Antonyms: expert, veteran, professional
4. *Definition:* Pertaining to or limited by time; civil or worldly (as opposed to ecclesiastical or spiritual); transitory.
   Etymology: tempus, temporis (Latin), "time" + *-alis, -ale* (Latin), "connected with"
   Synonyms: impermanent, ephemeral; mundane, profane; secular, lay
   Antonyms: eternal, perpetual; spiritual, transcendental; ecclesiastical, religious
5. *Definition:* Of many varieties; having many forms or features.
   Etymology: manig (Old English), "many" + *feald* (Old English), "-fold; times"
   Synonyms: (adj.) diverse, varied, myriad, multifarious
   Antonyms: limited; single, few

6. *Definition:* Excessively boastful; overly self-important.
   Etymology: ego (Latin), "I" + *ism*
   Synonyms: conceited, vainglorious; self-centered, egocentric
   Antonyms: modest, self-effacing, selfless
7. *Definition:* Impervious to light; difficult to understand.
   Etymology: opacus (Latin), "dark"
   Synonyms: dense, murky, obscure
   Antonyms: clear, transparent, lucid, intelligible
8. *Definition:* Existing within definable bounds.
   Etymology: finire, finitus (Latin), "limit"
   Synonyms: limited, confined, circumscribed
   Antonyms: boundless, infinite, limitless
9. *Definition:* Of little or no value; having no force or power.
   Etymology: nugatorius (Latin), "trifling"; from *nugari* (Latin), "trifle" and *nugae* (Latin), "trifles"
   Synonyms: worthless; inconsequential, insignificant, inoperative
   Antonyms: valuable, worthwhile; significant, important; operative
10. *Definition:* Support or encouragement given to someone or something by a person of influence; customers collectively; the power to distribute government or political positions.
    Etymology: patronus (Medieval Latin), "patron" + *age* (Old French), "condition of"
    Synonyms: sponsorship, backing, support; clientele
11. *Definition:* (*adj.*) Traveling from place to place; (*n.*) a wanderer.
    Etymology: itinerans, itinerantis (Latin), "journeying"; from *iter, itineris* (Latin), "journey"
    Synonyms: (*adj.*) wandering, peripatetic, nomadic; (*n.*) nomad, gypsy
    Antonyms: (*adj.*) fixed, settled, stationary; (*n.*) a stay-at-home
12. *Definition:* Having the title but not the power; in name only.
    Etymology: titulus (Latin), "title" + *-aris, -are* (Latin), "relating to"
    Synonyms: nominal, token; formal, honorary
    Antonyms: real, actual
13. *Definition:* (*n.*) Militant adherence to a party, cause, idea, or person.
    Etymology: partigiano (Italian), "partisan"; from *pars, partis* (Latin), "part" + *ship* (Middle English), "state, quality, or condition of"
    Synonyms: (*n.*) supporter, follower
14. *Definition:* The state or quality of being full of longing or yearning.
    Etymology: blend of *wishful* and *wistly* (obsolete English), "intently"

Synonyms: melancholy, pensiveness, introspectiveness
Antonyms: blitheness, cheerfulness
15. *Definition:* A high degree of elegance or polish.
    Etymology: re (Latin), "again" + *finitus* (Latin), "finish" + *-mentum* (Latin), "state or act of"
    Synonyms: polish, finish; culture, sophistication; subtlety, delicacy
    Antonyms: roughness, crudeness; vulgarity

Lesson 23 (pages 371–388)

Exercise V.   Word Roundup (page 382)
1. a. A person who always agrees with an authority figure or superior, usually for personal advantage.
   b. A person who is obsessed with fantasies of having wealth or power.
   c. A person who is obsessed with one subject or idea.
   d. A person whose popularity, success, or fame is gone.
   e. A person who takes advantage of circumstances or opportunities for self-advancement with no regard for principles.
   f. A person afflicted with a mental illness characterized by delusions of being persecuted or being greater than he/she is.
   g. A person who conforms to the patterns of his/her time or superiors in order to gain advancement.
   h. A person who sets excessively high standards and is dissatisfied with results that do not meet those standards.
2. a. To shout a loud and public protest.
   b. To give in to or acknowledge defeat.
   c. To ignore or refuse to see something obvious.
   d. To act aloof in order to indicate disapproval.
   e. To seize the opportunity.
   f. To have a mind that is obsessed or preoccupied with a single subject.
3. a. See answer to V, 3, page 363 of the student text.
   b. A joke that is obscene or otherwise offensive.
   c. Automatic approval of something; someone who habitually gives such approval.
   d. A film that contains excessive violence, offensive language, or explicit sexual situations.
4. a. See answer to V, 2, c, page 319 of the student text.
   b. See answer to V, 4, f, page 251 of the student text.
   c. Abreast of times; up-to-date.
5. a. See page 372 of the student text.
   b. See page 373 of the student text.
6. See page 375 of the student text.

Exercise (page 385)

1. a. See e on page 383 of the student text.
   b. See f on page 383 of the student text.
   c. See b on page 383 of the student text.
   d. *Definition:* To prevent or dispose of effectively by previous action. *Meaning of* ob: against
   e. See b on page 383 of the student text.
   f. See a on page 383 of the student text.
   g. See d on page 383 of the student text.
   h. *Definition:* Excessively offensive or disagreeable. *Meaning of* ob: to; toward
   i. *Definition:* To haunt, harass, or bedevil. *Meaning of* ob: in front of; before; on
   j. See f on page 383 of the student text.
   k. See b on page 383 of the student text.
   l. *Definition:* To force oneself upon without invitation. *Meaning of* ob: against
2. a. See b on page 385 of the student text.
   b. *Definition:* A curve formed by points on a fixed line that are equidistant from other points not on the line. *Meaning of* para: beside
   c. See c on page 385 of the student text.
   d. *Definition:* An organism that is dependent upon another for survival while contributing nothing to its host; such a person. *Meaning of* para: beside
   e. See b on page 385 of the student text.
   f. See d on page 385 of the student text.
   g. *Definition:* A fixed limit or boundary; an arbitrary constant in a mathematical expression. *Meaning of* para: alongside
   h. *Definition:* (*n.*) A person the lower half of whose body is completely paralyzed; (*adj.*) completely paralyzed from the waist down. *Meaning of* para: beside
   i. See 3, a, on page 384 of the student text.
3. a. Paramilitary: Designating an extra-military group or force organized along military lines and often used as an auxiliary to regular military forces. *Para* ("alongside") indicates that the group in question is outside, but in many ways parallel to, the regular military.
   b. See 3, a, on page 384 of the student text.

c. Paramedical: Relating to auxiliary medical personnel (paramedics). *Para* ("alongside") indicates that the force in question is auxiliary.
   d. See 3, a, on page 384 of the student text.

Exercise I.   More of Our Greek Heritage (page 387)

1. *Definition:* The principal character in a drama or story; any principal or leading figure.
   Etymology: protos (Greek), "first" + *agonistes* (Greek), "actor"
2. *Definition:* Happening fitfully; convulsive.
   Etymology: spasmos (Greek), "spasm" + -*ikos* (Greek), "characterized by"
3. *Definition:* Having a severe mental illness, frequently involving withdrawal from reality.
   Etymology: psyche (Greek), "soul" + -*otikos* (Greek), "related to"
4. *Definition:* Despotic or oppressive.
   Etymology: tyrannos (Greek), "tyrant" + -*ical* (English), "like"
5. *Definition:* An argument or controversy designed to refute a specific opinion or doctrine.
   Etymology: polemos (Greek), "war" + -*ikos* (Greek), "having the quality of"
6. *Definition:* Extreme sluggishness or laziness.
   Etymology: lethargos (Greek), "torpor" + -*ikos* (Greek), "characterized by"
7. *Definition:* Having the power to heal or cure.
   Etymology: therapeutes (Greek), "healer" + -*ikos* (Greek), "characteristic of"
8. *Definition:* (*v.*) To copy or imitate, frequently with the intent to ridicule; (*n.*) one who copies or imitates.
   Etymology: mimos (Greek), "imitator" + -*ikos* (Greek), "characteristic of"
9. *Definition:* The study or act of correct speaking or writing; exaggerated or pretentious language.
   Etymology: rhetor (Greek), "orator" + -*ikos* (Greek), "characteristic of"
10. *Definition:* Rhythmic physical exercises performed to improve body tone and condition.
   Etymology: kalos (Greek), "beautiful" + *sthenos* (Greek), "strength" + -*ikos* (Greek). "characteristic of"
11. *Definition:* (*adj.*) Speaking, writing, or composed in several languages; (*n.*) a person with a knowledge of several languages; a book in several languages; a mixture of languages.
   Etymology: polys (Greek), "many" + *glotta* (Greek), "tongue"
12. *Definition:* Harmful or poisonous.

Etymology: toxicum (Late Latin), "poison for arrows"; from *toxon* (Greek), "bow" + *-ikos* (Greek), "relating to"

13. *Definition:* Fearful or contemptuous of foreigners or strangers.
Etymology: xenos (Greek), "stranger" + *phobos* (Greek), "fear"

14. *Definition:* An image that is only an illusion and not real.
Etymology: phantasma (Greek), "specter"; from *phantazein* (Greek), "make visible"

15. *Definition:* A prayer consisting of phrases recited by a leader alternating with responses by a congregation; a repetitive recital.
Etymology: litaneia (Greek), "entreaty"

16. *Definition:* Native to a particular place; aboriginal.
Etymology: autos (Greek), "same" + *khthon* (Greek), "earth" + *ous*

17. *Definition:* A complete suit of armor or ceremonial dress; any magnificent array.
Etymology: pan (Greek), "all" + *hoplon* (Greek), "weapon; instrument"

18. *Definition:* Pertaining to a figure of speech that uses a comparison or analogy to suggest a likeness.
Etymology: meta (Greek), "involving change" + *pherein* (Greek), "bear" + *ikos*

19. *Definition:* A surface decoration created by setting small pieces of colored material into mortar.
Etymology: mouseion (Late Greek), "mosaic"; from *mouseios* (Greek), "belonging to the muses"

20. *Definition:* Relating to moving bodies and the forces and energy they create.
Etymology: kinetikos (Greek), "moving"; from *kinein* (Greek), "move" + *ikos*

21. *Definition:* A traditional story or popular tradition dealing with heroes, ancestors, or supernatural beings that reflects a people's beliefs or practices; any fictitious story, person, or thing.
Etymology: mythos (Greek), "myth"

22. *Definition:* Consisting of diverse parts or elements; mixed.
Etymology: heteros (Greek), "other" + *genos* (Greek), "kind, sort"

23. *Definition:* (*adj.*) Having a musical or poetic quality; (*n.*) a lyric poem; the words to a song.
Etymology: lyra (Greek), "lyre" + *ikos*

24. *Definition:* See page 462 of the student text.

25. *Definition:* A serious drama or literary work that describes the downfall of the protagonist as the result of his/her own weaknesses or mis

deeds; any dramatic calamity, especially if it has moral overtones.
Etymology: tragos (Greek), "goat" + *oide* (Greek), "song"

26. *Definition:* Needless repetition of a word, phrase, or idea.
Etymology: tauto (Greek), "the same" + *logos* (Greek), "word"

27. *Definition:* Showing a slow and sluggish temperament.
Etymology: phlegma, phlegmatos (Greek), "flame; body heat" + *-ikos*

28. *Definition:* A tubular optical instrument constructed with mirrors and bits of colored glass that, when rotated, creates an endless variety of patterns.
Etymology: kalos (Greek), "beautiful" + *eidos* (Greek), "form" + *skopein* (Greek), "see"

29. *Definition:* A specifically defined division within a group or classification.
Etymology: kategoria (Greek), "public accusation"; from *kata* (Greek), "against" + *agora* (Greek), "assembly"

30. *Definition:* The outward limits or region within a precise boundary.
Etymology: peripheres (Greek), "a carrying around"; from *peri* (Greek), "around" + *pherein* (Greek), "carry"

Exercise II.   Ecclesiastically Speaking (page 388)

1. *Definition:* The misuse or desecration of something sacred.
Etymology: sacer (Latin), "sacred" + *legere* (Latin), "gather; steal"

2. *Definition:* A formal religious rite, such as baptism or matrimony.
Etymology: sacer (Latin), "sacred" + *-mentum* (Latin), "-ness"

3. *Definition:* A clergyman of high rank.
Etymology: prae (Latin), "before" + *ferre, latus* (Latin), "carry"

4. *Definition:* The people of a religious faith, as distinguished from the clergy.
Etymology: lay (from *laos* [Greek], "people") + *ity* (from *-itas* [Latin], "state of")

5. *Definition:* Pertaining to a church or established religious group.
Etymology: ekklesia (Greek), "assembly of citizens; church" + *-astos* (Greek), "one who" + *-ical*

6. *Definition:* Pertaining to the spiritual care and guidance of a congregation; pertaining to shepherds and rural life.
Etymology: pastor (Latin), "shepherd" + *-alis, -ale* (Latin), "relating to"

7. *Definition:* The established form of a religious service.

Etymology: leitourgia (Greek), "public service"; from *laos* (Greek), "people" + *ergon* (Greek), "work"

8. *Definition:* Worldwide in influence; relating to the cooperation or unity of all churches.
   Etymology: oikoumene (Greek), "inhabited world"; from *oikein* (Greek), "dwell; inhabit"

9. *Definition:* The district under the jurisdiction of a bishop.
   Etymology: diokesis (Greek), "administration"; from *dia* (Greek), "through; apart" + *oikein* (Greek), "dwell, inhabit"

10. *Definition:* Relating to monasteries, monks, nuns, or other persons living in religious seclusion.
    Etymology: monazein (Greek), "live alone" + *ikos*; from *monos* (Greek), "alone"

11. *Definition:* Pertaining to or required by the established religious code.
    Etymology: kanon (Greek), "model" + *-ical*

12. *Definition:* See answer V, 8, page 368 of the student text.
    Etymology: pente (Greek), "five" + *konte*, "times ten" + *-alis, -ale* (Latin), "relating to"

13. *Definition:* The study of God and religious belief.
    Etymology: theos (Greek), "god" + *logia* (Greek) "study of; science of"

14. *Definition:* The customary or prescribed form for a religious ceremony.
    Etymology: ritus (Latin), "rite"

15. *Definition:* Relating to a bishop or church government by bishops.
    Etymology: episkopos (Greek), "overseer"; from *epi* (Greek), "over" + *skopos* (Greek), "watcher"

Exercise III. Manias (page 388)

1. *Definition:* An irresistible impulse to start fires.
   Etymology: pyr (Greek), "fire" + *mania* (Greek), "madness"

2. *Definition:* an exaggerated preoccupation with acquiring books.
   Etymology: biblion (Greek), "book" + *mania* (Greek), "madness"

3. *Definition:* An obsessive impulse to steal, especially when there is no great need or desire for what is stolen.
   Etymology: kleptein (Greek), "steal" + *mania* (Greek), "madness"

4. *Definition:* An insatiable craving for alcoholic beverages.
   Etymology: dipsa (Greek), "thirst" + *mania* (Greek), "madness"

5. *Definition:* An excessive preoccupation with oneself; extreme egoism.
   Etymology: ego (Latin), "I" + *mania* (Greek), "madness"

6. *Definition:* A psychopathological condition characterized by delusions of power, greatness, or wealth; an obsession with doing grand or extravagant things.
   Etymology: megas, megalos (Greek), "great" + *mania* (Greek), "madness"

Exercise IV. Expanding Your Word Power (page 388)

1. *Definition:* Appealing to or stimulating sexual desire.
   Etymology: salax, salacis (Latin), "lustful; fond of leaping"; from *salire* (Latin), "leap"
   Synonyms: lustful, libidinous; bawdy, ribald
   Antonyms: decent, decorous, dignified, tasteful

2. *Definition:* greasy or oily; insincerely earnest.
   Etymology: unctum (Latin), "ointment; oil" + *-osus* (Latin), "full of"
   Synonyms: slippery, smooth; glib; fawning, obsequious
   Antonyms: dry; rough; sincere

3. *Definition:* Compelling; caused by an irresistible impulse.
   Etymology: cum (Latin), "together; completely" + *pellere, pulsus* (Latin), "drive" + *-ivus* (Latin), "relating to"
   Synonyms: obsessive, overwhelming

4. *Definition:* No longer living or in existence.
   Etymology: de (Latin), "completely" + *fungi, functus* (Latin), "discharge"
   Synonyms: obsolete, extinct, dead
   Antonyms: extant, living, alive, operational

5. *Definition:* Thrusting in rudely or inappropriately.
   Etymology: in (Latin), "in" + *trudere, trusus* (Latin), "thrust" + *-ivus* (Latin), "inclined to"
   Synonyms: intruding, interruptive, meddlesome, interfering
   Antonyms: discrete; aloof, standoffish

6. *Definition:* A prophetic sign of good or evil.
   Etymology: omen, ominis (Latin), "portent"
   Synonyms: portent, foreboding, presentiment

7. *Definition:* Occurring at an inappropriate time.
   Etymology: un + time + ly
   Synonyms: inopportune, ill-timed
   Antonyms: timely, opportune, well-timed

8. *Definition:* (v.) To claim or profess to be; (n.) the apparent meaning, significance, or purpose of something.
   Etymology: porporter (Old French), "embody"; from *pro* (Latin), "forth" + *portare* (Latin), "carry"
   Synonyms: (v.) allege; (n.) import, sense, gist

9. *Definition:* (v.) To banish from one's home or country; (n.) forced removal from one's home or country; a person so banished.
Etymology: exilium (Latin), "exile" and *exul* (Latin), "an exiled person"
Synonyms: (v.) expel, deport, expatriate; (n.) outcast, expatriate, émigré

10. *Definition:* Din or commotion.
Etymology: tumultus (Latin), "commotion"; from *tumere* (Latin), "swell"
Synonyms: uproar, hubbub; disturbance, ruckus; agitation, disquiet
Antonyms: silence, calm, tranquility, placidity; orderliness

11. *Definition:* Pertaining to an island; having a restricted or isolated outlook.
Etymology: insula (Latin), "island" + *-aris, -are* (Latin), "relating to; like"
Synonyms: detached, isolated; parochial, provincial
Antonyms: cosmopolitan, catholic

12. *Definition:* A literary work that attacks or ridicules human vice and folly by means of irony and wit.
Etymology: satura/satira (Latin), "medley; full plate"; from *satur, saturis* (Latin), "full of food"
Synonyms: parody, travesty, burlesque, lampoon

13. *Definition:* (v.) to make an identical copy of; (n.) an identical copy; (adj.) identical
Etymology: duo (Latin), "two" + *plicare, plicatus* (Latin), "fold"
Synonyms: (v.) copy, reproduce; (n.) facsimile, replica; (adj.) twin, same
Antonyms: (v.) vary, change; (n.) an original; (adj.) unalike, different, dissimilar

14. *Definition:* Full of significance (either good or bad) for the future.
Etymology: portentum (Latin), "omen" + *-osus* (Latin), "full of"
Synonyms: momentous; ominous
Antonyms: insignificant, nugatory

15. *Definition:* Carefully considering or examining one's own thoughts.
Etymology: intro (Latin), "inside; within" + *specere, spectus* (Latin), "look" + *-ivus* (Latin), "tending to"
Synonyms: reflective, thoughtful, contemplative
Antonyms: extroverted, outgoing, gregarious, unself-critical

Lesson 24 (pages 389–405)

Exercise V. Word Roundup (page 398)

1. In the selection of a jury, the right of either of the lawyers involved in the case (*i.e.*, prosecution. defense) arbitrarily to refuse to accept a prospective juror without offering any reason for this refusal.

2. See page 391 of the student text.
3. See page 392 of the student text.
4. a. To admit or concede defeat.
   b. To maintain an opinion, position, or course of action despite a great deal of opposition from others.
   c. To take foolhardy or unnecessary chances or risks.
   d. To feign grief.
5. a. An exceptionally talented youngster.
   b. A shortage or deficit, especially of money; the amount of the deficit.
   c. A person whose skills, talents, or beauty develop later in life than is customary.
   d. A short sketch performed on the stage before the main production begins; any preliminary event.

Exercise I. Common Phobias
(page 402)

1. *Definition:* Fear of cats.
   Etymology: ailouros (Greek), "cat" + *phobos* (Greek), "fear"
2. *Definition:* Fear of being alone.
   Etymology: monos (Greek), "alone" + *phobos*
3. *Definition:* Fear of water.
   Etymology: hydor (Greek), "water"+ *phobos*
4. *Definition:* Fear of being in high places.
   Etymology: akros (Greek), "topmost; highest" + *phobos*
5. *Definition:* Fear of open spaces.
   Etymology: agora (Greek), "open space; marketplace" + *phobos*
6. *Definition:* Fear or dislike of strangers or foreigners.
   Etymology: xenos (Greek), "foreign; stranger" + *phobos*
7. *Definition:* Fear or dislike of women.
   Etymology: gyne (Greek), "woman" + *phobos*
8. *Definition:* Fear of darkness or the night.
   Etymology: nyx (Greek), "night" + *phobos*
9. *Definition:* Fear or dislike of the people or culture of England.
   Etymology: Angli (Latin), "the English people" + *phobos*
10. *Definition:* Dislike of books.
    Etymology: biblion (Greek), "book" + *phobos*
11. *Definition:* Fear of the number thirteen.
    Etymology: treis (Greek), "three" + *kai* (Greek), "and" + *deka* (Greek), "ten" + *phobos*
12. *Definition:* Fear of dogs.
    Etymology: kyon, kynos (Greek), "dog" + *phobos*
13. *Definition:* Fear of spiders.
    Etymology: arachne (Greek), "spider" + *phobos*
14. *Definition:* Fear of thunder.
    Etymology: keraunos (Greek), "thunder" + *phobos*

15. *Definition:* Fear of snakes.
    Etymology: ophidia (Late Latin),
    "snakes" (from *ophis* [Greek],
    "snake") + *phobos*

Exercise II.   Words Based on Philos
(page 402)

1. *Definition:* The love and pursuit of
   wisdom by intellectual means;
   the investigation into the nature
   of things; a synthesis of beliefs
   and theories.
   Etymology: philos (Greek), "loving" +
   sophia (Greek), "wisdom"
2. *Definition:* A stamp collector.
   Etymology: philos (Greek), "loving" +
   ateles (Greek), "tax-free" (a
   learned translation of words on
   old postmarks); from *a* (Greek),
   "without" + *telos* (Greek), "charge"
3. *Definition:* A person who loves or
   admires the people or culture of
   France.
   Etymology: Francus (Latin), "French-
   man" + *philos* (Greek), "loving"
4. *Definition:* A hereditary blood defect
   (primarily affecting males) characterized by excessive bleeding
   and difficulty in blood clotting.
   Etymology: haima (Greek), "blood;
   bleeding" + *philia* (New Latin,
   from Greek), "tendency toward"
   (from *philos* [Greek], "loving")
5. *Definition:* Love of mankind; the
   effort to promote human welfare
   by charitable acts.
   Etymology: philos (Greek), "loving" +
   anthropos (Greek), "man; human
   being"
6. *Definition:* The study of language,
   including literature.
   Etymology: philos (Greek), "loving" +
   logos (Greek), "word"
7. *Definition:* Devoted to or apprecia-
   tive of music; relating to a symphony orchestra.
   Etymology: philos (Greek), "loving" +
   harmonia (Greek), "harmony" +
   -ikos (Greek), "relating to"
8. *Definition:* A person who collects
   phonograph records.
   Etymology: diskos (Greek), "disc" +
   philos (Greek), "loving"
9. *Definition:* A person who loves or
   admires the people or culture of
   England.
   Etymology: Angli (Latin), "the
   English people" + *philos* (Greek),
   "loving"
10. *Definition:* To engage in casual love
    affairs.
    Etymology: philos (Greek), "loving" +
    aner, andro (Greek), "man; male"

Exercise III.   A Verbal Diversion
(page 402)

1. Pertaining to cats; supple, sly, or
   stealthy.
2. Pertaining to dogs; faithful, affectionate.
3. Pertaining to horses.
4. Pertaining to cows; patient, stolid.
5. Pertaining to lions; strong, majestic,
   fierce.
6. Pertaining to foxes; cunning, artful.
7. Pertaining to wolves; ravenous,
   fierce.
8. Pertaining to rabbits or hares;
   timid, skittish.
9. Pertaining to sheep; docile, stupid.
10. Pertaining to elephants; huge,
    massive, ponderous.
11. Pertaining to pigs; chubby, sloppy,
    self-indulgent.
12. Pertaining to peacocks; colorful,
    vain, ostentatious.
13. Pertaining to serpents; sinuous,
    undulating.
14. Pertaining to bears; awkward, gruff.
15. Pertaining to monkeys; antic, zany.
16. Pertaining to bulls; large, strong,
    aggressive.
17. Pertaining to fish.
18. Pertaining to geese; stupid, silly.

Exercise IV.   Colorful Phrases
(page 403)

In addition to an unabridged dictionary,
the following may prove helpful in doing this exercise; *Morris Dictionary of
Word and Phrase Origins*, 2d ed.;
Brewer's Dictionary of Phrase and Fable,
16th ed.; Makkai, Boatner, and Gates:
A Dictionary of American Idioms, 3d ed.

1. To make an excessively careful
   examination of the value of a present and complain if it is not perfect.
2. A nasty person who will prevent
   another from using or having something and yet refuses it him/herself.
3. To lose esteem in the eyes of others.
4. To take from one person in order to
   give to another; to pay one debt by
   incurring another.
5. To reprimand or scold someone.
6. To be satisfied with what one has
   already achieved and refrain from
   making further efforts.
7. A hidden enemy or danger.
8. To put all one's time, energy, money,
   or hopes into one enterprise, person,
   or thing to the exclusion of all else.
9. To find and argue about insignificant matters as if they were really
   important.
10. To forget about one's pride; to
    humble oneself.

11. To pay far too much for something.
12. To become uncontrollably angry or excited.
13. In a few words; concisely; briefly.
14. To use whatever money one gets as quickly as it comes in without having any extra for luxuries or the future.
15. To buy something sight unseen.
16. To give something low priority; to put aside until a future time.

Exercise V. Expanding Your Word Power (page 403)

1. *Definition:* Likely but not certain to happen; dependent upon other circumstances.
   Etymology: contingens, contingentis (Latin), "touching"; from *cum* (Latin), "together" + *tangere* (Latin), "touch"
   Synonyms: possible, provisional, tentative, dependent
   Antonyms: sure, certain, definite; unlikely, improbable, impossible
2. *Definition:* Having no exceptions or qualifications.
   Etymology: categoria (Greek), "affirmation" + *-ikos* (Greek), "like" + *-alis, -ale* (Latin), "relating to"
   Synonyms: absolute, unequivocal, unconditional
   Antonyms: qualified, provisional, conditional
3. *Definition:* Ruling with absolute power and authority.
   Etymology: despotes (Greek), "master; lord" + *-ikos* (Greek), "like; relating to"
   Synonyms: autocratic, tyrannical, dictatorial
   Antonyms: kindly, merciful, tolerant, indulgent
4. *Definition:* To wet thoroughly; to influence or penetrate deeply.
   Etymology: imbuere (Latin), "moisten; stain"
   Synonyms: saturate, permeate, pervade, tinge; inculcate, implant
5. *Definition:* Conducive to health and well-being.
   Etymology: salubris (Latin), "healthy" + *-osus* (Latin), "full of; pertaining to"
   Synonyms: healthful, beneficial, salutary, wholesome
   Antonyms: harmful, detrimental, deleterious
6. *Definition:* To stop doing something.
   Etymology: de (Latin), "from" + *sistere* (Latin), "stop; stand"
   Synonyms: cease, quit, refrain from, abstain
   Antonyms: persist, persevere, continue
7. *Definition:* A natural attraction or similarity between two things.

Etymology: affinitas (Latin), "marital relationship; neighborhood"; from *ad* (Latin), "near to" + *finis* (Latin), "border" + *-itas, -itatis* (Latin), "state of"
   Synonyms: predilection, penchant; resemblance, likeness
   Antonyms: aversion, distaste; dissimilarity
8. *Definition:* Mournful to a laughable degree.
   Etymology: lugubris (Latin), "mournful" + *-osus* (Latin), "full of"
   Synonyms: lachrymose, doleful, funereal
   Antonyms: merry, jocund, cheerful
9. *Definition:* (v.) To supply to excess; (n.) an excess;
   Etymology: sur (Old French), "over" + *faire, fait* (Old French), "do; make"
   Synonyms: (v.) cloy, glut, satiate; (n.) glut, superfluity, superabundance
   Antonyms: (v.) want, lack; (n.) scarcity, paucity, deficiency
10. *Definition:* Expressing sorrow or mourning; relating to such poetry.
   Etymology: elegeia (Greek), "elegy" + *-ikos* (Greek), "like; related to"
   Synonyms: poignant, mournful, melancholy
   Antonyms: upbeat, cheerful; humorous, funny
11. *Definition:* Unable to be captured, shaken, or criticized.
   Etymology: in (Latin), "not" + *prehendere, prehensus* (Latin), "capture" + *-abilis, -abile* (Latin), "able to"
   Synonyms: invulnerable, unassailable
   Antonyms: vulnerable, open to attack
12. *Definition:* To rob or seize by force; to despoil.
   Etymology: piller (Old French), "tear up; maltreat" + *-age* (Old French), "act of"
   Synonyms: plunder, loot, sack
13. *Definition:* Collectively, the consequences or results of something, especially a disaster or misfortune.
   Etymology: aefter (Old English), "after" + *maeth* (Old English), "mowing"
   Synonyms: effects, outcome, upshot, repercussions
   Antonyms: prelude, preliminaries
14. *Definition:* A theory or conjecture designed to account for a set of facts and used as the basis for further investigation; an assumption used as the basis for action.
   Etymology: hypothesis (Greek), "proposal; suggestion"; from *hypotithenai* (Greek), "suppose"; from *hypo* (Greek), "beneath" + *tithenai* (Greek), "place"

Synonyms: theory, premise; assumption

Antonyms: a fact, a certainty

15. *Definition:* To put forward as fact or truth.

   Etymology: ponere, positus (Latin), "put, place"

   Synonyms: postulate, propound, assert

Lesson 25 (pages 406–425)

Exercise V.   Word Roundup (page 416)

1. a. See answer to IV, 3, page 368 of the student text. Latin.
   b. Authoritatively. (The expression is most often used of solemn or official papal pronouncements.) Latin.
   c. A pseudonym used for literary purposes. French.
   d. See answer to V, 2, a, page 319 of the student text. French.
   e. A fictitious name taken by a soldier who for some reason wishes to conceal his/her true identity; any fictitious name taken in pursuit of a particular course of action. French.
   f. See answer to V, 2, b, page 319 of the student text. French.
2. a. Samuel Langhorne Clemens (1835–1910)
   b. William Sydney Porter (1862–1910)
   c. Jean-Baptiste Poquelin (1622–1673)
   d. François-Marie Arouet (1694–1778)
   e. Mary Ann Evans (1819–1880)
   f. Hector Hugh Munro (1870–1916)
3. a. See page 420 of the student text.
   b. See page 422 of the student text.
   c. See page 414 of the student text.
4. a. One of the twelve peers of Charlemagne's court; any heroic champion.
   b. See page 408 of the student text.
   c. See page 462 of the student text.
   d. A figurative purification or purging of the emotions, often through art; a psychoanalytical technique for relieving anxiety or tension by bringing repressed material to the surface; a purging of the digestive tract.
   e. Spirit; pluck; mettle.
   f. A semicircular instrument used for determining angles in geometry.
5. a. A high-minded but impractical proposal that will therefore never come to fruition; an empty promise.
   b. Deceit or trickery, especially in business dealings.
   c. To put aside the draft of proposed legislation for future consideration.
   d. A political campaign launched against one's opponents on the pretext of investigating activities subversive to the state.

Exercise (pages 421–422)

1. a. See 1, a on page 417 of the student text.
   b. See 1, a on page 417 of the student text.
   c. See 1, b on page 417 of the student text.
   d. See 1, b on page 418 of the student text.
   e. See 1, c on page 418 of the student text.
   f. See 1, d on page 418 of the student text.
3. a. See 3, a on page 419 of the student text.
   b. See 3, a on page 420 of the student text.
   c. See 3, a on page 420 of the student text.
   d. See 3, b on page 421 of the student text.
   e. See 3, d on page 421 of the student text.
   f. *Definition:* In favor of the philosophy of Karl Marx and its goals.
   Meaning of pro: in favor of
5. See pages 418 and 421 of the student text.

Exercise I.   Our Latin Heritage (page 424)

1. *Definition:* To renounce under oath; to repudiate.
   Etymology: ab (Latin), "away" + *jurare* (Latin), "swear"
2. *Definition:* (*adj.*) Not yet mature or fully developed; young or youthful; (*n.*) a youngster.
   Etymology: juvenis (Latin), "young; a youth" + *-ilis, -ile* (Latin), "related to; like"
3. *Definition:* Present and capable of activity but not yet evident or active.
   Etymology: latens, latentis (Latin), "lying hidden," the present participle of *latere* (Latin), "lie hidden"
4. *Definition:* Imperviousness to light; impenetrability or obscurity.
   Etymology: opacus (Latin), "dark" + *-itas, -itatis* (Latin), "state of"
5. *Definition:* Lying; deceitful, false.
   Etymology: mendax, mendacis (Latin), "lying" + *-osus* (Latin), "full of"
6. *Definition:* To force oneself on others with undue insistence or without invitation; to push forward.
   Etymology: ob (Latin), "against" + *trudere* (Latin), "thrust"
7. *Definition:* A long duration of life; length of life.
   Etymology: longus (Latin), "long" + *aevum* (Latin), "age; lifetime"
8. *Definition:* To swing back and forth in a steady rhythm.
   Etymology: oscillare, oscillatus (Latin), "swing"

9. *Definition:* To provide with a reason to act.
   Etymology: movere, motus (Latin), "move" + *-ivus* (Latin), "causing" + *-are, -atus* (Latin), "make; do"
10. *Definition:* The path of one celestial body or man-made satellite as it revolves around another; (*v.*) to revolve around.
    Etymology: orbita (Latin), "track; rut"; from *orbs, orbis* (Latin), "circle"
11. *Definition:* Afflicted with rabies; fanatical or uncontrollable.
    Etymology: rabidus (Latin), "raving"; from *rabere* (Latin), "rave"
12. *Definition:* The point where two things are joined or come together; a point or interval of time; the transition from one sound to another.
    Etymology: jungere, junctus (Latin), "join" + *-ura* (Latin), "that which"
13. *Definition:* Able to cause death.
    Etymology: lethum (Latin), "death" + *-alis, -ale* (Latin), "relating to"
14. *Definition:* A person who wields power and influence in business or industry.
    Etymology: magnas, magnatis (Latin), "great person"; from *magnus* (Latin), "great"
15. *Definition:* Emitting light, glowing; clear and intelligible.
    Etymology: lumen, lumenis (Latin), "light" + *-osus* (Latin), "full of"
16. *Definition:* Pertaining to, active during, or occurring at night.
    Etymology: nocturnus (Latin), "at night" + *-alis, -ale* (Latin), "relating to"; from *nox, noctis* (Latin), "night"
17. *Definition:* An opening, such as a mouth, vent, or hole.
    Etymology: os, oris (Latin), "mouth" + *facere* (Latin), "make"
18. *Definition:* To ripen or mature; to discharge pus.
    Etymology: maturus (Latin), "ripe" + *-are, -atus* (Latin), "make"
19. *Definition:* A person who is authorized to act on behalf of another; a substitute.
    Etymology: proxcy (Middle English), a contraction of *pro* (Latin), "on behalf of; for" + *curare, curatus* (Latin), "care" + *-(t)io, -(t)ionis* (Latin), "act of"
20. *Definition:* Foul-smelling, rotten; morally corrupt.
    Etymology: putridus (Latin), "rotten"; from *putrere* (Latin), "be rotten"
21. *Definition:* To accost or harass; to disturb or annoy.
    Etymology: molestus (Latin), "annoying; burdensome"; + *-are, -atus* (Latin), "make"
22. *Definition:* The state of not supporting, favoring, or being allied with either side in a conflict.

Etymology: neuter, neutri (Latin), "neither of two" + *-alis, -ale* (Latin), "relating to" + *-itas, -itatis* (Latin), "state of"
23. See answer to IV, 8, page 388 of the student text.
24. *Definition:* To name or list; to count one by one.
    Etymology: enumerare, enumeratus (Latin), "count out;" from *ex* (Latin), "out" + *numerus* (Latin), "number" + *-are, -atus* (Latin), "make"
25. *Definition:* (*adj.*) Unable to speak; unspoken or not expressed; (*n.*) a person who cannot speak; a silent letter; a plosive letter (stop); (*v.*) to soften or tone down.
    Etymology: mutus (Latin), "silent; dumb"
26. *Definition:* Commonly assumed or supposed.
    Etymology: putare, putatus (Latin), "think; consider" + *-ivus* (Latin), "inclined to"
27. *Definition:* To crush into fine powder; to demolish.
    Etymology: pulvis, pulveris (Latin), "dust; powder" + *ize*
28. *Definition:* A person who lives completely withdrawn from society or the world.
    Etymology: re (Latin), "completely" + *claudere, clausus* (Latin), "close"
29. *Definition:* Tasting or smelling foul or unpleasant from decomposed oils or fats.
    Etymology: rancidus (Latin), "smelly; rotten"; from *rancere* (Latin), "stink"
30. *Definition:* An authoritative command or order; a statute or regulation; a long-established custom.
    Etymology: ordinans, ordinantis (Latin), "putting in order"; from *ordo, ordinis* (Latin), "order" + *-are, -atus* (Latin), "make"

Exercise II. Verbal Pollution
(pages 424–425)
1. a. Intentional confusion or obscurity.
   b. False and misleading; not genuine.
   c. To disguise or conceal the real nature of; to feign.
   d. Contamination with noxious substances.
   e. Here, the proper balance or relationship between language, meaning, and communication.
   f. Unjustified; groundless
   g. To twist or misrepresent.
   h. Unusual; unparalleled.
   i. Power; influence.
   j. Unhealthy side effects or developments.
   k. Vague; hazy.
   l. Relating to language and word usage.
   m. Unintentional; accidental.

n. To add to or append in order to improve or make more complete.

o. Here, nonmilitary.

2. a. I lied, so ignore what I said.

   b. Many people are going to lose their jobs during this recession.

   c. We must simply accept the fact that industrial development inevitably results in increased pollution.

Exercise III. Expanding Your Word Power (page 425)

1. *Definition:* Profit or privilege received in addition to regular wages or salary; something claimed as an exclusive right.
   Etymology: perquisitum (Medieval Latin), "an acquisition"; from *per* (Latin), "thoroughly" + *quaerere* (Latin), "seek, search"
   Synonyms: bonus, fringe benefit
   Antonyms: occupational hazard, disadvantage

2. *Definition:* Underhanded or unscrupulous behavior; trickery.
   Etymology: Origin unknown.
   Synonyms: sharp practice, chicanery
   Antonyms: fair play; honesty, rectitude

3. *Definition:* To compromise or act evasively in order to gain time; to behave as circumstances dictate or to yield to current conditions.
   Etymology: temporizare (Medieval Latin), "wait one's time"; from *tempus, temporis* (Latin), "time"
   Synonyms: stall, procrastinate, shilly-shally
   Antonyms: take action on, settle, decide, dispose of, make up one's mind

4. *Definition:* A person with an extraordinary talent or skill; a marvel.
   Etymology: prodigium (Latin), "omen; marvel"
   Synonyms: genius, Einstein, wunderkind; phenomenon, wonder

5. *Definition:* To grow new buds or greenery; to expand rapidly.
   Etymology: burjon (Old French), "bud"
   Synonyms: sprout, bloom, proliferate, mushroom
   Antonyms: wither, dwindle

6. *Definition:* To spread or scatter broadly.
   Etymology: dis (Latin), "in different directions" + *semen, seminis* (Latin), "seed" + *-are, -atus* (Latin), "make; (here) cast"
   Synonyms: disperse, broadcast, circulate
   Antonyms: conceal, supress, withhold

7. *Definition:* A natural inclination towards something.

Etymology: pro (Latin), "forward" + *clivus* (Latin), "slope; hill" + *-itas, -itatis* (Latin), "state of"
   Synonyms: propensity, tendency, predilection
   Antonyms: aversion, repugnance, antipathy

8. *Definition:* Moral uprightness; correctness of judgment.
   Etymology: rectitudo, rectitudinis (Late Latin), "correctness"; from *rectus* (Latin), "straight; right"
   Synonyms: probity; impeccability, soundness, accuracy
   Antonyms: unscrupulousness; inaccuracy, unsoundness

9. *Definition:* To shorten by cutting off the extremities.
   Etymology: truncare, truncatus (Latin), "shorten"; from *truncus* (Latin), "trunk" + *-are, -atus* (Latin), "make; do"
   Synonyms: abbreviate, abridge, condense
   Antonyms: expand, augment, elongate, prolong

10. *Definition:* Spirit; courage and fortitude.
    Etymology: a variant of *metal*
    Synonyms: pluck, backbone, valor, hardihood
    Antonyms: pusillanimity, cowardice, faintheartedness

11. *Definition:* To remove harmful or objectionable material from a literary or artistic work.
    Etymology: ex (Latin), "out of" + *purgare, purgatus* (Latin), "purge; cleanse"
    Synonyms: censor, bowdlerize

12. *Definition:* To drive or throw out forcibly.
    Etymology: e(x) (Latin), "out" + *jacere, jactus* (Latin), "throw"
    Synonyms: expel, evict; reject
    Antonyms: accept, receive, welcome; absorb

13. *Definition:* To make amends for; to atone for.
    Etymology: ex (Latin), "completely" + *piare, piatus* (Latin), "appease"
    Synonyms: remedy, redress, redeem, satisfy

14. *Definition:* To suppress forcibly; to annul by judicial action.
    Etymology: casser/quasser (Old French), "annul"; from *quassare* (Latin), "shake violently" and *cassare* (Late Latin), "nullify"
    Synonyms: quell, squelch; annul, invalidate
    Antonyms: investigate, foment, provoke, incite; uphold

15. *Definition:* (*adj.*) Ideal but existing in theory only; (*n.*) a zealous but impractical reformer.
    Etymology: ou (Greek), "not" + *topos* (Greek), "place" + *(i)an* (English,

from Latin), "relating to; like." See also answer to II, A, 13, page 308 of student text.

Synonyms: (*adj.*) pie-in-the-sky, idealistic; (*n.*) visionary

Antonyms: (*adj.*) down-to-earth, realistic; (*n.*) pragmatist

Lesson 26 (pages 426–443)

Exercise V. Word Roundup
(pages 435–436)
1. See page 426 of the student text.
2. See page 427 of the student text.
3. See page 428 of the student text.
5. a. A person who resists change or refuses to give up a position or attitude.
   b. See page 431 of the student text.
   c. More nuclear power than is actually required to destroy an enemy completely; any excessive reaction or response.
   d. See page 427 of the student text.
   e. A person who renounces a faith, cause, or principle.
   f. A sudden reversion to an event or situation that happened or was depicted earlier.
6. a. To retract a statement that is embarrassing or humiliating.
   b. To disagree, oppose, or be in conflict with.
   c. To retaliate in kind; to give like for like.
   d. To adjust the circumstances or situation so that it is bearable or acceptable to a person in a helpless or disadvantaged position.
   e. To be penitent or contrite.
   f. To have an unemotional or unyielding disposition.
   g. To be flexible; to respond to difficulties or situations in a way that provides the utmost self-protection and least discomposure.
   h. To destroy, wreck, or leave in ruins.
7. a. Something in return for something given; a trade-off. Latin.
   b. A complete reversal; an about-face. French.
   c. A bitter feud. Italian.
   d. See page 429 of the student text.

Exercise I. Adjectives Derived from Proper Names (pages 439–440)
1. George Gordon, Lord Byron (1788–1824), English poet.
2. John Maynard Keynes (1883–1946), English economist.
3. Geoffrey Chaucer (ca. 1342–1400), English poet.
4. James Joyce (1882–1941), Irish author.
5. Karl Marx (1818–1883), German political philosopher and economist.
6. Aristotle (384–322 B.C.), Greek philosopher.

7. Edward VII (1841–1910), King of England (1901–1910).
8. Franz Kafka (1883–1924), Austrian novelist.
9. Thomas Jefferson (1743–1826), American author, scientist, architect, educator, diplomat, and third president of the United States (1801–1809).
10. Elizabeth I (1533–1603), Queen of England (1558–1603).
11. Plato (ca. 428–347 B.C.), Greek philosopher.
12. Saint Thomas Aquinas (1225–1274), medieval Christian theologian and philosopher.
13. Charles Dickens (1812–1870), English novelist.
14. Moses (fl. 13th century B.C.), Old-Testament Hebrew prophet and lawgiver.
15. Napoleon Bonaparte (1769–1821), emperor of France (1804–1814).
16. Socrates (ca. 470–399 B.C.), Greek philosopher.
17. Sigmund Freud (1856–1939), Austrian physician and pioneer psychoanalyst.
18. Nicolò Machiavelli (1469–1527), Italian statesman and political theorist.
19. George Bernard Shaw (1856–1950), Irish-born English playwright.
20. Charles Darwin (1809–1882), English naturalist and scientist.
21. François Rabelais (ca. 1483–1553), French satirist and humorist.

Exercise II. Our Celtic Heritage
(page 440)
1. A three-leaf clover, considered the floral emblem of Ireland.
2. A female spirit whose wailing warns a family of the impending death of one of its members; figuratively, a woman who complains too much.
3. A steep and projecting cliff or mass of rock.
4. Several families descended from a common ancestor; a large group of relatives, friends, or associates united by common interests or characteristics.
5. A dialectal or regional Irish or Scottish accent; a coarse shoe made of untanned leather.
6. A mischievous elf who, if caught, can reveal the whereabouts of treasure; figuratively, any sprightly person.
7. (*n.* and *adj.*) Cloth with a tartan or checked pattern; any pattern of unevenly spaced stripes crossing at right angles.
8. A phrase describing the nature or purpose of an organization; a catch-phrase or motto; a battle cry of the Scottish clans.

9. (*n.*) Soft, waterlogged ground; a marsh; (*v.*) to cause to sink into; to hinder or slow down.

Exercise III.   Thanks to the French
(page 441)
1. An official bulletin or announcement.
2. The body of practices or conduct prescribed by social convention; any special code of behavior or courtesy.
3. The emotional state of an individual or group, as shown in confidence, cheerfulness, willingness to perform duties, or the like.
4. A person whose career or welfare is furthered or protected by the power, influence, or wealth of another.
5. The main course of a meal; access to something desirable or normally inaccessible.
6. In relation to; face to face.
7. A talent or aptitude for something; a knack.
8. A level expanse of land elevated above the surrounding terrain; a stable period or condition; any level.
9. A large amount of water kept for future use; a place where something is stored; a reserve.
10. (*n.*) A demand by an audience for an additional or a repeat performance; the additional or repeat performance in response to audience demand; (*v.*) to give such an additional or repeat performance.
11. A strong inclination; a definite liking.
12. A distinctive class of literary, artistic, or musical composition; any type or category; a style of art concerned with scenes or subjects of everyday life.
13. Several separate elements that blend or perform together harmoniously; a coordinated outfit or costume.
14. (*n.*) A private conversation between two people; (*adv.*) in private.
15. A means of communication between different groups or organizations; a close connection or relationship.

Exercise IV.   Expanding Your Word
Power (page 441)
1. *Definition:* To take apart or tear down; to strip of.
   Etymology: dis (Latin), "apart; away" + *mantellum* (Latin), "covering"
   Synonyms: destroy, demolish; disassemble, undo
   Antonyms: assemble; erect, construct
2. *Definition:* To lay waste to; to confound.
   Etymology: de (Latin), "completely" + *vastus* (Latin), "waste" + *-are*, *-atus* (Latin), "make"
   Synonyms: ravage, wreck; flabbergast, nonplus

Antonyms: build up, establish; cheer, gladden, exhilarate
3. *Definition:* Stubbornly disobedient and rebellious.
   Etymology: contumacia (Latin), "stubbornness" + *-osus* (Latin), "full of"; from *con* (Latin), "very" + *tumere* (Latin), "swell; be proud"
   Synonyms: insolent, defiant, insubordinate
   Antonyms: cooperative, compliant, agreeable; obsequious
4. *Definition:* Using or containing too many words.
   Etymology: verbum (Latin), "word" + *-osus* (Latin), "full of"
   Synonyms: wordy, prolix; loquacious, garrulous
   Antonyms: concise, succinct; laconic
5. *Definition:* To pay back or return; to avenge.
   Etymology: re (Latin), "back" + *quiter* (obsolete English), "pay"
   Synonyms: repay, reciprocate; retaliate; get even with
6. *Definition:* (*v.*) To reply sharply or wittily; (*n.*) a sharp or witty reply; a kind of laboratory vessel.
   Etymology: re (Latin), "back" + *torquere, tortus* (Latin), "twist"
   Synonyms: (*v.*) respond, answer; retaliate, reciprocate; (*n.*) response, answer, rejoinder
7. *Definition:* involving unnecessary repetition of a word or idea.
   Etymology: tauto (Greek), "the same" + *logos* (Greek), "word" + *-ia* (Greek), "condition, state, act" + *ical*
   Synonyms: redundancy, pleonasm
8. *Definition:* Grief and repentance for sins or faults.
   Etymology: con (Latin), "thoroughly" + *terere, tritus* (Latin), "rub; wear away"
   Synonyms: penitence, sorrow, regret, remorse
9. *Definition:* A written account of experiences the author has lived through; a biographical sketch of someone the author knew.
   Etymology: mémoire (French), "memory"; from *memoria* (Latin), "memory"
   Synonyms: reminiscence(s), account, record, confession(s)
10. *Definition:* Able to float in liquid or rise in air; cheerful.
    Etymology: boyante (Spanish), "light-sailing"; ultimately from *boie* (French), "buoy"
    Synonyms: light, weightless; lighthearted, sprightly.
    Antonyms: leaden, weighty; melancholy, dejected, morose
11. *Definition:* To use up.
    Etymology: de (Latin), "un-" + *plere, pletus* (Latin), "fill"
    Synonyms: exhaust, consume, dissipate, squander

Antonyms: increase, augment; restock, replenish

12. *Definition: (n.)* A sudden and violent backward movement; an adverse reaction to a prior development; *(v.)* to cause or result in such a reaction.
    Etymology: back + lash
    Synonyms: (n.) outcry; uproar; *(v.)* boomerang, backfire

13. *Definition:* To sign; to endorse or assume financial responsibility for; to guarantee; to insure.
    Etymology: under + write
    Synonyms: initial, countersign; back, support; certify, assure

14. *Definition:* Capable of being formed, shaped, changed, or influenced.
    Etymology: malleus (Latin), "hammer" + *-abilis, -abile* (Latin), "able to"
    Synonyms: plastic, pliable, flexible, tractable
    Antonyms: inflexible, intractable, recalcitrant

15. *Definition: (n.)* A person who renounces a faith, cause, or principle; *(adj.)* guilty of renouncing a faith, cause, or principle.
    Etymology: apostates (Greek), "a deserter"; from *apo* (Greek), "away" + *histanai* (Greek), "stand"
    Synonyms: (n.) defector, renegade, traitor; *(adj.)* perfidious, unfaithful, recreant
    Antonyms: (n.) loyalist, adherent; *(adj.)* faithful, loyal

Lesson 27 (pages 444–461)

Exercise V. Word Roundup
(pages 454–455)
1. See page 451 of the student text.
2. See page 446 of the student text.
3. See page 448 of the student text.
4. a. See answer to III, 30, page 168 of the student text.
   b. A person who commits acts of sabotage.
   c. A pompous or sanctimonious person.
   d. See page 449 of the student text.
5. a. See page 445 of the student text.
   b. See page 445 of the student text.
   c. Intense reverence and admiration for a person considered to be a hero or idol.
   d. A book that teaches the basics of something.
   e. See answer to III, 1, page 96 of the student text.
   f. A strike or slowdown by workers to protest against a company practice or to enforce worker demands.
   g. See answer to V, 2, c, page 363 of the student text.
   h. An area in which one powerful nation exerts paramount influence.

6. a. To talk too much, often injudiciously.
   b. To follow conventional social rules; to conduct oneself in a stiff, formal (rather than a relaxed or natural) manner.
   c. To make oneself inconspicuous.
   d. To betray or harm a trusting or unsuspecting person, especially in a clandestine way.

Exercise (page 457)
1. a. *Definition: (adj.)* Opposing progress or liberalism; ultraconservative; *(n.)* an opponent of progress; an ultraconservative.
   Meaning of re: back; backward
   b. See 1, b on page 456 of the student text.
   c. *Definition: (n.)* To pay back; *(n.)* payment in return or compensation for a service or a favor.
   Meaning of re: back
   d. See page 446 of the student text.
   e. *Definition:* To cut down or reduce; to economize.
   Meaning of re: very, completely
   f. See 1, a on page 455 of the student text.
3. a.–d., f. See bottom of page 456 of the student text.
   e. See page 450 of the student text.
5. a. A bunt or ground ball that allows a base runner to advance though it retires the batter.
   b. The holy of holies; a private room or study where a person can remain undisturbed.
   c. See answer to III, 20, page 96 of the student text.

Exercise I. Myth and Ritual
(pages 459–461)
A.
N.B. Words are defined as used in the passage on pages 459–460.
1. Customary; established; conventional.
2. To claim.
3. Pertaining to the universe; infinitely vast.
4. A sudden large-scale calamity or disaster.
5. A rescue; salvation.
6. A buildup; an extraneous addition.
7. See fourth paragraph of the passage (top of page 460 of the student text).
8. Exacting; strict.
9. Of unknown authorship.
10. Collective; expressing the whole community's attitude.
11. Embodiment, attribution.
12. Final and therefore most significant or dearest; fundamental.
13. Artistic; relating to beauty.
14. An associate or coworker.
15. Group or class unity.
16. Relating to a society or community; social.

17. Whimsical or imaginative rather than realistic.
18. See paragraph 9 of the passage (bottom of page 460 of the student text).
19. See paragraph 8 of the passage (bottom of page 460 of student text).
20. Bigoted; prejudiced; discriminatory.
21. Dictated or ordained by custom, law, or a higher authority.
22. Breed; disseminate.
23. Broadened or increased in meaning, scope, or application; figurative.
24. Aggregate; combined.
25. Figurative; metaphorical.
26. See paragraph 9 of the passage (bottom of page 460 of the student text).
27. To contain or embrace.
28. Involving comparison; relative to something else.
29. The soul or spirit, as distinguished from the body; the mind.
30. Resulting from the practical application of scientific or industrial developments or discoveries.

B.
1. The Norse god of light; son of Odin and Frigg; regarded as the most beautiful and gracious of the gods. (The name is also spelled *Baldur.*)
2. The Toltec and Aztec god of civilization, the planet Venus, and the wind; represented the forces of good; depicted as a feathered serpent; also reputed to be a legendary ruler of the Toltecs.
3. Legendary ruler of predynastic Egypt and Egyptian god of the dead or ruler of the underworld; variously identified with the Nile, grain, the sun, the moon; represented the creative forces of nature and the imperishability of life.
4. Legendary hero of Ulster, Ireland; noted for his prodigious strength and remarkable beauty. (The name is also spelled *Cuchulain.*)
5. The Hindu god of destruction and regeneration; one of the three supreme Hindu deities. (The name is also spelled *Siva.*)
6. The Babylonian god of light and life and the creator of humankind; was the chief god of the Babylonian pantheon.
7. In Greek myth, the Titan (Giant) who stole fire from the gods, gave it to humans, and also taught humans how to use it (along with other useful arts and sciences).
8. The lengendary founder (along with his brother Remus) and first king of Rome.
9. Legendary American lumberjack; noted for his prodigious strength and enormous size; ruled a gargantuan lumber camp and owned a huge blue ox called Babe.
10. Legendary folk hero of early and medieval Germanic literature and myth; slew the dragon Fafnir, married Kriemhild (Gudrune), loved and betrayed Brünnhilde; figures prominently in both *Volsungasaga* (Norse) and *Nibelungenlied* (German).

Exercise II. A Verbal Diversion
(page 461)
1. Eloquent.
2. Reluctant to speak; reticent.
3. Stubborn; hardheaded.
4. Having flat feet; being steady on one's feet; forthright; unprepared; clumsy or awkward.
5. Impetuous or rash; easily excited.
6. Generous.
7. Overly sensitive to criticism; touchy.
8. Harsh, critical, or sarcastic.
9. Secretive; not disposed to talk.
10. Having a sincere or open face or expression; (of a sandwich) with one side uncovered by bread.
11. Having a quick or nimble touch; skilled at petty thievery.
12. Stingy; frugal; reluctant to part with money.
13. Giddy; dizzy.
14. Innocent; with the eyes completely open in wonderment.
15. Easily excited or angered; ardent or passionate; rash or reckless.

Exercise III. Expanding Your Word Power (page 461)
1. *Definition:* Wordy and tedious.
   Etymology: prolixus (Latin), "abundant"; from *pro* (Latin), "forward" + *liquere, lixus* (Latin), "be liquid; (here) pour"
   Synonyms: verbose, garrulous, loquacious
   Antonyms: concise, succinct; taciturn, laconic
2. *Definition:* To think carefully about.
   Etymology: cum (Latin), "completely" + *agitare, agitatus* (Latin), "turn (in the mind)"
   Synonyms: meditate, ponder, ruminate
3. *Definition:* The return of like for like.
   Etymology: re (Latin), "back" + *talio, talionis* (Latin), "recompense" + *-are, -atus* (Latin), "make"
   Synonyms: requital, revenge
4. *Definition: (adj.)* Reviewing or surveying the past; *(n.)* an exhibition reviewing an artist's achievements to date or in the past.
   Etymology: retro (Latin), "backwards" + *specere, spectus* (Latin), "look" + *-ivus* (Latin), "tending to"
   Synonyms: (adj.) looking back; *(n.)* review
5. *Definition: (v.)* To shrink back in fear or repugnance; to spring back; to fall back; *(n.)* the act or state of springing back.

Etymology: reculer (Old French), "spring back"; from *re* (Latin), "back" + *culus* (Latin), "buttocks"
Synonyms: (*v.*) rebound, kick back; flinch, wince; (*n.*) rebound, kick; flinching, wincing

6. *Definition:* The system of rites for public worship belonging to a religion.
   Etymology: leitourgia (Greek), "public service"; from *leos, leitos* (Greek), "people" + *ergon* (Greek), "work" + *-ia* (Greek), "things belonging to"
   Synonyms: ceremony, ritual, observance, rite

7. *Definition:* Relating to an embryo; in an early stage of development.
   Etymology: embryo, embryonis (Medieval Latin), "embryo" + *-icus* (Latin), "relating to"; from *en* (Greek), "in" + *bruein* (Greek), "grow; swell"
   Synonyms: undeveloped, incipient, rudimentary
   Antonyms: advanced, mature, full-fledged, fully developed

8. *Definition:* A tricky move designed to gain an advantage over or frustrate an opponent.
   Etymology: ploy (Scottish), "business; trick"; short for *employ*
   Synonyms: ruse, maneuver, subterfuge

9. *Definition:* (*n.*) One of the two tendons at the back of the human knee; (*v.*) to cut the hamstring of; to make ineffective or powerless.
   Etymology: ham (English), "thigh" + *string* (English), "(here) tendon"
   Synonyms: (*v.*) frustrate, thwart, sabotage, cripple, incapacitate
   Antonyms: (*v.*) facilitate, expedite; abet, assist

10. *Definition:* To speak irreverently of.
    Etymology: blasphemein (Greek), "speak evil"
    Synonyms: profane; abuse, vilify, curse
    Antonyms: praise, laud, glorify, extol

11. *Definition:* (*n.*) A person lacking in moral principles and, from a theological point of view, destined to damnation; (*adj.*) morally unprincipled; (*v.*) to disapprove of
    Etymology: re (Latin), "un-" + *probare, probatus* (Latin), "approve"
    Synonyms: blackguard, miscreant; (*adj.*) degenerate, depraved; (*v.*) reprove, censure, condemn

12. *Definition:* (*n.*) Monotonous and mechanical speech; hypocritically pious language; the special vocabulary of a particular group; (*v.*) to speak tediously; to whine; to moralize.
    Etymology: cantare (Latin), "sing"
    Synonyms: (*n.*) jargon, argot; mummery, bunk

13. *Definition:* Claiming or pretending to hold feelings or beliefs that one does not really hold.
    Etymology: hypokrites (Greek), "actor"; from *hypokritein* (Greek), "play a part"; from *hypo* (Greek), "under" + *kritein* (Greek), "separate"
    Synonyms: phony, dissembling

14. *Definition:* Unnaturally pale; languid or melancholy.
    Etymology: wann (Old English), "dusky; dark"
    Synonyms: sickly, pallid; haggard, gaunt
    Antonyms: rosy, ruddy, glowing; vibrant, lively

15. *Definition:* Predominating influence or authority, particularly of one nation over another.
    Etymology: hegemon (Greek), "leader" + *-ia* (Greek), "state or act of"
    Synonyms: dominance, suzerainty, domination, supremacy
    Antonyms: subjugation, bondage, enslavement, thralldom, subjection

Lesson 28 (pages 462–479)

Exercise V.   Word Roundup (page 473)

1. See page 462 of the student text.
2. a. The problems of aging and old people.
   b. The acquisition, maintenance, and transport of (usually) military materials or personnel.
3. a. See page 464 of the student text.
   b. See page 372 of the student text.
4. See page 467 of the student text.
5. a. A scapegoat; formerly a boy raised with a prince and punished for the prince's misdeeds.
   b. A small group or faction that for some reason breaks away from a larger group, party, or organization.
   c. See page 465 of the student text.
   d. A landlord who allows the property he/she owns to deteriorate to slum conditions.
   e. A strategy created before, and put into effect during, a sports event; any strategy designed to achieve a specific goal.
   f. Organized surveillance of an area, building, or person by the police.
6. a. See page 465 of the student text.
   b. The union of two or more companies or organizations; the absorption of one company or organization by a larger one.
   c. A refractive defect of the lens of the eye that prevents sharp focusing.
   d. Spying to obtain confidential information about a competitive business.
7. a. An essential condition or element. Latin.
   b. See answer to I, 17, page 273 of the student text. Italian.

c. A clause (in a contract or document) that stipulates a qualification or restriction; any stipulation. Latin.

8. a. To categorize something; to ignore or put aside something.
   b. To do something in a hasty, careless, or superficial way; to pay scant or cursory attention to something.
   c. To scrutinize or look over very carefully.
   d. To have someone followed. (This is a police expression.)

Exercise I. Fairness in Language
(pages 476–477)
1. Discrimination based on sex, particularly discrimination against women.
2. The doctrine that advocates for women the same rights and privileges as men have; the movement supporting this doctrine.
3. See page 467 of the student text.
4. The air of mystery supposedly surrounding women; the particular attitudes, ways of thinking or behaving, and aspirations that come with being a woman.
5. A practice or procedure that custom or general acceptance has dictated.
6. A career path allowing a mother flexible or reduced hours but having an adverse effect on advancement.
7. See page 192 of the student text.
8. The principle that every group within the society should have the same rights and opportunities as every other group.
9. See page 468 of the student text.
10. An attitude of superiority that some men have toward women.
11. An intangible barrier that keeps women or minorities from top-level positions in a company.
12. The process of achieving an increasing awareness of one's needs in order to fulfill one's potential as an individual; the technique by which a person is made aware of discrimination against a particular group.
13. A distressful circumstance or situation considered to be just cause for protest or complaint.
14. Development to one's full potential; full use of one's talents or skills.
15. The distinct character or personality of an individual; a person's individuality.
16. Setting top priority on the pursuit of a profession or occupation (for which one has been educated or trained) as a permanent source of income and satisfaction.
17. To belittle, defame, or deny the validity or significance of.
18. Making one's character, behavior, or the like correspond exactly with current customs, rules, or styles.
19. The act of freeing; the state of being free; the process of trying to achieve equal rights and status.
20. A condition in which men rank higher than women in power and authority in, or dominate, a society.
21. The state of being controlled by or subordinate to someone or something else.
22. (adj.) Relating to one's own household, family, or country; (n.) a household servant.
23. Of or relating to jobs traditionally filled by women, such as nursing and clerical positions.
24. See page 138 of the student text.

Exercise II. "Sound" Words (page 477)
1. *Definition:* To cry out loudly in protest; to clamor.
   Etymology: vox, vocis (Latin), "voice" + *ferre* (Latin), "carry" + *-are, -atus* (Latin), "make"
2. *Definition:* A grating, coarse, and irritating sound.
   Etymology: rasper (Old French), "scrape"; from *raspon* (Old High German), "scrape together" + *ing*
3. *Definition:* Having or producing a rich, deep sound; impressive.
   Etymology: sonor (Latin), "sound" + *-osus* (Latin), "full of"
4. *Definition:* (v.) To cry like a sheep or goat; to whine or whimper; (n.) the cry of a sheep or goat; a whine or whimper.
   Etymology: blaetan (Old English), "bleat"
5. *Definition:* (v.) To make a quivering sound; to tremble; (n.) a trembling or quivering sound.
   Etymology: quaveren (Middle English), "tremble repeatedly"
6. *Definition:* (adj.) Producing a hissing sound; (n.) a hissing sound; the sound of s or sh.
   Etymology: sibilans, sibilantis, the present participle of *sibilare* (Latin), "hiss; whistle"
7. *Definition:* (v.) To produce a sharp, piercing sound; (adj.) high-pitched or piercing.
   Etymology: shrille (Middle English), "shrill" and *shrillen* (Middle English), "shriek"
8. *Definition:* Quivering or vibrating; trembling; timid.
   Etymology: tremulus (Latin), "trembling"; from *tremere* (Latin), "tremble"
9. *Definition:* To lament or mourn loudly over the dead.
   Etymology: caoine (Irish Gaelic), "lamentation"; from *caoinim* (Gaelic), "I lament"
10. See answer to I, 15, page 289 of the student text.
11. *Definition:* (n.) The gentle murmur or movement of water; (adj.) to

make a soft murmuring or rippling sound.
Etymology: purla (Norwegian), "ripple"

12. *Definition:* Melodious; pleasing or soothing to the ear.
Etymology: learned respelling of *doucet* (Middle English), "sweet"; ultimately from *dulcis* (Latin), "sweet"

13. *Definition:* (*v.*) To growl viciously; to speak with anger or hostility; (*n.*) an angry growl.
Etymology: snarle (Middle English), "growl"; from *snarren* (Middle Low German), "growl"

14. *Definition:* Harsh or dissonant; disagreeable in sound.
Etymology: dis (Latin), "apart" + *cors, cordis* (Latin), "heart" + *-ans, -antis* (Latin), "causing; promoting"

15. *Definition:* With a repetitive metallic ringing sound.
Etymology: clangor (Latin), "noise; din" + *-osus* (Latin), "full of"

Exercise III.   Expanding Your Word Power (page 477)

1. *Definition:* (*adj.*) Split or divided; (*n.*) a crack or division.
Etymology: cleofan (Old English), "split" and *geclyft* (Old English), "a crack or rift"
Synonyms: (*adj.*) detached, separated; (*n.*) rift, fissure, crevice, break
Antonyms: (*adj.*) fused, joined, connected; (*n.*) connection, junction

2. *Definition:* A joining or blending thoroughly.
Etymology: fundere, fusus (Latin), "pour; melt"
Synonyms: union, merging
Antonyms: separation, severance

3. *Definition:* (*n.*) A critical review or commentary; (*v.*) to review or criticize.
Etymology: critique (French), "critical review"; from *kritike* (Greek), "art of criticism"
Synonyms: (*n.*) report, analysis, commentary; (*v.*) review, analyze, comment on

4. *Definition:* Careful and detailed observation.
Etymology: scrutinium (Latin), "examination"; from *scrutari* (Latin), "examine"
Synonyms: examination, study, perusal
Antonym: a lick and a promise

5. *Definition:* Ineffective or unqualified because of advanced age; retired or discharged because of advanced age; obsolete.
Etymology: super (Latin), "over" + *annus* (Latin), "year" + *-atus* (Latin), "made" + *-ed*
Synonyms: antiquated, worn-out, over-the-hill; pensioned off; outmoded, antiquated

Antonyms: fit; still working; up-to-date, brand-new

6. *Definition:* (*n.*) Help in time of distress; (*v.*) to help or solace.
Etymology: sucurs (Middle English), "help; aid"; from *succurrere, succursus* (Latin), "run to the aid of"; from *sub* (Latin), "under" + *currere* (Latin), "run"
Synonyms: (*n.*) aid, assistance, relief; (*v.*) aid, assist, relieve
Antonyms: (*n.*) vexation, aggravation; (*v.*) aggravate, vex, upset

7. *Definition:* Dirty or wretched; morally repulsive.
Etymology: squalidus (Latin), "filthy"; from *squalere* (Latin), "be filthy"
Synonyms: filthy, grimy; sleazy, sordid
Antonyms: clean, tidy; noble, lofty

8. *Definition:* Impairment of strength.
Etymology: de (Latin), "not" + *habilis, habile* (Latin), "able" + *-itas, -itatis* (Latin), "state of"
Synonyms: weakness, feebleness, infirmity
Antonyms: strength, vigor, energy

9. *Definition:* To put into a classification or category.
Etymology: category (see answer to I, 29, page 387 of the student text) + *-ize* (Late Latin; Greek), "make"
Synonyms: classify, pigeonhole
Antonyms: scramble, mix up, jumble

10. *Definition:* To accuse or condemn publicly or formally.
Etymology: de (Latin), "completely" + *nuntiare* (Latin), "announce"
Synonyms: censure, decry, reprove, castigate
Antonyms: praise, extol

11. *Definition:* (*v.*) To look over quickly; to analyze verse into metrical feet; (*n.*) an instance of scanning; the act of scanning; a field of vision.
Etymology: scannen (Middle English), "scan"; from *scandere* (Late Latin), "scan"
Synonyms: skim, peruse, browse
Antonyms: scrutinize, pore over

12. *Definition:* Alert watchfulness.
Etymology: vigil, vigilis (Latin), "alert" + *-antia* (Latin), "state of being"
Synonyms: caution, wariness, watchfulness, attentiveness
Antonyms: carelessness, disregard, negligence

13. *Definition:* Sounding pleasant or agreeable.
Etymology: eu (Greek), "good" + *phone* (Greek), "sound" + *-osus* (Latin), "full of"
Synonyms: melodious, dulcet, mellifluous
Antonyms: dissonant, discordant, cacophonous

14. *Definition:* (*v.*) To keep track of for a particular purpose; (*n.*) someone who keeps track of or observes; someone who cautions or reminds.

Etymology: monere, monitus (Latin), "warn" + *-or* (Latin), "one who"
Synonyms: (*v.*) observe, supervise, check; (*n.*) observer, advisor, counselor; helper, assistant

15. *Definition:* Pertaining to the internal affairs of a state or nation; pertaining to the civilian population; characteristic of the regular administration of government; polite.
Etymology: civilis, civile (Latin), "relating to a citizen, public life, of the state"; from *civis* (Latin), "citizen"
Synonyms: civic; lay; internal; mannerly, courteous
Antonyms: military, ecclesiastical; external; rude, impolite

Lesson 29 (pages 480–495)

Exercise V.   Word Roundup
(pages 488–489)
1. a. See page 487 of the student text.
   b. See page 485 of the student text.
2. a. Awkward; lacking in social grace or experience. French.
   b. The sudden and violent overthrow of a government by people in subordinate positions. French.
3. a. A partner who invests financially in a business but who does not actively participate in the management of the concern.
   b. A small receptacle with a hinged cover used for collecting table crumbs or cigarette/cigar butts and ashes.
   c. An experimental program.
   d. See page 483 of the student text.
   e. See page 481 of the student text.
   f. Plans that provide for an emergency or for an unforeseen situation.
   g. Odd or peculiar notions, or whimsies.
   h. Internal peace, prosperity, and general well-being. (The phrase comes from the Preamble to the Constitution of the United States.)
4. a. To steal the show or spotlight from someone.
   b. Accepting or seeking to accept bribes.
   c. To remain calm despite confusion or disturbance.
   d. To put out feelers in order to determine other people's opinions.
   e. To stop something at an early stage; to destroy something before it develops fully.
   f. To purchase something without obligation to keep it or with the stipulation that it can be returned if it does not provide satisfaction.
   g. To ignore or avoid someone in order to express disapproval or contempt.

Exercise (page 492)
1. a. See a on page 489 of the student text.
   b. See c on page 490 of the student text.
   c. See b on page 490 of the student text.
   d. See e on page 490 of the student text.
   e. See f on page 490 of the student text.
   f. See a on top of page 490 of the student text.
   g. *Definition:* A secondary, often explanatory title of a literary work; the printed translation of the dialogue in a foreign-language film usually shown at the bottom of the frame.
   Meaning of sub: Secondary in rank; under
   h. See d on page 490 of the student text.
   i. See g on page 490 of the student text.
2. a. A memory that holds or remembers information easily.
   b. A persistent or stubborn grip that cannot be released easily.
   c. To have a permanent position. Tenure is usually granted to an employee (*e.g.*, a university professor) after the completion of a specified number of years' service.
   d. Money paid to engage the services of a lawyer, consultant, or other professional.
3. a. Showing tact, consideration, and discretion.
   b. An accomplishment.
   c. See top of page 492 of the student text.
   d. See bottom of page 491 of the student text.
   e. See top of page 492 of the student text.
   f. A future possibility; something dependent upon chance.
   g. See top of page 492 of the student text.
   h. See page 481 of the student text.
   i. Inconsiderate; discourteous or gauche.

Exercise I.   Is There a Doctor in the House? (pages 494–495)
1. *Definition:* See answer to I, 13, page 167 of the student text.
   Etymology: dia (Greek), "apart; completely" + *gignoskein* (Greek), "perceive; know"
2. *Definition:* Evidence of a disease; an indication of a condition or event.
   Etymology: symptoma (Greek), "phenomenon"; from *syn* (Greek), "together" + *piptein* (Greek), "fall"
3. *Definition:* Treatment for a disease or condition; healing power.

Etymology: therapeia (Greek), "service"; from *therapeuein* (Greek), "be an attendant"

4. *Definition:* See answer to I, 15, page 239 of the student text.
Etymology: pathos (Greek), "suffering" + *logia* (Greek), "science"

5. *Definition:* To worsen or intensify.
Etymology: ad (Latin), "in addition to; (here) more" + *gravis, grave* (Latin), "heavy; serious" + *-are, -atus* (Latin), "make"

6. *Definition:* The period of recovery to health after an illness.
Etymology: cum (Latin), "completely + *valescere* (Latin), "grow strong" + *-antia* (Latin), "state of; act of"

7. *Definition: (adj.)* See answer to IV, 2, page 258 of the student text.
Etymology: psyche (Greek), "soul; spirit" + *soma, somatos* (Greek), "body" + *-ikos* (Greek), "relating to"

8. *Definition:* Relating to or derived from living organisms; pertaining to a bodily organ; free from chemical additives; forming an essential part of.
Etymology: organon (Greek), "instrument" + *-ikos* (Greek), "relating to; serving as"

9. See answer to I, 11, page 72 of the student text.

10. *Definition:* To impair the strength of.
Etymology: de (Latin), "not" + *habilis, habile* (Latin), "able" + *-itas, -itatis* (Latin), "state of" + *-are, -atus* (Latin), "make"

11. *Definition:* Causing or capable of causing death.
Etymology: fatum (Latin), "fate" + *-alis, -ale* (Latin), "connected with"

12. See 4 on page 421 of the student text.

13. *Definition:* To introduce the virus of a disease into the body in order to immunize or cure.
Etymology: inoculare (Latin), "engraft"; from *in* (Latin), "in" + *oculus* (Latin), "eye; bud" + *-are, -atus* (Latin), "make"

14. See answer to III, 15, page 241 of the student text.

15. *Definition:* Causing, pertaining to, or containing cancer; malignant.
Etymology: cancer (Latin), "crab; creeping ulcer" + *-osus* (Latin), "full of"

Exercise II. Some "Tricky" Words
(page 495)

1. *Apparent Meaning:* To scare; to frighten.
Real Meaning: To wound or lacerate.

2. *Apparent Meaning:* Historical.
Real Meaning: Relating to actors or the theater; deliberately affected or overdramatic.

3. *Apparent Meaning:* Relating to tests or examinations.

Real Meaning: Puzzled, derisive.

4. *Apparent Meaning:* Noisy.
Real Meaning: Noxious; offensive to the smell or other senses.

5. *Apparent Meaning:* Presenting queries or questions.
Real Meaning: Irritable; tending to complain.

6. *Apparent Meaning:* Full; complete.
Real Meaning: Nauseating; sickening; offensive to moral or aesthetic sensibilities.

7. *Apparent Meaning:* To connect; to join.
Real Meaning: To forbid; to restrain, as by judicial decree.

8. *Apparent Meaning:* Official.
Real Meaning: Meddling.

9. *Apparent Meaning:* Engaged in competition; satisfied or content.
Real Meaning: Quarrelsome; likely to cause disagreement.

10. *Apparent Meaning:* Praiseworthy; meritorious; based on merit.
Real Meaning: False; lacking in genuine worth or validity; based on pretense or insincerity.

11. *Apparent Meaning:* Adventurous.
Real Meaning: Chance; accidental.

12. *Apparent Meaning:* Moment; momentary.
Real Meaning: Impetus.

13. *Apparent Meaning:* A female egret.
Real Meaning: An exit; to exit.

14. *Apparent Meaning:* Bombing; abomination.
Real Meaning: A buzzing or droning sound.

15. *Apparent Meaning:* Wrathful, irate; ironic
Real Meaning: Peaceful, tranquil, placid, serene

Exercise III. Expanding Your Word Power (page 495)

1. *Definition:* Serving for the time being.
Etymology: provisio, provisionis (Latin), "foresight" + *-alis, -ale* (Latin), "marked by": from *pro* (Latin), "fore" + *videre, visus* (Latin), "see"
Synonyms: temporary, transitional, interim; tentative, contingent
Antonyms: definite, permanent, finalized

2. *Definition:* Having a rapid flow of words; garrulous.
Etymology: volvere, volutus (Latin), "roll" + *-abilis, -abile* (Latin), "able to"
Synonyms: verbose, long-winded; loquacious, talkative
Antonyms: succinct, concise; taciturn, laconic

3. *Definition:* Able to be touched, handled, or perceived.
Etymology: palpare (Latin), "touch" + *-abilis, -abile* (Latin), "able to"

Synonyms: tangible, material, physical, obvious, manifest
Antonyms: intangible, imperceptible
4. *Definition:* Impossible to prove false or wrong by argument.
Etymology: irrefutabilis (Late Latin), from *in* (Latin), "not" + *re* (Latin), "back" + *futare* (Latin), "beat" + *-abilis* (Latin), "capable of"
Synonyms: corroborative, confirmable, substantiable
Antonyms: disprovable, rebuttable, confutable
5. *Definition:* (*n.*) A time period between one event and another; (*adj.*) taking place between two time periods.
Etymology: interim (Latin), "meanwhile; in the meantime"
Synonyms: (*n.*) interval, interlude; (*adj.*) temporary, stopgap
6. *Definition:* To counteract the effect of; to make ineffective.
Etymology: neutral + *-ize;* from *neuter* (Latin), "neither" + *-alis, -ale* (Latin), "pertaining to"
Synonyms: offset, counterbalance, nullify
7. *Definition:* Tranquil; unruffled; fair and bright.
Etymology: serenus (Latin), "clear; serene"
Synonyms: calm, composed; halcyon
Antonyms: agitated, hysterical, distraught; cloudy, stormy
8. *Definition:* Disagreeably harsh and rough-sounding; noisy.
Etymology: raucus (Latin), "hoarse"
Synonyms: grating, strident, boisterous, disorderly
Antonyms: mellifluous, euphonious; quiet, tranquil
9. *Definition:* Intense stimulation of the mind or emotions; someone or something that moves the intellect or emotions; a bright idea or action.
Etymology: in (Latin), "into" + *spirare, spiratus* (Latin), "breathe" + *-io, -ionis* (Latin), "process; state or act of"
Synonyms: stimulus, goad, spur; invention, conception
10. *Definition:* (*adj.*) bitingly sarcastic; incisive or trenchant.
Etymology: mordant (French), "biting," the present participle of *mordre* (French), "bite"
Synonyms: acrid, acidulous, scathing
Antonyms: bland; pleasant
11. *Definition:* Present everywhere.
Etymology: omnis, omne (Latin), "all" + *present;* from *prae* (Latin), "in front; before" + *esse* (Latin), "be"
Synonyms: ubiquitous, pervasive, universal
Antonyms: localized; nonexistent; rare, scarce
12. *Definition:* International in scope;

comfortable in many parts of the world or with many spheres of interest.
Etymology: kosmos (Greek), "world; universe" + *polites* (Greek), "citizen" + *-anus* (Latin), "relating to"
Synonyms: sophisticated, urban
Antonyms: parochial, provincial, insular, narrow
13. *Definition:* To claim or seize without right.
Etymology: arrogare, arrogatus (Latin), "claim for oneself"; from *ad* (Latin), "to" + *rogare, rogatus* (Latin), "ask"
Synonyms: usurp, expropriate
14. *Definition:* A small hook; an odd or eccentric idea.
Etymology: crochet (Old French), "hook"
Synonyms: vagary, whim, quirk
15. *Definition:* In a vertical position; morally respectable.
Etymology: upriht (Old English), "upright"; *up + right* (=*straight*)
Synonyms: perpendicular, erect; honest, upstanding
Antonyms: prone, prostrate, horizontal; dishonest, depraved, corrupt, immoral

Lesson 30 (pages 496–514)

Exercise V.   Word Roundup (page 507)
1. a. See page 501 of the student text.
   b. See page 502 of the student text.
2. The process by which a president may prevent a bill from becoming a law by failing to act on it. This applies if Congress adjourns within less than ten days (Sunday excepted) after submitting the bill. Some governors also have the pocket-veto power.
3. See page 504 of the student text.
4. a. A region in the world that is politically unstable and volatile or where military outbreaks within or among nations occur frequently.
   b. The hymn accompanying the exit of the clergy and choir after a church service; the exit itself; any recession.
   c. Mischievous and zany pranks.
   d. The period of a tide between high water and the succeeding low water.
   e. A quick temper.
   f. An elderly, respected, and usually retired political leader who acts as an unofficial adviser on national problems.
5. a. In an angry and indignant emotional state.
   b. Tied, or very close together, in a race or contest.
   c. Very enthusiastic.
6. a. To have a feeling of resentment or ill will toward.
   b. To reject, refuse, or disapprove of.

c. To forget about all previous disagreements; to stop fighting and make peace.
d. To behave foolishly or frivolously.
e. Any fatal personal flaw that proves to be a person's undoing; a disappointing weakness of character in someone previously admired or in a prominent position.
f. To grant permission to proceed.

Exercise I. Misusing Words: A Look Back (pages 511–512)

Student answers may vary.
1. Our furniture prices are the lowest in town.
2. Please turn off/out the lights when you leave for the day.
3. simulated.
4. The bed was so comfortable that I fell asleep quickly and slept soundly all night.
5. respectively.
6. virtuoso; enthusiast; *possibly* buff.
7. fled, beat a hasty retreat.
8. This company has always been willing to promote deserving employees to more responsible positions.
9. beeline.
10. by genocide.
11. authority; expert.
12. most beautiful.
13. I was extremely upset (with myself) because my own stupid mistakes had (fouled up the job and) gotten me into a lot of trouble.
14. flouted.
15. We worked hard to make the party a success.
16. We hope shortly to conclude an agreement (clinch a deal) that will prove very profitable to everybody concerned.
17. Our team looked pretty fit after its (grueling) workout before the game with its archrival, State. Even after a grueling workout, our team looked ready to take on its archrival, State.

Exercise II. Expanding Your Word Power (page 512)

1. *Definition:* The front or face of a building; a false or artificial appearance.
   Etymology: façade (French), "face of a building"
   Synonyms: exterior, veneer; false front, illusion, pretense
2. *Definition:* Inspiring admiration or awe; venerable.
   Etymology: augustus (Latin), "venerable; magnificent"
   Synonyms: majestic, grand, noble, sublime, imposing
   Antonyms: uninspiring, unimposing, unimpressive; humble
3. *Definition:* Misleading.
   Etymology: decipere, deceptus (Latin), "deceive" + *-ivus* (Latin), "tending

to"; from *de* (Latin), "away" + *capere, captus* (Latin), "take"
   Synonyms: illusory, fraudulent, deceitful
   Antonyms: truthful, honest, candid
4. *Definition:* Able to act effectively, even in difficult or challenging situations.
   Etymology: resource (Old French; from Latin), + *ful* (Old English)
   Synonyms: inventive, ingenious, clever, quick-witted, handy
   Antonyms: unimaginative, uninventive
5. *Definition:* (*v.*) To prohibit by civil or ecclesiastical authority; (*n.*) a court- or church-ordered prohibition.
   Etymology: interdicere, interdictus (Latin), "forbid"; from *inter* (Latin), "between; against" + *dicere, dictus* (Latin), "say"
   Synonyms: (*v.*) forbid, ban, proscribe; (*n.*) ban, taboo, prohibition
   Antonyms: (*v.*) approve, permit, allow; (*n.*) approval, sanction, authorization
6. *Definition:* Openly expressed anger.
   Etymology: ira (Latin), "anger"
   Synonyms: wrath, rage, choler
   Antonyms: favor; delight, pleasure
7. *Definition:* Filled with or showing malice and the urge to humiliate.
   Etymology: (de)spite (Old French; from Latin), "insult; ill will" + *ful* (Old English)
   Synonyms: malicious, malevolent
   Antonyms: kindly, benevolent
8. *Definition:* (*v.*) To touch or affect slightly with something spoiled or corrupt; (*n.*) a stain or defect.
   Etymology: teint (Old French), "color; tint"; from *tingere, tinctus* (Latin), "dye"
   Synonyms: (*v.*) stain, contaminate, infect; (*n.*) spot, blemish
   Antonyms: (*v.*) purify, cleanse, purge
9. *Definition:* (*adj.*) Showing little or no change or movement; (*n.*) random noise, as from a radio or television; back talk or opposition.
   Etymology: statos (Greek), "placed; standing" + *-ikos* (Greek), "relating to"
   Synonyms: (*adj.*) quiescent, dormant, stationary; (*n.*) crackling; conflict, disagreement
   Antonyms: (*adj.*) active, moving, mobile; turbulent; (*n.*) agreement, support, approval
10. *Definition:* (*adj.*) An addition or increase in number, size, or extent.
    Etymology: incrementum (Latin), "growth; increase"; from *in* (Latin), "in" + *crescere, cretum* (Latin), "grow, increase" + *mentum* (Latin), "process; state; condition"
    Synonyms: accretion, augmentation, enlargement

Antonyms: reduction, decrease, cutback

11. *Definition:* To make thinner; to reduce the strength or purity of.
Etymology: diluere, dilutus (Latin), "wash away"; from *dis* (Latin), "apart; away" + *lavere* (Latin), "wash"
Synonyms: attenuate, weaken, water down
Antonyms: fortify, strengthen, reinforce, bolster, boost

12. *Definition:* See answer to I, 20, page 257 of the student text.
Etymology: nazir (Arabic), "opposite" + *as-samt* (Arabic), "zenith; top"
Synonyms: bottom, depths
Antonyms: zenith, summit, apex, pinnacle

13. *Definition:* Gray or white with age; covered with gray or white hair; ancient.
Etymology: har (Old English), "frost" + *ig* (Old English), "full of"
Synonyms: grizzled; aged, elderly
Antonyms: beardless; youthful, young, adolescent, juvenile

14. *Definition:* To separate or cut off from association with.
Etymology: des, de (Old French), "apart; un-" + *estachier* (Old French), "attach"
Synonyms: disconnect, disengage, unfasten
Antonyms: join, attach, connect

15. *Definition:* Intense joy, delight, or emotion.
Etymology: ekstasis (Greek), "state of being driven out of one's senses"; from *ek, ex* (Greek), "out of" + *histanai* (Greek), "place"
Synonyms: rapture, frenzy
Antonyms: despair, melancholy, misery, depression

Review (pages 515–521)

Exercise IX. Word Roundup
(pages 518–519)

1. a. See page 372 of the student text.
   b. See page 373 of the student text.
   c. See page 464 of the student text.
   d. See page 487 of the student text.
   e. See page 485 of the student text.
   f. See page 484 of the student text.
   g. See page 502 of the student text.
   h. See page 501 of the student text.
2. a. See answer to V, 3, c, page 345 of the student text.
   b. See answer V, 3, a, page 345 of the student text.
   c. See answer to V, 1, g, page 382 of the student text.
   d. See page 408 of the student text.
   e. See answer to V, 1, d, page 382 of the student text.
   f. See answer to V, 5, d, page 473 of the student text.

3. a. See answer to V, 5, a, page 473 of the student text.
   b. See answer to V, 5, a, page 346 of the student text.
   c. See answer to V, 3, g, page 489 of the student text.
   d. See answer to V, 3, b, page 345 of the student text.
   e. See answer to V, 5, c, page 455 of the student text.
   f. See answer to V, 5, b, page 473 of the student text.
   g. See answer to V, 5, h, page 455 of the student text.
   h. See page 500 of the student text.
   i. See answer to V, 1, h, page 363 of the student text.
   j. See page 481 of the student text.
4. a. See answer to V, 5, a, page 363 of the student text.
   b. See answer to V, 6, a, page 436 of the student text.
   c. See answer to V, 6, c, page 507 of the student text.
   d. See answer to V, 6, c, page 455 of the student text.
   e. See answer to V, 4, d, page 489 of the student text.
   f. See answer to V, 4, d, page 398 of the student text.
   g. See answer to V, 4, a, page 398 of the student text.
   h. See answer to V, 8, d, page 473 of the student text.
   i. See answer to V, 5, a, page 507 of the student text.
   j. See answer to V, 2, d, page 382 of the student text.
5. a. See answer to V, 4, b, page 382 of the student text. French.
   b. See answer to V, 7, c, page 436 of the student text.
   c. See answer to V, 6, a, page 346 of the student text. Latin.
   d. See answer to V, 7, b, page 473 of the student text.
   e. See answer to V, 4, c, page 363 of the student text.
   f. See answer to V, 7, a, page 473 of the student text.
   g. See answer to V, 4, b, page 363 of the student text.
   h. See answer to V, 2, b, page 489 of the student text.
   i. See answer to V, 7, a, page 436 of the student text.
6. a. See page 342 of the student text.
   b. See page 342 of the student text.
   c. See page 449 of the student text.
   d. See page 414 of the student text.
   e. See page 420 of the student text.
   f. See page 504 of the student text.

Exercise X. Etymology (page 519)

1. a. See answer to 1, a, page 348 of the student text.
   b. To act on each other or one another.

c. See answer to 2, d, page 348 of the student text
d. See answer to 2, c, page 348 of the student text.
e. See top of page 347 of the student text.
f. See answer to III, 5, page 495 of the student text.
2. a. See 1, a, page 383 of the student text.
   b. See 1, d, page 383 of the student text.
   c. See 1, b, page 383 of the student text.
   d. See 1, e, page 383 of the student text.
   e. See 1, c, page 383 of the student text.
   f. See 1, f, page 383 of the student text.
3. a.–c. See page 418 of the student text.
5. a. See answer to 3, a, page 492 of the student text.
   b. See top of page 492 of the student text.
   c. See top of page 492 of the student text.
   d. See answer to 3, b, page 492 of the student text.
   e. See top of page 492 of the student text.
   f. See answer to 3, f, page 492 of the student text.

Cumulative Review (pages 522–533)

Exercise VIII.   Look Alikes
(pages 528–529)
1. See page 28 of the student text.
2. See page 38 of the student text.
3. See page 40 and answer to III, 7, page 37 of the student text.
4. See page 112 of the student text.
5. See page 29 of the student text.
6. See page 263 of the student text.
7. See page 310 of the student text.
8. See page 173 of the student text.
9. See page 191 of the student text.
10. See page 230 of the student text.
11. See page 373 of the student text.
12. See page 484 of the student text.
13. See page 485 of the student text.
14. See page 487 of the student text.
15. See page 501 of the student text.

Exercise X.   Word Roundup
(page 529)
1. a. See page 29 of the student text.
   b. See page 30 of the student text.
   c. See page 101 of the student text.
   d. See page 40 of the student text.
   e. See answer to I, 6, page 203 of the student text.
   f. See answer to V, 2, c, page 268 of the student text.

g. See answer to VI, 2, a, page 285 of the student text.
h. See answer to V, 2, d, page 268 of the student text.
i. See page 153 of the student text.
j. See answer to V, 7, a, page 162 of the student text.
k. See answer to V, 1, g, page 382 of the student text.
l. See answer to V, 1, d, page 382 of the student text.
m. See page 408 of the student text.
n. See answer to VI, 2, b, page 285 of the student text.
o. See answer to V, 3, c, page 345 of the student text.
2. a. See page 30 of the student text.
   b. See page 100 of the student text.
   c. See page 111 of the student text.
   d. See page 39 of the student text.
   e. See page 156 of the student text.
   f. See page 195 of the student text.
   g. An exact duplicate but in reverse (page 246 of the student text).
   h. See answer to V, 5, c, page 455 of the student text.
   i. See page 500 of the student text.
   j. See answer to V, 5, b, page 473 of the student text.
3. a. See page 41 of the student text.
   b. See answer to IV, 6, page 403 of the student text.
   c. See answer to V, 2, d, page 45 of the student text.
   d. See answer to V, 3, d, page 302 of the student text.
   e. See answer to V, 3, e, page 302 of the student text.
   f. See answer to VI, 1, a, page 284 of the student text.
   g. See answer to V, 1, f, page 233 of the student text.
   h. See answer to V, 6, c, page 507 of the student text.
   i. See answer to V, 4, a, page 398 of the student text.
   j. See answer to V, 4, d, page 398 of the student text.
4. a. See page 102 of the student text.
   b. See page 124 of the student text.
   c. Sec page 392 of the student text.
   d. See pages 340, 341 of the student text.
   e. See page 414 of the student text.
   f. See page 504 of the student text.
5. a. Environment;   surroundings. French. (page 52 of the student text)
   b. See answer to V, 2, a, page 301 of the student text.
   c. See answer to I, 13, page 184 of the student text.
   d. See answer to I, 4, page 273 of the student text.
   e. See answer to V, 2, b, page 489 of the student text.
   f. See answer to V, 7, a, page 436 of the student text.

Answer Key to Supplementary Testing Program

Lesson 1
Exercise I. Parts of Speech (page 1)
1. v.   2. adj.   3. v.   4. v.   5. n.

Exercise II. Words in Phrases (page 1)
1. b   2. d   3. c   4. a   5. c

Exercise III. Completeing Sentences (page 1–2)
1. abets   3. abstain   5. abject
2. abhorrent   4. accedes

Exercise IV. Antonyms (page 2)
1. b   2. c   3. a   4. d   5. d

Exercise V. Word Associations (page 2)
1. c   2. b   3. d   4. a   5. c

Lesson 2
Exercise I. Syllabication and Pronunciation (page 3)
1. ad'-verse,   3. af-fec-ta'-tion
   ad-verse'   4. a-gen'-da
2. aes-thet'-ic   5. ag'-gre-gate

Exercise II. Words Out of Context (page 3)
1. d   2. b   3. a   4. e   5. d

Exercise III. Completing Sentences (pages 3–4)
1. affluent   3. adjourned   5. agile
2. advocating   4. aggregate

Exercise IV. Antonyms (page 4)
1. d   2. a   3. e   4. c   5. b

Exercise V. Word Associations (page 4)
1. a   2. c   3. b   4. d   5. c

Exercise VI. Framing Sentences (page 4)
1. adjournment   3. affluence
2. affability,   4. agility
   affableness   5. adversity, adversary

Lesson 3
Exercise I. Parts of Speech (page 5)
1. v.   2. n.   3. adj.   4. n.   5. n.

Exercise II. Words in Phrases (page 5)
1. b   2. d   3. a   4. c   5. d

Exercise III. Completing Sentences (pages 5–6)
1. anarchy   4. amnesty
2. ambience   5. ambivalent
3. anathema

Exercise IV. Antonyms (page 6)
1. c   2. b   3. d   4. a   5. c

Exercise V. Word Associations (page 6)
1. a   2. d   3. b   4. d   5. c

Lesson 4
Exercise I. Syllabication and Pronunciation (page 7)
1. ap-pall'   4. ar-tic'-u-late
2. ar'-bi-trar-y   5. as-sim'-i-late
3. ar-ray'

Exercise II. Words Out of Context (page 7)
1. a   2. d   3. a   4. c   5. d

Exercise III. Completing Sentences (pages 7–8)
1. apprehend   3. askew   5. anomaly
2. articulating   4. arbitrary

Exercise IV. Antonyms (page 8)
1. e   2. d   3. b   4. a   5. c

Exercise V. Word Associations (page 8)
1. d   2. b   3. c   4. a   5. c

Lesson 5
Exercise I. Parts of Speech (page 9)
1. n.   3. v.   5. n.
2. n., v.   4. n., v.

Exercise II. Words in Phrases (page 9)
1. c   3. d   5. c
2. a   4. b

Exercise III. Completing Sentences (pages 9–10)
1. augment   3. augurs   5. authentic
2. asylum   4. atrocities

Exercise IV. Antonyms (page 10)
1. a   2. e   3. d   4. c   5. b

Exercise V. Word Associations (page 10)
1. d   2. c   3. b   4. d   5. a

Review
Exercise I. Syllabication and Pronunciation (page 11)
1. ab'-di-cate   4. ar-tic'-u-late
2. ad'-vo-cate   5. at'-ro-phy
3. am-biv'-a-lent

Exercise II. Parts of Speech (page 11)
1. v.   2. adj.   3. n.   4. v.   5. n.

Exercise III. Words Out of Context (page 11)
1. d   2. b   3. b   4. a   5. e

Exercise IV. Words in Phrases (pages 11–12)
1. b   2. a   3. c   4. a   5. d

Exercise V. Completing Sentences (page 12)
1. acclimating   4. abject
2. atone   5. addiction
3. asylum

Exercise VII.   Antonyms (page 13)
1. d   2. c   3. a   4. e   5. b

Exercise VIII.   Related Forms (page 13)
1. academy,   3. apprehensive
   academician   4. atrocious
2. adjournment   5. anathematize

Exercise IX.   Look-Alikes (pages 13–14)
1. See page 38 of the student text.
2. See page 40 of the student text.
3. See page 52 of the student text.
4. See page 28 of the student text.
5. See pages 65 and 66 of the student
   text.

Exercise X.   Word Associations
(page 14)
1. c   2. d   3. a   4. b   5. c

Lesson 6
Exercise I.   Syllabication and Pronunciation (page 15)
1. av'-a-rice   4. ba'-nal or ba-nal'
2. badg'-er   5. bi-zarre'
3. baf'-fle

Exercise II.   Words Out of Context
(page 15)
1. d   2. b   3. b   4. a   5. c

Exercise III.   Completing Sentences
(pages 15–16)
1. bland   3. badgering   5. bizarre
2. avarice   4. benign

Exercise IV.   Antonyms (page 16)
1. a   2. d   3. b   4. e   5. c

Exercise V.   Word Associations
(page 16)
1. c   2. d   3. c   4. b   5. a

Lesson 7
Exercise I.   Parts of Speech (page 17)
1. adj.   4. adj.
2. v., n.   5. n.
3. v., n.

Exercise II.   Words in Phrases (page 17)
1. b   2. a   3. d   4. a   5. c

Exercise III.   Completing Sentences
(pages 17–18)
1. brusque   3. brash   5. bombastic
2. boisterous   4. blighted

Exercise IV.   Antonyms (page 18)
1. b   2. e   3. c   4. a   5. d

Exercise V.   Word Associations
(page 18)
1. d   2. b   3. a   4. c   5. b

Lesson 8
Exercise I.   Syllabication and Pronunciation (page 19)
1. bu-reauc'-ra-cy   4. cap'-tious
2. ca-jole'   5. cath'-o-lic
3. can-tan'-ker-ous

Exercise II.   Words Out of Context
(page 19)
1. c   2. a   3. e   4. b   5. d

Exercise III.   Completing Sentences
(pages 19–20)
1. buttress   4. calumnies
2. catholic   5. cantankerous
3. candid

Exercise IV.   Antonyms (page 20)
1. b   2. d   3. c   4. e   5. a

Exercise V.   Word Associations (page 20)
1. a   2. c   3. b   4. b   5. a

Lesson 9
Exercise I.   Parts of Speech (page 21)
1. adj.   3. n., v.   5. adj.
2. n., v.   4. adj.

Exercise II.   Words in Phrases (page 21)
1. a   2. d   3. b   4. b   5. d

Exercise III.   Completing Sentences
(pages 21–22)
1. charlatans 3. circuitous 5. caustic
2. clandestine 4. censure

Exercise IV.   Antonyms (page 22)
1. e   2. d   3. a   4. c   5. d

Exercise V.   Word Associations (page 22)
1. d   2. c   3. b   4. c   5. a

Lesson 10
Exercise I.   Syllabication and Pronunciation (page 23)
1. col-lab'-o-rate   4. con-done'
2. com-pat'-i-ble   5. con-jec'-ture
3. con-fron-ta'-tion

Exercise II.   Words Out of Context
(page 23)
1. e   2. b   3. d   4. a   5. c

Exercise III.   Completing Sentences
(pages 23–24)
1. cogent   4. condone
2. collaborated   5. compatible
3. conjectured

Exercise IV.   Antonyms (page 24)
1. e   2. b   3. c   4. d   5. a

Exercise V.   Word Associations
(page 24)
1. a   2. c   3. d   4. b   5. d

Review

Exercise I. Syllabication and Pronunciation (page 25)
1. be-nign'
2. boy'-cott
3. ca-jole'
4. clan-des'-tine
5. co'-gent

Exercise II. Parts of Speech (page 25)
1. v.   2. adj.   3. adj.   4. n., v.   5. v.

Exercise III. Words Out of Context (page 25)
1. a   2. d   3. d   4. b   5. d

Exercise IV. Words in Phrases (pages 25–26)
1. b   2. a   3. d   4. b   5. c

Exercise V. Completing Sentences (page 26)
1. bickering   3. charlatan   5. callous
2. compatible 4. blithe

Exercise VII. Antonyms (page 27)
1. d   2. b   3. a   4. e   5. c

Exercise VIII. Related Forms (page 27)
1. bafflement   4. coherent, cohesive
2. bombast   5. calumniate
3. circumspection

Exercise IX. Look-Alikes (pages 27–28)
1. See page 87 of the student text.
2. See page 101 of the student text.
3. See page 115 of the student text.
4. *Chronic* means "continuing over a long period of time or recurring often"; *chronological* means "arranged in order of time of occurrence."
5. See page 137 of the student text.

Exercise X. Word Associations (page 28)
1. c   2. b   3. a   4. b   5. d

Lesson 11

Exercise I. Parts of Speech (page 29)
1. v.   3. n., v.   5. v.
2. adj.   4. n.

Exercise II. Words in Phrase (page 29)
1. b   2. d   3. a   4. c   5. a

Exercise III. Completing Sentences (pages 29–30)
1. culpable   4. consummate
2. connoisseurs 5. cursory
3. counsel

Exercise IV. Antonyms (page 30)
1. e   2. b   3. d   4. a   5. c

Exercise V. Word Associations (page 30)
1. b   2. c   3. a   4. a   5. d

Lesson 12

Exercise I. Syllabication and Pronunciation (page 31)
1. de-ject'-ed
2. de-lin'-e-ate
3. de-lude'
4. de-noue-ment'
5. de'-fect, de-fect'

Exercise II. Words Out of Context (page 31)
1. e   2. a   3. c   4. c   5. b

Exercise III. Completing Sentences (pages 31–32)
1. defer   3. deviation   5. demure
2. delinquents   4. desultory

Exercise IV. Antonyms (page 32)
1. d   2. b   3. e   4. a   5. c

Exercise V. Verbal Analogies (page 32)
1. d   2. b   3. c   4. a   5. b

Lesson 13

Exercise I. Parts of Speech (page 33)
1. v.   2. n., v.   3. adj.   4. adj.   5. v.

Exercise II. Words in Phrases (page 33)
1. a   2. d   3. b   4. d   5. c

Exercise III. Completing Sentences (pages 33–34)
1. dilapidated   4. duplicity
2. dormant   5. distraught
3. divulged

Exercise IV. Antonyms (page 34)
1. a   2. d   3. c   4. e   5. b

Exercise V. Verbal Analogies (page 34)
1. b   2. d   3. a   4. b   5. c

Lesson 14

Exercise I. Syllabication and Pronunciation (page 35)
1. e-clec'-tic
2. ef-fron'-ter-y
3. e-lic'-it
4. em'-a-nate
5. en-dem'-ic

Exercise II. Words Out of Context (page 35)
1. d   2. c   3. a   4. b   5. d

Exercise III. Completing Sentences (pages 35–36)
1. endemic   3. empathize   5. enigma
2. effete   4. elite

Exercise IV. Antonyms (page 36)
1. e   2. d   3. a   4. c   5. b

Exercise V. Verbal Analogies (page 36)
1. b   2. a   3. d   4. c   5. b

Lesson 15

Exercise I. Parts of Speech (page 37)
1. v.   2. adj.   3. n.   4. adj.   5. n.

Exercise II. Words in Phrases (page 37)
1. a   2. c   3. b   4. d   5. b

Exercise III. Completing Sentences (pages 37–38)
1. exacerbate
2. ethical
3. esoteric
4. entreat
5. envisaged

Exercise IV. Antonyms (page 38)
1. d   2. d   3. d   4. a   5. d

Exercise V. Verbal Analogies (page 38)
1. c   2. d   3. b   4. a   5. c

Review

Exercise I. Syllabication and Pronunciation (page 39)
1. cul'-pa-ble
2. dex'-ter-ous
3. dis-par'-i-ty
4. ef-fi-ca'-cious
5. e-qua-nim'-i-ty

Exercise II. Parts of Speech (page 39)
1. n.   2. adj.   3. v.   4. n.   5. adj.

Exercise III. Words Out of Context (page 39)
1. a   2. c   3. e   4. d   5. b

Exercise IV. Words in Phrases (pages 39–40)
1. d   2. b   3. a   4. c   5. d

Exercise V. Completing Sentences (page 40)
1. emanate
2. drastic
3. criterion
4. devout
5. enticed

Exercise VII. Antonyms (page 41)
1. e   2. a   3. d   4. d   5. b

Exercise VIII. Related Forms (page 41)
1. consummation
2. deletion
3. embellishment
4. duplicitous
5. exigent

Exercise IX. Look-Alikes (pages 41–42)
1. See page 156 of the student text.
2. See page 172 of the student text.
3. *Divulge* means "to make known": *diverge* means "to move or extend in different directions; to deviate; to differ in opinion."
4. See page 208 of the student text.
5. See page 228 of the student text.

Exercise X. Word Associations (page 42)
1. c   2. d   3. b   4. d   5. a

Lesson 16

Exercise I. Syllabication and Pronunciation (page 43)
1. ex-ploit',
   ex'-ploit
2. fab'-ri-cate
3. fat'-u-ous
4. fe-lic'-i-tous
5. fet'-ish

Exercise II. Words Out of Context (page 43)
1. c   2. a   3. d   4. e   5. b

Exercise III. Completing Sentences (page 43)
1. exotic
2. facsimile
3. expound
4. expedients
5. fatuous

Exercise IV. Antonyms (page 44)
1. a   2. c   3. d   4. c   5. b

Exercise V. Verbal Analogies (page 44)
1. d   2. c   3. b   4. b   5. a

Lesson 17

Exercise I. Parts of Speech (page 45)
1. adj.   2. n.   3. adj.   4. v.   5. v.

Exercise II. Words in Phrases (page 45)
1. c   2. b   3. d   4. a   5. d

Exercise III. Completing Sentences (pages 45–46)
1. flout
2. forestall
3. fortuitous
4. fulsome
5. flaunt

Exercise IV. Antonyms (page 46)
1. e   2. a   3. d   4. b   5. e

Exercise V. Verbal Analogies (page 46)
1. b   2. d   3. a   4. c   5. d

Lesson 18

Exercise I. Syllabication and Pronunciation (page 47)
1. gar'-ble
2. gra-tu'-i-tous
3. gul'-li-ble
4. ha-rangue'
5. har'-bin-ger

Exercise II. Words Out of Context (page 47)
1. c   2. e   3. b   4. a   5. d

Exercise III. Completing Sentences (pages 47–48)
1. gregarious
2. grope
3. grimace
4. gruesome
5. grueling

Exercise IV. Antonyms (page 48)
1. e   2. b   3. d   4. a   5. c

Exercise V. Verbal Analogies (page 48)
1. c   2. d   3. b   4. a   5. c

Lesson 19
Exercise I. Parts of Speech (page 49)
1. adj.   2. n.   3. n.   4. adj. 5. n., v.

Exercise II. Words in Phrases (page 49)
1. c   2. d   3. b   4. a   5. c

Exercise III. Completing Sentences
(pages 49–50)
1. illicit   3. impervious   5. implicit
2. impasse   4. incensed

Exercise IV. Antonyms (page 50)
1. b   2. c   3. a   4. e   5. c

Exercise V. Verbal Analogies (page 50)
1. c   2. b   3. d   4. a   5. c

Lesson 20
Exercise I. Syllabication and Pronunciation (page 51)
1. in-gen'-ious   4. jeop'-ard-ize
2. in-veigh'   5. jus'-ti-fy
3. in-cep'-tion

Exercise II. Words Out of Context
(page 51)
1. e   2. b   3. a   4. c   5. b

Exercise III. Completing Sentences
(pages 51–52)
1. inception   3. inherent   5. judicious
2. justify   4. inveighed

Exercise IV. Antonyms (page 52)
1. e   2. d   3. c   4. c   5. a

Exercise V. Verbal Analogies (page 52)
1. a   2. d   3. b   4. d   5. c

Review
Exercise I. Syllabication and Pronunciation (page 53)
1. fe-lic'-i-tous   4. im-plic'-it
2. foi'-ble   5. jet'-ti-son
3. graph'-ic

Exercise II. Parts of Speech (page 53)
1. v.   2. adj.   3. v.   4. adj.   5. n.

Exercise III. Words Out of Context
(page 53)
1. e   2. a   3. b   4. e   5. d

Exercise IV. Words in Phrases
(pages 53–54)
1. b   2. c   3. d   4. a   5. d

Exercise V. Completing Sentences
(page 54)
1. feigned   3. immaculate 5. irony
2. haggard   4. fickle

Exercise VII. Antonyms (page 55)
1. d   2. e   3. a   4. b   5. d

Exercise VIII. Related Forms (page 55)
1. frugality, frugalness 4. immune
2. gullibility, gull   5. innovate
3. exploitable

Exercise IX. Look-Alikes (pages 55–56)
1. See page 247 of the student text.
2. See page 265 of the student text.
3. See pages 208 and 294 of the text.
4. See page 310 of the student text.
5. See page 316 of the student text.

Exercise X. Word Associations
(page 56)
1. d   2. c   3. b   4. a   5. b

Lesson 21
Exercise I. Parts of Speech (page 57)
1. n.   2. n., v. 3. v.   4. adj.   5. n.

Exercise II. Words in Phrases (page 57)
1. b   2. c   3. a   4. d   5. a

Exercise III. Completing Sentences
(pages 57–58)
1. lucrative   3. liability   5. malice
2. mammoth   4. libel

Exercise IV. Antonyms (page 58)
1. b   2. e   3. a   4. c   5. c

Exercise V. Verbal Analogies (page 58)
1. b   2. d   3. a   4. c   5. d

Lesson 22
Exercise I. Syllabication and Pronunciation (page 59)
1. mer'-ce-nar-y   4. nom'-i-nal
2. myr'-i-ad   5. nos-tal'-gia
3. neg'-li-gi-ble

Exercise II. Words Out of Context
(page 59)
1. b   2. d   3. a   4. a   5. c

Exercise III. Completing Sentences
(pages 59–60)
1. mercenaries 3. nominal 5. mundane
2. motley   4. nuances

Exercise IV. Antonyms (page 60)
1. b   2. c   3. e   4. a   5. d

Exercise V. Verbal Analogies (page 60)
1. b   2. a   3. b   4. c   5. d

Lesson 23
Exercise I. Parts of Speech (page 61)
1. n.   2. adj.   3. v.   4. n., v. 5. adj.

Exercise II. Words in Phrases (page 61)
1. d   2. b   3. a   4. d   5. c

Exercise III. Completing Sentences
(pages 61–62)
1. paradox   3. paraphrase 5. pensive
2. obsequious 4. obsolete

Exercise IV. Antonyms (page 62)
1. a   2. c   3. d   4. e   5. b

Exercise V. Verbal Analogies (page 62)
1. c   2. a   3. d   4. a   5. d

Lesson 24
Exercise I. Syllabication and Pronunciation (page 63)
1. per-se-vere'   4. pre-car'-i-ous
2. pho'-bi-a   5. pre-co'-cious
3. poign'-ant

Exercise II. Words Out of Context
(page 63)
1. c   2. e   3. c   4. e   5. a

Exercise III. Completing Sentences
(pages 63–64)
1. plaintive   4. peremptory
2. permeated   5. predatory
3. plethora

Exercise IV. Antonyms (page 64)
1. c   2. b   3. e   4. a   5. b

Exercise V. Verbal Analogies (page 64)
1. a   2. c   3. b   4. c   5. d

Lesson 25
Exercise I. Parts of Speech (page 65)
1. n.   2. adj.   3. n.   4. adj.   5. v., n.

Exercise II. Words in Phrases (page 65)
1. b   2. c   3. a   4. d   5. c

Exercise III. Completing Sentences
(pages 65–66)
1. purge   3. probity   5. quixotic
2. promulgated 4. prowess

Exercise IV. Antonyms (page 66)
1. e   2. b   3. a   4. d   5. c

Exercise V. Verbal Analogies (page 66)
1. c   2. b   3. b   4. d   5. a

Review
Exercise I. Syllabication and Pronunciation (page 67)
1. mal'-a-prop-ism   4. pleth'-o-ra
2. myr'-i-ad   5. pro-pen'-si-ty
3. par'-o-dy

Exercise II. Parts of Speech (page 67)
1. n.   2. adj.   3. n.   4. adj.   5. n.

Exercise III. Words Out of Context
(page 67)
1. d   2. a   3. e   4. b   5. d

Exercise IV. Words in Phrases
(pages 67–68)
1. b   2. c   3. d   4. a   5. b

Exercise V. Completing Sentences
(page 68)
1. pusillanimous   4. kudos
2. ostracized   5. pernicious
3. nebulous

Exercise VII. Antonyms (page 69)
1. d   2. a   3. e   4. b   5. c

Exercise VIII. Related Forms (page 69)
1. perseverance   3. litigious
2. narcissism,   4. propitiatory
   narcissist   5. obsess

Exercise IX. Look-Alikes (pages 69–70)
1. See page 372 of the student text.
2. See page 378 of the student text.
3. *Plaintive* means "mournful"; a *plaintiff* is a person who brings charges against another in a lawsuit.
4. *Poignant* means "keenly touching"; *pungent*, "sharply penetrating."
5. *Foment* means "to promote the growth of, to incite" (*verb*); *ferment* means "to agitate" and "to be agitated" (*verbs*) and "turmoil" (*noun*).

Exercise X. Word Associations
(page 70)
1. b   2. c   3. b   4. c   5. b

Lesson 26
Exercise I. Syllabication and Pronunciation (page 71)
1. re-crim-i-na'-tion 4. re-per-cus'-sion
2. re-lent'   5. re-plen'-ish
3. ren'-e-gade

Exercise II. Words Out of Context
(page 71)
1. b   2. c   3. a   4. e   5. e

Exercise III. Completing Sentences
(pages 71–72)
1. recalcitrants   4. relents
2. remorse   5. recriminations
3. reprisal

Exercise IV. Antonyms (page 72)
1. d   2. a   3. d   4. e   5. a

Exercise V. Verbal Analogies (page 72)
1. d   2. b   3. c   4. c   5. a

Lesson 27
Exercise I. Parts of Speech (page 73)
1. adj.   2. v.   3. n.   4. v., n.   5. adj., n.

Exercise II. Words in Phrases (page 73)
1. a   2. d   3. c   4. b   5. a

Exercise III. Completing Sentences
(pages 73-74)
1. salients   4. ritual
2. sabotage   5. sanguine
3. reverberated

Exercise IV. Antonyms (page 74)
1. d   2. e   3. b   4. b   5. c

Exercise V. Verbal Analogies (page 74)
1. b   2. d   3. d   4. c   5. a

Lesson 28
Exercise I. Syllabication and Pronunciation (page 75)
1. sec'-u-lar   4. strat'-e-gy
2. stig'-ma-tize   5. syn'-drome
3. stip'-u-late

Exercise II. Words Out of Context
(page 75)
1. b   2. d   3. d   4. a   5. c

Exercise III. Completing Sentences
(pages 75-76)
1. secular   3. solace   5. stamina
2. senile   4. sordid

Exercise IV. Antonyms (page 76)
1. d   2. c   3. a   4. b   5. e

Exercise V. Verbal Analogies (page 76)
1. a   2. c   3. b   4. a   5. d

Lesson 29
Exercise I. Parts of Speech (page 77)
1. adj. 2. v.   3. adj.   4. v.   5. n.

Exercise II. Words in Phrases (page 77)
1. c   2. b   3. d   4. a   5. c

Exercise III. Completing Sentences
(pages 77-78)
1. venal   3. taciturn   5. tenable
2. tacit   4. trenchant

Exercise IV. Antonyms (page 78)
1. a   2. c   3. b   4. e   5. c

Exercise V. Verbal Analogies (page 78)
1. b   2. c   3. a   4. b   5. d

Lesson 30
Exercise I. Syllabication and Pronunciation (page 79)
1. ve-neer'   4. vin-dic'-tive
2. ven'-er-a-ble   5. vi'-ti-ate
3. ver'-sa-tile

Exercise II. Words Out of Context
(page 79)
1. d   2. a   3. e   4. b   5. c

Exercise III. Completing Sentences
(page 79)
1. yoke   3. zany   5. veneer
2. zeal   4. vindictive

Exercise IV. Antonyms (page 80)
1. d   2. b   3. c   4. e   5. a

Exercise V. Verbal Analogies (page 80)
1. c   2. d   3. a   4. c   5. b

Review
Exercise I. Syllabication and Pronunciation (page 81)
1. re-cal'-ci-trant   4. tan'-gi-ble
2. sanc-ti-mo'-ni-ous 5. ve-rac'-i-ty
3. sur-veil'-lance

Exercise II. Parts of Speech (page 81)
1. n.   2. v.   3. v.   4. adj.   5. n., v.

Exercise III. Words Out of Context
(page 81)
1. b   2. c   3. a   4. b   5. c

Exercise IV. Words in Phrases
(pages 81-82)
1. d   2. b   3. a   4. c   5. b

Exercise V. Completing Sentences
(page 82)
1. repercussions   4. turbulent
2. vitiated   5. sacrilegious
3. scrutinized

Exercise VII. Antonyms (page 83)
1. c   2. a   3. e   4. a   5. d

Exercise VIII. Related Forms (page 83)
1. stridency,   3. retributive,
   stridence   retributory
2. urbanity   4. zealous
                     5. reminisce

Exercise IX. Look-Alikes (pages 83-84)
1. See page 426 of the student text.
2. See page 451 of the student text.
3. See page 464 of the student text.
4. See page 480 of the student text.
5. See page 502 of the student text.

Exercise X. Word Associations (page 84)
1. c   2. a   3. d   4. b   5. c

Cumulative Review
Exercise I. Syllabication and Pronunciation (page 85)
1. a-bet'   9. cir-cum-vent'
2. ad-journ'   10. com-pat'-i-ble
3. a-nach'-ro-nism   11. cri-te'-ri-on
4. as-sim'-i-late   12. de-noue-ment'
5. aus-tere'   13. dras'-tic
6. av'-a-rice   14. em'-pa-thy
7. bois'-ter-ous   15. ex-em'-pla-ry
8. bu-reauc'-ra-cy   16. fac-sim'-i-le

17. for-tu'-i-tous
18. har'-bin-ger
19. im-per'-vi-ous
20. in-cep'-tion
21. li-a-bil'-i-ty
22. no-mad'-ic
23. op-por-tune'
24. pla'-gia-rism
25. pro-tract'-ed
26. rem-i-nis'-cence
27. sa'-li-ent
28. stam'-i-na
29. ten'-a-ble
30. ver'-sa-tile

21. recant
22. urbane
23. condone
24. implacable
25. officious
26. zeal
27. dejected
28. ostensible
29. gratuitous
30. renegades

Exercise II. Parts of Speech (page 85)

1. v.	11. n., v.	21. n.
2. v., n., adj.	12. adj.	22. adj.
3. n.	13. adj.	23. n.
4. v., adj.	14. v.	24. v.
5. n.	15. v.	25. n.
6. v.	16. n.	26. v.
7. v., n.	17. v.	27. n., adj.
8. adj.	18. adj.	28. n.
9. adj.	19. adj.	29. adj.
10. v.	20. v.	30. v.

Exercise III. Words Out of Context
(pages 85–87)

1. e	11. a	21. d
2. c	12. d	22. d
3. a	13. c	23. c
4. a	14. c	24. e
5. d	15. d	25. b
6. b	16. e	26. a
7. c	17. b	27. e
8. e	18. a	28. d
9. e	19. b	29. a
10. b	20. b	30. c

Exercise IV. Words in Phrases
(pages 87–88)

1. b	11. d	21. a
2. d	12. d	22. b
3. a	13. c	23. b
4. b	14. b	24. d
5. b	15. a	25. c
6. d	16. a	26. d
7. c	17. b	27. a
8. c	18. c	28. b
9. b	19. c	29. b
10. a	20. d	30. c

Exercise V. Completing Sentences
(pages 88–90)

1. discomfited	11. schism
2. adverse	12. banal
3. ingenious	13. lackadaisical
4. persevere	14. prodigious
5. reticent	15. erudite
6. arbitrary	16. candid
7. eclectics	17. mercenaries
8. jettison	18. propitiate
9. satellites	19. strident
10. poignant	20. felicitous

Exercise VI. Synonyms and Antonyms
(pages 90–91)

1. A	11. S	21. S
2. S	12. A	22. S
3. S	13. S	23. S
4. A	14. S	24. A
5. S	15. A	25. A
6. S	16. S	26. S
7. A	17. A	27. S
8. A	18. A	28. S
9. S	19. A	29. A
10. S	20. S	30. S

Exercise VII. Related Forms (page 91)
1. cynicism, cynic
2. fickleness
3. narcissism, narcissist
4. obscenity
5. predator, predatoriness
6. ruminant
7. conjectural
8. enigmatical
9. libelous
10. confront
11. immunize
12. recriminate
13. apathetically
14. disparagingly
15. ironically

Exercise VIII. Look-Alikes (page 91)
1. See page 52 of the student text.
2. See page 62 of the student text.
3. See page 88 of the student text.
4. See page 101 of the student text.
5. See page 112 of the student text.
6. See page 137 of the student text.
7. See page 156 of the student text.
8. See page 169 of the student text.
9. See page 210 of the student text.
10. See page 226 of the student text.
11. See answer to V, 1, a, page 251 of the student text.
12. See page 314 of the student text.
13. See page 316 of the student text.
14. See page 426 of the student text.
15. See page 451 of the student text.

Exercise X. Word Associations
(page 92)

1. b	5. b	9. c
2. d	6. a	10. b
3. c	7. b	
4. a	8. d	